THE
COLLECTED LETTERS
Dylan Thomas

Volume II

1939–1953

Dylan Thomas was born in Swansea on 27 October 1914. After leaving school he worked on the *South Wales Evening Post* before embarking on his literary career in London. Not only a poet, he wrote short stories, film scripts, features and radio plays, the most famous being *Under Milk Wood*. It was in New York, during his fourth US tour, that he fell ill shortly after his 39th birthday, dying there on 9 November 1953. In 1982 a memorial stone to commemorate him was unveiled in Poets' Corner in Westminster Abbey.

Also available from Orion

A Dylan Thomas Treasury
Portrait of the Artist as a Young Dog
Collected Stories
Dylan Thomas Omnibus
Selected Poems
The Love Letters of Dylan Thomas
Under Milk Wood

THE
COLLECTED LETTERS
Dylan Thomas

Volume II

1939–1953

Edited by Paul Ferris

WEIDENFELD & NICOLSON

A W&N PAPERBACK

First published in one volume in Great Britain in 1985 by J. M. Dent
Revised edition first published in Great Britain in 2000 by J. M. Dent
This two volume edition first published in Great Britain in 2017
by Weidenfeld & Nicolson
an imprint of the Orion Publishing Group Ltd
Carmelite House, 50 Victoria Embankment
London EC4Y 0DZ
An Hachette UK Company

1 3 5 7 9 10 8 6 4 2

Introduction and notes © Paul Ferris 1985, 2000

Letters © 1957, 1966, 1985, 2000, The Trustees for the Copyrights of Dylan Thomas

A CIP catalogue record for this book is
available from the British Library.

Volume I
ISBN (trade paperback) 978 1 4746 0799 5
Volume II
ISBN (trade paperback) 978 1 4746 0800 8

Printed in Great Britain by Clays Ltd, St Ives plc

MIX
Paper from
responsible sources
FSC
www.fsc.org   FSC® C104740

www.orionbooks.co.uk

Contents

For Caitlin

Chronology

1914 Born 27 October, Swansea.

1925 September, enters Swansea Grammar School.

1927 14 January, newspaper *Western Mail* publishes Thomas's poem 'His Requiem', discovered (forty-four years later) to be plagiarised from a *Boy's Own Paper* of 1923.

1930 27 April, date of the first surviving poem in a poetry notebook, 'Osiris, Come to Isis'.
December, correspondence with Percy Smart begins.

1931 Summer, leaves school to be a reporter on the local newspaper, *South Wales Daily Post*.

1932 Joins Swansea Little Theatre's company of amateur players.
?December, leaves newspaper.

1933 18 May, *New English Weekly* publishes 'And death shall have no dominion'.
Summer, first visit to London.
3 September, *Sunday Referee* publishes 'That sanity be kept', which leads to correspondence with Pamela Hansford Johnson.

1934 23 February, first meeting with Pamela Hansford Johnson, in London.
13 November, moves into London lodgings.
18 December, *18 Poems*.

1936 17 July, first letter to Caitlin Macnamara.
10 September, *Twenty-five Poems*.

1937 21 April, first radio broadcast, 'Life and the Modern Poet'.
11 July, marries Caitlin Macnamara, Penzance register office.

1938 May, moves to Laugharne lives there intermittently from now on.
August, applies unsuccessfully for help to Royal Literary Fund.

1939 30 January, Llewelyn Edouard Thomas born, Hampshire.
24 August, *The Map of Love*.
20 December, *The World I Breathe* (USA).

1940 4 April, *Portrait of the Artist as a Young Dog*.
Summer, with John Davenport at Marshfield, Gloucestershire.

1941 January, applies successfully to Royal Literary Fund.
?Autumn, joins Strand Film Co in London as scriptwriter.

1943 February, *New Poems* (USA).
15 February, 'Reminiscences of Childhood', first of his nostalgic radio talks.
3 March, Aeronwy Bryn Thomas born, London.

1944 September, moves to bungalow at New Quay, Cardiganshire.

1945 Autumn, completes 'Fern Hill' at Blaen Cwm, Carmarthenshire.

1946   7 February, *Deaths and Entrances*.
8 November, *Selected Writings* (USA).

1947   April (until August), in Italy, with family.
15 June, 'Return Journey' (to Swansea), radio feature.
September, moves to South Leigh, Oxfordshire.

1948   Writing feature films for Gainsborough.

1949   March, commissioned by BBC Television to adapt *Peer Gynt*.
March, in Prague, guest of Czechoslovak Government.
April or May, moves to the Boat House, Laugharne.
May, accepts invitation to read at the Poetry Center, New York City.
24 July, Colm Garan Hart Thomas born, Carmarthen.

1950   20 February, flies to New York: first US trip.
1 June, sails for England.

1951   January, in Iran, to write film script for Anglo Iranian Oil Co.
December, living briefly in Camden Town, London.

1952   20 January, arrives in New York, with Caitlin: second US trip.
28 February, *In Country Sleep* (USA).
16 May, leaves New York for England.
10 November, *Collected Poems*.
16 December, Jack Thomas, his father, dies.

1953   31 March, *Collected Poems* (USA).
21 April, arrives New York: third US trip.
14 May, first performance of *Under Milk Wood* with actors, New York.
14 May, *The Doctor and the Devils*.
2 June, returns to London.
19 October, arrives New York: fourth US trip.
5 November, collapses at Chelsea Hotel, New York City.
9 November, dies at St Vincent's Hospital.

Acknowledgements

Many people have taken time and trouble to help me find, date, assess and annotate letters. I mention especially Professors Walford Davies of Aberystwyth and Ralph Maud of Vancouver, the leading authorities on Dylan Thomas texts. Gwyn Jenkins and Dr Ceridwen Lloyd-Morgan at the National Library of Wales. Andrew MacAdie, who made available Dylan's first letter to Caitlin and other items in his collection; Jim Martin also let me see letters. Michael Rush, senior trustee of the Dylan Thomas copyright estate. Meic Stephens, writer and editor. David N. Thomas, who showed me the MS of his *Dylan Thomas. A Farm, Two Mansions and a Bungalow*, before Seren Books published it (2000); the information in n. 2, page 218, is his. Jeff Towns of Dylans Book Store, Swansea, who has an unrivalled knowledge of the market in Thomas holographs; I also adapted some of his footnotes to the letter to Loren MacIver, published by his Salubrious Press. Gwen Watkins, widow of the poet Vernon. John Whitehead of Moffat, Dumfriesshire, who wrote to me after the first edition with useful corrections.

For other assistance I am grateful to The Astrology Shop, Richard Atkinson (Casenove), Lady Avebury (daughter of Pamela Hansford Johnson), Barclays Bank (Human Resources), Michael Basinski (State University of New York at Buffalo), Dr Peter Beal (Sotheby's, London), Gilbert Bennett, Brighton Public Library, Kathleen Cann (Cambridge University Library), Chris Coover (Christie's New York), Wystan Curnow, Roy Davids, Michael Davie, Baldwyn Davies, Jane Davies (Tenby), Esmond Devas, Reg and Eileen Evans, Charles Fisher, Mark Fisher, Dr Chris Fletcher (British Library), David Gascoyne, General Dental Council, Elva Griffith (Ohio State University Libraries), Ken Hewlings (Tenby), Mary Johnson, Paul Johnson (National Library of Wales), Marilyn Jones (West Glamorgan Public Library, Swansea), Ed Knappman, Mark Le Fanu (Society of Authors), J. C. Wyn Lewis, Ray Lovell, Ann McKay (BBC), Nancy MacKechnie (Vassar University Library), Mexican Consulate, Dale Miller (Christie's East), Sarah Mindham, Leslie A. Morris and Melanie Wisner (Houghton Library, Harvard University), Timothy Murray and Rebecca Johnson Melvin (University of Delaware Library), Maurice F. Neville, Aedin O'Carroll (Location Register, University of Reading), Sonia Richmond (Phillips), Caroline Roberts (Brewers' and Licensed Retailers' Association), William Roberts (University of California at Berkeley Library),

Royal Pharmaceutical Society, Louise Ryan (Authors' Licensing & Collecting Society), Jay Satterfield and Krista L. Ovist (University of Chicago Library), Lorraine Scourfield (Boat House, Laugharne), Fiona Searle, Michael Snow, Neil Somerville (BBC Written Archives), Shayera Tangri (Wilson Library, University of North Carolina), Michael Taylor, Tenby Public Library, Aeron Thomas (Dylan's daughter), Clem Thomas (Laugharne), Dewi Thomas (Carmarthen Public Library), Kim Thomas (India Office Library), Llewelyn Thomas (Dylan's elder son), Tony Vilela (Laugharne), Tara Wenger and Cliff Farrington (Harry Ransom Humanities Research Center), Helene Whitson (San Francisco State University Library), Robert Williams, Bill Willis (Swansea), Joan Wintercorn, Sarah Wombwell (Christie's, South Kensington), Professor John Worthen, Stephen Young *(Poetry,* Chicago).

For help with research, proof-reading, indexing and general attention to the text, I am indebted as always to my wife Mary.

The following list repeats personal acknowledgements from the 1985 edition.

Graham Ackroyd, Ben Arbeid, Eric Barton, John Bayliss, Sir Theodore Brinckman (Monk Bretton Books), John Malcolm Brinnin, Victor Bonham-Carter (Society of Authors), Julian Chancellor (Society of Authors), Douglas Cleverdon, John Crichton (The Brick Row Book Shop), Roger Davenport, H. W. E. Davies, Sean Day-Lewis, Nicolette Devas (sister of Caitlin Thomas), Sheila Dickinson, Lawrence Durrell, Valerie Eliot, Charles Elliott, Frances Freeth, Jean Overton Fuller, Roland Gant, Clive Graham, Thomas B. Greenslade (Kenyon College archivist), Bernard Gutteridge, Desmond Hawkins, Ian Henderson, Nigel Henderson, Robert Hewison, Jane Aiken Hodge, Barbara Holdridge, G. Thurston Hopkins, Hubert Howard (the Camillo Caetani Foundation), Lord Howard de Walden, Dr Cyril James, Fred Janes, Glyn Jones, Professor Gwyn Jones, Mimi Josephson, P. J. Kavanagh, Ellen de Young Kay, James Laughlin, Laurie Lee, John Lehmann, Michael Levien, Mervyn Levy, Jack Lindsay, Brigit Manlier (sister of Caitlin Thomas), R. B. Marriott, Douglas Matthews, Barbara Noble, John Ormond, Ruth Wynn Owen, Ken Pearson, P. E. N., Hermann Peschmann, Gilbert Phelps, Douglas Phillips, Peter Quennell, Keidrych Rhys, Anthony Rota, Charles W. Sachs (The Scriptorium), D. S. Savage, Rupert Shephard, Philip Skelsey, Elizabeth Reitell Smith, John Sommerfield, Sir Stephen Spender, Professor Jon Stallworthy, Derek Stanford, Harald Sverdrup, Amelia Taylor, Professor Christy M. Taylor, Haydn Taylor (brother-in-law of Dylan Thomas), David Tennant, Georgia Tennant, Molly Murray Threipland, Dr Kerith Trick, Meurig Walters, E. W. White, John Wilson (bookseller).

The author and publisher thank the following corporate holders of Dylan Thomas letters for access to material; all are identified where the letters appear.

We are especially grateful to the Harry Ransom Humanities Research

Center of the University of Texas at Austin—which has the largest collection of Thomas letters—and to the State University of New York at Buffalo—whose Poetry and Rare Books Collection at the University Libraries contains the Pamela Hansford Johnson letters and the Thomas Notebooks—for their help with many inquiries.

We also formally thank the BBC Written Archives Centre; University of Birmingham Library (UK); Bodleian Library; the British Library Board; the Syndics of Cambridge University Library; the Joseph Regenstein Library, University of Chicago Library; Columbia University Libraries; University of Delaware Library; Houghton Library, Harvard University; Lilly Library, Indiana University; Chalmers Memorial Library, Kenyon College; University College of Los Angeles Library; Pierpont Morgan Library; Mount Holyoke College Library; Henry W. and Albert A. Berg Collection, New York Public Library, Astor, Lenox and Tilden Foundations; Fales Library, New York University; Ohio State University Libraries; Oxford University Press; Rosenbach Museum and Library; Royal Literary Fund; Paul Sacher Foundation, Basle; National Library of Scotland; Morris Library, Southern Illinois University at Carbondale; the Department of Special Collections, McFarlin Library, University of Tulsa; National Library of Wales; University of Washington Libraries; West Glamorgan Archive Service.

Laurence Pollinger Ltd, Viking Penguin Inc. and the Estate of Mrs Frieda Lawrence Ravagli kindly gave permission to use the three verses from 'Another Ophelia' and the two verses from 'Obsequial Ode', by D. H. Lawrence, which Thomas quoted in a letter dated 30 July 1945. The British Library and Mrs Gwen Watkins gave permission for the reproduction in facsimile of a letter from Thomas to Vernon Watkins.

Abbreviations

BBC	BBC Written Archives Centre, Caversham
Berg	Berg Collection, New York Public Library
Buffalo	University Libraries, State University of New York at Buffalo
Chicago	University of Chicago
Carbondale	Morris Library, Southern Illinois University at Carbondale
Delaware	University of Delaware
Houghton	Houghton Library, Harvard University
Indiana	Lilly Library, Indiana University
Ohio	Ohio State University Libraries
Texas	Harry Ransom Humanities Research Center, the University of Texas at Austin
Victoria	University of Victoria, Canada
Washington	University of Washington, Seattle
CP	*Dylan Thomas. Collected Poems 1934–1953*
The Poems	*Dylan Thomas: The Poems*, edited by Daniel Jones
'Notebooks'	The four surviving 'Poetry Notebooks' with Thomas's adolescent work, at Buffalo.
SL	*The Selected Letters of Dylan Thomas* (1966), edited by Constantine FitzGibbon
VW	*Dylan Thomas. Letters to Vernon Watkins* (1957), edited by Vernon Watkins.

When the whereabouts of a letter, as given in the first edition, is no longer certain, the original location is in brackets, eg *MS: (Thomas Trustees)*.

———

The approximate value of money in Britain since Dylan Thomas's time:

Past value	*Value in year 2000*
£1.00 in 1939	£27.00
£1.00 in 1945	£23.00
£1.00 in 1950	£19.00

Majoda
New Quay
Cards
26 2 45

Dear Vernon,

I was very very glad to hear and see from you; it's been a long and complicated time since we disappointingly met, and I'm happy and relieved to think that the offence, (for my lost, preoccupied manner must really have been that), I gave when we did meet in that gabbling drunk-gray crush, the worst of the town, has, if never to be forgotten utterly, lost some disfavour. (I have just been writing at length to Llewelyn, on the occassion of a fall from a tree and a split tongue, and the effort of not talking to a boy of six has made me adopt the claptrap periods of a leader-writer under gas.) I have found, increasingly as time goes on, or around, or backwards, or stays quite still as the brain races, the heart absorbs and expells, and the arteries harden, that the problems of physical life, of social contact, of daily posture and armour, of the choice between dissipations, of the abhorred needs enforced by a reluctance to "miss anything", that old fear of death, are as insoluble to me as those of the spirit. In few and fewer poems I can despair and, at rare moments exult with the big last, but the first force me every moment to make quick decisions and thus to plunge me into little hells and rubbishes at which I rebel with a kind of truculent acceptance. The ordinary moments of walking up a village streets, opening doors or letters, speaking good-days to friends or strangers, looking out of windows, making telephone calls, are so inexplicably (to me) dangerous that I am trembling all over before I get out of bed in the mornings to meet them. Waking to remember an appointment at X that coming evening is to see, before X, galleries of menacing common places, chambers of errors of the day's conventions, pits of platitudes and customary gestures, all beckoning, spurning; and through, over, & out of these I must

A troubled letter from Thomas to his friend, the poet Vernon Watkins. It is printed on pages 151–2.

2.

somehow move before the appointment, the appointment that has now become a whining grail in a dentist's surgery, an almost impossible consummation of illegal pleasure to be achieved in a room like a big gut in a subterranean concentration-camp. And especially, of course, in London. I wish that I could have met Gwen "properly", and glad that she wanted to; I was "myself" in the sense that I was no-one else, but I was broken on a wheel of streets and faces; equally well, I may be just as broken in the peace — what peace? — I the country, hysterical in my composure, hyena-ish in my vegetabledom. I will, if I may, try to come to stay in the pub in Stony Stratford when next I come to London: but oh the bony cupboards and traps and vats before that.

I wish I could see your new poems. The translation in Horizon I did, & remembered much of it; it was beautiful.

I am glad Francis is alive, well, and happy.

I have lost Dan's address again. Will you tell him that we are not going to Ireland for a long time, perhaps not even this year, as another film has risen out of some fool's mind and must be written so that we can eat and tremble at the approach of each quiet, unsensational & monstrous day? The studio is being carefully looked after. I'll write to Dan this week & will send the letter to you.

          Love to you and Gwen from us both.

                    Ever,

                         Dylan.

I wish I could understand your letter from Heatherslade. It was dated the 24th, which was Saturday, but said that you were afraid we would be unable to meet as you were leaving on Friday. If that was not also, and unfortunately, typical of myself, I should say it was a piece of genuine-accept-no-other Vernon.

Don't mind this silly letter. It was lovely to have yours.

THE
COLLECTED LETTERS

Volume II

A Writer's Life
1939–49

The Second World War made the publishing of books and magazines more difficult, and interfered with the livelihood of many 'literary' writers. Thomas, who was determined to avoid military service, spent the early part of the war drifting from place to place, but later found work writing scripts for the propaganda films then being mass-produced in London. In the middle years of the war he wrote little or no serious verse, but made up for this with a dozen or more poems in 1944 and 1945; some of them made vivid use of images from air raids. A year after the war ended, *Deaths and Entrances* (1946) was well received. Thomas was now a notorious literary figure: drinker and half-hearted womaniser, as well as craftsman obsessed with his vocation. To some he was a scrounger and a liar, but he had loyal friends as well as brigades of hangers-on. As a freelance writer he was successful and well-paid. He wrote, read and acted for radio, and worked on film scripts; the immediate postwar years were spent mainly in Oxfordshire, within easy reach of London and the broadcasting studios. He attracted loans (rarely repaid) and gifts from friends and patrons. None of this gave Thomas the freedom from debts and anxiety, which—he complained—stood between him and his work. In 1946, 1947 and 1948 he wrote only one poem, 'In country sleep'.

DESMOND HAWKINS
September 3 1939   Sea View   Laugharne   Carmarthenshire

Dear Desmond,

Yes, terrible, terrible. Being my hero, my chief concern, too, is to keep out of death's way. And no, I don't know what to do either: declare myself a neutral state, or join as a small tank.

Hope you do my story, I want a pound badly. I liked your review very much, and thank you. I want to see Muir's review, too.[1] Hope he agrees that the poems, as a whole, are better than any I've written. But a filthy time for a book. Only my Aunty Polly's bought one, I think.

And I want a pound quickly, too. No, sorry the short poem isn't finished yet. If it is, you must have it straight away.

Dylan

MS: National Library of Wales

DAVID HIGHAM
11 Sept 1939   Sea View   Laugharne   Carmarthenshire

Dear Higham,

I wonder—without bothering you too much—whether you could find out for me, from Dent's, whether they are going to send me the press-cuttings about my new book as they did about my last one? I've heard that several reviews have appeared, but I take no papers. It is, apart from anything else, very useful to me to see what things the reviewers say.

I'm extremely glad that you believe my Dent's monthly-arrangement is bound to continue.

Yours,
Dylan Thomas

MS: Texas

1 Edwin Muir reviewed *The Map of Love* for the October–November issue of *Purpose*.

GLYN JONES
11 September 1939   Sea View   Laugharne   Carmarthenshire

Dear Glyn,
    Thank you for the Miller book back. I'm glad you enjoyed most of it, and I mostly agree that it is not the super book I sometimes blurb it to be to fellows who haven't read it. As writing, it *is* unoriginal, but it has, sentimentally speaking, more guts & blood in it than new English prose books have. The only recent prose I've had as much pleasure out of, loud meaty pleasure, has been another American book—Nightwood (far different, with original writing too).[1] I remember you said, in Laugharne, that you hadn't read it: would you like to? I like the *idea* of Miller's anti-literature, but it is a pity he writes, so often, in the old literary way to try to achieve it. He's always got the same cracks to grind, but, after all, good fucking books are few & far, & if you look at *Tropic of Cancer* as the best modern fucking book, & not—perhaps my sincere enthusiasm misled you—as a universal life-&-death book, then I know you must enjoy & admire it enormously. (The adverb is also, I notice, on the back of the book.) Yes, it is, to date, his best *book*, but passages from *Tropic of Capricorn* which I've read in magazines are really much better, wider, less repetitive, & contain the best descriptions of America I've ever read.[2] But I'm too annoyed & unsettled to write clearly, even about Miller's books which I do know well & feel about clearly. I want to get something out of the war, & put very little in (certainly not my one & only body). I'm trying to get some profitable civilian work; that will probably be impossible. Does your School go on? Do tell me what you intend doing when, after registration, you are called up? Prison & the Medical Corps are both disagreeable to me. Regards to your wife, from us both.
Dylan

I want to see your review in Welsh Review. Will it appear now?

MS: Carbondale

1 *Nightwood*, a freakish novel by the American writer Djuna Chappell Barnes (1892–1982), was enthusiastically reviewed by Thomas in 1937 in the magazine *Light and Dark*.
2 Miller's *Tropic of Cancer*, a novel based on his adventures in Europe, and first published in Paris in 1934, was seen for many years as pornographic. It didn't appear in Britain until 1963, though many copies were smuggled in. *Tropic of Capricorn*, also banned for years, was published in 1939, again in France.

DAVID HIGHAM
12 Sept 1939   Sea View   Laugharne   Carmarthenshire

Dear Higham,
    Here are the filled-up forms. I hope, very much indeed, something will come of it.[1]

Yours sincerely,
Dylan Thomas

MS: Texas

SIR EDWARD MARSH[2]
September 14 1939   Laugharne   Carmarthenshire   S Wales

Dear Sir Edward,
    I am writing to you, a patron of letters, to ask for any help that you may be able to give me. You may have read some of my work, or heard it spoken of. If not, I can refer you to Miss Edith Sitwell and Mr. T. S. Eliot, who will tell you that I am a poet of some worth and deserving of help. I have a wife and a child and am without private means. For the last few years I have been earning just enough money to keep my family and myself alive by selling poems and short stories to magazines. These sources of income are now almost entirely dried up. It has occurred to me that you, with your connections with the Government, might be able to obtain some employment for me, either in the Ministry of Information—though that, I am told, is overrun with applicants, stampeded by almost every young man in London who has ever held a pencil or slapped a back—or elsewhere, any other place at all. I have been a journalist and an actor in a repertory theatre; I have broadcast, and lectured. I am 25 years old.
    I suspect that this letter is one of many similar that you are receiving, and must apologise for giving you this additional trouble.
    I have never, even in my most desperate moments, begged or attempted to seek any employment outside my own limited and underpaid profession. But now I must have work—I want to be able to go on writing, and conscription will stop that, perhaps for ever—and I beg you to help me.
    I would very much like to give you, if you wanted it, any information about me and my work. Or I could, again if it was needed, attempt to come to London.

Yours sincerely,
Dylan Thomas

MS: Berg

---

1 Perhaps the questionnaire mentioned on page 13.
2 Sir Edward Marsh (1872–1953), scholar, translator and civil servant.

JOHN DAVENPORT
14 September 1939   Sea View   Laugharne   Carmarthenshire

Dear John,
   Although you haven't answered any of my letters since you came down
here in June—and one of the letters was important, about the 5 bob flotation
scheme which has now come to nothing; I don't know if it would have come
to anything even if you *had* helped me—I'm still trying to get a word out of
you, and this time again writing for advice or assistance. If you don't answer, I
shall know Something is Wrong, though I shan't know what the Something
is, unless, as I said before in one of my letters-to-the-void, you were so
unspeakably bored with your visit that you've decided not to speak. It's this
War. I am trying to get a job before conscription, because my one-&-only
body I will not give. I know that all the shysters in London are grovelling
about the Ministry of Information, all the half-poets, the boiled newspaper-
men, submen from the islands of crabs, dismissed advertisers, old mercuries,
mass-snoopers, and all I have managed to do is to have my name on the crook
list and a vague word of hope from Humbert Wolfe.[1] So I must explore every
avenue now, I can't afford to leave an Edward Marsh unturned. Because along
will come conscription, and the military tribunal, & stretcher-bearing or jail
or potato-peeling or the Boys' Fire League. And all I want is time to write
poems, I'm only just getting going now, and enough money to keep two and a
bit alive. The only thing I can do, apart from registering myself on the official
list of writers to be kept available for possible abuse by the government, is to
write to people, friends and acquaintances or just people who might be able to
help, and to ask them, on knees not yet broken, whether they can give me a
job or suggest to whom or what I should apply. For my little money-sources—
(apart from anything else)—are diminishing or dying. Soon there will not be a
single paper paying inadequately for serious stories & poems. Do you know
of anything for me? I can speak & act too. Does the film-world want an
intelligent young man of literary ability, 'self-conscious, punch-drunk', who
must (for his own sake) keep out of the bloody war, who's willing to do any
work—provided of course that it pays enough for living? I'm not expecting
plums from the war—after all, they must go to the kind of chaps who refused
to give me anything out of the Royal Literary Fund—but I do want
something. Will you tell me if you know of any chances, if, in your clubman
rambles, you meet persons who might be just even likely to consider me for
some job, if there is, to your knowledge, any vacancy in films of any sort, and,
most important, if you are willing, after such a long silence, to try to help me?
Otherwise, I don't see how I am to continue here, or anywhere else, even for a
very short time. As soon as war was, bills were popped in; the attitude of the

---

1 The poet Humbert Wolfe was an official at the Ministry of Labour, a useful man to
   know at the start of a war.

tradesmen is changing rapidly; there's a great difference between a rich pacifist & a poor coward. Is it worth, (do you think, & also, of course, if you are willing to think), my coming to London to pull, lick, and see? Please write to me.

Love from us both to you both,
John & Clement,
Caitlin & Dylan

MS: Texas

DESMOND HAWKINS
Sept 14 1939   Sea View   Laugharne   Carmarthenshire

Dear Desmond,

So you've been trying to pull strings too, have you, you old racketeer? You should be ashamed: go on and fight for culture like a fool: don't attempt to get anything out of the fucking war. I wrote to Mr. Humbert Wolfe, and what does he do but send me a copy of a letter he wrote to you. So you were there first; alright, then, I shan't tell you the famous man *I'm* writing to. (If he sends me a copy of a letter to you, we may as well send out circulars signed with both our names.) But do you think there's any possibility at all of wheedling oneself—whining, under protest—into any governmental job. I wrote to Norman Cameron who told me that every literate or semi-literate party-goer in London is stampeding the Ministry of Labour, willing to do anything from licking stamps & bums to writing recruiting literature or broadcasting appeals for warm bodies to become cold. The question of conscience *can*, apparently, be ignored, even among our honourable intelligentsia. And what work would there be, even if we did manage to fawn in, in the Government? Principle prevents us, I hope, from propaganding; I personally know nothing of any foreign language except a very little about the sanitary-towel of the gardener's wife & a few Welsh dirty words. I can't decipher anything, not even poems. What I'm doing is writing urgent & bad-tempered letters to everybody who has ever said publicly that I am a better poet than Alfred Noyes, & telling them that, unless someone does something soon, there'll be one better-than-Alfred poet less, that the Armed Forces are not conducive to the creation of contemplative verse, and that all my few sources of income are drying up as quickly as blood on the Western Front. Though it will probably leave my correspondents unmoved, there is nothing else that I can think of to do. The Army Medical Corps is presumably admirable, but I don't want to help—even in a most inefficient way—to patch poor buggers up to send them out again into quick insanity and bullets. Have you any suggestions? I know you must be trying too, all that you can think of. (The literary Left, I suppose, is having a loud whack at the Nazi nightmare; or can it do its work better in safety? Auden is in America, isn't he? And the very best place, too, for a militant communist at this time.) Come & stay here, completely out of harm's way, and help compose letters to the Big Boys. It's speed that counts now; jobs must be obtained, or exemption promised, before conscription & military—'what would you do if you saw a soldier raping John Lehmann?'—tribunals. And what—as a matter of interest—did you reply to Wolfe?

Love,
Dylan

MS: National Library of Wales

JAMES LAUGHLIN
15 September 1939   Sea View   Laugharne   Carmarthenshire   S Wales

Dear Laughlin:
That was an awful bother with agents and contract, but it was taken right out of my hands—I have to show all business dealings to them—and it's settled now and that's alright.

40 poems, you say, and 10 stories. Right. But perhaps you could allow just one more story. I've gone carefully through all my prose, and the eleven I have chosen do seem, to me, pretty unalterable—that is, I shouldn't like any one to be omitted. Simple sentimental stories, melodramatic stories, apocalyptic stories, all the kinds I write and have written are represented.

I hope you like my selection of poems. If, by any chance, you want to substitute one poem for another, do let me know, won't you? But I do think I've chosen the best: by the simple process of not allowing the worst.

Reavey, as you might have heard, was unable, owing to the squeamishness or carefulness of printers, to bring out my book of stories, and J. M. Dent's bought the mss. back from Reavey and included some of the stories in a prose-&-verse book of mine, *The Map of Love*, which they have just published.

You will see that I have given the numbers, & pages on which they are to be found, of all 40 poems. You have my first two books, & I'm enclosing the proof-sheets of the third (corrected).

You may have copies (in magazines) of some of the selected stories, but I'm enclosing more copies of them anyway. Do you mind, some time, returning these magazine copies?

I suggest—and I am sure you too have decided on this—that the poems come first & the stories second.

As to the arrangement of the poems: do you think it would be best to print them in strict chronological order (with a note saying, at the beginning, that the first group are from a book published in 1934, the second from a book in 1936, the third in 1939)? Or do you think it would be more effective to print the 1936 & 1939 poems first, in the order in which they appear in the books, & then print the 1934 poems? I am in favour of the first arrangement, but it is, after all, up to you. What I would *not* agree with would be to print the poems just anyhow (according to editorial taste), with no mention of their dates. (And no aspersions against your taste.) The stories you can arrange as you like, though obviously *The Enemies* must come some time before *The Holy Six*, which is a kind of continuation.

I think that 'The World I Breathe' is a good title. I've been considering 'These Ancient Minutes', (from the poem on page 19 of 25 Poems).[1] What do you think? I don't mind which.

One story, 'The Prospect of The Sea', which I believe to be one of the best, is not among the selected material I am suggesting & sending. I'll post it to you tomorrow: I know where it is, but I can't get hold of it today.

Would you like me to send you, for any publicity purposes, extracts from reviews of the 3 books in the English press?

The fragment, 'In The Direction of the Beginning', which you printed in N.D. 1938 must not, by the way, be included, as it is the beginning of a new book not yet finished (a book I shall send to you next year).

I think that's all for the moment. Any questions?

Do write to me soon.

> Best wishes,
> Dylan Thomas

Will you, if you see him, tell Kenneth Patchen[2] that I am writing to him this week, & that I'm sorry for the delay. It's this war you might have heard.

MS: Houghton

SIR EDWARD MARSH
September 19 1939   Laugharne   Carmarthenshire   S Wales

Dear Sir Edward,

I know you'll forgive me for not replying at once to your very kind letter and for not thanking you, very sincerely, for your gift. A friend called here and drove me to see my father: I don't often have the chance of seeing him, as he lives fifty miles away and we're both too poor to move much, and I stayed with him until yesterday. Your letter was waiting for me. It was most generous of you to assist me. I had, as you knew and said, no thought at all of asking anything other than advice, but I am very grateful and your gift was welcome indeed and will help us *considerably* over a bad time.

I was afraid that the Ministry of Information would be crowded with staff and that it would be useless for me to apply, but I must thank you for

---

1 'Hold hard, these ancient minutes in the cuckoo's month'.
2 The poet Kenneth Patchen (1911–72) was published by New Directions.

mentioning my name there. I do hope that, if anything does come to your notice, you will let me know. For the present I can only wait; and will, if necessary, when the time comes, register myself as a conscientious objector and see what national work I will be directed to do by the tribunal.

Thank you again.
Yours sincerely,
Dylan Thomas

MS: Berg

DAVID HIGHAM
21 September 1939   Sea View   Laugharne   Carmarthenshire

Dear Higham,
  Thank you for enquiring about the cuttings. A pile have already been sent to me from Dent's.
  It is indeed extremely unlikely that I shall do any work of national importance, & Dent's can continue to pay me without fearing that the Government is making me a profiteer. I am, as you might have seen from my letters, an objector.

Yours,
Dylan Thomas

MS: Texas

JAMES LAUGHLIN
22 Sept 1939   Sea View   Laugharne   Carmarthenshire

Dear Laughlin,
  Here's the other story I promised. I hope you'll be able to include 11 stories in the book; otherwise I think that the *Burning Baby* is, perhaps, the one to omit.[1] Certainly not this tale.
  Hope to hear from you soon.

Yours,
Dylan Thomas

You will, whatever else, see, won't you, that it is made clear which groups of poems belong to the certain dates.

MS: Houghton

---

1 *The World I Breathe* was published on 20 December 1939, and included 'The Burning Baby'. The 'other story' was 'A Prospect of the Sea'.

DESMOND HAWKINS
24 September 1939   Sea View   Laugharne   Carmarthenshire

Dear Desmond,
  I've filled up that questionnaire from David Higham. A lot of good will
come from that. My only special qualification I put as reading poems aloud.
Not 'If' to the troops, either. I've no wish to propagandise, nor to do anything
but my own work. I'm Mr. Humanity and can't kill or be killed (with my
approval). Like you, I shall wait, register as as an objector, and see. Chapel
Wales is down on conscription alright, but my objection can't be on chapel-
religious grounds, and I'd have little support. What have we got to fight for or
against? To prevent Fascism coming here? It's come? To stop shit by
throwing it? To protect our incomes, bank balances, property, national
reputations? I feel sick. All this flogged hate again. We must go on with our
out-of-war life. It's a temptation, in the pubs, on Saturday nights, in the
billiard saloon, to want to allow myself to get that fuggy, happy, homosexual
feeling and eat, sleep, get drunk, march, suffer, joke, kill & die among men,
comrades, brothers, you're my pal, I'm with you son, back to back, only die
once, short life, women and children, here's a photograph of my wife, over
the bloody, down the bloody, here's to the bloody, shit and blood. But the
temptation's not too strong, and the sanity of the imagination is. I'd like you
very much to send me your collected advice; there must be lots of tips. Thank
you for your letter. Write soon.

                                                    Dylan

Tell me, please, about my story & Purpose. I haven't got one penny, and
unless Purpose can send me a quid or 30 bob straight away I must send that
trivial story to Herring.

MS: National Library of Wales

DESMOND HAWKINS
[Sept/Oct 1939]   Laugharne

Dear Desmond,
  Sorry to rush you: but what about the pacifist tips and the fate of my story?
The local PPU reply was very vague.[1]

                                                    Dylan

MS: National Library of Wales

1 Hawkins had advised him to contact the Peace Pledge Union. See page 19.

VERNON WATKINS
Thursday [postmarked 29 September 1939]   Sea View   Laugharne

But is there
any reason
against you
coming down here in the weekend?

Dear Vernon,

We were all ready to come when bills came too, and, to our disgust, we felt we should pay them at once with the money we were intending for our Swansea visit. We did. Caitlin and I were very sorry to miss Dot once again. Just as we're about to come, we have a wire from you saying 'Dot is here', & our plans, quite soon after, are changed. Just as we used to leave the day before she came.[1] All that's unfortunate & accidental, as you might know: we'd love to see you & Dot right now but we have to stay here with a baby and a new kitten called Pussy. I hope a lot we can come to see you soon. Write to me. Poems? I want to have everything (except aeroplanes)

Love, to all,
Dylan & Caitlin

MS: British Library

A. E. TRICK
29 September [1939][2]   Sea View   Laugharne   Carmarthenshire

Dear Bert,

And I never managed to see you in Swansea after all. I was there for a few days about 2 months ago, but stuck all the time in Bishopston pennilessly. I didn't write asking you if you could come down to see *me*, because I didn't know when my pennilessness would end and allow me suddenly to come to Swansea and Brynmill[3] for the day. The state did not end, and hasn't ended yet. Now it's harder than ever, poor or not, to move from this cockled city even to Carmarthen overrun with soldiers and war urgers and rememberers. I wish it were possible for you to visit us: Laugharne is sweet and quiet, and our house big enough to conceal all the Tricks in the world. How are wife and children? Tell Kerith I agree with him when he said 'Damn that' about my being a poet. Damn it forever, it makes uncomfortable life even harder and bonier and gives a poor man a wild beast for a conscience.

How does the body-snatching go? Be quick, there'll be less bodies soon. I

1 Dot was Watkins's sister. It was a standing joke that she and Thomas always missed one another by a day.
2 Thomas wrote '1929' by mistake.
3 The suburb where Trick lived.

live from poem to mouth, and both suffer. Now I am trying to complete, by December, a book of short stories, mostly pot-boilers, called, temporarily, 'Portrait of the Artist as a Young Dog: stories towards a Provincial Autobiography'. They may be amusing eventually, but the writing of them means the writing of a number of poems less; they're all about Swansea life, the pubs, clubs, billiard saloons, promenades, adolescence in the suburban nights, friendships, tempers, and humiliations. The book is on contract: I get too little regularly for the job: I am commissioned to write another prose book by the middle of next year, but there is, apparently, no clause in the contract forbidding obscenity and I'll give Dent the whole fucking works.[1] Hope you get hold of my autogeographical book; you knew all the stories, but the poems were new. I'd love to know what you think of them.

Llewelyn is bursting with energy; soon he probably *will* burst. He's 8 months, just 8 months, old now & has the familiar Thomas puffed innocence about him, lollypop eyes, and nose that looks to heaven. His eyes are blue. If I can find one later, I'll send a photograph of him discussing philosophically with himself the alternatives of crowing or blowing.

As one Daddy to another, what are you doing in the War? I'm very puzzled. When it is necessary, I am going to register as an objector, but also, because I want to get something out of the mess if possible, I'm trying to get a mild job, in the film-writing racket, before conscientious-registration is forced on me.[2] My little body (though it's little no longer, I'm like a walrus,) I don't intend to waste for the mysterious ends of others; and if there's any profiteering to be done, I, in my fashion, wish to be in on it. But my natural, &, to me, sensible, greed & opportunism will unfortunately come to nothing; I'm sure of that: I know a few wires but they only tinkle when I pull them. So I'm afraid that I shall *have* to take the Tribunal. Is there any possibility of getting a soft job in Swansea? I don't know how you feel about all this, but I can't raise up any feeling about this War at all and the demon Hitlerism can go up its own bottom: I refuse to help it with a bayonet. To talk about keeping Hitlerism out of this sink of democracy by censorship and conscription, mystery-mongering, umbrella-worship, atrocity-circulation, & the (thank God mostly unsuccessful *so far*) * [*circled addition:* * how long?] fostering of hate against a bewildered, buggered people, is only to encourage the rebellious pacifism of anti-social softies like myself. *Write soon* and tell me all about the War: I've only my feelings to guide me, & they are my own, and nothing will turn them savage against people with whom I have no quarrel. There's a need now for some life to go on, strenuously & patiently, outside the dictated hates & pettinesses of War, & that life I, for my own part, shall

1 Thomas may have been looking ahead to *Adventures in the Skin Trade*, the book he began to write the following year; Dent were duly disturbed when they saw the result.
2 Thomas toyed with the idea. But even trying to register as a conscientious objector was a serious business that meant pleading before a local tribunal presided over by a judge. Artists of one sort or another sometimes succeeded.

continue to support by my writing and thinking & by living as coolly, hotly, & as well as I know how.

Our love to you all,
Dylan

And do tell me all the news too. I miss the boys & the smoky nights. Here everything is so slow and prettily sad. I'd like to live in a town or a city again for a bit. Let there be one town left, & we'll fill it with ourselves.

MS: Ohio State University

VERNON WATKINS
September 29 1939   Sea View   Laugharne

Dear Vernon,

I haven't written all this month because there's been no news of any importance—only the War—and I've been busy, too, with my innocent stories. I've written to a few people, asking them about the difficulties, you know which ones, but nothing has come of it, and I intend registering as a conscientious objector as soon as necessary.

I suppose you've heard that Keidrych is to be married in Llanstephan next Wednesday.[1] She's a curious girl, a poet, as they say, in her own right, with rich Welsh parents in South America (oil-diving or train-wrecking) and all the symptoms of hysteria. She was here a few days ago & she said that Life was too hard for an artist and I said that for 'an artist' of the sort she meant nothing was too hard, and she burst into tears and told Keidrych to protect her. Keidrych was asleep on the settle at the time. I don't suppose you'll be able to come to the wedding, which is a pity because we will make a party to go over to Ferryside and get silly. Send your rice anyway. Keidrych's parents are making difficulties, will not speak to the Bride, (she's very untactful, & talked to K's mother, who's a hard-fisted old Welsh farming bitch, about colour-values. She doesn't know yet how to behave. Will Keidrych teach her, do you think? He's a very nice chap. He should tell [her], 'One more colour-value from you & into the Ferry you go.'), are talking of disowning their only son & won't attend the ceremony. I am to be best man. Have you got a respectable suit you can lend me, or, rather, trust me with? I'll return it, unegged, straight after the wedding—the next day, really, I can't undress in the church porch. I shall hardly ever, if ever, need a respectable suit again & it would be silly of me to put myself in more debt by getting a new suit for this one remarkable occasion. You're the only chap about my size. Two men could go in one of Hughes's suits, though he has offered me one with tails. (that looks like rails, doesn't it?) I'll take great care of it if you would lend one? Caitlin, who has a very odd creation to wear, with different coloured sleeves

1 To Lynette Roberts.

& frills,—she had it made some time ago, by mistake—promises her personal supervision of the suit. And its neatly-packed, punctual return.

I don't know if anyone else will be there. Nasty Heseltine perhaps—though he's trying to be a bomber. Some glamorous friend of Lynette's (that's the girl). One uncle of Keidrych's, (the black sheep). Mrs Williams from the pub here. Llewelyn, unavoidably.

My Collected Works—or, really, 40 poems & 12 stories—are to be published in America in December with the pathetic title of 'The World I Breathe'. I objected to the title, but was told it would sell like cakes there. It's a title, I believe, based on Gone With The Wind. Did you read my 'Cough' story in Life & Letters?[1] The others in my coming book are all like that, though not exactly. Your *Rough Sea* looked splendid. I read it aloud again & woke the baby.

Have you seen Taig recently? Is there a chance of the show coming off this year?

Caitlin (and I) wants to tell Dot that she is very something or other not to come down and visit us & stay with us for as long as she can bear it. September is by far the loveliest month here. Make her come, please. And when are you coming. I haven't seen you for more than a day & a bit for more than a year or more.

Do see if you can lend me a suit. All care and gratitude too. I've only got a pair of baggy trousers & a damp leather coat.

Love to you,
Dylan

Regards to your family.

MS: British Library

VERNON WATKINS
Sunday [postmarked 8 October 1939]   Sea View   Laugharne
                                                      Carmarthenshire

Dear Vernon,

First: many, many thanks for the supersmart suit in which no moth-holes could be seen and which suited me, apart from a hesitation at the waist, very well indeed. I looked neat, clean, and quite prosperous. It's grand of you to let me keep it: I am now ready for all sartorial occasions, so long as at some of them I can appear in jersey & corduroys & at others in a smart brown suit, slightly open in the middle, with its pockets full of rice.

Perhaps you've been seeing Keidrych; when he left us, he didn't know whether they were going to Swansea or Cardiff; but I imagine Swansea won. If you have seen him, you know all about the wedding; if not, I can tell you that it was distinguished mostly by the beauty of the female attendants, the

1 'Extraordinary Little Cough'.

brown suit of the best man, the savage displeasure of Keidrych's mother, &
Keidrych's own extremely hangdog look & red-rimmed eyes:—he reminded
you of all the old marriage musichall jokes in the world: I've never seen any
one so miserable. The female attendants were really lovely to look at—it
wasn't just my spite. There were two & Caitlin, all with long curly hair,
black, gold, & silver. The clergyman was illiterate & apoplectic.

We're hoping to come to Bishopston for a few days very soon: mostly to
have a bath, as there's no water in Laugharne & I smell like an old beaver. I'll
try hard to get there: it'll be good to see you again & talk & listen.

Thank you again, &
our love & mine,
Dylan

MS: British Library

HENRY TREECE
13 October 1939   Sea View   Laugharne   Carmarthenshire

Dear Henry,
This is a very short note to say how sorry I am for the long delay in writing
and to promise a long news letter this week. There's plenty to tell you. I've
got out of the habit of writing letters, but I must write to you. I'm fairly busy
all the time writing sentimental stories for a kind of provincial autobiography I'm doing for Dent's & which has to be finished by Christmas: not a
serious book. I think it's about time that I produced a purely-entertainment
book now; a series of obscure poems is too much & too thick.

I haven't been sent, yet, any of the monthly magazine reviews—which are
bound to be the most full & intelligent. Life & Letters, Wales, etc. have
delayed their reviews. Here however are a few daily & weekly ones, for what
worth they are to you. Return them sometime. The Cutting Agency shd be
sending me some more soon, & I'll let you have them at once.

I'd love to see the Adelphi & Welsh Nationalist reviews of yours: I'm afraid
the Agency won't send me these, they're very uncommercial papers. Could
you let me have copies for a day or two? I'd be very very grateful. Here's the
Voice of Scotland: sorry, again, it's so late.

I'm compiling an article to be called Objection to War—the objections of
writers etc. who will *not* assist the war in any way. Just General objections
not wanted.

Can you suggest anybody?
I'll be writing with full news & arguments.
Regards to Nelly, from us both.

Dylan

Thanks for the check.

MS: Andrew MacAdie

LAURENCE POLLINGER[1]
14 October 1939   Sea View   Laugharne   Carmarthenshire

Dear Mr. Pollinger,
    Here is the Dent's contract, initialled & signed.

Yours sincerely,
Dylan Thomas

MS: *Texas*

DESMOND HAWKINS
14 October 1939   Sea View   Laugharne   Carmarthenshire

Dear Desmond,
    Thank you for the tribunal talk. I'll be wary.
    I wrote to the Welsh secretary of the Peace Pledge Union. He said that membership of the PPU would be an advantage, as tribunals are often impressed by the fact that one is associated with people with similar opinions. But it wouldn't be of much help to say one joined the PPU in October, 1939.[2] Anyway I'd prefer to be alone. You know, don't you, that a written statement will have to be sent in first, & then read aloud by the objector. If I write a statement soon, in preparation, I'll send you a copy for criticism etc. And you do the same. This Welsh secretary man says that he does not think it advisable—unless one is quite inarticulate—to be represented by a lawyer. I'm getting in touch with a barrister I know, just in case, & will tell you if he tells me anything interesting. I'm trying hard to think of respected gentry to get testimonials from. I know one defrocked bard.
    This Welshman also says that, in his opinion, a few testimonials as to my literary capabilities, invaluableness and/or etc would be of great assistance too—as well as testimonials as to my sincerity & hate of killing. Any very respectable literary testimonialist that you can think of? *Do tell me a few people.*
    I'm afraid I couldn't with honesty *plead* as a Christian, although I think I am one.
    Yes, please, I should like to do some reviews of novels. Any chance of getting some of the novels about Wales that are coming out now—in particular, 'How Green Was My Valley' by Richard Llewelyn (Michael Joseph)?[3] I could do a snappy article. But any novels will do.

---

1 David Higham was in the Army, and Laurence Pollinger looked after Thomas at the agency for the next six years.
2 The Peace Pledge Union was founded in 1936 and grew into a modest-sized pacifist movement that claimed 112,000 members by September 1939.
3 Richard Llewellyn Lloyd (he omitted his surname), 1908–83, published his first and best-known novel, *How Green Was My Valley*, set in an idyllic coal-mining community, in 1939.

Wales will do that little story of mine.[1] Sorry about *Purpose*.

Dylan

Oh, I forgot. I'm thinking of compiling for *Life & Letters* a thing called 'Objection to War'. Objections, not generalised but whole-heartedly practical, of various people, mostly writers. *Not* a Pacifist, proRussian, Mosleyite or literary peace-front, but the individual non-party non-political objections of people like you & me. I think, at this time, when many people who appeared trustworthy are turning out as penny heroes, guttersnipes, rattlesnakes, mass-minded fools or just lazy buggers, it would be valuable. Will you write your Objection—to war, to this war, to any war—briefly. Will Barker write too? I'm getting in touch with him. *Life & Letters* will give the Objection a few pages. Write soon.

Dy

MS: *National Library of Wales*

GLYN JONES
October 14 1939   Sea View   Laugharne   Carmarthenshire

Dear Glyn,
I've thought of compiling, or some other word, an article to be called Objection to War which I hope Robert Herring will print. A collection of individual nonpolitical (but political opinions can colour what they like) objections to war, this war, any war. Objections mostly from writers. Will you write your objection, briefly, and let me have it? I don't mean the thing to be any pacifist united front, but merely the individual views of several people put together. Now, when so many hitherto trustworthy people are ratting, backing out, being heroic or lazy, I think it would be good to have printed, in a good magazine like Herring's, the sincere objections of people who help to keep papers like Herring's going. Will you do this?

Love,
Dylan

Sorry I lost your address.
Can you give me Rayner's?
I had a quick glimpse of your
Welsh Review review, but haven't had
a copy yet.

MS: *Carbondale*

1 'Just like Little Dogs.'

*HERBERT READ

*HERBERT READ
25 October 1939   Laugharne   Carmarthenshire   S Wales

Dear Herbert Read,

I have just been sent Seven,[1] with your review of my book in it. Thank you very very much for the review, which is the best I have ever had, could have, or could want. I'm glad and proud to know that you like my work.

I've been meaning to write to you for some time, but haven't had such an opportunity as now. I wanted to know if you could help me to obtain some reviewing on any paper or papers that would pay. I've been reviewing novels, off and on, in the New English Weekly for a long time, but that can pay nothing and now I will not work unless I get at least a little for it. I have no private means at all, and live entirely by what I write and support my small family, too, by it. I do not know who to approach to ask for reviewing, and I wonder if you know somebody or some paper you could ask for me. I should be extremely grateful. Day by day I find it harder to live; and the war, in which I will take no part, does not help. I couldn't review poetry— shouldn't—but anything else at all. For about a year I did all the crime and detective stories for the Morning Post, and know quite a bit about that. Do you think there's any chance? And please forgive my bothering you. I do really need help now. Thank you again for your review. I should very much like to send you some of my new poems, if you'd care to see them.

                                        Yours sincerely,
                                        Dylan Thomas

MS: Victoria

GLYN JONES
27 October 1939   Sea View   Laugharne   Carmarthenshire

Dear Glyn,

Thank you very much for the letter, and for the statement which I thought was grand, just the thing for this intended collection & probably far more suitable than a possibly seditious article such as the other one you talked about. I'm writing to Rayner & to Savage, & will be seeing Keidrych tomorrow. I've had a little thing from Desmond Hawkins, & expect to hear soon from Barker, MacDiarmid, & H. Read. I do hope Herring *will* print them.

I'm glad your book's coming out—the poems. The Fortune Press do them nicely, don't they? And thank you a lot, I'd love to have a copy. I'm looking forward to it.

I'm afraid there's little chance of us coming to Cardiff for a while: I can't

1 Read's review of *The Map of Love* in the literary magazine *Seven* (No. 6, autumn 1939), spoke of Thomas's 'poetic genius' and 'the most absolute poetry that has been written in our time'.

move an inch now. I'm broker than I've ever been—which means I'm ordinarily penniless but also in debt. I wish to the lord it were possible to get something out of Wales. Things are getting worse here every day.

Love to you & family,
Dylan
& Caitlin

I'd like to send you the more-or-less complete edition of my poems which New Directions are publishing in December.

MS: Carbondale

RAYNER HEPPENSTALL
27 October 1939   Laugharne   Carmarthenshire   S. Wales

Dear Rayner,
  Glyn Jones gave me your address. How are you? I've wanted to write to you for a long time, but for the moment let me ask you this.
  I'm trying to get together, for publication in any unsqueamish paper (preferably Life & Letters To-Day), a collection of objections to war from writers mostly of our age. Not just general objections, but the statements of fellows who aren't going to support the war at all. I don't know how you stand now, but, if you do thoroughly object and intend to stay by your objections, will you write your reasons in a fairly brief statement?—in any way you like, of course. I think the publication, especially in a widely circulated popular-literary magazine such as Life & Letters, will, or might, do, at this time, a lot of good. This is not meant to be a Peace Pledge front, it's no party or union thing at all, just the statements of individuals. Whatever your feelings, do write anyway. I'd love to hear from you. I've had statements from Glyn Jones, Desmond Hawkins, Keidrych Rhys, MacDiarmid, and hope to have them from Barker, D. S. Savage, Durrell, & others. Any names to suggest? This, my dear old Rayner, is no racket, & I don't care a bugger how well or not the chaps write. Objections from *individuals*. Be in the army & see the next world.

from Dylan

MS: Texas

D. S. SAVAGE
27 October 1939   Sea View   Laugharne   Carmarthenshire

Dear D. S. Savage,
  I'm trying to get together a number of statements of objection to war from young writers. These I want to get printed in Life & Letters Today: or, if they become squeamish, in some smaller, independent paper. I don't know how

you feel about this, so, in a first letter, will only say that the objections must not be just *general* ones:—'war is bloody, criminal, & absurd, everybody knows that, & I object to it heartily but I suppose I shall have to do something when the time comes'. Now, more than at any other time we have known, *definite* objections are needed. If you intend *not* to support the war and to take no part in it, will you write, fairly briefly, your reasons?—in whatever way you like, of course. I have written to several people, and have had statements of objection, so far, from Desmond Hawkins, Glyn Jones, Keidrych Rhys. I've been promised statements, too, from Barker, Heppenstall, N. Moore, MacDiarmid, and others. Any names—whether or not you yourself are a thorough objector—you can suggest? I needn't tell you that, if you are an objector, the fact that you contributed to a thing of this sort, in face of public opinion, and against most even of the intelligentsia, will *not* be in your disfavour if, & when, you appear before a tribunal. Glyn Jones told me that he believed you stood with us. I do hope so. Write to me, if you will, anyway.

Yours,
Dylan Thomas

MS: Texas

DESMOND HAWKINS
Nov 2 [1939]   Laugharne   Carmarthenshire

Dear Desmond,
    In your last letter, which I had Friday, you said the novels from the New English would probably have reached me by that time. Not a sign of them—though what sign they are supposed to make I don't know. Will you see what's happened? I want a fortnight to do them in—& *from* the date they arrive.
    By the way, do you know what periodicals there are nowadays which print longish stories? I've got a good one, & I want some crinkly for it.

Dylan

Rayner Heppenstall tells me his novel 'The Blaze of Noon' is due out now. I don't know the publishers. Do you think I could have it for review?

MS: National Library of Wales

RAYNER HEPPENSTALL
November 2 1939   Laugharne   Carmarthenshire   S Wales

Dear Rayner,

I am not 'making a stand against war'—which I doubt was the expression I used; if I did use it, it was for convenience quickly and not for argument, not to be offered as an expression of my own thinking or feeling for you to put into inverted commas and throw back to me; certainly not as a militant priggishness. I am banging no drum for a Right, right, left, or wrong; I am not forming fours to oppose sixes and sevens—to 'justify my existence' (back the phrase comes, dolled up in selfconscious punctuation. I too can recognise a cliché & must let you know, as you let me know, that I recognise it as one) but to prolong it. In asking you to 'contribute to my symposium' I was merely asking you, as a man I know who writes, to let me have your individual objections to war; these objections, if they existed, could take any form; I was not attempting to form a common or rarefied front or backside; because I thought people might like to read them, I set out to collect individual objections from some of my friends & acquaintances. Also, of course, because I wanted to read them; I wanted to know what my friends and acquaintances are going to do when they are told by the State to fight not their enemies [sic]. My own 'stand' is a sit, and it will be on my own sit me down.

I'll certainly use your 'bit of nonsense'—which is what I do believe it to be—and thank you for bothering. Your question, 'who's to stop me letting my rifle off up the colonel's arse?', has only one answer: 'Plenty of people'.

And it's no use telling me, with heavy underlining, that you *won't* have an *attitude* to the war, much less to WAR. I don't care a bugger whether you won't or will: I wanted to know if you objected to war & why & whether you were going to 'serve' or not. My curiosity, I imagined, might have a journalistic interest. Others might like to be told that the only pacifists you come across are sexual perverts (crossed out & tut tut) or elderly ladies worried about dividends. You must have been living in a curious world—and there's no reason why you shouldn't have—to come across no other kinds of pacifists. Those are the kind that Beachcomber hopefully imagines make up the whole 'forces for peace' in this country. Perhaps the only socialists you come across are teetotal fruitarians.

When you come to talk about one's duty as a writer, then *one* can only say that his duty is to write. If to undergo contemporary reality to its most extreme is to join in a war—the evil of which is the war itself & not the things it is supposed, wrongly, to be attempting to exterminate—against people you do not know, and probably to be killed or maimed, then one can only say flippantly that the best poems about death were always written when the poets were alive, that Lorca didn't have to be gored before writing a bullsong, that for a writer to undergo the utmost reality of poverty is for him to starve to death and therefore to be, as a writer, useless.

Three more reasons of yours why you will probably join up are, to me, even more doubtful; and by that I mean that the honesty that made up those reasons is in doubt. You say you may join up because you *could not* cash in on the Ministry of Information. Does that mean you *can* not? Is it any worse to receive a good salary for muddling information, censoring news, licking official stamps, etc. than it is to kill or be killed for a shilling, or less, a day? You say you *could not* work on the land as one of a chaingang. Again, I do not see how that is any worse. One large lot of people is nearly always as 'congenial' as any other lot, & the matey folk-warmth of the trenches can only make for hysterical friendships, do or die companionships, the joking desperate homosexual propinquity of those about to die: the joy of living and dying with a Saturday football crowd on an exploding ground. You say you *could not* languish like a martyr in jail. Why a martyr anyway? The only reason one will go to jail is if a tribunal refuses to register one as an uncondition[al] objector & then if one will not do the services, substitute for military service, which the tribunal enforces. The individual can do what he likes: whatever he does, he is punished. I wanted to know which punishment *you* preferred.

How is the nest of fairies? Dan Jones told me something or other. Nice to hear you're having a baby. You or Margaret? Take no offence, Mr. H., but you said in your letter that you were pregnant. I'll get the Blaze of Noon, if I can, for review in the New English Weekly.

I'm living extremely quietly here, with Caitlin & Llewelyn. No money, of course, and we can't, even if we wanted to, move. I've nearly finished a book of straight, autobiographical stories: Portrait of the Artist As a Young Dog. Dent's give me a little miserable allowance which pays for cigarettes, lights, & coal. We're always warm, but badly in debt.

If you see Dan Jones ever, ask him to write. He's one of my oldest friends, but an angry boor, a conceited fool, and I like him a *lot*. He was down here in the summer, drinking & posturing.

Will you be in London in December? I hope to come up for a week. And is Durrell there too? I'd like to see you very much.

Love to you & Margaret.

Dylan

I'll let you know the hour of my birth after I see my mother. The date is 27 October, 1914. The place, Swansea.[1]

MS: Texas

---

1 Heppenstall was interested in astrology.

DESMOND HAWKINS
Saturday [November 1939]   Sea View   Laugharne   Carmarthenshire

Dear Desmond,
The review. Is it too long? Perhaps my autobiographical introduction should be cut, I don't know.[1]
Can I have Rayner Heppenstall's Blaze of Noon? I've read some of it, & want to give it a good notice.
And have you, by any chance, a copy of Purpose with Muir's review of my book in it.[2] Laughlin of America wants some good review extracts for preliminary publicity to my American book coming out sometime in December.
I haven't numbered the pages of this present review consecutively, in case you want to chop it about. Hope it can stand. It's not v good but I'll get better when I get more into novel-reading—I'm out of practice.

Dylan

MS: National Library of Wales

HERMANN PESCHMANN
November 6 1939   Sea View   Laugharne   Carmarthenshire

Dear Mr. Peschmann,
I don't suppose you've kept them for a moment, & I certainly don't blame you, but:—have you, by any chance, got those few random notes of mine that I used when I talked, a couple of years ago, to Goldsmiths' College? Perhaps you remember them:—notes about Hardy etc. I'm preparing a paper for a Cambridge lecture, & those old notes may help a little. Sorry to trouble you, & if you haven't the notes it doesn't matter a bit.

Best wishes,
Dylan Thomas

MS: the recipient

VERNON WATKINS
Monday [?6 November 1939]   Sea View   Laugharne   Carmarthenshire

Dear Vernon:
I'm going to talk to the English Club at Cambridge on December 7. Not talk, but read poems. I want to read one of yours—what do you suggest?—and some of the very last Yeats, some of those lovely poems you said down here a few months ago when we were walking down a hill. Could you copy a few of

1 The review, 'Novels and Novelists', appeared in the New English Weekly on 14 December, and included notices of books by Frederic Prokosch and Dorothy Parker.
2 Edwin Muir, reviewing The Map of Love, October-December issue.

those Yeats out for me—& also one or two recommended poems of your own. I'm going to read some Hardy, one Ransom, one Hart Crane, one Auden, one Spender, some Henry Miller, a bit of Nightwood, one or two of my own, one decorative Wallace Stevens.[1] Any suggestions? Would you like to copy out a few odd poems, anybody's? But anyway do send the Yeats, & yours.

News in another letter.

Love,
Dylan

MS: British Library

JAMES LAUGHLIN
Nov 8 1939   Sea View   Laugharne   Carmarthenshire   S Wales

Dear Laughlin,
Thank you for your letter. And thank you too, very much, for the cheque. I'm looking forward to having a copy of N.D. 1939, and also to seeing Patchen's new book. It's very kind of you to promise to send it to me.

Here are 2 reviews of *The Map of Love*. Read's review is particularly good, & I hope it's not too late for you to be able to use extracts for advertisement. Will you send back Seven—it's the only copy I have—along with the other magazines I asked you to return when you had finished with them?

No, I haven't been told to fight yet, &, when I am told I shan't. Though whether it's going to be more hell as an assured objector than as a bewildered fighter, I don't know.

Best wishes,
Dylan Thomas

MS: Houghton

VERONICA SIBTHORP
November 8 1939   Laugharne   Carmarthenshire   S Wales

Darling Veronica,
It's nice to know where you are, even though you say no news and may be staying with Aleister Crowley and Thuell Roskelly. You never answered my last chatter letter which was an answer to your letter saying you would be able to come down to see us very soon. That was months and months ago. Now comes a brief note saying nothing out of, if I may coin a, the blue. What have you been doing all the time? How are Archies & Jakes[2] and their mistakes? Have they married them? Write, please, a long letter; and in return I'll send you, as soon as I can get hold of it, a copy of my slim volume. At the moment I've only got my own love-stained copy which I've lost. I'll try to be

1 Wallace Stevens (1878–1955), American poet.
2 Archie McColl; John (Jake) Sibthorp, who knew Aleister Crowley.

brave enough to write to Dent's—to whom I owe a book—and ask them to send you a complimentary copy with a view to you reviewing it in the Taltz Mill Times. Is that really the name of the house? O Christopher almighty who sees each Robin fall, Pooh to you and Pooh to me and swing on my tilty ball.[1] Llewelyn our son is a nice boy: you must come & stay with us, do, and we'll all play with the woozikins. (Oswell & Max,[2] by the way (of all flesh) send me occasional letters still, with cigarette-cards of Hedgerow Horrors from Player's: signed Sister Bats, or Brother Badgers, whatever the card may be. We laugh until we die.) Caitlin, who is well & strong & who just, a few minutes ago, bounced the baby's head on the brick floor like a ball, sends her love & would love to see you: I am trying to finish, by Christmas so that we may spend a Christmas not to be remembered, my adolescent autobiography entitled Portrait of the Artist as a Young Dog. It will, I hope, be out next spring. My only War joke is that I have been thinking of volunteering as a small tank. Really, I am going to do nothing at all. Do tell us everything you know about everything: we're miles from anywhere or anyone here, and sometimes, on lucky days, we're miles from where we are. More elbow to the Power of Love. Write soon.

My love to you,
xxxxx Dylan xxxxx

MS: National Library of Wales

*HERBERT READ
November 8 1939   Laugharne   Carmarthenshire   S Wales

Dear Herbert Read,
    Thank you for your letter. I do agree with you that the mistake is to do any kind of intellectual jobbing—reviewing, BBC script writing—and I am, or was, only attempting to resort to it because I need money and don't want to polish lenses for it. I don't think that reviewing—especially, if one can get hold of it, of popular books—need be a self-destructive activity; it can be done with a bit of the mind, & the rest needn't be hurt even if it is bound to be touched. It's possible, I think, to review, say, novels as a more-or-less ordinary novel reader who enjoys reading novels & talking about them afterwards & who writes down his opinions to increase his enjoyment by getting a bit of money for it. Considerable regular reviewing would, I suppose, prove a bad hindrance; but all I'm looking for is the promise of a few books, preferably not highbrow ones, every now and then. Thank you for promising to ask the Listener people for me. I don't expect anything, but it's very kind of you to try.
    Dent's are sending me a few quid a month, but that doesn't cover much more than milk and rent. And for those quids I've got to turn out two prose books, which I think is a mistake. I've nearly finished one now—a vulgar

1 Veronica Sibthorp's third husband, John Armstrong, lived in Essex, at Tilty Mill House, presumably the address from which she wrote to Thomas.
2 Oswell Blakeston; Max Chapman.

book of stories about provincial life, I mean an obvious book & one that prevents me writing poems. But I'm not a grumbling garreteer and I don't mind being very poor; I'd rather not be, but poverty is not going to kill me, and it's not very bad not writing poems for a bit—there's plenty where they came from. Perhaps that's a wasteful attitude, & I lay it at poverty's door. Being poor is a waste of money, that's my chief grumble at it, I think. I hope something comes of your asking Ackerley,[1] and I am really grateful that you should bother. I hope you will be able to write to me if anything does happen.

Yours,
Dylan Thomas

I'll send you on the poems I mentioned as soon as I can type them. Thank you, again, for wanting to see them.

MS: Victoria

VERNON WATKINS
Nov 10 1939   Sea View   Laugharne   Carmarthenshire

Dear Vernon,
    Thank you a great lot for the present—for the poem and the money. I liked both immensely. The poem, I think, is altogether successful.[2] And thank you for the great Yeats poems; I'll read them all, of course. The poem of yours that you sent with them is a serious failure, I think—I mean it is a serious poem which fails. *The Windows*, I can't say much about it here and now, but I'll be coming to Swansea at the very beginning of December, all being well & I'd like very much to go through it with you then. The fifth verse particularly struck me as ugly & over-worked. The whole poem, to me, creaks & blunders, although some isolated bits I like & remember. It's altogether too ponderous & stuffy for me; it *is* a camphored elegy—mothballs. But don't mind my rudeness, I'll tell you my real & detailed objections to the poem later. They might amuse you anyway. This is a dirty note—I can't find a pen. Better one coming *before* we meet, & that should be on the 1st of December.
    Thank you again for the terribly kind postal order, the Yeats, The Windows (an admiring boo from me) & Life & Letters which I thought had only your poem to redeem it this month; but what a grand redemption.

Very much love to you
from
Dylan

Love from the family to yours.

MS: British Library

1 J. R. Ackerley (1896–1967) was literary editor of the BBC's magazine, the *Listener*, 1935–59.
2 Vernon Watkins's 'Portrait of a Friend', about Dylan Thomas. It was prompted by the photograph—'The face of this cracked prophet'—sent him the previous year; see page 315, Vol I.

JOHN DAVENPORT
16 November [1939]   Sea View   Laugharne   Carmarthenshire

Dear John,
   We're going to be able to get away from here, which is killing us a bit this winter, for a week in December, might go to Ringwood, and would be delighted to be invited to stay with you for a day or two. My previous letters weren't answered, and this is a last request for a little word. It would be nice to have somewhere to go; & we'd like to see you. Do you know Frederic Prokosch's poem, The Dolls? I've seen it in lots of anthologies lately. Do try & get hold of it for Spender-voice reading. I've done an almost *exact* imitation of it which you might like: but you must see the original by its side:

The Molls

I found them lying on the floor,
Male shapes, girl-lipped, but clad like boys:
Night after night their hands implore
Emetic Percies for their joys.

They retch into my secret night
With stale & terrifying camp
And offer as the last delight
A crude, unhappy, anal cramp.

Gently they sigh to my behind
Wilde words, all buttered, badly bred,
And when I dream of them I find
Peacockstein's poems on my bed.

   The real last line of the poem is: 'Small tears of glass upon my bed'. I couldn't beat that & didn't try.

Love to all,
Dylan

MS: Texas

D. S. SAVAGE
24 November 1939   Sea View   Laugharne   Carmarthenshire

Dear D. S. Savage,
   So very sorry. Yes, I did get your letter and the admirable peace offering. And I thought I *had* acknowledged it, so perhaps it's my letter that's gone astray. But most likely I'd meant to write, thanking you, & then thought that I'd posted what I'd never written. But, anyway, thank you now: the contribution to my intended peace demonstration was grand. I'm very glad,

personally, that you feel like that. So do I. I was going to come to Cambridge early in December, & was looking forward to meeting you. The university English Society asked me to speak there, & I said yes—providing you pay my expenses. Then they pleaded poverty, the rogues & liars, & wanted to postpone the meeting, or whatever it was going to be. Fuck them all. Sorry to miss you—I did hope we could have arranged to meet, if only for a drink.

I'll let you know more about this peace thing when it gets going—not many people have replied yet. Thank you for suggesting some names—I've written to Miller.

Yours,
Dylan Thomas

MS: Texas

*KENNETH PATCHEN[1]
27 November 1939   Sea View   Laugharne   Carmarthenshire   S Wales

(12th week of the war
to end war to save my
democramatic Aunty Titty.)

Dear Kenneth Patchen,
    I'd have written before, long before, I've been meaning to write, every day I sit down, etcetera, but my troubles as one of those who is always with us and as one who tries in a temper always to live up to a standard of comfort and pleasure I have never been used to—in my poorest and most nagged days it's my only wealth to remember, with self-deception and envy, those rich days past which never were—have spoiled my natural politeness (another imagined quality of the unborn, never-forgotten past) and pinned me down, like a frog with ideas above his suction, on to a tableful of halfmade stories, semi-white pages waiting for wheedle—'Dear—, I'm hoping that this may move you (though nothing will, I know, but the last dynamite trumpet) to help me, in my present desperate [?situation] with a small [?loan] (big, big, damn your breath) which I will [?repay] instantly, as soon as my ship (if it came home with a deck of poundnotes and a golden captain, I'd blow it up to the sky rather than let you put your HongKong foot or Hottentot apron on the gangway')—old poems, flies-by-night, hack-to-come. With neither faith nor hope, and despising the charity I seek, I'm working quickly and mostly badly on a book of stories so that I may work slowly on poems, and, at the same time, whining, with my tongue in their cheeks, to a few old-fashioned humbugs for enough money to live better than they do. I'm not angry because the large public does not support me; I give the large public very little, probably nothing, and there is every reason against them supporting me. As a

1 See page 11.

public entertainer who entertains very few, I cannot grumble—or, rather, I can grumble but only for the pleasure of grumbling—and must either change my entertainment, take up some other occupation or be angrily content (which I am) with my present one. And I don't want you to imagine me— thank God none of us knows how extremely little the other one ever thinks of him at all, let alone imagines him as this or that—as a whiner *against* people with money; I whine, among other noises, *for* their money, which is quite different. The Welsh have money under their skins and that's all you see of it, their dried and stunted bodies rustle when they squat, their bad teeth chink when they bite on a pinched turnip, they piss a stream of coins which they at once suck down again. (This last cheapness is what I think the boiled string and lobster on my colonel school might say about the Welsh, or about anybody else, at length and with suet pictures. I remember somewhere in Miller's Tropic of Cancer, a man pissing gold coins at a wall, but I've plenty of cracks to grind with Miller.) They're mean. This morning I asked a Welsh farmer to lend me half a crown for a lying purpose and my expectations were realised: I got nothing and a long lie back. He said he had no money, he was very poor. He has two large farms, no wife, no good habits to waste anything on, lorries, a motorcar, and thousands of crinklers in God's hands (in the Bank). His name, oddly or not oddly, was Henry James. I offered him a good lie for half a crown—not 'a good lay' as our American cousins put it, as they express themselves 'over the pond', and mind the inverted commas, Mrs. Ratface—and a good Welshman, that heavenly devil, should stump up readily. I could have told him the truth and he'd have believed I was lying; we respect each other so much for our capacity for lying that we would never insult each other by imagining we were telling the truth. But the roguery, the wild eye (nearly always ingrowing), the sly and vicious tribalism, the imaginative deceits, the revivalist rhythms, the conscience-wallow, the occasional inverted miserdom ('having a good spend'), the comic religious hysterical churning together of false thoughts and genuine emotions (the Welsh equivalent of Irish blarney) are very lovable. You have to put up with them all, and smile, too, smile, if you still want to weep over the Celtic onion. That because Henry James refused me half a crown to waste carefully. Money again. I'm smoking a halfpenny, writing with twopence on sixpence, sitting on three and six—the chair was bought at a sale; the Welsh like sales almost as much as funerals; in either case you're getting something cheap, and in one case, brassbound, you're getting a lot for nothing, even if you get nothing after all, which is a matter of opinion, and that, in my opinion, is precisely what the hereafter is. In Welsh sales, by the way, I've seen farmers buy dirty and warped junk at twice or three times its doubtful value; a Welshman will buy a bargain at *any* price. When I lived in London a few years ago, in the bedsitting-room with the scribbled card on the door, cultivating a number of voices and obtaining at considerable cost the clap and the itch, first at the bottleparty and last to go, paying for the rent and the kippers on the gas fire with a pound a week from my parents, determined to get there, not knowing where 'there' was but having a very good idea, covering with crabs and cracks and wild dirt, with eccentricities I had long possessed but had never, until that monent, been frightened enough to expose and expand, my confusion at the shockingly liberated behaviour of other young men and women two stages further, from the provinces into another conventional life, than myself, enviously scorning the well-poised manner of the intelligent well-to-do, racing against time as though time were another young writer with a suburban home address, but always, in myself, naturally and fortunately thick-skinned and stubborn, I decided never to forget the importance of money and to devote all my spare time to gathering it from other than literary sources, and never to live below the imagined standard I had set myself, and always to live within those luxuries I enjoyably deceive myself into thinking I was born to enjoy. Although I have never forgotten the importance, the rest of my monetary decisions have come to little. Sometimes, indeed, I think I am living far *above* the standard I imagine myself to have been born to deserve; but that soon grows into an unworthy thought, and the wind again, blowing from penniless places, is thick with rich cigar smoke. Now I live only three times above my salary, & still badly, above, that is, what I earn through writing—an occasional drop of milk from Life & Letters To-Day, 10 shillings a poem from the New Curse,[1] love and some stamps from the red monthlies—what I am fobbed off with by (as Charles Morgan would say) friendly conscience-smoothers, what I cajole, extract. I cannot, as Balzac wrote on the bare walls of his attic, write Rosewood Panels on the crumbling walls of this tall, thin, nibbled & neglected, mouseful, sea-staring house, nor turn my water into wine, nor tear the invisible cigarbands off my Player's Weights.[2] Angrily satisified with the shape of things as they should not be, a man used to riches but born poor, I continue to think of money as it moves about beautifully beyond my reach, money that burns and multiplies and smells of hot food.

Interval for thinking of food and drink. Today it is indecently cold & I have no fire in this rotting room. Where are my London plans now? Gone up in the smoke that should be going up the chimney. Now, through some dull work, I'm trying to move towards a respectable financial safety which I must immediately make perilous. I must be moving all the time, even if it's down. But that's more than enough of this. I've got some very thoughtful things to say about money, if I could only think of them.

I had a letter from you, dated Christ knows when, somebody tore off the top of the letter and I'm the only one here who touches my papers—failing very very successfully to get enough money to live on (how am I living then? anyone's hand to my mouth) is my excuse for never having answered it, and so the embroidered money-talk—in which you said that it might be interesting for us to exchange perhaps fifty letters about work and living and then publish them. Yes, I think it would be interesting; at any rate, I'd like to read them. Let's go on writing to each other for a bit and see what happens.

1 *New Verse*, edited by Geoffrey Grigson, no longer a friend of Thomas.
2 A brand of small, cheap cigarettes.

When I read letters I nearly always whizz through the explanatory parts and the arguments and am really excited to know what the person writing has been doing with himself & with others lately, where he's been to, who he's met, what he feels like the moment he's writing, and, if I don't know him personally, what sort of person he actually is, what sort of face has he got, who he loves and doesn't, is his Sex Life a Mystery, has he got any money and if so does he want to share it, where he comes from, what sort of parents did he have, what does he do most evenings, does he know anything about the private lives of film stars, even what he had for breakfast so that I can compare. So if I was reading, in a book, this letter I'm just writing, I'd say to the devil with all the twisted sentences and why doesn't he talk about the things that happened. Or an emotional gush is very nice too. It's like wanting paragraphs and conversations and a lot of moving about in stories, rather than studied settings, atmosphere, and morals expressed without people. I don't know what a reader of a letter like this could get out of it. But let's see what happens, write as we like, about anything or anybody, and if after some time we get the letters together and can find someone to sell them to the public—then let's hope he sells them well and that we can buy another yacht. In that letter of yours you said too that if you get a renewal of your Guggenheim Fellowship you'll be able to send me something for bread and potatoes, beer & cigarettes, bus-rides & cinemas, all the essentials, and *thank you, thank you,* and if I catch a rich widow or write a book in a trance and the Book Societies recommend it then I'll send you something that matters—I've never felt more worldly than today; I want to go on with a poem some time, but it will be all stocks and shares, even if it looks just zoological about bears & bulls; Anna Wickham, a large, frenzied poetess I used to know sold her little poems, & some of them were fine, as she wrote them, for a shilling each to a young relic called John Gawsworth, and once she rebelled and wrote a long, indignant poem about love entitled 'Advance to 1/3d'—and you send me some cigarettes in a letter and I'll send you some cockles. But what I need right now is a lump of money to pay my fare and the fares of my family to Corfu where we want to live for a while with the Durrells and, if he remains there, Miller. I've got to get out of England before I'm called upon to join the army and see the next world or—and that's much more likely—before I object to fighting & having to fight and am sent either to jail or to a working camp (concentration camp, but run on British lines) with a lot of other jesusing, vegetarian, socialist, mother-stuck nancies and fanatics. I want to get out of the war: to America best of all but nobody, possibly quite rightly, will help me to.

A man I wrote to recently about objections to fighting answered that, though he was, by nature & conviction, a coward and a pacifist, as I am, he would probably join up & fight—bayonetting included—because he believed that a writer should undergo contemporary experience to the uttermost. This seemed to me hysterical and pernicious misreasoning. To undergo contemporary experience to the uttermost, he would have to be bayonetted, he would have to starve to death, and as a dead man what use could he possibly be, either as a man or writer. He's a young man, and what's the good of dying for your writing before you've begun? And to call me an escapist is no insult. As far as a country at war goes, I'm hermetic. I want, among other things, to go on working, and I know I can work only in peace; I can't do a Brooke[1] in a trench; mud shells shit and glory will make me swear & vomit, not write. So I want to be where there still is peace, peace at least from the propagating of hate, the enforcements of military discipline, the extraordinarily rapid growth of dictatorship all around me, and the immediate prospect of a noble death ha ha or ignoble detention ho ho as an anti social shirker and—worse still—unrepentant individualist. At a recent London tribunal for conscientious objectors, the presiding Judge refused to register one man as an objector because he refused to fight 'only on *moral & ethical* grounds'. The only two men they totally exempted were: one 'mentally retarded', and one who was already working in an aeroplane factory. Tribunals, in South Wales anyway, still ask: 'What would you do if you saw a German . . . rape . . . kill . . . mother . . . sister?' If you come across, or can think of, any would-be patron who'd like to aid a poet's flight from war to work, mention (without success) my name. Wouldn't American Societies like me to come over, at their expense, and read poems to them in my passionate voice? I can't think why they should.

Now I know what you look like. I don't mean I know what you resemble: you look like a young man with a big nose and an open shirt, suspicious, broad, and rather angry, to me. I'm thanking you for the photograph. The only likenesses of me that I can find are tucked away, scowling, in groups. So, until someone appears with a camera, I'll just send on a photograph that was printed in some newspaper; I've lost the original, though not of myself: I wake up with that, with delight and repugnance, every morning or afternoon.

I'd like you to have this silly letter before Christmas; though again I don't know why. So I'll send it off now—without a word about your grand, exciting book which I liked more than any new book of poems for years.[2] I want to write a lot to you about it, but it'll keep. Thank you for the copy. More, lots more, again.

Yours,
Dylan Thomas

MS: Location unknown

RAYNER HEPPENSTALL

Nov 27 1939   Laugharne Carmarthenshire S. Wales

Dear Rayner,

Just to let you know that I was born *about* 11 p.m. Monday October 27 1914.

1 Rupert Brooke (1887–1915), whose poem 'The Soldier' is an elegy for a dead Englishman sanctifying 'some corner of a foreign field'.

2 Patchen's second verse collection, *First Will and Testament*, was published in 1939.

This would look a very curious note to someone who didn't know why I was telling you.

Hope to see you soon.

Ever,
Dylan

MS: Carbondale

VERNON WATKINS
30 Nov 1939   Sea View   Laugharne

Dear Vernon,
Would you mind forwarding this letter to Taig? I've been asked to do a one-act play here for something or other, & can't think of a play—I want Taig's advice. Lost his address.

We'll be seeing you v. soon now, I hope.

Love,
Dylan

MS: British Library

LAURENCE POLLINGER
December 9 1939   Sea View   Laugharne   Carmarthenshire

Dear Mr. Pollinger:
I'm enclosing the manuscript of my new book: a book of autobiographical stories called, for the moment, 'Portrait Of The Artist As A Young Dog'. About 55 to 60,000 words. My contract of 12th of October this year, says that, on the receipt of my manuscript, to be delivered before December 31 (not less than 50,000 words), Dent's will let me have at once the £45 advance which is the balance due to me in accordance with a contract of March 7, 1937. Will you see to it that Dent's do let me have this money immediately. I am writing to Richard Church about details of the book, but I do not suppose that he is responsible for paying out the money. I must have the £45 *before* Christmas. Actually I need it on the 20th, to pay off large & pressing debts. I don't see why there should be any difficulty about this, do you? Please do stress the urgency of this, to Dent's. Before Christmas. On the 20th.

Do you think you could also buck them up, unless you've already got it, about my December cheque. I'd like to have that always in the first week of the month. I rely on it to live.

Yours sincerely,
Dylan Thomas

From a typescript. MS location unknown

HENRY TREECE
13 December 1939   Sea View   Laugharne   Carmarthenshire

[*In the margin: Sketch of a man in a hat. Below:* I don't know why I cramped this so much. Does it mean that I always sleep on the edge of the bed? Or perhaps the grandmother I secretly lust after had one eye.]

Dear Henry,
    I wish I could be up in London Christmas week, when you're there: I haven't seen a town for 12 months. But I'm afraid we have to spend the holiday with parents, Caitlin's or mine, in Hampshire or Swansea: probably Swansea, with Vernon Watkins and other queer men for company. Do you know Vernon's poetry? Sometimes it is, I think, very good. Always unfashionable, but I don't mean that that's why it's good. How are you and Nelly? Perhaps next year, before being conscripted, I may manage to come up to see you. I hope so. Do you? About this anthology for the Virginia Spectator: I think you'd better count me out. I don't like the company—in print, I mean—of Moore, Cooke, Heseltine, and anyway I'm not an advanced writer in the way that the inclusion of those names suggests. Besides, I've nothing new except straight stories. When is your book coming out in America? Do let me see it. Merry Christmas, and love. There's no news I can remember for the newsy letter I want to write, so I'll have to make up news and write to you quickly. This is only an answer about Virginia.

                                                    Dylan

[*On the envelope:* So very sorry. Just found this in a drawer. Thought it was posted 10 days ago. Try to make up for this by writing soon & at length, with poems etc.]

                                                    Dylan T

MS: Texas

CHARLES FISHER
[December 1939]   Sea View   Laugharne   Carmarthenshire

Dear Charles,
    I did enjoy hearing from you about yourself and the local lads with whom, in the intervals between Fitzrophobia, attempted 19th century dissipation, artgraft, amateur poncing, I condescended to muck provincially about. But the lads themselves are splitting up, perhaps even cracking up. Vernon should write the Glamorgan Lad and tell how, one by one, we reach the gallows, the marriage bed, the grave,[1] Harrow, Windrush, or the Air Force. I'm coming to Swansea, to swell your numbers, in Christmas week, or, if I happen to see an old blind lady crossing Laugharne High Street and I rush to

1 An echo of A. E. Housman's *A Shropshire Lad.*

her aid and later she turns out to be Lady St. Clears and leaves her fortune to the last person who did her a service, earlier. I am, at last, fed up with this retreat, the day has come, the castle and the pretty water make me sick. I want to see our beautiful drab town, I want to have smuts in my eye in Wind Street, I want to hear the sweet town accent float into my ears like the noise of old brakes. Keep some days for us when we arrive; show us round the town; reserve two seats (and one seat specially sawed down) in the Kardomah my Home Sweet Homah. Perhaps Mabeley will be about too, unless he's almost a Warden.[1] I'm glad the Spy Service didn't take you: you would always have given up your papers to Dolores (the password is cocksnap, knock a hundred times on the onionseller's door, his name is Tabash, call him Dickinson) even if they were the wrong papers. I like your standard war joke; you should give the healthier-looking waitresses white feathers. I'm not doing anything about the war; resigned to personal neutrality, I wait until I am called up, and then I will probably scream and wheedle and faint.

There's a story of mine about me and Dan in the December Life & Letters, by the way.[2]

See you all, or both, soon. Love, to you & Fred.

Dylan

We never see the Keidrych Rhyses now. I'm number one on the list, Mrs. R's list, of people who have a bad effect on hubby. That's what she thinks. I tell him bad things about poetry; such as that his isn't poetry at all.

MS: the recipient

VERNON WATKINS
December 13 1939   Sea View   Laugharne   Carmarthenshire

Dear Vernon,

What do I want for Christmas? Oh, that's nice. I want a war-escaper—a sort of ladder, I think, attached to a balloon,—or a portable ivory tower or a new plush womb to escape back into. Or a lotion for invisibility. I don't want a cathedral—you said I couldn't have one—so can I have a dear book? If you like best giving toys or games, could I perhaps have The New Yorker Annual (published by Hamish Hamilton at, I believe, ten & six) which is all funny drawings, half a game, half a book? I should like that very much indeed.

As for Llewelyn, a poem in his stocking is more than he deserves—unless you think, as I think, that everybody deserves everything or nothing. And if you want to add a croaking duck or floating frog, that'll be lovely, the boy is no zoologist and likes, better than anything else in the world, sucking. I can't pretend that he will admire the poem, even if it's grand which I hope and

1 Part-time air-raid wardens were being recruited in thousands.
2 'The Fight.'

wish, but we will. We send our love, and will be coming up next Thursday. My sister is going to drive us. Of course we're looking forward to seeing you: a silly way of saying we'd fly up if we could, before that. But there will be Christmas Eve for us, and we'll smoke your ridiculous cigarettes and buy bathfuls of cointreau, bitter, biddy, or ink. For you this Christmas a record: which? The land, the air, Elizabeth, Trouts or Surprises? Thank you for the New Yorker Annual.

Dylan

I'm so glad you liked the fresh, Dan story. I've finished the book now and have nothing to do but wait for Swansea, marble-town, city of laughter, little Dublin, home of at least 2 great men.

MS: British Library

LAURENCE POLLINGER
29 [probably December 1939]   As from Marston   Bishopston   nr Swansea

Dear Pollinger,
    Thank you for getting the Dent's cheque through so quickly. I'm v grateful. Sorry not to have acknowledged it before.
    I wonder if you'd ask Dent's what so far are the sales of my Map of Love. I asked once before, but someone forgot to tell me.
    Some of the stories I've included in 'Portrait of The Artist As A Young Dog' I want to sell to American papers—New Directions have just brought out my book there, & it would probably be a good time, and the stories, as well, might appeal to some of the better-paying magazines there.[1] Shall I send the stories on to you when they are typed?

Yours sincerely
Dylan Thomas

MS: Texas

LAURENCE POLLINGER
Jan 3 1940   Blashford   Ringwood   Hants

Dear Pollinger,
    Just to let you know that I am staying at the above address for a few weeks. When my monthly Dent cheque comes to you, will you send it on here?

Sincerely,
Dylan Thomas

MS: Texas

1 The *Portrait* book was not yet published, either in Britain or the U.S. The book that had just appeared in the U.S. was *The World I Breathe*.

LAURENCE POLLINGER
Jan 10 1940   Blashford   Ringwood   Hants

Dear Pollinger,
    Thank you for getting the sales of *Map of Love*. I shall blame the war for them.[1]
    The Dent's cheque has arrived: very punctual.
    No, New Directions has not had any sort of a copy of *Portrait of The Artist As a Young Dog*. Do they want one straight away? I haven't got a duplicate typescript, nor a typewriter, and I can't afford to employ a professional. So *what can be done*? I've got copies of a few of the stories which I'll send on to you once I return to Wales—for magazine selling in America.
                                    Yours sincerely,
                                    Dylan Thomas

MS: Texas

VERNON WATKINS
[postmarked 30 January 1940]   Blashford   Ringwood   Hants

Dear Vernon,
    Thank you for typing the poem. And for wanting to get Llewelyn something for his birthday. That's tomorrow. I wish I could have written to you, asking, from him, what he wanted before this, but we've been staying with Joey the ravisher. You will be interested to know that she is appearing in a pantomime—Cecil Beaton's snob show for the troops—dressed as a scarlet & gold satin admiral. She'd knock you cold. Caitlin says that Llewelyn needs most of all: undervests and/or nappies. Is that too dull? she asks. Perhaps it would be easier for her to get them in Ringwood—unless you feel strong enough to ask for such things in the Kiddies' Department, and anyway it's difficult to tell you what size he is. So, if, again, you don't think underwear a very happy present for a one year old boy, perhaps you'd like to send a little bit of What Matters on to Caitlin [*marginal note:* I'm not sure if these negatives make sense] & she'll buy the things & you shall see Llewelyn in them—if you've got eyes that penetrate outer wrappings, or even if Caitlin shows you—when we return to Bishopston in about 10 days time. Llewelyn says Ta to you—*and* ba, da, ma.
    I agreed with your criticism of the 'lubber crust of Wales' but have, so far, done nothing about altering it. Gaels is good, but that sounds to me facetious.[2] Actually, although I thought the pun out quite coldly, I wanted to make the lubber line a serious one, and I'm glad that you like it apart from its joke. I'll tell you, later, what I do about it: I shall probably use Gaels, anyway. Now I'm working on a new poem, a poem which is giving me more

1 Pollinger had written that sales were only 280 copies, adding, 'Pretty discouraging, eh?'
2 The poem was 'Once below a time'. The line in question remained 'Up through the lubber crust of Wales'.

pleasure than I've got out of any work for months, or even years.[1] Yes, the Lawrence calling-up-of-memory in the kangaroo lines was intentional,[2] but if in any way it seems feeble, perhaps a little tame, in such a poem (strenuously resisting conventional associations) then, of course, I must change it. I'll let you know when I come back to the poem. As it is, changing only the word 'Wales' I might print the poem in L & Letters just as it is, alterable bits & all; & then work on it later. I see nothing silly in that. I didn't like much 'I do not regret the bugle I wore' but its omission makes the end too vague. I'll either retain the line or alter it—alter it, that is, in a worked-on version later. I'll send you the new poem v. soon. I've just finished my Portrait... Young Dog proofs. Out in March. I've kept the flippant title for— as the publishers advised—moneymaking reasons. I'll be writing when the poem's finished. Love, & thanks for poem, criticism, & godfatherliness.

D.

MS: British Library

J. M. DENT
30 Jan, 1940   New Inn House   Blashford   Ringwood   Hants

Dear Sir,
    Here's the corrected marked proof.
    In the tablet opposite title page I've put down my first book, 18 Poems, which was not produced by Dent's but by a private firm—& is now out of print. I don't know what the rule of the House is, but I should v much like this title to be included.

Yours truly,
Dylan Thomas

MS: National Library of Wales

LAURENCE POLLINGER
Jan 30 [1940][3]   at New Inn House   Blashford   Ringwood   Hants

Dear Laurence Pollinger,
    Here are 9 stories—from my Portrait of Artist As Young Dog book—for you to send to your American branch to distribute among magazines there. Do you think some of them will appeal to good-paying papers? I do hope so, & I hope the American branch will try: I'm tired of appearing in American highbrow papers that pay with love & stamps. I think some of these stories might go down well commercially.

1 'There was a saviour.'
2 In 'Once below a time', a passage in the second stanza, which includes the line 'From the kangaroo foot of the earth', has an echo of D. H. Lawrence's poem 'Kangaroo'.
3 Thomas wrote '1939' by mistake.

I'll send you on a complete spare proof copy—corrected—of the book, for you to send to New Directions, in a few days.

Somebody told me, by the way, that, if an author's name was down on that Ministry of Labour list your office sent around to its people—the official questionnaire—it would be unlikely that he would be ordinarily conscripted into the Army. Is that true? I doubt it. I'm due to be conscripted in a few months' time, & by Christ I want to avoid it. Do please tell me about this.

Yours,
Dylan Thomas

MS: Texas

DESMOND HAWKINS
Jan 30 1940   at Blashford   Ringwood   Hants

Dear Desmond,

Terribly sorry about the lateness of the review. To make up, in some way, may I give this story to the New English? Five bob, if they can afford it, just so that I can keep up to my promise to myself that I wouldn't write anything for nothing ever any more. If they can't, okay.

Do write to me.

Yours,
Dylan T

MS: National Library of Wales

VERNON WATKINS
Feb 3 1940   Blashford   Ringwood   Hants

Dear Vernon,

Thank you—Caitlin is writing separately—for the present for Llewelyn, who is an intolerable dandy and shames his stained and smoky father. He also had a suit from grandparents, and a musical box, and the most menacing, lunatic doll, half Mervyn Levy, half Harpo Marx, that I have ever seen—with a twitching head and revolving ears—and some napkins and barley sugar and a cake (with one candle) which his cousin ate.

For 'I do not regret' in my much discussed poem[1] I have put 'Never never oh never to regret the bugle I wore' (all one line), so that the repetition, the pacific repetition, of 'I would lie down, lie down, lie down and live' is loudly and swingingly balanced. When you see the poem again, I think you'll like the alteration.

I'm glad Herring is going to print some Llewelyn poems. Little the little one knows. Our family is very proud of the poems.

1 'Once below a time.'

The dim snaps were liked a lot.

Is Dot still with you? We will miss her easily this time. Our love to her & you, and all.

Dylan

P.S.
This all is
shockingly late
because Caitlin
thought I'd
posted it &
I thought she
had. Also
I've been in
bed for 3
days—just
up now—with
a huge cough &
cold.
Write soon, & I
will too.

MS: British Library

DESMOND HAWKINS
Feb 13 1940   Blashford   Ringwood   Hants

Dear Desmond,

I sent you a short story a few weeks ago, for the New English Weekly. Do you or they want it? If not, *do chuck it back*.[1] Someone may pay me for it.

I'm going up to London this Thursday. Any chance of seeing you?

Dylan

MS: National Library of Wales

LAURENCE POLLINGER
13 Feb 1940   at Blashford   Ringwood   Hants

Dear Laurence Pollinger,

Here's the proof copy for New Directions.[2]

I haven't got my New Directions contract at hand, but I remember that no detailed arrangement for payment of royalties, advance etc on my new books

---

1 No story appeared in *New English Weekly*.

2 *Portrait of the Artist as a Young Dog*, which New Directions published in September 1940.

was mentioned. A new contract was to be made for each book. I should like you to stress to New Directions, when you send off these proofs, that, if they accept the book, I require a decent advance on royalties. On the first book of mine that they printed, I was advanced £10 only, which was absurd. But it was an 'advanced' book mostly, & as this book should be much more popular I obviously expect better treatment. James Laughlin will, of course, send his draft of a contract (if he takes the book) directly to you; so please don't forget a nice advance sum.

Dent's cheque just arrived. Thank you.

Sincerely,
Dylan Thomas

MS: *Texas*

LORNA WILMOTT[1]
28 February 1940   c/o New Inn House   Blashford   Ringwood   Hants

Dear Lorna Wilmott,
    Thank you very much indeed for lending us your flat. We left London yesterday, Tuesday, but in such a hurry that I forgot to call at the delicacies shop and leave the key. I hope that, if you did return to London yesterday, it didn't make any trouble. Actually, we found the front door open every night, &, though we closed it, someone else always opened it again. So I don't think my carelessness could have kept you out of your own flat. We left so hurriedly, & with so little time to think, that we mayn't have tidied everything up. I hope not, though, and I hope too that you won't think we're too messy. It was very kind of you. I do hope we'll all be able to meet when we come up to town next.

Yours sincerely,
Dylan Thomas

MS: *Ben Shephard*

1 First wife of the painter Rupert Shephard (1909–92). They were friendly with the Thomases, both of whom Shephard painted in Laugharne, at Sea View (the paintings are in the National Portrait Gallery), early in 1940. Shortly afterwards Thomas was in London, seeking work that would keep him out of the Army, and Lorna Wilmott let him borrow her flat. She and her husband returned to find that Thomas and friends had pawned gramophone, typewriter, cutlery, family silver and fur coat. Shephard said that the episode took place in April 1940, and that Thomas's 'very feeble little letter', complete with false date, was written as part of a retrospective attempt to cover his tracks. When Lorna Wilmott wrote threatening to tell the police, Thomas sent a telegram saying, 'Call off hounds, will restore everything'. After much trouble, most of the effects were recovered.

JAMES LAUGHLIN
March 5 1940   Laugharne   Carmarthenshire   S Wales

Dear Laughlin,

I've just remembered that, very rudely, I haven't yet acknowledged my book, which you sent me. Or the Virgil ode.[1] I thought you made a marvellous job of the book: probably the handsomest I'll ever have, unless, as I hope, you'll do another of mine. The paper & the print and the cover, I liked everything a great lot. You sent me only one copy, and we'd arranged that I be sent six. Do let me have the others soon, because I want to give them away as presents. The book's much admired, and I must give copies to friends. Please don't forget. How is it, or was it, selling? And what kind of reviews did it, or didn't it, have? Could you send me some copies of the reviews, or at least of some of them? I do *very much* want to see them. If you don't want to part with the actual reviews, knowing my carelessness—although I do promise that I would return them very quickly—perhaps you wouldn't mind copying out a few of them, or bits of them: the most interesting fors and againsts. By this time, you'll probably have received a corrected proof copy of my book of straight autobiographical stories. Do you like & want it? It's just about to appear over here; the publisher's very hopeful of it. I'll send you copies of its reviews straight away. Did Patchen ever get the long over-literary letter I sent him? I'd like to hear from him again. Is he still with you? I shall be conscripted in about a month now, and am worried. I won't fight, and I don't want to object. Wish I was well out of it. Do write to me, & don't forget the other five copies of my book or—if you'll be kind enough—some copies of reviews. I'll send reviews of Portrait of The Artist As a Young Dog as soon as they come out.

                                        Best wishes,
                                        Dylan Thomas

MS: Houghton

VERNON WATKINS
March 6 [1940]   Blashford   Ringwood

P.S. The Virgil ode[2] I said I was
enclosing won't fit in the
envelope. Sorry, I'll buy
a big envelope this week.

Dear Vernon,

I'm so glad you liked my lyrical poem, that you thought it was one of my

---

1 Laughlin had translated Virgil's Fourth Eclogue and used it on a New Directions Christmas card.
2 See preceding letter.

best.[1] I'll think of 'stupid kindred', which is right, of course, in meaning and which prevents any ambiguity, but kindred seems a little pompous a word: it hasn't the literal simplicity of hindering man. No, I can't see 'seep' with dust, & unless a better word can be made will remain true to 'fly'. But about line 3 of the last verse, you're right as can be and somehow I must make 'death' the second word. I'll let you know what I can work out. I like the word 'blacked', by the way, in spite of its, in the context, jarring dissonance with 'locked'. I had, quite apart (that is absurd, I mean secondarily to) from the poem, the blackout in mind, another little hindrance on the scene, & the word seemed, to me, to come rightly. But I'll think about it. Your criticism's always terribly suggestive, & in that particular 'death line' you showed quite clearly to me the one big misbalance in the poem. Ta. I'm writing an awkward, satirical poem about war-time London now: a kind of elaborate, rough, angry joke which Keidrych would like a lot. You shall see it, of course; you might like it too, with all the proper reservations: I had to have a change after my austere poem in Milton measure.

And now I want very much to see the long-waited-for Ballad.[2] Would it be too much work for you to copy me a copy? I thought I'd be back in Wales early this month, but I may have to go up to London to see about a possible, but very improbable, job that would keep me from pleading or soldiering. To do with films: I shan't get it. But if I do have to go up to town, it means I shan't be home for a bit of time & I must see the Ballad before that. Do, please. I'm glad you're happy from it. It must be very good.

Has Life & Letters come out yet? I haven't been sent my copy. Thank you for wanting to give Llewelyn the quid from the Llewelyn poems. But Caitlin says he's got plenty of clothes now; and if you'd like to send me the quid, or 14/- of it, you'd save us losing our bed. The bed on which you have slept in Laugharne is being bought on hire-purchase from a shop in Swansea, at 7 bob a month, and we owe them 2 months on it—no, 3 including this, I forgot— and they're going to do something cruel with solicitors unless we pay immediately. And I'm without a penny and hopelessly in debt, here as well as in Laugharne. I think it would be very nice for Llewelyn's poems to save our bed. (Our cardboard bed, do you remember it?) Llewelyn's bronchitis is better, and today he is out in the sun. I'll send you my awkward poem in a day or two. But let me have the ballad. I'll recite it to the collected household. Caitlin's mother is waiting, too, to read the poems to her grandchild: I have only the prologue with me here. I'm enclosing Laughlin's Christmas card.

Love to you from Caitlin & me,
& to your family

Since this—I lost the post—I've been reading the (my) poem very carefully, and have made these slight but, I think important (relatively) alterations:

---

1 'There was a saviour'.
2 Watkins's 'Ballad of the Mari Lwyd'.

'*And laid your cheek against a cloud-formed shell*'. This harder word, 'formed', balances the line, avoids the too-pretty internal rhyme of 'laid' & 'made', & stops the too easy flow, or thin conceited stream.

To avoid ambiguity, & also the use of the word 'kindred', I've turned 'his' in line 6 of verse 2 into 'that'.

In the last verse, the 3rd line now is: 'Brave deaths of only ones but never found', which I believe to be right. Do look at it carefully. For 'fly' in last line but 2 of last verse I have now 'ride'. I'm sure of that: it's mysteriously militant, which is what I wanted.

MS: British Library

LAURENCE POLLINGER
March 6 1940   Blashford   Ringwood   Hants

Dear Pollinger,

Sorry I missed you in London.

Would it be asking too much of you *not* to take out the three quid I owe your firm from my about-to-come March cheque? I want very much to return to Wales, and am relying on the Dent money to get me there. Minus the three quid, I'd have only four and a bit left, which isn't enough to take myself & family back & settle up the few odds & ends I have to before going. Perhaps you could deduct what I owe you either from my April cheque or from any American money—I'm looking forward to having Laughlin's offer—that might come before then? I hope you can do me this favour.

Thank you for your kindness in town.

Yours sincerely,
Dylan Thomas

MS: Texas

STEPHEN SPENDER
March 7 1940   Blashford   Ringwood   Hants

Dear Stephen,

Thank you for writing, and for having written to Marsh. I thought he could do nothing for me, so I was not disappointed. I'll have a medical examination when I have some money, and try to get a certificate. Augustus John has told me that Kenneth Clark, of the National Gallery,[1] is in charge of some film board, and tries to help young men who paint or write; he, John, is writing to him for me. Do you know Kenneth Clark, or know anybody who knows him and might press my claims or whatever is the right thing to do? I hope you do:

1 See page 50.

I'm in such a hurry, and anyway I want a job. Thank you so much, as well, for writing to Eliot: I hope Faber will let me do the selection.[1] Here is a poem you might like to use, or anyway read.

I'll send along another—if you don't, or even if you do, like this one—when it's finished. Probably at the end of next week.

Yours,
Dylan

Don't forget to try to do a little Clarking around for me, if you can.

MS: Houghton

VERNON WATKINS
[March 1940]   Blashford   Ringwood

Dear Vernon,
Thank you so much for the bedsaver; it has. Lovely of you, and one day I will buy you a bank all for yourself.

I've no news. We're just hanging on here until I hear, or don't, from London where I *may* be offered a job, though it's improbable.

I've not finished my satirical poem yet, & have, for the want of satirical feeling, left it for a time to begin an ambitious new[2] poem. Sorry you can't send the Ballad, I must see it soon.

Thank you—I nearly forgot—for Life & Letters; mine came today. The Llewelyn poems were appreciated by everyone; I liked, myself, the Dalai Lama poem particularly. Apart from you & me, I didn't like much in the number, & thought Glyn Jones's story affected & imitative. Peter Helling's got something, hasn't he? Why no Caradog?[3] 'Got something', my God. Am I trying to be a Little Master.

Thank you again, & love from the both of us. News, I hope, soon; & we're longing to return. South England is a flat green plate covered with soldiers.
Dylan

MS: British Library

LAURENCE POLLINGER
March 13 1940   Blashford   Ringwood   Hants

Dear Laurence Pollinger,
Thank you for making an exception, and not deducting from my March cheque the money I borrowed from you in advance.

I haven't been able to return to Wales yet, as I've been waiting to hear from

1 Perhaps *A Little Book of Modern Verse*. Anne Ridler edited it for Faber in 1941.
2 'Into her lying down head'.
3 Presumably Caradoc Evans.

London whether there was the possibility of me getting a war job. I've just heard there is a possibility, and I have to come to town to see about it. Can I be a nuisance again? Will you make another exception? I've had £3, which leaves £4.4.0 (that includes your agency deductions) to come to me next month. Can you advance me that 4 guineas straight away, and take the whole of Dent's next cheque? I may have a little money next month, of my own, but I haven't any this & I've got to get to town. I apologise for making our small transactions so complicated, but I do hope you will let me have, in advance, that remaining 4 guineas. Then everything will be quite clear: Dent's April cheque goes straight to you. I'll be terribly grateful. This job, if I get it, will probably mean a lot to me.

Yours sincerely,
Dylan Thomas

MS: Texas

VERNON WATKINS
March 19 [1940]   Blashford   Ringwood

Dear Vernon,
Here's my 100 line satirical poem.[1] I'm sure you won't like it. Or am I sure? It isn't, by a long something, your favourite kind, but you like all kinds and may appreciate—(not the word)—this half-comic attack on myself. I've got very little to say about it myself: you'll see the heavy hand with which I make fun of this middle-class, beardless Walt who props humanity, in his dirty, weeping, expansive moments, against corners & counters & tries to slip, in grand delusions of all embracing humanitarianism, everyone into himself. The first 'Cut' in the last verse is, of course, cinema. And a loud Stop. The heaviest satire against myself (or the figure I have made myself into) is in the 7th to the 13th line of the last verse. Then, in the very last part, by a change of rhythm I try to show the inevitability of my unrepentance of the charges that the rollicking attack has made. The whole thing's bristling with intentional awkwardnesses, grotesque jokes, vulgarities of phrasing; but I know it *is* a whole thing, & that's *some*thing. Tell me. I shan't alter much of it anyway: it's not the sort of poem to try to polish; in fact, I've tried to avoid most slicknesses, which might have come so easily. This proud talk is only because I've just finished.
   I may be back on Thursday, unless I'm called to town. I'll let you know.

My love,
Ever,
Dylan

1 'The Countryman's Return', published that summer in a magazine, *Cambridge Front*, but not included in *CP*. Thomas caricatures himself as suburban man 'from the mower / And jerrystone trim villas / Of the upper of the lower half', adrift in the 'dirtbox' of the city before returning disconsolately to the 'wasteful hushes among trees' of the countryside.

Could you type all this? I've no-one else to help me in *any* way about poems.

MS: British Library

*HERBERT READ
March 25 1940   Laugharne Carmarthenshire S. Wales

Dear Herbert Read,
   I'm going to be conscripted very shortly, early next month, and I don't want to be. I refuse to fight, but I'm willing to do some kind of work, any kind of work of which I'm capable. I've written to Sir Kenneth Clark, on the recommendation of Augustus John, and he's apparently willing to help me find some kind of exempting work, but so far hasn't answered or done anything. And time's terribly short. Do you know Clark? And, if you do, would you help me, and I'll be very very grateful, by dropping him a line and telling him that I told you I was trying to get in touch with him and that you thought I was the kind of person who should get some work outside the army or the pacifist camps? Will you write to him, even if you don't think I *am* the kind of person? I've no-one to turn to for advice or for anything. Please, if you can help. I'm halfway through a lot of work now, poems and stories, and I know that conscription would stop that altogether, and probably for ever. And I don't want that, either. Sorry to bother you.
                                            Yours,
                                            Dylan Thomas

MS: Victoria

SIR KENNETH CLARK[1]
25 March 1940   Laugharne Carmarthenshire S Wales

Dear Sir Kenneth,
   I wonder if you got my letter of just over a week ago? I sent it to a Portland Place address, which Augustus John had given me, and which was in the telephone book. Augustus wasn't sure, though, whether you still lived there. If you have had my letter, I apologise for bothering you again; but I daren't take the chance that you have [?not] had it. I do hope this reaches you through the Ministry of Information; I wanted to write to your private address, because you must be bombarded with letters at the other place.
   Augustus said he'd written to you and talked to you about me, about my chances of getting a job, any kind of job I'm capable of doing, to avoid

---

1 Kenneth Clark (1903–83), later Lord Clark, art historian and writer, in 1940 Director of the Film Division at the Ministry of Information.

conscription. And he told me that you'd said you'd look out for a job, but that, anyway, you didn't think I would be conscripted. In my letter, which perhaps has gone astray, I asked you if you'd be kind enough to tell me how probable my exemption was, and, if it wasn't very probable, could you help me to get some work, which would exempt me? I'm to register on April 7, which leaves me hardly any time, and if I do have to register it will have to be as an objector.[1] I don't want to do that, because, though I will not fight, I am perfectly willing to do some kind of work; and I think it would be wasteful and silly for me to be made to work at something I know absolutely nothing about and at which I would probably always be inefficient. Augustus told me, too, that you knew some of my writing. I've got a year's work planned out, I'm halfway through a long book, and I do very much want to go on with my work. Conscription, or objection, must, I know, stop that work altogether—objection too, because I hardly think a tribunal, especially in Wales, would pay much attention to my nonreligious, nonpolitical reasons. I know it's presumptuous of me, as a complete stranger to you, to worry you with my worries, but I've no-one at all to turn to, no-one to advise me, and very little time left. Also, Augustus said that you were very willing to help me; and I shall be grateful for ever if you can.

I wrote my first letter to you from Hampshire, where I was staying, and asked you if you could arrange to meet me in London; if there would be a reason in my coming to London; if you would care to see me. I waited in Hampshire until the end of last week, hoping to hear from you, but now have had to come home to Wales. Will you let me know if I shall come to London to see you? Or, anyway, tell me about the possibilities of exemption or any kind of exempting work? I wish I could have made this letter shorter. I do hope you will answer me.

Yours sincerely,
Dylan Thomas

Only source: SL

SIR KENNETH CLARK
April 1 1940   Laugharne   Carmarthenshire   S Wales

Dear Sir Kenneth,

I don't know which of my two rather silly, and almost duplicate letters, you got first, but thank you very much for your answer. I quite understand that jobs can't be found—I wasn't asking for a bogus job; quite willing to work

---

1 Thomas's age-group, consisting chiefly of those born in 1914, was the sixth to be called up, and contained a third of a million men. Of these, 4,772, 1.4 per cent, declared themselves conscientious objectors; about two-thirds of those were granted some form of exemption, mostly to do civilian war work or serve as non-combatant soldiers. Only a handful were accepted unconditionally as objectors, although in that respect the South Wales tribunals were comparatively lenient.

at almost anything—for every poet and painter and dancer: it was just that Augustus had given me a little personal hope. I also asked Herbert Read to write you a line for me, and by this time you've probably received it. I didn't know then that getting a job was quite hopeless, and I'm sorry to bother you with these odd recommendations etc. I'll join up, now, with my age-group, and trust to God and other people that I may get a non-combatant job within the army. My great horror's killing.

Thank you again,
Yours sincerely,
Dylan Thomas

From a typescript. MS location unknown

LAURENCE POLLINGER
4th April 1940   Sea View   Laugharne   Carmarthenshire   S Wales

Dear Laurence Pollinger,
Just to let you know I'm back in Wales, so that any news etc you might have [for] me can be sent direct. Anything from America? I'm relying on magazines there (heard from Ann Watkins?) or on Laughlin, New Directions, for some money soon.

Yours,
Dylan Thomas

MS: Texas

LADY CLARK
4 April 1940   Laugharne   Carmarthenshire   S Wales

Dear Mrs. Clark,
Thank you for your letter. I'm very grateful to Sir Kenneth for trying to get me exempted; I know it must be almost impossible now, but it's grand he had a shot at it.
I should very much like to join your friend Captain Cazalet's lot[1]—I couldn't quite read if you wrote 'battery', and, if you didn't, I don't know if it's the right word—and it would be a nice consolation to be among people I knew slightly, etc. And thank you for writing to him to see if it's possible. If it *was* possible to get in there, would it also be possible, do you think, to get— eventually, of course—a nonfighting job: anything, dishwarden, dishwasher, latrine minder? There must, surely be little jobs in the army, like cook or storeboy. If there's a chance of that, I should far far prefer to be in Captain Cazalet's problematical battery than among complete strangers. *Far.* Do let

1 Victor Cazalet, one-time Member of Parliament, who organised his own unit of anti-aircraft gunners, 'Cazalet's Battery'.

me know, soon, if you can, whether or not I can join them.

> Yours sincerely,
> Dylan Thomas

From a typescript. MS location unknown

LADY CLARK
12 April 1940   Laugharne   Carmarthenshire   S Wales

Dear Lady Clark,

Thank you a lot for sending on Captain Cazalet's letter. You've been most kind to me. This is certainly a great help. I've written to Captain Cazalet, and, if that suits him, will go to see him next week.

I'm glad you like my new book. I've just started a kind of sequel to it—hope I'll be able to get a little time to finish it too.

> Thank you very much again
> Yours sincerely,
> Dylan Thomas

From a typescript. MS location unknown

VERNON WATKINS
Tuesday [?April 1940]   Laugharne

Dear Vernon,

TA for the great pound. I heard it singing in the envelope.

Be an R.A.F. officer. You're too senile to be made to fly, and there's obviously more time to write poems when you're an officer than when you're creeping round corners slow as snails on your motorised scooter.

Ring up Laugharne 3 and say that you'll come *this* weekend. We want you to very much.

TA again, & be sure to come down, please.

> Love,
> Dylan

MS: British Library

JAMES LAUGHLIN
April 15 1940   Sea View   Laugharne   Carmarthenshire   S Wales

Dear Laughlin,

Thanks for the letter; and for the Nation review: far more sensibly serious or vice bloody versa than most I get in England. Yes, please do send on some other reviews as they come, I want very much to see them.

I'm glad you liked my Portrait of the Artist As A Young Dog,[1] and that you want to do it. I hope you can get an answer soon from Dent's about sheet prices, because I want to arrange a contract with you quickly as I must have some money. Since the war, all my little sources of money have dried up, I haven't seen one penny now for over a month and am living on suspicious credit, I'm badly in debt and there's nothing at all coming unless it is from the American sale of these new stories. Do, please, see if you can settle with Higham, Pollinger and Pearn to arrange an advance for me straight away. Things haven't been worse ever.

The stories from the Portrait by the way, have been sent by Higham, P and P to Ann Watkins, who's trying to place them. So it's best not to try to have them placed twice.

I'm sending some new poems to the Southern Review.

Not many reviews of the Portrait have come along yet; the weeklies and monthlies haven't had time, and it's only the once-a-week book pages of government newspapers[2] that have noticed it so far. On a separate sheet I'll copy a few bits from them, but probably they won't be much good. As soon as serious reviews appear, I'll send them on.

I thought I had sent Herbert Read's review, in the little paper Seven, of my Map of Love, but you said it hadn't reached you so I'll also copy out some of it. Read told me that he wrote about me in the Kenyon Review *before* reading the Map of Love, and that if he'd read it then he'd have altered much of what he said.

Doings and plans: I'm writing poems, trying to keep small wolves from the door and trying not to think of the Big Bad Wolf. I registered on April 6 on the military register, and will, if I pass the medical test, join an anti-aircraft battery early next month. Alone, I would object, but there is almost no chance of my being exempted by a Carmarthen chapel-headed tribunal and the most that I could hope for would be civilian non-combatant work: this would pay me nothing, and my family would be left destitute. By going into the army, I can keep them in food, & shelter them. Or the dear government can. I am disappointed that I cannot object, because the Germans are not my enemies, I do not want to die or kill, freedom's only a word and I'm a thinking body. Sentimentally, I prefer to be in the army than in the pacifist camps, to be among other poor buggers having a bad time. I shall be an abominable

---

1 The book had been published in Britain on 4 April.
2 There were no 'government' newspapers. But they had fewer pages and were subject to censorship.

soldier. I hope I shall have enough cynicism to carry me through, but all I can feel are personal loves and hates.

I had wanted to write a sequel to the Portrait: a year in London, but written as a continuous story: the flight into another convention: a proper city book, and far free-er in style than the slight, 'artful' other stories.[1] But this will have to wait, I write very slowly & need quiet & will be able to do very little in the army; after the war after the after lord god almighty perhaps I won't want to do that book at all, and am writing poems now to get them, excuse me, off my chest while there's a chest to get them off from.

I'll send some poems for the next number of N. D. before the army calls and snivelling I obey, and perhaps you'd like to use one of the Portrait stories too: I think the last one's best.

Do try to arrange some advance soon.

Dylan Thomas

Tell Patchen to write.

MS: Houghton

STEPHEN SPENDER
May 6 1940   c/o Marston   Bishopston   nr Swansea   Glam

Dear Stephen,

Just to let you know that this will be my address for a couple of weeks—in case anything comes, & lord it *must* come—out of the letters you terribly kindly wrote for me.[2] This is my father's house & it's very awkward to stay any length of time, so I do hope the patrons unbutton quickly.

I went, by the way, to have another army medical examination, this time in Wales, & was found to be Grade III, which will keep me out of all the main army nastinesses and perhaps out of the army altogether.

Yours,
Dylan

MS: Houghton

---

1 The 'city book' was *Adventures in the Skin Trade.*
2 Spender had enlisted the help of Herbert Read, the critic, and Henry Moore, the sculptor, in raising money for Thomas.

GWYN JONES[1]
May 6 1940   c/o Marston   Bishopston   nr Swansea

Dear Gwyn Jones,
    Excuse my not answering before: I've been away.
    I'm very glad you're going to include my story 'The Tree' in your Penguin anthology,[2] and of course you may do so and I hereby give *my* formal assurance about copyright. The story was published by Dent.
    I don't suppose there's a chance, is there, of my getting the four guinea fee beforehand? Do you think you could try for me? I'm in a very tough spot at the moment, I've had to take my family away from home until I can get enough money to pacify the tradesmen, and every penny I can get in advance for work I do want badly. And after all, the Penguin's very rich. Anyway, will you have a shot? It means a lot to me.
    I hear they're doing a play of yours in the Swansea Little Theatre next week. Are you coming along to see it? If you'll tell me the night, perhaps we could meet afterwards. I hope so.

                                            Yours sincerely,
                                            Dylan Thomas

MS: National Library of Wales

STEPHEN SPENDER
13 May 1940   c/o Marston   Bishopston   nr Swansea   Glam

Dear Stephen,
    Thanks for the letter, I do know it isn't an easy job for you to work out and carry out this appeal. But I misled myself and you when I told you that, as the medical board had graded me 3, I wouldn't be called up for a long time. I've been told now, authoritatively, that grade 3 people will be called up exactly the same time as the other, 1 & 2, people in my age-group—though, of course, for different work: mostly, I gather, noncombatant. It was the first kind of excitement following the result of the medical examination that led me to wish-imagine I wasn't, therefore, wanted for the army. But in your letters, surely none of these details need be gone into: the fact is that I *shall* be called up when the rest of my age-group is.[3] That can be said truthfully and simply; whether I'm called up to fire bullets or peel spuds doesn't, for the sake of this appeal, make much difference, does it? I didn't realise, anyway, that the whole grounds of your appeal would be that I was being called up. I thought

1 See note, page 386, Vol I.
2 In the event, *Welsh Short Stories*, edited by Gwyn Jones, printed Thomas's 'A Prospect of the Sea'.
3 Thomas was not called up. Whether he avoided military service by guile or incapacity has never been established. He told Dan Jones that he did it by turning up drunk for medical examinations.

that the filthily desperate state of my money life at the moment was the important reason for help. You asked for a few particulars:—

I've had to sneak my family away from our home in Carmarthenshire, because we could no longer obtain any credit and it was too awful to try to live there, among dunning and suspicion, from hand to mouth when I knew the hand would nearly always be empty. I've had to leave all our books and clothes, most of my papers etc., and unless I pay our most important debts quickly, everything will be sold up: the beds & china & chairs & things that we've managed, with difficulty, to collect over three years. Now, until some money comes, we're staying here in my father's house: he's a very poor man and finds it, himself, hard to live: we're almost an intolerable burden on him, or, rather, we will be very very soon. I'm writing only poems now, those extremely slowly, and can expect very little money for them. I do not want to write another straight prosebook yet; it would eventually get me some money, I suppose, but it would mean ten or more poems less, which, I think, would be sad and silly for me. And when I am called up, if only to be latrine-minder, I shall obviously have less and less time in order to gain me even a few occasional pounds. My wife & myself have not a private penny. I do, a lot, want to return to Laugharne, Carmarthenshire, pay our debts, find ourselves in our own home again, live there working quietly until I am needed; & then to leave my family there, knowing they are, at least, clothed and housed. My debts amount almost exactly to £70. If I could get £100, I could settle everything & make a new start there: ensure food for the two others for a long time to come. If I cannot pay these debts & have a little to live on, there's no hope at all: everything we have collected and built up will go & I do not see where & how my wife & child can merely live. I cannot go away, leaving them nothing but debts & their lodging in another's poverty. I'd sooner die with them, & this little money worry is making a nervous fool of me when I want to be, and can be, solid and busy.

Thank you & Herbert Read & Henry Moore. I do hope something will happen from your kindness. And I hope this letter explains.

Yours,
Dylan

MS: Houghton

PETER WATSON[1]

June 2 1940   Laugharne   Carmarthenshire   S Wales

Dear Peter Watson,

Thank you very much for sending on the two cheques.[2] I never thought I'd have so much, and was frightfully pleased: I'll be able to settle everything now. As you see, I've gone back to this place.

1 Co-founder (with Cyril Connolly and Stephen Spender) of *Horizon*.
2 Part of the response to Spender's appeal.

You said, by the way, that the £10 cheque came from Lady Clark. Should I thank her personally? I can't, of course, thank any of the others because I don't know who they are.

Yours,
Dylan

MS: *Houghton*

STEPHEN SPENDER
June 4 1940
[extract from letter written at Laugharne][1]

... The results were wonderful ... life's quite different now, and I'm beginning to work like a small, very slow horse.

SIR EDWARD MARSH
4 June 1940   Laugharne   Carmarthenshire   S Wales

Dear Sir Edward,
I've just been given the names of the very generous subscribers to Stephen Spender's fund for me. Thank you, greatly, for your kindness. The result of the appeal was wonderful, I had never hoped to receive such help. It has made every difference to me, settled all my debts and enabled my family to go on living here certain of food and shelter for a long time to come. For your grand help in the past and now, I shall always be grateful.

Yours sincerely,
Dylan Thomas

MS: *Berg*

LAURENCE POLLINGER
4 June 1940   Sea View   Laugharne   Carmarthenshire

Dear Mr. Pollinger,
I wonder if you could get Dent's to send me on the rest of the reviews of my last book. They've been very good about it, & you sent me a lot from them about 2 months ago—or less. But I know that several more have come out lately. I find the cuttings of great value, & *would* like to see them.
I know this isn't the time to think about poetry-publishing now, but would you sound Dent's as to the possibility of reprinting, some time, my *18 Poems*, which was originally published by The Parton Press. The copyright is mine.

1 Spender had this letter in 1976, when the extract was copied, but it disappeared.

I'm wanting to know about the possibility of this, as a man called Tambimuttu, editor of some Poetry magazine & beginner of some small press, has asked me whether he can republish the poems in a very cheap edition. And obviously I'd prefer to have Dent's do them—for, say, 2/- or 2/6. I think they'd sell: I'm often having enquiries about them.

Yours sincerely,
Dylan Thomas

MS: Texas

VERNON WATKINS
[postmarked 5 June 1940]   Sea View

Dear Vernon,
   The first word since the death of our date in No. 10,[1] when pimples would have put us in our places—though I think Caitlin would have frightened them, not frightened them away, perhaps, but certainly made each blush. What a lot of pities we never could arrange longer and noisier evenings: noisy with our own poems, and even with poor Yeats's or done Pound's. ('Well, what do you think of Paradise Lost?' 'It was the title got me.') But we had our moments, I heard Baille's Strand and two, at least, fine ones of your own, we heard Figaro and 'I am' very very high up in the Empire roof, Beethoven accompanied our croquet, you nearly caught us napping on the Worm—and what would a stranger, hearing suddenly, make of that?—and, of course, we carefully missed Dot.[2] Is she still in Pennard? Give her our love and tell her that God must consider us allergic: we don't. Can you come down here soon? You & Dot? You? We've distempered the rooms & made a cosy home: come and sit down, talking, on our deceptive chairs, and lie in the stormy bed of which Llewelyn now, most indirectly, owns half a leg—it was the proceeds of a poem to him, do you remember, that saved it.
   Here's a poem.[3] I showed you the beginning, or *a* beginning, months—is it?—ago in Laugharne. Tell me straight away. I consider, at the just-finished illusionary glowing moment, it's good. I've never worked harder on anything, maybe too hard: I made such a difficult shape, too. Points: (1) I want a title for it. Can you suggest? Modern Love?[4] Wd that be affected? I've often wanted to use other people's titles, & once began my Ode On The Intimations Of Immortality. It is a poem about modern love. For some reason, I wrote a note under the poem in my copybook:

1 A pub near the Swansea town centre.
2 Dylan and Caitlin, staying with his parents at Bishopston in May, frequently saw Vernon Watkins, who lived nearby at Pennard. *On Baile's Strand* is a late play by Yeats. The Empire was Swansea's principal theatre, where they all went to hear *The Marriage of Figaro*. Croquet was played on the lawn at Pennard. On a visit to the Worm's Head, they were nearly cut off by the tide.
3 'Into her lying down head.' The version that Thomas enclosed, printed in *VW*, differs from the *CP* version.
4 'Modern Love' is a poem about an unhappy marriage by George Meredith (1828–1909).

All over the world love is betrayed as always, and a million years have not calmed the uncalculated ferocity of each betrayal or the terrible loneliness afterwards. Man is denying his partner man or woman and whores with the whole night, begetting a monstrous brood; one day the brood will not die when the day comes but will hang on to the breast and the parts and squeeze his partner out of bed. Or, as a title, One Married Pair. It's a poem of wide implications, if not of deep meanings, and I want a matter-of-fact, particular title.

(2) 'Helled and heavened shell'. Is this too clumsy? I like it, but it may be. (3) The longest line in the last verse: is this too—prosy? I wanted a very direct statement, but perhaps this straggles.

Write soon & tell me about yourself your poems & this.

Love,
. Dylan

Will you type the bleeder? It's not so easy to type either. Hope you can see the arrangement of the length of lines.

MS: British Library

SIR HUGH WALPOLE[1]
8 June 1940   · Laugharne   Carmarthenshire   S Wales

Dear Sir Hugh,
I suppose that Stephen Spender has told you by this time of the terribly good result of his appeal for me; he raised more lovely, important money than I'd dared to hope; people's kindness has changed everything for me except the war: now I can live here, working, for as long as I'm allowed, with certain food and shelter for a long time for my family, and sure small luxuries. Thank you, very much, for your generosity. It was very good to think that you wished me so well, and I'll always be grateful.

Yours sincerely,
Dylan Thomas

MS: Texas

CLEMENT AND JOHN DAVENPORT
June 8 1940   Laugharne   Carmarthenshire   S Wales

Dear Clement and John,
I don't know if you're still in Marshfield: Roger told me in a letter just about Christmas that you might be moving. How are you both?

1 Hugh Walpole (1884–1941), novelist.

The author Hughes here is going to Bath, he's on the Admiralty now. His wife wants to go with him. There's nowhere to stay in Bath. I told her you lived—or used to live—a few miles outside, and she asked me to ask you if you'd think of—if only for a week—swapping houses, hers for yours. A week would do fine, or any time longer. She's got a nice house: I hope it's possible for you to come, though I don't suppose it is. Do let me know.

Yours,
Dylan

MS: Texas

JEAN OVERTON FULLER[1]

19 June 1940   Laugharne   Carmarthenshire   S. Wales

Dear Miss Fuller,
I hadn't heard anything about Vicky and Runia[2] for years, until a fortnight ago. Then Pamela Johnson wrote to tell me that Vicky had just died. I was very grieved to hear it: he was a sweet, wise man. Runia's address is 84 Boundary Road, N.W.8. At least, I suppose she's still there: I wrote her a letter, but haven't had a reply yet: probably she's too sad to write.

Yours sincerely,
Dylan Thomas

MS: the recipient

JAMES LAUGHLIN

20 June 1940   Laugharne   Carmarthenshire   S Wales

Dear Laughlin,
Thanks for the last letter you wrote dated exactly a month ago. Yes, do try to speed the agents on the new book contract so that I can have some money. It's getting harder to live here. And what bits there might be from the first book—as you suggested there might by now—I can do with. Hope the agents have heard from Dent's.

Here are some more bits from English reviews. A few new ones, and old ones I found. Some of them may be of use to your collection: how's it getting on? I don't quite understand what it is to be. Copying these reviews out makes me feel like a crab; and certainly no good.

Let me have, please, some American reviews to make me feel worse. I've

---

1 Jean Overton Fuller (b. 1915), author, was a member of Victor Neuburg's literary circle in the mid-1930s. Her book *The Magical Dilemma of Victor Neuburg* deals with the period, as well as with Neuburg's involvement with Aleister Crowley.
2 Runia Tharp, Neuburg's companion.

only had that one in the Nation—was it?—and particularly want to see Aiken's.

I'm not in the army yet. I was passed unfit. I've got an unreliable lung. But I'll probably be used for something. Anyway, we're all in it. Or will be soon. No bombs here yet. Twenty miles away, though, last night.

I'll type some new poems today and let you have them separately. For Partisan Review, or whatever you think best. For the New Yorker, perhaps the poem beginning: 'There was a saviour'. What do you think?

Don't forget money. Try to make it soon.

Yours,
Dylan T

MS: Houghton

LAURENCE POLLINGER
22 June 1940   Sea View   Laugharne   Carmarthenshire

Dear Laurence Pollinger,

Here is a copy of *18 Poems*. I hope you can persuade Dent's to republish it. If they will republish, I suggest that I add *ten recent—& unpublished*, except in magazines—poems, which should help the sale. Auden did the same with his republished first poems (Faber) & the result was very successful: more for the money, & a fine contrast of the new & the old. I do think this would make a good book.

I can, if necessary, send along some reviews of *18 Poems*; by Edwin Muir & others; for the (possible) book jacket.

You will see that the *18 Poems* were published by the Parton Bookshop and the Sunday Referee. All this means is that the Sunday Referee, who were then running a weekly Poets' Corner or something silly like that, helped, a little, to finance the printing of the book. No contract was made, & the Referee, of course, took no royalties &, for that matter, no interest. The Parton Press no longer exists, & the copyright of the poems is mine. I made no contract, either, with the Parton Press. I can get, if Dent's should want it just for safety, a note from the chap who used to run the Parton Shop & Press corroborating me.

I'm not in the army—yet. I took Higham's advice & went before the military board who found me 3. Whatever that will come to mean.[1]

No word from America? I heard from Laughlin a week or two ago. He said that he was trying to find out at what price Dent's would make sheets, of the *Portrait of the Artist as a Young Dog*, for him, but that Ann Watkins & Co. hadn't given him, up to May 20, any reply. I hope this can be speeded up a bit; I need money.

Try to press these 18 Poems plus 10 new poems on Bozman,[2] won't you?

1 Later Higham was unable to remember what his advice had been.
2 E. F. Bozman (1895–1968), editor-in-chief at J. M. Dent.

Yes, thank you. Dent sent on the rest of the reviews. Some very nice, some snooty.

> Yours,
> Dylan Thomas

MS: *Texas*

*ROBERT HERRING
[?June/July 1940]   c/o The Malting House   Marshfield   Chippenham
Wilts

Dear Robert Herring,
  Would you like to use this poem? If you would, I could use a guinea.[1]
> Yours,
> D.T.

The poem may look very sprawly, but it's really properly formed.

MS: *Rosenbach Museum and Library, Philadelphia*

FRANCIS BRETT YOUNG[2]
4 July 1940   Laugharne   Carmarthenshire   S Wales

Dear Mr. Brett Young,
  Stephen Spender has just sent me the wonderful result of his appeal for me. Thank you very much indeed for your generosity. I had never hoped that the appeal would be so successful. Now I have been able to get out of miserable debt, and begin again with money behind me. People's kindness to me, a stranger, has altered everything, made me happy, & allowed me to begin my own work again, knowing that knocks, bills, tradesmen and a hundred impossible calls will not interrupt at every second or nearly so. Thank you very much.

> Yours sincerely,
> Dylan Thomas

MS: *University of Birmingham (UK)*

1 The letter is written at the foot of a damaged two-page typescript of the poem 'Into her lying down head', to which Thomas appended his name in handwritten capitals. It was published in Herring's *Life and Letters Today* for November 1940.
2 Francis Brett Young (1884–1954), novelist.

LAURENCE POLLINGER
[late July 1940][1]   at The Malting House   Marshfield
                                                     nr Chippenham   Wilts[2]

Dear Laurence Pollinger:
   I'm sorry that Dent's won't do the Eighteen and Ten poems.[3] I haven't any
work fit for them to see yet, other than poems, as I find I have to rewrite the
short novel I have been working on. There should be enough, in revised form,
for Dent's to see quite soon.[4] This isn't an easy time to work in, and I find I
have to revise thoroughly everything I do. But there will be some stuff. It's
coming on.
   I think that Laughlin's royalty offers are bloody, and his idea of an advance
preposterous. 50 dollars, about twelve quid, for a whole book of stories that
might sell very well in America, in spite of what dear little Laughlin says,
seems to me to be absolutely unfair. I'm sure another American publisher
could be made to offer a more honest advance than that. However,
I'll probably have to sign Laughlin's filthy contract as, oddly enough, I can't
live without money in my pocket. And the stopping of Dent's monthly
cheque will just about make me sign my entire future writings away for a
guinea.
   No news, I suppose, from Ann Watkins about placing the stories in
American magazines? If she can't do anything with them soon, I should like
to have them back as John Collier has written to me from America to say that
he thinks he can place some of the stories himself.
                                                     Yours sincerely,
                                                     Dylan Thomas

MS: Texas

1 The letter was received on 30 July.
2 John Davenport's house, a handsome building in the main street of Marshfield (which
   is in Gloucestershire; the postal town was in Wiltshire), was briefly a refuge for writers
   and musicians in the first summer of the war, while the Battle of Britain was being
   fought over south-east England.
3 In 1942 Thomas sold the rights in 18 Poems to the Fortune Press, who reissued the
   book that year. The rights had to be repurchased in 1949, before Dent could plan the
   Collected Poems.
4 Dent were asking for the prose book that was due to be delivered at the end of June.
   The unfinished 'short novel' (which was to remain unfinished for ever) was Adventures
   in the Skin Trade. All Thomas's references to 'novel' and 'prose book' over the next few
   years are to the Adventures.

MISS M. CRANSTON (Secretary to Laurence Pollinger)
Aug 6 1940   at The Malting House   Marshfield   nr Chippenham   Wilts

Dear Miss Cranston,

Thank you for your letters. Yes, of course quote Methuen a fee & give them permission to include my three poems in Day Lewis's & Strong's anthology. Do you think you could see if I could get the fees for the poems paid *before* publication? Preferably straight away? I need money urgently.

If you haven't yet written to your New York people asking for a report on Laughlin, please don't bother. I have heard from him, he has sent me the $50 dollar cheque &, because of my present position, I will have to accept it. But I should like to hear about the short story situation: if Ann Watkins can't sell them, I should like them returned to me.

Yours sincerely,
Dylan Thomas

MS: Texas

LAURENCE POLLINGER
[August 1940]   Malting House   Marshfield   nr Chippenham   Wilts

Dear Pollinger,

Here is the contract, signed.

As to clause 15: Laughlin says 'on terms to be arranged', & if, over my next books, his terms are awful—can I refuse them? Because my next prose book might sell well.

Sincerely,
Dylan Thomas

Hope you can get the Methuen fee. And that I can hear about Ann Watkins & those stories.

MS: Texas

VERNON WATKINS
8 August, I think [1940]   at The Malting House   nr Chippenham   Wilts

Dear Vernon,

It shows what a terribly long time we haven't written each other: I've been here for nearly 2 months, and you still think I'm in Laugharne. So I can't come this weekend, however much I want to, and I do want to very much. What a sensational postcard you sent me, & only comfortable, wild Pwll Du[1] on the front. Dot going to Japan & you joining the army; dear God. Have

1 A small bay with a pub and a few houses near Watkins's home.

you joined, or are you conscripted? Do tell me everything about it. And why a motorcycle driver? I know what your motor-driving's like from Pendine sands.[1] I'm not going to say *you're* barmy, but the chaps who engaged you to drive on the public roads must be very strange little men with curling beards & tall white hats. But I want to know *all* about the decision & mystery. Please write soon.

I'm staying here in John Davenport's house. He's an amateur writer & musician, extremely able, weighing nineteen stone. It's a big house, full of books & pianos & records. There are lots of other people staying here too: Lennox Berkeley, Arnold Cooke (who remembers you very well at Repton. Do you remember him?) who are both professional composers, Antonia White, and William Glock.[2] Aren't they nice names? Davenport & I are writing a fantastic thriller together,[3] so I haven't done a poem for a long time although there are 2 I want to write badly: both nightmares, I'm afraid. Oh Europe etcetera please do be bettera.

A great old friend—he's neither great nor old—came for last weekend: Jim Thornton.[4] And his wife. I gave him your address. Perhaps you've heard from him by this time. I hope so.

The other Llewelyn poems are in Life & Letters, are they? I'll get a copy. I want to see them a lot. Llewelyn is with Caitlin's mother at the moment, but we'll have to have him back soon because we both miss him, especially Caitlin.

I don't know what my own plans are. I want a job very badly, because I haven't a penny: quite as a matter of fact, not a penny. If you ever have 5 shillings you hate, I shan't. I've applied for a BBC job, but I think my lack of university will spoil it. It wd be a very well paid job, but boring: making preces (I mean summaries) of the world's news for Empire bulletins.

Caitlin & I go bicycling nearly every day. I love it. I wish you could come here, I wish I cd see you. Do write straightaway & tell me the whole stories. I'll write a long letter by return.

Love from C & me,
Dylan

Remember me to your pa & ma, please

MS: British Library

---

1 Watkins had applied to join the Army's field security police, which involved motor-cycle maintenance. Pendine, in Carmarthenshire, has a beach used for motor-racing events. Thomas and Watkins once tried unsuccessfully to drive a friend's saloon car on the sands.

2 Antonia White: see page 275, Vol I. William Glock (1908–2000), musician later, the BBC's Controller of Music.

3 The *King's Canary* spoof. Davenport had replaced Charles Fisher as collaborator.

4 James Thornton had been a publisher's reader for Dent. He joined the BBC in 1936.

J. ROYSTON MORLEY, BBC[1]
August 20 1940 [telegram]

SCRIPT ARRIVING PADDINGTON BETWEEN 2.30 AND 3
WEDNESDAY AFTERNOON SORRY FOR DELAY. DYLAN THOMAS.

Original: BBC

J. ROYSTON MORLEY
Wed [August 1940]   Malting House   Marshfield   nr Chippenham   Wilts

Dear Morley,
    Here's nearly all the abomination. The last bit of a scene—about a typed
page—I'll send on tomorrow: you'll have it first post Thursday. If this stuff is
really *too* bad, do tell me straight away.[2]
    On the telephone you said this morning that we'd arranged to have lunch
Thursday. Was it just a slip? Friday you told me was the best day to come. I'll
ring you Friday morning.
    Do have this typed before you read it: it will look a little less bloody.
                                                    Yours
                                                    Dylan Thomas
MS: BBC

BBC
21 August 1940   at The Malting House   Marshfield   Gloucester

Dear Sir,
    I agree to the fee of 12 guineas for the broadcast of my script on the Duque
de Caxias; and with the script rights you detailed.
    I should be very glad if I could be paid the fee fairly soon—I have written the
script & delivered it—as I have already had to make one journey to London in
connection with the script & will have to make another journey tomorrow. I
can't really afford these visits.
                                                    Yours faithfully,
                                                    Dylan Thomas
MS: BBC

1 John Royston Morley, then at the BBC, had known Thomas before the war. As editor of
  a literary magazine, *Janus*, he printed a story by Thomas, 'The Horse's Ha'.
2 Morley had commissioned a short script about the Duque de Caxias, to be broadcast to
  Brazil. This was the start of Thomas's career as a scriptwriter.

VERNON WATKINS
[early September 1940]   Malting House   Marshfield   nr Chippenham
                                                                Wilts

Dear Vernon,
  God, yes, how awful it must have looked. But I didn't get the 2 quid. Mad
things have been happening to letters: I've lost one before, about 3 weeks ago.
I think this house must be marked, & the letters opened. Really. The house,
as I told you, is full of musicians, all are young men, not one is in the army,
one has a German name, there *was* a German staying here some time ago,
and there have also been five lighting offences in about six weeks. Perhaps a
lucky censor got your lovely present. I am so sorry, for you & for me.
2 crinklers. And at bank-bombing time too. I thought that your not
answering my letter was because you'd been hijacked into the army. I
couldn't realize *you* were waiting for an answer from *me*.
  I can't imagine Gower bombed. High explosives at Pennard. Flaming
onions over Pwlldu. And Union Street ashen.[1] This is all too near. I had to go
to London last week to see about a BBC job, & left at the beginning of the big
Saturday raid. The Hyde Park guns were booming. Guns on the top of
Selfridges. A 'plane brought down in Tottenham Court Road. White-faced
taxis still trembling through the streets, though, & buses going, & even
people being shaved. Are you frightened these nights? When I wake up out of
burning birdman dreams—they were frying aviators one night in a huge
frying pan: it sounds whimsical now, it was appalling then—and hear the
sound of bombs & gunfire only a little way away, I'm so relieved I could laugh
or cry. What *is* so frightening, I think, is the idea of greyclothed, grey-faced,
blackarmletted troops marching, one morning, without a sound up a village
street. Boots on the cobbles, of course, but no Heil-shouting, grenading,
goosestepping. Just silence. That's what Goebbels has done for me. I get
nightmares like invasions, all successful. (Ink gone)
  I saw, and of course liked for I'd known nearly all of it before, the Llewelyn
poems. Have you any time for writing now? Will you let me see something
new? I've collaborated in a detective story and am just about to begin a short
story. I do scripts for the BBC, to be translated into, & broadcast to, Brazil. I've
got an exciting one to do next, on Columbus. But I haven't settled down to a
poem for a long time. I want to, & will soon, but it mustn't be nightmarish.
  I just looked again at your last letter, and you said in it that bombs were
falling on the cliffs. I hope they missed you. Where is the nearest air-raid
shelter? Singleton?[2] You must run very fast. In this house Caitlin & I have
our bedroom on the top floor, and so far we haven't got up even when the
German machines are over us like starlings. But I think we'll have to, soon.

---

1 The first heavy air-raid on Swansea was on the night of 1–2 September, when thirty-
  three people were killed and more than a hundred injured. This must be the raid
  referred to.
2 Singleton Park, the town's largest open space.

My mother wrote & told me that people are sleeping on the Gower beaches, in barns and hedges. I went to see a smashed aerodrome. Only one person had been killed. He was playing the piano in an entirely empty, entirely dark canteen.

What are our Swansea friends doing? Is Fred still crossgartering fruit and faces? drilling? objecting? I don't hear from him ever. Life & Letter, of course. My father said he saw him in an airbattle over the town, standing in the middle of the street, his long neck craned.

I don't know at all when we'll be back in the ruins. I'll have to go to London so often, once—& if ever—this job gets really going. I'd love to see you before you undrive your motorcycle. No chance of us meeting in London? We've never done that. That would be lovely.

Write soon. Forgive this unavoidable & rude-appearing delay. Sorry, very sorry, sorrier than I can tell you, about the death of the pounds.

Lower me immediately on the equinoctial list of dislikes.

Love from Caitlin & me.
Remember me to your people. I hope the
bombs won't touch the croquet lawn.
We must all play next summer.

Dylan

MS: British Library

VERNON WATKINS

[September 1940]   [postmarked Chippenham]

Dear Vernon,

It was lovely to hear from you. Thank you for the rest of the lost present. It was needed, alright: by others. I'm in debt, & need my job quickly. Perhaps we're both marked. You translate Hölderlin & swear in German to the Home Guards; I have no visible means of support, & have been known to call the war bloody and silly. I hope there's a special censor for our letters: a man who keeps a miserable family on the strength of attempting to decode our innocent messages.

I hope Dot will like Japan. Would she care for me to write to Empson, asking him for addresses of some of his friends? He was there for years, & knows a lot of people. He'd like to. Old Japanese professors. Pale tea & poetry afternoons. I wish we were going there too, I could do with a bit of inscrutability. Europe is hideously obvious and shameless. Am I to rejoice when a 100 men are killed in the air?

Is the Pioneer Corps non-combatant? Was Fred happy about it?[1] Do you know his address? I'd like to write to him, even tho he won't answer. I'll enjoy seeing his war-pictures: the veins of a leaf that blew from a shelled tree; the crisscrosses on the head of a spent bullet. He should do widespread camouflage work, & make Oldham look like the back of a herring.

1 Fred Janes had joined the Pioneer Corps.

I can't do much work, either. I go for long bicycle rides, thinking: 'Here I am on a bicycle in a war.' I play whist with musicians, & think about a story I want to call 'Adventures in the Skin-trade'. I've finished my poem about invasion, but it isn't shapely enough to send you yet.[1]

Caitlin dances every day in a private Roman Catholic chapel.

Remember me to your mother & father.

Don't forget: cover the croquet lawn, bury your poems in a stout box, & don't stare at the sky too much. The wrong wings are up there.

Thank you again. I'll come to Wales soon.

Love,
Dylan

MS: British Library

*NANCY PEARN

20 Sep 1940   The Malting House   Marshfield   Chippenham   Wilts

Dear Miss Pearn,

Thank you for your letter. I'm sorry none of my stories have yet been placed in USA, but glad the editors you mentioned are interested.

Would you tell your American associates that I shall try to do some stories especially for the New Yorker? and let you have them as soon as possible.

Yours sincerely
Dylan Thomas

MS: Texas

BBC

28 x 40   At The Malting House   Marshfield   Chippenham

Dear Sir,

I thank you for your cheque for twelve guineas (12.12.0.); but feel you must have overlooked the payment for 'COLUMBUS', which was written for Mr. Morley's production about three weeks ago. The fee agreed upon was fifteen guineas (15.15.0).

Yours truly,
Dylan Thomas

MS: BBC

---

1 'Deaths and Entrances.'

JOHN LEHMANN
11 Nov 1940   c/o   Malting House   Marshfield   Chippenham
                                                                    Wilts

Dear John Lehmann,
    I'll be very glad to be a contributor to the Penguin New Writing.[1] Thank
you for writing. I haven't finished any new stories yet, but I hope I will have
by the time you've fixed the publishing details.
    I'm glad you like my Portrait of the Artist as a Young Dog. I'm going to start
soon to write a continuation of it: one long story about London.

Yours sincerely,
Dylan Thomas

MS: Texas

M.J. TAMBIMUTTU
Monday 11th Nov '40   Malting House   Marshfield   near Chippenham
                                                                    Wilts

Dear Tambimuttu:
    Sorry I wasn't able to reply before. I haven't been at any of the addresses you
wrote to, & some of them were very slow being forwarded.
    And I'm sorry I haven't a poem for the November number. The last poem I
did I've just sent away somewhere else: before hearing from you. It's a pity; I
should like very much to be included.
    I'll certainly be able to send you a poem or two for the Jan 15th number. I'm
glad you're beginning again.[2]

Good luck,
Dylan Thomas

MS: Texas

BBC
24 November 1940   The Malting House   Marshfield   Gloucestershire

Dear Sir,
    I shall be glad to accept a fee of twelve guineas for the feature programme
on the march of the Czech Legion across Russia in the last war, which is to be
broadcast in your Overseas programmes.
    I have not, by the way, been paid yet for a programme I did several weeks

---

1 The influential *Penguin New Writing* first appeared in 1940. It developed from the
  periodical *New Writing* which began in 1936, with Lehmann as editor.
2 After the first three issues in 1939, *Poetry London* had failed to appear.

ago on Christopher Columbus, broadcast Overseas. The sum Mr. Harding[1] and I had agreed upon was fifteen guineas, as the programme lasted nearly an hour. I should be extremely grateful if you could arrange to have this paid me.

Yours faithfully,
Dylan Thomas

MS: BBC

ROYSTON MORLEY

24 Nov 1940   The Malting House   Marshfield   Gloucestershire

Dear Royston Morley,
   Thank you for your letter. It'll be nice doing another programme. I'll remember what you said. I haven't got much interesting material yet—can't find, in Bristol, any books in which the march is fully written up—but I'm writing to the Czech Legation. If you do happen to come across the name of any book or article, do let me know.

Best wishes,
Yours sincerely,
Dylan Thomas

MS: BBC

ROYSTON MORLEY

[?1940]

Dear Morley,
   The last page. Is this kind of propaganda too sticky? I hope to be able to know soon much more exactly what's wanted. Could I have a script to do without battles, d'you think? Or perhaps with only 20 or 30?

Yours,
Dylan T

MS: BBC

1 Archie Harding was a BBC features and drama producer.

LORD HOWARD DE WALDEN[1]
24 December 1940

c/o Marston   Bishopston   Gower
near Swansea   Glam

Dear Lord Howard

I've just posted to you, separately, a copy of my American book. I thought it had been sent a long time ago, but I found it at the bottom of a suitcase I was packing this morning before leaving here. It's very very careless of me, and I think it must look ungrateful too. And it can't even reach you for Christmas; it'll have to be a very small thank-you for the New Year.

I've left the place I was staying at in Wiltshire for many weeks now, as the friends who were putting us up couldn't afford to any longer. We—that's my wife & myself and our son—must leave here too, straightaway, because this is my mother's house and she can't afford us either. We can put the baby with someone, and then go to London which is the only place I know where there are a couple of friends with spare rooms.

You said, in your letter, that you hoped you would be able to help me again sometime; and I'm desperately sorry that the sometime I do need help again should be so very soon after your last great kindness. I'll understand at once, of course, if you're quite unable to spare anything, at this ghastly time, to someone who can have no claim at all upon you and to whom you've been so good already and so recently. All I can do is to tell you how I'm fixed. We are now quite homeless. What I need is just enough to let me look around for a cottage somewhere in Wales where we can begin again to try to live and work alone. We could, perhaps, get along for a little time in London—I don't know how—but obviously couldn't have our baby there. I have begun a prose book, and will be paid for it quite well when it's finished, but I must have somewhere to live quietly until it is. And I don't think London—even if we could manage to exist there—is the right place. There's sure to be a cottage in Pembrokeshire or Carmarthenshire I could hire cheaply, but as it is I can't even go to look for it let alone pay the first month or so's rent. I believe my book could be good, and I want to write it more than anything else in the world. I'm not in debt now—your cheque settled most of that months ago—so that we could begin without any arrears and shadows, if we *could* begin.

If you were able to help me, I should like very much for you to consider it as a loan to be repaid on the finishing of my book. And, please, I don't mean that to be presumptuous or impertinent. Perhaps I would be able to repay the loan even earlier, as I'm trying to put my case in front of the Royal Literary Fund who have refused me, in the past, on the grounds, mainly, that I am not old enough to need support.

Will you write to me? Your letter will be forwarded to London from this address.

---

1 Thomas Evelyn Scott-Ellis, 8th Baron (1880–1946), patron of music and drama in Wales. The family has Welsh connections.

I'm really deeply grateful to you, and I hope you like some of the things, in the American book, that you haven't read before.

I'm enclosing several poems done during the last six months. I hope you'll be able to find enough time to read one or two of them anyway.

Yours sincerely
Dylan Thomas

MS: Texas

JAMES LAUGHLIN

25th December 1940   c/o Marston   Bishopston   near Swansea   S Wales

Dear Laughlin,

It's my Saviour's birthday today, and I'm reminded of what's owed to me. You never sent my six authorised copies of the Portrait of the A as a Y.D. Nor the reviews of The World I Breathe (which I particularly want to see; Aiken's[1] very much so), nor the pamphlet you were bringing out. For my side of it, did I ever acknowledge the cheque on advance of royalties for the Portrait? I've got an idea I didn't, owing to the bombs. Anyway, thank you. Will you send your things along as soon as you can? I'd like to hear from you, too.

Fortunately I'm not in the army yet. I've been living in London,[2] which is exciting, and writing a few poems and trying to get hold of some money.

Hope to hear soon.

Yours,
Dylan Thomas

MS: Houghton

---

1 Conrad Aiken, American author, in *Poetry* (Chicago).

2 Thomas's movements, never easy to follow, become baffling in wartime. He wrote fewer letters than before, and shuttled between Wales and London, seeking work and avoiding bombs. Constantine FitzGibbon and others thought that he was writing scripts for propaganda films—his bread and butter for several years—from 1940. Theodora FitzGibbon said (in her autobiography *With Love*) that Thomas went to see Donald Taylor of Strand Films on 8 September that year. But the scriptwriting didn't begin until late 1941. Once he was at Strand Films, Thomas was paid £8 or £10 a week, an income that doesn't agree with the poverty evident in surviving letters through 1940 and into 1941. See his letter to Vernon Watkins, 28 August 1941, where he is 'still looking for a film job'.

SIR HUGH WALPOLE
27 December 1940   temporarily c/o Marston Bishopston Gower
                                                                            Glamorgan

Dear Sir Hugh,

I'm trying to get a grant from the Royal Literary Fund. I tried about two
years ago, but I'd published only two books then and the granters didn't think
that that was enough or that the books were good enough. Now I've
published three more, and I've been told my chances are much better—if I
can get one or two strong recommendations. You were extraordinarily
kind to me when Stephen Spender was collecting some money for me once,
and I wonder if you'd be kind enough to help me again by writing a little letter
saying that I deserve a grant.[1] The committee—who've been acquainted with
the details—are bound to see that I need money, but it's going to be harder to
persuade them that my poems and stories are worth it.

Perhaps you'll wonder why I'm broke again after Stephen's fund. All that
that collected went almost at once on old debts for rent & tradesmen, and I've
been living since then with some friends who can't afford us any longer. Now
we're homeless. I must look for a cottage but can't travel to look and couldn't
pay a week's rent if I found one. I was going to go into the army, but the
Medical Board rejected me at the last moment. I've begun a prose book but
it'll take a good time to finish & I've nowhere to live & nothing to live on
until it is.

If you could spare the time to write a letter I know that it would have a
tremendous influence, and I'd be very very grateful. The address is: H.J.C.
Marshall Esq. Royal Literary Fund, Stationers' Hall, E.C.4.

I'm awfully sorry to bother you. I wouldn't if my need wasn't great to me.
I'll always appreciate your kindness.

Yours sincerely,
Dylan Thomas

MS: Texas

H. J. C. MARSHALL (Royal Literary Fund)
January 1 1941   c/o Marston Bishopston near Swansea Glamorgan

Dear Mr. Marshall,

Mr. Astbury,[2] whom I saw some weeks ago, has just written to tell me
that you are willing to put forward to the Committee of the Royal Literary
Fund a further application on my behalf.

1 Walpole obliged with a letter to say he thought Thomas 'a genuine and promising poet
  with, I think, a touch of something like genius'.
2 B. E. Astbury, of the Charity Organisation Society.

The Committee did not grant my previous application, and you told me, in a letter, that their main reason was that I had not produced enough literary work of sufficiently high merit. I had then published only two books. Three new books of mine have been published since, however: two in England and one in the U.S.A. The titles of my books are:

18 Poems (1934)
25 Poems (1936)
The Map of Love (1939) (Poems & Stories)
Portrait of the Artist As A Young Dog (1940) (Stories)
The World I Breathe (1940) (Poems & Stories).

I am collecting another book of poems—which should be ready in the spring of this year—and have just begun a long prose book.

I am married, and have a son aged two.

For the last six months we have been staying with some friends who can no longer afford to support us. Now we are quite homeless and haven't one penny. We are staying temporarily with my father, who is a poor man and not really able to feed, even for a short period, three more mouths. We have nowhere at all to go when we leave here, which must be very very soon.

I need urgently to find somewhere in the country, rooms or a cottage, where I can keep my family and work on the prose book I have just begun. I have a contract with J. M. Dent's, and will be paid for this book when it is finished, but I do not know how or where to live while I am writing it nor how to support my wife & son.

I am medically exempted from the Army because of my lungs.

I have written already to Sir Hugh Walpole, Mr. J. B. Priestley, and Mr. Edwin Muir, asking them if they would be so kind as to recommend my work to your Committee, and I will ask some other writers too to say a word for me.

If they are needed, I could send you a selection of press cuttings about my work; also some articles on it which have been printed in periodicals recently.

My need is really great. I do not see how we can continue to live unless I am given some support. If I can be given money enough to feed and shelter us & to enable me to work hard without the ceaseless worries caused by our homelessness and pennilessness, I know I can produce two books this year: poems & prose. I want to write these books, and to feed and shelter my family while I am writing them, more than anything in the world.

If you want any other details about me or my work, I shall be very glad to send them to you.

Yours sincerely,
Dylan Thomas

MS: Royal Literary Fund

JOHN DAVENPORT
Jan 8 1941   c/o Marston   Bishopston   Glamorgan

Dear John,

I had a telephone by my side last night so I had to ring you up. It was lovely to hear Clement. It was good to see you in London too, and I liked the Queens lunch with rednose and his belonging girl, and shabby humped elegant Pulham,[1] and barmy Archer[2] apologising for eating, and us, and port and mussels. It was grand, just like the old times we never really had together in London. But the second meeting was an absolute daze to me, and I slept in the dark bombed room like a pig and I was obstreperous and over-confident, closing one eye, and weepy and repetitive, during the moments awake. I hope I wasn't too much for you, for a rather sinister countryman in his town club, menacer of Churches,[3] of devious and improbable connections, living up to de Walden's income, the largest host in London. 'So this is what they call a host. I'd forgotten.' Remember that architectural beard at the beginning of the 4 hour lunch? I rang you up the next morning, but you'd gone with Dawes to the country, so we went after lunch, travelling for about nine hours, and some officers in the restaurant car thought I was a spy—me—and asked to see my identity card which I didn't have all because I wore a black hat and because a young Welsh boy in naval uniform was sitting opposite me, copying out his poems on small bits of paper and handing them to me slyly across the table.

After buying a few useless things—did Clement get her salonscene?—the Watson money[4] disappeared, quick as a sardine, and we've been cooped up here, in little, boiling rooms, for nearly three weeks, quite broke, waiting for the second instalment: or, anyway, waiting for little sums to carry us over while we wait. Today the pipes burst, and Caitlin, in a man's hat, has been running all day with a mop from w.c. to flooded parlour, while I've been sitting down trying to write a poem about a man who fished with a woman for bait and caught a horrible collection.[5]

I finished the Czech script, three weeks late, and sent it on to Morley with a rude note, as though it were his fault. The script uses five announcers, and if Archie Harding doesn't fall for that I'll lie down with his wife's hobby. 'War. The shadow of the eagle is cast on the grazing lands, the meadows of Belgium are green no longer, and the pastures are barbed with bayonets. War. War.' Five announcers, and a chorus of patriots crying 'Siberia', 'Freedom of Man', 'Strengthen us for the approaching hour' like a bunch of trained bulls.

I told Clement on the telephone that we were thinking of going back to

1 Peter Rose Pulham, painter and photographer.
2 David Archer.
3 No doubt a gibe at Richard Church.
4 Peter Watson of *Horizon*. The magazine published the poem 'Deaths and Entrances' in January.
5 'Ballad of the Long-legged Bait.'

Laugharne to live, for a time; sharing a house there with the owner of the buses, the garage, the pub, the electric plant, the cockles, and, no doubt, eventually, us. As soon as I can I'm going down to inspect. Perhaps you & Clement will come to see us, once, and if, we're settled?

I know I did apologise, in town, for my not writing after that morning rush away from Marshfield, but I haven't apologised to Clement. All I can say is: I was very muddled and unhappy, and didn't feel a bit like having any contact at all—until the muddles were straightened in my head—with anyone in the place where for so many months I had been so happy.[1] You gave me a wonderful time; the summer talked itself away; and our book was the Best of its Kind or unkind, and Arnold and Lennox and Eric Dawes were fine new friends, and I loved our Club of Bad Books, and Antonia, buttoned, unbuttoned, dame, flapper, was always a charmer and a caution. I had the nicest, fullest time for years. Thank you both.

If I can—and Clement said I may—I'll try to come to Marshfield next weekend. We must do the last pages of the Canary then, and have it published quickly and make some money and enemies.

I heard yesterday from Frank Swinnerton[2] about my application to the Royal Literary Fund. He's on the Committee, but won't be able to attend the January meeting although he's written a letter supporting me. Priestley & Walpole have also written.[3] But Swinnerton says I must try to canvass some of the other members so that they'll appear at the meeting and squash the opposition of the older boys who would rather give compassionate help to a poor old bedridden girl who once wrote an ode to the Queen than to an unintelligible young man who should be earning his living by bum or stamp licking, national service, family name etc.

He tells me to write immediately to de la Mare,[4] J. C. Squire, Alec Waugh.[5] The main thing is to write very quickly, to get them there for the meeting rather than to get them to write a few words; & I haven't any of their addresses. Could you drop a line to Waugh and/or Squire? Where

---

1 Perhaps Thomas was distressed because that summer he detected Caitlin in a love affair. She was infatuated with one of the Davenport guests, William Glock (so was Clement Davenport), and arranged to spend a night with the young music critic at a Cardiff hotel. Covering her tracks by visiting Thomas's parents in Swansea, she sold some of the household effects at Laugharne, bought pretty clothes, and went to the assignation. It was a disappointment, according to Caitlin—'We just lay there and nothing happened'—although they were more successful at Marshfield later. Thomas, left behind in the Malting House, found out, probably from his mother, that a night was missing from Caitlin's itinerary, and for a while he refused to sleep with her.

2 Frank Swinnerton (1884–1982), novelist.

3 The novelist J. B. Priestley (1894–1984) wrote to Marshall (6 January) that he thought it unfair of them to have refused Thomas in 1938: 'his work may be difficult, obscure and not to the taste of most of the Committee, [but it] is taken very seriously by the younger critics'.

4 The poet Walter de la Mare (1873–1956) supported the application, but with less enthusiasm: the obscurity of Thomas's poems ('which personally I think is rather excessive') restricted their appeal to a narrow audience.

5 Alec Waugh (1898–1981), novelist.

could I get hold of de la Mare? It's a bother for you, I know, but if I can get a grant straight away I'll be able to settle my debts. If I don't get a grant, the debtees will have to wait until my Watson comes in. Swinnerton seems to think that de la Mare (who we must have in our parodies, by the way) and Sir Frank Knight wd go *specially* to the meeting if they were given enough warning. Can you help?

How are Clement's angels and devils? Kingsmill-shockers?[1] horned or Samite Davenports?

My mother says she re-addressed several letters to Marshfield *before* Christmas: a registered couple of quid, a tiny cheque from the College of Wales. And you said there were one or two things, askings for anthologies, from America. Do forward them if you can find them, John, as we want the little sums dreadfully to carry us over until Watson & grant. As it is, we can't go out in the evenings at all, can't go to Swansea, buy fags, see a film.

I told Vernon Watkins about Arnold wanting to set songs. Would Arnold like to still? I'll get Vernon to send some if he does.

Much love to Clement, Arnie blarney, and you.

Dylan

MS: Texas

H. J. C. MARSHALL
9 Jan 1941   c/o Marston   Bishopston   nr Swansea   Glamorgan

Dear Mr. Marshall:

I hope you received my letter early last week, in which I applied for a grant from the Royal Literary Fund. I have been worried about it, as Stationers' Hall, E.C.4. didn't seem a detailed enough address, although it was the one Mr. Astbury gave me.

I omitted, in that letter, to say this:

After being rejected by the Army, for which I volunteered, I tried hard to get some work of national service, and, when that failed, mainly owing to my illhealth, I tried to get work of any kind. I tried to get into the monitoring service of the BBC, for example,—a job that illhealth wouldn't bar me from—but my application wasn't answered. So I realised that I would have to live, & to support my family, entirely on my writing. And only when we found ourselves homeless, and without any money at all—as we are now—did I turn to the R.L.F.

I'm mentioning this because I do think that the Committee should know that I *have* tried to make my living by non-literary work, as most young writers have done in the past, and that I still hope I may find some national work to do. My troubles are now immediate—I do not think we can stay here more than another week, and, after that, there is nowhere for us at

---

1 Hugh Kingsmill (Lunn) (1889–1949), author and journalist, another occupant of Thomas's derisive gallery of 'men of letters'.

all—and that is why I am asking the R.L.F. for a grant.

I would very much appreciate it if you would let me know whether my previous letter, and, of course, this letter, have arrived safely.

Yours sincerely,
Dylan Thomas

MS: Royal Literary Fund

JOHN DAVENPORT
16th January 1941   c/o Marston   Bishopston   nr Swansea

Dear John,

Sorry not to be able to manage this weekend to finish off the book and see to the collecting & sending here—or somewhere else—of our goods. I've just heard from Laugharne that there are some other rooms vacant there, and that we should go down to have a look at them, and to reserve them if they're all right, before soldiers or evacuees come along. I must go; although there's no chance yet of my doing anything but promising to take the rooms 'sometime', even if they were entirely suitable.

I've written to de la Mare. No answer yet. Thank you for wiring. I'm glad you think you've roused Squire & Waugh.

The cheque was kind and grand. It will take us to Laugharne & perhaps pay a first instalment on the possible reservation. What writing? It's the only money I've had since Christmas.

About money, all I can say is, quoting, more or less, your letter: If, and when, I get money from any of my possible sources, I do really feel that you ought to have some of it. I'll try, as soon as, and if, the money comes, to give you a share of it; and of any other monies, soon or future, that might, and will, I hope, be coming. That *is* all I can say, apart from: whatever, of course, comes from our joint book shall be all yours. Now, I have in the world only some of the fiver, most of it, you sent me, and a few dim possibilities. I've Caitlin to keep, and a home to find, and Llewelyn to take away at once from Ringwood. We *must* leave here by the beginning of February; it's extremely awkward staying here at all. My gratitude to you & Clement is not 'dim or fading', and soon I hope I'll be able to show you practically. All I don't want you to imagine is that, having partially helped to impoverish you, I am now living in a conscienceless luxury. I am penniless & homeless. Asking me for money seems a not very kind joke now. *My* responsibilities, too, are growing & heavy. I do appreciate your position, John, and I'm sure you'll appreciate mine. All I can do now is to wait & hope. I want to pay you just as much as I must keep Caitlin, Llewelyn, & myself. I hope I can do both, & soon too.

Love to Clement. Remember me to Arnold again.

Dylan

MS: Texas

H. J. C. MARSHALL
16th Jan 1941   c/o Marston   Bishopston   nr Swansea   S Wales

Dear Mr. Marshall,
  Thank you for the form. The post had been held up, and the first form arrived only a day or two before the second.
  I am sending you two of my last three published books under separate cover.
  I see that you have marked clause I of the Regulations.[1] I understood that the first long letter I sent you—plus the added note of January 9—would be sufficient; but if it isn't, I would be grateful if you would let me know, so that I can detail again the causes of distress etc.

                                   Yours sincerely,
                                   Dylan Thomas

MS: Royal Literary Fund

H. J. C. MARSHALL
17 Jan 1941   Marston   Bishopston   Swansea   nr Glamorgan

Dear Mr. Marshall,
  Enclosed, two of my last three published books, as requested.
                                   Yours sincerely,
                                   Dylan Thomas

MS: Royal Literary Fund

JOHN DAVENPORT
27 January 1941   Marston   Bishopston   Swansea

Dear John,
  No, the sneer wasn't justified. My silence has been accidental, not a dignified or otherwise reproof for your Financial Times. We had to go to Laugharne, to see about lodgings for the future, and we've only just come back, having failed to find them. Before I went, I wrote you a letter in answer to your first long one, and caught a bus in such a hurry that I had to leave the letter, with apologies for the silly, careless delay.
  Thanks v much for writing to Sir Frank. I enjoyed his knightly note to you. What is he: author or gentleman? To me he said only that I could take his support for granted—(but not along the street?)—and that my handwrit-

---

1 The applicant was required to write a letter 'stating the *causes of his (or her) Distress* ...'

ing had almost ruined his already failing eyesight. De la Mare has also promised support at the Meeting of the Burke & Hare Peerage. And, thanks, too, for talking to Alec Waugh. I don't know how I've 'offended him in some way', considering that I've never met him. I offend enough people I meet, especially my friends, without giving annoyance to total strangers. I'm glad he wrote to Marshall, but I hated his note to you: 'advise Dylan to write more stories and fewer letters.' I should like to write to the Petroleum Department—what's he doing there? gathering material for another oily novel?—advising 'Alec to write fewer stories and more letters', always supposing that there could be anyone who wanted to receive them. When I want advice from Alec Waugh, I'll go to his brother.[1] Perhaps I did write to too many English authors, but it was at Swinnerton's suggestion; and Swinnerton, by this time, must know the English Literary Scene like the back of his crossed palm.

As you'll see from the delayed letter, I have already surrendered to you all problematical rights & monies of the Canary without a tail. So that leaves a sum which, in time, I hope to be able to pay off.

I'm thinking of trying to live, eventually, somewhere in Cornwall. Come to St. Ives & see the bigbrimmed ghost of Laura Knight,[2] the flesh of Lamorna Birch,[3] the absence of flesh of Dod Procter, and the authentic hole in the wall where Wallace B. Nichols pulls the glowingly alive pageant of history out of his little ear. I know a man who keeps a pub in St. Ives, and might stay there.

I'll try my best to come along on February 7. If I can't come, it will only be because I can't move from here—here where it is growing more intolerable every minute—or can only afford to move Caitlin & myself to another temporary lodging.

I've asked Vernon, whose poems Faber's might be doing in the spring, to send Arnold his songs. Less lumbago to Arnold.

Yours ever,
Dylan

MS: Texas

LAURENCE POLLINGER
27 Jan 1941   c/o Marston Bishopston nr. Swansea Glamorgan

Dear Pollinger,

Many apologies for not writing sooner. Everything's been very muddled for me, and I've been living, or trying to live, all over the place for several

---

1 Alec Waugh wrote to Marshall to 'strongly support' the application, adding, 'I don't like his work and I don't like anything I hear about him as a person. But he is producing work that is respected by people competent to judge . . .'
2 Dame Laura Knight (1877–1970), painter.
3 Samuel John Birch (1869–1955), painter, adopted the name 'Lamorna' from the Cornish village where he worked.

months now. I hope to have those books ready to send you soon. As soon as, in a less temporary home than this, I can get down to finishing them.

Will you send, in the future, whatever is to be sent to me c/o the above address? *Not* Marshfield, Chippenham, which is now a dead address.

I wonder if you could find out for me how my 'Portrait of the Artist' went, as regards sales? And whether there's any money due to me on it yet? I need all I can get, badly.

Yours,
Dylan Thomas

MS: Texas

M. J. TAMBIMUTTU
19 February 1941   Marston   Bishopston   Glamorganshire

Dear Tambimuttu,
Here are some poems by a friend of mine. Will you read them, please, carefully, and consider them for publication in 'Poetry'? I like them a lot.

Will you return the ones you don't want to
                     Veronica St. Clear Maclean,
                     Monmouth House
                     24 Lawrence St
                     S.W.3.

Best wishes,
Dylan Thomas

P.S. I haven't finished my own thing for the next number. Will it do for the number after next? Sorry.

MS: Texas

H. J. C. MARSHALL
2 March 1941   c/o Marston   Bishopston   nr. Swansea

Dear Mr. Marshall,
Sorry not to have acknowledged the R.L.F. cheque before.[1] I've been away from this address, and the letter wasn't forwarded.

Thank you for the trouble you've taken.

Yours sincerely,
Dylan Thomas

MS: Royal Literary Fund

---

1 The Fund made a grant of £50.

JOHN LEHMANN
13 March 1941   Marston   Bishopston   nr Swansea

Dear John Lehmann:
Thank you for writing, and for wanting to know about my new book. I'm afraid I haven't got anything much of it done; I'm still looking for somewhere to live on extremely little—do you know of anywhere?—and have been so homeless and penniless and uncertain lately that I've only been able to write little bits of the story; I hope very soon to find a place to live in, really to live in for perhaps even two months, and then I can get it going. I'll let you know as soon as there's enough to print. I'm very glad you want it for New Writing. Staying, on sufferance, with parents and unfortunate friends, wanting to get away but quite unable, it's hard, I find, to settle to writing anything continuous.
And I'm very glad that you want to print some of the stories from Portrait of the Artist As A Young Dog. I wish I had sent some of them to you in the first place. I'd like, a lot, to see them come out in New Writing. Will you let me know which ones you're thinking of printing? I'm sure Dent won't raise any objection. The book sold hardly at all. Three or four hundred copies, I think. And if Dent do agree, any chance of a few quid soon?
I don't know when I'll be in town next, but I'll drop a line to Atheneum Court when I do come. I'd like to see you.

                                        Sincerely,
                                        Dylan Thomas

MS: Texas

CLEMENT DAVENPORT
April 2 [1941]   Marston   Bishopston   Glamorgan

Dear Clement,
Sorry to write only when we want things. I owe you and John a letter or letters, among other things. But I'm awfully busy with a long poem, and I've just borrowed this typewriter to type out the never-ending Canary, God moult it, and I'm helping about the house, shuffling and breaking, and I think that unless I'm careful and lucky the boys of the Government will get me making munitions. I wish I could get a real job and avoid that. Clocking in, turning a screw, winding a wheel, doing something to a cog, lunching in the canteen, every cartridge case means one less Jerry, bless all the sergeants the short and the tall bless em all blast em all,[1] evenings in the factory rest centre, snooker and cocoa, then bugs in digs and then clocking in and turning and winding and hammering to help to kill another stranger, deary me I'd rather be a poet anyday and live on guile and beer.

1 'Bless 'em all, bless 'em all, the long and the short and the tall', etc, was a 1940 song
(Jimmy Hughes and Frank Lake) about fighting men.

In the pink bedroom we slept in and stored apples in and knocked about, you'll find unless they've moved a number of, I think, red small exercisebooks full of my old poems and stories. Would it be a lot of trouble for you to send them to me? I mean, will you? I've got a chance of selling all my mss,[1] for about the price of two large Player's after the next budget, and it's easier, and more honest too, to send the real mss rather than to copy out the copies in different coloured inks and with elaborate and ostentatiously inspired corrections. Will you send them here, and not to Laugharne as we haven't reached there yet though we should very shortly. I've got to send them off in the next few days. Thanks very much.

How's everything? Give my love to Arnold, if he's still with you, and tell him that the weather down here is quite middling and sometimes we have rain and sometimes we don't. I'm going to write to him soon, too. Love to yourself,

Dylan

I'm sending a note to John the same time as this.

MS: Texas

JOHN LEHMANN
April 3 1941   Marston   Bishopston   Glam

Dear John Lehmann:
I'm very glad Dent's okayed the stories for New Writing. Hope I'll get my 75% in time.

I don't know what to put in Notes on Writers, about myself. Will just this do: '26 year old poet & short story writer, born & living in South Wales. Author of 18 Poems, 25 Poems, The Map of Love, Portrait of the Artist As A Young Dog, and, in America, The World I Breathe, a collection of poems and of several stories not published in the English volumes. Contributor to periodicals in England, U.S.A., South America, & France.'

It's very feeble.

Yours,
Dylan Thomas

MS: Texas

1 See page 542.

BERTRAM ROTA
8 April 1941   Marston   Bishopston   Glamorgan

Dear Mr. Rota,[1]

Thank you for your letter. I am very interested in selling my manu-scripts.[2] The trouble is that most of my poems I write into exercise books, and that each exercise book contains a lot of poems, including utter failures that I shall never print. The same goes for my stories. If you would care for me to send a few of these books along, I'd be delighted. I think it would be a pity to disfigure the books by tearing a few poems out. I do not know, of course, if there would be a market for such work in bulk, as it were. Will you let me know soon? I should like to sell them, if possible, as I am in need of money.

In the meantime I enclose, for your offer, a small group of manuscripts: five poems and a story.

Yours very truly,
Dylan Thomas

PS. I have almost completed what I think is my best work so far: a long Ballad, which *Horizon* is printing next month.[3] The manuscript of that, comprising a great deal of drafts, corrections, & alterations, is certainly the most interesting I have. Perhaps you would tell me if you'd like to see this, too?

D.T.

MS: Texas

CLEMENT DAVENPORT
23 April [1941]   Marston   Bishopston   Glam

Dear Clement,

Sorry not to have thanked you before for sending on my manuscript books. I wanted to write to you from Laugharne, and so put it off every day. Now we won't be in Laugharne until, definitely, the end of the month. No, May the second. Caitlin says: Will you send the gramophone & the records

1 The name of Rota, a London dealer in books and manuscripts, had been removed from the holograph before it reached Texas.
2 Thomas sold Rota the core of his early manuscripts, in the form of four exercise books containing poems, and one with stories. Other similar notebooks with early poems are known to have existed; they may have been lost before this date, although they must still have been in his possession a couple of years earlier, because he incorporated Notebook poems, otherwise unknown, in the *Portrait* stories. Rota sold the five notebooks, together with other manuscripts, to the Lockwood Library of the State University of New York at Buffalo. The library paid Rota just over $140. Whatever Thomas received, it was far less than that.
3 'Ballad of the Long-legged Bait'.

on to her, c/o Laugharne Castle, Laugharne, Carmarthenshire, because she says how nice it would be to have it there when we arrived.[1] Will be very grateful. How are you? and how is John? I haven't heard from him yet. Vernon Watkins hasn't heard from him either, and wants to know very much if John still wants him to go up to talk in Repton.[2]

I envy you terribly the dream of Mexico City. All I can see is a high-explosive factory on the horizon. I met a man yesterday who worked in a high-explosive factory in the last war, & he said, 'Oh, don't you worry about it. Everything's all right. I lost the sight of my right eye but I got the O.B.E.'

Love to Arnold, to whom I still haven't written a promised letter, if he's still with you.

Love to you from Cat & myself. Will we see you one day?

Dylan

MS: Texas

JOHN DAVENPORT
25? April 1941   Marston   Bishopston   Glam

Dear John,

Deeply, really distressed to hear about poor, dear, old Roger.[3] Although I hadn't seen him for more than two years, and wasn't likely to see him for years to come, if ever, I've always known that he was about somewhere with his little eyes and his cigarette, calm and treble in the middle of the crumbling system; I knew that he was always somewhere, perhaps driving a Bugatti with the radio full on, or riding a ladies' broken bicycle. It was nice to know that one always *could* see him. Now I find that, straightaway after your letter, I miss him an awful lot. I can understand how upset you are. You won't forget, will you, to let me know how he died, and as much of the why as we'll ever be able to know.

There won't, I suppose, be a single obituary line anywhere. I think we should do something, John. It may be silly, but I think it would be right. A letter—New Statesman?—saying that there are so many deaths now that the death of Roger Roughton will perhaps pass unnoticed, and that we, the undersigned, don't want it to. We could say that his paper[4] was the most lively & original for years and years. We could say just a few things about him, his work for the Communist Party, his publishing, his parties, his

1 The Thomases had arranged to stay with Frances Hughes in Laugharne while Richard Hughes was away at the war.
2 Repton was the public school where Watkins had been educated. Davenport, no longer affluent, probably taught there for a few terms. He taught at Stowe for a year from autumn 1941.
3 Roughton had committed suicide in Ireland.
4 *Contemporary Poetry and Prose.*

poems, himself. And get a few chaps—Bert Lloyd,[1] maybe Enoch Soames, & Henry Moore, you'll know who to get—to put their names. What d'you think? You'll know better than I would. Roger shouldn't be allowed to pass out, in the middle of a bad war, in dirty Dublin, without his friends publicly recording it and their gratitude to him. We should do it quickly, too. Do let me hear from you very very soon.

I've nearly finished the Canary typing now. I'd have been quicker, but have had to borrow Vernon's typewriter for short, irregular periods. Can you send me, or ask Clement to send me, the last few pages of the last part? Do you remember, we did a little that pre-Repton weekend? In small exercise books. I wrote about half a dozen pages, nearly up to the Blackpool dinner from which Chronos escapes. The exercisebook is probably in the pub room somewhere. When I've finished all the typing, & the quick end of the book, I'll write or wire you, & then perhaps you'll be able to ask me up to Repton & we can correct it all.

I told Vernon that a stamped envelope to him had probably been on your desk for weeks. He quite understood. Faber's are bringing out his poems this year. I'm very glad. Provisionally titled 'Gratitude of a Leper', though I'm not quite sure myself.[2]

I've just finished my ballad. Too late, unfortunately, for the May Horizon. It's about 220 lines long, a tremendous effort for me, & is *really* a ballad. I think you'll like it. At the moment, I think it's the best I've done.

I'll write to Antonia today about the script. Thanks.

Sorry not to have written before, about a number of things. I'll get them in order, and tell them to you very soon. Now I want to get this off so that we can pay our tribute to Roger.

I wish I knew what your life in Repton was like. Mine here is almost intolerable. We're leaving on May 2 to stay some weeks in Laugharne. Caitlin thanks you very much for the gramophone, and for the arrangements you're making. She's having a worse time here than I am; at least I have my corner and my web.

> Love from us both.
> Dylan

MS: Texas

BERTRAM ROTA
May 5 1941   Laugharne Castle   Laugharne   Carmarthenshire

Dear Mr. Rota:

Can you tell me what modern novelists' first editions are worth selling now? I should like to get rid of some of mine, which include William

1 A. L. Lloyd, folk-singer and musicologist.
2 It appeared as *Ballad of the Mari Lwyd*.

Faulkner, Richard Hughes—High Wind in Jamaica, and the plays—H. G. Wells—first private printing, in New York, of the Country of the Blind—Evelyn Waugh etc. But I have a lot of first edition novels, and would be very glad to hear which names might fetch money nowadays. I'd also be extremely obliged if you would tell me whether you would be prepared to buy any of them. I shall send you, if I may, some more of my own mss very shortly.

Yours sincerely,
Dylan Thomas

I am not sure if I acknowledged your last letter, and the enclosed money. I have been moving to the above address since then, and may have forgotten. Anyway, thanks very much.

From a typescript. MS location unknown

ARCHIE HARDING (BBC)
May 6 1941   Laugharne Castle   Laugharne   Carmarthenshire

Dear Mr. Harding:
      Thank you very much for your long, and extremely helpful, letter about the amount of backing the B.B.C. could give me if they were questioned by the Ministry of Labour as to whether I was doing any work for you that could be called valuable. I understand, naturally, that you could not support me *in full*; but what you said in your letter, and what you said you could say to the Ministry of Labour if necessary, will, I hope, do the trick:—that is, keep me for a while longer out of the factories.
      Thank you for sending on the reports from the Czech Legation. I'm afraid I found them pretty useless: just dry accounts, with no personal detail to speak of, of the taking of towns and military positions. 'Then we took Omsk and Tomsk and Bomsk. We lost 40 wagons and 3 men. This was in April.'
      I have added one scene to my previous script, but really cannot see how to add any more. The only things I could add would be figures and place-names. The Czech officers who so very kindly wrote their reminiscences have apparently so little dramatic feeling that they could make their reminiscences of Dunkirk as uneventful as a meeting of the Coke Board.
      I hope the script is not too unsatisfactory.
      Thank you again for your letter. I apologise for not answering before but I have been moving about a lot, trying to find somewhere to live, and have only just managed to settle down here for a few weeks.

Yours,
Dylan Thomas

MS: BBC

M. J. TAMBIMUTTU
May 21 1941   at: Laugharne Castle   Laugharne   Carmarthenshire

Dear Tambimuttu,
   I haven't heard a word from you yet about the poem I sent you at the end of last month. You did agree that you would pay me at once. I don't wish to be a nuisance, but I must ask you again. *Could you pay me by return?*
   Hope you've come through all the bombing all right.

                                             Yours,
                                             Dylan Thomas

MS: Carbondale

VERNON WATKINS
22nd May 1941   Laugharne Castle   Laugharne   Carmarthenshire

My dear Vernon:
   It's been a long pause. And, apart from the loss of your company, a great, sighing relief. I hope we can stay here for a good bit: I have the romantic, dirty summerhouse looking over the marsh to write in, and Caitlin an almost empty, huge room to dance in. Also, we have lots of records now, and we hear, quite often, another word than 'ration'.
   Is Dot home? Our love if she is; or isn't, of course, though it is hard to think with affection of someone in S. Africa. Or to think, perhaps I mean, without envy.
   My prosebook's going well, but I dislike it.[1] It's the only really dashed-off piece of work I remember doing. I've done 10,000 words already. It's indecent and trivial, sometimes funny, sometimes mawkish, and always badly written which I do not mind so much.
   Any more about your leprous collection? Perhaps the volume should be surgically bound. I do hope it comes out this summer, just before the gas.
   When can you come down? There's no room in this house—there are 10 children under 10—but there is in the pub, cheap. Write quickly, and say. You must; we must see you before your new 'Confession of a Dirt-Track Rider'. Because we'll never come back to Bishopston, God's least favourite place. Write this week. Thank you for everything you gave us on our long visit. A little money has arrived for me since your last pound for the road; now that has gone. But anyway we can get so very few cigarettes down here. None now for days. I have taken to biting my nails, but they go down so quickly, and one has only 10.
   Well, well, look at the world now.

                                             Love,
                                             Dylan

MS: British Library

1 *Adventures in the Skin Trade.*

LAURENCE POLLINGER
May 23 1941   at Laugharne Castle   Laugharne   Carmarthenshire

Dear Laurence Pollinger:
  I am so sorry—mostly, I'm afraid, for myself—that I never managed to
send on any of the promised books. Something went wrong with the lot of
them, and the prose book, the novel, I scrapped entirely just a short time
ago. Now I have started it again, and it seems to be going really well. But I
do want some money to carry me over while I am completing it. Would
you be so kind as to find out from Dent's whether they would be prepared
to give me an advance—they owe me 40 quid, don't they—on receipt of not
less than *ten thousand words* and a *detailed synopsis* of the rest. It would
be ordinary novel length. When I saw you last year, you did, I believe, tell
me that you thought a forty quid advance on such an instalment would be
possible. Or have things changed since then?
  If you could possibly get them to agree, I'd revise and type ten thousand
words straight away and let you have them.
  I do hope you'll do your damndest for me.

                                        Yours sincerely,
                                        Dylan Thomas

I shall be at the above address for some weeks.

MS: Texas

VERNON WATKINS
28 May 1941   Laugharne Castle   Laugharne   Carmarthenshire

My dear V:
  Thank you for the letter with Jammes in it.[1] And the round silver trash.
Filthy, damned stuff, the halfcrown[2] was the only lovely money I'd seen
for a week and more. And it's still all I've seen. This is getting ridiculous.
The joke has gone too far. It isn't fair to be penniless *every* morning. Every
morning but one, okay; but no, *every* morning. If you do have a tiny bit to
spare, whether it clinks or tinkles, let alone rustles, *do* send it, Vernon.
This is absurd. Anything, bled boy, leper, from a penny to a pound. My
head's been whirling with wondering how to get twopence, fairly or foully,
to put on this nearly a letter. If I fail, it must go naked. Here we are, safe
and quiet, and should be happy as cabbages, but it's hard—for me—without
a single hour's, halfhour's, minute's, going out in the long, social evening.
So if you can don't forget, oh quickly quickly don't forget. I get in such a
nagged, impotent, messy state when I'm like this; sit and snap and worry

1 Watkins's translation of a poem by Francis Jammes.
2 The half-crown coin was worth thirty old pence, something over three pounds at end-
of-century values.

all day; can't be easy, can't work hard, just sit by myself saying 'Fuck it' in a flat voice. I *do* like that wonderful independence of being able to walk across the road *any* time and buy an envelope or some Vim.[1] Don't forget, like lightning, yours ever,

Dylan

My dear V:

I liked the translation enormously much. What a poem! Of course, 'behoves' is right. I read it aloud, slowly, to Caitlin. The music is beautiful. Two possible exceptions: 'poverty' and 'limpidity' so close together; and 'infatuated flies'. Especially the alliteration seems uncertain to me. I'm going to read it again in a minute. Get on with your slow giant Sleeper, I loved the bulls I saw for a moment on the typewriter. And the opening, old lines. You must—can you?—finish it this month, because of the advent of mechanical death. (What a lot of trouble it would have saved if We had sunk the Hood and They the Bismarck).[2] I'm glad you wrote, telling the officials you can only just turn on a bathroom tap. Be a censor: pry and erase. Don't be a cyclist or a parachutist or a mine-tester or the first man on the *very* edge of Dover cliffs.

No, I couldn't do that Ackerley article.[3] I'm not going to talk about poetry now that I have had to, temporarily, stop trying to write it. Besides, he would not print one's truth, because it *would* blast the B.B.C. and every other government institution.

My ballad will be in the June number of Horizon. They haven't printed it nicely: it's in double columns. They wanted more space for an article called 'Whither Solidarity?' or 'An Analysis of Prokosch's Rhythm In His Middle Period'.

My novel blathers on. It's a mixture of Oliver Twist, Little Dorrit, Kafka, Beachcomber, and good old 3-adjectives-a-penny belly-churning Thomas, the Rimbaud of Cwmdonkin Drive.

I was terribly sorry you didn't come down last week-end. It would have been really good. Come down *as soon as* you can. Bring Dot if she's about & will come. Give her our love. I'm afraid I won't be able to meet you in London, or to meet you anywhere further away than walking distance from here. I wish we could meet in the bombs there. But visit us, please.

See if you can squeeze another drop from your borrowed-to-death body. I'm not going to tell you how grateful I am and have always been; or how vile I feel when I ask you again. Really vile. Weazels take off their hats as I stink by. No, I am sorry. I have no right. I hope I am spoiling nothing. It is just that I am useless, & have nowhere to turn.

I have told Caitlin about Kierkegaard, & he will be sent on,[4] with thanks for him, & love, when we are bloated enough with pennies to be

1 Vim, a household detergent.
2 The German battleship *Bismarck* sank the British battle-cruiser *Hood* in the north Atlantic, then was itself sunk on 27 May.
3 For the *Listener*.
4 A borrowed book that Watkins wanted back.

able to bluster into the p-office & say, 'Post this, you fool. *All* of it. *All* the way.'

Remember us to your mother & father and Dennis.[1] Tell him all the boys here fight with hatchets.

Love,
Dylan

MS: British Library

BERTRAM ROTA

June 3 1941   Laugharne Castle Laugharne Carmarthenshire

Dear Mr. Rota:

Thank you for your letter and for the catalogue. I have some of the things you seem to be requiring, but haven't got them out of storage. I am enclosing a few volumes—one or two of them rather badly looked after, I'm afraid—which I hope you'll be able to give me a price for, soon. They aren't much, I know. And I'll send others on later, along with some of my own mss.

Yours sincerely,
Dylan Thomas

From a typescript. MS location unknown

LAURENCE POLLINGER

9 June 1941   Laugharne Castle Laugharne Carmarthenshire

Dear Pollinger:

Did you get my letter? About the novel? I've written separately to Richard Church, but have had no answer yet. I do hope you'll buck Dent's up for an *immediate* advance. I now have over 15000 words to show them, which I'll send you as soon as I know what they are prepared to advance.[2]

Sincerely,
Dylan Thomas

MS: Texas

1 An evacuee from south-east England, living with Watkins's parents.
2 Dent disliked what they saw of *Adventures in the Skin Trade*. An editor wrote to Pollinger on 10 July: 'This material is not good enough; and we would like you to put this fact plainly before the author. It seems to us that Dylan Thomas has reached a crucial point in his literary career. He made a flying start, and there has been no lack of recognition of his uncommon talent ... In our view, however, he has not maintained the position which he gained by his early work.' The letter quoted some damning comments by the firm's readers—'more coprolitic than ever, and seems to be quite without intellectual control ... Thomas cannot build a literary career merely on the miniature furore created by his early work ... Unless he pulls himself together he is going to fizzle out as an author most ignominiously ...' Dent said they still had faith in his future, but 'it seems to us that he is now slipping into a state of literary irresponsibility'. Presumably Pollinger didn't pass on such painful opinions to his client.

M. J. TAMBIMUTTU
June 9 1941   Laugharne Castle   Laugharne   Carmarthenshire

Dear Tambimuttu,

Thank you for the post-dated guinea; and sorry to have been a bother about it, but even in a castle one must eat and smoke. I suppose.[1]

I hope number six goes well, though I'm not looking forward to Treece's article after his ridiculous overpraise of Read:—[2]

'*All* Elizabethan tragedy, *all* the colour and violence of the ballads,' or whatever the words were, in some such ice-cream line as 'O O Antonio'. I think the article did Read a disservice, for the natural reaction to it was ridicule and that, unfortunately, might embrace Read's own dull, honest poetry too. If someone says a line is better than Shakespeare, and it's really just an ordinary, pleasant line, one's inclined, I think, to pass over the ordinary pleasantness of it by attacking the humbug, or gutter eye, that sees it as superb. I hope Treece doesn't say that there's *all* metaphysics in some ordinary line of mine. Although I am a friend of Treece's, I think he is a loud and brawling hypocrite. This isn't for print; I don't like magazine quarrels, I can have as many as I like outside. Also I think it's a mistake for one young poet to shout at length, in print, about the works of an almost exact contemporary, good or bad. Young poets don't want praise, they want money. Treece has been climbing for some years now, and he isn't even in sight of the ladder yet. And he's surely old enough now, you'd believe, to realise that he won't get anywhere up those snob-snotted rungs by licking the bums of his creative friends or by describing, incorrectly, the contours of them for the benefit of other blind and mouthey climbers.

I don't think it's a bad thing to be a climber, so long as you make sufficient entertaining noises as you slime your way up. Grigson did make some sort of simian show, but you can't see Treece for the wood, the numb and solid wooden front against all sensitivity or intelligence.

A thing I don't like about 'Poetry', now that I'm feeling like this, is its plague of dedications: 'For Nigel', 'To Nicholas', 'From Basil', and the letters with all the Christian names and the back-pats and kicks. It's too much like 'Hi Gang' on the wireless.[3] The intimate magazine should be circulated only among the family, and I'm damned if I belong to your family or Nigel's or Basil's. The public's got a right to demand that its entertainment should be public; and if the public likes all this matey to-you for-you we're-all-poets-together hugging and buggering party exhibition, then the public, as nearly always, is wrong.

1 Issue No. 6 of *Poetry London*, May/June 1941, printed 'Love in the Asylum'.
2 In 'Herbert Read—A Salute', *Poetry London* No. 4, Jan/Feb 1941.
3 'Hi Gang!', a popular radio comedy show 'coming to you from the heart of London' in the early years of the war: noisy, amiable and Americanised.

What I do like about 'Poetry' is some of its poems; which is as it should be. Let's have less about them and more of them.

I'll write again when I get number six. Best wishes for it.

Yours,
Dylan Thomas

Sorry, I haven't got a copy myself of my 18 Poems. And I'm sorry some cad removed yours, but if your copy was inscribed by me to Runia—an old friend—then some cad must have removed it from her.

Yes, I'd love to send you some drawings, or illustrations. I'll have a shot right away.

MS: Texas

VERNON WATKINS
Sunday 21 June 1941   Laugharne

My dear Vernon:

It was very nice seeing you those days. I loved Rilke and the scrabbling in the shrubbery and your Sea Music. I wish you could have stayed longer. Sorry for being so huffish and insultable that last night: you know how it is.

Ackerley has been in Laugharne for the last 3 days; or four. Funny, after our talking about him. Someone who stayed here last year told him about the place; he'd never heard of it before. He was sorry to miss you, here and in London: I told him you'd been in London & that you missed him here by one day only. He's quite a charming man, rather grey and tired, with a nice smile and a lazy, affected, very pleasant voice. About 50. He said he liked your poems a great deal. Most of the time he was here he spent doing great walks, but I met him every evening in the pub and he came to the house for drinks.

Here is a tiny poem I've just done. Not very well formed; just a poem between bits of my unfortunately forced novel, a breathing space between mechanizations; & I think I agree with you about that destination phrase.

Do write soon; and tell me about going to London. We're just the same.

Love,
Dylan
Poem on back.

[*Written on back of letter: first verse of 'The Marriage of a Virgin' = 'On the Marriage of a Virgin'.*]

MS: British Library

VERNON WATKINS
[4 July 1941][1]   Laugharne

Dear Vernon:

A wonderful surprise present. Thank you. I could buy Laugharne, but it would be ostentatious.

A great pity you couldn't come this weekend. Beforehand I miss you. And you'd have had the pleasure of Hughes's company. He's been aloofly here for some days. I don't know what he does on the Admiralty, but I can imagine him being introduced: 'Ah, Admiral, and here's Hughes, Richard Hughes, you know, our Out of Contact man.'

I'll try to come down next weekend, and thank you. If I don't it will be because I'm in London; or, of course, because Marjorie's with you. I must go to London quickly, to see what honey of a ministerial job is open for a man of the strictest obscurity and intemperance: £1000 a year, excluding tips, bribes, blackmail, bloodmoney, petty cash, and profits realized by the sale of female clerks into the white slave traffic and the removal of office furniture.

I look forward to the new poem.

I'll write as soon as I know about my London visit.

Anyway, next weekend or the weekend of the 20th.

                                        Thank you again,
                                        Love,
                                        Dylan

I'm enclosing the short, now finished, poem.[2]

MS: British Library

CHARLES FISHER
July 15 1941   Laugharne Castle   Carmarthenshire

My dear Charles,

While looking through a drawer to find something—it was not my drawer so I did not know what the something would be though I hoped for tinned food—I came across an old letter of yours to me, and with your home address which I'd lost. It really took the wind out of my sails (I was a yacht at the time), finding your handwriting in somebody else's drawer where peas at the very least should have been. It was like, not very much

---

1 Thomas wrote 'Friday June 4 (?)41'. 4 June was a Wednesday; 4 July was a Friday. The latter seems more likely.
2 'On the Marriage of a Virgin.'

like, I admit, burgling a safe and finding an old friend inside it not a day older than one foot two. I thought I'd better write at once, before I found a drawing of Fred's (Still Life: One Egg. June 1936–June 1940) behind the hatrack in the music room or a manuscript of Tom's (Mabinogion, a Tone Poem for Horn and Kardomah) behind the butler in the cook's room. Especially as there is no music room and no butler and the only hatrack is a bust of Dante on which some child has written 'Odd Job'.

I saw too little of you in Swansea last time; hat and moustache for half a quick evening among the good-shows of the young lieutenants and Peggy and Betty and Babs the dancing dailies. I remember reading some of my unfinished Ballad—the whole is coming out in this month's Horizon—in a thick, confidential voice, being bought two pints at a time, giving my belly what-for; but the date we made for later I forgot at once, and spent the next evening trying to be in three Gower pubs at the same time, waiting, wondering which of them I had arranged to meet you in, then remembering too late that the meeting was to have been in Swansea, a large town. After months and months, and if you remembered the date yourself, forgive me, and do write.[1]

I think that quite soon I'll be made to do work in a factory, so this is my last bit of as much freedom as one can expect to enjoy without any money. I haven't seen a coin for weeks. Do they still sing as you spend them? Jesus, I loathe my poverty. Caitlin will, I hope, be able to stay on here while I am being thrown to the high explosives. My upper lip is a board, but still I am very miserable.

I'm writing, now, a long story about London, called 'Adventures In The Skin Trade'. Miller and Wodehouse.

Do you know Tom's address? I want, through him, to find where Daniel is, that Lost Tribe in himself.

Tell me how you are, what you're doing, and be good to the Generals.

Love,
Dylan

And just a poem, finished today.[2]

MS (incomplete): the recipient

VERNON WATKINS
Tuesday [?15 July 1941]   Laugharne

Dear V.

Here are two poems of very different kinds. That is to say, here are two poems. Do tell me at *once* what you think of them. I am a bit dubious

---

1 To this point, the only source is *SL*. Fisher's MS begins at page 2.
2 'The hunchback in the park', revised from the original version, which Thomas wrote when he was seventeen.

about 'Through ruin' in the third line of the sextet. Originally I had 'All day.'[1]

Looking forward to the weekend. As I told you, the only 2 things that will prevent me coming are London & utter poverty (in which I am now, having to borrow 2½d for this stamp). But I do want to come. I'll ring up either on Thursday evening or Friday morning. What's the trainfare?

Much love,
Dylan

MS: British Library

VERNON WATKINS
Wednesday [?23 July 1941]   Laugharne

Dear Vernon:

Thank you for the lovely weekend. A pity we couldn't have done more, but I liked very much what we did. I *must* have a copy soon of the Foal which I remember, lots of it, by heart on a first hearing: nothing, perhaps, to old Datas Watkins but a great deal for me. I hope the Money poem goes well, and probably 'Earth-winged mortal' is right. It's just that to me it doesn't express the meaning you originally told me.[2]

Thank you for the croquet & the poems & the kindness & the money; and thank your mother for me, very much, for the superabundance of far-too-good-for-the-war food. Remember me to your mother & Mr. Watkins & Dennis.

Yo— etc Lederer came down with me for 2 days & is returning tomorrow. He *walks*. A nice boy, but terribly affected in many ways. Dante is boring. Eliot is dry. Gorki is a journalist. But I think that what he really thinks, & will one day be brave enough to say, is simple, unaffected, & right.

Thank you for 'Assembling'.[3] Of course.

A proper letter soon when I know more plans. And I hope I can send you a poem soon.

I liked everything.
Love,
Dylan
& Caitlin
& Llew

MS: British Library

1 The poems were 'Among those Killed in the Dawn Raid was a Man Aged a Hundred' (which in Thomas's draft contained the words 'Through ruin') and 'The hunchback in the park'. Both were published in *Life and Letters Today* before the end of the year.
2 'Foal' and 'Money for the Market' are poems by Watkins.
3 Watkins's suggested replacement, which Thomas accepted, for 'Through ruin'.

BERTRAM ROTA[1]
[Summer 1941] [fragment]

[. . .] I mean, not that the poems are good or bad, but only that they show the growth of poems over a period of just more than a year, one extremely creative, productive year, in all their stages and alterations, and—in many instances—show how a quite different poem emerges, years later, from the original. [. . .] The majority of them have not been printed anywhere yet, though I'll quite probably print some of them in my next collection due some time this year[2] and in altered form perhaps in future books. [. . .]

From a typescript. MS location unknown

VERNON WATKINS
28 Aug 1941

c/o Horizon   6 Selwyn House   Lansdowne Terrace
WC1

My Dear Vernon,
    A tiny note to tell you where, if you write, I can be got hold of. It's only a forwarding address, I haven't moved into the editor's chair. The place I'm staying in in London with Caitlin is closed after tomorrow or Friday and we haven't yet found anywhere new. We've been having an awful time, and I have felt like killing myself. We arrived with no money, after leaving Llewelyn in Ringwood,[3] and have had none since. In Laugharne that was not so bad. In stinking, friendless London it is unendurable. I am still looking for a film job, & have been offered several scripts to do 'in the near future', which might mean weeks. In the meantime, we sit in our bedroom and think with hate of the people who can go to restaurants. Have you written? Frances Hughes has, as yet, forwarded no letters. I would have written to you long before, but have been too miserable even to write Poem at the top of a clean page and then look out of the window at the millionaires catching buses. Are you, I don't hope, in the army? Write soon. Soon perhaps this will have been worn away, hunger, anger, boredom, hate and unhappiness, and I will be able to write to you about all the things we have always had, and will always have, to talk about together. We are prisoners now in a live melodrama and all the long villains with three halfpence are grinning in at us through the bars. Not the best bars either. Bless you,

Dylan

MS: British Library

1 This extract is taken from Thomas's letter that accompanied the MS poems sent to Rota, who quoted it when he wrote to Charles D. Abbott of the Lockwood Memorial Library, Buffalo, 1 September 1941.
2 No new collection of poems appeared during the war.
3 Llewelyn spent much of the war staying with his maternal grandmother at Blashford, near Ringwood.

BBC
[?September 1941]   Mars Hotel   Frith St   Soho

Dear Sirs,
I apologise for the delay in returning the contract sheet signed. It was not forwarded to me here immediately, by some mistake.

Yours faithfully,
Dylan Thomas

MS: BBC

JOHN LEHMANN
[early October 1941]   c/o   Horizon

Dear John L.
Here are the proofs. Sorry so late. You wanted me to say something about the book as a whole. Will just this do?
'A Fine Beginning' is the first chapter of a novel in progress to be called 'Adventures In The Skin Trade'.[1] The novel is a semi-autobiographical continuation of 'Portrait of The Artist As A Young Dog' and takes the principal character of that book of stories up to the age of twenty.

Dylan T

MS: Texas

JOHN SOMMERFIELD[2]
[6 January 1942][3]   Strand Film Company[4] Filmicity House
                            5a Upper St Martin's Lane   London   WC2

Old John,
My first letter, too. After all these pints. It was better than a Pimm's to hear from you, and especially to hear that you'll be in London so thirstily soon. I look forward, my constitution is not so happy. And get me here, will you, TEM. 1891, as quickly as you can once they let you out. We'll make a date straightaway, for that moment. Why can't you desert for a bit? Or is this scrap and scribble bluepencilled? We'll choose a good—quali-fied—place, but that doesn't mean we won't visit all the qualified bad

---

1 It was published in Lehmann's *Folios of New Writing*, autumn 1941.
2 John Sommerfield, novelist and documentary-film writer. He was in the RAF.
3 Thomas wrote '1941'. Sommerfield had no doubt that it was the following year.
4 Thomas was now on the payroll as a writer/director, making documentaries for the Ministry of Information.

places too. Glad you liked my winter verses,[1] very quickly produced from my tame Swinburne machine, and don't forget: TEM 1891, or above address, and we'll be quietly noisy together for as long as you like and we can. All my lack of news *then*. Caitlin sends best love. Send ours to Molly.

I'm still helping to produce those things that Beachcomber calls the series of priggish, facetious shorts extolling the virtues of sad girls in unfitting uniforms and the vices of happy thinking, moving, and x-ing—the word I must use. How are you?

Always,
Dylan

MS: (the recipient)

LAURENCE POLLINGER
19 Jan 1942   Strand Film Co   1 Golden Square   W.1.

Dear Laurence Pollinger,

Sorry not to have got in touch with you for so long. So many reasons for my carelessness about this & about so many other quite urgent things; so many reasons, & all too dull to bother you with.

About the new poems Laughlin is bringing out in America. They are, so he told me some months ago, only a very small collection of poems that have appeared, since my last book, in periodicals here & in America. They are to make up a pamphlet, or more-or-less a broadsheet, in a series rather insolently called 'Poet of the Month'.[2] In no way can the little selection be called a *book* of poems; and I see no point in letting Dent's have a copy as there are far too few poems for them to make a commercial book out of it. I would prefer to wait a short time until I had added to the little American broadsheet the rest of the poems I have written & written in periodicals since my last Dent-volume appeared.

Agree terms with Laughlin, certainly; & I hope you can get the cheque through as soon as possible. Will you let me know—at the above address, which will always find me now as I have turned into a script-writer—what happens?

Sorry again for my long absence from any correspondence with you.

Sincerely,
Dylan Thomas

MS: Texas

---

1 Thomas wrote eight verse captions for a photo-feature, 'A Dream of Winter', in the January 1942 issue of the magazine *Lilliput*.
2 The series was 'Poets of the Year'. The slim volume, which contained seventeen Thomas poems, was published in February 1943 as *New Poems*. In the first edition of these Letters, this item was wrongly dated '19 Jan 1943'.

*JOHN LEHMANN
27 Jan 42   Strand Films   5a Upper St. Martin's Lane   WC2

Dear John L,
Here's the Dent letter. I do hope we can do business about the book[1] very soon. Given an advance etc, I can definitely undertake to finish the book by a date to be arranged. I want to get on with it, but obviously wouldn't until publication was assured.

                                                Good wishes
                                                Dylan Thomas

MS: Location unknown

OSCAR WILLIAMS

The American Oscar Williams (1900–64) wrote poetry but was best known as an anthologist. He acted as an unofficial literary agent for Thomas, selling manuscripts as well as poems.

April 5 1942   13 Hammersmith Terrace   London W6[2]

Dear Mr. Williams:
I got your second letter—thanks very much—but I'm afraid your first *must* have gone down. I'm glad you want to use some of my poems in New Poems 1942. Looking forward to seeing it.
Horizon will be sending on those signed sheets. When I signed them, only Spender & Empson had been there before. I hope the other chaps you want are obtainable. Rodgers[3] is somewhere in Northern Ireland.
I'm sorry, but I believe my signature got a bit strange at about the 50th sheet. I'd forgotten everything about the person whose name I was signing; and eventually even his name. The weather, or war, or London, perhaps.
I haven't any new poems at the moment, as I'm working on a long story which takes most of the time that's left over after half-earning a daily living in a film company: a company that works on shorts for the Ministry of Information. When I have some, I'd be glad to send them along.
Delighted to hear from you.
Good luck.

                                                Dylan Thomas

MS: Houghton

1 *Adventures in the Skin Trade.*
2 Sir Alan Herbert, the author, lived next door. The Thomases borrowed a studio through the intercession of John Pudney, the Herberts' son-in-law.
3 W. R. Rodgers (1909–69), poet and radio scriptwriter, was a Presbyterian minister in Northern Ireland before joining the BBC.

*MR WELLS[1]
May 20 1942   13 Hammersmith Terrace   London W6

Dear Mr. Wells,
   Sorry not to have answered before, but I've been away, out of London,
and your letter wasn't forwarded.
   I was very interested to hear about Poetry Folios and what's behind it,
and will certainly send you a poem when I have one. At the moment I
haven't got anything new at all: I'm writing a lot of prose, for a bit. But
perhaps you'd like me to contribute to a later number?
   Anyway, the best of luck with the first number.
                                              Yours sincerely,
                                              Dylan Thomas

MS: Buffalo

BBC
20.5.42   13 Hammersmith Terrace   W6

Dear Sir,
   Enclosed, the signed copyright form. I hope the cheque for the agreed
amount can be sent on very quickly, as I am trying to settle all my
accounts etc. before moving. I would appreciate it this week if possible.
                                              Yours faithfully,
                                              Dylan Thomas

MS: BBC

RUTH WYNN OWEN

Ruth Wynn Owen was an actress, originally from North Wales. Thomas met her in Bradford
in 1942 when she was with a touring company, and he was making a film documentary
about the theatre in wartime. She said that she fell in love with him but refused to become
his mistress.

[?May 1942]   [headed paper: Strand Film Co, etc]
                                    as from 13 Hammersmith Tce   W6

                                    no, not any longer after Saturday.
                                    So will you—if you will
                                    write, please—please write
                                    to the film address.

   Your letter—thank you very, very much for it; I was terribly glad to

1 Unidentified correspondent.

hear—came just after I had been seeing you on the films, you with your wand, showing a ladderless leg in the wings. You looked, if I may or mayn't say so, pretty good to me, and I wish you were in London, where even the sun's grey and God how I hate it, and not in Preston with a lot of sillies. I do hate the life here, the grey gets in your eyes so that a bit of green nearly blinds you and the thought of the sea makes you giddy as you cross the road like a bloody beetle. You wrote to me on a moor, and I write to you in a ringing, clinging office with repressed women all around punishing typewriters, and queers in striped suits talking about 'cinema' and, just at this very moment, a man with a bloodhound's voice and his cheeks, I'm sure, full of Mars Bars, rehearsing out loud a radio talk on 'India and the Documentary Movement'. I wish I were on the Halifax moor talking to you, not to dishonest men with hangovers. Perhaps I shall be able to give a long-postponed talk to the Cambridge English Society during the week of June 8, which would be wonderful because perhaps you don't work all day and perhaps you would come out with me, walk somewhere, watch me drink a pint, and talk and talk and talk. Would you like that? If you would, then I could try very hard to come up for a day. Let me know will you?

You said you wrote a bad letter, and you wrote a lovely one, though too short. I said, horribly, that I wrote a good letter, and I'm almost inarticulate. What's a good letter anyway? To put down a bit of oneself to send to someone who misses it? To be funny and selfconscious or selfconsciously formal, or so very natural that even the words blush and stammer? I only know I'd prefer to talk to you, but as I've got to write because you're a million miles away, in the mild and bitter north, [at the head of second page: terribly late letter] then I must write anything, anything or everything, just as it comes into the thing that keeps my collar from vanishing into my hat. First, how very very odd it was, coming across you out of the blue, out of the black, out of the blue-and-black bruise of a smutty town at the end of a witless week, when everything had gone wrong, had gone wrong, as I didn't know then, only to come extravagantly right. I saw, suddenly, a human being, rare as a Martian, an actual unaffected human being, after months and months, and years indeed of meeting only straw men, sponge and vanity boys, walking sacks full of solid vinegar and pride, all the menagerie of a world very rightly at war with itself. (And now even the ink is spitting.) I felt, at once, so at ease with you that I can still hardly believe it.

Thank you for saying about Llewelyn. He's going away, tomorrow, for a few weeks to his grandmother, quite near Salisbury. Just outside Fording-bridge. I have to move from Hammersmith Terrace, and am trying to get a house in St. Peter's Square to share with some people who have furniture. You don't know, I suppose, anyone who has any furniture stored in London and who would want to give it a good home? The only things I have are a deckchair with a hole in it, half a dozen books, a few toys, and an old iron. These would not fill even a mouse's home. It is very good sometimes to have nothing; I want society, not me, to have places to sit in and beds to lie in; and who wants a hatstand of his very own? But sometimes, on raining, nostalgic Sunday afternoons, after eating the week's meat, it would, however cowardly, whatever a blanketing of responsibility and conscience, be good to sprawl back in one's own bourgeois chair, bought slippers on one's trotters. But to hell with it, I want to talk about you, I know too much about myself: I've woken up with myself for 28 years now, or very nearly. But I can't write about you—and now the spitting pen is broken and the ink over documents ostentatiously and falsely called Important—because, though I feel much, I know so little. So goodbye for a time, and the smaller the time the better—at least for me. You will write? And I will see you?

love,
Dylan

MS: Location unknown

RUTH WYNN OWEN
Monday July 6 1942   [headed paper: Strand Film Co etc]

My Dear Ruth,
    A very tiny note to thank you most properly and deeply for your lovely letter. A tiny note because I'm just off to Scotland. I'll be back in about a week. I want to write a full, long letter full of love and nothing, and I will from perhaps the wet, never-so-good-as-I-probably-think Highlands. I couldn't manage Cambridge, mostly because, as you told me, the boys had come down. I shan't tell you how much I am looking forward to seeing you when you come to London in 14 days' time. I shan't but I'd like to. Let's paint this foul town the colour we like the best.

X
Dylan

MS: Location unknown

CAITLIN THOMAS
Sunday [?1942][1] [incomplete]   84 Old Church St   SW3

Caitlin,
    I love you.
    I am desperate without you. I love you, more and more and more the longer I am without you. I cannot go on without you, for you are forever

---

1 The date could be 1942 or 1943, and in any case is before the birth of the Thomases' second child, Aeronwy, in March 1943. Caitlin was often in Wales, either in Laugharne or with friends in Cardiganshire, where she may have been at the time of this letter. Thomas went down when he could.

too wonderful and I can only say Cat my darling you are my sweetheart and nothing can come between us. God, Catly, if only I could see you now. I want to touch you, to see you, you are beautiful, I love you.

Why I had not written was because of money,

[four pages, 2 to 5, are missing]

money that the Accounts deducted; so that, if you still want me, which is unlikely, and if the presence of Elizabeth etc. does not overcrowd the house, I could come down on this Tuesday. Will you wire? Wire me at the office: Strand Films, 1 Golden Square, W.1. Or to the office telephone number: GER 6304. As soon as you get this letter. And tell me if you want me to come down. I can't describe to you, I never will be able to describe to you, how much I love you, my own wife and Llewelyn's mother, my own Caitlin, and how much I want to see you terribly terribly soon. Forgive. How can I tell you the kind of money panic I got into? You weren't there to hold me & tell me, every day you went further as I could not write, I don't know *why* I thought I couldn't write & tell you the truth. I am telling you the truth now. And I love you so very much that even in writing gabblingly, desperately, like this, I can somehow come near you and kiss your heart.

Please, my very own dear, tell me that you want me to come down. It is the only thing on the earth that I have to look forward to. And if, because of the other visitors, I cannot come down this week, wire all the same & tell me when I can. I saw the Roberts this morning who told me they have written to you to say that *they* cannot come go down [*sic*] to Wales for another week. Perhaps you may think it best—if you want me to come, and, O my darling, please do—for me to come with them: that is, if I can. But I want to come as soon, as soon as I can: if ever I can now, but I know that I must be with you, live with you, always. Why I wired to say that I could come down *this* weekend was that I had heard that Taylor[1] was returning and I knew he would, at once, straighten things out. But, when he returned, he asked me to stay on until Tuesday to do some small special job. And I couldn't refuse. Then, at the end of the small job, I have to do another, longer one; but this he has agreed to let me take away with me for a week to do. I could come to you now. I love you. I love you. Love me, Caitlin. You will always be my

[end of page 9]

MS: *(Maurice Neville)*

---

1 Donald Taylor was managing director of Strand Films.

CAITLIN THOMAS
[undated fragment, probably wartime][1]

[page headed 3] that I could borrow. I was ashamed to write without sending anything to keep you going on—I know you will say I am a bloody fool, but you know too that that, justly bugger me, is what I unfortunately am—and, as the days went on and I could not write, I became desperate, I became ill with wanting you, with being ashamed that I could not write, with being ashamed that I was too much of a money headed fool to write, with thinking of you 200 miles away thinking that I had, as you said, a

MS: Texas

RUTH WYNN OWEN
28 August 1942   Talsarn   Cardiganshire[2]   as from Strand Films [etc]

Ruth my dear,
I missed you; and I think that I must have willed myself to miss you that night after the theatre; not of my thinking self, whatever that vain, paste and cotton-wool wad of my self may matter, for I tried hard to reach the Salisbury or the stagedoor; I think I must have willed my lateness and weakness, willed it because, simply, I was ashamed of my hysterical excitement of the wet-eyed and over-protesting night before. I remembered losing my head in Piccadilly, which left very little for my heart had gone two months ago, gone into your by-me-unkissed breast. And you'll have to forgive now, along with my tears, protestations, and denials, my almost archly over-writing writing in this late, loving letter. I can be natural—my behaviour, then, in the black streets was as natural as my too-much drink and my giddiness at seeing you again allowed me—but perhaps my nature itself is over-written and complicate me out of this, you Ruth in a well. Was there something a little clinical in your attitude, or was it my windy head that blew your words about and got me dancing with love and temper among the bloody buses? I'm sure, and this isn't a mockmodest wish to be stroked back into vanity, that you were all right and I was all wrong. I had time wrong, I was thrusting its hands, instead of letting it move passionately gently until we could in time's good time be as near as we wished and we must. So forgive me: I'll follow the ticking old fossil until it's the Now Now hour, I'll follow it through the provincial towns and sail with it under the stagey bridges.

1 This item belongs to the previous letter. Texas acquired it about 1958 with the collection owned by T. E. Hanley of Pennsylvania.
2 Talsarn is a village in west Wales. From time to time Caitlin Thomas, and less frequently her husband, stayed with a Swansea family called Phillips, who had moved to a large house in the village, Plas Gelli, to escape the air raids. Vera Phillips, one of the daughters, had known Dylan since childhood, and was friendly with Caitlin.

Believe me, I love you too.

And when will you be back in London? I shall go back from Wales on Tuesday. Will you wire me? I think that is the best: everything that comes here is unopened except bottles. And if you don't, or forget to, I will phone the stagedoor. We must find each other again and when we meet again I'll be more controlled and, indeed, even sane.

The cocks are crowing in the middle of the afternoon, and the sun is frying.

Will you trust me?

It is grand and lovely to have known you for even a little for such a little time.

I hope you are well and I know you are sweet and more than sweet to *me*.

When we are together next, let it be on your whole free day or at least on your whole free evening. Time will not let me say or ask more than that.

Dylan

MS: Location unknown

T. W. EARP

Tommy Earp (1892–1958) was an art critic and hard drinker; Thomas was very fond of him. They shared the crossword puzzler's weakness for anagrams and double meanings. Among the topical ingredients in the poem is a local joke (not Thomas's) to the effect that Marshal Semyon Timoshenko, a Russian commander often in the news, had a Welsh grandmother and was really called Timothy Jenkins. Fedor Bock was a German field marshal.

30 August 1942   Gelli   Talsarn   Cardiganshire as from Strand Films [etc]

Dear Tommy:

On-and-on General Bock is driving a wedge among pincers,
Timothy Jenkins feints on the flank and the rouged Duke is wan,
The war is sweet with the summer breath of the panzers
And the dehydrated choirs of day welcome the dawn.

As I tossed off this morning over Talsarn Bridge to the fishes,
At war myself with the Celtic gnats under a spitfire sun,
Reading that twenty poems make fifteen cartridge cases,
Commandos are trained to be cannibals and bombs weigh a hundred ton,
Poison is dropped from the sky in the shape of hipflasks and cheque-books,
Pigs can be taught to firewatch and hens to lay handgrenades:
O the summer grew suddenly lovely as the woodland rose in a phalanx
And the painted privates I thought were bushes moved in their Nash
                                                                    parades.

I have been here for over a week with Caitlin, with milk and mild and cheese and eggs, and I feel fit as a fiddle only bigger; I watch the sun from a cool room and know that there are trees being trees outside and that I do not have to admire them; the country's the one place you haven't got to go out in, thank Pan. I missed you last Friday, and was not in time, (as I thought, up until the last moment, that I would be able to catch the Thursday-night train), to let you know. I hope you did not wait nor were cross, and that the Monico made up for the lack of green tooth and pot belly, for the absence of one ventripotent scortatory Krut.[1] I'm returning tomorrow, Tuesday, and will be in London until Friday night. Can you come up during the week, or on Friday? A visit will make up for London after Wales. I want to bring my bit of a novel with me, and let's try the Ladder & the Jubilee and have a gala climb, without banting and unanned.[2] I do hope you can manage it. Will you write or wire?

Ever,
Dylan

MS: Ohio State University

CAITLIN THOMAS
[1943]   8 Wentworth Studios   SW3[3]

Monday, in misery in our leaking
studio, among vermin and falling
plaster & unwashed plates.

My Own Caitlin, my dear darling,
It's never been so useless and lonely away from you as it is this time; there is nothing to live for without you, except for your return or when I can [come] down to Laugharne which must, somehow, be this week because I love you far more than ever and I will not exist without your love and loveliness, darling, so please write and tell me you miss me, too, and love me, and think of us being, soon, together for ever again. By the time you get this, you'll also have got, I hope, *a bit more money* which I will wire either tonight or tomorrow morning. I could not send any more on Friday as there were so many things to pay; & some rent, too.

There is *nothing* to do without you; so terribly terribly sad to come back to our empty barn, lie all night in our big bed, listening to the rain & our

---

1 Del Monico, where Earp had been waiting for him, was a pub in Soho. 'Ventripotent' means gluttonous, 'scortatory' means fornicating. 'Krut' might be an anagram for 'Turk', or could be associated with the American slang 'crut' for excrement, but in any case implies Thomas.

2 Ladder, Jubilee: drinking clubs. 'Banting': John Banting was a painter and illustrator. 'Unanned': which 'Ann' is undiscoverable.

3 The Thomases occupied this unglamorous Chelsea apartment (in Manresa Road) at intervals from mid or late 1942. Visitors remember Caitlin's vegetable stew bubbling on the stove when she was there, and squalor when she wasn't.

mice and the creaks & leaks and the warnings;[1] so sad I could die if I hadn't got to see you again & live with you always & always, when I woke up without you, think of you hundreds of miles away with Aeronwy Lil[2] at your breasts that I want to kiss because I love you, my Cat. I hope to God I can come down for 2 or 3 days at the end of the week.

Last night I called on pudding Vera who has been in bed for over a week with apathy and illusions and who said she'd written to you about Gelli.[3] She did not know you were in Laugharne,[4] & when I told her she said could she spend a week or a bit *in* Laugharne with you before going on *with* you to Gelli for a week or a bit? And I said I'd tell you, I knew nothing about it.

How is it in Laugharne? Tell me everything; and especially that you love me & want me as I love & want you now, at this moment, and for every moment of my life & yours always. How is Frances, Mrs Wood (?), & Ivy?[5]

I have seen some, not too many, of the usual people: Dan. The Rat who has now sold everything in his den or hole except that double revolting bed. My office horrors. Nobody I want to see at all because there is only one person I ever want to see and that is you darling oh oh darling I love you I want to be with you.

I'm going to the Chelsea tonight. Alone. And then back to think about you in bed. Give my love to Aeronwy. Every bit of my love to you, every substance & shadow of it, every look & thought & word. Oh I hate it without you.

xxxxxxx
Dylan

PS I work in Elstree,[6] have to leave Chelsea frightfully early. I hate Elstree & Chelsea, too; very much. I have seen one or two films, halfquarrelled again with J. Eldridge,[7] & over-wound the clock which I shall take to a man.

PSS What do you want me to send you? Books? Shawls? Skirts? Napkins? Cloak? Shoes I see on the floor? I'll send money anyway, and, I hope to God, myself. Kiss me. I'll say your name *very loudly* tonight as I put out the light.

PSSS Are you going to go over to Blaen-Cwm again? I'll write to them tomorrow.

PSSSS No more, dear, until I send a few pounds.

OH DARLING. X

MS: Tony Vilela

1 'Warnings' in those days meant air-raid warnings.
2 Aeronwy was born in London, 3 March 1943.
3 'Pudding Vera' was Vera Phillips, then in London. 'Gelli' was the house in Cardiganshire.
4 Caitlin was staying with Frances Hughes.
5 Ivy Williams of Brown's Hotel.
6 Strand Films used studios at Elstree.
7 John Eldridge directed films for Strand.

HERMON OULD[1]
31st May 1943   [headed paper: Strand Film Co etc]

Dear Mr. Ould,
Thank you for your letter. I am most interested in the scheme of Mr. Olaf Stapledon's enquiry and in the statement you enclosed, and I will try, as soon as possible, to send along what I myself think about them.

I would also like to become an ordinary member, and would be grateful if you would tell me the exact procedure.

Yours truly,
Dylan Thomas

MS: Texas

CAITLIN THOMAS
Thursday [?1943]   King's Arms   Stirling Corner   Barnet   Herts[2]

Darling:
Darling:
Caitlin my dear dear Cat.

It's awful to write to you because, even though I love writing to you, it brings you so near me I could almost touch you and I know at the same time that I *cannot* touch you, you are so far away in cold, unkind Ringwood and I am in stale Barnet in a roadhouse pub with nothing but your absence and your distance, to keep my heart company.

I think of you always all the time. I kiss my uncharitable pillow for you in the nasty nights. I can see you with our little Mongolian monkey at your breast; I can see you in that unfond house listening with loathing to the News; I can see you in bed, more lovely than anything that has ever been at all. I love you. I love Llewelyn & Aeronwy, but you above all and forever until the sun stops and even after that.

And I cannot come down this weekend. I have to work all day Sunday. I am working, for the first time since I sold my immortal soul, very very hard, doing three months' work in a week. I hate film studios. I hate film workers. I hate films. There is nothing but glibly naive insincerity in this huge tinroofed box of tricks. I do not care a bugger about the Problems of Wartime Transport.[3] All I know is that you are my wife, my lover, my joy, my Caitlin.

Oh Cat darling I miss you too much to bear.

1 Hermon Ould was general secretary of P.E.N., the writers' organisation. Thomas was elected to membership two years later, on 2 May 1945, but there is no further trace of him in P.E.N. records.
2 Barnet is near Elstree and the film studios.
3 The film was probably *Is Your Ernie Really Necessary?*, its title a parody of the wartime slogan, 'Is your journey really necessary?' It was filmed but not released.

Come Back on Wednesday. I'll send you another inarticulately loving letter tomorrow, with some money. You should have it by Saturday morning. No, it's better that I wire the money so that you can have it for the weekend. Even though I dislike Blashford very much, I envy it because all my love is there with my children and with you.

Come back on Wednesday. *Please.*

I haven't been in London at all as I have to start working unlikelily early in the morning & carry on until six o'clock.

I love you more, even, than when I said I loved you only a few seconds ago.

I think I can get Vera a little part in this film: a tiny part as a pudding-faced blonde sloth but I shan't tell her that.[1]

Write to me telling me two things: that you love me & that you are coming back on Wednesday which is like a day full of birds & bells.

I am writing on the back of a script by Mr. J. B. Priestley.[2] But that doesn't spoil what I have to say to you. I have to say to you that I love you in life & after death, and that even though I drink I am good. I am not drinking much. I am too lonely even for that.

Write.

Give my love to the pigmy baby & kiss Llewelyn on the forehead for me.

Touch your own body for me, very gently. On the breast & the belly. My Caitlin.

Your

Dylan

X

MS: Tony Vilela

T. W. EARP
July 1 1943 [incomplete]   Ger. 6304 [the Strand phone number]

Dear Tommy:

When next shall we stumble to the stutter of our lewis-gun carols
From bombazine-bosomed bar to a bliss of barrels,
Two period percies friscoed with ladders and banting,
Two spooneered swiss pillars, tumble falsetting and ranting?

O when, marcel-bound, shall we ruth our swine's way to the many-johned
Penny-fond antelope's cavern from the royal back-bar of beyond,

---

1 Vera Phillips had done some acting.
2 The author J. B. Priestley became a popular wartime broadcaster, giving man-of-the-people homilies in his weekly 'Postscript' after the Sunday evening news bulletin.

Or, sinister self-mabuses ripe for the phelan of the withy,
Peggy-legged limping in bottle-dress be hooved from the Wardour-street
smithy?[1]

MS: Ohio State University

WYNFORD VAUGHAN-THOMAS[2]
[?September 1943]

This is, I think, the first time I've written to you—treasure the paper,
boy!—and, oh, for what a reason. I'm whimpering in bed, with mumps and
gout, the music-hall duo, and cannot work and am, quite suddenly, utterly
without money and horribly in debt. My face is a sad bladder and my big
toes full of teeth. And tradesmen bludgeon the door all day and summonses
fall like grouse. There is no one here to borrow a mite from [. . .][3] and I am
writing to ask you if you could temporarily (oh cringing word) help me
with a little money however little. If you can I will send you a cheque post-
dated eight weeks hence when I begin again to write film-scripts in London
where, God, I must spend the winter. Snarl and throw over the Devonshire
Castle[4] if you must, but try your best, and do not think too hardly of your
lumpish and gehenna-toes Dylan.

From a typescript. MS location unknown

RUTH WYNN OWEN
September 19 1943   Carmarthenshire
                              as from Strand Films 1 Golden Square W1

Ruth, my Dear,
    It's over a year, I think, or know, since I wrote to you with my heart on
my sleeve; now the shape of the hidden heart is arrowed, bloody, with a
children's on-a-tree inscription under it: X loves Y, though those aren't the
names. I've been in Wales for some weeks now, and have had time and a
rinsed head enough to be able to write what I want. In London, I mean to

---

1 A crossword-puzzle poem. Line 1 is a pun on the Lewis Gun, a type of machine-gun,
  and Lewis Carroll. Line 3, 'ladder' is the Ladder club and 'banting' is John Banting
  again. Line 4, 'swiss' is a Soho pub, the Swiss Tavern, and 'spoonered' suggests a
  spoonerism, to turn 'swiss pillars' into 'piss swillers'. Line 6, the Antelope is a
  Kensington pub. Line 7, *Dr Mabuse* was an early horror film. Line 8, FitzGibbon said
  there was a drinking club in Wardour Street run by a woman called Smith. And so on.
2 Wynford Vaughan-Thomas (1908–87), broadcaster and writer; he was from Swansea. He
  received the letter 'just after I returned from reporting the raid over Berlin in September
  1943'. He sent £10.
3 Vaughan-Thomas supplied a typescript copy of this letter but withheld the MS because
  it contained 'a remark' about Dan Jones's wife, Irene. Apparently Dylan had referred to
  her as 'the dam of Wales'.
4 A London pub.

write you every day, but the laziness, the horror and selfpity, that London drizzles down on me, stop everything but the ghost of a hope that perhaps you will ring, will drop a postcard to say you have come to town and would like to see me, or, ghostliest of all the half-hopes, that you might turn the corner of a street I am walking and that all the traffic will stop and the sirens suddenly sing sweetly, At last! at last!

Not that I had any right to think that you might write me, ring me, meet me; it was my turn, but I was too cowardly to go on, thinking that you might tire or say, forever, go away and no more.

But I want to forget the falsities and lazinesses and evasions and pretences of the oh-dear-crying past—oh, the mountainously pretentious want—and to say only what I think and feel now at this moment which, deep down, has been the same long moment for a year and more. But why do you want to hear from me? and how do I know that you do? I don't know, but I hope. Will you write and say that you still want to hear? to see me? And come to London—I'm going back tomorrow—or let me come to you. I can come anywhere. At any time. Tomorrow.

Thank you for your card at Christmas. Such a nice, prim, nothing-at-all remark it is—'thank you for your card at Christmas'—to end an inarticulate little letter on; because I must end, because I do not yet know if, after such a silent time, you want me to go on or want to see me. Perhaps you've forgotten. I am short, snub, unsteady, moles on my cheek, in a check suit. Of you I have only the still picture from the silliest film in the world, which is still the best film for the one reason that it allows me to send you now, with all my heart, my love.

Dylan

MS: Location unknown

T. W. EARP
4 October 1943   Strand Film Co   1 Golden Square   W1

Dear Tommy,

Your letter to me, when I was in Wales, was waiting for me, too late, when I came back from Wales; and, since then, I have not heard a word from you or seen you, and London is empty of everyone except the unseeable ubiquitors, our gumfed Allies.

When are you coming up next? I hope it's very soon. Bill Gaunt[1] wants to make a bad day for all three of us. Anyway, we must have a good bad day. Please do wire or write. Can you bring some Pera?[2] I am pretending to be busy now.

Yours
Dylan

MS: Ohio State University

1 William Gaunt (1900–80), painter and writer.
2 Verse written by Earp using the joke-name Pera, another anagram.

CAITLIN THOMAS
[?1943]   [headed paper: Strand Film Co etc]

My dear darling:
   It's the same; but true again. True as God, even though the ink, for some
reason, has changed. But if we're to spend the rest of our life in Wentworth
Barns, let us at least pay to have Van and Grada on the telephone. It's hell
trying to get hold of you, to tell you, Cat, that I couldn't get home—home,
Wentworth, but still our big gay bed—because, if I had done so, it would be
only for quarter of an hour or less. I'm tangled with doctors and M and B;
one doctor is facing me as I write.[1] I left Barker after a few minutes: he'd
had a letter from Donald making a date for next week, so that he felt he
needn't come along to get messed about *before* then. I am going, as you
know, to meet another doctor—someone called Peter Gorer—at the
Gargoyle[2] at 7 o clock tonight; I won't be finished until 6; and it would,
however, my darling, lovely to come back before then, [be] useless,
unprofitable, (from the point of view of us being together), and just silly. I
will stay in the Gargoyle until 7.45 (quarter to eight) & then taxi back.
Unless, unless, Cat, you can come up to the Gargoyle for a drink before
that. I'd love you to, not because of the horrid, low-ceilinged, devil-
enveloping Gargoyle Club itsbeastlyself, but because you and I have not
been together—even for a moment, apart from badly-acted Chekov—for
what seems months & months. So if you can, please come along to the
above horrible Gargoyle on, or after, just after, seven; & then we can go and
have a look at the big naughty world of the Café Royal or the Wheatsheaf,
just for a tiny bit before going back together. If you can't, or if you dislike
me, I'll be back just after eight. Do what you like. Only remember I like
you. I am sorry to write to you only by such plutocratic methods as
messenger-boy-sending. I love you.
                                         Dylan

Our money will be up tomorrow early evening at the same time as my not-
enough-pittance comes. Dear Cat.

MS: (Maurice Neville)

1 'M and B' was the popular name for one of the early antibiotics, manufactured by May
  and Baker. Thomas was working on *Conquest of a Germ*, a film released in 1944.
2 The Gargoyle Club, above a printing works in Soho, was opened in 1926 by David
  Tennant as a non-profit-making venue for writers and artists. By the 1940s there was
  less culture and more drinking.

T. W. EARP
Friday [?October 1943]   [headed paper: Strand Film Co etc]

Dear Tommy,
   I hope that a week today'll see you in Finch's with Normal and me; and
many apologies for having been late & self-fuddled after my rover's
Jamboree last Tuesday, the Tuesday the Gargoyle was so usually foul,
Tennant[1] trembling in the twenties, and Caitlin and myself still
boycotted and scouted after our paid-in-the-bowel sing-sing, our brownied-
off boy and girl bushranging, round the nightclub log. And I don't forget
lovely Virginia[2] having arrived in at the back door of a foreign society
from the front door of the Parson's house. I saw you go in a daze of night,
and could not remember if I had made our next Friday appointment, for by
that time I was odd God wot and all I could think of, nearly, was how
quickly to get out after getting another in: one of those brandy-and-milk-
and-thunders. So please do write. By another post as they say I am sending
you the very hard to read because of the typewriting and crossing out only
copy of the first half or so of the comic novel I've been telling you about for
too long.

                                        Yours ever,
                                        Dylan

MS: Ohio State University

T. W. EARP
23 12 43   Film Centre   34 Soho Square   W1

Dear Tommy,
   I did get your letter at the address you find, and I find, though differently
perhaps, it hard to credit; but a day late. Letter or message would, I think,
arrive even on time at my older, above, address, rather than at that House I
try to visit only on money-for-jam-and-ham-days.[3] I missed the Hole;[4]
and missed you, too, on returning, after about an hour of recrimination, not
self, to Sloane Square that last happy stagger.
   Thank you for the Chinese Serenade, Yai Sigh, sing low, prang gong, ring
high, me too in admiration and in pride at being present at that excellent
poet's appearance.
   What a pity you can't manage Boxing Day (which was not at Basing-
stoke). If, however, you feel that we could meet in any town between

1 David Tennant (1902–68), a younger son of the first Lord Glenconner.
2 Mrs Tennant.
3 Perhaps Filmicity House, one of Strand's addresses. Does 'jam-and-ham' mean that the
  Accounts Department was there, paying him for writing commentaries that 'hammed
  it up'?
4 'The Coal Hole' was a popular pub in the Strand.

Salisbury & your nearest, ring me at East Knoyle 83.[1] I'd jeep along at once.

Will you be in London soon? I hope v much.

Dylan

MS: Ohio State University

MAJOR PETER BAKER[2]
[?26 January 1944]   Film Centre W1

Dear Peter Baker,

Here is the manuscript of the first thirty thousand words of the novel we were talking about.[3]

This represents roughly a half of what the whole novel will be. It may look a little formless now, but actually the whole conception of the book is made to a most formal pattern.

It might be worth while my saying in a few lines what happens in the rest, the unwritten, as yet, part of the story. The hero, as you will notice is in the gradual process of losing his clothes; and as the story progresses so he loses more and more clothes, bit by bit. He loses these clothes through a series of incidents and in a number of places that are not connected by content or atmosphere with any of the incidents that came beforehand. That is, he does not progress through any ordinary drunken romantic picaresque movement, but through all kinds of sober, grisly, embarrassing, mortifying, but always readable, I hope, adventures in the wilderness of London—from Kilburn to Cockfosters.

Eventually, of course, he winds up without any clothes at all, and finds himself outside Paddington station a moment before dawn. Standing there naked, having had every garment fall from him simultaneously with the acquisition of every new experience, he wonders: 'Now I am here, outside Paddington station, just from where I began my pilgrimage, as naked as the day I was born. What'll happen to me? Will a very rich woman in a Rolls-Royce and a fur coat pass me by in the almost dawn, stop her chauffeur, and befriend me and lard me with charity and nymphomania? Or will a policeman pick me up for indecent exposure, my having shed all the skins

---

1 David Tennant's country home was at East Knoyle, in Wiltshire. Thomas used to stay there.

2 Presumably the Peter Baker (d. 1966) who became a publisher after the Second World War, and was Conservative MP for South Norfolk from 1950 to 1954, when he was gaoled for forgery. But in January 1944, Baker, an acting major in the Royal Artillery, was a prisoner of war. The letter, at Buffalo, is only a typescript, so the date shown may have been miscopied. A more likely date would be January 1946, when Baker had just started his Falcon Press. But 'Film Centre' had ceased to be a Thomas address by 1946. Baker's father, also a Major Baker, was general manager of Ealing Films. Unfortunately his first name was Reginald.

3 Adventures in the Skin Trade.

of my semi-proletarian, bourgeois, provincial upbringing? Or will a romantic tart clutch me to her used bosom, in the Catholic tradition of Francis Thompson? Or will, when dawn breaks, I see everyone walking about the streets, going to work, conducting traffic, going about their daily dulness, as naked, as utterly naked as I?'

That's how the book will run. Sorry if it sounds pretentious, but it's difficult to summarise the plot of something that's supposed to be nasty *and* funny.

Will you write me at the above address when you've read this; and I do hope you can do something about it.

Details, if any, until then.

Sincerely,
Dylan Thomas

TS: Buffalo

JOHN BAYLISS[1]
[?1944]   64 Grove Park Road   Chiswick   W4

Dear Mr. Bayliss:

Have I written to you? I know I did write, but have I posted it? If not, do please accept my apologies. Everything's in such a muddle here, as you probably saw even from the outside of the vicarage. Do use those two poems of mine that you want. On the same understanding as the other contributors of course: drop of royalties, if any.

Sorry I was away when you called. Call in if you're round here again, won't you?

Yours sincerely,
Dylan Thomas

MS: Texas

T. W. EARP
[postmarked 1944 ?9 Feb]   Far End   Bosham   Sussex[2]

Dear Tommy:

Everything went wrong last lost London meeting. Jobs came up and Tennant fell down and I couldn't reach the Ladder and Tennant couldn't

1 John Bayliss, writer and editor, serving in the RAF, was compiling an anthology that appeared yearly (as did many others, to circumvent the wartime ban on new magazines), *New Road*. He had visited a vicarage in Chiswick where Thomas was staying. The poems, published in the 1944 volume, were 'Dawn Raid' and 'On the Marriage of a Virgin'.

2 A bombing campaign on London, the 'Little Blitz', began in January 1944 after three years of relative freedom from air attack. The Thomases moved to a cottage at Bosham, Sussex, for several months.

remember if it was the Ladder we were to reach and I looked-in at the Antelope and it drawled with moustaches. An awful day. Now we're moved to a house in Bosham—very nice, too, looking over water and perhaps Russell Flint[1]—but I'm keeping the Manresa Studio on. I'll be up in London twice or more a week, but always on payday Fridays. Let me know, at Film Centre 34 Soho Square, when you're coming up. We must meet.

Almost as important—but perhaps a thing to be talked about when we meet in London—is that Petersfield is on the main London line from Bosham. Isn't Petersfield your market-town? And I would, I would like to meet there one morning.

Please don't forget to write. We have a dog now.

Dylan

MS: Ohio State University

DONALD TAYLOR[2]
Monday morning. 11 [?Spring 1944]   8 Wentworth Studios
                                        Manresa Rd   off King's Rd   Chelsea

Dear Donald:

I was going to hold up M & B anyway, in spite of Elton's demands,[3] as you suggested; but now the holding-up's unavoidable for a day or two as I've got laryngitis or bronchitis or asthma or something: a complaint, whatever it is, that makes your chest like a raw steak, prevents breathing, & produces a food-losing cough. Caitlin's going to leave a message for Elton this morning.

I tried to get hold of you Saturday in order to take you at your word about money. Five pounds was sent by Davies, but that had to go immediately on rent, debts, etc; the other salary money, which didn't, of course, arrive, was to have kept us for the rest of the week. I'm seeing an income-tax man tomorrow who will, I hope, be able, quickly, to arrange that I'm paid my ordinary salary 'pending I.C. discussions.' In the meantime, would you, as you said, lend me the salary-making-up money? I do need it so urgently.

I phoned Paddock (is that his name? I forget for the moment) & have sent the ms along. He sounds very promising.

When I received my fiver—from Ossy's own hands, as everything must now pass through him—I was told that a Parish memo had arrived to state that taxis should not be taken on jobs, people shd be interviewed in the office and not taken out to lunch, regular hours observed etc—*when can I resign, please!*

1 Sir William Russell Flint (1880–1969), painter, best known for his watercolours.
2 Thomas's employer at Strand Films.
3 Arthur Elton was supervisor of films at the Ministry of Information.

Do hope you can send that dough along by hand. Sorry to be a nuisance.

Dylan

MS: Buffalo

T. W. EARP
[postmarked 13 April 1944]   Far End   Bosham   Sussex

Dear Tommy,

Very very disappointed I couldn't manage our Petersfield meeting. Donald wired urgently for my help on the rebuilding of Coventry Cathedral,[1] so I had to hurry up and help him rebuild it in Henekey's. I do hope the wire, my wire, reached you before you started out.

When can the next date be, in Petersfield? Tuesday would suit me, this coming Tuesday, admirably, at the same time, 12.20, in church or pub opposite. Would it suit you? There'll be no cathedral-call this time; a country-town few hours would be very pleasant.

I'm looking forward, so is Caitlin, to your coming down here. I have found some nice places, and there are no Pauls or Ninas, however goodhearted, at all: only the worst people I've ever met and not to talk to. Grand if I could bring you back here with me after Tuesday's Petersfield.

Write or wire about Tuesday.

And will you ask May, please, about Bosham, and send her my love?

I have poems to bring on Tuesday, and hope Pera has been busy too.

Yours,
Dylan

MS: Ohio State University

T. W. EARP
Sunday 15 or 16 April '44   Far End   Old Bosham   Sussex

Dear Tommy:

It was distressing not to meet you so many times. I can't remember in detail how we missed each other so successfully; once, I think, I wired confirmation of a wrong Petersfield date too late, and, by going to town, missed your wire confirming the right one. Then I was sent to Coventry, a visit of a few days which confused things for many more, and went to a wedding, and had such a fall into melancholy I couldn't even get round to Lysol or the utility blade but could only whimper in bed and fail to understand detective stories. In one communication you too hinted at the coming on of coma from which I hope you've now recovered enough to meet either this Tuesday or this Friday. On Tuesday I shall be, anyway, but

---

1 Thomas was working on a film about the much-bombed city of Coventry called *Building the Future*.

with hope, in Mooney's Cambridge college[1] from half past twelve. On Friday I can be anywhere you like at any after-twelve time if you'll write, or wire, before then to Bosham. But Tuesday will be best, of course, because it is nearest.

Here is a poem in three parts. One part, the second, I've already shown you in London when I probably forgot to mention that it was incomplete. Also another short poem.[2] I would love to hear what you think about them when, at last, our bi-paths join in some coal-hole, some cheese-hole, or in any other reputable and, almost essential, acquaintanceless sewer.

Yours,
Dylan

MS: Ohio State University

M. J. TAMBIMUTTU
[?1944][3]   [headed paper: 24 Culross Street W1]

Dear Tambi,
My price has gone up, you mink! It's *thirty* shillings now.

Yrs,
Dylan

MS: Carbondale

LAURENCE POLLINGER
Wed 28th June 1944   Gryphon Films[4]   Verity Films
Filmicity House   2–6 West Street   WC2

Dear Laurence Pollinger:
Sorry not to have answered your letter before this: the letter about James Laughlin of New Directions and his wish to know what the hell I'm doing.

I'm glad Laughlin's working towards plans for the issue of my first American book, THE WORLD I BREATHE, in a cheaper form. Does this mean any money for me? Hope very very so.

Incidentally, I have never had my agreed-upon so-many copies of the pamphlet (Poet Of The Month) NEW POEMS that he published fairly recently.

1 One of the 'Irish houses', London pubs run by the J. G. Mooney company.
2 'Ceremony After a Fire Raid' is a poem in three parts, and was published the following month in the magazine *Our Time*. The 'short poem' was probably 'Lie still, sleep becalmed'.
3 *Poetry London* printed two Thomas poems in April 1944.
4 Gryphon was the successor to Strand, and had ambitious plans to make feature films. Donald Taylor was still in charge.

I haven't a new *book* ready for him, but I have got some work on the way. Perhaps you will tell him that I shall finish a short novel this year: the novel [*six words are deleted*: Dent turned down some time ago:] ADVENTURES IN THE SKIN TRADE. Just in case he wants to mention it in some advertisement of his. And there will be a new collection of poems but probably this won't be much good for him as quite a number of them will have already been published in the NEW POEMS pamphlet. How many I can't know until I am sent my copies of the pamphlet.

I'm writing films now, and have almost completed a feature film based on the lives of Burke and Hare. This film will be put into production by the Gryphon Films, for which I work, some time this year; but I do think that it might be a good idea to publish the script separately, perhaps with an introductory essay. I'll let you have a copy of the script very soon.[1]

I shall also send you a book of poems, for Dent's. Can you tell me what advance I can expect on a book of poems from J.M.D.? Ordinary poem-book length. Size of my TWENTY FIVE POEMS, about. I'd like to know what I could expect so that I can plan my financial embarrassments for the winter.

Hope to hear from you, and sorry about my delay.

Sincerely,
[no signature]

MS: Texas

T. W. EARP
12 July 44   Hill Cottage   Hedgerley Dean   near Slough   Bucks[2]

Dear Tommy:
Haven't seen you for so long. When will you be up, or are the flying bombs keeping you out of town altogether?[3] I don't go up myself unless there's a real reason. Give me a real reason to come up next week. Can you make it Monday or Tuesday or Wednesday? I'm going to Wales for a few weeks quite soon and *should* like to see you before I go. Could you come to Wales? Anyway, let me know at the above, Donald's, address whether you can come to town next week. We must meet, if you can come, in an underground bar: Ward's, Piccadilly; Coal Hole; Falstaff; Piccadilly Hotel American Bar; or any other really low place you can think of. Hope to hear.

Yours
Dylan

MS: Ohio State University

1 Taylor never succeeded in making the film, *The Doctor and the Devils*. Thomas's script ('from the story by Donald Taylor') was published in 1953. The film (written by Ronald Harwood) was finally made in 1986.
2 Another temporary address, this time west of London.
3 Attacks by the pilotless weapons began in June and drove a million people out of London.

VERNON WATKINS
27 July 1944   Blaen Cwm   Llangain   near Carmarthen

Dear Vernon,

I didn't think it was so long since we saw each other, or since I wrote to you. We were three months in Sussex, and two months near Beaconsfield.[1] So it's nearly half a year and what a year and what a pity and what the hell. We must (always my fault that we haven't) write regularly to each other now, if only to report that a little tepid blood is still trickling, that there is still a faint stir somewhere in the chest, that we can still put pen to paper, paper to bottom, thumb to nose, the world to rights, two & two together, put and take.

The Sussex months were beastly. When it wasn't soaking wet, I was. Aeroplanes grazed the roofs, bombs came by night, police by day, there were furies at the bottom of my garden, with bayonets, and a floating dock like a kidney outside the window, and Canadians in the bushes, and Americans in the hair; it was a damned banned area altogether.[2] They worshipped dogs there, too, and when a pom was born in one house the woman put out the Union Jack.

Near Beaconsfield, where Chesterton sat on his R.C.,[3] it was better. We stayed with a man who runs the film company I fool for, and the country was green and okay, but the well-off people were dry and thin and grieved over their petrol-less motorcars and played bridge like ferrets, and the poor snarled and were all named Body.

Now we're with my mother and father in Llangain, near Llanstephan where everyone goes into the pubs sideways, & the dogs piss only on back-doors, and there are more unwanted babies shoved up the chimneys than there are used french letters in the offertory boxes. It's a mean place but near Laugharne where we will go next week.

Is Dot in Carmarthen? Let me know. We'd love to see her.

I've found that I can do most of my filmwork outside London, (which soon will be shelled terribly by things that scream up into the stratosphere, passing the queen bees, and then roar down on to Manresa Road),[4] and so we are looking, again, for somewhere to live in the country. In Laugharne, if possible. In Wales, preferably. And we'll stay here, getting on my father— for he's one bald nerve—until we find a house, a flat, a room, a sty, a release.

By the way, I have a new complaint. Itching feet. There is nothing to see, the feet just itch. I have to take my shoes off many times a day and rub my

---

1 With Donald Taylor, whose house 'near Slough' (see previous letter) was also near Beaconsfield.
2 Bosham is on the Channel coast east of Portsmouth. When the Thomases were there, the invasion of Europe was imminent.
3 A pun. The author G. K. Chesterton (1874–1936) had lived at Beaconsfield. He was a convert to Roman Catholicism. 'Sat on his R.C.' sounds like 'sat on his arse'.
4 There were rumours in London of forthcoming attacks by German rockets.

soles with my socks. Ask Dan if he knows what it is—he's learned in little woes. How *is* Dan? I'd write to him but have lost his address. Ask him to write to me; I feel very Warmley to him all the time, and would very much love to hear.

Here is a poem (printed in 'Our Time') which perhaps you haven't seen.[1] I didn't print the Lorca lines above the poem. Will you tell me about it? It really is a Ceremony, and the third part of the poem is the music at the end. Would it be called a voluntary, or is that only music at the beginning?

Keidrych & Lynette are in Llanybri. I always knew Keidrych was a turnip, and now there are little turnips growing all over his top. Lynette, who cannot read Welsh, is revising the standard nineteenth-century book on Welsh prosody, and also annotating a work on the Hedgerows of Carmarthenshire. I hope she becomes famous, & that they will name an insect after her.

I am writing poems, and have three new ones I'll send you when they are typewritten and after I have heard from you about the Ceremony.

Write very soon, please, & tell me everything.

Love,
Dylan

MS: British Library

VERNON WATKINS
26 August 1944   Blaen Cwm   Llangain   near Carmarthen

Dear Vernon,
I'm so very glad that you are going to Pennard on September 2nd, and that Gwen[2] is coming down too and that we shall be able to see both of you. Do you think that you could come to Carmarthen town to meet? It's only an hour by bus from Swansea. We would come to Pennard but it's a nuisance taking the baby on crowded buses and my mother is never very well and it's rather a strain for her to look after Aeronwy for a whole day. If you come to Carmarthen we could meet in the Boar's Head or somewhere and have some beer in a corner and a long lunch. So please do try. I'll look forward to hearing from you. Bring a poem. I've just finished two poems, one over 200 lines and I'm excited by it. The other is a Laugharne poem: the first place poem I've written. I'll bring them both along.[3]

1 'Ceremony After a Fire Raid.'
2 Gwen Davies, Watkins's fiancée.
3 'Vision and Prayer' and 'Poem in October'. Thomas was enjoying a new burst of creativity. Blaen Cwm, where 'Poem in October' was completed, was the family cottage where he had been writing poetry since adolescence. Watkins said that the poem had been 'contemplated' since 1941, and originally the first line read, 'It was my twenty-seventh year to heaven'.

We may be living in New Quay in a week or two, & are trying to get a house. If we do—the house will be right on the sea—you *must* come down to stay after you are married. Or before, of course, but I mean as a special bit of holiday. Caitlin sends her love to both of you. And mine is sent always.

Dylan

No word from Dan. Do you see him? Or will you send his address?
I saw Mervyn Levy. He's stationed at Llangennech.
Keidrych is living in Llanybri again, but I don't see him much.
Our dog has got mange.
Aeronwy cannot walk but she climbs rocks.
And of course we are coming to your marriage, in our brightest colours.

MS: British Library

VERNON WATKINS
Wednesday [30 August 1944]   Blaen Cwm   Llangain   near Carmarthen

Dear Vernon,
    A complication. On Monday Sept. 4 we are moving into a new house—we call it a house; it's made of wood and asbestos—in New Quay, Cardiganshire. It's in a really wonderful bit of the bay, with a beach of its own. Terrific. But it means that we're much further from Carmarthen. Now how can we meet? Can you come down here? You said you didn't want to spend your leave outside Pennard, but couldn't you spare us just *one* night in New Quay? We would love it so. Anyway, write. After Monday, our address will be Majoda, New Quay. The name is made of the beginnings of the names of the three children of the man who built the questionable house. I may alter the name to Catllewdylaer.[1]
    Here is a new poem.[2] It's a month & a bit premature. I do hope you like it, & wd like very much to read it aloud to you.
    Will you read it aloud too? It's got, I think, a lovely slow lyrical movement.
    Write as soon as you can.
    We must all meet.

Love,
Dylan

In the poem, I notice, on copying out, that I have made October trees bare. I'll alter later.[3]

MS: British Library

1 Majoda was a bungalow, meant for summer visitors, not residents. Thomas rented it for a pound a week.
2 'Poem in October'; it celebrates Thomas's thirtieth birthday.
3 'Bare' became 'winged'.

T. W. EARP
September 1st 1944   Majoda[1] New Quay Cardiganshire

So much Meux has flowed under the bridges
You could drown London town, which would be just,
Since we met in the spring and drank religious.
If we don't meet again I shall throw away my trust.
And bitter's gone up and bombs have come down
Since Pera and pal like a pair of mouse
Squeaked in the liquorish wainscots of the town
And thumbed their whiskers at Philmayicity House.[2]
It's a long way from London, as the fly bombs,
And nothing of Donald's guile can lug me
Away from this Wales where I sit in my combs
As safe and snug as a bugger in Rugby.
We've got a new house and it's called Majoda.
Majoda, Cards, on the Welsh-speaking sea.
And we'll stay in this wood-and-asbestos pagoda
Till the blackout's raised on London and on me.
But meet we must before the dove of peace
Drops in my eye his vain and priggish turd,
And England's full of cultural police,
(For you, at once, a sentence of three months Heard,
For me a year on bread and de Polnay, Peter),
And verse inspectors kick up a mingy din
Demanding, at pistol point, to read your metre,
And oh the significant form troops mincing in!
How shall we meet, then, since countries lie between
The Rimbaud of Ockham and Swansea's Villon?
O fly the miles in Stephenson's machine
And spend a month with

                                        Yours ever
                                        Dylan

MS: Ohio State University

1 See previous letter.
2 Filmicity House had been one of Strand's addresses. Other parts of the pun might be
  Phil May, the cartoonist; Philip Lindsay, the writer, who worked for Strand; Earp's
  wife, who was called May. In line 1, Meux is a brew of beer. Line 11, 'Combs', which
  rhymed with 'bombs', was short for 'combination garment', old-fashioned underwear
  incorporating vest and drawers. Line 20, perhaps Gerald Heard, writer, friend of Aldous
  Huxley. Line 21, Peter de Polnay, novelist. Line 26, Earp lived in a house in Hampshire
  called Ockham Cottage.

DONALD TAYLOR
4th September 1944   Majoda   New Quay   Cardiganshire

Dear Donald,

Here is Resistance:[1] or, at least, the commentary minus the concluding chorus (I'll explain that in a moment). Writing it was made more difficult by my not knowing for what countries the film is intended, nor whether it will be shown before the war is over or after. I have worked on the assumption that it *will* be after—or, anyway, after all the chief countries of resistance have been freed; and so the Resistance story must be told in the past tense: 'we were free; we were occupied; we were maltreated; we made sporadic attempts at revenge; for these we suffered; we learnt that Resistance must be organised; we became a movement; we became an Army; we fought and won. Now we are free again.' Following that rough line, I have, as you'll see, stopped short at 'we won.' I wanted to hear from you before writing the short section of 'now we are free again': to hear whether the treatment is in accordance with the plan we roughed out together. I haven't put in any visual indications at the side of the commentary. You know all the material there is at hand, and I, of course, don't. When the 4th Voice begins there is, I remember, a Russian resistance-meeting sequence which would go well. I don't know if you agree, but I haven't *mentioned* underground press, telephone-exchanges etc but have indicated, perhaps sufficiently, in the commentary towards the end where the press etc shd be seen.

Do let me know if it's at all satisfactory: and what to write at the end. Just the 'now we are free again' stuff?

Anyway, I do hope it is something to work on. It is in a sufficiently loose form for me to be able to change it around drastically at a moment's notice.

Looking forward to hearing from you.

I've found a bungalow right on the Atlantic, with a beach of its own, & moved in today. Want a holiday? Tell me when you need me in London. I pay my own fare, of course.

Waiting to hear to work to do anything.

Ever,
Dylan

On reading through, I see a couple of rather too-literary phrases which I shall cut out in next (& final?) version. 'Steely sea,' for instance. Out!

MS: Texas

1 Thomas enclosed a seven-page MS headed *The Unconquerable People*, written for four Voices in fiery prose or perhaps verse: '. . . Men cannot chain / forever the fury of Man / against their evil / though they break his bones. / Resistance began. / Resistance began / clumsily, hastily, with a knife in the dark . . .'

LAURENCE POLLINGER
Sept 12 1944   Majoda   New Quay   Cardiganshire

Dear Laurence Pollinger,
    I was glad to hear that Laughlin of New Directions wants to bring out a
Selected Volume of my stuff. Yes, please do go ahead & draw up a contract
with Laughlin. Is a 'flat 10%' good? What's it mean, really? Any advance?
    I'll be sending along a new book of poems for Dent's next (I hope)
week.[1]
    Has Laughlin answered you about my enquiry as to what has happened
to my copies of New Poems ?[2] I've never seen a single copy. Do ask him to
let me have some, will you?

                                              Sincerely,
                                              Dylan Thomas

MS: Texas

DONALD TAYLOR
19 Sept 44   Majoda   New Quay   Cardiganshire

Dear Donald,
    Wonderful news—or half-news. I have my fingers, legs, and eyes, crossed.
    Do write or wire me once you know the best/worst.
    I hope you're not quite so penniless, & in debt, as I am, but, anyway, the
dough from B & H will be, I'm sure, welcome.[3] And oh the difference to
me!
    I've read through Resistance many times and added a valediction. I can't
do more until I know more of your, & M.O.I., reactions. Your wire about it
was so hopelessly muddled by the P.O. people here that all I could clearly
make out was that you hoped the MOI would consider making a more
ambitious film than they'd intended. This commentary can be expanded,
contracted, rewritten or thrown away & started again at a moment's
notice, as you know.
    Do tell me: has V.2. really arrived? Here there are rumours.[4] I'm coming
up, unless you call me earlier, at the end of the month. Want to discuss
many things urgently.

                                              Ever,
                                              Dylan

You'll notice I've suggested that we cut out the opening lines 'We were
free'. Surely, 'we' weren't?

MS: Texas

1 The volume being planned was Deaths and Entrances.
2 The 'Poets of the Year' volume, published 1943.
3 'B & H': Burke and Hare (the film about the body-snatchers) = The Doctor and the Devils.
4 German rockets, 'V2s', had begun to bombard London. The first landed on 8 September.

PETER LUNN LTD[1]
20 Sept '44   Majoda   New Quay   Cardiganshire

Dear Sir,
   Thank you for your letter of the 15th.
   I am very interested indeed in the idea of editing, and writing the
commentary for, the book of photographs you mention.
   I shall be in London at the end of the month—on the 28th, I think—and
will be staying up for some time. If you would write me, making an
appointment for any day after the 28th, I should be grateful.
   I could, if it was really urgent, come up a few days beforehand. Anyway, I
hope you'll let me know.

                                          Yours faithfully,
                                          Dylan Thomas

MS: National Library of Wales

T. W. EARP
[postmarked 21 September 1944]   [Cardiganshire]

          Dear Tommy, please, from far, sciatic Kingsley[2]
          Borrow my eyes. The darkening sea flings Lee
          And Perrins on the cockled tablecloth
          Of mud and sand. And, like a sable moth,
          A cloud against the glassy sun flutters his
          Wings. It would be better if the shutter is
          Shut. Sinister dark over Cardigan
          Bay. No-good is abroad. I unhardy can
          Hardly bear the din of No-good wracked dry on
          The pebbles. It is time for the Black Lion
          But there is only Buckley's unfrisky
          Mild. Turned again, Worthington. Never whisky.
          I sit at the open window, observing
          The salty scene and my Playered gob curving
          Down to the wild, umbrella'd, and french lettered
          Beach, hearing rise slimy from the Welsh lechered
          Caves the cries of the parchs and their flocks. I
          Hear their laughter sly as gonococci. . . .
          There slinks a snoop in black. I'm thinking it

1 A small publishing firm that wanted Thomas to write an illustrated book about the
  streets of London. It had been impressed by captions he wrote for the magazine *Lilliput*.
2 Line 1, Earp lived in a village called Kingsley. Lines 2 and 3, Lea and Perrins Worcester
  sauce. Lines 11 and 12, Buckley's is a Welsh beer, as Worthington is an English. Line
  17, parch, a Welsh clergyman, literally 'reverend'. Line 33, Augustus John.

Is Mr. Jones the Cake, that winking-bit,
That hymning gooseberry, that Bethel-worm
At whose ball-prying even death'll squirm
And button up. He minces among knickers,
That prince of pimps, that doyen of dung-lickers.
Over a rump on the clerical-grey seashore,
See how he stumbles. Hallelujah hee-haw!,
His head's in a nest where no bird lays her egg.
He cuts himself on an elder's razor leg.
Sniff, here is sin! Now must he grapple, rise:
He snuggles deep among the chapel thighs,
And when the moist collection plate is passed
Puts in his penny, generous at last.

On Saturday Augustus comes, bearded
Like Cardy's bard, and howling as Lear did.
A short stay only but oh, how nice. No
One more welcome than the oaktrunked maestro—
No-one but you who'll never come unless
I send the million-miscarriaged Welsh Express,
A train of thought run on wheels within wheels.
But on October 1 I show my heels
To New Quay, Cards, and then shall brave V.2.
And come to London. Remember me to
May. Is there a chance of one I never see
Coming up, also? Write me: Ever,

D.

MS: Ohio State University

PETER LUNN LTD
25 Sept 44   Majoda   New Quay   Cardiganshire

Dear Sir,
    Thank you for your note.
    I shall call at your office on Friday, Sept. 29, at 3 p.m., as suggested.
                              Yours faithfully,
                              Dylan Thomas

MS: National Library of Wales

PETER LUNN LTD
6 October '44   Guild House   2–6 West St   London   WC2

Dear Sirs,

Re Book on Streets. I am in receipt of your letter of October 6 and confirm that the terms contained in it are in accordance with our arrangements.[1]

I hope that it is possible for me to let you have the completed manuscript in about three months.

Yours faithfully,
Dylan Thomas

MS: National Library of Wales

DONALD TAYLOR
[?October 1944]   Majoda   New Quay   Cardiganshire

Back in the bosom, repentant and bloodshot,
Under the draper-sly skies,[2]
I try to forget my week in the mudpot
And cottonwool it in lies:

'I do not, my dear, pretend that I mastered
Altogether the intemperate vice.
I may in the Gargoyle have fallen down plastered,
But I did see my publishers—twice.

You wouldn't believe me were I to aver
That I never went out "on the bust".
You'll pardon the phrase? Ah, thank you, my dear,
And I did see an editor—just.

Now let us be frank. I behaved, I'm afraid,
Like a squalid and tiddly dunce.
But I really was brave in that *terrible* raid,
And I did make some money—once.'

Dear Donald,

I'm sending you the words for 'Our Country'.[3] I took away a typed copy but, as most of the corrections to be made were only of punctuation, I made such a mess of the typesheets I decided to write out the whole thing afresh. Going through it, as I did, carefully, it's my opinion that it may be a

1 Thomas was paid an advance of £50.
2 Cardiganshire people, the butt of many Welsh jokes, are supposed to have a sly streak, and also to thrive as drapers.
3 Another rhetorical film for the Ministry of Information, released in 1944. Texas has Thomas's eleven-page MS.

mistake to have the words printed in the premiere programme. For two reasons. First: the cuts you made in the verse-commentary, which, from the point of the film, were essential, did destroy some of the continuity of the verse *as verse*. The words were written to be spoken & heard, & not to be read, but all the same there was in the original version—before your most necessary cuts—a literary thread, or, at least, a sense-thread, which is now broken. And, second: I think that, to many people, a reading of these words before the film will presuggest an artiness that is not, I think, in the film. If, for instance, Alf Burlinson, who is loud in his praise of the film and of the verse (inseparable, we hope), had first of all seen the words written or printed down his reactions to the film would, I think, have been different. Written down, the verse looks a little chaotic—as it's bound to be. And, to Alf & others, 'modern'. Heard spoken to a beautiful picture, the words gain a sense & authority which the printed word denies them. I don't make myself very clear, but these are two quite relevant points. If you *are* going to print the words, perhaps Miss Harrington, who now knows my kind of punctuation or lack of it, could do them? Anyway, whatever you think best is alright by me.

I am just starting to go through 20 Years[1]—the book, John's selection of passages, & my own notes. I shd start on the real work this week.

I hope to hear from you soon about B & H. Passed? Hope to God so as the money I collected in London is all gone in debts. And new ones are rising.

I enclose, for your private interest, Watt's letter on the Dickens script.[2] Not much there, once it has been threed up. Could you return it some time?

Yours ever,
Dylan

Thank you for London kindness & help with the scrappy Streets synopsis. I saw some of Banting's suggested drawings for it. Very nice. Very sweet. Very unsuitable.

P.S. On page 6 of the 'Our Country' verse: I know that the place-name Shipbourne is wrong, but can't remember what was right. It might have been Shibbon. Perhaps Colin could find out if there *is* such a place as Shibbon-in-Bredon, for I seem to remember that the penultimate line of the list of place-names was only one word. May be wrong, though. Anyway, Shipbourne is wrong.

MS: Texas

---

1 A film was projected (but never made) based on Maurice O'Sullivan's book about the Blasket Islands, off the south-west tip of Ireland, *Twenty Years A-Growing*.
2 A film on the life of Charles Dickens that Thomas was to write with Philip Lindsay. It was not made.

VERNON WATKINS

TO BE READ FIRST

28 Oct 1944   as from Majoda   New Quay   Cardiganshire

My dear Gwen and Vernon,

What on earth can you think of me?[1] It is the last, last, last thing of all—on top of all the other things—that the hasty letter I should scribble in such a panic to you, while on the train away from London where we never met, should remain unposted until today: 26 days after your wedding. I have no excuses, but that I was so flurried and anxious, so tired, so miserable, that I put the train-letter into my pocket, arrived in New Quay after an 8 hour journey, imagined, in a kind of delirium, that it was posted; & then waited, perhaps without much hope of ever hearing, to hear from you that, though I was not forgiven, my explanation was understood. What can you think of me? Today I found the letter, crumpled, unposted, in my overcoat. Please, please do try to understand. I shall let you have these two letters now, & a poem I meant also to send weeks ago,[2] without another word of apology or abasement. All our love to you both, for your happiness forever.

Your worst man,
Dylan

[Sent with letter dated 28 October 1944.]

The Train to Wales, 1.30 Wed.

On Not Turning Up To Be Best Man
At The Wedding Of One's Best Friend

Reeking & rocking back from a whirled London where nothing went right, all duties were left, and my name spun rank in the whole old smoky nose, I try, to a rhythm of Manchester pocket-handkerchers, and Conk him on the mousetrap, Conk him on the mousetrap, from the London-leaving wheels, to explain to you both, clearly & sincerely, why I never arrived, in black overcoat & shiny suit, rose-lapelled, breathing cachous & great good will, at lunch and church. But the train's stacked tight, I'm tabling a bony knee for this little pad, and am stuck, in the windy corridor, between many soldiers, all twelve foot high & commando-trained to the last lunge of the bayonet. It's not easy to think, or write, or be, and my explanations, true as air, sound, when I try to marshal them, like a chapter of accidents written in a dream by a professor of mathematics who has forgotten all formulas

---

1 Thomas had failed to appear at Vernon Watkins's wedding in London, where he was supposed to be best man, on 2 October. According to Gwen Watkins, Vernon said, 'That's the end of Dylan as far as I'm concerned.' But when this letter arrived, he was quick to forgive. The enclosure, written in pencil on well-creased paper, has many alterations; Mrs Watkins thought its appearance was faked, to make it look as if it had lain in Thomas's overcoat pocket for weeks.
2 'Vision and Prayer'.

but the wrong one that 2 & 2 make 5. First, then, I arrived in London on Thursday & was sent straightaway, that is, on Friday morning, to Coventry: the City of Coventry, where the company who pay me occasionally are making a film called 'Building The Future', a subject on which I particularly should have no say. In Coventry I arranged to catch a train back on Sunday night, which would carry me to London in time to meet you both at the station. That train, owing to no fault of my own but to callous & diffident members of the hotel staff, who did not trouble to get the train-times straight, but only late, I missed. There was no other train until the next morning, which was Monday, & that train would reach London at an hour just convenient for me to be able to get into a cab & race for the church. I could not, at that hour of Sunday night, reach my office to leave a message for someone there to spend Monday morning ringing up you & your people & making my—by this time—frantic excuses; I could, indeed, have reached the office by telephone, but there would be no-one there to answer, except some celluloid rat or other. So I waited until Monday morning & then, before catching the train, rang up the office & told a secretary girl to ring Charing Cross Hotel straight away, get in touch with anyone called Watkins, & explain the whole position to him or her. I had not, myself, got the time to ring up Charing X Hotel, as it wd take hours, & as my call to the office could be, & was, made Priority, thereby saving those hours during which, by the nicotine-stained skin of my few teeth, I caught the wedding-going & troop-crammed horribly slow train. On arriving in London I managed, by the fervour of my heart only, I am sure, to snatch a cab. I sat back, wheezing, in it. 'Where to?' the driver said. And—this is the real God-help-me—I couldn't remember the name of the church. It was after half past one. I looked in all my pockets but had left your last letter, I suppose, in wood-&-asbestos Majoda, New Quay. I tried, in my head, every church name I knew. I explained to the driver: 'A Church in the City. Very old.' Suddenly something came & I said, 'I think it's Godolphin. Or something like that. Yes, Godolphin.' We went to the City, the driver was dubious. We asked policemen: they were certain. By now, after two, & you too, I feared & hoped, married without my presence but with all my love, I went back to the office to find the secretary-girl out for lunch & the few people still there surprisingly cool and ignorant of all the infernal muddle that had been clotting up the wheels of the world for over a day. There was nothing to do. When the girl came in I asked her, though I was terrified to ask, if her little side of the whole business had gone well. She had tried the Charing X Hotel all the morning. The Watkins were out. She had left my name. The Watkins were out.

Later that evening, feeling wretcheder than ever before, alone in my beast of a studio, I remembered the church. Of course I remembered the church. Not Godolphin but St. Bartholomew the Great—too late! O what a prize of prize pickles & I'll understand always if you never want to see me again. I know this hasty jumble can't explain all the somersaulting & backspinning of circumstance against my being where I most wanted to be:

at your wedding. God bless you both, & do try to forgive me.

All my love,

Dylan

MS: British Library

T. W. EARP

28 October 1944   Majoda New Quay Cardiganshire

Dear Tommy,

I came up to town for a week but it was sudden and accidental and I made no arrangements & hoped to see you only by hanging about some of the places in which sometimes we hang about together. But at the end of November, when I can move next, we must & will meet. I'll send you a string of wires beforehand, none of them contradictory. Oh I do wish you & May could come down here before then—won't you ever?

I've just had a birthday & here is a poem.[1] I hope you'll read & like.

Tell me about it when you write; & write soon.

Yours,

Dylan

MS: Ohio State University

DONALD TAYLOR

28 October 1944   [headed paper: Gryphon Films etc]

as from Majoda New Quay Cardiganshire

Dear Donald,

Now who could be writing to *you* from Gryphon? Why, bless my soul, it's the little Welsher. This is only to thank you for your wire, and to tell you that though work on *20 Years* has been going so slowly & badly that at one time I thought we'd have to alter the title to *40 Years*, now I believe I can get ahead with it properly. Reason for the badness & slowness is that this little bungalow is no place to work in when there's a bawling child there, too: the rooms are tiny, the walls bumpaper-thin, & a friend arrived with another baby with a voice like Caruso's. Now, however, I have just taken a room in a nearby house: a very quiet room where I know I can work till I bleed. So little's been done on *20 Years*—I've spent my time running out to look at the sea, away from the greater sea of noise within—it's not really worth discussing or sending. But now I shall get down to it with axe, concentration, and blow-lamp.

I hope the censors have finally come to heel. Let me know what happens

---

1 'Poem in October'.

from time to time about all our films, made, halfmade, unmade, readymade, secondhand, if you can.

A very nice fellow here, who runs a Nautical School, asked me how to get 16 mm films to show. All kinds: they're tough boys. I asked him to get in touch with you, who would—I hoped—tell him, in turn, who to get in touch with. Hope you can help him.

The Dickens terms are indeed scandalous. I would like to have nothing to do with them at all—they really are almost insolently puny—& I won't if some other book-money I'm expecting comes along before the contract. Otherwise I'm afraid I'll have to sign as even the preliminary £20, which is all I'll get out of the first £100, will settle a debt & take this bungalow for another three months. I hope not to have to sign, though, damn their meanness.

How are things? Have a drink for me, only make it beer, as a new resolution, now a fortnight, nearly, old, has banned all other drinks—for a long time, I trust & believe.

Ever,
Dylan

Will write again soon, with *much more encouraging* Twenty Years news.

MS: Buffalo

LAURENCE POLLINGER
28 Oct 44   Majoda   New Quay   Cardiganshire

Dear Pollinger,
    Enclosed title page of book of poems. Forgot to put it with the manuscript which I hope now is in your hands—along with explanatory letter.[1]

Yours sincerely,
Dylan Thomas

P.S. Have just received the copy of *New Poems* and Laughlin's letter. I'll reply personally to Laughlin, at once. Would you send the remaining presentation copies of *New Poems* to me here at New Quay? I want to make some alterations in them before sending them on to friends.

MS: Texas

---

1 *Deaths and Entrances* was not published until 1946, when it included poems still unwritten in October 1944.

VERNON WATKINS
Nov 15 1944   Majoda   New Quay   Cardiganshire

Dear Vernon,

I was so very pleased to have your letter last week, your letter this morning, and, best, yours and Gwen's (even in 1980) pardon. I can now take my head out of the grubby lining of my overcoat pocket, where I have been keeping it for weeks along with a beetle, something that looks like porridge and smells like the Underground, and an unposted letter. I can take my head out now and face the perpetual rain.

I like your address, especially if it is Story Stratford.[1] What kind of a house have you, or is it a room, or rooms, or a flat, or the use of somebody's old larder to live in? I should like very much to visit you, if I may, if Gwen will bury her sten-gun[2] in the garden before I come, one day, soon, in December. Caitlin and I are going to London the first week of December. Caitlin will leave Aeronwy with her mother, at Ringwood, and we will probably stay in an hotel for a week or two. Caitlin hasn't had a holiday away from Aeronwy since Aeronwy appeared with pain and trumpets. So we want to go to cinemas & theatres and eat nice spicy meals and meet you and Gwen and go to see paintings and drink in the Eight Bells and Claridges like improper people and sneer at the V.2. and come back here for Christmas. (I didn't tell you that Vera Phillips, now Killick, for she has married a man called Killick but who, for years, we thought was called Waistcoat, is living in the next bungalow to us on this ratty cliff. She lives alone except for her baby daughter who is five months old and, during all that time, has screamed only twice. Vera says it is because of character. We say it is because of laziness. Vera lives on cocoa, and reads books about the technique of third-century brass work, and gets up only once a day to boil the cat an egg, which it detests.) So we must meet in London. Is it possible for you & Gwen to have leave together & come up and see a play in a theatre, or outside a theatre, with us? And a real meal, not a crawl on bent minds round the Tambied pubs?

Has Dot told you yet that we met in Cardigan, filthy town, for a, on my part, rather rambling hour? I had been to a farmers' fair. Dot looked awfully well, and was lovely to meet. I hope I'll see her again when she comes billeting.

I am so glad you liked the 'Vision & Prayer' poem; and that the diamond shape of the first part seems no longer to you to be cramped & artificed. I agree that the second part is, formally, less inevitable, but I cannot alter it, except, perhaps, in detail. I will read the very last line again, & see what, if anything, can be done about the stresses. I haven't a copy of the poem

---

1 The address was Stony Stratford, in Buckinghamshire. Vernon and Gwen Watkins, both in the armed forces, were billeted there. Both worked at nearby Bletchley Park, the code-breaking centre. So did Captain Dan Jones.
2 A type of sub-machine-gun.

with me but, as I remember, I liked the last line *for* the awkward stressing, for the braking, for the slowing up of the last two same-vowelled words (I wrote 'birds' instead of 'words'). But I'll read the whole poem again, most carefully. Yes, the Hound of Heaven is baying there in the last verse, but, at the moment, and again from memory, I don't remember seeing any Hopkins after the poem was finished.

I'll look out for the David poem[1] in the Listener, if I can get a copy from our newsagent who closes nearly all day and sells, I think, only the Western Mail and ink.

Here is a poem of mine which I started a long time ago but finished very recently, after a lot of work. This poem, the Vision & Prayer, & the birthday poem are coming out together in the January Horizon.[2] I hope you'll be able to get a copy & see them in pretty print.

How is Dan? Is he a new father? Do you see him? Send him my love, if you do.

And love from Caitlin & myself to you and Gwen.

> Ever,
> Dylan

MS: British Library

*LOUISE VIDAUD DE PLAUD[3]
15 November 1944   Majoda   New Quay   Cardiganshire   Wales

Dear Louise

I missed you, time after time, since we met first, lost your address, your number, and my way anywhere, and I've been living here for many months, with only short and rowdy hours in London. I'm so glad to hear from you, and I'll be in London again the first week of December. We *must* meet. I'll wire you at the Essex address, and arrange—where? your club, or is it very stiff? But wherever you like. I shan't be able to tell you anything about the 'younger poets', but that won't matter much, will it? Thank you for saying lovely things about my poems, and for wanting to see some new ones. I do hope you'll let me see what you're going to write about me. Here are a few recent poems—most of them are coming out in the January

---

1 Watkins's poem 'Reprisals of Calm'.

2 The January 1945 *Horizon* contained 'Holy Spring', which was enclosed with the letter, and 'Vision and Prayer'. The 'birthday poem', 'Poem in October', was in the February issue.

3 A French journalist who worked in London during the war.

Horizon, but I'd rather you read them straightaway.[1] Tell me about them when, and if, and I do hope you do, write.

Ever,
Dylan

MS: Andrew MacAdie

LAURENCE POLLINGER
17 November 44   Majoda   New Quay   Cardiganshire

Dear Laurence Pollinger:
You'll have received, I hope, my wire before this, accepting Dent's offer and asking you to get the agreement sent to me for signature as soon as possible. I'm glad you will be able to arrange for the £50 to be paid upon delivery to Dent of my signed copy.[2] So do please let me have the agreement very quickly. I must have the £50 on or before the 24th of this month. That is a very fateful date.

I was hoping for a larger royalty, and would, I know, have been able to get a substantially larger one from Nicolson and Watson.[3] Probably not on such good royalty terms, but, then, I never expect my poems to sell very much. Immediate money is, at this stage, what I need for work done. However . . .

I shall look forward to hearing from Church about those 'points of detail' you mention. And also to seeing a specimen of the 'small and attractive format' in which my book will be published. But the latter can wait until I come up to town the first week of December when, I hope, we can meet. I will ring you then. I do hope you'll be able to spare a few minutes to come out and talk over a drink, as even the friendliest office drenches me with dread.

About Mr. Gottlieb:[4] I am sure I have behaved naughtily, but I could not, really, wait for un-naughty arrangements to be made. I was then, as ever, and as, again, particularly now (until the coming of Dent's £50 which *must* be before the 24th), tangled in debts, and Mr. Gottlieb's ready cheque book tempted me too much. I will bring up his letters of contract and agreement to show you.

About Laughlin: there is no point in sending him a duplicate complete typescript of *Deaths & Entrances* as at least half of the poems in it

1 Enclosed were typescripts of four poems: 'Ceremony After a Fire Raid', 'Love in the Asylum', 'Holy Spring' and 'Vision and Prayer'. The last two appeared in the January *Horizon*.
2 The publisher's contract for *Deaths and Entrances* is dated 24 November.
3 A small firm of publishers with whom Thomas had had dealings.
4 Gottlieb, of Peter Lunn, had commissioned the 'Book of Streets'.

appeared in the New Directions publication of *New Poems*. Several of the poems Laughlin published I have, for the Dent's book, extensively revised, but not *so* extensively as to warrant their publication, in America, *as* new poems. The best thing to do, I should think, would be to wait until I have another half dozen poems to add to the ones, in the Dent book, which have not appeared in *New Poems*.

I am writing to Laughlin about the *Selected Works*, answering all his points. I shall, at the same time, enclose the additional poems, included in Deaths & Entrances, for him to see. He can then decide whether he would prefer to include these in the *Selected Works* or wait (as I have suggested above) until there are sufficient new poems added to them to make a separate new book worth while. However, again . . .

I shall definitely ring you when I'm in town early in December.

And I await eagerly the Dent agreement to sign.

Yours sincerely,
Dylan Thomas

MS: Texas

[?JOHN BAYLISS][1]
25 Nov 44   Majoda   New Quay   Cardiganshire

Dear John,

Thank you for the copy of New Road, I was very glad to have it. I haven't read much of it yet, but it seems a fine job. It was good to see Antonia White's poem reprinted, I had been trying to remember it all on and off for years.[2]

Sorry I haven't a story; I haven't written one now for a long time, but I shall try again soon and if it works I'll send the result along. I'm writing filmscripts for a living & the time—the work time, I mean—left over from that I try to spend on poems: a miserable arrangement, which should be reversed. But I *have* collected a book of poems together & Dent will be bringing it out early next year at the very sane price of 3/6: it'll be called Deaths & Entrances: I hope you'll manage to get a copy.

I'll see what I can do about a story in the next month, if that's not too late, but I can't promise anything for the only stories I've written since the war, & very few, have been straightforward anecdotes (not, I'm glad to say, of the 'Then he downed a bloody pint, see' kind). Be seeing you some day.

Yours,
Dylan

MS: Texas

1 Texas suggests this is John Lehmann. John Bayliss is more likely.
2 The Antonia White poem was 'Epitaph'. The 1944 number of *New Road* contained, besides two poems by Thomas (see page 118), poems by Vernon Watkins and John Ormond (Thomas).

VERNON WATKINS
Tues Nov 28 44   Majoda   New Quay   Cardiganshire

Dear Vernon,

I hope you find the poem[1] visible this time.

I will be in London from December the first: for, say, ten days. (Though I don't know why, 'say'.) Will you wire me, any day after the first, at GRYPHON, 2–6 WEST STREET, W.C.2, and say when you & Gwen can come up. I suggest either Monday, Dec. 4, Tuesday, Dec. 5, or Wednesday, Dec. 6. I suggest one o'clock (1 p.m.) as the time, and the Back Bar of the Café Royal (table facing the door) as the place. If you can meet *there*, at *that* time, on *any* of the three days suggested above, your wire need contain only the one word—Monday (or Tuesday, of course, or Wednesday)—and I shall be there—(Back Bar of the Café Royal, table facing door, one p.m.)— henna'd, camelia'd, & smelling of moths.

I shall buy the December Horizon for your poem. How big is it? Send, by rail, or carrier pigeon, or in a plain man, a prose summary of all your poems and a pocket bicycle and a machine for draining witches and oh God help me I should never write letters after lunch: I am whimsical, I am porky, there are peas in my ears & my smile is gravy.

Yes, we could see 'Night at the Opera', I should love that, or a murder film called 'Laura', or even Henry V.

I am *very* frightened of the rockets.

There is no news here: a woman called Mrs. Prosser died in agony last week, there has been a coroner's inquest on a drowned coastguard (verdict suicide), Vera's cat was wounded by a rabbit trap & died, all night long we hear rabbits shrieking like babies in the steel jaws in the hedges, Caitlin killed five mice in one day by traps, but, still, I am quite happy and am looking forward to a gross, obscene and extremely painful middle-age.

Did I tell you I was going to Ireland early next year: to an island off Kerry? Well, I am, & I shall tell you about it when we meet.

Wire me after the first, at the unlikely address of GRYPHON, 2–6 West St., W.C.2.

Love to you both from Caitlin & myself.

Ever,
Dylan

MS: British Library

1 'Holy Spring'.

D. GOTTLIEB (Peter Lunn Ltd)
19th December 1944   [headed paper: Gryphon Films, etc]

Dear Mr. Gottlieb,
   After our explosive interview on the telephone this morning, I have
thought it best to write to you this brief and sincere explanation of my
point of view, while apologising for my rudeness and carelessness in not
replying to your correspondence and for the shifts and evasions that my
laziness and neurotic fear of telephones and telegrams have reduced me to.
   In our letters of contract and agreement, there is no mention made of any
definite date upon which the manuscript is to be delivered.[1] But we did
have a verbal understanding to the effect that I would endeavour to
produce some work—part, if not whole—by the 6th of January 1945. This I
will still endeavour to do, and have every hope of succeeding on or near
that date. The work I have so far done is only in form of notes but these I
hope to resolve into something concrete by or near the verbally agreed
date.
   I hope this may be satisfactory to you and that my not replying before
may be forgiven.

                                        Yours sincerely,
                                        Dylan Thomas

MS: National Library of Wales

OSCAR WILLIAMS
31 December 44   as from Gryphon Films   Guild House
                                      2–6 West Street   London W

Dear Oscar,
   The signed anthology for 1942 has arrived, and the Man has come
Towards me.[2] Thank you very much for both. I haven't yet read more
than a scattered few of the poems in your own book, stopping with delight
and surprise at many knock-me-down lines, and shan't try to write
anything to you until I have read the whole book carefully, and more than
once, through from torpedo to cloudburst. Of the 1944 anthology I like a
great deal. I like all that I have read of Alfred Hayes: has he had a book out
there? And Shapiro's poem, and most of W.R. Rodgers's, and, as always, the
lovely poems of my friend Vernon Watkins (who certainly should be
published in book-form in America). And much more, of course. I don't
agree with you at all about Timothy Corsellis, and think that you have
anthologised, in Henry Treece's poem, two of the worst lines since man
began to write:

1 All Thomas ever produced was a three-page synopsis headed, 'A Book of Streets. Words
  and Pictures about Streets. Streets in London.'
2 Williams's first book of poems was *The Man Coming Toward You.*

'And the green shark-cradles with their swift
Cruel fingers setting the ocean's curls.'[1]

Treece has written his own criticism in one almost comparably bathetic line: 'In the beginning was the bird'.

Oh yes, and while I'm feeling like that, let me curse you to the company, eternally, of novelists and actors for tacking on to the end of my poem, 'When I Awoke' the last verse of my poem, 'On A Wedding Anniversary'. I do not like either poem, but they *are* better apart. I expect a printed apology and an orange.

I am looking forward to a few cheques from magazines to which you sent my new poems. Thank you so much. I'm very glad to be able to send things to you, knowing that you'll get them printed. I am extremely poor at the moment; there is no chance of getting any money out of poetry in this country, no Guggenheims, no literary dibbers, only a few magazines, which pay nothing or a pound, and a handful of greyfaced young men with private incomes, weasely habits, and no inclination to give one anything but melancholia or dysentery.

I'll try to write something on war and poetry during the next week, but can't promise anything. I shan't know until I start writing whether I have any clear ideas on this, or on any other, subject. I prefer what I think about verse to be *in* the verse.

I meet Dunstan Thompson sometimes in London, and find him quite charming.[2] I asked him what you yourself were like & he made an elegant movement of his long sea-green hands, signifying, to me, nothing but the efforts of a man to play the flute without using his mouth.

Thank you, again, for the books & the good wishes, & for sending my poems around.

It is the last evening of the bad year and I am going out to celebrate myself sick and dirty.

Make what you can of 1945.

I shall try to write soon, sending the letter by airmail (or in a sealed man).

Yours,
Dylan

MS: Houghton

1 From Treece's poem 'The Dyke Builder'.
2 Dunstan Thompson, American poet. In 1944 he was in the U.S. Army, stationed in Europe.

D. GOTTLIEB
3rd January 1945   Majoda New Quay Cardiganshire

Dear Mr. Gottlieb,
Thank you for your considerate letter and for your acceptance of my apologies for behaving in a quite uncivilised manner.

I'm afraid I have nothing of consecutive value to send you by the suggested near-date of January 6th, owing more to domestic troubles beyond my control—my wife has influenza and I am trying to combine the duties of housekeeper and children-minder along with my own work—than to the difficulty, however pleasurable, of the job itself. I suggest that we move the date forward one month: to the end of the first week of February. The plan for the book that I had started work upon I've decided to scrap, as a much better plan came to my mind; and this change necessitates far more work & will result, I think, in a far more original book. Roughly, my plan is this: to call the book *Twelve Hours In The Streets* and to take the life of the streets from twelve noon to twelve midnight. Thus the street can fit the hour, and vice versa; streets that to my mind, & perhaps to the minds of many others, recall instantly some specific hour of day or night will fit naturally, & not artificially, into the structure of the book. And the whole might well be an imaginative, picaresque perhaps, cross-section of the life of the English streets for a whole modern day. (There is a *kind* of Elizabethan analogy to this in Nicholas Breton's 'Elizabethan Day' reprinted in Dover Wilson's Penguin book on Elizabethan England.)[1]

I hear that Banting's drawings were considered too gay for such a book as I have in mind; & perhaps this is so. Have you another illustrator in mind?

I hope to hear from you soon.

                                           Yours sincerely,
                                           Dylan Thomas

I should add that I am, of course, as desirous as you of having the book published in the early, rather than in the late, part of 1945 (other conditions, as you say, permitting) and that I intend working on nothing else for the next month.

                                           DT.

MS: National Library of Wales

D. GOTTLIEB
6 February 1945   Majoda New Quay Cardiganshire

Dear Mr. Gottlieb,
Thank you so much for your letter of January 6th. I would have replied sooner, but I was waiting—rather vainly, as it happened—for my nasty attack of gastric 'flu to disappear—a 'flu I caught from my family (as I think

1 Nicholas Breton (?1555–1626), English writer.

I told you my family was suffering from, the last time I wrote).

I came up to London last month, with the intention of seeing you and talking over the book with Games, but, almost as soon as I was up, I got caught with this annoying trouble & was forced to travel back, through snow, in an ice-bound train, in order to get a little nursing attention from an already flu-fed-up family.

I hope to come up to town in about 10 days time—when I will ring you at once &, I hope, arrange for a lunch & discussion as soon as it suits you.

I have one or two new ideas which I think are essential to the artistic success of the book.

Regards,
Yours sincerely,
Dylan Thomas

MS: *National Library of Wales*

T. W. EARP
6 Feb '45   Majoda   New Quay   Cards

Dear Tommy,
Very deeply sorry to have missed you in the Bell, that Monday. I was, strictly, in bed, in Chelsea, in London, in pain, with gastric flu; and alone, so that I could not get to the telephone to leave a love and a sorry message. I came back, as soon as better, here, in order to get nursed and cursed. How is May? I still hope you and she may be able to get down here soon, when May can travel. We may, by that time, have a better (or worse) house, near here. Write when you can, and do tell me about the enclosed poems:—I enclose them in case, as rightly, you have not seen the January Horizon. One, the triangular looking poem (though badly typographed here) I have shown you the beginning of.[1] Now the beginning is different, & the rest, which you have not seen, obviously so. All regards from us both, and *please* don't insult us by not visiting us very soon.

Dylan

MS: *Ohio State University*

DONALD TAYLOR
8 February 45   Majoda   New Quay   Cardiganshire

Dear Donald,
I feel very badly about it that our conversation some evenings ago should have disturbed you, and I do apologise now and immediately, knowing that the disturbing influence was, however it sounded, quite unintentional. I

1 'Vision and Prayer'.

can only say that I'd just come out of a gastric chamber, had had a few hurried drinks to see if I were still alive, and then spoke to you, not in a quiet box as I usually do when I ring up, but against a background of maudlin sea-captains and shrewd, if stunned, travellers in petrol. One ear was hearing you and the other ear busy shutting out the buzzing of those Cardy drones, and I spoke, I know, hurriedly & stupidly. Please take no notice of what I said about Labour: I'm proud to be asked to try to do the script: my only fear is that I shall not do a very good job of it: I am not, as you know, politically very acute, and will have to rely, as always, upon emotionalism. But I will send off the opening sequences in a few days, and you will be [?able to] tell from them whether I should go on alone with the scripting or whether I should work at it closely with you and, alone, do only the dialogue (whose indications we could map out together) and the descriptive-visual writing. Another reason for my unfortunately—and, again, really unmeant—disturbing conversation, was that I was enormously pleased by the good news of the 'Suffer Little Children' film,[1] and very very keen on getting on with it at once. I know the short films have to be done, and I am sorry that I gave the impression of wanting to get away from them; it is, of course, the big-scale film of ideas that we both wish to work at, work hard & work soon, but 'Labour', too, is a job of work and I have, in my proper self, no intention of trying to escape it. I do want to say again that I think 'Suffer Little Children' a superlative idea, and I am longing to talk about it in detail and around it, to discuss it at great length with you, and to work upon it as soon as possible & to produce the completed script more quickly than any other we have done.

I'll come up as soon as you want me, but you will have the opening Labour sequences in your hands first.

Sorry again.

What news of B. & H.? I think I forgot to tell you the new name I had thought of for Dr. Robert Knox: *Thomas Rock*. This is very near, in vowels & general feeling, to the original, and does, I think satisfy Bridie's[2] complaint: it does sound the name of a man who could be very distinguished & great in science. What do you think?

Let me know if you wish me to ring you again soon; & this time I shall choose the privacy of a public booth not the propinquity of a public bar.

Ever,
Dylan

I have just finished reading—and will send on under separate cover—the autobiography, called *The Islandman*, of Tomás Ó Crohan (The Blaskets, 1856–1937). It is *the* very first book about the Blaskets, written in 1926,

---

1 *Suffer Little Children*, alternatively *Betty London*, was to be a feature film, the kind that Donald Taylor hoped to produce after the war. It was not made. Some of Thomas's dialogue is said to have been used in a Diana Dors film, *Good Time Girl* (1948).

2 James Bridie (1888–1951) wrote a comedy about Burke and Hare, *The Anatomist* (1930). Taylor had been in touch with him to allay fears of plagiarism.

published 1929. Ó Crohan was, apparently, a great & famous man, a Celtic scholar & authority, & lived all his 81 years on the Blaskets. It is most extraordinary that O'Sullivan makes no mention of him: he was, of course, very much alive on the Island *all* the time O'Sullivan was living there; it is also very odd that George Thompson should study Irish under a boy like O'Sullivan when there was already on the Island an acknowledged (by Yeats & everyone else interested in the folklore & the language) Irish scholar & taleteller.

There is no mention, either, of O'Sullivan in Ó Crohan's book.

'The Islandman', 'Twenty Years', and Robin Flower's own book—the 'West Island' is it—represent all the available written literature of and upon the Blaskets; literature, that is, of general appeal, for there must be many, & probably untranslated, essays & papers on folklore, dialect, etc. etc., written by visiting scholars. But we should be able, from those 3 books, to tell the story of life on the Island *in its entirety*. I do not suggest that we use the actual material of Ó Crohan's & Flower's books, but that we study them as background. I should very much like to see a copy of Flower's when I come up to town.

D.

MS: Buffalo

JAMES LAUGHLIN
10th February 1945   as from Gryphon Films [etc]

Dear James Laughlin,

I haven't written to you for a very long time.

I got your letter, dated Sept. 18. '44, which first mentioned the volumes of SELECTED WRITINGS you were bringing out in your New Classics Series, and I was proud and glad you were going to do a volume of mine.

I've been all those months replying because I couldn't find anyone here who could really do the job you wanted—'a sort of "warm" account of what you yourself are like, what you are working toward in your poetry and that sort of thing'. The main difficulty was that the people who do know what I'm like don't know what I am working toward in my poetry, and don't care anyway. And most of the people here who write about poetry can't tell one person from another. So I was glad to hear today from Pollinger that you had found your own man over there, J. L. Sweeney, to write the introduction, and that the personal account is necessarily cut out as Mr. Sweeney & myself are unknown to each other except through our writing.[1]

---

1 John Lincoln Sweeney (1906–86), author and curator; member of the English faculty at Harvard.

Have you any idea when the book will be coming out? And do you want a portrait for it? I seem to remember, in another, now unfortunately lost, letter, that you did mention it. If you do, will you tell me and I'll have a new photograph taken by a good man in London and sent to you immediately. Only for God's sake, please don't use any of the two or three old portraits that Oscar Williams dug up out of somewhere and has used in his Poems of The Year series. All those were at least five or seven years ago, and I'm much fatter and coarser now: and that, if my face is to appear at all in the Selected volume, is how it should look.

You asked me to tell you what I consider are my best 20 odd poems, my best 4 stories, and the 2 best chapters of the autobiographical Portrait.

These I have written down on a separate sheet, enclosed,[1] and I do very much hope you will be able to stick fairly closely to it. They are my considered opinions after re-reading all the stuff. (But don't let that worry you.) Pollinger also told me today that he had himself written to you, explaining that I had no new stories I thought worth including in the Selected volume but that there were a few new poems I wish most urgently to be included. These I enclose—they are coming out sometime in American periodicals—and have also written their titles down in my enclosed list of personal choices for the volume.

My opinion as to what is my best mayn't, on the whole, agree with yours & Sweeney's. Will you tell me, before publication, which you both have chosen? I shan't, of course, mind a bit: I'm probably blind about most of the poems; the only ones I feel most strongly about are the last nine from the books, & the four new ones; but that's probably because they *are* new.

I hope to hear from you soon, though I don't know how long air-mail letters take these days.

Do forgive me for not writing before this: I've been very busy at my wartime job, which is writing filmscripts, and also trying to think of someone who could, as you asked, do the introduction. If you *did* want a personal note to add to Sweeney's introduction, I should suggest either Vernon Watkins, whose poems you probably know & who was brought up in the same town as me, or one of my best friends T. W. Earp, who is quite well known here as a painting critic and a general dear old talking body about the place.

Will you give my regards to J. L. Sweeney, whose job I don't envy a bit?

Wishes,
Yours,
Dylan Thomas

I should like to come over to the States after the war for a few months. Any chance of getting a job to keep me while over there? Reading, talking?

A note about the typography of the poem 'Vision and Prayer'.

In the corrected proofcopy—corrected, that is, in detail—I am enclosing,

---

1 The list was sent with the letter of 16 February.

the lines are not spaced as they must be. The point is that each stanza of Part One starts, in the first line, with one beat and goes up to nine beats in the ninth line, & then decreases regularly down to one beat again. Up to line nine, each line should be one exact space to the left of the preceding line, the line above it, & should then decrease space by space. (Sorry this is so confusing to write down; it's simpler to explain in conversation to the printer; but you probably get it anyway). Thus, each stanza of Part One should look like this, as far as possible.

There must be no variations in the straight diamond lines of the left hand side of the poem, as—in the proofcopy—there are in, for example, lines 6, 7, 8 of stanza one.

Who

Are you

Who is born

In the next room

So loud to my own

That I can hear the womb

Opening   and   the   dark   run

Over the ghost and the dropped son

Behind the wall thin as a wren's bone?

In the birth bloody room unknown

To the burn and turn of time

And the heart print of man

Bows   no   baptism

But dark alone

Blessing on

The wild

Child.

is a bit nearer to what I want. I wish I had a typewriter here, I could show you exactly. But I'm sure you get it now.

In Part Two of the poem, the lines should go—absolutely symmetrical again—from nine beats in line one to one in line nine & increasing to nine in line seventeen: a complete reversal of Part One.

Sorry to bother you.

Dylan T

Looking again at my copying out of stanza one I see that I've made a balls of it, but I know you see what I'm after.

MS: Houghton

JAMES LAUGHLIN
16 Feb '45   as from Gryphon Films [etc]

Dear Laughlin,
    Here is my suggested—& very shakily suggested—list of contents for the Selected Writing volume.[1]
    Hope you've had my long letter & enclosed poems, or, anyway, that they arrive the same time as this.
    I'm more & more doubtful about the *beginning* of my list.

Yours,
Dylan Thomas

POEMS

[*in the margin:* From 'The World I Breathe' and 'New Poems']

I See The Boys Of Summer In Their Ruin
The Force That Through The Green Fuse Drives The Flower
When Like A Running Grave Time Tracks You Down
I In My Intricate Image Stride On Two Levels
A Grief Ago
Then Was My Neophyte
Sonnet IX
Sonnet X
I Make This In A Warring Absence When
It Is The Sinners' Dust-Tongued Bell Claps Me To Churches
The Spire Cranes. Its Statue Is An Aviary
After The Funeral, Mule Praises, Brays
How Shall My Animal
A Saint About To Fall
If My Head Hurt A Hair's Foot
There Was A Saviour
Among Those Killed In The Dawn Raid
Love In The Asylum
Ballad of The Long-Legged Bait
Deaths & Entrances.

[*in the margin:* Unpublished in Book Form in America]

Ceremony After A Fire Raid
Holy Spring
Vision and Prayer
Poem In October.

---

1 *Selected Writings of Dylan Thomas* [New Directions, 1946] included the material on Thomas's list, plus a further twenty-five poems and stories.

PROSE

[*in the margin:* From 'The World I Breathe']

The Orchards
A Prospect Of The Sea.

[*in the margin:* From 'Portrait of the Artist']

The Peaches
One Warm Saturday.

MS: Houghton

BBC
16 Feb '45   Majoda   New Quay   Cardiganshire

Dear Sir,
    I enclose the Reply Sheet, signed.
    The bus fare from New Quay to Carmarthen—return—is five shillings.
                                                    Yours faithfully,
                                                    Dylan Thomas

MS: BBC

VERNON WATKINS[1]
26 2 45   Majoda   New Quay   Cards

Dear Vernon,
    I was very very glad to hear and see from you; it's been a long and
complicated time since we disappointingly met, and I'm happy and
relieved to think that the offence, (for my lost, preoccupied manner must
really have been that), I gave when we did meet in that gabbling drink-grey
crush, the worst of the town, has, if never to be forgotten utterly, lost some
disfavour. (I have just been writing at length to Llewelyn, on the occasion
of a fall from a tree and a split tongue, and the effort of not talking to a boy
of six has made me adopt the claptrap periods of a leader-writer under gas.)
I have found, increasingly as time goes on, or around, or backwards, or
stays quite still as the brain races, the heart absorbs and expels, and the
arteries harden, that the problems of physical life, of social contact, of daily
posture and armour, of the choice between dissipations, of the abhorred
needs enforced by a reluctance to 'miss anything', that old fear of death, are
as insoluble to me as those of the spirit. In few and fewer poems I can

---

1 Not in *VW*: Gwen Watkins found the letter in a kitbag after her husband's death. She
  suggests that Thomas's statement in it of his difficulties with 'the problems of physical
  life, of social contact', constitute 'his real letter of apology for letting Vernon down [at
  the wedding]—real, in the sense that he is now telling the truth'.

despair and, at rare moments, exult with the big last, but the first force me every moment to make quick decisions and thus to plunge me into little hells and rubbishes at which I rebel with a kind of truculent acceptance. The ordinary moments of walking up village streets, opening doors or letters, speaking good-days to friends or strangers, looking out of windows, making telephone calls, are so inexplicably (to me) dangerous that I am trembling all over before I get out of bed in the mornings to meet them. Waking to remember an appointment at X that coming evening is to see, before X, galleries of menacing commonplaces, chambers of errors of the day's conventions, pits of platitudes and customary gestures, all beckoning, spurning; and through, over & out of these I must somehow move before the appointment, the appointment that has now become a shining grail in a dentist's surgery, an almost impossible consummation of illegal pleasure to be achieved in a room like a big gut in a subterranean concentration-camp. And especially, of course, in London. I wish that I could have met Gwen 'properly,' and glad that she wanted to; I was 'myself' in the sense that I was no-one else, but I was broken on a wheel of streets and faces; equally well, I may be just as broken in the peace—what peace?—of the country, hysterical in my composure, hyena-ish in my vegetabledom. I will, if I may, try to come to stay in the pub in Stony Stratford when next I come to London: but oh the bony cupboards and traps and vats before that.

I wish I could see your new poems. The translation in Horizon I did, & remembered much of it; it was beautiful.

I am glad Francis[1] is alive, well, and happy.

I have lost Dan's address again. Will you tell him that we are not going to Ireland for a long time, perhaps not even this year, as another film has risen out of some fool's mind and must be written so that we can eat and tremble at the approach of each quiet, unsensational & monstrous day? The studio is being carefully looked after. I'll write to Dan this week & will send the letter to you.

Love to you and Gwen from us both.

Ever,
Dylan

I wish I could understand your letter from Heatherslade. It was dated the 24th, which was Saturday, but said that you were afraid we would be unable to meet as you were leaving on Friday. If that was not also, and unfortunately, typical of myself, I should say it was a piece of genuine-accept-no-other Vernon.

Don't mind this silly letter. It was lovely to have yours.

MS: British Library

---

1 Francis Dufau-Labeyrie.

LAURENCE POLLINGER
24 March 45   Majoda   New Quay   Cards

Dear Laurence Pollinger,
    Just a note to say that I've lost Dent's address & am writing to R. Church
care of you. I do hope you'll get the letter to him straight away. Sorry for
the bother.

                                        Sincerely,
                                        Dylan Thomas

MS: Texas

DONALD TAYLOR
Tuesday March 28(?) 45   Majoda   New Quay   Cards

Dear Donald,
    Today, limp in the hut, watching the exhausting sea, lost in our Betty—
Betty dark?—drowned in our Sophie—Sophie fair?[1]—but writing little
until tomorrow, first, cold thing in the morning, with the dew on the grass,
and the Captains in bed, and the trees talking double rook. I was so very
sorry you went back. Did you get a sleeper? And even the Captain is gone,
with all his wheezy rumbling as though he were trying to bring up from his
cavernous inside a very old, rusty, seaweedy anchor. Frank sparkles still,
but the Lion lies down.[2] This is only to say (1) I hope you'll be back soon,
(2) I *do* hope you can, somehow, manage a little money this week, by some
not-so-Verity ruse,[3] (3) I'll work as hard as I know on the synopsis or
whatever we call it, as long as we call it good, and (4) Please don't forget to
have a shot at doing those 'personal' thousand words for the introduction
to my American Selected Writing. Let me see what you bang out. If you're
too busy, I can ask Tommy E. to do something, but I hope you aren't.
You've got Laughlin's letter, haven't you? He wants the thing very, very,
very soon. Let me know.
    Tomorrow morning I shall be fit as a tuba again, and will work, work,
work,

                                        Ever,
                                        Dylan

MS: Buffalo

1 Betty and Sophie were characters in the projected *Suffer Little Children*.
2 The Black Lion, a local pub.
3 'Verity' was a film company associated with Gryphon.

VERNON WATKINS
28 March 1945   Majoda   New Quay   Cardiganshire

My Dear Vernon,
   Lovely to hear from you. I'd have written before this but am, unfortunately, caught, however innocently—and it will [be] the sweet job of the
defending counsel to impute guilt to my every innocent thought and
action—in a Case of Attempted Murder, Caitlin, I, and three others being
the attempted murderees (though that isn't quite right, as we certainly
didn't attempt to be murderees). Vera Phillips' husband, called Killick,
though that's not what I call him, started a fight in the local hotel, in
which I took a small part, lost, returned home to the bungalow next to
mine, and, when I also had returned home and was talking to Caitlin & 3
others, fired many rounds from his Sten gun through our paper-thin walls,
missing us by inches and Aeronwy by feet. It's all very nasty, and I'm as
frightened as though I had used the Sten gun myself. He also had a hand
grenade. He is now on bail—the first stage of the case coming off next
Thursday, the 5th of April—and Caitlin and I go to bed under the bed.[1]
The last letter I wrote to you, at Pennard, told of my daily terrors, my
everyday traps & pits etc. I'm sure you thought I was exaggerating. At
debts' and death's door I now stand with a revolving stomach, waiting for
V.1000[2] and the Bubonic Plague.
   I'm so delighted you and Gwen are going to have a child this summer.
Do give Gwen my congratulations; you yourself shd have received mine as
soon as I opened your letter, by telepathic pigeon.
   How are you both? I miss seeing you, but then I have missed seeing you
properly for—what is it—years; at least, since we left our studio, where we
did have some proper evenings. The war's over soon, let's see each other
then, a lot. You'll be going back to Swansea, of course. I want to stay in
Wales for a bit, too. The Irish trip is off until the summer, & perhaps until
even later.
   Give my love, when you write, to your Mother and Father. My Father is
awfully ill these days, with heart disease and uncharted pains, and the
world that was once the colour of tar to him is now a darker place.

1 The man, William Killick—who had married Vera Phillips, Thomas's childhood friend,
  two years earlier—was a captain, aged twenty-eight, in the Royal Engineers, seconded
  to the Special Operations Executive. He had not long returned from a gruelling tour of
  duty in Greece, where he was dropped behind German lines, and for more than a year
  trained partisans and took part in sabotage attacks. The trouble at New Quay began
  with a brawl on 6 March in the Black Lion between Killick and some film people from
  London, friends of Thomas. The shots, about eighteen rounds from the automatic
  weapon, were fired at, and in, the bungalow later that evening. Thomas behaved coolly,
  Killick went away and the police were called. At Lampeter Assizes in June, Killick said
  that 'the whole affair was a bluff'. The judge suggested there was no evidence of
  attempted murder, and the jury found him not guilty. Thomas told marvellously
  embroidered versions of the tale for years.
2 An uneasy joke about a successor to 'V2', the German rockets.

I'm sending some new poems. The long one doesn't, I think, come off, but I like it all in spite of that. It isn't really one piece, though, God, I tried to make it one and have been working on it for months.[1] Do tell me all you think of it, and of the others. And do let me see some of your new poems, please. Write very soon.

Love from both to both,

Ever,
Dylan

Urgent Postscript

James Laughlin, of New Directions, America, who is going to bring out a book of mine, 'Selected Writings', in America, wants, from a friend of mine over here, a short, 'personal introduction' to the book, of *not more than 1000 words*. There is a 'critical introduction', but that Laughlin is having written by an American, J. L. Sweeney. Laughlin has just written to me to say that he must have this 'personal' thing *at once*. Could you do it, or, rather, would you like to do it, or, rather, have you got time to do it, or, again, could you make or find time to do it. What Laughlin means by a 'personal introduction' is, roughly, this—I quote from memory as I haven't got the letter here—: 'an idea, in non highbrow language, of what you yourself are really like; a human portrait of the poet written by a close friend of his or by one who has known him for a long time.' You'll have to excuse phrases like 'non highbrow language', 'human portrait', etc, but what he really wants is clear, I think. American readers of poetry seem never to be really satisfied unless they have portraits—photograph or words—of the writers; and they like them as candid and intimate—comic, if you see me that way, & you must do, sometimes—as possible. To me, of course, that introduction coming from you, as my friend and as—we've both said this, with a kind of giggling gravity—the only other poet except me whose poetry I really like today—would be the best in the world. Let me know if you would do it; and, if you would, could you do it *terribly* quickly and let me have it so that I can send it off almost at once. It's a lot to ask, and you hardly ever write prose, but. . . . Well, I'll hear from you. We know each other by doing so many things together, from croquet to bathing (me for the first time) in the icy moon, poetry and very high teas, getting drunk, reading, reading, reading, sea staring, Swansea, Gower, Laugharne, London . . . I've written thousands of letters to you; if you've kept some you could use what you liked to help build up this 'human portrait' of this fat pleader,

Dylan

Write very soon.

MS: British Library

1 The long poem was 'A Winter's Tale'; the others were 'The conversation of prayers', 'This Side of the Truth' and 'A Refusal to Mourn the Death, by Fire, of a Child in London'. *VW* has details of small variants from the *CP* versions.

GWYN JONES
28 March '45   Majoda   New Quay   Cardiganshire

Dear Gwyn Jones,
   I should have written long before to say how glad I was to meet you that
booming afternoon in Carmarthen,[1] and to thank you for the copies of
Wales which I have now read from eagle to Corona.[2] Who is William
Morgan? I like his Working Day poem very much indeed. I'd not seen any
of Alun Lewis's Indian poems before, and could see, as you said, his death
walking through them.[3] I think your goodbye to Caradoc was fond and
just.[4]
   Are you staying in Aberystwyth for a few weeks? I hope to come along
soon, and am looking forward to a few drinks in the town with you. At the
moment I am caught in a policecourt case; someone fired a Sten gun at us; I
hope he missed.

                                           Best wishes. Yours,
                                           Dylan Thomas

I'll write you a note a good time beforehand about meeting in Aberystwyth.

MS: National Library of Wales

OSCAR WILLIAMS
March 28 '45   Majoda   New Quay   Cardiganshire   Wales

Dear Oscar,
   Many thanks for the letter and for Poetry's cheque. I'm very glad you
don't mind sending my stuff to the magazines. Here are another five
poems: one longish one, four short ones.[5] The longish one, I'm glad to say,
has taken a great deal of time and trouble, and has prevented me from
writing filmscripts on Rehabilitation, Better Housing, Post War Full
Employment, etc. for the socialist film department of the Ministry of
Information. If it surprises you that the Ministry, or any Ministry, should
have a socialist department, I can say that none of the scripts approved by

1 Thomas was at the BBC in Carmarthen (the Swansea studios had been bombed) on 23
   February to record poems by Welsh writers. Gwyn Jones introduced the programme.
2 The magazine was not *Wales* but the rival *Welsh Review*, which Gwyn Jones edited.
   The cover featured a small dragon that might have been mistaken for an eagle in a poor
   light. 'Corona' was a fizzy drink, made in Wales, that loyally advertised at the back of
   the magazine.
3 The Welsh poet Alun Lewis committed suicide while in the Army in 1944.
4 An obituary of the writer Caradoc Evans.
5 The 'longish one' was probably 'A Winter's Tale'. *Poetry* (Chicago) published it in July.
   Three other poems (see n.1, page 611) appeared in quick succession in issues of *The
   New Republic*.

that department get further than the next where they are shelved among a million dead ideas and periodically reshuffled by dead young men with briar pipes that are never lit in the office but which they always have protruding from their mouths like the cocks of swallowed bodies. By such so-quickly-to-be-buried work I earn enough to live on if I do without what I most like. So I'd love a little ladleful from the gravy pots over there—a lick of the ladle, the immersion of a single hair in the rich shitbrown cauldron—though naturally I expect nothing. It is very very good of you to try to fish something up for me. In this country, it would be the skull of a boiled fawner who, smelling the gravy steam, fell in and died, to the especial pleasure of his mother who had borne him piping. The war, they say, is all over bar the dying; and, when it is, I want to come over to America. How could I earn a living? I can read aloud, through sonorous asthma, with pomp; I can lecture on The Trend of Y, or X at the Crossroads, or Z: Whither? with an assurance whose shiftiness can be seen only from the front row; I can write script and radio films, of a sort; I can— and so on with the list that could be, and is, supplied by every person fit for nothing but his shameful ability to fit into the hack ends of commercial, intellectual, or personal, advertisement. I hope you'll get the five poems printed. Perhaps 2 or 3 of the short ones together in one magazine? You know. I hope you like them, or some of them. I've forgotten if the address you have of mine is the one at the top of this letter or the one of the Gryphon Film Company. If it *is* Gryphon, please do use that when—and I do hope you do, soon—you write. That is more-or-less permanent. The Welsh address I leave, for nowhere, some time in June. My poems are coming out this spring and, though by that time you will have seen all the poems in it—several, however, in very altered versions—I'll send it on at once. I'm looking forward to yours, and to the War Poets. Laughlin is bringing out a 'Selected Writing' of mine—when, I don't know—with a critical introduction by J. L. Sweeney. Though I know his name, I don't know his writing. It is very lovely here; I have a shack at the edge of the cliff where my children hop like fleas in a box—in London, the only remaining flea-circus I have seen is pushed about the streets in one half of a child's pram—and my wife grumbles at me and them and the sea for the mess we all make, and I work among cries and clatters like a venomous beaver in a parrot house. A letter full of nothing.

> Yours,
> Dylan

MS: Houghton

DONALD TAYLOR
Tuesday [April 1945]   Majoda

Dear Donald,
I'm sorry that my telephone calls are always about the same dear little thing, but I can't help it. I just can't get straight, ever since five pounds was, quite justly, deducted from my weekly pay: the week you were down. I really am in a mess, and am likely to get in more of one. And I must say that I *can't* live on eight pounds a week. Can't. Ten is hard enough to get on with, with a pound worth about eight shillings, but eight pounds is impossible, and I don't know what to do. If only somehow one could manage until this film is sold—as it really should be, it seems to me to have everything. But on eight a week, one can't. It seems I cannot do anything that requires more than about a pound; I can't get Llewelyn down for this incredible April, I can't buy a pair of trousers though my bum is bare to the sun, I can't join a library, & I *shouldn't* even smoke. All the eight, or even, really, the ten does, is to pay rent, food, oil, & coal. Enough? No, Christ no. There are a hell of a lot of other essential things, and I can't get them. And, once in debt for anything over a pound or so—as I am, as I am—that debt can never be paid, and grows & grows into proportions beyond any hope. All this is, I know, familiar to you; but things have reached a climax for me, & I can't go on with this amount of money. I don't know what the hell to do, & wish to the Lord we could fix something together. I've got such great faith in the films we'll make together, it seems so silly to be grumbling about money now when, soon, we should be crinkling all over. But there it is.
I hope the script will be finished in a week.[1] The trial, necessitating my getting my mother here from another county to look after the children, hindered it a lot;[2] as all this petty hell about money is still doing. But I do think: a week. I'll send it off with notes; there are, I think, 4 or 5 sticky constructional points, but I have only in one case altered a constructional detail from our original. I have, too, cut out the jewels in the empty house that B. & S. & the boy break into. It seems to be too forced, too much of a coincidence, that Betty's downfall shd come, both times, through jewels left so *absurdly* open for anyone to take. So I think that just 'breaking & entering' is enough to send B. & S. to School for three years. Other suggestions etc. I'll write about at length when I send the complete MS.
Sorry for most of this letter, but I had to say it. And I still don't know what to do.

                                                              Ever
                                                              Dylan

MS: Buffalo

1 'Suffer Little Children.'
2 Thomas gave evidence when Captain Killick made a preliminary appearance before the local magistrates.

VERNON WATKINS
April 19 45   Majoda

Dear Vernon,

It was so good of you to write that little personal—what?—thing, then, so quickly and so very nicely. Just, I should imagine, what New Directions want, and I have sent it off *just* as it is, not even altering 'good' to 'great' or putting in a paragraph about my singing voice or horsemanship.[1] Thank you a lot. It did, I know, sound rather awful: Write about me. If you had asked me to do it about you, I think I should have pleaded everything from writer's cramp to never having met you except in the dark, & then only once. I'm so glad you wrote the last bit about the poems: how you so much more liked the latest to the earliest. Wouldn't it be hell if it was the other way around, and the words were coming quicker & slicker and weaker and wordier every day and, by comparison, one's first poems in adolescence seemed, to one, like flying-fish islands never to be born in again? Thank God, writing is daily more difficult, less passes Uncle Head's blue-haired pencil that George Q. Heart doesn't care about, and that the result, if only to you and me, is worth all the discarded shocks, the reluctantly-shelved grand moony images, cut-&-come-again cardpack of references.

And I'm very glad you liked the new poems I sent, especially A Winter's Tale. I won't be able to test your suggestions for myself until I have the proofs back from Dent: I seem to have lost other copies. My book should be out this spring, costing, luckily, three and six so that perhaps lots of people can buy it and pass it on.

Yes, Captain Waistcoat[2] has nearly put me off drinking, though, indeed, the night of the shots of the dark I had drunk only some bottled cider and talked morosely to retired sailors in dusty corners, provoking nobody, so I thought.

I do hope I see you soon in Stony Stratford. I am going to London the end, perhaps, of next week.

Thank you again for the little personal what; it was, I thought, nice, funny, and, as far as I know, right.

I'll write again, very soon, and more.

Love,
Dylan

MS: British Library

---

1 When *Selected Writings* was published in the U.S., it had the introduction by Sweeney, but not the 'personal' note by Watkins.
2 Thomas's nickname for Killick.

LAURENCE POLLINGER
27 April 45   Majoda   New Quay   Cardiganshire

Dear Laurence Pollinger,
   Very sorry not to have answered your letter of Feb. 6 about Laughlin's
edition of *Selected Works*. I thought I *had* answered: I should have my head
read: my books won't be.
   I've sent the poems—the additional poems for the *Selected Works*—on to
Laughlin direct, & have had a letter back from him.
                                              Yours sincerely,
                                              Dylan Thomas

MS: Texas

VERNON WATKINS
May 21 1945   Majoda   New Quay   Cardiganshire

Dear Vernon:
   Lovely to hear from you. I wish I could come to Pennard to see you, but I
am broke & depressed & have just returned from London & hated it more
than ever & though it is lovely here I am not. Oh, I do wish *you* could come
down here. There is room, rest, food, & sea. Can't you?
   Dot is engaged to—who? I couldn't read. *SANTI!* Never heard of him, if
that is the name. Write clearly & jog my old man's memory. Where did I
live with him, & when? Has he two names? What nationality is he? Give
me clues, I'll give you the frankest low-down in the world. Anyhow, I hope
Dot will always be happy.
   Just a tiny note. I'm worried about things. I think I'll walk & grieve and
scowl at the unmitigated birds—the first adjective, of any kind, I cd think
of.
   Can't you come down? *Try.*
   My love, & Caitlin's, to your people and yourself.
   Write soon with S. clear & clued.
                                              Dylan

MS: British Library

JULIAN ORDE[1]
May 21st 1945   Majoda   New Quay   Cardiganshire

I'll send away, at once, the poems you sent me, to the few editors I know:
Herring first, then Cyril C., then Muir of Orion—though you probably
know him as well as I do—, then Quennell of Cornhill; and will let you
know. Here I am efficient. There, inefficient but not poppycock, or, at
least, not very much, and what there was was not directed at—if that's
what you do with poppycock—anything that matters. I liked all the poems,
but am not going to say anything about them yet because I am down,
down, down among the live men, drowned in writs, terrified of the past,
the knock, the crunch on the gravel, even the baying of the sea a little
distance from my hand. I missed you, in fact, in theory, in every way,
dearly. Next time I'll see more of you, may I? Have you got any more that I
am allowed to see? No laughing at you, now or ever. The opposite, which
isn't crying. Are you being a subconscious girl for Donald? He is cross with
me, I am cross with him, but we will live to kill another pig. It is very quiet
here; only the hunting noise of the hard-away sea, the throbbing of tractors,
the squealing of rats and rabbits in the traps, the surging of seagulls,
thrushes, blackbirds, finches, cuckooing of cuckoos, cooing of doves,
discussion of works, crying of babies, blinding of wives, sputtering of
saucepans and kettles, barking of dogs, voices of children playing trumpets
on the beach, bugling of sea cadets, naying, chucking, quacking, braying,
mooing, rabbit-gunning, horse trotting, scraping of magpies on the roof,
mice in the kitchen: an ordinary day, nature serene as Fats Waller in
Belsen.[2] I'll be up again in about a month. I hadn't your address, knew it
just as Charlie, Highgate, or I would have written. Horror came over me,
and I went into a basement. How are you? Believe me, I will write soon,
and tell you about the poems.

Love, always,
Dylan

MS: Location unknown

---

1 Poet and sometime actress (1917–54), married to Ralph Abercrombie, who was
connected with the Parton Bookshop. Thomas is said to have spent 8 May, the day of
celebrations to mark the end of the war in Europe, with her. The text of the letter is
taken from an unreliable typescript copy, made after it was sold at Sotheby's.
2 The Nazi concentration camp near the village of Belsen, in north Germany, was one of
the first to be liberated. British troops reached it shortly before the war ended.

*[T. W. EARP][1]
May 28 '45   Majoda   New Quay   Cards

Sooner than you can water milk, or cry Amen,
Darkness comes, psalming, over Cards again.
Some lights go on; some men go out; some men slip in;
Some girls lie down, calling the beer-brown bulls to sin
And boom among their fishy fields; some elders stand
With thermoses and telescopes and spy the sand
Where farmers plough by night and sailors rock and rise,
Tatooed with texts, between the atlantic thighs
Of Mrs Rosser Tea and little Nell the Knock.
One pulls out Pam in Paris from his money-sock;
One, in the bible black[2] of his back, mothy house,
Drinks paraffin and vinegar, and blinds a mouse;
One reads his cheque book in the dark, & eats fish heads;
One creeps into the Lion Inn to foul the beds;
One, in the rubbered hedges, rolls with a bald liz
Who's old enough to be his mother (and she is);
The grocer lies in ambush in his smelling shop,
Praying for land-girls, and the preacher lies on top;
In snug and public, hunched by the gob-green logs,
The customers are telling what they do to dogs;
The chemist is performing an unnatural act
In the organ [loft][3] and the lavatories are packed.

MS: Ohio State University

1 The letter lacks a salutation, but so do other verse letters written by Thomas—to Earp
(page 582) and Donald Taylor (page 630). It is shown as part of the Thomas–Earp
correspondence at Ohio. According to Daniel Jones, who printed a version of it in the
1978 edition of *The Poems* under the title of 'A Pub Poem' (and says nothing about
either a letter or Tommy Earp), it was written jointly with Wynford Vaughan-Thomas
in a pub. This account probably originated with Vaughan-Thomas himself. In a letter of
June 1984 he told the present editor, more reliably, that '[Dylan] gave me his splendidly
bawdy pub-poem on the night life of New Quay' when the two of them were getting
drunk in Chelsea, some time after September 1943. The implication was that the poem
was by way of thanking him for an earlier loan or gift of ten pounds. By 1945, when the
poem was sent to Earp, Thomas had made changes to the earlier version.
2 The phrase, and the poem in general, have a ring of *Under Milk Wood*, which was yet
to come. That play belongs to Laugharne, where it was written. But its origins were in
Thomas's fantasies of a wider West Wales countryside, and New Quay did much to
incubate them.
3 The manuscript is torn at this point, removing part of the last line, but the version in
The Poems has 'organ loft'. On the edge of the tear are traces of words below, now
illegible.

CAITLIN THOMAS
Sunday night [24 June 1945]   26 Paulton Square SW3[1]

My dear my dear my dear Caitlin my love I love you; even writing, from a universe and a star and ten thousand miles away, the name, your name, CAITLIN, just makes me love you, not more, because that is impossible, darling, I have always loved you more every day since I first saw you looking silly and golden and much much too good forever for me, in that nasty place in worse-than-Belsen London, no, not more, but deeper, oh my sweetheart I love you and love me dear Cat because we are the same, we are the same, we are the one thing, the constant thing, oh dear dear Cat.

I'm writing this in bed in Constantine's and Tony's at about one o'clock Sunday morning—I mean after midnight. You are the most beautiful girl that has ever lived, and it is worth dying to have kissed you. Oh Cat, I need & want you too, I want to come to you, I must be with you, there is no life, no nothing, without you: I've told you, before, in the quiet, in the Cardy dark, by the sea, that I adored you and you thought it was a word. I do. I do, my love, my beautiful. I can see your hair now though I can't see it; & feel your breasts against my stupid body; I can hear your voice though you aren't speaking except to—who? Mary? Bloody Mary?[2] Did you see the thing in News of the World?[3] 'Among those not to be congratulated after the trial were Cat Thomas & her vile Dylan who loves her so much he is alone alone in a big room in London in England and yet he lets her live 300 miles away.' Oh, be near me, tonight, now, Sunday, 300 miles away. I kiss you. I love you.

I'll try to come back Wed or Thur but may have to put it off until the end of the week. I've been told of a few flats & houses & am looking for them. Now I must try to sleep because I can only say I Love You My Own Heart My Little One Caitlin my Wife and Love & Eternity.

X Dylan

Monday morning.

Still in bed. About eight o'clock in the morning. Found it terribly hard to sleep. Said your name a thousand times, my little dear. In a few minutes I'll get up and go to work: to write, still, about Allied Strategy in Burma: oh why can't they get someone else.

Tony has promised that *she* will look, for us, at the few addresses of flats I've been given. I'm thinking it is by far the best thing to get a very temporary furnished flat—however not nice—rather than an unfurnished

---

1 Constantine FitzGibbon, then serving in the U.S. Army, and his wife Theodora (sometimes 'Tony' or 'Toni') lived in part of the house, which was owned by the writer Maurice Richardson.

2 Mary Keene, wife of the film director Ralph Keene, was staying at Majoda with her baby, and had been there on the night of the shooting.

3 The *News of the World*, reporting the Captain's acquittal on 24 June, began its report, 'Officers and civilian friends congratulated a captain in the Royal Engineers renowned as a guerrilla and sabotage expert in Greece after he stepped from the dock ...'

one; so that we can leave it any time we raise enough money to go to America. I'll let you know if anything comes of it. I've been doing very little except work with Eldridge & Donald; anyway, I've only been here two days. Leaving you was like cutting my body in half; and yours. I LOVE YOU. That's as sure as the earth's turning, as the beastliness of London, as the fact that you are beautiful, as that I love Aeronwy and Llewelyn too— Caitlin my own my dear—Wire me TEM 5420 to say if you want to speak on the telephone to me. I'm going to the Zoo tomorrow, with a Lilliput photographer, to write captions for his pictures: What Animals Think. I don't know if it's Brandt;[1] rather hope not. If they commission me straight away, I'll send on half the money. I think, by the way, that our court expenses will be sent to me at Majoda. If they are, you'll be okay. Wire or phone me about it. I'll come back as soon as I can: certainly this week. I am longing for you. That's such a little understatement. I want you. You're the whole of my life. The Rest is nothing. Believe me, Cat, forever, and write or wire & phone & let me hear your voice because I love you. I want to be in your arms.

    Always & always and always & always

X
Dylan

MS: Maurice Neville

SHEILA SHANNON[2]

5 July 45   Majoda   New Quay   Cardiganshire   Wales

Dear Miss Shannon,
    Your letter asking me about those two poems was, as you thought, waiting for me here at home. In case spoken consent to your including them in your anthologies isn't enough, here it is in writing. Grand: print what you like of mine.
    I hope to see you some time again. Perhaps we could have lunch? I'll ring when I get back to town.

Yours sincerely,
Dylan Thomas

MS: National Library of Wales

---

1 Bill Brandt.
2 Sheila Shannon was helping to edit two anthologies published by Frederick Muller, *Soldiers' Verse*, which included Thomas's 'The hand that signed the paper', and *Poems of Death*, which included 'And death shall have no dominion'.

OSCAR WILLIAMS
July 30 1945   as from Gryphon [etc]

My dear Oscar,
    Many thanks for many things.
    For the cheques from periodicals, they couldn't have been more welcome, they seethed in their envelopes, which sounds like Lawrence, and burst in a shower of drinks and cabrides and small hospitalities to the dour and filmy mackintoshed bar-flies who work, or don't, with me.
    For the anthologies, all of them so heavy and in such large lovely type, so dear, and with such lovely ladies and gentlemen to be seen out at the back: all portentously smoking (the pipes of bedpan), prinking, profiling, horizon-eying, open-collared and wild-haired in the photographer's wind, facing America and posterity and the music, shy as professional novelists caught accidentally in an arc-lamp, framed against rock and ruin, musing in cactused, glass-haired, first-editioned, (oooh, Cyril, a Kafka's missing), Paul-Kleed brown studies, some smelling visibly of just-a-little-rice-and-bamboo-shoot-dish-my-wife-found-in-Mexico, or of peanut butter and homebrewed cider, some painted, some by painters, some by themselves, some just painted, one self-drenched and solemn under a coat of Celtic jam, one bow-tied to his explosive cross, the pin-up poets, oh how I love you all.
    For your own book of poems. You've let down your hair hard and loud on the one real ground, and sometimes you fall over it into a boiling black Belsen of your own. The poems never relax or play fair or explain or whine about their condition or are ashamed, but conduct their prolific unpretty lives in front of the nose of your nerves. They are pieces that fly, hot and violent and exuberantly unhappy, off a poem in the making. The wheels go round, crying, protesting, denying, on rails that are laid out only as the wheels express towards them. The rules, the form, spring up urgently as the temper of making needs them.
    For your letters, too long unanswered but cherished next to my heart, hair, identity disk, razor scar from a Poetry Tea, the tattooed hoofprints of Dali's mother—It is hysterical weather where I am writing, Blaen Cwm, Llangain, Carmarthenshire, Wales,[1] in a breeding-box in a cabbage valley, in a parlour with a preserved sheepdog, where mothballs fly at night, not moths, where the Bible opens itself at Revelations; and is there money still for tea? My son, in the nonstop probably frog-filled rain, is performing what seems, from this distance, to be an unnatural act with a beaver. Looking closer, I see he is only destroying his sister's doll—the little pixie. I can hear, from far off, my Uncle Bob drinking tea and methylated spirits through eighty years of nicotine-brown fern. My father, opposite, is reading about Hannibal through a magnifying glass so small he can see only one

---

1 They had left New Quay.

word at a time. I could lie down and live with Hannibals. And my wife is washing an old opera.

For the crust you offer in America. It is already nibbled, and I am the mice. Hands, and teeth, across the ocean.

For reading this.

Next morning. Still raining, and not daffodils. A farmyard outside the window, sows and cows and the farmer's daughters, what a day of dugs. I've been reading all Lawrence's poems, some aloud to no-one in this bombazine room, and liking them more & more. Do you remember:—

> O the green glimmer of apples in the orchard,
> Lamps in a wash of rain!
> O the wet walk of my brown hen through the stackyard!
> O tears on the window pane!
>
> Nothing now will ripen the bright green apples
> Full of disappointment and of rain;
> Blackish they will taste, of tears, when the yellow dapples
> Of autumn tell the withered tale again.
>
> All around the yard it is cluck! my brown hen.
> Cluck! and the rain-wet wings;
> Cluck! my marigold bird, and then
> Cluck! for your yellow darlings.[1]

Yes, there's his brown hen cluck in the gambo-swished mud,[2] scratching for Christ, cackling in droppings, Gladys's pet lamb-now-sheep follows here maaa-ing for poor, unloved Gladys's unmade milk, an Italian prisoner is scraping hay off a hedge, one Fontamara[3]-brown-sly-innocent eye in the back of his head fixed on her black bloomered bottom as she bends to scatter grain for the yellow darlings. The rainy robin tic tac at the pane. Over the hill, the hoarse noise of a train carrying holes to Hugh's Castle. Near, a grey gulled estuary, and sheepshanks, corpses of cats, cowteeth, bottles of ether, jellyfish, frenchletters, indecipherable messages in jars (the secret of the Marie Celeste, the Number of the Beast, the name of Cain's wife, pyramid riddles, Tibetan acrostics, next year's newspapers) on the foreshore. I'm trying to establish my geography. Up the hill-lane behind this house too full of Thomases, a cottage row of the undeniably mad unpossessed peasantry of the inbred crooked county, my cousins, uncles, aunts, the woman with the gooseberry birthmark who lies with dogs, the farm labourer who told me that the stream that runs by his cottage side is Jordan water and who can deny him, the lay preacher who believes that the war was begun only to sell newspapers which are the devil's sermon-

---

1 From D. H. Lawrence's 'Ballad of Another Ophelia', slightly misquoted.
2 A gambo is a cart.
3 See page 212, Vol I.

sheets, the man who, when his pony could work no longer because of old age, hanged it on an apple-tree to save a bullet, the woman who cries out 'Cancer!' as you pass her open door.

I should have written long before this, but couldn't bring myself to write only Thank you so very much for distributing my poems and for the sweet money, or to send you grunts of salutation from my trough. I have been trying to find out what legal etc. complications I will have to go through before leaving this country for America. First of all, because I have no financial independence, I have to be assured—or, rather, the American Embassy over here will have to be assured—that, on arriving in America, there is a job, or there are jobs, waiting for me; that I will not become a liability to the United States. There must be a sponsor, or sponsors, who will sign a declaration saying that I & my dependents will *not* be allowed to become liabilities. So what is my first step? The American Embassy has given me several printed forms to be sent to whoever I imagine will employ me in the States & guarantee me a living. If I send those official forms to you, could you do anything about them? That is, could you approach TIME—whom you suggested as possible employers, if only for part of my time—and get some definite promise, however small, from them? If that *could* be arranged, then, after the returning to the American Embassy here of the signed 'We-won't-let-the-bugger-starve' declaration, and after the final examinations, interviews, and okayings, physical & political, I could sail within three months. So that, supposing with your help some job, appointment etc. could be fixed, I should be able to arrive, a Migrained Father, in the early spring of next year. I have not yet written to Theodore Spencer,[1] because I have lost your letter with his address in it, and with the particulars of the work he might be able to give me in Harvard. Also, I did not quite know how to approach him. I have found that he is an old friend of a very old friend of mine here, Augustus John, who sends him every greeting and asks him to do what he can. Perhaps Augustus has already written, I wouldn't know, when I saw him last he was chasing a woman in uniform through the Zoo, horned & goat-bearded. If Spencer could assure me—that is, again, if he could assure, on a form I could send you to send him, the Embassy here that Harvard will engage me in any lecturing or librarying—of some work, it would work wonders. Otherwise, a patron would do just as well, to say that he will look after me & mine in luxury, New York, or even in a kennel, Texas. I should most like to read, library, or lecture at Harvard. Time & Harvard. A promise of work from T & H from next spring on would settle, I think, everything—apart from money to travel with, & this I must try to rake up from the gutters in which I pretend to work. I'm asking you a lot, causing you bother, heaping responsibilities on your shoulders, prematurely crust-gulping. Will you do

---

1 Theodore Spencer (1902–49), poet and critic, member of the Harvard faculty.

what you can? If you say yes, I will send the Embassy forms to you straightaway. I shall not write to Spencer until I hear from you.

I should bring my wife, my son aged now $6\frac{1}{2}$, my daughter aged now $2\frac{1}{2}$. Their names are Llewelyn and Aeronwy. *They are quite nice hell.* My wife's name is Caitlin, she is Irish. We would all come together because I do not want to return to this country for a long time.

The rain has stopped, thank Jesus. Have the Socialists-in-power-now stopped it? An incometax form flops through the window, the letter box is choked with dockleaves. Let's get out, let's get out.[1]

Later. I have been out. I went to the Edwinsford Arms, a sabbath-dark bar with a stag's head over the Gents and a stuffed salmon caught by Shem and a mildewed advertisement for pre-1914 tobacco and a stain on the wall, just above my head, that I hoped was beer. I had some beer with a man who said he was shot in the groin in the last war, and who, unable to have a woman ever since, blames it on the dirty Jews. He said, 'Look what they did, the moochin',[2] and showed me a scar on his calf. I said that I thought he said he had been shot through the groin. 'And the calf, and the calf', he said in a terrible temper. 'And the calf, the bloody yids.' He is an official in some Department—a Department set-built for the early German films— that investigates the authenticity of discharged soldiers' pension-claims. 'Every time I see "Psycho-neurosis" on a discharge paper, I say, Lead- Swinger.' He told me the best way to boil lobsters, which was detailed and painful. I told him Norman Douglas's[3] recipe for raping a dog: Catch the dog, open the drawer of a desk, put the dog's head in the open drawer, and then close the drawer. He told me how he had once made a child of six dead drunk. It began to rain again, great wrathful drops. We parted enemies. I rode back on a bicycle through the justice-must-be-done-let's- rain-on-sinners rain, and the bicycle wheels through the pools & slush on the roads asked the same monotonous & inane questions as the boiler- pipes once asked Gorki: Have you got any rubber? Do you want some fish? Cows under crying roadside trees, looking over the estuary, weed and webfoot mud, waited for Royal Academicians. Snails were coming out; a P.E.N. Club of slugs crossed the road; Manchester, Manchester, fetch a pocket handkercher, said the engine over the hill; you could hear little boys in desolate back-gardens facing the depressed water slapping each other on the stomach.

And back to a cardtable holding up a jamjar full of cigarette-ends, the rough draft of a ten minute film on the Kitchen Front, your War Poetry anthology, a spool of film showing a pair of hands over a sink, Why Birds Sing, Llewelyn's stampalbum, a large sheet of paper with the first line of a poem at the top: 'O'. I must, this week, at this table, finish the Kitchen

---

1 The result of the first postwar general election in Britain, announced on 26 July, was an overwhelming victory for the Labour Party. Thomas expresses the middle-class fears of rampaging socialism that were abroad in 1945.

2 'Mochyn' is Welsh for 'pig', colloquially 'dirty pig'.

3 Norman Douglas (1868–1952), novelist and travel writer.

Front, write a broadcast talk to be called 'Memories of Christmas' for the Children's Hour, write a begging letter to a Sir, write another line to come after 'O', fill up my £1000 People's Crossword, observe ill-nature, stop doodling, be natural, not sniff, not put ash in my coatpocket, remember that we all are brothers—'but not a trace of foul equality, nor sound of still more foul human perfection. You need not clear the world like a cabbage patch for me. Leave me my nettles, let me fight the wicked, obstreperous weeds myself, & put them in their place. I don't at all want to annihilate them, I like a row with them, but I won't be put on a cabbage-idealistic level with them.' I don't agree. Judy O'Grady and the Colonel 's Lady[1] and Lamarr Hedy[2] and the Workers' Mayday, we're all bothers and blisters under unoriginal sins. For Whom Omar's Bowl Tells. The Censury of the Common Man. All Men My Enemas. O God, O Aren'tweall.

I liked the War Poetry immensely. Everything I liked, much I didn't know. I could have done with some Lawrence, though.

> Surely you've trod[den] straight
> To the very door!
> You have surely achieved your fate;
> And the perfect dead are elate
> To have won once more.
>
> Now to the dead you are giving
> Your last allegiance.
> But what of us who are living,
> And fearful yet of believing
> In your pitiless legions?[3]

But, probably no, he is too unequal. Thank you for the *two* copies, one for each eye. And I don't like the verses I have quoted above, either. Some of the contributors' views on War & Poetry I was glad to read; by others, especially by Treece's, appalled. War can't produce poetry, only poets can, and war can't produce poets either because they bring themselves up in such a [?way] that this outward bang bang of men against men is something they have passed a long time ago on their poems' way towards peace. A poet writing a poem is at peace with everything except words, which are eternal actions; only in the lulls between the warring work on words can he be at war with men. Poets can stop bullets, but bullets can't stop poets. What is a poet anyway? He is a man who has written or is writing what he, in his utmost human fallible integrity, necessarily communal, believes to be good poetry. As he writes good poetry very rarely, he is most often at peace with the eternal actions of words and is therefore very likely to be caught up in any bang bang that is going. When he is fighting, he is not a poet. Nor is a craftsman a craftsman. I think capital-lettered War can only

---

1 From Rudyard Kipling, 'The Ladies': 'For the Colonel's Lady an' Judy O'Grady / Are sisters under their skins!'
2 Hedy Lamarr (1913–2000), Hollywood star of the 1940s.
3 From D. H. Lawrence's 'Obsequial Ode'.

in subject matter affect poetry. Violence and suffering are all the time, & it does not matter how you are brought up against them. And so on. But this is all vague and loose, like myself this rainy moment, and all I want to say before we bid a reluctant farewell to colourful Carmarthenshire is: Thank you again for books, periodicals, letters, cheques, friendship, and the help I know, I hope, you will give me in trying to get to America—which can succeed only if the authorities are informed that a position or positions— cut-glass for job or jobs—is or are waiting me in America, in your more- than-European idealism, like a beaureoled bleached skeleton hovering its cage-ribs in the social heaven, beneficent. Lawrence again; oh leave me, you talking prick; oh to be where the Lady Loverlies shatter and the blackguards ride no more. Write soon.

Dylan

[*On reverse of sheet: a drawing of three men in tall hats, fighting.*]

MS: Houghton

LORRAINE JAMESON[1]

4 August 45   Blaen Cwm   Llangain   near Carmarthen

Dear Miss Jameson,
    I'm so sorry not to have replied sooner to your letter. I've changed my address, and the letter has only just been forwarded to me.
    Thank you for wanting me to do something else for the Children's Hour. I think 'Memories of Christmas' a perfectly good title to hang something on, and I'll get down to it soon.[2] Is there a closing date? If I have any other ideas, I'll let you know.
    I wonder whether you'd be interested in my reading a short story of mine—'A Visit to Grandpa's'—that was included in my book of stories called 'Portrait of the Artist As A Young Dog' (Dent)? I'm afraid I've no copy of the book or the story, but perhaps the BBC Library has—though I doubt it. Anyway, if you could get hold of it & read the story, perhaps you'd let me know what you think? I think it would go well, very well.
    Thanks again, & apologies for the delay.

Yours sincerely,
Dylan Thomas

MS: BBC

1 Lorraine Jameson ran the 'Children's Hour' programme at the BBC in Cardiff.
2 Thomas had read a radio talk, 'Reminiscences of Childhood'—a revised version of a broadcast on 14 February 1943—in Children's Hour on 21 March 1945. Jameson's suggestion (on 17 July) that he write about 'Memories of Christmas' was to prove lucrative after Thomas's death. In 1950 he combined the 1945 radio talk with a 1947 article that he wrote for the magazine *Picture Post*, 'Conversation about Christmas', to produce 'A Child's Memories of Christmas in Wales' for an American magazine. As 'A Child's Christmas in Wales' this probably has come to appeal to a wider audience, both in print and as a recording, than anything else he wrote.

J. M. DENT
8 August 45   as from Gryphon [etc]

Dear Sir,

I must apologise for not having returned the proofs of my book of poems—'Deaths & Entrances.' I see they were sent to me on 30th of May, but they have only just been forwarded. I will correct them & send them on in a few days. I do hope this very long delay will not prevent the book being published this year.

Apologies again for being, unavoidably, a nuisance.

Yours truly,
Dylan Thomas

MS: (J. M. Dent)

CAITLIN THOMAS
[after 15 August 1945]   M[ervyn] Peake's flat

My dear
My Caitlin
    darling more times than ever before to me, I love you. And this time has seemed the very longest since we haven't been together all the time, since I've had to leave you alone, or with parents, for weeks & ten-days and eternities:—the *very* longest; I have never missed you more nor loved you more, and every long night without you has been sleepless and fear-filled, and I've cried to be with you. I've said to you, all these hours away, Oh be around the next corner, Caitlin my own, climb up the stairs of the next bus I'm in, be waiting, somewhere, somewhere very near, for me. But I knew you were in a hutch in a field, so far away, with two neurotics & a baby and a dog, bound to Daddy-likes-his-dinner and eternal afternoon walks.[1] I do, I do, I do think of you all the time. And I love you. I've been having an awful time, too, looking for a house, a flat, a room, a hole in the wall. One excellent thing *might* happen. I said 'House news tomorrow I hope' at the end of a money wire, but the news is put off till next week. It's a house about 30 miles from London, near Bovingdon, in Herts, & we could have it free for 3 months, furnished. Isn't *that* better than me having to jog back & forth to you in Wales, every few days or so it seems, & better, much better, for you? But God knows, nothing might happen. And there's the *chance* of a flat somewhere in Chelsea, very small. Nothing else, & they're both chances.
    I hung on because all V.Day Week was impossible to travel. You had to

---

1 Caitlin was at the Blaen Cwm cottage with her parents-in-law.

get to the station last night to get a train next morning. The second V.Day I've not had the luck to avoid: London was terrible, terrible, terrible.[1]

And I've no extra money. No house, as yet, no money, as yet. But good chances of money, at least, from the BBC. But *that's* not much good if we can't live in, or near, London to do it. It's acting in plays, especially verse plays for the Empire Service: & they pay well.

So I'm not much good to you, coming home, (not home), but I hope, oh God I hope, you'll say you *are* & kiss me. I want you holding on to me, & me on to you. I love you I love you I love you dear sweet Cat, dear mine.

Think that I think of you.

Feel that we know each other forever.

Know that I love you.

Tomorrow I'll see you, poor & a bit dirty but oh so glad.

X

& to Aeron   Dylan

MS: Tony Vilela

FRANCIS BUTTERFIELD[2]
[August 1945]

Dear Francis,

Just as Caitlin was about to send off her letter to you, this Electric bill came. I suppose it's a bill that Fred Brown owes: it certainly has nothing to do with me, as I haven't been in the studio for over a year. Will you hand it on to Fred & get him to settle it? Or arrange it somehow—to hell with old bills that are no concern of mine, I've enough new ones that are.

I'll be up in about a fortnight. Hope to see you.

Yours,
Dylan

MS: Jim Martin

VERNON WATKINS
22 Aug 45   Blaen Cwm   Llangain   nr Carmarthen

My Dear Vernon,

How happy and glad Caitlin and I are that Gwen and you have Rhiannon. Every love and good wish for ever and ever from us both to the three of you.

---

1 'VE Day', 8 May 1945, had marked the end of the war in Europe. 'VJ Day', victory over Japan, was Wednesday 15 August, but there was a two-day public holiday, the Wednesday and the day after.

2 The letter was found in the grate of the house in Twickenham where Butterfield, a painter, died.

There could never be fonder and truer parents, and never more loving well-wishers. This isn't word day. God bless you all.

Dylan

MS: British Library

DAVID TENNANT
28 August 1945   as from Gryphon [etc]

My dear David,
   Across the counties, from mean, green, horsethieving Wales, I raise one Playercoloured aspen hand to salute and supplicate. The last time I saw you, you had just gone from the Prince of Wales, and who am I to blame. The rest of the day was dark, shot with fire, a hummingtop of taxis and glasses, a spinning sight of scowls and leers seen through the wrong end of a telescope made of indiarubber, a rush of close-ups, strange mouths and noses flattening themselves on one's own in places that seemed to be now a turkish bath, now a lavatory, now a gymnasium for midgets, bar, hothouse, hospital, knockshop, abattoir, crematorium, revolving cathedral and, at last, a bed only an inch from the ceiling. I'm coming to town again on Thursday, and would love to see you. This time I shall be collected, calm but gabbling, a patient on a monument: beer only, for me, for weeks, for health, forgive me, for Christ's sake, for sanity, four freedoms. Can you ring me? A City, or at least a Fleet St, morning would be lovely. Do you know of any flat, small house, in London or fairly near that I could rent? I am getting desperate here. We *have* to move. There has never been, for me, anything more urgent than this. I have to find somewhere to live in, if only for a few months. Do you know of anybody? Would you ask some of the people you see? God, I'd be grateful. I'm going out of my mind here, and can do no work. There *must* be somewhere. Do do do do do ask and see for me, David. I can't go on like this, travelling eight hours to spend a weekend with Caitlin. We must be somewhere fairly near London, if not in it. This is the supplication I referred to at the beginning. Can you, will you, help in any way by asking any who might know, who could know, who would be kind? It is spoiling everything, having nowhere permanent to live. I want so much to work, and cannot without some certainty of surroundings. A house, a flat, two rooms. I have managed to write one new poem and will bring it up to show you when we meet. I think you will like it, it's a poem for evenings and tears.[1] I shall look forward to you ringing. Don't forget, please. Let's hug the counters of nasty reporters' pubs, and drink to the Only Atom. I think I could lie down and live with men, they are so

1 'Fern Hill'.

unplacid and so unselfcontained, they sweat and whine about their condition; I like that. I'll be, I hope, seeing you soon. Do your best for me, about finding some hole in the wind to lay down my two heads.

Everything to you.

Dylan

MS: Victoria

DONALD TAYLOR
Tuesday [August 1945]   [Blaen Cwm]

The postman knocks. By Cain, he knocks once more![1]
I spring from bed. Then, rising from the floor
Where I have fainted, rush to the door and fall
Again. Youth, what a joy is youth! The hall
Is dark with dogs. They bite me as I pass.
My dear dumb friends! I'll put some powdered glass
Today in their Bob Martin's. That'll teach
Them manners. And now at long last I reach
The dog-and-child-chewed mat and find?—yes, yes!—
A bunch of letters from the far U.S.
Ah, what epistolary pearls unseen
Blush in these envelopes! what hippocrene!—
'Be my pen-pal' from Truman. Or 'Dear Friend,
Shall we arrange a *personal* Lease-Lend?'
From Betty Hutton. Or 'Will you play for me
An Air on my G. String?' signed Gypsy Lee.
Or 'We salute you, Script-King!' from MacArthur,
Hecht, and Wilder. Or a plea to bath her
From Miss Colbert.[2] But, alas, vain hopes!
There's nothing in those Sam-stamped envelopes
But a request to write on 'Whither Art?'
For 'Cyclorama', 'Seed', 'Rubato', 'Fart'
'Prognosis', 'Ethic', 'Crucible', and 'Clef'—
And other small reviews that pay sweet F.

In other words, none of the money I expected to come did come, and I am broke and therefore unable to buy a ticket to come to London. Can a few pounds expenses be arranged somehow and wired on to me on Wednesday? My own expense account is fairly clear, and I could settle up with the accounts department when I arrive. I should very much like to come up on Thursday, the first train, arriving lunchtime. *Can* it be managed? I'll ring

1 James M. Cain wrote *The Postman Always Rings Twice*, a novel of 1934.
2 Harry S. Truman was American President from 12 April 1945. 'Lease-Lend' was the 1941 agreement by which Britain leased overseas bases to the United States, and was loaned destroyers in return. Betty Hutton, Gypsy Rose Lee and Claudette Colbert were movie actresses. Charles MacArthur, Ben Hecht and Billy Wilder were screenwriters.

you Wednesday afternoon. But, if possible, I'd like to have the expenses (?) wired before that, as the Thursday train leaves 7.30 in the morning. Sorry to be such a nuisance. I very much want to discuss this film with you—or, rather, the tentative idea I've been working a bit at. And there are tons of other things. No V. Days. All work and discussion. Hope you can send on the fare etc.

Ever,
Dylan

MS: Texas

T. W. EARP
28 Aug 45   as from Gryphon [etc]

Dear Tommy,
    I'll be in London from Friday, August 31st, for a week. Can we meet? Will you let me know, by wire, phonecall, note, or sealed man, when and where? It's been a long time.
    Anyone want to let a house in your district? We're getting desperate. I hope May is better.
    Perhaps we could have a Hants tiny party this time?

Ever,
Dylan

MS: Ohio State University

T. W. EARP
Monday [postmarked 3 September 1945]   Gryphon

Dear Tommy,
    Too gastric to write anything except 1 o clock Wednesday at the Salisbury will be fine & lovely.

Ever,
Dylan

MS: Ohio State University

CAITLIN THOMAS
Thur [6 September 1945]   Gryphon   Guild House

My darling dear, my own, my poor, beautiful Caitlin, this is only a little note because I want you to have this money straightaway. I have been waiting every day for money to come from the BBC; it still hasn't come;

this was a cheque from the agents for poems in anthologies. I will send the BBC money as soon as it comes. I love you forever, &, though I thought last time, & the time before that, that I never in all our lovely life together missed you [?so] desperately, & loved you more dearly, this is the worst time of all. I love you & need you, dear my dear & think of you in that grave & look around me at mine. I am terribly sorry not to have sent you money sooner; I had none. I hope this will help, & there shall be more. The Electricity Summons, supposed to be paid by Fred months ago, I [?telephoned] Fred about [it] this afternoon & [?will] get the money at once from him & send it off to the electric buggering people.[1] There are 2 chances of a house, & I have had a message from Miss Griffiths we met in Llanstephan asking me to ring her at home this evening. Perhaps she will have something definite, please our Lord & preserve our sanity. Do not be too depressed, my sweetheart, though you've every right to be. I shall be back on Monday, arriving in Carmarthen at six. I should love you & love you & love you to meet me. I hope to God I shall be able to say, We can go up to town almost at once. Donald is going on holiday—*not* to N. Quay—& I needn't return anyway for a fortnight. But I told him, quite definitely, I wouldn't return at all unless there is a house but would live in Majoda again. I love you. I am so glad you liked the two broadcasts. Do listen on Sunday at 11 p.m. & less than a day after I shall be with you, my true love until death & forever afterwards.[2] I want to hold you & kiss you. Kiss Aeronwy for me. Say that you love me. Wait for me. I love you & though I am wild unhappy think of you every second. You are everything that is good. I love you.

Dylan

MS: (Maurice Neville)

LORRAINE JAMESON

12 Sept '45   Blaen Cwm   Llangain   near Carmarthen

Dear Miss Jameson,

Thank you for your letter. I'm sorry you had such difficulty getting hold of my book of stories. I'm sure you're right, & that 'A Visit To Grandpa's' is not really suitable for children. Thank you, though, for mentioning it to Aneirin Davies.[3] I should like very much to read it from the West Regional one evening, & will give Aneirin a ring next week.

I've been away for a little time, but shall get down to writing 'Memories

1 Some words are illegible in the MS.
2 'Quite Early One Morning' read by Thomas (in a BBC recording made the previous December) was broadcast on 31 August, and on 2 September he read three of his poems on the radio; these are the 'two broadcasts' referred to. On Sunday 9 September he was to read poems by D. H. Lawrence at 11 pm, returning to Blaen Cwm on 10 September.
3 Aneirin Talfan Davies, talks producer at the Cardiff BBC.

of Christmas' straightaway, & will send it on in plenty of time—I hope.

Yours sincerely,

Dylan Thomas

MS: BBC

A. J. HOPPÉ[1]

18 September 1945   as from Gryphon [etc]

Dear Mr. Hoppé,

I am returning herewith the corrected proofs of my book of poems, *'Deaths and Entrances'*. Thank you very much for sending on the new set of proofs; I'm afraid I made a terrible mess of the other two.

And you'll see that I've made, and am making, a nuisance of myself over these proofs. Let me try to put my points in order.

(1) The poem on pages 16 and 17 I have completely rewritten, retaining only the title line and one or two others.[2] The poem in its final, revised form—exactly the same length as the original—I am enclosing.

(2) The poem on page 32 is substantially altered. In form, it is now three stanzas of four lines each.[3]

(3) I have crossed out the poem on page 36 *entirely*, and am substituting another, and shorter, poem—*'In My Craft or Sullen Art'*—which I enclose.

(4) The poem *'Vision and Prayer'* on pages 43-50 is not set typographically as I wish and as I tried to explain in a letter to my agents which was forwarded to Mr. Richard Church. I am enclosing a copy of the Sewanee Review, in which the poem is printed *exactly* as it should be. I do hope, & beg, that the poem will be printed in the book just as it is in the magazine.

(5) I am enclosing a further poem, *'Fern Hill'*, not so far included in the book, which I very much *want* included as it is an *essential* part of the feeling & meaning of the book as a whole.[4]

As so much re-setting etc. will have to be done anyway, I do most earnestly hope that *'Fern Hill'* can be included in the book. I myself would be very unsatisfied were it omitted. (I realise, naturally, that it should have been sent along in the first place with the others, but it was not at that time completed.)

(7) [*sic*] I have not corrected the title-page as the numbers will nearly all have to be altered if, as I very much hope, *'Fern Hill'* can be added to the book.

I'm sorry there has been such a delay in my returning the proofs, and that such an amount of additional work—for which, of course, I will pay—is involved.

1 Hoppé was a director of J. M. Dent.
2 'Unluckily for a death'.
3 'On a Wedding Anniversary'.
4 The poem was written at Blaen Cwm in the summer; see letter to Edith Sitwell, page 197.

I am sorry too that I cannot send the revised form of '*Unluckily For A Death*', & the substitute-poem, '*In My Craft or Sullen Art*', in typescript. I am on holiday in Wales & far away from typewriters.

I am looking forward to hearing from you, and apologise again for all inconveniences etc.

Yours very truly,
Dylan Thomas

MS: (J. M. Dent)

FRANCIS BUTTERFIELD
Friday 21 [Sept] '45   Blaen Cwm   Llangain   near Carmarthen   S Wales

Dear Francis,

Caitlin and I are sending up some things to London—a trunk or two and a single bed among them—which we want temporarily put among our other things in the studio. A van is bringing them up from Wales this coming Wednesday (26th), and will deliver them at the studio sometime late afternoon. As I don't suppose you'll be in then, would you tell the van Hengelaars that a van *will* be arriving then & that the few things are to be put in the studio? I don't know how the key-arrangement is now, but in case it's altered since my time & the key no longer hangs on a string through the door, would you—if there is a new key—let the van Hengelaars have it on Wednesday afternoon so that the vandriver can shove the stuff in without any bother?

This note *might* be unnecessary; we might be in London before then, staying temporarily with Toni[1] and if we are will look out for you around Chelsea. I hope to see you very soon anyway, about a couple of things. Where d'you go? The Black Lion?

Ever,
Dylan

MS: Andrew MacAdie

LORRAINE JAMESON
25th September 1945   [headed paper: Gryphon Films, etc]

Dear Miss Jameson,

Here is the script of 'Memories of Christmas', which you invited me to do. I do hope you like it.

---

1 See n.1, page 163.

I've been sent a contract, applying to the story alone, for 'A Visit to Grandpa's', which is also, so my Agent's note said, to be included in the Children's Hour, but I've had so far, no contract about my reading of it. I want, of course, to read the story, and the 'Memories of Christmas', myself.

Will you write and let me know?

Yours sincerely,
Dylan Thomas

MS: BBC

ANEIRIN TALFAN DAVIES[1]

28th September 1945   [headed paper: Gryphon Films, etc]

Dear Aneirin,

Thank you for your letter. I should like very much to record that story of mine called 'A Visit to Grandpa's'. I've had a contract about the copyright of it, from the B.B.C., but I gather it was for the Children's Hour. Still, I'd rather me read it than anybody else. Could I do that and then talk with you about some of the other broadcasts that you suggested? There is one that I have already sent to Miss Jameson; and I agree with you that a talk in justification of 'penny horribles' would be lovely to do. So if you would let me know I would be very grateful.

Do you ever come to London nowadays? My telephone number is TEMPLE BAR 5420.

Best wishes,

Yours,
Dylan Thomas

MS: BBC

A. J. HOPPÉ

28th September 1945   [headed paper: Gryphon Films, etc]

Dear Mr. Hoppé,

Thank you for your letter. I think the poem 'Vision and Prayer' must be set-up as it was in the Sewanee Review. I wish it were easier for me to say that I should like the book to be kept to its sixty-four pages, but I'm afraid

---

1 Talfan Davies wrote to Thomas on 25 September to say he wanted to record 'A Visit to Grandpa's'. He asked for more scripts because Thomas's last talk (presumably 'Reminiscences of Childhood') had 'taken very well with our listeners. I wonder could you repeat the miracle with a talk on a Welsh country village? Or does this idea appeal to you?—a talk in justification of "penny horribles"—"The Magnet" and so on. I think I heard you once defend this type of literature for children . . .' The scripts were never written.

that I can't think how four pages could be well omitted. If it is any help, the poem called 'On a Wedding Anniversary' could be cut out, but that, after all is only one page, so, if you don't mind, the best thing seems to me that 'Vision and Prayer' should be printed as in the American magazine and that the further additional poem 'Fern Hill' should be put at the end of the book.[1]

You said that you would be prepared to do that, if necessary, and I would be awfully glad if you would.

Yours sincerely,
Dylan Thomas

MS: (J. M. Dent)

A. J. HOPPÉ
6 Nov 45   39 Markham Square   London   SW3[2]

Dear Sir,

Here enclosed are the corrected *final* proofs of my book of poems Deaths & Entrances. Thank you for printing the poem as it is on pages 43–54.[3] I do hope something can be done about page 45.

Yours faithfully,
Dylan Thomas

MS: (J. M. Dent)

LORRAINE JAMESON
7th Nov '45   39 Markham Square   Chelsea   London   SW3

Dear Miss Jameson,

Thank you for your letter of October 23, which has just been forwarded to me, saying that my talk on 'Memories of Christmas' will be used in the Children's Hour on Sunday December 16 at 5.15 p.m.

I shall be in London all December, & would very much appreciate it if you could, as you suggested, arrange for me to broadcast from here.

Apologies for the unavoidable delay in my answering your letter, & I hope it hasn't inconvenienced you too much.

Yours sincerely,
Dylan Thomas

I wonder if it would be possible for me to have a copy of my Christmas

1 'On a Wedding Anniversary' wasn't deleted. 'Fern Hill' was printed as suggested.
2 A basement flat in a house owned by the writer Noel Blakiston. Caitlin's sister Nicolette Devas, who also lived in Markham Square, found it for them. Nicolette's husband, the painter Anthony Devas, didn't want the Thomases in his own house if he could help it.
3 'Vision and Prayer'.

script sent to me, at the above address, before the broadcast? I haven't got a copy, & should like to have a look at it before reading it.

MS: BBC

BBC
November 10th 1945   39 Markham Square   SW3

Dear Sir,
    I regret not having been able to answer your contract letters of 23rd October and 1st November concerning the two scripts on, 'Augustus John' and 'Nationalism in Poetry.'[1] Illness prevented me from answering, as, unfortunately, it also prevented me from writing the script on John—as, perhaps, you might have heard by this time.
    I do not quite know, therefore, what position this leaves me in. In your letter of November 1st, you said that though six guineas is actually your standard rate for a 10-minute talk that is not read by the author, you felt that, in my case, a higher rate—that of seven guineas—should be paid. As, unavoidably, I failed to turn out the script on John, I wonder whether the seven guinea rate still applies for the script I am in the process of writing on Nationalism in Poetry. I should be very grateful to hear from you, and to sign a new contract for the Nationalism talk, and apologise for any inconvenience caused you by my delay in answering your letters.

Yours sincerely,
Dylan Thomas

TS: BBC (copy made for Legal Section)

ANEIRIN TALFAN DAVIES
Nov 11 '45   39 Markham Square   Chelsea   London   SW3

Dear Aneirin,
    I've only just found your letter dated 29th Sept; I must have put it aside, meaning to answer it directly, and then mislaid it in the bother of moving. The above is now my address, and *not* c/o Gryphon Films.
    You said in your letter you were hoping to come to London before long, and that then I could record 'A Visit to Grandpa's'. I do hope I haven't missed you. Will you let me know?

1 The Augustus John script was commissioned for a 'Famous Contemporaries' series in the BBC's Eastern Services. 'Nationalism in Poetry' was for the Belgian Service.

I haven't written the penny-horrible script yet but will get down to it next week.

How are you?

Yours,
Dylan

MS: BBC

LORRAINE JAMESON

30 Nov [1945] [postcard]   39 Markham Square   Chelsea   London   SW3

Sorry not to reply before to your letter of 26th. Yes, 11.0. a.m. December 6th at Broadcasting House, London, will be fine for me to record my Children's Hour talk, 'Memories of Christmas'. Shall I receive further notification or shall I just turn up? If I don't hear from you, I'll turn up anyway.[1]

Sincerely,
Dylan Thomas

MS: BBC

BBC

November 30th 1945   39 Markham Square   Chelsea   London   SW3

Dear Mr. Alexander,

Thank you for your letter saying that, in spite of my failure, through illness, to turn in the script on Augustus John for the Hindustani Service, the fee of seven guineas, rather than six, which you kindly arranged for me to receive for a 1,200 word script in English on 'Nationalism in Poetry' for the Belgian Service, still stands.

I return, signed, the corrected contract, and corrected from 6 to 7 guineas, as you suggested.

Yours sincerely,
Dylan Thomas

TS: BBC

BBC

Nov 30 '45   39 Markham Square   Chelsea   London   SW3

Dear Sir,

I apologise for not having replied before to your letter of Nov 19 '45 in which you said that you had enclosed two contracts in another letter to 37

---

1 Unknown to Thomas, the head of 'Children's Hour' in London had insisted that he be prerecorded—'As you are aware,' he told Cardiff, 'there is tremendous risk in taking Dylan Thomas "live" in the programme for reasons which I do not think I need enlarge upon. He is notoriously tricky ...'

(not my address) Markham Square. You enclosed, in yours of the 19th, two duplicate contracts which I now sign and return.

I take notice of the fact that the contract for my selection & presentation of an half hour programme of Welsh Poetry to be recorded on 2nd January '46 has been sent to me on condition that you receive my script on or before the 15th of December '45.

Yours faithfully,
Dylan Thomas

MS: BBC

CYRIL CONNOLLY
Dec 5 1945   39 Markham Square   SW3

Dear Cyril,
Do you remember our conversation if that is the word in the Gargoyle some nights ago about fifty pounds that I think you said you thought I should have for my poem but for your fear that I should spend it?[1] Spend it of course I would, but certainly not all on what I don't know why I shouldn't spend it on anyway. I'm so much in worry and debt that the money would be wonderful *now*. Without it, or some other, I shall have to leave here for nowhere: our landlord's a vampire and strangers call every day baying. Is there any chance? If not of that, then of something reasonable down for future poems all of which you may have? Every day is worse and worst. Do try, please.

Ever,
Dylan

MS: McFarlin Library, University of Tulsa

OSCAR WILLIAMS
December 5th 1945   39 Markham Square   Chelsea   London   SW3
                                                        England

New address, for as long as
I pay the rent to our vampire,
the only one that garlic does
not keep off.

Dear Oscar,
In front of me, two unanswered letters from you dated October 2 and November 1. Behind me, two months when there was nothing in my head but a little Nagasaki,[2] all low and hot. I've lurched and boasted and lied

---

1 Perhaps 'A Winter's Tale', which appeared in a special French issue of *Horizon*.
2 A nuclear bomb, the second, was dropped on the Japanese port of Nagasaki on 9 August 1945.

through eight weeks of my allotted spin, at war with the lining of my stomach. Now I have won and am ill at peace again, in bed with a poultice called Mrs Hyam, I can write to thank you for your letters and their bangs of good news and to try to answer all the importents in them.

Poems Here is the signed form ('authorizing', my my!) about the nine poems you want for the Scribner anthology.[1] I hope, if this is too late, that you took my authorisation for granted. For you, for Poetry, and for money, I'd sign up for the Dynamos.[2]

Also, here are two new lyrical poems which I hope you'll send to the magazines. I like the long one, and may be given an Horizon award for it.

And about awards: Thank you, an awful lot, for getting the Levinson Prize from Poetry (Chicago) for me. I'd love to see it and stroke its little front: the cheque's, not Poetry's[3]—I know what's in front there. Will it come one day? No sign of the cheque yet, nor any official notification. 'View' has written asking for poems. Who's View? I didn't gather from their letter that they'd like the two poems I [sent] you. They sounded as though they liked their poems inside out. I like to see the outsides of poems, knowing there's an inside in.

George Barker and I read some poems on a platform yesterday to twenty or so communists and a couple of people. He sends his love.

I do quite a lot of reading of poetry on the radio here. I've read a lot of Elizabethans lately, & Lawrence, and Hardy. And some of my own next week. Do you think there will be any chance of my reading verse, or prose, on the American radio? I'm quite good; at least I'm often allowed to do it, though late at night: at hours carefully arranged so that no-one can be offended except those who like hearing verse read aloud and who also like going to bed early.

America: My Going, or Coming, To It

After much formfilling and dirty-questions-answering at the front door of the American Embassy, I am now going to try the back, hoping that consular Sweeney is in residence. The position, so far, is this: I must have, or the American Embassy must have, a letter or letters from responsible people, or authorities, or institutions etc, in America to say that I am being *invited* to America to take up a position as X, Y, or Z. And the more pompous the position (or 'appointment', I think, is the better word) can be made to sound, the better. Lecturer, adviser, critic, etc. is the kind of thing, I believe, that gets them. Yes, the letter or letters must invite me to take up an appointment, on my arriving in the States, with, or under, the signers of the letter or letters. This straight letter approach is better than the ordinary formfilling which relatives & near friends etc. are usually asked to

---

1 *A Little Treasury of Great Poetry*, published 1947.
2 The Moscow Dynamos, the Soviet Union's premier football team, had been playing in Britain. They gave a farewell party in London on 5 December.
3 The prize was worth $100.

do. The letter, or letters, can either, formally, invite *me*, or, formally, tell the Embassy that I am being invited. If this invitation is found to be genuine—as, *of course*, it will—then they'll see about granting me visas. These will have to be special visas. Or, alternatively, I take out immigration papers, insisting, I trust, that I can return to this country. But the thing is: LETTER, or letters, STRAIGHTAWAY. Can you get this done? You said, in yours of Oct. 2, that J. L. Sweeney 'has promised to do something very definite about getting me here.' And that you are to 'bring the forms to be filled by him, and that Something Will Be Done.' Your capitals. Okay and marvellous. Does that still stand? If so, (pray God), you have only to tell J. L. Sweeney that a letter from him or from someone else important has to be written to me or the Embassy inviting me to a post, position, appointment, or bit of money, in the States, and the worst may be over. I haven't written to Theodore Spencer or to Professor Morrison. Should I? Or should you again—I'm relying entirely on your kindness and on our transatlantic friendship—tell them the position. Anyway, so far as I can see it, one single good, important-sounding invitation will do. Once over there, I can try, with God's help & yours and the help of any old poetasters etc. to get other positions, appointments & other money (films, radio).

(I think, incidentally, I shall be fixing up, for an American publisher, with Reynell & Hitchcock who have written very sweetly & whom I have just answered.)

So my future is in your hands. BUT DON'T WORRY. Next: The visas obtained one day next year perhaps, how the hell do I raise the passage fare (one way) for myself and wife & two children? Maybe I can do something about that this end. Maybe. I'm not thinking of *that* yet. I'm just rushing down, I hope not too incoherently, the *real important things*.

Now I'm going to airmail this off at once, and wait, shaking, to hear from you, J. L. Sweeney, & anyone else who wants me to come, poor sod.[1]

I'll write another letter, about other things, once this is mailed. Take my usual flowery letter as being written.

Ever,
Dylan

MS: Houghton

MAURICE CARPENTER[2]
[?late December 1945]   39 Markham Square   SW3

Dear Maurice,

Sorry not to have answered before, but thanks a lot for the poem which I liked on a first reading and want to read many times again.

About this poetry reading. Is it the one I got a letter about from J. P.

1 The plans came to nothing, and it was more than four years before Thomas reached the promised land.
2 Poet and critic.

Tredgett, Croydon, a reading to be given at the Ethical Church on January 21? It sounds a bleeder. Do give me a ring and tell me: any time before eleven in the morning.

Thanks again for the poem. See you soon. Best wishes New Year etc.

Dylan

MS: National Library of Wales

*JOHN ARLOTT[1]

[late December 1945]   39 Markham Square   SW3

Dear John,

Here are the two returned Horizons, and my two poems copied out from them. I don't know what I could have been thinking about when I suggested, for inclusion in the Welsh programme, these *two* poems of mine: I must have forgotten they were both so very long. Surely they'll take a disproportionate amount of our time? And surely, again, they're very much alike in feeling and would give a monotonous effect?—even if a reader read one of them and I the other. But it's up to you. I suggest that only the *Poem In October* is selected. Let me know what you think on Wednesday. You shall have the last word.

Even though we talked for a second, on the phone, about excluding any V. Watkins, do bring along his book 'Ballad of the Mari Llwyd' if you can get hold of it—just for us to look at.

See you about 2.15 next Wed.[2]

Yrs,
Dylan

MS: Location unknown

MARGARET TAYLOR

Margaret Taylor (1905–80), who claimed Celtic origins, was brought up by British parents in India, and then in an English convent. She married the historian A. J. P. Taylor in 1931. Taylor disliked Thomas almost from the moment he met him in 1937. Mrs Taylor, on the other hand, was inordinately fond of him. She had a little money of her own, and after the war she began a career as patron of the poet that was of great benefit to the Thomases but had disastrous consequences for her marriage. She wrote poetry.

1 Arlott (1914–91), author and cricket commentator, was a police detective before he joined the BBC as a producer. He regularly used Thomas to read poems for a long-running series in the BBC's Eastern Service, 'Book of Verse'.

2 Programme No. 65 in 'Book of Verse' dealt with 'Welsh Poetry', and was recorded on Wednesday 6 January. Thomas wrote the commentary. Among the poets represented were Henry Vaughan, Edward Thomas, Wilfred Owen, W. H. Davies, Idris Davies, Glyn Jones and Alun Lewis. He included his own 'Poem in October'. Script and reading fee: 20 guineas.

[?late December 1945] Holywell Ford.[1] Guests' Bedroom

My dear Margaret,

I was so glad to be allowed to see the poems and to keep them for such a long time: too long a time, perhaps, though we did talk about them for a little and (on my part) a mostly inarticulate minute. I kept them so long, not because I had nothing to say about them but because I had so much. I find it awfully hard to say, about another's poems, just 'I enjoyed them', or 'I didn't like them', or, humming and ha-ing, to mumble something about 'the influence of X' or how much 'you could learn from Y'. The only way I know to talk about poems—another's poems—(unless they are *all* perfect, which means unless they are written in Heaven with a Gabriel-winged-Waterman dipped in nectar and God's blood)—is to try to go through them in detail for sound and shape and colour. The *meaning* of a poem you cannot, as a poet, talk about in any way constructively: that must be left to theoreticians, logicians, philosophers, sentimentalists, etc. It is only the *texture* of a poem that can be discussed at all. Nobody, I think, wants to talk, either, about how a poem *feels* to him; he finds it emotionally moving, or he doesn't; and, if he does, there's nothing to discuss except the means, the words themselves, by which this emotional feeling was aroused. It is, of course, far easier to point out what one disagrees with than it is to comment sensibly upon what one finds good. One disagrees with a line of poetry because one discovers, immediately or after re-reading, that it is not inevitable, it could be changed, the wrong words have been used or the right words in the wrong order, indeed one changes them about in the mind as one reads; but when the inevitable line appears, what is there to say? The music is made, the magic is done, the sound and the spell remain. This is only a (I'm afraid) repetitive, pedantic, platitudinary preliminary (God help us) apology for the few comments I want to make on each of the poems. I'm very conscious of how little, if at all, I can help to make these poems, or your future poems, nearer, in texture and intensity, to what you yourself would wish them to be. I can only burble, like an old bird with its beak full of bias and soap; and you can but curse yourself for ever having given your poems to such a turgid rook.

First Poem:

I find all such descriptive pieces, such nostalgic time-and-place evocations relying on the impressionist expression of remembered detail, always rather baffling to read unless the actual objects—trees, river, wings etc—are *re-created* for me in a new light. I mean, unless the writer remembers that he is not re-creating *for himself alone* those objects he remembers in such a place and at such a time. He has been there before; I haven't. And therefore he must depict his recollected landscape (or whatever it may be)

---

1 A house in the grounds of Magdalen College, Oxford, where Alan and Margaret Taylor lived; Taylor was a Fellow of the college. The Thomases took refuge there in March 1946. This letter seems to have been written on an earlier visit, probably just after Christmas 1945.

at several levels: he must see it, as it was, through his own eyes, and also make *me* see it as he saw it *then*; and, either afterwards or simultaneously, he must make us *both* see it freshly and anew.

And so, in this poem, though the words make me begin to *feel* what you felt when you saw that emerald river and those feathered trees, yet I cannot *see* them clearly. And the reason for that is because of the word 'impressionist'. I think it always unsatisfactory to put down the general word rather than the particular: in this instance, the river you describe as being 'spread impressionist' should be *defined* impressionistically. It may become, as it has become in the writing of many poets, a lazy mannerism to describe an object by a kind of group-word: 'cubist fields', 'symphonic rivers', 'architectural mountain': in those tiny examples, all of which have probably been used, there is no clarity of vision at all. To bring it down to complete absurdity: If a certain hill that you wish to describe seems to you architecturally composed and reminiscent of a certain style, it's laziness to say 'the Wren hill'. You should describe that hill in terms of pillar, dome, spire-like trees etc. I don't want to go on plugging this, and it may appear relatively trivial: all I want to do is to emphasise the need, in natural descriptive verse, of a fresh *conceiving* of each object. Emerson said to readers, 'You must read proudly.' I think he meant that readers should not be expected to do the writer's work. And when you use the word 'impressionist', you're asking the reader to project *his own images* into that word and to derive [from] them, what satisfaction he can. 'Here's a suggestion', the poet says, 'of what I mean. Now you work on it.' 'No,' the reader should say, 'take it back and give it again when *you've* put all you know and feel into it. I'll do the rest.'

In two other words of the first verse of poem one, I find rather a discordant ambiguity: the words are '*scorpion*' swans and '*crop*'. It's difficult, I think, leaving a queer, however good, adjective like 'scorpion' all alone in the air. And the verb 'crop', coming almost immediately after, does nothing to add to this word, to strengthen or illuminate it; indeed the verb contradicts and denies the adjective. And so both words lose their meaning.

The second verse has lovely movement, the floating and drifting of the mists implicit in the long-drawn rhythms. But, again, the word 'counterpoint', like the word 'impressionist', halts and hinders me. As a 'proud reader', I have to decline to accept a word upon which I myself have to work unduly. I'm prepared to accept, and to work upon, a difficulty, of meaning, syntax, image, symbol, but, not an evasion of a difficulty. Don't merely tell me there *is* a counterpoint: show it to me in words.

Will you take for granted my same criticism of each undefined generalisation, each group-word, each indefinition, each take-it-or-leave-it vagueness, each arbitrary abstraction, as it occurs in the rest of the poems? I wouldn't have laboured the point so, didn't I think it important and didn't I feel how a really lovely verse (verse two) could be marred by one inexactly realised word.

I like the last verse, though there are memories in it, for me, of passages in Eliot: particularly of passages in 'Burnt Norton' where he writes of 'at the still point of the turning world'. The resemblance, mostly of mood, was probably fortuitous, and matters very little anyway.

Poem Two. Here again, the question of texture is all-important (says Doctor Sneezer, failed B. A., Swansea). The deliberate movement and the careful grouping of words in the first four lines dwindle away as they reach the last, long 'impenetrable'. I should infinitely prefer here an *image* of impenetrability. A vague, unspecific word at the end of a verse in which all the other words are distinguishable objects moving harmoniously, can easily obfuscate, and nullify, them. It's impossible, of course, for me to suggest in what way you could objectify, make real, the 'impenetrable'. And the only general advice I can, misgivingly though sincerely, give is that you try to Think in Things.

In the second verse, I must merely repeat that the 'inner vision' should be particularised. What is it? If it is too vague to define, set down what *things* come nearest to being part of that vision. Sooner one solid glimpse of the inner world, [than] an amorphous statement of its existence.

The third verse is beautiful. (Mind, by the way, the spelling of 'bare'. What is this verse: a menagerie?) You can see in this how you have kept everything concrete to the very end. Here are no 'impenetrable visions' but honey, lion, and rose: all acquaintances, and given a new kind of life and meaning here. I do think, I do really think, you should work more, and very hard, on this poem, so that the third verse does not shine right out of it, as it does now, but is part of the whole radiance.

In verse four, a thousand times no! to 'ethereal as a dream'—phrases like that are written forever in the Oliver Sandys of time.

Poem Three:

I think that if you use this regular tumpty-tum beat (and, Lord knows, no disrespect to it, it can do wonderful things), you inevitably lead the ear to expect rhymes or assonances. And when, in lines three and four of each verse, and especially in line four, you give no rhyme or assonance, the ear, disappointed, rejects what it has already heard. The fourth line, in a verse using this metre, should tauten the whole verse, not leave it loosely unresolved. 'With every cloud that rides the skies,' though an absurdly banal line and only thrown out as a tentative first-thing-that-came-into-my-head suggestion, is the kind of line, only because of its ultimate rhyme, that shapes the verse as a whole. I like all the substance of the poem a great deal; it is only my ear, that red-lobed carper, that finds it unsatisfactory. I think the poem could be reshaped and rhymed to beautiful effect.

Poem Four:

From here, to Thirteen, it is, of course, quite a different kettle of poems. And I have far less to say about these poems in any detail.

I think that if you go on writing poetry, as I hope exceedingly you will, and indeed as I am sure you feel you must, you will find yourself writing in a kind of way which combines the full-imaged natural world of the first descriptive poems with the frail (but never weak) inner world of those very feminine (but *never* poetess-y) extracts of experience.

In this second group of poems, there is very little for me to criticise. More than the others, more than any kind of poem, these rely upon the immediate transference of an isolated emotion—though 'transference' is probably the wrong word. These poems must be *felt at once*; there is no time for them to creep in at a side-door, or seep down the chimney: they've got to come *right* in, without a waste syllable, expression, or gesture. Once they arouse in one any desire to analyse them, they fade. They're not written in invisible ink, but neither are they written in everybody's. There's a thin ice over the ink, and if one unbalanced word breaks that ice, down you go, poem and all, into a big blank blot. In this poem, beginning 'Dear Love, if you should cease to be', the word 'frightfulness' almost tips the whole thing into tenuous oblivion; but not quite. My objection to that word is the same as to the rest of the undefined generalisations etc of the earlier (in the folder, not by date) descriptive poems. I'm sure the one rule that can properly help, is: *Never* put down a word such as 'frightfulness'. Put down, instead, a frightful thing, symbol, image, or the precise words for a frightful feeling.

Poem Five Only two tiny points. Qualify, define, particularise—yes: but don't do these things to something that needs none of it. There is no need to say of a vacuum that it is 'where nothing is'. The Mediterranean is also tideless and parallel lines, except to some scientists, do not meet.

And again I find the memory coming up of Eliot's 'at the still point of the turning world'. But I'm sure it's my memory, not yours. The words are common words.

Oh, and a third carp. *What* 'mysterious world'? You must say more. Neither does 'infinite space', 'celestial light' etc. mean anything to me.

Poem Six. 'The music in the hall' is, I think, almost exactly what you wish it to be, because it *is* exact.

Poem Seven, 'A Dedication'. I believe you could clarify the first verse, but the second is perfect: particular, minute, 'justly' observed, and not for a second's second is it petty.

(Incidentally, the 'pealing' of potatoes is most strange vegetable campanology.)

Poem Eight needs more concentrated working-upon. The words seem to me thinly spaced and to have relationship to each other only through superficial *meaning*, not through texture: the sound, shape, weight, colour, density of language. Too often (in what one might call poems of emotional immediacy and what appears to be, but rarely is, spontaneous growth), unmarried words limp together towards the consummation of the last line only to find it entirely unsatisfying, unrewarding of the intensity that has forced them towards the end.

I hope, in commenting so heavily, almost so blunderbussily, on a short and simple poem, that I'm not giving the idea that I would wish you to burden it with any intricate technical apparatus. All I mean is that a poet must endeavour to feel & weigh the shape, sound, content etc. of each word in relation to the words surrounding it—and that of however simple a nature the poem he is working upon. It isn't only the *meaning* of the words that must develop harmonically, that must weave in and out of each other, each syllable adding to the single existence of the next, but it is that which also informs the words with their own particular life: the noise that they make in the ear and the air, the contours in which they lie on the page and the mind.

Poem Nine, 'So quiet and still', is quiet and still as the breath itself; and beautiful, & not to be touched.

Poem Ten Only the same now nearly threadbare criticism: 'Hardship's fierce frustration' has no place in any poem because it *escapes* the work of defining, poetically, the hardship and the frustration.

In *Poem Eleven*, 'The Sunday Street', there is something wrong, grammatically, with the first verse. This wouldn't matter if it did not hold one up.

I find the phrase 'with pleasurable surprise' a little too ingenuous, and would be inclined to write here a phrase reflective, in some slight, subtle way, of the character—as you see it in the poem—of the 'you'. But the end is lovely, & does so need lovely language—as simple as possible—to flow up to it.

Poem Twelve, 'Who Can Hear The Stars Sing', seems out of keeping with the rest of this very moving group; to have slid in from another world of experience; and from *another* need to write. Also, I think it too obviously reminiscent of Donne's 'Go and catch a falling star'.

Of the last poem, I have nothing to say except that I like it very very much. I told you, at the beginning of this letter, that I could never speak commonsensibly about what moves me & what seems to me inevitable. So I shan't *try* to speak about this. Maybe 'agitated breath' for a moment disturbs my appreciation: two words set together as one: a cliché, rather tired. But, maybe again, I am wrong. It *is* a good poem.

Thank you for letting me have the poems, and I hope you found *something*, of even the frailest value, in all these argeybargeying pages of Sneezer's Manual.

May I see some more poems when they are ready?

Love to you,
Dylan

I haven't read this over, so you must forgive, please, all the slips & redundancies etc.

MS: Texas

*CHARLES FISHER
2 2 '46   39 Markham Square   SW3

Dear Charles,
   Well I'll be damned. A filthy waste of time. I'm sorry for you and me. But
the photographer should have his plates removed. What's the matter?
Can't he see through his little box? My cat could get someone in the
middle of the picture, with a broken Brownie. Could you, as you promised,
and as I subsequently promised the Markham Arms people themselves, get
a couple of copies made up—however bad they may be as pictures—of the
photographs of Mrs Andrews the landlady and the hippo-Colonel and
myself (though that doesn't matter) playing shove-ha'penny? They ask me
about it very often, and, until your letter, I assured them that, though the
pictures were not going into Illustrated, you were getting a few copies
made. You did promise, & I'll be scorned if I fail to produce them. The two
we chose, or any others. *Please.*[1]
   Have you sent the copies of my 25 Poems and Map of Love back to
Stephen Spender? His address, in case you haven't yet, is: 15 Loudoun
Road, St. John's Wood, N.W.8. He's asked me about them again.
   I'm very glad there's a chance of you & Joanna getting a cottage soon, and
thank you a lot we'd like to come down & see you when you're installed. I hope
you'll be there in the Spring; I could do with a weekend out of this filthy city.
   Don't forget the pictures of Mrs A. & the Colonel.

                                                         Yours,
                                                         Dylan

MS: Jim Martin

JOHN DAVENPORT
February 13th 1946   Holywell Ford   Oxford

My Dear John,
   Wd you do me a favour? Could you send on the enclosed letter to
Norman? Or if you haven't his address, do you know who would have? It's
rather urgent, in a way. I'll tell you when we meet.
   And let's meet soon. I'll ring Bush House next week. Probably Tuesday
morning. And hope you're about. Terribly sorry to have missed you last
time. I rang your office. E. Lutyens told me I had lost £500, but I think that
was malice.[2]

                                                         Love,
                                                         Dylan

MS: Texas

1 *Illustrated* was a topical magazine, which evidently had commissioned an article from
   Fisher. The Markham Arms was a pub in the King's Road, near Markham Square.
2 Norman: Norman Cameron. Bush House: a BBC building where Davenport was then
   employed. E[lisabeth] Lutyens (Mrs Edward Clark) (1906–83): the composer, a friend of
   the Thomases.

*SOCIETY OF AUTHORS
[card, postmarked 5 March 1946]   39 Markham Square   London   SW3

Thank you for your letter. I'll be delighted to serve on the Selection Committee to help choose the poems and the people to read them.[1] Any date early in March—except the 11th—will be quite convenient for me.

Dylan Thomas

My address from Monday the 11th of March will be Holywell Ford, Oxford.[2]

MS (photocopy): British Library

T. S. ELIOT
24 March '46   Holywell Ford   Oxford

Dear Mr Eliot,
    Thank you for sending me the letter about Ezra Pound. I return it, signed.
    And thank you for letting me have that dreadful, unutterably moving statement made by Pound's attorney.[3]

Yours sincerely,
Dylan Thomas

MS: Valerie Eliot

1 The Society of Authors planned a poetry reading at the Wigmore Hall on 14 May. Kilham Roberts, still secretary of the society, had an apartment in Middle Temple, where the committee was to meet. Others expected to perform were Walter de la Mare, John Lehmann and Edith Sitwell.
2 The Thomases were leaving Markham Square. Margaret Taylor persuaded her husband to let them occupy a damp summerhouse in the garden, on the banks of the Cherwell. It had gas and electricity, but no water, which had to be fetched a hundred yards from the house, where the two Thomas children slept.
3 The poet Ezra Pound (1885–1972), charged with treason against the U.S. for wartime broadcasts from Italy, was deemed unfit to stand trial on 13 February, and committed to a psychiatric hospital.

*SOCIETY OF AUTHORS
25 March '46   Holywell Ford   Oxford

Dear Sir,
  I regret not having been able to attend the first meeting of the
Committee responsible for the programme arrangements in connexion
with the forthcoming Poetry Recital. I was ill in hospital.[1]
  I shall, however, manage to be present at the meeting at Mr Kilham
Robert's flat at 2.45 p.m. Thursday March 28.

                                        Yours sincerely,
                                        Dylan Thomas

MS (photocopy): British Library

DAVID HIGHAM
March 25 '46   Holywell Ford   Oxford   Ox: 47549

Dear David,
  Thank you for your two letters, March 5th and 13th. I would have
answered them straightaway, but I've just had a short spell in hospital—
since seeing you, but nothing, I assure you, to do with that—and am only
now about again. It was very nice to see you again after so long.
  (1) I have a copy here of your letter of Feb. 21st, about the Mondadori
proposal; but I know nothing more about it than is contained in your letter.
I should, of course, like to be published in Italy, and especially in a de-luxe
edition such as you believe Mondadori to be proposing.[2] Can you go ahead
and find out whatever there is to be found? And might there be some real
money.
  (2) About the BBC and your talk with Nancy Pearn about improving
prices for my work there. I am writing to the BBC, (Contracts) as you
suggest, to notify them that from now on all my financial arrangements
with them are to be arranged with you. I'll send the letter off today. I (a)
gather that this—i.e. the financial arrangements to be taken over by you—
applies also to my work *as an actor* reading the work of others. (b)
Contracts for my work as an actor have in the past been sent to me from
the Talks Department. But the Dramatic Dept. obviously pays higher fees.
How does Equity fit, or not fit, in with this?
  (3) About your talk with Bozman concerning the book to be called
provisionally, either *Top Hat & Gasworks* or *Bob's My Uncle*. I note that
Bozman agrees the book might well consist of BBC childhood reminiscen-

1 St Stephen's Hospital, London. He is alleged to have been suffering from 'alcoholic
  gastritis'.
2 No such edition seems to have been published.

ces plus short stories, straight & fantastic. I'll get together, from the BBC & odd periodicals etc, all the material there is to hand as quickly as possible, & let you have it with an indication of what I intend to add.[1]

(4) Good news, to me, about the new edition of *Deaths & Entrances* of 3,000;[2] and also the binding of the sheet stock of the *Young Dog* book, the *Map of Love*, & the 25 *Poems*. How soon do you think you can touch Dent's for some more money for me on account of the new printing of Deaths & Entrances?

Hoping to hear from you soon.

> Yours,
> Dylan

MS: Texas

T. W. EARP
Tuesday March 26th 1946   Holywell Ford   Oxford

Dear Tommy,

Will you write to me some time at this address? If you give me, say, 2 days' notice, I can come up any day you like. And then we'll both have trains to catch and maybe that'll be good though at the moment I can't think why. Anyway, it's been a long time and let's meet in ... Coal Hole?—anywhere in town when you come up please. Only 2 days' warning, and up I come from bore's hill,[3] out of hospital fresh as a fresh as a

> Yours
> Dylan

MS: Ohio State University

EDITH SITWELL
Sunday March 31st '46   c/o A J P Taylor   Holywell Ford   Oxford

Dear Miss Sitwell,

It's nine or ten years, I think, since I last met you, though we did write some letters after that; it is, anyway, a long long time, and all that time I've very much missed being able to write to you occasionally and to send you poems and to ask you about them, for I value, with all my heart, what you

---

1 The book didn't appear until after Thomas's death, and then became two books, *Quite Early One Morning* and *A Prospect of the Sea*.
2 *Deaths and Entrances* had been published on 7 February.
3 Boars Hill, a select residential district of Oxford.

have said about them in the past. I find it so easy to get lost, in my actions and my words, and I know that, deeply lost so many times, I could have, through writing to you and through your writing, come somehow out and up, so much less sufferingly than I did, into the miraculous middle of the world again.

I think that, in some way, I offended you, through some thoughtless, irresponsible written or spoken word, on some occasion, those nine or ten years back. And I can't forgive myself that I can't remember what, exactly, the offence was, how crude or ignorant. Whatever it was, it seemed to stop, as though for ever, our writing to one another, let alone our meeting. May I say, now, as I know I should have said many years before, how sorry and, inarticulately, more than that, I am that some minor (oh, I hope so, minor) beastliness of mine, presumption, conceit, gaucherie, seeming-ingratitude, foul manner, callow pretension, or worse, yes, indeed, or far worse, interrupted our friendship, just beginning, and lost for so long, to me, the happiness and honour of being able to send my work, as it was written, to you, and to write to you of the never-ending-circling problems and doubts of craft and meaning and heart that must always besiege us. If my apology, true as my love of your Song of the Cold, reads to you as stiltedly as, quickly writing, it sounds to me, I'm sorry again and can only say how hard I find it to move naturally into the long silence between now and nine beautiful, dreadful years ago.

I'm daring to write to you now because I have been reading, in Our Time,[1] your passages, or message, about my new poems, all those words glowing out of the paper like caves and eyes, full of understanding and mysteries:—though that may sound, God knows, affected, but how can I say how profoundly I was moved by the expression of your profound & loving understanding of the poems I've worked upon for so long and through so many giant and pygmy doubts, high and low darknesses, ghastly errors and exaltations? The poems you liked least were of course the worst in the book: they were worked at intermittently, out of changing values, there was no cohesion in them, poems of bits, or bits of poetry sliced off at the intellectual end of a series of conflicting, locked, and lost-before-they-were-begun, arguments. 'Paper and Sticks' was a 'light relief' where none was wanted; and I am always light as a hippo. But your quickening to the best of the poems came across to me like a new life of sympathy and mystery; to share the joy you express at the joyful poem, Fern Hill, is a new joy to me, as real as that which made the words come, at last, out of a never-to-be-buried childhood in heaven or Wales.

I hope you will write to me, forgive me for a long-gone never-meant boorish blunder or worse. Am I better now, I can ask only the never-telling tides of war and peace and duties around me? I hope you will let me meet you again.

For months and months and grey months I've been basemented in

1 *Our Time* ('incorporating *Poetry and the People*'). Sitwell reviewed *Deaths and Entrances* in the April 1946 issue.

London. Now we can stay here, in a kind of summerhouse by the river, for a few green months (I trust). We are so miserably poor, blast and blast it, but the spring's singing all over the place, and, between scraping and hacking and howling at my incompetence, I've time to listen and, soon perhaps, to work again. 'Fern Hill' was the last poem I've written, in September, in Carmarthenshire, near the farm where it happened.[1] I want very very much to write again. And I should like to write to tell you how I feel about all your poems written during the war, if one day I am forgiven and I may. There is no: 'There is no need to say what I feel about poems whose beauty is true and strange and clear to all *and* the blind'. There's always need to say what great work means to one man, how your creation of revelation and his revealed acceptance meet in a point—did Yeats say it?—of light.

But I've written enough and too much—pass over, if you can, all the tongue-knotted awkwardnesses, these stammers for nine years back—and I must wait now hoping, all the time, to hear from you.

Yours sincerely,
Dylan Thomas

MS: Texas

DAVID HIGHAM
April 5 '46   Holywell Ford   Oxford

Dear David,
   Thank you for yesterday's letter. I'm delighted you managed to get Dent to make the £24 odd up to £50.[2] Can you really get the cheque as *quickly as possible*? I've just been sent urgent school-bills etc for loud & all too quickly growing children, & must pay them *at once*. I *do* hope you will be able to: otherwise I'm sunk.
   Thanks again.

Yours,
Dylan

MS: Texas

MAURICE CARPENTER
April 5 1946   Holywell Ford   Oxford

Dear Maurice,
   Nice to hear from you. And I'm glad you've managed to get a 2 page May Day space for poems. I'm awfully sorry, but I haven't got a poem. The one I

1 A draft, at least, must have been finished by 28 August when Thomas sent it ('a poem for evenings and tears') to David Tennant, page 173.
2 A payment for *Deaths and Entrances*.

mentioned on St. Patric's night has become very odd & foggy; and I'm afraid there's no chance of finishing it under a couple of weeks.

I hate the title Flame Bird, and don't like The English Helicon. I like, as a title: 'Danger Men Writing'.

Hope to see you soon. Thank you a lot for what you said about Edith Sitwell's review. There's a new edition of my poems—3000—being printed now.

Give me a telephone number, if there is one. I come up once a week, but not on a fixed day.

Yours,
Dylan

MS: National Library of Wales

'JOHN'[1]
April 5 '46   Holywell Ford Oxford

Dear John,
Thanks for the letter. I'm sorry, but I haven't a poem at all. When is your *final* date? If it's a reasonable way off, I might be able to finish, in time, one I'm trying to work on now. If it isn't, I'm glad you invited me anyway, and I hope you'll get a good page together.

I haven't been able to get to Dublin yet, but I hope this spring. I'd cut my toes off to go.

Yours,
Dylan

Do you ever come up to Oxford? Do drop me a line if you do. We're here for quite a bit, I think.

MS: Texas

NANCY PEARN
April 15 '46   Holywell Ford Oxford

Dear Miss Pearn,
Thank you for your letter of April 11th; I'd have answered at once, but have been in town.

I'm glad that you have made the Features Contract department agree to pay at the rate of 33 & $\frac{1}{3}$ per cent above the standard rate as arranged with the Authors' Society.

---

1 Unidentified recipient. It is not John Lehmann, John Bayliss, John Ormond or John Waller. It might be the late John Pudney.

I note also the payments due to me for the use of 4 of my poems in the Italian Service on 10th April.

The letter I'd thought I'd send to the Talks Contract Dept authorising the BBC to deal with you on this side, I mislaid somehow & am writing to them again & will post it with this letter.

Yours sincerely,
Dylan Thomas

MS: Texas

BBC
15 April '46   Holywell Ford   Oxford

Dear Sir,

This is only to corroborate the letters you have already received from my agents, Pearn, Pollinger & Higham Ltd., of 39–40 Bedford Street, Strand, W.C.2., that contracts & payments for my future Talks & Reading engagements should be sent to them.

I had written to corroborate this some days ago, as Miss Pearn told you, I believe, when she spoke to you on the phone, but the letter was somehow mislaid.

Yours truly,
Dylan Thomas

MS: BBC

*CHARLES FISHER
April 15 '46   Holywell Ford   Oxford

Dear Charles,

Thank you very much for the other Illustrated prints of our dear and, I thought, forgotten faces. That large c.u. of me is still out of picture: I suspect the photographer of some kind of secret thinking.

As you see, we've moved from London, & will be staying here for a few months. But I come up to town about once a week, & hope to see you soon. Where do you go in the evenings?

Thanks again,
Yours,
Dylan

MS: Jim Martin

*MARY FIELD (Society of Authors)
April 15 '46   Holywell Ford   Oxford

Dear Miss Field,
   I suppose Mr Kilham Roberts wants to know what poems of *my own* I'll be
reading at the recital on May 14th, as the other poems I'm to read, 'Snake' by
Lawrence, & 'Tyger Tyger' by Blake, have, I think, already been settled by the
committee whose last meeting I couldn't attend.
   I want to read, of my own, one poem only, 'Fern Hill' which takes three
minutes to read.[1]

                                        Yours sincerely,
                                        Dylan Thomas

                        It is true, is it, that the Committee
                        decided not to include the Hardy lyrics
                        which I was to have read? I heard, or
                        thought I heard it, only over the
                        dinner-table & should be glad to know
                        yes or no officially.
                        DMT

MS: British Library

JEAN LEROY[2]
15 April 1946   Holywell Ford   Oxford

Dear Miss LeRoy,
   Thank you for your letter of April 12.
   I see that the Head of the Talks Contract Dept. of the BBC says that I do
not qualify for professional actor's fees when I read other people's work on
the air, but that 'naturally all fees are subject to negotiation.'
   Yes, I have already done two of the three readings you mention, in the
'Book of Verse' programmes, & will be doing the third tomorrow.
   I see that the BBC have sent you the three contracts with them,
proposing a fee of 5 guineas plus 13/2 fare from Oxford to London for each
broadcast; & you want to know how these fees compare with the ones I
have been paid for similar jobs in the past. For all 'Book of Verse'
programmes I have, in the past, received 5 pounds each.
   I think we shd accept this difference, don't you? I'm urgently in need of
the money & further discussions will probably make little or no odds. So, if

---

1 According to *The Times*, which reported the event, Thomas, Day Lewis and
  MacNeice were much better at reading their work than de la Mare, Eliot and Edith
  Sitwell. It was a royal occasion, with the Queen, Princess Elizabeth (later Elizabeth II)
  and Princess Margaret present.
2 Jean LeRoy joined the firm of Pearn, Pollinger and Higham after the war.

you think it advisable, I say go ahead & collect what they offer. But what d'you think?

Yours sincerely,
Dylan Thomas

MS: Texas

W. EMLYN DAVIES[1]
April 26th 1946   Holywell Ford   Oxford

Dear Emlyn Davies
   What a wonderful gift. A very, very lovely book, eye-and-I delighting, and, to me, a great tribute. I shall always keep and treasure it. Dent's didn't send it along until last week, and then I was away. I came back to find this burningly good present waiting. Dent's had kept it in their office for days, to show everyone; they wrote to tell me, as indeed they should write to tell you, however well you *must* know it, what a splendid piece of craftsmanship they thought it was, and how much everyone there appreciated it. No-one can appreciate it as I do, except perhaps my children when they're old enough. And no, they couldn't either.
   Of course I remember you, and well, though it was such a short friendship owing to all kinds of reasons—mostly, I think (and hope) to my going away. It's strange to think of you living in the house where I was born. If I come to Swansea, as I certainly shall do one day, though, as you probably know, my mother and father are now in Carmarthenshire and I have very few home associations in the town, may I call and see you?
   A very good friend of mine lives in Swansea; he's just returned after five and a bit years in the Air Force: Vernon Watkins. Do you know him? I'm sure you know some of his poems. He lives at 131 Glanmor Road, Sketty. If you don't know him, I wish you would. I'm writing to him, and may I give him your address too? He has great powers and profound poetical sincerity, an ear for all music and a tongue against all humbug; he's a pretty marvellous chap, but don't tell him I said so.
   It would be silly to say that I'm glad you like my poems; glad's a spindly little [word], and there is no such thing as 'like' in the splendidly loving care of your beautiful penmanship. But I am glad, anyway. Glad that you remember that evening, years ago, in Cwmdonkin Drive. Glad to think that the first printed poem of mine, Light Breaks, must have said to you what it meant to me.
   My wife, whose name is Caitlin, wants to say with me again: Thank you for the book.

All good wishes,
Yours,
Dylan Thomas

MS: National Library of Wales

1 Emlyn Davies, a schoolmaster, moved to 5 Cwmdonkin Drive in 1937, when the Thomases left, and lived there with his family until his death in 1973. He used compasses and coloured pens to make abstract 'calligrams' or patterns: in this instance to illustrate Thomas poems.

VERNON WATKINS
April 27th 1946   Holywell Ford   Oxford

My dear Vernon,
  There's never been such a long time between our letters, and I hope,
atom willing,[1] there won't be again. (Somewhere in the wet Magdalen
trees a bird makes a noise exactly like Doctor Ludwig Koch.)[2] It's been my
fault of course, that goes without whining, but I'm heavy with reasons like
Doctor Magnus Hirschfeld.[3] Right below where we live—it is, I think, a
converted telephone kiosk, with a bed where the ledge for directories used
to be—there is a vole-run. (Do not tell this to Fred who said that I could not
speak for half a minute without mentioning vermin or Dracula, and that
was five years ago.) The run is so narrow that two voles cannot pass each
other. Suddenly, an elderly, broad vole with a limp came quite fast down
the run from the left just as an elderly, broader vole with a limp came from
the right. From where I am sitting, expectantly nervous and ill like patients
on an imminent, I could see what the voles were thinking. They never
stopped running as they thought, as they neared one another. Who was to
turn back? should they both turn back? should they fight, kiss, call it a day,
lie down? They never stopped their limping running as I saw and heard the
decision made. With a wheezing like that of a little otter, with a husky
squeaky updrawing of shining arthritic legs, the elderly broader limping
vole jumped over the back of the other. Not a word was said.
  We've been here about six weeks, just behind Magdalen, by river and
vole-run, very quiet, Aeronwy in a day-nursery near and sleeping in the
next-door house or house-proper, Caitlin and I going our single way into
the vegetable kingdom. I haven't worked for a long time, apart from
reading, every week, over the air to the Indians: an audience of perhaps
three, and all of them bat-or-Tambi-voiced. I'm reading Hardy on the
ordinary service on May 19th. Probably about eleven at night. Try to
remember to listen. I've written a long comic poem, not to be published, to
keep the uttermost cellarmen of depression away and to prevent my doing
crosswords.[4] I've written a few pieces, nearly all quotations, for the
Eastern radio, on Edward Thomas, Hardy, and some others. And I'm going
to do a programme on Wilfred Owen: though all my job is the selection of
the poems for professional readers to (badly, usually) read, and the
interpolation of four-line comments between each. I'd love to see your
essay on Owen. Could I? I'd be very careful with it and return it spotlessly

1 The atomic bomb, increasingly on people's minds.
2 Dr Ludwig Koch (1881–1974), author and naturalist. He recorded birdsongs and
  broadcast them.
3 Dr Magnus Hirschfeld (1868–1935), German sexologist.
4 A satirical piece with melancholy undertones about himself and academia—'Oxford I
  sing, though in untutored tones, alack! / I heard, long years ago, her call, but huffed it
  back; / In vain her chiming cloisters claimed this callow calf / From his rude rut. Ah,
  not for me the windblown scarf . . .' Texas has the ms.

unAeronwied. And I want to write a poem of my own again, but it's hard here with peace and no room, spring outside the window and the gascooker behind the back, sleep, food, loud wireless, broom and brush all in one kiosk, stunted bathing-hut or square milkbottle.

About Owen: Siegfried Sassoon has a lovely chapter about him, completely new, in his latest book, Siegfried's Journey. You would like it very much.

It's strange to think of you, and Fred, and Tom sometimes, in Swansea again. How is that blizzardly painter, that lightning artist, that prodigal canvas-stacker? Has he reached the next finbone of the fish he was dashing off before the war? Please give him my love.

And Cwmdonkin Park. I wish we were there now. Next month sometime I'm going down to see my mother, who has been very very ill, outside Carmarthen, and will stop at Swansea on the way back? Have you a little sheetless, must be sheetless, dogbox with nails for me to sleep in? Any shelter for a night? Unless you've been mending the roof. Then we could, maybe, all spend one evening together, wipey-eyed, remembering, locked in these damned days, the as-then-still-forgiven past.

You and Fred and Tom and, shame, no Dan whose future's stranger than ever, his multiplying harassed women trailing children like seaweed, his symphonies shouldering out in his head to unplayable proportions, his officer's trousers kept up now by three safety-pins. And me too: I had a little time in hospital but I'm out again now and fit as an old potato.

Love to you all, Gwen, Rhiannon, yourself, from Caitlin, Llewelyn [*in margin, arrowed from* 'Llewelyn': in Cornwall for a month], Aeronwy and myself. Please do send a photograph of Rhiannon. And the Owen?

Dylan

MS: British Library

DAVID HIGHAM
April 27th 1946   Holywell Ford   Oxford

Dear David,

Same wolfish cry, I'm afraid, for money, though I need it really for other wolves. I wrote to Miss LeRoy telling her that, as far as I was concerned, the extra bit she'd obtained for me for reading poetry on the radio was acceptable. That immediately covered three small contracts. There were, too, a few other BBC copyright fees that had come or were coming. Also, there may be a few other bits and pieces.

I'm really in a hell of a way for money at this *very moment*, fearing that cheques may even be returned to my landlords unless I bung in something to the bank at once. That's bad enough, indeed it's fatal, but there's worse which wouldn't, I know, interest you: I mean, the worse is embarrassingly intimate. I can hear it howling now from 50 miles away. You said, in your last note, when sending me your pro-Dent's cheque for £50, that that left me £16 still in your debt. Could you, oh please, take the £16 off our next piece of real or real-ish money and let me have some now, straightaway? I can't write URGENT big enough; there isn't enough paper in Oxford to contain the letters.

I've got quite a lot of those stories—provisionally 'Bob's My Uncle'— together, & a friend of mine is trying to collect the rest out of miserably forgotten advanced quarterlies etc. I'll let you have, *quite* soon, what there is plus indication of additions.

But, immediately, it is, on my word, a desperate matter of having money. Will you see what you can do?

When—as I hope to God—that's somehow settled, I should very much like to see you for a few minutes about films.

And excuse this franticery.

Yours,
Dylan

MS: Texas

GODFREY THURSTON-HOPKINS
April 27th 1946   Holywell Ford   Oxford

Dear Sir,
Please do forgive me for not having answered your letter of March 15. I've been changing my address too often for the BBC to keep up with me, & your letter arrived only a day or two ago.

The 'Memories of Christmas' was printed in the Listener of December 20 1945. The recording you heard was called, I think, 'Second Hearing.' I haven't a copy myself, but the BBC is sure to have a back number.

I am very glad you enjoyed the talk, and I am really grateful to you for writing & wanting to see it in print.

Yours truly,
Dylan Thomas

MS: (the recipient)

JOHN ORMOND [THOMAS][1]
30 May 1946   Holywell Ford   Oxford

Dear John Ormond Thomas,[2]

I think I owe you two apologies.

First, for being so unhelpfully, even helplessly, comatose when you and the Picture Post photographer came along to that Time for Verse reading on May 19th. I had a really sickening bout of gastric 'flu, and only wanted to lie in a corner, whimper, and die: I don't know how the hell I managed to read aloud at all; I know I couldn't speak. And God knows what the pictures looked like. If they're *too* frightful, I do hope you can take them again. Patric Dickinson's always about at the BBC, and I'm more than willing and will co-operate to the extent of as many grimaces and standings-on-the-head as you like. Could one see what was taken before, if ever, they appear? I really *don't* want to appear as a liverish, green, sulky, hunched and glazed man—as most often I am very well indeed, and suffer from nothing more than the occupational complaints of nervousness and high blood-pressure. Do let me know.

And the other thing is, that I was introduced to you wrongly; or, rather, not rightly enough. I caught, on our first and second meeting, only the words 'Thomas' and 'Picture Post'. And it wasn't until I got home, after the photographic evening, and read your preliminary letter that was waiting for me there, that I knew really who you were. You must, after our letters etc. of the past, our common town and school background, and, of course, my knowledge of your poems, have thought me offensively rude. Do forgive me. Perhaps we can meet one day, in Fleet Street, for a drink or six?

Don't forget to drop me a line, if you can, about the photographs; and, if possible, let me have a shuddering glance at them before they appear.

Yours,
Dylan Thomas

MS: Glenys Ormond

HARRY KLOPPER
May 30th 1946   Holywell Ford   Oxford

Dear Mr. Klopper,

Thank you for your letter, and for letting me see the nine short poems from your long poem to be called 'The Vision'. I meant to reply long before

1 Poet (Cholmondeley Award, 1975) and BBC film producer (1923–90), of Swansea, who had corresponded with Dylan Thomas before they met. His later films included studies of Thomas (*A Bronze Mask*) and Vernon Watkins (*Under a Bright Heaven*). In 1946 he was a writer on the staff of the magazine *Picture Post*. 'Time for Verse' was a BBC series for which Dylan Thomas often read. Patric Dickinson was the producer. The article that appeared in *Picture Post*, 'A Nest of Singing Birds', 10 August 1946, featured a number of 'BBC' poets.
2 Later known as 'John Ormond'.

this, but have been away. Do forgive me: the delay wasn't caused because I could think of nothing to say about your poems, but because I had too much to say and too little time to sit down and say it. Even now, I'm very much rushed for bread-and-butter work, and can put down only a few short and, I'm afraid, inadequate comments on the poems. Perhaps, if you'd be kind enough to let me see the second part of the long poem, when it is finished, I could write my own, frankly personal, impressions of it at greater length.

Let me say, first of all, that I do appreciate the difficulties you must feel in writing poetry in a, comparatively, recently acquired language, especially when you are, as you mentioned in your letter, cut off from all literary activities. This last, in the case of a poet writing in his native language, might indeed be more of an advantage than a hindrance; but, in your case, I can see that it must be grievously hard not to be able to share, with anyone sympathetic to the writing of poetry, in some discussion of the problems that arise out of it. I can imagine that one of the gravest disadvantages you encounter is that of feeling yourself—even though temporarily, and at inevitable moments of depression and self-mistrust—incapable of appreciating how an ordinary reader of English poetry would react to the texture and movement of your words, not to their meaning (for the meaning that any poetry can convey is common to all readers and writers in every language) but to the *stuff* itself out of which the poetry is made. Though you may be certain of the logical development of the argument of each poem, you are, I believe, *un*certain of the *feel* of it. Too often, unmarried words limp together towards the consummation of the last line, only to find it entirely unsatisfying, unrewarding of the intellectual passion that had forced them towards that end.

All I can say that might be interpreted as even remotely constructive is that you must endeavour to feel and weigh the shape, sound, content of each word in relation to the shape, sound, content etcetera of the words surrounding it. It isn't only the *meaning* of the words that must develop harmonically, each syllable adding to the single existence of the next, but it is that which also informs the words with their own particular life: the noise, that is, that they make in the air and the ear, the contours in which they lie on the page and the mind, their colours and density.

So that in these poems—no, not individual poems but pieces of poetry moving towards a poem—I see that the abstract words rarely harmonise, or live together, with the concrete. In piece I, for instance, the 'avarice of shuffling feet' is, to me, quite discordant. I always feel that one should be very reluctant of putting down any abstract words at all, or at least of abstract words that one has not previously, or is not going to later, define. I believe, referring to the line in piece I, that it is better to put down an avaricious word, an avaricious image, than the vague abstraction, the undefined word that means so many different things to so many different people. That is, to put down something like 'where all the shuffling feet are misers' (that's only the first tentative suggestion that came into my head) rather than 'the avarice of shuffling feet'. I admit this is an absurd suggestion: I'm not attempting to rewrite your poem, God forbid, but merely to instance, concretely, something of what I mean by saying that the juxtaposition of a vague word and a particular word is, to me, nearly always unsatisfactory.

Later, in the second piece, I confess that I can never make anything much of such a phrase as 'the measureless depth of fears'. I like, in poems, to be told why or how this 'depth' is full of fears, and even exactly what the 'depth' is. Such a line as 'the untellably deep, squid-crowded sea' would, in spite of its impromptu silliness, mean more to me.

Certain lines of the second piece I like; and the repeated lines, though they do contradict what I said about the juxtaposition of vague and particular, are moving.

The opening of piece III seems, to me, to be intellectually confused, the images mixed in some sort of evocative pudding.

It is, of course, far easier to point out what one disagrees with than it is to comment sensibly upon what one finds good. One disagrees with a line of poetry because one finds that it is *not* inevitable, it could be changed, the wrong words, quite simply, have been used; but when the inevitable line appears, what is there to say? The music is made, the magic is done, the sound and the spell remain.[1] And so it is easy for me to say that I find most of piece IV unreal: the words speak to a dictionary-in-the-head, even to a dictionary of synonyms for I do not believe the words to be exact, to be 'just'.

But pieces VI and VII, because the words are objects, make an immediate impact. 'Yes', one says, 'this is what it is about; he is looking through windows at the rocks; I can understand, I think, his grief and transitory omnipotence.'

And I think the rhythms of *all* the pieces could be tautened; but that tautening will emerge itself as each word is valued according to its individual life.

But how little I can help you! How profoundly difficult it is! I can only burble like an old bird with its beak full of bias and soap; and you can but curse yourself for ever having given your poetry to such a turgid rook.

Send me some more any time you like, and believe me that, in spite of what I have said or only half said, I was grateful to you for having read them.

And do let me know if you want the poems back.

Yours sincerely,
Dylan Thomas

MS: Carbondale

1 Thomas is repeating much of this paragraph (and the 'turgid rook' analogy below) from his letter to Margaret Taylor, page 187.

JEAN LEROY
May 30 1946   Holywell Ford   Oxford

Dear Miss LeRoy,

Yes, I agree to the BBC fee of 5 guineas and 13/2 fare—retrospectively—for my 7-minute reading in 'The World Goes By' series recorded on May 6th.

Incidentally, a travel voucher for return fare from Oxford to London for my participation in a 'Time for Verse' programme on May 19th I never used, having mislaid it & bought a ticket myself. Now I've found the voucher and enclose it. Perhaps you can get the BBC to cancel it and allow me the return fare in exchange?

Last Monday, the 27th, I went up to London to take part in a $\frac{1}{2}$ hour programme on the National Insurance Bill[1] (fee 7 guineas & 13/2 fare). You had already sent me notice of the engagement. In London, I found that the programme had been put off a *week before*, and that, owing to some hitch of a newly-engaged secretary's, it had been forgotten to notify me of the postponement. The producer, R. D. Smith, wired his apologies afterwards, but I had *wasted* a whole day and been forced to pay travelling expenses etc. *for* that day. I don't know what the BBC ruling is in cases like this, but I do hope you can get me, at least, my out-of-pocket expenses. Okay?

                                        Yours sincerely,
                                        Dylan Thomas

MS: Texas

DAVID HIGHAM
June 10th 1946   Holywell Ford   Oxford

Dear David,

Hindle, of Henry Holt,[2] told me he'd had a talk with you about my publishing-position in America; and that you believed *New Directions* to have an option on my next books. I told Hindle that I'd unfortunately mislaid my last *N. Directions* contract, but that *I* believed I was entirely free of them after the publication of my *Selected Writings*, which shd be out any time now. And I promised Hindle that I wd let him know *definitely*, by the time he returned at the end of this week, whose belief was correct: yours or mine.

Can you dig up the Laughlin contract & find out, for good & all, whether we did allow him option on any future work of mine—and, if so, on how many books? I do hope *I'm* right, & that I'm no longer bound to that mean

1 Probably a dramatised documentary.
2 A firm of American publishers.

Laughlin. Even if I am, Hindle says that Holt will try to get me away from *N. Directions*. But until it's known, obviously he, Hindle, can't make any actual offer for future work. Could you let me know very soon?

No news yet from Harper's magazine, I suppose, about my proposed visit to, & article on, Puck's Fair?[1] If they don't want it, is there any English newspaper or magazine?

Yours
Dylan

MS: Texas

ALEC CRAIG[2]

July 2 1946   Holywell Ford   Oxford

Dear Alec Craig,

Thank you for your nice letter, & for what you said about my reading at the Wigmore Hall.

I'd like very much to come & read again at Bayswater.

Monday, Sept. 16, will suit me perfectly well.

I see you want me to read for 2 sessions. Again, I'd be delighted.

Let's fix up a place for meeting before the reading, shall we, a little later on.

Hope to hear from you soon.

Oh, by the way: could I, on the 1st occasion, read the poems of *other* poets?

Sincerely,
Dylan Thomas

MS: Thomas Trustees

JOHN ARLOTT

Monday 22 July 1946   Holywell Ford   Oxford

My dear John,

I forgot, last Yeatsday, entirely, to ask you to have lunch with Margaret Taylor, Roy Campbell, & myself—& any young man of Margaret's—on Wednesday of this week, the 24th, at the White Tower, Percy St. It's Margaret's lunch & she's very keen on it. She wants us to meet about a quarter to one in the Wheatsheaf pub next door.

---

1 The three-day Puck Fair, with echoes of fertility cults, is held annually at Killorglin, Co. Kerry, and features a billy-goat crowned 'King Puck'. *Picture Post* advanced £50 in hope of an article, but got nothing. The Thomases went with friends, Bill and Helen McAlpine, travelling via Dublin.

2 Alec Craig, author, ran a poetry circle.

I had to tell Margaret T. that I'd asked you, as she'd been at me to do so for days & days. So, if you can't manage it, will you ask—as a special favour—Sylvia to wire deep regrets for inconvenience etc. to Margaret at Holywell Ford tomorrow, Tuesday.

Sorry to be such a nuisance, but I *had* to tell Margaret I'd asked you & you'd said yes. I've put you in a false position, but it's only a tiny one, I hope. Will you do it for me? That is: either turn up—the lunch will be good—or wire apologies, impossible, sudden call to work etc. to Margaret. I hope you can manage it, of course.

I hope you get this note before you go Test-wards.[1] If you do, will you leave all information & details with Sylvia or at the reception-desk on TUESDAY. I'll be in town & I'll ring Sylvia. If there's no reply, I'll call at Oxford St.

But do your best. I'll be seeing you Friday.

Ever,
Dylan

From a typescript. MS location unknown

JEAN LEROY
July 22nd 1946   Holywell Ford   Oxford

Dear Miss LeRoy,

Sorry not to have answered your enquiries about the 30 minute BBC Feature Programme for the *This Is London* series. But I am very glad to hear that the BBC are now going to pay forty (instead of thirty) guineas for *one* broadcast use of my script.[2]

Incidentally: surely your information that the script was broadcast in the African Service on Friday, July 12, is wrong? I didn't hand in the script until late on Thursday the 11th. And also I was the narrator, myself, in the recording of the script on Monday July 15th. You *must* be wrong; but if, by some most improbable chance you aren't, then I need to be paid for *two* broadcasts: the July 15th recording was, I gather, for the North American etc service.

And, incidentally again, I've not yet had word of your receiving an actor's contract for me for my part in that recording of the 15th.

But this is what I'm really writing about:—I'm going away to Ireland for a

---

1 England was playing India in the second Test match of the tour at Old Trafford, Manchester.

2 By now Thomas was in demand for many kinds of radio work. In 1946 he was involved in more than fifty radio programmes, which earned him about £700, say £16,000 in the year 2000. For 'This is London', a series broadcast overseas, he wrote *The Londoner*, an account of a day in the life of a working-class street. Although plainly written, it points towards the fantasy of *Under Milk Wood* a few years later. 'It is a summer night now in Montrose Street,' says the closing passage. 'And the street is sleeping. In number forty-nine, all is quiet. The Jacksons are dreaming.'

holiday on August 4th. And I must have, well before then, the outstanding money due to me from the BBC.

This outstanding money now includes:

1) *20 guineas* (plus railway fares) for programme on *Wilfred Owen* recorded June 19.

2) *15 guineas* for *Time For Verse* broadcast July 15th.

3) *40 guineas* for *This is London* recorded July 15.

There are also: 7 *guineas* (plus fare) for my part in *Book of Verse* in the Far East Service on July 18; and 7 *guineas* (plus expenses)—this is the usual fee, at any rate—for my part as narrator in my script recorded on July 15th.

But for these two last, I have not yet heard of your having had contracts sent to you.

It is items 1) 2) and 3) that are, to me, enormously important. Without them I can't go away.

Will you, *please*, collect those *three* outstanding fees for me *straight-away*. There is such little time. I will be so grateful.

I'll give you a ring, tomorrow, Tuesday, to see if you've had this letter and to press its urgency even further.

And a last, tiny thing. I didn't use my BBC travel-voucher from Oxford to Birmingham for a broadcast on *Lord Byron*, in the Midland Regional, on July 16th—(cheque for broadcast already received). I was working in London & had to travel from London to Birmingham, having left the voucher in Oxford. I return the voucher herewith, hoping—though only dimly, not at all urgently—that the BBC will accept it and refund me the railway fare. Will they do that, I wonder?

But urgent, really, are the seventy-five odd quid. Which I *must* have almost straightaway.

I'll be ringing you.

Yours sincerely,
Dylan Thomas

MS: Texas

LAURENCE GILLIAM[1]
July 23 '46   Holywell Ford   Oxford

Dear Laurence,

Thank you very much for your letter. I was sorry about the recording-car for Puck Fair, but I knew it was terribly short notice.

I'm so glad you liked the 'Portrait of a Londoner' programme, and I'll let you know some script-suggestions as soon as I can. If, in the meantime, you think of any that I could have a shot at, I'd be very grateful.

1 Laurence Gilliam (1907–64) was Head of Features in BBC radio, an innovator who filled his department with poets and journalists. He had written to say that the London programme was 'a most sensitive and successful piece of radio'.

But I'll be suggesting something very soon anyway.

Yours,
Dylan

MS: BBC

LORRAINE JAMESON
July 23 1946   Holywell Ford   Oxford

Dear Miss Jameson:

Thank you for your letter of the 17th. I hope this answer won't be too late: your letter's only just been forwarded to me.

Yes, I should like very much to do a Children's Hour talk for the next quarter's programmes. (I didn't know, by the way, that Aneirin Davies had left Talks, and was expecting, a long time ago, to hear from him.) But I think 'Penny Dreadfuls', as a subject, would be a little too narrowing [?harrowing]: I've forgotten nearly everything about them. I suggest a talk on memories of books I read as a young boy: this would include Penny Dreadfuls, & Chums & Tiger Tim's Weekly & the B.O.P. & the Magnet & the Gem etc., but also Henty & Marryat, Swiss Family Robinson, Jules Verne, Water Babies, etc etc etc: a talk, of course, not overmuch keeping to its subject and certainly not just a literary record: just a bit of nostalgic knockabout.[1]

Can you give me a dead-line date for receipt of the M.S.? Any other suggestions for further talks—Children's Hour or not—would be most welcome.

Yours sincerely,
Dylan Thomas

MS: BBC

DANIEL JONES
Monday [July] 24 '46   Holywell Ford   Oxford[2]

My dear Dan,

I've only just got, dear God, your letter.
I've been in London & Birmingham and jeopardy & hazard.
I'm eely and oily.
I'm hot trottered toast.
I'm my cup of toe.
I hate the earth: oh to hell with that incommensurable cowpad.

1 The script was not written.
2 Thomas wrote 'June' in error. The letter mentions a visit to Birmingham, and says he had 'a job' every day the previous week. He was in Birmingham for a broadcast on 16 July. Altogether that week he was at BBC studios on the Monday, Tuesday, Wednesday and Friday. Nothing comparable happened in June.

Cleopatra smells of Marmite.

Come again, King Cain, and have a cosh, I'm Abel.

It was terrible to miss you. I wanted so much to help with mothers, aunts, children, luggage, eartrumpet.

In my reeking way, I'd forgotten you were going so soon.

I'm weevil.

I haven't forgotten the other help and shall send it as quickly as possible. Or, best, give it to you here.

I had a job every day to do, last week, shouting 'Hi' in the North & 'Varlet' in Portland Square.[1]

How long will you be in Swansea? *Will you write by return?*

And this is important. When can you *come, alone or with your piece of Exeter oatcake, to Oxford?* It *must* be in the next fortnight. Margaret Taylor, my hostess, has an empty (but for 5 children) house for a fortnight and sends an invitation: there's a big bedroom waiting, & three lavatories.

I have a cricket bat & a hard ball and a choice of lawns.

I wish beyond anything you would come.

I have a room in Magdalen to read, write, dance & destroy poems in.

I am negotiating the purchase of a barrel of Flower's Best Bitter.

There is a grand piano, a harpsichord, & a large library of records (*with* gramophone).

We are on the river, & there is a punt.

I shall have some money.

Will you write at once?

Caitlin is looking forward very much to seeing you & Irene; or you alone; or Dan first & then Jones after.

If you cannot *possibly* come, I will try to come to Swansea.

[*A sentence has been deleted:* But, for the next few weeks, I have to do a few hours' work every day, & I know I will not work in Swansea.]

But for the next few weeks I think it will be difficult for me to move all that way from London, as I am waiting for a job.

Oh, it *will* be good here if you come.

My love for always, & my truly deep apologies for not being able to come down with them, to your mother & Aunt Alice. I am so glad they are home again, at last.

And I *will* see them soon.

But we *must* be here first.

I shall sharpen the cricket-bat in anticipation.

We have a tame robin, & the swan calls on Mondays.

Love from your old friend,
Dylan

By return, write.

And all regards to Vernon & Fred.

MS: Texas

1 The BBC's Broadcasting House is in Portland Place.

VERNON WATKINS
26th August 1946   Blaen Cwm   Llangain near Carmarthen

My dear Vernon,
   I'm a little nearer Swansea, anyway, and I hope to see you and Gwen and
Rhiannon at the end of this week or the beginning of next. I'd have written
from Ireland but I didn't take letters or anything with me and couldn't
remember your address. V. Watkins, Swansea, looked presumptuous.
Ireland was lovely. We spent all our time in Dublin and in Kerry. We ate
ourselves daft: lobsters, steaks, cream, hills of butter, homemade bread,
chicken and chocolates: we drank Seithenyns[1] of porter and Guinness: we
walked, climbed, rode on donkeys, bathed, sailed, rowed, danced, sang. I
wish you'd been there. I didn't write anything, but here in Wales I will—all
about Ireland. It'll be lovely to see you all, and so soon. I'll let you know
exactly when.

                                        Best love,
                                        Dylan

MS: British Library

JOHN ARLOTT
26th August '46   Blaen Cwm   Llangain near Carmarthen

My dear John,
   I tried to get hold of you as soon as I got back from Ireland but you were
always out. I don't know if you'd written while I was away, because my
letters haven't been forwarded yet:—I expect them tomorrow. I should,
anyway, have given you my Irish address. I saw Reggie Smith,[2] and was so
disappointed I wasn't there for the Lawrence programme. Ireland took all
my money in the world—and some of other people's money, too—so I
must get as much work now as I possibly can. Will you help? Any scripts
and/or readings you can manage will be terribly welcome. I'll do you a
script in a few days if you can get me one, or can come up to town for a
reading at a day's notice—provided the BBC will pay expenses to & from
Wales. I have to spend 10 days or a fortnight here with my mother, who is
ill, and after that will go back to Oxford. Do your best for me, please, John:
I'm in a real spot and simply must have a lot of work to do. How did the
Lawrence go? Ireland was grand: I ate myself daft, but have now recovered.
When do you go abroad? Hope to hear from you very soon. And *any* work:
the bigger, of course, & the higher paid, the better.

                                        Ever,
                                        Dylan

From a typescript. MS location unknown

1 Prince Seithenyn was a legendary Welsh alcoholic whose lack of vigilance let the sea
  breach a dyke.
2 R. D. Smith, BBC radio producer.

DONALD TAYLOR
26th August 1946   Blaen Cwm   Llangain near Carmarthen

Dear Donald,

I haven't written to you for many months. I realised that, if ever there were any news to tell me, you would write. I'm here for a week or so, and, in this tremendous quietness, feel lost, worried about the future, uncertain even of now. In London, it doesn't seem to matter, one lives from day to day. But here, the future's endless and my position in it unpleasant and precarious. Do write and tell me if there are any hopes of our ever selling our pictures, old or new? I've reached a dead spell in my hack freelancing, am broke, and depressed. A word would help.

                                        Yours,
                                        Dylan

MS: Buffalo

D. LEWIS-JONES
28th August 1946   as from Holywell Ford   Oxford

Dear Sir,

I am sorry not to have answered, before this, your letter of August 9th. I've been away.

By all means, send me your manuscript book of plays; I'll be pleased to read them and, if I can, comment on them. But I should warn you that I know nothing whatsoever about Welsh History: perhaps your plays will help to fill a lamentable gap in my already gap-filled knowledge.

                                        Yours sincerely,
                                        Dylan Thomas

MS: Carbondale

E. J. KING-BULL[1]
28th August 1946   as from Holywell Ford   Oxford

Dear Mr. King-Bull,

Thank you for your letter of the 23rd of this month.

The new series of poetry broadcasts,[2] which are to form part of the new

1 King-Bull was a BBC producer.
2 'The Poet and His Critic.' See letter to King-Bull, 223.

'Third' Programme beginning at the end of September,[1] does indeed sound elaborate and ambitious. I hope it has every good luck.

I should be most glad to be one of the poets in the series, and thank you for wanting me to be. And I should, I think, be very happy collaborating with G. W. Stonier.[2]

You suggest that, once I accepted the invitation generally (which I do), the three of us might meet soon for lunch and get down to it. I'll be back from holiday in about a week's time. Shall I give you a ring, then, or drop you a card? My address, for the next week, is: BLAEN CWM, LLANGAIN, near CARMARTHEN. After that, as above. If I don't hear from you while I'm in Wales, I will, anyway, get in touch with you as soon as I return. I'm sure that the three of us could beat four programmes into shape in a very short time.

Yours sincerely,
Dylan Thomas

MS: Texas

MISS PEARCE (at Pearn, Pollinger & Higham)
28th August 1946   Blaen Cwm   Llangain   near Carmarthen

Dear Miss Pearce,

I've just got your letter of August 21st. In it you say that you have arranged for me to take part in the programme, *COMUS*, to be broadcast on Monday, Sept. 30th from 9.45 to 10.45 p.m.—rehearsals 28th Sept, 29th Sept, 30th Sept, times & studios for these rehearsals to be arranged.[3]

The fee offered, you say, is 12 guineas plus 15/- fare & £2 subsistence.

Yes, do accept the proposal on my behalf, but: is the 12 guinea fee offered that which is offered to actors and not just to non-acting readers? I do a great deal of BBC readings, and have been trying for some time to get my position straight. 12 guineas for a programme which necessitates rehearsals on 3 days does not seem particularly generous to me. I have been told by a BBC producer with whom I am in touch that he is trying to get better fees for non-acting readers—needless to say, I cannot tell you his name, as the producers are not supposed to talk to the people they employ about money—and I would be very much obliged if you could find out how my 12 guinea fee compares with the fees offered to acting-readers. But, in any case, accept this. I should only like a little investigation to be done on account of future work.

1 The BBC's Third Programme, so called because it supplemented the existing domestic channels, 'Home Service' and 'Light Programme', set out to be cultural and élitist; at one time it was proposed to call it 'The Arts Programme'.
2 George Stonier, writer and critic.
3 Milton's *Comus*, a pastoral verse-play, was one of the first offerings of the Third Programme, which began on 29 September.

I shall be at the above address for another week. After that, the address is, as usual, HOLYWELL FORD, OXFORD.

Yours sincerely,
Dylan Thomas

MS: Texas

DAVID HIGHAM
29th August 1946   as from Holywell Ford   Oxford

Dear David,

Thank you for asking Ruthven[1] to dig up my old stories. I'll get busy and do my share, too, though what I must really do is to start writing a few new stories to add to the old ones. And I will.

My address, until Sept 7th, is Blaen Cwm, Llangain, near Carmarthen, Wales. But any ordinary communications, if there are any, can wait for me at Oxford.

I enclose a letter from Harper you might think worth answering for me. Is it?

Yours,
Dylan

MS: Texas

MARGARET TAYLOR
29th August 1946   Blaen Cwm   Llangain   near Carmarthen

My dear Margaret,

It was lovely to have your letter. But it was sad to miss you in Wales; and this is the second time, for we called at Laugharne, once, just after you'd gone. One day, how odd and good it would be to spend together, in this timeless, drizzled, argufying place, some very unOxford days. I wish New Quay had had more sun for you, though Jack Pat loves it as it is for then he has his guests all trapped and cosy in his godly grot. Time has stopped, says the Black Lion clock, and Eternity has begun. I'm so glad you met and like Dai Fred who bottled your ship. Did you come across Dewi, the battery-man? Evan Joshua of the Bluebell? The Norman you know is New Quay's noisiest and least successful fighter; every summer he starts a fight, & every summer some tiny little ape-man knocks him yards over the harbour-wall or bang through the chemist's window. Did Mrs Evans the Lion twitch, wink, and sip? Did Pat bring his horse in the bar? Jack the Post

1 Ruthven Todd.

is an old friend: he once married a pretty widow in London & everything was fine, he said, except that wherever they went they were followed by men in bowler hats. After the honeymoon, Mrs Jack was arrested for double bigamy. And all the husbands appeared in the court and gave evidence as to her good character. But I do hope you and Alan and Giles and Sebastian[1] enjoyed some bits of the rainy time. I'd be so ashamed, after our lauding, if the place had let you down with a wet Welsh bump. Did you meet Taffy Jones, the stuttering ace? He's not very nice. Or Alistair Graham, the thin-vowelled laird?[2] Was the red plywood bungalow, where we lived for a year and where the machinegun incident took place, pointed out to you? I should have told you to take Sebastian to the back room of the Commercial public house, where there are two very large & very fine coloured prints of Louis Wain cats: do you know his cats? Very alive and odious, capering, creeping, sneaking, ogling & dancing, arch as Eliot's.[3]

We had breathless days in Ireland: four in Dublin—oh the steaks, the chickens, chocolate, cream, peaty porter, endless blarney of politics never later than 1922—& the rest in Kerry, all wild sea and hills and Irish-reeling in kitchens. And a day on the Blasket: a very calm day, they said: the wind blew me about like a tissue-paper man, and dashed us against the donkeys.

We'll be staying here for another week, though I've got to go to London on Sunday to read in the Time for Verse programme at 10-30. Do listen if you can. Val Dyall and I are reading sea-battle poems: 'Of Nelson and the North', Tennyson's 'Revenge' etc. But we'll be in the studio when you come back from France. I can't tell you how much we're looking forward to being there again. We love it; and can never thank you both enough for having let us descend on you, you being so kind every way. Let's have some little journeys, foot and bus, round Oxford when you come back, please. We've hardly been on any; & perhaps September will be good.

Roy Campbell told me, when I saw him for a moment in London on the way here, that he likes Robert's reading very much. He wants us to read in a programme together, soon: a Milton programme, I think. Robert's done some work for him—and very well—already.

Aeronwy, in a fortnight with the Leahys, has developed a powerful, whining Oxford accent: and not the musichall sort.

Thank you for forwarding my letters. Could they go on being forwarded until the end of next week? But if it's a trouble, with you away, let them

---

1 Margaret Taylor's husband and their sons, Giles (b. 1937) and Sebastian (b. 1940).
2 Among the local characters Thomas mentions: Dai Fred was David Frederick Davies, a mariner's mate. Mrs Jack, perhaps a *Milk Wood* character in the making, was married to Jack Lloyd the postman. Taffy Jones was Ira Jones, a fighter pilot of the First World War. Alastair Graham, Evelyn Waugh's lover when they were at Oxford, was a reclusive figure who had gone to New Quay after a sex scandal in London, and remained there; he was at the Thomas bungalow on the night of the shooting.
3 T. S. Eliot's book of children's verse, *Old Possum's Book of Practical Cats*, was published in 1939.

stay till we come. So many were out of date, but I only lost one job, and that a perniketty one.

I do hope you have a lovely holiday in France.

And we'll see you soon, which will be splendid.

> Love from us both.
>
> Dylan

I'm glad about the Lyric man; & thank you. Will he write to me?

MS: Texas

DONALD TAYLOR

23 9 '46   Holywell Ford   Oxford

Dear Donald,

Thanks for writing.

I'm up in town at least two days a week, doing things for the BBC—and will be able to make quite a good thing of it.

If you ever come up nowadays, do let me know, at this Oxford address, & perhaps we can meet & have a drink.

I should like to talk about, among other things, turning B & H[1] into a full-length radio play—they want them now, however experimental or unsqueamish, up to an hour and a half—for the Third Programme.

Pleasant to meet again anyway.

Love to your family.

> Dylan

MS: Buffalo

*MR WAITS

27th October 1946   Holywell Ford   Oxford

Dear Mr Waits,

Thank you very much for your letter, which has just been forwarded to me by the BBC. I was very glad to hear what you so kindly said about my work, and very glad you took the trouble to write and tell me.

I've autographed the card you enclosed.

> Yours sincerely,
> Dylan Thomas

MS: Jim Martin

1 Burke and Hare.

JEAN LEROY
Nov 6th 1946   Holywell Ford   Oxford

Dear Miss LeRoy,
I see from your letter of the 5th that you've accepted, on my behalf, two invitations from the BBC: the first, to play in two live performances of *In Parenthesis*; & the second, to play the chief part in two live performances of *Aristophanes*.[1] And the fees you have accepted are twenty guineas *inclusive* for each.

I think these fees absurd; and though I've previously agreed with the producers of these two shows to play in them, I really do object to accepting the money offered.

Take *Aristophanes*. There are 3 whole days' rehearsals, plus one rehearsal from 2 p.m. onwards, *plus* two one-hour-&-a-half performances. Thus, four whole days (minus one morning) are to be spent on this show. Living in London for four days will cost me at least five pounds. Add to this my railway fare, & it works out that for four whole days work, including two live performances, I am offered about £14: £7 for each long feature performance, in which I am the principal character.

The same, except that I am not in this the principal character, applies to *In Parenthesis*.

Perhaps the trouble is that I am still being booked through Talks Dept. If that's so, it really must be seen to at once. In these two shows, & in very many others, I am a radio actor & *must* be contracted through Drama Dept.

But, even for Talks, £20 *inclusive* for 4 whole days' work is unacceptable. Absolutely unacceptable.

I do hope you'll do something about it straightaway.
                                    Yours sincerely,
                                    Dylan Thomas

MS: Texas

DAVID HIGHAM
23 11 46   Holywell Ford   Oxford

Dear David,
Re letter re Vogue.
Sorry, but I was away and got your original letter of the 4th of November—asking me to get hold of a copy, for Vogue's American editor,

---

1 David Jones's book, *In Parenthesis*, had been adapted for radio by the BBC's Douglas Cleverdon; Aircraftman Richard Burton, waiting to be demobilised from the RAF, was also in the cast. 'Aristophanes' was 'a panorama of Aristophanic comedy', *Enemy of Cant*, by Louis MacNeice. Both were Third Programme productions.

of my BBC script on *Memories of Bank Holiday*—too late to do anything about it. So glad you managed to get the *Listener* to her.

Re second par. re the possibility of my writing an article for English *Vogue*: I've had a letter from Audrey Withers wanting to fix up a meeting to discuss the article, & I think it's probably best for me to answer her myself as the next week or ten days are in a hell of mess for me with lots of jobs big & little:—but I'll be able, with a bit of fiddling, to fix a meeting.

Nice to be so busy—(I suppose).

Will get down to Dent book *very* soon.[1]

Yours,
Dylan

MS: Texas

JAMES LAUGHLIN
Nov 24th 1946   Holywell Ford   Oxford

Dear James,

I'm so sorry we didn't manage to have, together, quieter drinks, or less, or more, and that, before you went off to Paris, we hadn't advanced very much my America-ward plans. What I do really remember is that you did promise to look out for a house in the Adirondacks where I could live for some time with my wife & two children; and that pretty soon. Of course I believe your promise, but this letter's only to tell you again that I want to be writing—poems, stories, scripts—and broadcasting—poems, stories, scripts,—and that I must be fixed up, somewhere in the country, up the hills, and fairly near a city (New York, in this case) before I can. So this is only to tell you (again) that I am very much relying on your true and proper promise. All I write in America is yours for America, (and I want, and mean to, write a lot), but until that is settled I have no intention of writing anything at all. I think I can, from this side, with the active help of Edith Sitwell, manage to get jobs—lecturing, reading, etc—to be awaiting me in America. But from *your* side, and from you personally, I want to know that there is *immediate temporary accommodation* for the four of us (Dylan, Caitlin, Llewelyn, Aeronwy) when we arrive in New York, and a house in the country for us pretty soon afterwards. I hope I'm not being dictatorial. What I want to say, again, is that I want to work a lot and very much, but that those things have got to be seen to (as you promised) before I leave here.

And the other importance: Even if, from this side, Edith contrives to get for me a few American lectures etc, I still won't have the money to take the four of us on ship, plane, raft, or even by carrier pigeon. Caitlin is insisting that I write to you in this way: if she did not insist, I would still be writing this way. I hope that we, together, have a successful author-and-

1 Probably the projected collection *Bob's My Uncle*.

publisher existence: but it *must* be in America, and it *must* be through you. Can you write, or cable, me as soon as possible. These, to be dull, are the facts once more:

(1) I want to come early in the New Year to the States.
(2) I will not come unless I bring my family with me.
(3) I need the money to take us over.
(4) I want somewhere temporary for us to stay when we reach N. York.
(5) I want somewhere, after that, preferably in the hills, and certainly in the country, where we can live.
(6) Where we live must be somewhere near whatever place you think that I best can earn my living (mostly by broadcasting) in.
(7) I want to write a lot.
(8) What I write is, by our agreement, yours without any condition to print, publish, in America.
(9) And this, most importantly, must be soon.

Please, James, what can you do about it? And, please, make it quick. I hope to see you soon—but not here. And this, on my heart, is urgent. Don't forget.

Yours,
Dylan

MS: Houghton

CAITLIN THOMAS
Monday afternoon [2 December 1946]   as from Garden Flat
                                        45a Maresfield Gardens   Hampstead[1]

Darling my dear darling Cat, my love, I love you for ever, please my sweet think of me I love you Catty darling I love you. I'm writing this, very quick, very short, in the bloody BBC Maida Vale Studio where Louis's *endless* play is going on. And tonight—8.30 about—I'm reading Edith's vast bad poem.[2] Try to listen, dear. It *was* recorded, but I'm going to do it, 'live', again. Here's a tiny cheque. I daren't do any more until I get the letters sent to me (c/o Bill) that I hope are in Holywell Ford now. Please *do send* them, Cat my beautiful darling. Then I can send another cheque immediately. I don't want to phone because of maudlin Magdalen Maggie. Will you phone me before you take Aeron (how is she?) to school? About 9-ish. HAM 1483 (Bill's number). I love you I love you I love you.

Dylan   XXX & all in the world

Back Thursday afternoon. But do, dear, phone *tomorrow morning* about 9.

MS: (Maurice Neville)

1 Bill and Helen McAlpine lived there.
2 Thomas had recorded Edith Sitwell's 'The Shadow of Cain' a few days earlier, but for technical reasons the broadcast on 2 December was live (see page 479).

JOHN DAVENPORT
[about 22 December 1946]   [headed paper: TELEPHONE MESSAGE] 3.30

Dear John,

Terribly sorry missed you today: I had an idea I'd, myself, look for that abominable briefcase. So I went round, feeling hopeless, with Louis's Pinkerton clueing, found it. I'll write to the cops tomorrow, putting them off. Hope to see you just after Christmas in London. Many thanks. I'll get that poem shipshape for Jan 1.

Yours ever,
Dylan

Can't wait. Have got to catch 4.45 Padd for Oxford where, tomorrow, I pick up Llewelyn to take him to that Ringwood hell-hole.

MS: Texas

E. J. KING-BULL
December 26 1946   Holywell Ford   Oxford

My Dear King-Bull,

A very late indeed, but most sincere, apology for not turning up, as I promised, and as I so much wanted to, at our Earp meeting.[1] I got caught up, inextricably, with three dull, but urgent, things; and wasn't free until nearly three. That's no excuse—I could have rung. Please do forgive me. And thank you, a lot, for such a gentle reproof in your nice letter. I do hope you enjoyed Tommy E's company. I'm sure he'll do a thorough, and entertaining, job. I'm writing him by this post. He hasn't yet got in touch with me.

You ask whether I've any suggestions for readers. I think, emphatically, no woman. I can't, offhand, think of one poem of mine that needs a woman's voice; any poem, indeed, that wouldn't positively be better off for not having a woman's voice (I think I was caught in negatives, then, but you know what I mean). I think *two* men, don't you? I suggest, for one, John Laurie:—he does know my poems, though I can't tell if he'd care to read them aloud. I do really want a *masculine* voice. David King-Wood, as well? I don't, of course, know what poems Tommy E. is choosing, but for some of my poems I think Laurie's voice most suitable. And he's awfully intelligent.

1 The meeting was to discuss Thomas's contribution to 'The Poet and His Critic'. Each poet in the series was examined in four programmes, which contained examples of his work, together with critical appreciation and the poet's reply; they were expansive days for radio culture. T. W. Earp was to be Thomas's critic. In the event, due to the bitter weather and power shortages of early 1947—which shut down the Third Programme for two weeks in February—and to Thomas's illness, only three of the four programmes were broadcast.

You ask, too, about a copy of my 'Twenty Six Poems'. You mean, 'Twenty Five Poems', don't you? I've borrowed a copy from a friend, and am sending it, today, to T.W.E.

When is the first date of the series?

I'll give you a ring, if I may, as soon as I'm in town next.

And thank you very much for not being cross about my failure to turn up that day. I *did* miss it so much.

Dylan T

P.S. Again about readers: I have a friend, W. R. MacAlpine, 45a Maresfield Gardens, Hampstead, N.W.3., who knows more about my poems than I do and who reads them, aloud, extremely well. He has an Irish accent. Perhaps you'd think of trying him out?

MS: Texas

T. W. EARP
[about December 26 1946]   Holywell Ford   Oxford

My dear Tommy,

After months and months and months and months, I failed to turn up to meet you. Half it was that Commander King-Bull[1] frightens me, and half that I got held up in rehearsals for the part of a raven, and the bit of reason over was drink.[2] I was terribly, deeply, sorry to miss you. But I'm so glad you're willing to do those Critical Scripts. I had a note from K-Bull saying you had no copy of my '25 Poems'. Neither have I, but I borrowed one for you on big promises that it would be looked after (no Empson eggs between the pages) and returned. Have you got all the other books—particularly 'The Map of Love', which is hard to get hold of, and which has some of the poems I'm fondest of? When can we meet? Let's make it soon, and before the first broadcast. Will you wire me? I'll come up at once to town and turn up too early and wait biting my legs to the quick. So many things to tell you. I have missed you a great deal. Caitlin sends her love to you and May. So do I. Please wire soon as you can. What about Henekey's Holborn to meet in next week?

Yours,
Dylan

MS: Ohio State University

<hr>

1 King-Bull had been a naval Commander.
2 Thomas played a raven in *The Heartless Giant*, 'a Norwegian fairy story', by Louis MacNeice, broadcast on 13 December.

ARKIN COURTS & CO[1]
January 10 [1947]   Holywell Ford   Oxford

Dear Sir
    I enclose cheque for Fifty Six Pounds. I hope this covers the claim and
the costs and that further proceedings will now be stayed.
                                          Yours faithfully,
                                          Dylan Thomas

MS: National Library of Wales

GRAHAM GREENE
[early January 1947]   At Holywell Ford   Oxford

Greene was a director of Eyre & Spottiswoode, the publishers, and was known for his
interest in the cinema; Thomas hoped he might publish *The Doctor and the Devils*.
Margaret Taylor had made the initial approach.

Dear Graham
    Thank you so very much for troubling about all this. I fear two things:
first, that the script's no good, and second that, even if it were, it would be
impossible to release it from whoever owns the copyright.
    I looked the script over again—and it looks amateurish: the dialogue's
over wordy, and the construction badly needs pulling together. Probably a
good subplot's needed; probably nothing is needed but 'No!'
    Anyway, I'm so grateful to you for telling Margaret—whose idea it was
that I should dig it out of justified darkness—you'd read it.
    Will you let me know?
    I'm so sorry to have missed you & Walter Allen[2] that morning some
weeks ago. I found I had to work in Maida Vale that morning: too far to
come to town.
    And thank you very much for sending 'The Little Kingdom' & Mervyn
Peake's Grimm. Lovely drawings. I haven't read the Emyr Humphreys
yet.[3] It was terribly kind of you.
    I do hope we can meet soon.
                                          Yours,
                                          Dylan Thomas

MS: Theodore Brinckman

1 A firm of solicitors who had issued a writ on behalf of John Westhouse, a firm
  associated with Peter Lunn Ltd, when it became obvious that no 'Book of Streets' was
  forthcoming. Thomas had avoided the writ since the previous May. It was served early
  in January 1947, as he left the BBC after reading 'A Visit to Grandpa's'. The letter is in
  another hand, with Thomas's signature appended.
2 Walter Allen, author and journalist.
3 Emyr Humphreys (b. 1919), novelist. *The Little Kingdom* was his first book.

GRAHAM GREENE[1]
[1947]

The brief and, I'm afraid, ignorant history of a script, tentatively called 'The Doctor & The Devils', about Dr. Knox, the Edinburgh anatomist and Burke & Hare, the murderers.

This script was written by me when I was employed as a script-writer by a small company called Gryphon Films which was formed as a result of the dissolution of the documentary-making Strand Film Company.

The director of the Gryphon unit was Donald Taylor. (His private address is Hill Cottage, Hedgerley Village, near Slough, Bucks.) He resigned from Gryphon Films at the same time as myself: September, 1945, just as the Film Producers' Guild Ltd was being formed.

Gryphon Films had its offices in Guild House, (which now houses the Film Producers' Guild), St. Martin's Lane, W.C.2., and was somehow financially connected with Verity Films Ltd., which is still there. I do not know any details at all of the financial connection between Gryphon & Verity. But Donald Taylor, under whom I directly worked and on whose orders I wrote 'The Doctor and The Devils' must know. I have always been under the impression that the copyright is his.

Some of the research necessary for the scripting of this film was done by a member of Gryphon Films. And I also worked upon the preliminary roughing-out of the script with Taylor who took, throughout, a lively producer's interest.

The script was shown to a couple of wellknown producers, or companies, who—so I gather, but only at secondhand as Taylor told me little or nothing once the script was finished—were most enthusiastic about it and wished to do it but refused when Taylor demanded that he should direct it himself. I have, as I said, no firsthand proof of this.

I do know that Michael Redgrave, who read it, was extremely keen to play in it.

I also know that the script was sent to James Bridie whose play, 'The Anatomist', is on the same subject. Taylor wished to have it clear in writing that the script owed nothing to the play and that should the script be filmed Bridie could in no way object. Bridie replied satisfactorily.

When the script is seen, and if it is thought to have cinematic possibilities, Taylor is, of course, the one man to approach on the question of copyright.

Dylan Thomas

Only source: SL

---

1 Perhaps a memo that accompanied the previous letter. Graham Greene's MSS of this and the succeeding item were loaned and copied for *SL*. Later he said they had disappeared.

GRAHAM GREENE
January 11 1947   Holywell Ford   Oxford

Dear Graham,

Thank you such a lot for your letter. And, please, forgive me for not having answered it straightaway. I've been working in London, and very muddled too about where to live—here is feverish—and how and why. And about many other things, one or two of which I want to worry you with if you don't terribly mind. I know you're so busy, as publisher, writer, man and all, but if you could, though I've no right in the world to ask you, help, I'd be grateful always. I'm so sorry Margaret Taylor nagged you about the filmscript over Christmas: I only heard afterwards how she had written and phoned and plagued and plugged, all through kindness towards me I know; I didn't realise she was making such a business of it. I felt and feel, vague and nervous about it myself, and about sending it to you and trying to make some of my problems, if only for a moment, yours.

But, first, thank you very very much indeed for reading the script. I am so glad you liked it—if anyone could *like* such a nasty thing. And for writing to say what you thought about it. And for getting in touch with Michael Redgrave: it's good to think he hasn't forgotten the script & still wants to do it, in spite of the old B picture and Tod Slaughter's Plans.

About publishing the script. I'm pretty sure Dent's wouldn't touch it with a pole, and I'd very much like you to do it. But the question of copyright remains, of course, the same as when I wrote you about Donald Taylor and the other complications.

What I want, *frightfully urgently*—and this is the chief of the worries I want to worry you with—is some money for or from it or the chance of getting some, and ever so quickly, I can't tell you how quickly I need it, some money from Rank. I've got a pile of doctors' bills for Caitlin and for my son Llewelyn who is never, I'm sorry, well; and a looming writ; and another one on the doorstep. I'm in a hell of a mess. And *now*. So what I want to ask is, is there any chance of Rank[1] & his boys giving me some money at once, either on account of this script or on account of another script I could—and very much want to—write for them? I know that 'The Doctor & The Devils' might never, because of horror & copyright, ever be produced. But I should like it to be regarded as a *sample of what I can write for the films*. I want, naturally, to write a hundred-times-better script, and I'm sure I can. I can write other than horrible stories, and I want to. Would there be anything in the suggestion that I cd write a *film specially for Redgrave*? Would the reading of this D. & D. script make it clear to Rank and boys that I am capable of writing for the screen? and, if so, would they think of giving me some money, or putting me under contract?

On top of bills & writs, all howlingly pressing, I must get out of here &

1 J. Arthur Rank (1888-1972) was a home-grown British film tycoon, a God-fearing miller who initially saw films as a way to portray the 'great truths' of Christianity.

find somewhere else to live at once. And that will take money, which I haven't got. All I earn I spend & give to past debts. I'm in a mess all right. But I *know* I could write a good new script. And I wish Redgrave & Rank would pay me to do it.

Sorry about this breathless letter. Shall I ring you next week? and can you help, with the film boys, in any immediate way? Thank you again for your letter.

Yours,
Dylan Thomas

Only source: SL

URSULA KEEBLE[1]
January 11 1947   Holywell Ford   Oxford

Dear Mrs Keeble,
  Thank you very much for your letter of the [7th] suggesting that I might be interested in doing a poetry programme for one of the English Series (Dept. of School Broadcasting) in the Summer Term, 1947. I am indeed interested, and would be very glad to do a programme. I could discuss the details with you any time you like—either at B.H. or by correspondence. I haven't any definite ideas at the moment, but am very keen to try to put poetry over to these rather 'hostile' children:—or is that too harsh a word? I look forward to hearing from you, and shall in the meantime try to think up as many ideas and approaches as possible.

Yours sincerely,
Dylan Thomas

MS: BBC

AILEEN GOLDMAN
January 12 [1947][2]   Holywell Ford   Oxford

Dear Mrs. Goldman,
  Thank you very much indeed. I was delighted to have your letter, and so glad you liked my talk on 'Holiday Memories'. It was most kind of you to write. It's one thing to be moved by a broadcast—though that too rarely, I find; it's quite another thing to be moved to write to the chap who did it.

---

1 A BBC producer in schools broadcasting. A programme was scheduled for June but never made. Mrs Keeble wrote in an office memo, 'I feel that we cannot pander to his artistic temperament any further, and must give him up as a bad job.'

2 Thomas wrote '1946' in error. The talk, 'Holiday Memory. Dylan Thomas recalls many experiences of a holiday by the sea in his childhood days', was first broadcast (Third Programme) in October 1946, and repeated in November and on 7 January 1947.

I'm proud to think that the talk, or essay, or story, or whatever it is, did really mean something, at least to one listener. No, two: I was forgetting your son, whom I'd like to thank separately for having recommended it to you in the first place.

Thank you, again. I hope to do another South Wales 'Memory' quite soon; and I hope, too, you'll be able to hear it.

Yours sincerely,
Dylan Thomas

MS: Texas

D. J. AND FLORENCE THOMAS
January 12 1947   Holywell Ford   Oxford

Dear Mother and Dad,

I haven't written since before Christmas: it seems years ago. So much, and nearly all petty, has happened, so many plans made and broken. I wish I had written much sooner, to wish you a peaceful and well New Year, but I've been busy as a hive and mostly in London where, without a headquarters, I find it hard, even impossible, to settle down at borrowed desk or friend's table to write. Every proper wish now, though so late, and I *do* hope to see you soon. I'm glad you're back home; it's wicked weather to move about in. But I'm sure Hetty & Ken were awfully good and kind. How is Arthur?[1] I haven't seen him since—was it in London, when he & you came up about poor Will? How long ago? Will you send him Caitlin's love, and mine, when you write?

We had rather a gay and noisy Christmas here. Oxford's a very sociable place on occasions like that, and we went to several parties. We had Christmas Day lunch very quietly, just Caitlin & Aeronwy & myself in our snug summerhouse: we ate the biggest of the two delicious and tender chickens Mother sent, and a rich dark pudding made us by the Taylor cook, Florence, whose black-&-white baby is due any day now, and a bottle of caustic red ink called Algerian wine. Aeron had some crackers. She loved her teaset and gives an assortment of dolls & bears daily parties. She had quite a lot of presents altogether, including a tricycle from us, books, a little mangle, a Noah's Ark, a golliwog, and a stocking full of nonsense and tangerines. Then Christmas Day Dinner with the Taylors, with turkey. Boxing Day dinner with some friends of ours here called Veal—he's a young composer, and son of the University Registrar—and Saturday dinner with a Corpus Christi don called Stahl, & his wife. Our second fat and luscious chicken we added to the Veals' table. One of our troubles here is that we can't invite anyone back; so instead, we took along a few things to

1 Hetty and Ken Owen were family friends. Arthur, D. J. Thomas's brother.

their flats, rooms, or houses. The day after Boxing Day I had to go to London to give my after-the-news talk.[1] A lot of people found the talk eccentric; perhaps it was; it wasn't, certainly, what most people expected to hear after the news. I've had quite a big post from it: half of it enthusiastic, the other half calling me anything from obscurantist to poseur, surrealist comedian to Bedlamite. The Manchester Guardian reviewed it very cheeringly; the News Chronicle with boos.

On New Year's Eve we went, with lots of other people, mostly BBC, to the Chelsea Arts Ball at the Albert Hall. Never been to it before. 5000 people there, all in fancy dress. A tremendously bright affair. I went as a Chinaman, Caitlin as a grand Spanish lady. It really was very exciting: wonderful to look at: all the boxes round the great hall packed with pierrots, ballerinas, costermongers, Elizabethans, pirates, courtesans, tigers, Dutch Dolls, empresses, clowns, & the huge floor rainbowed with dancers. Valentine Dyall and Michael Ayrton—do you ever hear him on the Brains Trust?—were two of our company.

The day after that Dyall & I took part in 'Richard the Third' on the Overseas Service of the BBC. Eastern & Overseas Services I now do quite a lot of work for: scripting, acting, & reading. They do a potted Shakespeare play a week. Last week it was Titus Andronicus, which I'd never read and probably never will read again,—but it was great fun to do. There was a very fine actor, George Hayes once of the Old Vic, playing Aaron the damned Moor.

Last week I read my story 'A Visit to Grandpa's', too. Did you hear it? 10-30 pm on Wednesday, in the Home Service.

I haven't many reading engagements for the near future. I'm talking about Sir Philip Sidney on the 24th, from the West. Can you get that? It will be repeated later in the Third Programme. And, for the Shakespeare series I mentioned, I'm arranging the programme on 'Merchant of Venice'. But that's impossible to hear in England, without a short-wave set. I've finished, & recorded, the first of two programmes about Oxford—the first was an exchange programme with Princeton USA—and very soon will be able to do my 'Return Journey—Swansea' programme. A day in Swansea, & the rest in Blaen Cwm.[2]

Did I tell you about the opera-libretto I have been asked to write? A full-length grand opera for William Walton.[3] I have to turn out a very rough synopsis before I am definitely commissioned. This I hope to do next week. Michael Ayrton, who will do the decor, & I are going, on Wednesday, for a few days, to Gravesend, Tilbury, & all around there, as I want to set the opera in a near-docks area.[4] A very modern tragic opera, in the bombed slums of wharfland. If this ever comes to anything, it will be the biggest

1 'The Crumbs of One Man's Year'.
2 Thomas's feature-programme about the poet in search of his lost youth was researched in Swansea in February.
3 Sir William Walton (1902–83), composer. No libretto was written.
4 Michael Ayrton (1921–75), painter and designer.

English operatic event of the century. Really it will. A whole Covent Garden season in 1949 is contemplated. If, & when, I am commissioned to write the libretto, I should be able to stop doing any other work & devote about six solid months to it.

I've got a new book out in America: 'Selected Works'. I've had some good American notices—I enclose one from the New York Times. Can you return it afterwards, as I'm trying to file all American stuff for future use, when, one day, we go across there—but so far only one copy of the book which I can't, at the moment, find. As soon as other copies come, I'll send you one at once. It's a nice-looking book.

Do you ever listen to the series 'Poet & Critic' on the Third Programme? I'm the next Poet, the Critic being T. W. Earp. There'll be either three or four programmes, half an hour a week. Starting the end of this month. I'll let you know exact dates later.

As to domestic news: we're well on our way to getting a cottage here, in Magdalen grounds. But I shan't know finally for about six weeks. It will be fine, if it works. The cottage is an old mill-house, on the Cherwell, surrounded by gardens. It is Magdalen property, and, *if* I get it, it will be on a very long lease and at a very small rental. It will be a proper home for us. In the meantime: at the beginning of February, Caitlin & I think of moving to Richmond, to share a house—a big house—with Helen and Bill, the people we went over to Ireland with last summer.[1] It's a house just by Richmond Bridge, right on the river. I do hope you'll be able to come & stay with us in it in the early spring. There's tons of room, & it's extremely comfortable. I'll tell you more about this—an almost certain plan—later on. Our idea is to share both the Richmond house & the Oxford cottage with Helen & Bill, one part of the mixed family being, probably, 'in residence' in Oxford while the other part is in our 'town house'. The Richmond house belongs to Helen, so our rent will be most reasonable. It's all pretty ambitious, but may come off.

Caitlin & I are going to lunch with Edith Sitwell in London tomorrow. She's on her way to Switzerland.

Last weekend, we went down to Ringwood & brought Llewelyn back with us for a week or so. He likes it here, with the two small Taylor boys. It's Giles's birthday-party today, Sunday, & there's a hell of a row going on all over the house. They're playing Murder, by the sound of it. Llewelyn's very pale and frail, but full of life. Caitlin's taking him, this week, to see a Dr. Walker here, a famous children's specialist. He's been suffering all the winter from asthma, and he's frightfully nervous too and has a peculiar way of walking. If the Doctor says he needs a change of climate—which the Bournemouth Doctor recommended—Margaret Taylor has, voluntarily, promised that she will pay to send him over to, & keep him in, a kind of holiday-school in the Isle of Wight for about 3 months. But we'll know the Doctor's opinion on this on Wednesday. Whatever happens, we're [?not] going to allow Llewelyn to go back to Ringwood for any length of time. He

1 The McAlpines.

must have the company of children of his own age, & also he *must* get away from the flat, damp New Forest district.

Llewelyn's a great reader. He reads everything, except poetry which he 'hates'.

And now I can't think of anything else. Oh yes: interest has been revived in my filmscript. Did I ever thank Dad for sending it on? Anyway, thank you now, very much.

Caitlin will write this evening. Thank you for all the Christmas presents. I can't tell you how welcome they were. And for the pound, which filled Aeron's stocking full. Llewelyn was awfully pleased, too, by his Christmas gifts from you. I wish you could see him, & hope that you soon will.

I'll write later, with news of Llewelyn's Doctor & whether he'll be sent to the I. of Wight or not. And etcetera & etcetera.

Please write and tell me something, as soon as possible.

All love from
Caitlin & myself,
Aeronwy & Llewelyn,
Dylan

MS: (Thomas Trustees)

*J. MORYS WILLIAMS[1]
February 17th 1947

Holywell Ford   Oxford

Dear Mr Morris Williams,

I'm writing a script about Swansea for the B.B.C., as one of the series called 'Return Journey'. And I wondered if you'd be so good as to help me. I want the Roll of Honour of old Grammar School boys who were killed in the recent war. I hoped that you, as President of the Old Boys' Association, would be the proper person to approach.

The Roll of Honour is, I trust, very small; but I should be most interested to know if any of the names on it belonged to boys who were at School in my time—roughly, I should say, 1925–1931. But I would be extremely grateful if you could just let me have a copy of the Roll of Honour. The Swansea programme, by the way, is to be heard first on the Home Service (all regions *except* Wales) on February 28th; and on the Welsh Service a little time later.

I was in Swansea, on the programme, for a day, but unfortunately had no time to come up to the school—which I want to describe in the script. Does the Hut[2] still stand? And is it really true that soon there won't be a Grammar School at all, any more?

Please forgive me for bothering you like this. I do very much hope you

---

1 Classics master at Swansea Grammar school.
2 A 'temporary' single-storey structure, built when the school expanded earlier in the century, and used as classrooms. It was the object of long-running schoolboy jokes.

don't mind, and that you can help me. I've got such little time before the 28th.

Yours sincerely,
Dylan Thomas

MS: Location unknown

J. MORYS WILLIAMS
March 1st 1947   Holywell Ford   Oxford

Dear Mr Morys Williams,

Thank you very much indeed for your charming and most helpful letter, and for the Roll of Honour. I remember several of the names on it, of course:—Haines, Beer, Bucknell, Twford, Vagg, K. J. Evans. F. H. Bazzard was an old friend of mine, though several years senior to me.

I'd no idea the School was so very badly blitzed. Is the Hall utterly destroyed?[1] In my script I've had, unfortunately, very little opportunity to say more about the School except than to lament the destruction done to it, but, at the same time, to express my hope that the School itself will always continue. I assumed that the Hall was burnt out. If I'm wrong, would it be too much to ask you to let me know?

The Swansea programme was postponed because of the popularity of the five-editors' debate which was broadcast the week before & which public demand, as they say, wanted repeated. They will probably postpone my programme for a month.[2]

No wonder you get hot under the collar about the future, or no future, of the School. The decision of the local authorities seems a bit of vandalism, as you say, and also a precious piece of inverted snobbery. Thank you for your excellent letter to the Press. May it do some good.

It was good of you to answer my letter so fully & so quickly. Thank you again.

Yours sincerely,
Dylan Thomas

MS: Location unknown

KATHLEEN GURNER[3]
March 1 1947   Holywell Ford   Oxford

Dear Miss Gurner,

Thank you very much for your letter, & for enclosing the schoolgirls' letters. I did enjoy reading them.

About my poem 'October', which appears in '18 Poems'. Of course you

---

1 Only a couple of laboratories, the gymnasium and the headmaster's house survived.
2 *Return Journey* was postponed until June.
3 Letter addressed to her at Goldsmiths' College, University of London.

have *my* permission to use in it [it in] the series of anthologies of poetry for use in schools which a cte [committee] of the Training College Association is bringing out. But I'm afraid there are difficulties. The Fortune Press, which brought out my '18 Poems' some years after they were originally published, are making things difficult about copyright. Indeed, I believe they are trying to sue my agents. But this is something I understand little about & want to know less; so I'm sure the best thing for you to do, if you still want the poem in spite of these complications, is to write direct to my agent, telling him that you have my own permission to use the poem. He'll know what to say then about the legal position. He is David Higham, of Pearn, Pollinger, & Higham, 39–40 Bedford St. Strand. W.C.2.

Sorry about this bother. And thank you again for writing & for sending me those letters.

Yours sincerely,
Dylan Thomas

MS: Texas

CHARLES FISHER
March 1 1947   Holywell Ford   Oxford

My dear Charles,

Me too. I've thought, very often, during the last years, of writing, sending the letter somehow care of someone in the Army or in Swansea, but it came to nothing but 'My dear Charles' and a case-book doodle. The moment we met, when Dan was with me, in the Gargoyle, blew away like a butterfly cork, & I lost, or forgot, your address. So now I know where you are, and that's fine: I can write again & hope you'll write. Any sense or nonsense.

I went to Swansea a fortnight ago, for two nights, saw Fred, Vernon, Walter Flower, John Prichard, Bill Henry, Mrs Giles of the Singleton, the Borough Architect, and Mr Ernest Davies who wears very high collars, is, unlikelily, a fashion-designer, unless he was pulling my leg with a crane, and makes, out of cardboard & cellophane, very tiny naked women who do a kind of arthritic can-can when he lights a match behind them. Fred, I was astounded to see, was painting a rather careful picture of two herrings; Vernon, you would never believe, was writing a poem about spiritual essences; Walter, you'd hardly credit it, told me stories about councillors & trout.

Caitlin & Aeronwy & Llewelyn and Brigit and Tobias[1]—the last two are not really mine—and me are going to Italy, for six months we hope, in a

---

1 Tobias was the son of Brigit Marnier, Caitlin's sister.

month's time, where I hope to write poems, after a year's stop, which I will send to you. I have just had mussel-poisoning. All around us here, where we live by the river, frenzied voles are climbing the trees after the birds' bits. I have a black eye, too, which seemed to grow in the night. There is no news.

Write soon and tell me your no news. It was lovely to hear from you.

Ever,
Dylan

MS: the recipient

T. W. EARP
March 1st 1947   Holywell Ford   Oxford

My dear Tommy,

Thank you so much for your letter.

The people who told you about my health, when you were last in London, were *all* correct, & at the same time. I was roaringly well, then, some minutes after, a little mewling ruin. I would very nearly run down one street, to cringe, very nearly on my belly, up the next. In Finch's I was a lion; in the Duke of York's a piece of cold lamb with vomit sauce. Now I [am] back in ordinary middle health again, headachy, queasy, feverish, of a nice kind of normal crimson & bilious. I think that I am nearly well enough not to have to go out this morning in order to feel well enough to work this afternoon: a preposterous process, as it means I go to sleep with my face in the pudding & wake up sticky & fretful & bite my nails to the shoulder-bone. I hope, very much, that you are well too. I liked the first & second do's on me, & am looking forward to the third tonight which will be your fourth. I mean, the third section, supposed to be my reply, will now end the series. The Commander writes to tell me that, owing to rushed Third Programme planning, your 4th (now 3rd) section is cut to 15 minutes, which means the loss of 'Fern Hill' & 'Vision & Prayer'.

I found the greatest difficulty in writing my piece, & have become rather hysterical in my generalisations. My references to your critical remarks are warm-hearted and dull. So am I.

Write me when you'll be in London, and, unless some film-work I am rushing at the moment in order to get some money for Italy prevents me, I'll be there, fit as a fuddle.[1]

It was a great pleasure to me to hear you on the wireless; and thank you,

1 Edith Sitwell had decided that America, which Thomas was still anxious to visit, was not a wise choice for a poet who drank too much. She headed a committee of the Society of Authors that awarded travelling scholarships. It gave the whole of its 1947 grant, £150, to Thomas. The formal decision was taken on 26 March, and linked with 'a strong recommendation' that 'his travels should be in Italy rather than anywhere else'.

very deeply, for all the extremely kind & penetrating things you said.
I hope to see you very soon.

> Yours ever,
> Dylan

MS: Ohio State University

MICHAEL AYRTON
March 16th 1947   Holywell Ford   Oxford

Dear Michael,

I've let you down, and myself, and even if you can never forgive me, and I
don't see why you should, will you bury a hatchet in a glass with me? I'll
ring you at the end of this week, and get a nasty answer.

The books are being sent off this afternoon. I should have written the
thing at once. I'm sorry.

I hope your show went well. Is it still on? I should like a long peep. I saw
Martin Boddey,[1] for a few stolid, comfortable minutes, the first day, and
he said a lot had sold. I'm so glad.

A tree fell, last night, on our roof: a fir-tree.

> Yours ever,
> Dylan

From a typescript. MS location unknown

VERNON WATKINS
March 16 1947   Holywell Ford   Oxford

Dear Vernon,

It was lovely, all those weeks ago in the snow, to see you and talk and
laugh, Bush, water-pistol, Fred (Fish) Janes, and all. I was sorry not to be
able to come out to Pennard on my last evening: I lost the address, and had
to go and see a master from the Swansea Grammar School to find out how
much of the school was burned. 'Bloody near all', he said; then, with a
nasty sigh, he added, 'All except Grey Morgan'.[2]

Thank you very much for wanting to buy Llewelyn a book for his
Christmas Birthday. I'd like him to have a Bible too. But I'll ask him, in a
minute—he's downstairs, playing Demon Rummy—and I hope he won't
say Arthur Rackham [Ransome?] who he thinks is the best writer in the
universe except the writer of the Dick Barton series.

God brought a new one out of his bag of storms last night, tore down the
trees and dropped one on our roof, flooded the only path, drove the voles to

---

1 Martin Boddey was a singer.
2 Thomas had been in Swansea, researching the *Return Journey* script. The Bush was a
  pub in the High Street. J. Grey Morgans was still the Grammar School headmaster.
  Thomas's script described the ruined school: '... the echoing corridors charred where
  [young Thomas] scribbled and smudged and yawned in the long green days ...'

the trees, broke a window, sent Caitlin flying. I'd like to see Pennard now.

My Swansea programme was postponed because of fuel & weather, too little one, too much other, and can now be heard on April 2nd.

We go to Italy on April 8, but not to Florence: to a village near Rapallo. I shall ask about Pound.

I want very much to come & see you after April 2nd—the broadcast is from Cardiff—and will wire you at once if I can.

I'm looking forward to hearing 'Mari Lwyd' on Thursday. I'm one of the readers. I hope you won't mind too much.

Llewelyn's just sent his love, thanked you very much, and said:

I *do* hope I can see you soon.

Give our love to Gwen and Rhiannon.

Ever,
Dylan

MS: British Library

D. J. AND FLORENCE THOMAS
about 11 April 1947 [postcard]   From Villa Cuba
San Michele di Pagana   Rapallo   Italy

Arrived here a day ago, after fearsome three days travelling with Caitlin, Brigit, Llewelyn, Aeronwy, and Tobias. One night in Milan. Rapallo is very beautiful. Blazing sun, blue sea & sky, red, pink & white villas on fir-treed hills, orange-groves, olive-trees, castles, palaces. Our hotel small, v. pretty, fifteen minutes from Rapallo. Please write to above address. I am writing full letter this afternoon. All love to both from us all. I hope to God Dad's better.

X   Dylan

MS: Jim Martin

D. J. AND FLORENCE THOMAS
11th April 1947   Villa Cuba   San Michele di Pagana   Rapallo   Italy

Dear Mother and Dad,

I don't know which will arrive first: this letter, or a postcard of Rapallo. But the object of both is the same, and a pretty obvious one too: to tell you that we have all—Caitlin, Brigit, Llewelyn, Aeronwy, Tobias, & myself—arrived safely in Italy after three days' travel. Three very exhausting days. We had booked through from London to Rome—you *have* to book sleeping-reservations a long time ahead—before we knew where we were going. And so when we decided on Rapallo, we still had to travel on the Calais–Milan–Rome express, which meant that we had to go through Switzerland. If we had booked through to Genoa, we would have missed the whole Swiss loop. We'd have shortened the journey by a day. But it couldn't be helped. One of the nuisances was that our baggage got left behind at the Swiss–Italian frontier, and Caitlin & I had the hell of a job next morning, while Brigit looked after the three children, of chasing the baggage through the bowels of Milan station, endlessly interviewing bureaucratic officials in a jumble of languages, queueing up before wrong ticket-offices, bribing the Customs with English cigarettes, changing pound-notes into Black Market lire, dragging the children out of the hotel into rude & reckless taxis, & *just* managing to catch the train. Milan is a giant, nightmare city. The snow & the rain had just ceased before we arrived—a day or two before. The immensely long, wide streets, which run the entire length of the city, or seem to, were bakingly hot & dusty, clanking with great, packed, racing trams, buzzing with little toy motor-bikes; there were stop-me-&-buy-one bicycle-boys selling, not ice-cream, but bottles of Chianti, & set-faced sinister armed policemen. Brigit stayed in the hotel, and Caitlin & I went round the city & the cafés in the boiling sun, speaking our lame Italian. I have a dozen phrases, half probably wrong; Caitlin makes long & impressive-sounding speeches, which few can understand. But I hope we will pick up a working vocabulary fairly soon. Nouns I can remember; grammar, no. I shall have to learn it the dull way, I'm afraid, through a text-book.

The worst part of the journey was the shortest: from Genoa to Rapallo: an asthmatic train creeping & bumping over the bridges, over the bridges just erected or actually in the process of being erected. Nearly all the bridges along the Italian Riviera were blown up, but whether by the Germans or by the British I have not yet been brave enough to ask, or linguistically capable of asking.

San Michele is about a mile outside Rapallo: half way between Rapallo & Santa Margerita: not far from Portofino. It's a lovely village. Our little hotel—expensive; we can't stay *here* long—is right on the sea; our bedroom balconies are over the water. High hills above the village, covered with villas, fir-trees, olive-trees, wonderful villas, pink, red, white, turreted, pinnacled, baroque Christmas-cake; the sea's bright blue, the very bright blue sky cloudless. It's so lovely, lying by the sea in the sun; incredible after this winter. I wish you could both be here. Do please write soon, very soon, and tell me how you are. Especially Dad. The last time Mother wrote, he was ill again, and in pain. I do hope, above everything, that he is better now. Do let us know at once, now that you have our (temporary) address. It seems all wrong, us here in the great sun, on the Riviera, & Dad ill, who would, I'm sure, feel so much better for a complete change of climate.

We walked to Rapallo this morning, but didn't have much time there. The front is all enormous, expensive hotels & cafés, packed with the rich: like Nice, or Mentone. But the little of the town itself that we saw is heavenly. Max Beerbohm lives here, though I don't know where; in some wonderful villa up in the olive groves, perhaps. Here Ezra Pound used to live; here it was he went mad too.

I had a letter from Edith Sitwell this morning, who is mostly responsible for us being able to come here. She is the chairman of the Authors' Society Travelling Committee, which occasionally gives writers money to move about. Talking about money: the Bank gives you nine hundred lire for a pound; the Free Market, as it is known, gives you eighteen hundred. This part—indeed, much of the North, I think—seems well off for food. We have had excellent food, superlatively cooked, for the last two days: dinner being some form of very good spaghetti in a rich sauce, followed by white meat, artichokes, spinach, & potatoes, followed by bread & cheese (all kinds of cheese; my favourite gorgonzola), followed by apples or oranges or figs, & then coffee. Red wine always with the meal.

It's lovely to see the oranges growing around us.

Write soon, & so will I. Next week I am going, alone with Caitlin, to Rome, to see about British Council lectures. I have also an introduction to one of the heads of Italian films, an American Russian Jew. I'll let you know what happens.

Now write soon, & tell us everything. I hope to God Dad's better. All with me send their love. And I send all mine.

Dylan

MS: (Thomas Trustees)

EDITH SITWELL
11th April 1947   Villa Cuba   San Michele di Pagana   Rapallo   Italy

My dear Edith,

I owe you such a great deal of happiness, and so many apologies. First of all, let me thank you for persuading us to go to Italy, and for helping, wonderfully, to send us. I do not know how long we will be able to stay—perhaps for only a short time—but I am grateful to you every warm, blue minute, every orange and olive tree, every fir on a hill. And, second, let me, please, say how sorry I am, and how angry with me Caitlin is, for not having answered at once, except by cold telegram, your two letters, one of business, both of friendship. I wanted not to answer until the purpose of the letters was achieved, and I could say, writing in the sun, how fine & alive it was to be in the sun and how I and Caitlin thanked you for it & for everything. I should have written at once; this letter will take days & days to reach you; but I did so want it to come from here.

I was very, very sorry not to see you again in London. I had to go, for one thing, to Wales to read a script about childhood, which I hope, a lot, you will be able to hear. It will be on the Home Programme, under the title of Return Journey, but I am afraid I do not know when. It will be quite soon. I *did* want to see you again. Are you better now? You were ill at that lovely banquet after that over-long reading. Will you write a letter here, and tell us?

I went to see Denys Kilham Roberts, and got from him a letter to the Bank of England asking them, on behalf of the committee of the Travelling Fund, & of the Authors' Society, please to allow me to have, in Italy, that £150 on top of my ordinary, legal £75 allowance. It was then too late to do much about it, but I hope to hear, any day now, from *my* bank who are dealing with it for me. Kilham Roberts' letter seemed, to me, a model of tact and persuasion. I hope the Treasury is susceptible.[1]

We spent one night in nightmare Milan, which I enjoyed horribly, and came on here, over blown-up bridges, in a lame train, the children dirty, exhausted, excited, too many. But here is beautiful; the little pension's like a clean, pink ship in the sea. Everybody is kind, and oh the nice wine.

But, even if we could—the pension's expensive—we wouldn't want to stay on here for more than a couple of weeks. Rapallo *is* a Riviera rich holiday-place, isn't it, and we, I think, don't want to holiday but to stay, to live for a bit. I want, above all, to work like a fiend, a *good* fiend. And the pretty pension on the legendary water is *terribly* temporary. We want a small house to fill, cook in, work in, where the children can be noisy, where we can make a rhythm and a way of our own. Anywhere. Not at all necessarily by the sea. Osbert said, at that unforgettable after-Canticle supper, that he could write, perhaps, to find out whether, somehow, it would be possible to find a house somewhere that I could borrow or cheaply rent. I know he meant it, but I did not know if he would want me to write to him about it. So I haven't written. Shall I, do you think? I am writing, now, only to you, not to Osbert or to Sacheverell who, also, said that maybe he could help to find us a place of—for a time—our own. Shall I write to Sacheverell too, do you think? Or would you ask them again? I do not know what is best. A house, any kind, anywhere, would mean very very very much now.

And in the meantime, the sun *is* heaven. I'm going to walk to Santa Margarita tonight. Thank you because we are here. When I can write anything, I'll send it to you, if I may.

I have lost my copy of my Reply to T. W. Earp in the Poet & Critic broadcast series, but have written to King-Bull asking him to send a copy, urgently, direct to you.

I am *intensely* proud that you are writing an essay on my poems. I want to write so much better poems, though. Now, and all the time.

I will write again, very soon.

Love from Caitlin & me,
Yours ever,
Dylan

MS: Texas

1 Exchange Control made it illegal to move money out of Britain without official permission.

E. J. KING-BULL
[April 1947]   Villa Cuba   San Michele di Pagana   Rapallo   Italy

Dear King-Bull,

Would you do me a favour? Edith Sitwell has just written me asking for a copy of my Reply to Tommy Earp, the last in the Poet & Critic series about me. I haven't got a copy. Could you send her one, to Renishaw? She says she wants it urgently, as she's writing an essay about my poems for, I think, New Writing: & in a hurry.[1] I'd be awfully glad if you could.

Here I feel hot & lovely, though I look just hot.

Thank you so much if you'll do that.

How are you?

Dylan

MS: Texas

MARGARET TAYLOR
12th April 1947   Villa Cuba   San Michele di Pagana   Rapallo   Italy

My dear Margaret,

I was profoundly sorry not to see you; up to the last grey, ruinous moment I thought that, somehow, I could return to say au revoir, thank you for too many thousand things to count, above all your loyalty to me when I was wretched, ill, mean, drawn taut, lost, utterly unworthy of faith or affection, of anything but a kind of kicking pity. I wanted to thank you for your more than kindness to Llewelyn and Aeron, whom you helped to make well; to Cat and me, whom you housed when we were in a sick muddle; to me, to whom you were almost gentle. I do hope that you can help us to find a house in or near Oxford, so that we can see each other again. I want, so much to come back to Oxford. Oh, anywhere a house. I am lost without one. I am domestic as a slipper, I want somewhere of my own, I'm old enough now, I want a house to shout, sleep, and work in. Please help; though I deserve nothing.

The journey was first good, then baddish, then disastrous, then good again, then bad. The disaster happened at the Swiss frontier, when we lost our luggage. We should not have gone through Switzerland anyway. We found the baggage at last, after eternities deep, deep down *under* Milan

1 'Comment on Dylan Thomas' by Edith Sitwell appeared in *The Critic*, Vol. 1, No. 2, Autumn 1947.

station, through Ufa corridors,[1] in Kafka cells and temples of injustice. Our lack of Italian helped. In steel-barred rooms, where Mussolini personally had whipped and interrogated, we faced row after row of tiny, blue Customs-officers in wide hats, who smoked our cigarettes, spilt sugar on the clothes, joked at a great speed, ogled Caitlin, and cut our luggage labels off with scissors.

San Michele is a very pretty village; the sea's blue under our balcony; there's a wind, but the sun's hot; our pension is small, sweet, dear; there is lots of food & wine. The front at Rapallo, a mile away, is far too much of a rich playground, with enormous hotels, women from Phillips Oppen-heim,[2] international millionaires, &, this morning, us. But the town behind the swagger front is full of most lovely houses, cafés, chianti, gorgonzola, markets, orangetrees. We are going to Portofino tomorrow. I do not know if I can start working here. There is no escape in a small hotel from the too many children. And besides, we must live in the country. This is sophisticated as Nice.

Caitlin & I will go to Rome next week to see film-&-British Councilmen.

Write & tell me Nish-news. How are you? Don't, don't be unhappy, please. Write soon. And you will help about a house, won't you? I am as homely as a tea-caddy, but have no pretty pot.

Thank you, dear Margaret, for everything.

Yours ever,
Dylan

Caitlin sends her love. Could you, do you think, send a couple of thrillers or a magazine? I am forced to read poetry only.

Write soon,
D.

MS: Texas

DAVID HIGHAM
24 April 1947   Villa Cuba   San Michele di Pagana   Rapallo   Italy

Dear David,

My bank has just told me that it has obtained the authority of the Bank of England to transfer that Authors' Society £150 to me in Italy. Good. My bank also tells me that, as I drew out so much to pay for passages etc, I am much poorer than I thought & they cannot transfer to me more than just £50. Bad. You see, I had paid in, as soon as I received it, the Authors'

---

1 UFA, Universum Film Aktien Gesellschaft, the leading German film-making company before the Second World War; associated in its early days with bizarre and macabre movies.

2 E. Phillips Oppenheim (1866–1946) wrote romantic mysteries.

Cheque, & then drew on it. So will you please do what you said you could do: get £100 from Dent, for the Guild Books thing,[1] & push it into my bank (whose address Mr. Webb has) *straightaway*? I'd be enormously grateful. Then the bank could send me the £150, & I could stay on.

Heard anything from Taylor (Donald)?

It's very lovely here; I'm working on a long poem.[2] I hope Ireland was good too.

Yours,
Dylan

MS: Texas

RONALD BOTTRALL[3]
25th April 1947   Villa Cuba   San Michele di Pagana   Rapallo

Dear Ronald,

A very brief note. Will you, very much please, forward the enclosed letter, as soon as possible, urgently, to Maniani? From someone in your most pleasant party, Praz I believe, I got one version of his name and address. From Osbert Sitwell, who wired me this morning, another. Praz[4] (is that the name of the sidewhiskered chair-lover?) wrote down: Maniani, 6 Via Nibby, Roma. Osbert wired: Gino Magnani Rocca Via Antonio Nibby 16 Roma. Could you, from telephone book and staff, find out his correct name & address & *send off the letter at once, please please*?

I'm going to Florence on Monday and will see Francis Toye,[5] *if possible*. Then I'll write to you again, with worries & questions.

Thank you for being so nice to us in Rome.

I will see you again, for more niceness, shortly.

Yours,
Dylan

MS: Texas

---

1 A paperback edition of *Portrait of the Artist as a Young Dog.*
2 'In Country Sleep.' All the references while in Italy to work in progress (often 'long' or 'slow') are to this poem.
3 Bottrall was the British Council representative in Rome.
4 Mario Praz, critic and author.
5 Francis Toye had been director of the British Institute in Florence.

D. J. AND FLORENCE THOMAS
May 5th 1947   Villa Cuba   San Michele di Pagana   Rapallo   Italy

Dear Mother and Dad,

Since writing last, Caitlin and I have been to Rome & to Florence—not on the same visit. In between whiles, we came back to Brigit, Llewelyn, Aeronwy, and little Tobias: all of them fat and contented by the sea in the sun.

Rome is a frightful journey from Rapallo. All travelling, over any distance, is bad. There are few trains or buses, and all the bridges have been blown up, or nearly all, either by Allied bombers or by retreating Germans. We went by bus to Rome: four in the afternoon till eight the next morning. And a damned uncomfortable bus too. The children could never have done it in one go. Rome was, I am glad to say in my little travelogue letters, Rome. We stayed in the oldest hotel in the city, directly behind the Pantheon. We had about five days there altogether, but, most of the time, just wandered round rather than going on vast exhausting tours of inexhaustible galleries & churches. We did spend one morning in the Vatican City, dizzily moving down marble miles, craning and panting in the Sistine Chapel which is more wonderful than I could have believed, staring down from a great height into St. Peter's itself, from huge cool galleries that seemed the size of public squares and corridors like the terraces of gods. We met a great number of people, writers, painters, musicians, mostly through the good offices of the British Council who, housed in the Palazzo di Drago or Palace of Dragons in the Street of Four Fountains, give sumptuous parties, in tapestried rooms, to visiting intellectuals. The Council, whose director in Rome is a poet, Ronald Bottrall, whom I knew in London, gave a very good party for us; and after it we had the addresses of many people whom we met on subsequent days. They all talked English, which is shaming to foreigners who can only just catch buses, order wine, & count their change in Italian. There was one American writer, Frederic Prokosch:[1] has Dad read any of his novels? The one or two I've come across are very good. One most learned scholar, Mario Praz, author of 'The Romantic Agony' & an authority, abroad, on English metaphysical poets. I made a couple of film contacts—nasty word—but they have, so far, come to nothing. It was very lovely strolling about Rome in the bright bright sun. We couldn't face the bus back, and flew from Rome to Genoa in an old army-plane: nearly everybody got very sick. The dock-front of Genoa is marvellous. Such heat and colours and dirt & noise and loud wicked alleys with all the washing of the world hanging from the high windows. We were there only a few hours, but the next day I took

---

1 According to Prokosch in his memoir *Voices* (1983), he encountered Thomas in Rome and took him for a drunken day by the sea at Ostia. Prokosch doesn't mention Caitlin. He describes long, surreal monologues in which Thomas spoke of sexual problems and said that 'my balls aren't working', whatever that meant.

Brigit and Llewelyn there—it's an hour and a half from Rapallo—while Caitlin looked after the small children. Llewelyn was very excited, and ate much glorious ice-cream in garish cafés & felt like hell returning in the bus.

Then four days later, Caitlin and I went to Florence: not such a bad journey: 8 hours by bus through wonderful country. We stopped at Pisa, saw, of course, the Leaning Tower, & then, in Florence in the evening, met a lot of young Italian poets to whom, from Rome, we had introductions. Again, we were terribly lucky in our hotel, right in the centre of the city, in the Cathedral square, by the great Dome, and the Baptistry, and Giotto's Belltower. Next morning, we met, by accident, in a sidestreet, Stephen Spender, who was there, just like us, only for a few days. We had lunch & dinner together. We saw the Pitti Palace & the Uffizi. I'd just been reading Romola,[1] and could follow the city, almost, from my memories of that. The lovely, more than lovely, Ponte Vecchio was left untouched by the Germans, but the other lovely bridges were blown to hell, and also the little hanging houses round the Ponte Vecchio, old as Dante.

And the next day we rented, until the end of July, a little house some five miles from Florence, up in the hills, looking over the city, among pines and olives, beautifully green and peaceful, a cool, long house with a great garden & a swimming pool. The rent, in English money, was £25 for $2\frac{1}{2}$ months. If my money holds out until the end of July, we will, I know, be peaceful and happy there. The garden is full of nightingales and orange-trees. There are vineyards all around us. We move there next Monday, May the 12th.

The address is:

> Villa del Beccaro,
> Mosciano,
> Scandicci,
> Florence.

From there I will write again, at length, & tell you how we fare.

We *do*, with all our hearts, all of us, hope Dad is better & that Mother is able to carry on. Mother, in her letter, says the sun was shining. I hope it will be a lovely summer.

We are all well. Llewelyn is a fat boy now, but he misses the company of English boys of his own age to play with. He reads a lot. Now he is reading the Three Musketeers, in tiny print, in the same edition I read it in. Nelson's Classics, I think.

This afternoon, they are all out in a rowing boat in the still blue bay. I can see the boat from our window.

I'll let you know all about food etc. in my next letter.

The English tobacco situation is dreadful, isn't it. Here, there are nothing

---

1 *Romola* (1863), a novel by George Eliot, set in fifteenth-century Florence.

but Black Market cigarettes. We bought a pile of coarse black tobacco from a sailor in Genoa, and are rolling that.

Love from all to both. Caitlin is writing. And you, please, write soon.

Best love,
Dylan

P.S. When I can buy a big envelope, I will send on some American reviews of my Selected Writings, which Laughlin of New Directions has just forwarded.

MS: (Thomas Trustees)

D. J. AND FLORENCE THOMAS
[card, postmarked 19 May 1947]

This is our house. Really, it's a hundred times nicer than this picture, which gives little idea. It's on the hills above Florence, some five miles away or more from the centre, from the great Cathedral dome which we can see from the sunbathing terrace above our swimming-pool. And I hope that sounds grand enough. It's a very big villa, with huge rooms and lovely grounds, arbours, terraces, pools; we have a pinewood and a vineyard of our own. There are cypresses and palms all around us, in the wide green valley below with poppies among the vines and olives, and in the higher hills. Our garden is full of roses. Nightingales sing all night long. Lizards scuttle out of the walls in the sun. It is very lovely. I am writing a long letter, which may arrive the same time as this. We all send you our fondest love.

Dylan

MS: (Thomas Trustees)

MARGARET TAYLOR
May 20th 1947   Villa del Beccaro Mosciano Scandicci Florence

My dear Margaret,

At last we've found, in pinewoods on the hills above Florence, a house until the end of July. The pooled ponded rosed goldfished arboured lizarded swinghung towelled winetabled Aeronshrill garden leads into our own (dear God) olives and vines climbing to a mutes' conventicle, a Niobe's eisteddfod, of cypresses. What seem to be armoured belligerent emerald wasps bang and bully the bushes; one-noted birds blow their brains out in the pines; other very near birds, which I can see, birdily fox me with very distant cries from the wrong trees. I can smell the sun. There is a swimming pool into which I have been only once—by mistake. Caitlin,

Brigit, and the children are seals and newts there. Mosciano, the nearest village, is thin and tall, shouldered like Peter Quennell against the church. (The Marquis of Q I met in Rome. Recovering from a prolonged debauch in London, he was spending, at the expense of an airways company for whom he was writing a travelogue, a week with the British Ambassador,[1] drinking, by the gallon, grappa, which, to me, tastes like an axe.) Florence sparkles at night below us. In the day we see the Dome. It is perhaps five miles away. To get to the city we suffer by trap and tram. But there's so little need to move. The pinehills are endless, the cypresses at the hilltop tell one all about the length of death, the woods are deep as love and full of goats, the house is cool & large, the children beastly, the wine ample, why should I move at all until July the 31st. And then to the lovely unfound house in Oxfordshire, the house built round the desk you bought me? Oh I *do* hope so. And thank you thank you for the desk.

Did you receive the postcard, overcheerily scribbled with messages, after a big red dinner, by Caitlin, Natasha, Stephen and myself?[2] Stephen was very gay, Natasha British as a hockeystick: I hadn't seen her like that. In flatheeled shoes she thumped the hot Florence pavements, gawky as an Arthur Marshall schoolgirl, shouting English, elbowing the droll Florentines from her gym-knickered way.[3] I have met many of the young intellectuals of Florence, who are rarefied and damp: they do not write much but oh how they edit! They live with their mothers, ride motorscooters, and translate Apollinaire.[4]

And thank you, so very much indeed, for the books and papers which came to Rapallo and which were terribly welcome, all of them, Sunday papers, thrillers, Listeners. And for your lovely letter and for all it said. Do, do write again, and soon. Tell me all your news.

I wish I had heard you read my poems, and Vernon's, and Alun Lewis's, and Roy's[5] 'Skull In the Desert'. I wish I had heard you reading, on the Macedonian lake, from my orange stamp-book. And the changing fish and the living fossils of that deepest legendary water! God's pulling your leg.

It is all so widely quiet here, and the valley vining away to the church towers. In the next room, in her rest hour, Aeronwy is singing an obscene song. Brigit's Tobias, a spotty frog-boy, is screaming in the lavatory. Llewelyn, in the garden, is trying to cut a boat out of a pinecone with a breadknife and has several fingers left. Brigit is superintending the screaming of the boy-frog. Caitlin has shut herself away and is learning Italian—undoubtedly by looking through the window at the trees. I am sitting in a half-shuttered room over the vineyard, writing to you who are

1 Peter Quennell denied being at a debauch or writing for an airline.
2 Natasha Litvin, pianist, Spender's second wife.
3 Arthur Marshall (1910–89), originally a schoolmaster, was a humorous writer, female impersonator and broadcaster. His favourite subject was well-bred English schoolgirls and their teachers.
4 Guillaume Apollinaire (1880–1918), French poet.
5 Roy Campbell.

in Oxford, and thanking you for everything always, and sending my love. Write soon.

I read anything in English.

Yours ever,
Dylan

MS: Texas

BILL AND HELEN MCALPINE
May 20th 1947 Villa del Beccaro Mosciano Scandicci Florence

My dear Helen and Bill,

I'd written much, much sooner—did you get a postcard?—but waited until we had a house of our own to write from. Up to now, we've been staying in hotels and pensions: expensive and unsatisfactory. And the Riviera sea was too tidy. Now, on the hills above Florence, some five miles from the centre, we have found a lovely villa in the pinewoods: beautiful, nightingaled gardens, cypresses, pillared terraces, olive trees, deep wild woods, our own vineyard and swimming pool, very tasty. There is a big room waiting for you. The cellar is full of wine. We live on asparagus, artichokes, oranges, gorgonzola, olive oil, strawberries, and more red wine. We have the villa until the last day of July. Can you come? We'd love it, so much. Write at once, and forgive this delay. Best love from Cat and me.

Yours ever,
Dylan

I will let you know all, if any, details when you write.
I am writing poems.
Are you married?
Brigit's son Tobias has just fallen in the swimming pool.
Have you got your passports? Do hurry.

D.

MS: Buffalo

R. B. MARRIOTT[1]
May 24th 1947 Villa del Beccaro Mosciano Scandicci Florence

Dear Marriott,

So sorry not to have been able to answer, long before this, your letter of March 27th. I've been abroad for some time, and changing my addresses frequently, and letters follow me like incompetent snails.

I'm glad you've been asked to write about me for the Western Mail—it

1 Raymond Bowler Marriott, journalist, later drama critic of *The Stage*.

has dealt filthily with me in the past, mostly through reviews of A. G. Prys-Jones who merely pins on a few irrelevant labels, surrealism, etc., raises nonconformist hands and misquotes—and for a South African paper, and also to broadcast to France. Perhaps, so much time has gone, the articles and broadcast are over. If they're not, and I could be of any help by answering questions in a letter, please do write again—and I'll do my best.

Regards,
Yours sincerely,
Dylan Thomas

From a typescript. MS location unknown

DAVID HIGHAM
May 24th 1947   Villa del Beccaro   Mosciano   Scandicci   Florence

Dear David,
  This is only to give you our new address, which we hope to be at until the end of July. After that, unless a miracle happens, we'll have to come back to England. I hope to finish a radio play by the end of our stay here. But more about that later. The long poem is coming on slowly. No Donald Taylor news as yet?[1]

Yours,
Dylan

MS: Texas

JOHN DAVENPORT
  29th May 1947 Villa del Beccaro Mosciano Scandicci Florence Italy

My dear John,
  This pig in Italy bitterly knows—O the tears on his snub snout and the squelch in the trough as he buries his fat, Welsh head in shame, and guzzles and blows—that he should have written, three winevats gone, a porky letter to Moby D. or two-ton John; but with a grunt in the pines, time trotted on! The spirit was willing; the ham was weak. The spirit was brandy: the ham was swilling. And oh the rasher-frying sun! What a sunpissed pig I am not to dip a bristle in Chianti, and write. I have so many excuses, and none at all. A few days ago I climbed a tree, forgetting my shape and weight, and hung this shabby barrel from a branch by my white padded mitts: they were torn neatly up the middles. Also, very slowly, I am trying to write a poem, moping over it every afternoon in a room in the peasant's cottage: our little spankers make so much noise I cannot work anywhere near them, God grenade them. It was so good to hear from you, and to know you will be in Florence in July. Of course you must stay with us, but I had better explain that we are some miles from Florence itself, up in the hills. To get to the city, we go by horse-&-trap to Scandicci and then

1 Thomas still had hopes of *The Doctor and the Devils*, whether as book or film.

suffer in the tram for twenty-five minutes. One can order a car from Florence, but it costs about 3000 lire—thirty shillings. But we will, of course, manage somehow. We are all looking forward to you *enormously*. Will Rodney be with you?[1] If he has his car, everything will be so easy. If he hasn't, it won't be such a problem anyway. We are in very beautiful country, and there is lots of room and wine in the house. No, I don't know Edward Hutton, but we were going to see him when we first came here: he wanted to let half his villa to an English or American family. We have got to know lots of the young intellectuals of Florence, and a damp lot they are. They visit us on Sundays. To overcome the language, I have to stand on my head, fall in the pool, crack nuts with my teeth, and Tarzan in the cypresses. I am very witty in Italian, though a little violent; and I need space. Do you know anybody in Florence nice to have a drink with? I met Stephen Spender there a few weeks ago. It was very sad. He is on a lecture-tour. It is very sad. He is bringing the European intellectuals together. It is impossible. He said, in a lecture I saw reported: 'All poets speak the same language.' It is a bloody lie: who talks Spender?

I am going to write to Higham about Phillips & Green; this week. Thank you for sending Green's letter.

Write soon. It will be lovely to see you here. Love to all from us all here. And to Tommy, if you see him, to whom I must write.

I don't know what my plans are yet; they depend on money, and not on mine. We have been offered a house in Parma when we leave here on July 31st, and I should like to go. Also, the Oxford Taylors have wired about taking us a house in Witney, to which, I suppose, we'd have to return. It's very difficult. I am going to write a radio play when this slow poem is finished. How are you? Give Kingsmill[2] a punch for me.

> Yours ever, & see you soon.
> Dylan

MS: Texas

*CAITLIN THOMAS
[May, June or July 1947]

Written on small (10 x 6 cm) pages with vertical rules, evidently from a pocket diary, headed 'CASH ACCOUNT—APRIL 1947' and successively 'MAY', 'JUNE' and 'JULY'. It was one of five items that Caitlin retained after she sold the letters he wrote her.[3]

Caitlin my dear, dear, dear: I am writing this useless letter to you at a table

1 Rodney Phillips was financing a literary magazine, *Arena*, and Davenport was to be one of the editors.
2 Hugh Kingsmill.
3 The others were: [?February 1950], beginning 'Darling darling darling'; a version of a birthday poem written as an acrostic of her name, 8 December 1952; 7 May 1953, from New York; an undated fragment beginning 'I love you Caitlin'.

in the Giubbe Rosse[1] where, after I saw you go away in a tram, I went, sadder than anybody on the whole earth, to sit and wait. I can only say that I love you more than ever before; which means, I love you for ever & for ever, with all my heart & soul, but this time as a man who has lost you. I will love you. I do love you. You are the most beautiful woman who has ever lived. Every morning when I wake with you, it is like waking with the sun. Now if I am never to wake with you again, I shall die but that does not matter because all that matters is that I love you always, for ever, my own— though you are gone from me—my own true love. I am sorry for all the bad I have done to you and all the unhappiness I have made for you. I am grateful to you for the miraculous love you once, a million years ago, gave me, and will never, now, give me again. I have lost you because I am bad.

I said that waking with you was, all those million years ago, like waking with the sun. That isn't the kind of literary lie you hate. I mean, like the sun which gives life and makes things grow on the earth. I love you, since I was born. I know you in the dark. I can see you in the empty street. You are with me when you are gone away. And when you are with me really, when I can see you you [sic] with the eyes of my body, and touch your body with my rotten hands, and can hear you speak, I am so happy that I cannot write any words, in this useless letter, to tell you how happy, how blessed for a moment, and how proud and honoured for ever. I am the [four lines and his signature are crossed out] sore on your arm, which I made, your unhappiness & your pain. What I crossed out with my pen was too shameful. I want to keep a little dignity, not because I like it, but because, perhaps, you like me to have a little dignity. Or, you did like me to have that. I love you. That is all there is. There is shame, and disgrace, and grief, and despair, but there is only love about which I know nothing except that what I feel for you must be love because, to me, it is religion, and faith, and the world. I love you, Caitlin. I think you are holy. Perhaps that is why I am bad to you. I love you. I am holding you now, and you are beautiful.

Dylan

10 o'clock, alone, in
this place

On the reverse of the second sheet are draft lines of verse:

> It is night now.
> The ~~street is~~ fields are empty.
> The poor are sleeping.
> ~~Sleep~~ Poor sleep is plenty.
> ~~The rich sleeper~~
> ~~In the straw & the rags.~~
> ~~hay~~

MS: Berg

---

1 The Café Giubbe Rosse in Florence. The poet Mario Luzi saw him there 'entrenched behind a small forest of bottles, a full glass in his hand'.

MARGARET TAYLOR
[2 June 1947] [telegram from Scandicci]

LETTER ARRIVED HOUSE SOUNDS LOVELY PLEASE TAKE IT MANY
THANKS WRITING FULLY. DYLAN.

Original: Texas

MARGARET TAYLOR
June 4th 1947   Villa del Beccaro   Mosciano   Scandicci   Florence

Dearest Margaret,
How wonderful you are to me, and to us all here. I drink to you—or, I
have just drunk, because it is elevenses on a sizzling day—in our red, acid
wine which bites nice holes; but the spaghetti, later, will cover the holes
like elastoplast. Thank you, so very much, for the telegrams about the
Thomas Manor,[1] the books, the papers; and the letters. It is so good to hear
from you, to know that you will write again, to wait for the postman—a
small woman, who walks twenty miles a day and whistles uphill in the
sun—and your handwriting. I liked *all* the books: The Hole In The Wall
(like Jacobs in hell), Dialstone Lane, Deadlier than the Male, Almayer's
Folly,[2] the Tolstoi, the thrillers & the Onion. (Thrillers kill me in this
house, at night; huge birds, like Crow but which I hope are owls, beak at
the window and whoosh; mice behind the walls squeak round in their
divers' boots; men in distant cottages cry Ho; someone teehees in the
electric light bulb every time I turn the page of some unconvincing,
semiliterate blood—ooh! there's a tap dripping in that drawer—and
thunder). The book Graham published (did you read it?) seemed to me
really convincingly nasty: I shall never go to Joe's Club again, or Sam's, or
the Free Lance, or the White Monkey, or the M.L., or the Horseshoe, or
Peggy's, or Ma Hibbs': I shall even carry my knuckledusters into the
National Liberal.[3]
Our plans for the future: turmoiled. We have been offered, I think I told
you, by Gino Magnani Rocca, who came to Oxford, a composer, a friend of
Lizzie's,[4] a house near Parma, big, cool, green, when we leave here at the
end of July. But by that time, or before, our money will have run out, & I
cannot get any more. The British Council in Rome will lend me only the
money for our fares back. So we may be returning, some brown, one

1 To house the Thomases, Mrs Taylor had bought a cottage with the deceptive name of
   The Manor House, in the village of South Leigh, Oxfordshire. When they returned from
   Italy she rented it to them for a pound a week.
2 *Almayer's Folly* is by Joseph Conrad. Other titles: see page 257.
3 All the places mentioned were drinking clubs, except the National Liberal, of which
   Thomas was, improbably, a member.
4 Elisabeth Lutyens.

scarlet, at the beginning of August: not the right time at all. If we do, do you think our Manor will be habitable? Cookable in, I mean? And with water? We'd go to see my mother in Wales for a week or two, we always do in August, but after that . . .

Do write soon again. There are so many things. I love hearing from you. I rely on you, your help, your letters, so, so much. Do you mind this pin-nib? Can you read me?

And Aeronwy loved her animal book, & Llewelyn his Alice. They are falling in the pool at this moment; not the books. Aeron's making a noise like a female parrot locked in a room with Heath.[1] Caitlin is cutting something with a scythe. Brigit is resting; Tobias is kicking her. This afternoon I go on writing my poem, which is the slowest in the world.

Do you remember André Frenaux, who came with another Frenchman & a wife one evening to Holywell Ford? He recited a poem of his. I met him in Florence, & he spent two nights here, reciting a poem of his. He is like a fat owl, though lively, & very charming.

What are you writing for Roy?[2] And when, and what, do you read? I wish you were reading on the Overseas programme, which I can get here on a cross wireless that spits.

And the papers full of Xwords and cricket scores! O my liver and lights, my bird in three letters, my Wisden teeth!

And now the house, the home, the haven, the pound-a-week Manor! Thank you with all my heart, from the depth of my teapot, from the marrow of my slippers warm before the fire, for finding a house for us. It is what I most want. It sounds *good*. 20 minutes from Oxford, ten from Witney, a Free House in the village, a kind old couple, fields, a garden: all I want's a new body and an alchemist's primer. Will you come often, very often? I am so happy and glad about it.

RENT Shall I send, to you, a couple of months' rent in advance? Or more?
KITCHEN Will the Electric Company lend us electric stove, etc, as they did to the Little House?[3]
BATH Will it be terribly hard to get?
WATER Is there water? Can it easily be fixed?
FURNITURE Will you tell me when you have taken it? Then I can write to my mother who will, at once or as soon as it can be arranged from there, send on some furniture, some good, big, ugly things, dressing tables, dining table, etc, which she has for us?
LET Can I get the house for a long time? I want to send Llewelyn to school either in Witney or in Oxford, & Aeronwy somewhere near, and work at my crochet there.

I am so glad about it; and so profoundly grateful to you. It means a heaven of a lot.

1 Neville Heath, sadistic murderer, had been tried and hanged the previous year.
2 Roy Campbell.
3 The summerhouse in the Taylors' garden.

I am so glad you are seeing Roy, and dear Reggie, and Bertie,[1] and the ship-launching turtledove, and unconquerable Lizzie out of the Pit.[2] Do you like Parry? And how is the green & beige, brilliantined tapeworm in the Little House? Not a word about him. Does he have mincing, sibilant gin-giggles every night? And do the all-too normal voles approve?

I am looking forward such a lot to your next letter. And to all your letters. For the house: bless you for ever. It's made me so happy.

Now it is cold-lunch time, gorgonzola, wine, strawberries. Two foreigners—I think they must be Italians—are being loud, & perhaps indecent, on our seesaw. There is one thing: I *can* say, in Italian, 'Do not be indecent on our seesaw'. The opportunity to say it is rare.

And thank you for everything.

There's a cheque with this for school-car, gas, etc, mentioned in your last letter.

Yours ever,
Dylan

MS: Texas

D. J. AND FLORENCE THOMAS
June 5 1947   Villa del Beccaro Mosciano Scandicci Florence

Dear Mother and Dad,

How are you both? It's a long, long time since a letter came from you; or is [it] that time moves so slowly here and one looks forward as much to the postman? or postwoman, rather, a little woman, too, who walks about twenty miles a day, up & down these steep Florentine hills, in the baking sun. Whatever it is, we do want to hear from you soon. Letters from England seem to take, on the average, five days to get here.

I hope it is sunny in Carmarthenshire. I read in the Sunday papers Margaret Taylor sends me that it's going to be a wonderful year for fruit in England. Here we have had strawberries and cherries galore, lemons, and oranges from Sicily—too early for the more Northern oranges. Peas, beans, asparagus, artichokes. I don't know if we'll be here for the peaches. We do very well indeed for food, though it isn't cheap, by any means. You can get *anything*, if you have the money. Not as in England. Recently there was an English Exhibition in Rome, organised by the British Council, to show what goods etc. England was producing, what films it was making, pictures painting, books writing, etc; and how much food it was eating. One

---

1 'Reggie': R. D. Smith, of the BBC. 'Bertie': W. R. Rodgers.
2 Elisabeth Lutyens's dramatic work, *The Pit*, was given its first performance in London on 18 May 1947; Parry Jones sang the tenor part. According to Lutyens, Thomas had been paid £50, years earlier, to write the words, but failed to deliver. W. R. Rodgers did it for £5.

person's total rations for a week were exhibited.[1] And the reaction, even among the intelligent visitors, was: 'Yes, I see. That's the amount of sugar, or butter, or tea, one person's allowed in England. And very small too. How much does he have to pay for Free Market sugar, butter, tea, etc?' And everybody downrightly refused to believe that *that* was the amount you got, that and no more, and that you could not buy any more. They just did not believe that the Black Market in England is a tiny affair. In Italy, it is the White Market that is the tiny affair. The ration for cigarettes is 15 a week, I think. At *every* street corner, in *every* town, men, boys, & women, sit with great trays of cigarettes, English & American the dearest & the most popular. (We smoke the cheapest, rough Italian cigarettes: Nazionali, all stamped as the property of the Italian State. These we buy openly illegally at any shop, at any corner, for about 1/2 for twenty—twice the legal price.) Vegetables we get from gardens here, but they aren't cheap either. The pound is worth, officially, 900 to 1000 lire; but by some wangling I cannot follow, the Bank will give you about 2000 lire for it. If you walk down the street, however, you will be stopped by any amount of touts and offered—at the present moment—2,450 for it. Into whose hands the English Pounds & the 'hard' currency Swiss francs and Swedish money go, I don't know. Some speculators are hoarding them against preposterous inflation. It is almost impossible to achieve any money perspective here. A big glass of good wine costs 20 lire, about 2½d. A small bottle, less than half a pint, of extremely thin beer costs about 60 lire. The horse & trap we go in down the hill to Scandicci costs 350 lire each way. Sugar costs about 10/- a pound. I don't know offhand the price of rice & spaghetti, but I do know that the poor can afford to buy only the rationed amount per week, which is minute; & spaghetti is their staple dish. Nor can they buy more than the rationed amount of bread & flour: also tiny. And not only the real poor. It applies to the professional classes too. Only the profiteering rich, the already rich with well protected money, & foreigners can buy the goods with which the shops are stacked. And English foreigners, at any rate, not for long. The Americans, of course, can bring as much money as they like into the country. I hope to be able to last out, financially, until the end of our tenancy here: that is, the last day of July. But it won't be easy: neither Caitlin nor Brigit is a good manager. And, after the 31st of July, unless a miracle happens, we return. The best news is: We have a house. Margaret Taylor, a great friend to us, has found it. It is in South Leigh, which is 25 minutes by train from Oxford, 10 minutes from Witney. Eynsham is 2 miles away. Bablockhythe about 3½. South Leigh is on the branch line which runs from Oxford to Yarnton, Eynsham, Witney, Bampton, & on up the Thames past Kelmscot to Lechlade. The house is called South Leigh Manor, but Margaret says that its name must *not* give me a dream picture of a moated, mullioned grange with coats of arms etc., but that obviously the Manor itself has vanished long ago and the house must be the old

1 Rationing of some foods in Britain continued into the 1950s.

farmhouse that belonged to it. Its rent is £1 a week plus a couple of shillings a week rates. It has three bedrooms, two rooms downstairs, a tiny kitchen, & a washhouse where Margaret proposes installing a bath. It has a good garden in front & a bigger piece at the back. It is down a small farm drive. Attached to the house at the back is a cottage inhabited by an old couple who work for the neighbouring farmer—but looking the other way, and quite apart. The village is very small: one shop, one church (Margaret says it is lovely), one pub, and this a Free House. But Witney, quite big, is only 10 minutes away. The house is 5 minutes from the station. I think we are very fortunate. Margaret has been going around by car for nearly 2 months, looking all over Oxfordshire, and this was the *only* place. She says she is going to move our Wentworth Studio pieces into it very soon; they are stored with her at Holywell Ford. All except the big bed, the beautiful studio bed, which, as I think I told you, was stolen by our tenant. Also Margaret has several bits & pieces for us. Now as to the furniture in Waunfort. Shall I let you know as soon as Margaret lets *me* know that she has settled about the house? and can Hobbs then [move] the furniture to Oxford, picking up Margaret on the way? You must let me know what Hobbs will charge, and I will send a cheque. We need, of course, every stick of furniture, every cup or frying pan, we can lay our hands on. We will be starting, once again, with no utensils or anything; I'll write to you about all this immediately I have definite information from Margaret.

I think I told you, before, that an Italian composer, Gino Magnani Rocca, whom we met in Oxford—he is a friend of my friend Elisabeth Lutyens— has offered me part of his country house near Parma, after July, & is coming to Florence this month to see me & to talk about it. But obviously I cannot go there without money. Anyway, there is almost a stronger reason for our returning to England after our stay in this villa. Llewelyn *must* go to school; he *must* be with English boys of his own age. I'm afraid here he is getting very fed-up. There is so little for him to do, with only grown-ups and two small, bawling children. And, God, how they do bawl. They are, I'm afraid, bad for each other. Aeronwy is once more rather fractious and hysterical. There would be *so* much for Llewelyn to do with a boy of his own age here. The woods are beautiful; the garden one of the loveliest I've seen. There are wild groves and streams: paradise for cowboys & indians. But he can't play all day alone. He reads a great deal: Dickens, Marryat, Arthur Ransome, Encyclopedias, Captain Cook's Travels, Stevenson, & anything he can find here, thrillers included. But he can't read all day, either. He makes elaborate paper games of his own. We have just hired a wireless, & he footles with this, getting the BBC Overseas Service mostly— but it doesn't come through very well. It's not much of a life for him, though he is very well now, and brown, and fattening out. On Sundays, a family from Florence come out for the day with their two little boys: the man is editor of a literary quarterly here, and has translated lots of my poems. But the language barrier prevents Llewelyn & his boys really getting together.

It is terrifically hot to-day: ever since June began. It is useless to try to do anything between midday and 4 in the afternoon. And it will get hotter day by day. Florence lies below us, through the vines & olives, in a rippling haze.

Today there is a fiesta in Mosciano, & Brigit & Caitlin & the children are going. I am going to work. I cannot work usually in this house, even though it is large. Aeronwy & Tobias make a terrible din together, though Aeronwy is good enough by herself. So I work in a room in the peasant's cottage which is part of this estate: a good room, small & plain, looking into a wild wood. I am working on a long poem, but so slowly. And after it is finished, I want to write a radio play. Has my Swansea broadcast been on yet? I know it's due some time in June. Do tell me about it when you hear it.

My 'Portrait of The Artist' book of stories is also due this month on every bookstall in the shilling Guild edition. 50,000 copies to begin with.[1]

I enclose a few American cuttings.

Can you give me Nancy's address when you write? She wrote to me very nicely, but I lost the letter & want to reply.

How is Idris?[2] Remember me fondly to him.

Is Mabli a home dog again? Write soon.

And, so far as I know, & I hope, we will be seeing you, as usual, in August.

Caitlin is writing. She sends her love.

And all my Love,
Dylan

PS. I'm sorry: I can find only one American cutting, after all, from the best of the American University-sponsored quarterlies, the Southern Sewanee Review. Others when I can find them.

PPS. I have just had sent to me—Margaret again—'The Hole In The Wall' by Arthur Morrison, & W. W. Jacobs' 'Dialstone Lane'—both in the new Century Library. Both excellent. Also a very good thriller—'Deadlier Than The Male' by Ambrose Grant. Worth reading.

MS: Jim Martin

DONALD TAYLOR
June 7th 1947   Villa del Beccaro   Mosciano   Scandicci   Florence

Dear Donald,

I was very disappointed not to meet you that day, so long ago now, in the National Lavatory Club:[3] I should have rung you to try to fix another date,

---

1 The book wasn't published until March 1949.
2 Thomas's cousin, Idris Jones, of Fernhill, 'Gwilym' in his story 'The Peaches'.
3 The National Liberal Club.

but was whisked off by trolls. And I should have written, too, long before this, but have been soaking up the sun here, moving around a bit, and trying to work. We are staying high up in the hills above Florence, among vines & pines and olives & cypresses, and living extremely quietly, though the children would turn paradise into a menagerie—which perhaps it is— and I have a floating stomach because of too much oil. Are you in England? I hope Germany's over, for you. I had a letter today from David Higham, who said the film-agreement[1] was still being drawn-up by you and whoever-it-is, and that Dent's are going to publish the script. He has not yet arranged terms with Dent. About the version of 'Doctor & Devils' which is now with Dent: that is, I gather the copy you gave Higham. Is it the best version for publishing? i.e. is it the one with most descriptive writing? If it isn't, do you think you could send Higham the longer version straightaway? It will not affect the terms he will arrange with Dent's, who have taken the script on the version they were given, but they may as well have the longer version as soon as possible. Higham also said you would write a short introduction about the B & H Case & the history, such as it is, of the script. That's grand. Have you gone into the question of reproductions of Trial Documents, drawings of B & H, of Edinburgh, of Tanners' Lane, etc.? And do you think these really necessary? They might help.

I am probably coming back to England the first week in August; lire will almost surely have run out by then. I have got a cottage in South Leigh, about 25 minutes by train from Oxford, but of course shall be in London a lot. Do you think the film-agreement will be completed by that time? And do you want me to do any work on the script while it is in production? I'm afraid I shall be quite broke again when I return, and living on bits of broadcasting etc.

Do write, when you can.

And are we ever going to write a script together? A really good one, completely our own? I hope so. I do hope so.

There's a recorded thing of mine being broadcast on June 28, on the Home Programme, which I *would* like you to hear.[2]

The heat is sizzling, the wine overpowering, the villa enormous. We have no visitors, but one has invited himself in July. One guess; J. Davenport. My, he gets around. Our hill will kill him. One postwoman's died already this year (though it wasn't really the heat: a house fell on her).

Have you Ambrose Grant's 'Deadlier Than The Male'? Not half as good as Patrick Hamilton, but still good.

Looking forward.
Yours ever,
Dylan

MS: Buffalo

1 See letter of 14 June to Higham.
2 A repeat broadcast of *Return Journey*.

JOHN ARLOTT
June 11th 1947   Villa del Beccaro Mosciano Scandicci Florence

My dear John,

Thank you for writing. It was very good to hear from you. Though I hear your voice every day: from Trent Bridge, at the moment. You're not only the best cricket commentator—far and away that; but the best sports commentator I've heard, ever; exact, enthusiastic, prejudiced, amazingly visual, authoritative, and friendly. A great pleasure to listen to you: I do look forward to it. Here, in the hills above Florence, I lead the quietest life I ever remember leading: it is sizzling hot, the hill to the nearest village is a spinebreaker, I am far too limp and lazy to go often to Florence, and I can work only in the early mornings and evenings: never my best time: I'm used to working from after lunch until pub-time, which in the country used to be about seven. Here I drink in the garden, alone or with Caitlin: we have no social life: I am a sun vegetable: I live on red wine, cheese, asparagus, artichokes, strawberries, etc. The etc. is usually more red wine. We have our own vineyard. The villa is enormous. So, probably, am I, after two months. I'm coming back in August: if the lire last till then. I was given some travelling money by the Authors' Society; otherwise I'd have been back long ago. And I'll be broke when I return, so any bits of booming—I heard Rape of Lucrece today; is Shakespeare over? and what is the next series?—narrating, etc., will be very welcome. Also, I'd love to write any programme you think I could do: *and, scrupulously, on time.*

Yes, of course I'd love some dollars, but I have so far, no poem. It would be useless giving you a chunk of the long one I'm twisting and gnarling: it's got to be read as a whole. If I do manage to write any short ones in between, I'll send them to you straightaway.

I can't afford to go to Venice. I've spent some time in Rome, in Genoa, in Siena, and on the Riviera. But now I can just afford to stay here on my sunburnt behind. I *would* like to go to Venice though. Perhaps I can seduce your girl: or am I the wrong shape?

I'll be ringing you in August. Love to you & your family. Remember me to Val, when you see him. My daughter has fallen in a cactus bush.

                                        Yours,
                                        Dylan

From a typescript. MS location unknown

HERMANN PESCHMANN
14 June 1947   Villa del Beccaro   Mosciano   Scandicci   Florence   Italy

Dear Mr. Peschmann,
    Thanks for the letter, and, again, for the invitation.[1]
    Though it seems, now, such a terrible long way off, what about the first
date you suggest? Monday, September 15th. Perhaps you'd let me know.
    And what about a reminding p.c. nearer the date—though perhaps we
shall meet before then in the George. Anyway, I'll look forward to coming.
And would much rather be put up—which is very kind of you—than take
the last train back.
    I'd like to read poems by other people, too, if I may. More of them than of
me.

Yours sincerely,
Dylan Thomas

MS: the recipient

DAVID HIGHAM
14th June 1947 Villa del Beccaro   Mosciano   Scandicci   Florence   Italy

Dear David,
    Thank you for your letter of the 9th of June. *The Doctor & The Devils.*
Yes, please go ahead with the agreement.[2] It seems satisfactory.
    I have written to Donald Taylor, but perhaps you would drop him a line
too. I may have got his address wrong: I put Hill Cottage, Hedgerley
Village, near Slough, Bucks. I asked him about his introduction to *D. &
Devils*, and also about some prints he had of Burke & Hare at the trial, of
the School of Surgeons, of Doctor Knox etc. Also—& this is important, I
think—I asked him to send you, at once, the other version of the script: the
one with more descriptive writing. Dent should be given a chance,
obviously, of seeing both versions & printing the one they like best. So
would you send him a word about it?
    And what about *Doctor & Devils* in America? I don't think it's up
Laughlin's street, but he should have first refusal. Or should we wait,
before sending it to America, for Taylor's introduction?

Yours,
Dylan

P.S. Could I have a few copies of the Guild Book edition of my 'Portrait of
the Artist As A Young Dog' sent to me when it comes out?

MS: Texas

1 Thomas was to read at the Reigate Poetry Club. He cancelled the engagement at the
   last moment, but read there about a year later.
2 Taylor was selling the film rights of *The Doctor and the Devils* to Gainsborough, a
   subsidiary of the Rank film organisation. He agreed to pay a proportion of the money to
   Thomas, who later received £365 in twelve monthly instalments.

JOHN GAWSWORTH
[card, postmarked 18 June 47]

Dear John,
    Here's permission to print a digest of my broadcast, *In The Margin*,[1] in the Literary Digest. And thanks. Sorry I haven't got any new poems at the moment, but hope to have one or two soon. I'm having a long holiday over here, returning in the autumn. How are things?

Yours,
Dylan Thomas

Any little fee for the digest can be sent, please, to Holywell Ford, Oxford.

MS: Buffalo

MARGARET TAYLOR
20th June 1947   Villa del Beccaro   Mosciano   Scandicci   Florence

My dear Margaret,
    Parcels, books, magazines, papers, and lovely letters arrived, safe as houses, safe as our house to be for which never, till kingdom or atom come, can I thank you enough. 'A Child of the Jago' is savage and black and satisfying, like a rape in the Blackwall Tunnel.[2]
    This is only a little letter, and I'll write another, longer one this weekend, full of the almost nothing we do every day and how we like it. This is only to tell you about the beautiful parcels we'd be lost without, and the letters that mean so much. You are meeting so many people, and so many good ones. Good Bertie, still making his Ulster parish calls on an invisible bicycle.[3] And cornucopian Rosamond. Has she given birth to Day-Lewis yet?[4]
    I do like the sound of Mr. Hall, & Mr. Bob Russell, & the woman of 'San Remo', and 'The Retreat'. And yes, in spite of your most true and convincing exhortations to us to stay on in Italy, we have to, and will, come back in August. We'll have, for one thing, no more money by the end of July, and no way of getting any. I'll have to borrow, as it is, from the British Council to buy our return tickets. And, too, I want to get Llewelyn to school, and among boys of his own age and language again. For all its sun & splendour, and food and woods, this, with no children but our own

1 This was the series title. Thomas's contribution, 'How to Begin a Story', appeared in the *Literary Digest*, Autumn 1948.
2 *A Child of the Jago* (1896), a novel by Arthur Morrison, is a violent tale of London's East End.
3 W. R. Rodgers.
4 C. Day-Lewis, the poet, was the lover of Rosamond Lehmann, the novelist, during most of the 1940s. They didn't have a child, as Thomas seems to suggest.

Aeron and unpleasantly spoilt Tobias, is no place for him. For little children, yes. And heaven for us, who love to do nothing in the sun. But the days are swelteringly long for a friendless boy, and utterly without incident. His company is necessarily adult—which was so wrong when he lived with Cat's mother—or shrilly infant. How nostalgically he talks about Giles and Sebastian: the happiest time he ever spent was when he stayed with you and us and them. *So we'll return early in August.* Where will you be in August? We *must* see you before we go to Wales to see my mother. And then we'll want to come back to Oxfordshire in early September. There'll be so many hundreds of things to do for our house before then; and we must meet, in London or in Oxford or in both, and do, quickly, all we can. I want very much to see you apart from anything, from house, from bath, from windows & surveyors.

I am so smart in my Oxford clothes.

Poor Ruffini. The letter about him, the Rapallo pension has only just forwarded. Cat has written to his father.

I have written a hundred lines of a poem.

Today we have visitors from Florence: a brood of translators & their wives, & one American professor. I can hear them gaggling. I haven't gone out yet. Or perhaps it is frogs and cicadas, one with an American accent.

What a miserable little letter. I'll write on Sunday, among the bells.

God bless you. Write very soon.

Dylan

MS: Texas

RONALD BOTTRALL
June 20th 1947   Villa del Beccaro   Mosciano   Scandicci   Florence

Dear Ronald,

Thank you for, quite a long time ago now, forwarding my letter to Gino Magnani Rocca, a charming man, and for your note.

We found a villa here, on the hills over Florence, soon after seeing you—and how nice it was to see you—in Rome. Good country, big house, our own wine, a swimming pool (into which I have been only once, by accident), nightingales bawling their heads off, neighbours who do us with great charm, and eight miles away, by rack cart and iron maiden tram, Florence, which I don't like a lot. I mean, I like the people I don't know in the streets, but not the writers etc, who are nearly all editors, I meet in the cafés. So many live with their mothers, on private incomes, and translate Apollinaire. They talk of 'letters'. Montale[1] seems to be an exception, but

1 Eugenio Montale (1896–1981), poet and critic, 1971 Nobel Prizewinner.

smug, with his English horse or Sloane-street wife, warmed slippers, dry wit, like old Ryvita, aloof tolerance, cigarette-holder, and private God laid on. And why is the British Consul called, so nearly, Greenlees? It's confusing. And he's a porker. But of course there are pleasant ones; there must be; I wish I knew them.

Did an acquaintance of mine, from Paris, André Frenaux, call on you? I gave him your name and the Council address.

Two things, one of them extremely important, to us, and most urgent. The unimportant first. I've been asked to give, on the Florence radio, a reading of poems, by English poets, written in, or about, or connected with, Italy. Can you suggest some names and poems. I'm illread. I said, Browning, Shelley, (but what Shelley?), Pound (if they'll let me), D.H. Lawrence. What about others, lots of others to select from? Landor? I have no books here. I'll be awfully grateful if you can help.

And now the expressly urgent thing. It's money. We have this villa until the end of July, and hope, somehow, to last until then. And, at the very beginning of August, we must return to England. But we have no return-tickets, and no money to pay for our fares. Indeed, we haven't, really, enough money to last until the end of July. And I want to, I must, get the train-and-boat tickets *now*. Presumably a great lot of people will be travelling in August, and I should book as long ahead as possible. From England, I booked nearly two months ahead. And the tickets *have* to be for the beginning of August, the very beginning, as we shall be homeless and penniless. I want to borrow £100. I can give you a cheque for this immediately, though that, I suppose, is illegal. Legally, I can pay £100 into the British Council when I return to London; or into your English account, if you keep one now. There are six of us, and £100 will just buy the tickets and leave enough over for travelling and incidental expenses—The incidental expenses will all, I'm afraid, have to go on things smashed by children in this furnished villa. I want to be able to go to Florence *straightaway* & book our tickets for the first day, if possible, of August. We'd travel from Rome. (Incidentally, will you be in Rome at the very end of July? I do hope so.) There's no need for me to tell you how deeply important all this is to us. And until it's settled, & I have the tickets-to-England safe, I shall feel, as I do now, unsettled & rather miserable. If I can give you a cheque here in Italy, all the better. But, otherwise, I'll write a cheque, to you, or to the British Council, *as soon* as I arrive in London. Edith told me I must rush to you as soon as any really urgent need arose. And here I rush.

Need I come to see you in Rome to deal with this (unfortunately) breathless bit of business? or can it be done by letter? I don't want to move if I needn't, as I'm trying to work hard, & regularly.

I met Stephen Spender in Florence, as perhaps he told you. You are lucky: you must have had him for days.

Do write as soon as you can. I'm sorry this is nearly all about money.

Unless I can get tickets *at once*, I may have to wait in Rome, without any money, in August, for weeks. So please. And thank you a very great deal.

Caitlin and I both send our love to you and your wife.

Yours ever,
Dylan

And the English-Italy poems.
Any not-translation Rossetti?
Byron?
Yeats? I seem to remember some.
Swinburne?
Any Bottrall?

MS: Texas

DONALD TAYLOR
[card, postmarked 27 June 1947]

Thanks so much for the letter. You sound frightfully busy. I'm looking forward to meeting you, as many times as we can, early in the autumn, and to hearing some prison stories. Good news about The Importance of Being Earnest. You've probably had a note from Higham, whom I asked to write to you about which version. Dent's will want to go ahead with printing almost straightaway. So let Higham have The Business of Death, though we'll keep the other, D & D, title. Hope the contract's completed by end of July! This is our villa, but it's nicer than this. We are all devoured by mosquitoes. We are going for a week to the island of Elba. Good luck in the Shetlands, if you get there with all the children. I'll get in touch as soon as I get back.

Ever,
Dylan

MS: Buffalo

D. J. AND FLORENCE THOMAS
30 June 1947   Villa del Beccaro Mosciano Scandicci Florence

P.S. Can't find the Spectator cutting. Will look again.

Dear Mother and Dad,

Thank you for the long letter; I was so glad to get it, but distressed to hear that Dad was again so ill and suffering. I hope, with all my heart, he is better now, or, at least, that there is not so much pain. Caitlin, sending her love, hopes, too, he is a little better. It is dreadful, all this distance away, to think of him so ill; and for there to be nothing that one can do. Perhaps the good weather is some little help. Is it still good weather? I haven't heard the English radio news for a week or more. We get the Overseas programme quite well on our hired set, and I manage to hear a few programmes I like: the Eric Barker ones, and the Books of Verse; half hour readings & interpretations, which aren't heard at home but which are mostly very good. They're the series I contribute to a lot, in London. I couldn't hear my Swansea broadcast. It seemed to go well. I've had a few letters forwarded, & one tiny clipping (enclosed) from the Spectator, which Margaret sent. Did I tell you, by the way, that Dents are publishing that Burke & Hare script early next year? Also that my new book of stories is almost ready; will be quite ready, I hope, by the end of this year. I haven't got a title for it yet. The long poem I am working on here is going very slowly indeed. Now the heat is so intense I can work, properly, only a couple of hours a day. My regular time, from, roughly, 2–6, is quite hopeless. The nights are almost intolerably muffling, airless, mosquitoed. I can't budge out of doors after midday, & try to work in the evenings, behind shutters. But the whole 24 hours are hot as hell; and the children, I'm afraid, are rather wilting under them. In Florence, to which I had to go a couple of days ago, the heat's like a live animal you fight against in the streets. No one moves who hasn't got to. Here we are in the hills, but wish we were far far higher. If only the sea ran up the mountains! Our swimming pool is a blessing; Caitlin, Brigit, & the children are in & out all day, like seals. It has just gone midday; I'm writing, in my pyjamas, in a shuttered room, with a flask of fresh wellwater at my side; and sweat is running down my face. *Everybody* has a siesta after lunch; the shops in Florence close from one to four in the afternoons. There's fruit about— peaches and apricots—but the Sicilian oranges are finished. There are lemons, too, & soon will be plums & pears, in a week or less. Will you have lots of apples? I read somewhere it's going to be an apple-record year in England. Hope so.

Now: about our returning, and our coming down to see you. We hope to return in the first days of August, but have no proper plans as to what to do when we reach London. We should very much like to come down to Blaen Cwm, as we always do, but are worried that Dad's health is not up to it. Caitlin would help Mother all she can, of course, & I'll do everything I can—especially as I hope to have some more money than usual—but we mustn't land on you, with noise & children, if it's going to be a nuisance now that Dad is so frightfully unwell, & in pain, again. The strain of our visit might really harm him. I could come down myself for a week, after seeing Caitlin & the two children safe somewhere. But I must hear from you about that. And, please, under no circumstances whatever, (if that's grammatically right), say 'Yes, come', if Dad isn't fit enough to receive us. To say nothing of Mother.

Our house-to-be in South Leigh won't really be ready until September, though we could move in, in a rather camping way, earlier than that. Electricity can't be laid on till September; but Margaret has got hold of lamps & an oil stove for us. About furniture: Margaret says to do nothing about getting your furniture from Wales until we have seen the house & have seen what furniture she already has for us. So we will go to see it as soon as we get back, & then write, or tell you, fully. I realise that Hobbs will have to be given plenty of notice beforehand.

Margaret has invited Llewelyn to stay in Oxford [*the page has been cut*] [. . .] 2 boys until they go to France for a [. . .] know he would like [. . .] famous Dragon School in Oxford. He'll be fixed in some good place, anyway. He wants schooling, & the company of boys of his own age, more than anything else in the world. And wants it immediately.

We are getting frightfully short of money here; otherwise I would take the family to the island of Elba for a week or so, which, I am told, is cheap and beautiful. And, by the sea, there is always something for children to do. Here, Llewelyn, in particular, is getting restless &, in the boiling sun, listless too. And we are all bitten, by flies, ants, & mosquitoes. But I don't see how I'll be able to manage it. No film job has turned up; & only one broadcast, from Florence, which pays very badly. There'll be no work to do in July. Everything closes, for the summer. I'm hoping to hear from the British Council. It's such a nuisance, having a little money in the Bank in England & not being able to cash a cheque here. However.

Write soon. Tell me how Dad is. Tell me about August.

[*page incomplete*]

T. W. EARP

July 11 1947   Villa del Beccaro   Mosciano   Scandicci   Florence

My dear Tommy:

> In a shuttered room I roast
> Like a pumpkin in a serra
> And the sun like buttered toast
> Drips upon the classic terra,
> Upon swimming pool and pillar,
> Loggia, lemon, pineclad pico,
> And this quite enchanting villa
> That isn't worth a fico,
> Upon terrace and frutteto
> Of this almost a palazzo
> Where the people talk potato
> And the weather drives me pazzo—

I am awfully sick of it here, on the beautiful hills above Florence, drinking chianti in our marble shanty, sick of vini and contadini and bambini, and sicker still when I go, bumpy with mosquito bites, to Florence itself, which is a gruelling museum. I loved it in Rome, felt like Oppenheim on the Riviera, but we have been here, in this villa, two months and I can write only early in the morning, when I don't get up, and in the evening, when I go out. I've wanted to write to you, and have longed for a letter from you. We're coming back, some brown as shit, some bleached albino, one limp and carmine, all broke, early in August. Will you be in London, or visiting? I do hope we see each other often this autumn. I am told the bitter's better, and I will be writing a filmscript to buy same. We *really* do have an enormous swimming pool (into which I have been only once, by mistake), and our own vineyard, olives, mosquitoes, and small Italian mice with blue chins. I have written a longish poem which I'd like to send you when it is typed by an Italian professor of English in Florence. I asked the professor about Elba, where we thought of going, and he said—it was the first remark I heard him make—'Plenty di fish-dog'. He translates Henry James and Virginia Woolf. Give my love to May and to yourself. Write when you can, before August if possible, and tell me where, if you're in London, as you said, last time we met, you might be, I can write. Now I am going out to the cicadas to shake my legs a bit.

In the very opposite of haste,
Dylan

MS: Ohio State University

MARGARET TAYLOR
July 11 1947   Villa del Beccaro Mosciano Scandicci Florence Italy

My dear Margaret,
    Parcels, books, magazines, letters,—how many, how often, how good. You are the best friend that a stout—oh, I'd love some—temporary exile could hope to have; and better than I deserve, for I do not write half enough to you, though always I am wanting to spider-cover a hundred bedsized sheets with news and moonshine. Thank you for 'The Vet It Was That Died', and 'Poison in Jest', and 'High Table', and 'Keynotes'—a nineties Katherine Mansfield—and 'Ladies In Crime', and the Statesmen, Spectators, Tribunes, and soft Punches. I read Punch from the first advertisement for Old Skipper Tobacco and First Eleven cigarettes, through comic servants, zurring farmers, dropped aitches, motherly bodies, dear old parties, to the last advertisement for Three Nuns' Whiskey. It's rolling on croquetlawns in Wilts with Low Church curates called Sidebotham, or breathing deep the smell of lawnmowers, vicar's shag, rainwet marquees, hot deckchairs.
    Helen and Bill,[1] hotfoot, gooseberry-eyed, worn-tongued, all ears, in

1 The McAlpines.

literary London, cannot tear themselves away and will not be visiting. Bill is too busy pushing a peanut with his nose up a long, long hill, and Helen is helping: she cannot provide a peanut, but by God (who is, Bill has discovered, 'intellectually muscle-bound'), she can blow! She can puff!

And John D. can't come until the end of July, which is too late.

I wish you were coming.

I have written today to the Telephone Manager at Oxford. I want a telephone very much:—not that I think that Christ will ring.

And, yes, I shall keep the ditch as clean as clean, as pure as Stafford Cripps[1] (from whom salt comes).

Llewelyn has been sent, by Caitlin's mother, far too many books for us to be able to carry back. So he is making parcels of them, addressed to himself, and sending them to Holywell Ford. Will you keep them for him? Then he will pick them all up when we move to South Leigh.

What was the hitch-in-the-house, too silly to tell me, that needed a spade-chinned lawyer to clear up? Will you tell me, one day?

Llewelyn's education. It is lovely of you. He can go to Witney Primary County School for a term, and try, then, to get into Magdalen School. I'll see Mr. Stainer, and Mr. Busby. And Aeronwy can go to Witney too. Llewelyn is forgetting all he learned. Aeronwy has forgotten everything except songs about little white Jesus. I am so glad Llewelyn will go to Magdalen.

Thank you very much for your invitation to him to spend a time with Giles & Sebastian before you go to France. He would like it a lot, but I think he wants to go to Hampshire as soon as we return to get together old books & games to bring to the new house.

And, anyway, we will not be able to travel to England until after the 5th of August. Probably the 7th. Every place is booked till then. But I'll be back in time to see you before you go away. And, after you return, we'll be very near.

My mother has written to me to say that some furniture is waiting, in her cottage, ready for my (or your) word to have it vanned to South Leigh. There is one bed only, a kitchen table, a dining table, some chairs, two dressing tables. Odds & ends. Mostly odds.

I must see the house before I go to see my mother. (My father is very ill again.) And before the house, you. I shall wire as soon as we reach London.

Caitlin will buy a nice Italian purse as soon as she goes to Florence.

My poem, of 100 lines, is finished, but needs a few days' work on it, especially on one verse. Then I'll send you a copy. The manuscript is thousands & thousands of foolscap pages scattered all over the place but mostly in the boiler fire. What I'll have to send you will be a fair copy. I think it's a good poem. But it has taken so long, nearly three months, to write, that it may be stilted. I hope not. I want, as soon as the last revision is made, to write, quickly, some short poems. I can't think of anything else;

1 Sir Stafford Cripps, Labour politician, had the reputation of being irritatingly upright.

which isn't, of course, true. I mean, when I think, I think of the poems I want to write; not of their shape but of the feeling of them, and of a few words. But I can, in this blaring sun, creaked round by cicadas, write for so little of the day. By eleven in the morning I am limp as a rag or Stephen's rhythm. And I can't work again till the evening, when I want to go out. My social life: damp litterateurs pedal from Florence; neighbouring labouring men come in to dance; we walk, with Guido the gardener, or Eddo the tractor driver, or others with shining hair and blue cheeks, to village cantinas. The nearest café, at Mosciano, is no café but a wine-counter in a packed, tiny, fly-black general shop. Sometimes, an Australian professor comes from Florence to shout Dinkum and Good-oh in the garden. A Harvard professor of Romance languages came with rimless spectacles and no lips, and was nasty. Luigi Berti, a translator, editor, and expert on English literature, visits us on Sundays. He comes from Elba. He said—it was the first English statement I heard him make—'In Elba oo veel lak der skool di fishdog'. Or, 'In Elba you will like the schools of dogfish'. He translates, for a living, Henry James, Virginia Woolf etc.

Good old Normal. I can see his voice now.

I had a letter, about my Swansea broadcast, which I'm sorry you wouldn't hear, from the old lady who kept the sweetshop when I was a child. She said, Fancy remembering the gobstoppers, and the sherbet-suckers, and the penny piece-packets, and me, Mrs Ferguson. And a letter from the very old lady who ran the Dame School where I learned to do raffia work. She said, 'I think I must be getting old, but I don't like children very much these days.'

Has Lizzie been, drunk, and gone? I hear John Arlott's voice every weekend, describing cricket matches. He sounds like Uncle Tom Cobleigh reading Neville Cardus[1] to the Indians.

Is your house empty at last?

I'll send my poem this week. It isn't the one whose beginning I showed you.

I haven't thanked you for the plumbers, for the Dali bath, drains, pole-talk, & everything. But I thank you all the time.

I don't think we'll be able to go to Elba. We are down to our last ten pounds, & the British Council will give me none. Luckily, I can get my bank in England to forward, through Cooks, a voucher for return tickets. But I don't know how we carry on until August 7th. We leave here on July 31st. If you don't mind, perhaps you could put, in your next letter, five one pound notes which I shall pay you when we return. There is little chance of ordinary-looking letters, so long as they are *not* registered, being opened. Unfortunately, five or ten pound notes, which take so much less room, are not negotiable here.

I shall be seeing you now, soon, if only for a little time.

Dylan

MS: *Texas*

1 Neville Cardus (1889–1975), music critic and writer on cricket.

BILL AND HELEN McALPINE
July 14 1947   Villa del Beccaro   Mosciano   Scandicci   Florence

My dear Helen and Bill,

What a really big pity, and everybody waiting, from the torpedo lizards in the hairy pool—remind the gardener to change the water!—to the pickaxed and pneumatic-drilled mosquitoes in the guest's bedroom—remind the parlourmaid to take the bottles and the gorgonzola off the bed! We had planned such a lot of things to do, and all with wine: picnics, prickstrips, titlicks, nipsicks, gripwicks, slipthicks, tipsticks, liptricks, etcetera etcetera, parties, expeditions. Perhaps we can all come to Italy next year, and do things on a pig scale.

We are trying to arrange to spend our last weeks here in Elba, but have nearly exhausted our money and are twisting for more. We return on August 11th, and will be in London on the 13th. Will you be at home? And can you put us and our bags up for one night? Llewelyn, the next day, will go to his grandmother in Hampshire, & Cat, Aeron & I will go to Wales to see my mother for a fortnight. Then we return to a house Margaret has found us, in South Leigh, half an hour from Oxford: near Witney: small and a bit battered, but right in a village and in good country. I hope you'll be coming down, a lot, to see us there. We *are* looking forward to seeing you, so much, and having beer and words: no, not having words.

The first two parts of my poem are finished. I'm working on the third. It's not as long as it sounds. I'll show it to you, please, when I come back.

The Best to John.

What a pity you couldn't come.

Llewelyn is teaching English to some little girls nearby. As I write, in the garden, I can hear them doing their lessons, very loud: Funny bloody fart, funny bloody fart.

I do hope you'll be able to put us up that one night: we'll be rather lost.

Are you writing stories, Bill? I hope there's a lot for me to read.

> Love, from both to both,
> Dylan

MS: Buffalo

D. J. AND FLORENCE THOMAS
19 July 1947 Albergo Elba   Rio di Marina   Isola d'Elba   Livorno   Italy

Dear Mother & Dad,

We leave the Villa Beccaro tomorrow, Monday, for the island of Elba. And, above, is our address until the 10th of August. Elba is 12 hours by train & boat from Florence, but there are several changes: which, unusually, is a good thing, for we will eat at the towns at which we stop. Elba is a much larger island than I'd always imagined: someone told me it's as big as the Isle of Wight. We won't be staying at the principal town, Portoferraio—almost certainly misspelt, as our atlas is packed—but at a small fishing village recommended to us by a man in Florence, a translator & editor of a literary quarterly, whom we have grown to know quite well. He and his family will be in Rio di Marina too. The hotel, or boarding house, where we'll be staying, is so small that it can take no other lodgers but us.[1] There are only 3 bedrooms, & these our large family will fill. It'll be nice, though, having an hotel to ourselves. And it is, as Italian prices go, quite cheap. I didn't think we'd be able to go to Elba at all, but a man in Florence, who works for the Italian Radio & is going, in October, to the Italian Section of the BBC in London, helped me out (quite illegally) with money. If he hadn't, we'd have been in rather a mess; because we can't get a train for England until August 11th—& our tenancy expires here on July 31st. The children, Llewelyn especially, are very very keen on going to the sea again. There'll be lots of sailing & fishing, and—which the Riviera dismally lacked—sandy beaches to play on. The heat will almost certainly be too intense for me to be able to do much, if any, work, so I too shall sprawl in the sun & go out in little boats. I'll have to work like hell when I get back. I've written nothing since I've been here but one longish poem. And I'd intended to write also some stories & a radio play. My Swansea broadcast, by the way, has had a great reception: many, many letters, from Swansea people, from Welsh exiles, from Mrs Hole, of Mirador, & Mrs Ferguson, the Uplands sweetshop, & Trevor Wignall, the old sporting journalist from Swansea, and several producers on the BBC. Also some good press notices, three of which I enclose. I want very much to write a full-length—hour to hour & a half—broadcast play; & hope to do it, in South Leigh, this autumn.

I've been expecting a letter from you every day. I *do* hope no letter doesn't mean that Dad is seriously unwell again. Please write as soon as you can: I am very anxious for news of you. And we want, so much, to know if Caitlin, Aeronwy & I shall come down to Blaencwm for the second half of August. I wrote you about it in my last letter, saying that we wouldn't all come unless Dad were fit enough to have visitors—including such a rowdy visitor as Aeron. Llewelyn will go, when we return, to Blashford for a fortnight: mostly to collect his books & games to bring them, in September, to S. Leigh. So do write, please. Did I tell you that Llewelyn will be able, once he is 9 years old, to go to Magdalen School in Oxford: which is owned & governed by the College, & is said to be one of the finest schools in the country? We're very lucky, through the Taylors, to be able to get him in. And there are all kinds of special advantages

1 Caitlin Thomas took a fancy to the proprietor of the hotel, Giovanni Chiesa. Seven years later, after her husband's death, she returned to the Albergo Elba and began, or resumed, an affair with Chiesa.

connected with Magdalen College—use of its grounds, river, etc—and special scholarships from School to College, provided by an ancient Magdalen grant. Until he is 9, Llewelyn will go, from S. Leigh, to Witney County School; attached to the school there's a nursery school for Aeronwy.

Helen & Bill McAlpine, who were supposed to visit us here, had to call off at the last moment.

Tonight, to finish our supply of wine here, we are inviting the neighbouring peasants in. There will be music—fiddles & accordions—in the garden.

No other news. This is a dull letter. It's only to give you our new address, & to ask you please to write soon & tell us how Dad is & how you both are & whether we shall be seeing you in August. Caitlin & family send their love. All mine.

Love,
Dylan

MS: (Thomas Trustees)

DAVID HIGHAM
July 19 1947

Dear David,

My address until August 10, when I travel home, is: *Albergo Elba, Rio di Marina, Isola d'Elba, Livorno, Italy*—just in case anything urgent crops up.

Will drop you a line as soon as I return.

Yours
Dylan

MS: Texas

D. J. AND FLORENCE THOMAS
23rd July [1947] [postcard]

We came to this strange town yesterday. If you don't get my letter before, our address until August 10th is:—Albergo Elba, Rio Marina, Isola d'Elba, Italy. I might have given it to you wrongly in my letter, before we reached here. It's the 2nd largest place on the island: 27 miles, the length of the island, from where Napoleon was exiled. There are about 5,000 people here, living by fishing & mineral mining. It's not strictly beautiful, but it's odd & exciting. Very very hot and blue, wonderful bathing. A world by itself. I'll write a letter tomorrow. Love from all of us.

Dylan

MS: Jim Martin

MARGARET TAYLOR
[23 July 1947] [postcard]

Arrived here yesterday. Very strange town, second largest on Island of Elba.
Our address is: Albergo Elba, Rio Marina, Isola d'Elba, Italy. It's very very
hot, dusty, tortuous, grey & blue, full of fishers and miners, strong wine,
music at night. That's all I know so far. Tomorrow we [are] going all over
the island. Our train leaves August 11th. We'll just be able to see you
before you go to France.

Dylan

MS: Texas

BILL AND HELEN McALPINE
[card, postmarked 26 July 1947]

A message from Albergo Elba, Rio Marina, Isola d'Elba, Italy. Lucky
Napoleon! This is a most beautiful island; and Rio Marina the strangest
town on it: only fishermen and miners live here: few tourists: no
foreigners. Extremely tough. Something like a Latin Cahirciveen.[1] Notices 'Fighting Prohibited' in all bars. Elba cognac 3d. Of course, no licensing
hours. Bathing wonderful. Regret your absence. Looking forward letter.
Returning August 11th.
   Love to both from all.

Dylan

Only source: SL

BILL AND HELEN McALPINE
August 1 1947   Albergo Elba   Rio Marina   Isola d'Elba   Livorno   Italy

My dear Helen & Bill,
   What a nasty, really nasty, business for you. Ted I always loathed. I do
hope things work out as well as they can. I'm terrified of courts. A clever
solicitor could make me confess to being Jack the Ripper. As a witness in a
Juvenile Court in a case of the alleged dodging of tricycle tax, I would see
the shadow of the Black Cap and the smile of the American Army
hangman, Sergeant Dracula. I'm sorry, too, for Mary Rose,[2] living with
that viperish, Byron-skulled necrophile. Our best wishes for the most
favourable conclusion to a sordidness caused by kindness. One moral is—
you must only be kind to us, in future.

1   A town in south-west Ireland, not far from Killorglin and Puck Fair.
2   The McAlpines' daughter. Ted was her husband.

Elba is a wonderful island. One day we will come here together. Rio Marina is a communist town: communism in Italy is natural, national, indigenous, independent. And the green and blue transparent yachted winkled and pickling sea! We are rarely out of it, except to drink, eat, sleep, sing, fuck, walk, dance, ride, write, quarrel, climb, cave & café crawl, read, smoke, brood, bask in the lavatory over the parroty fruit-market. There is no winter in Elba; cognac is threepence a large glass; the children have web feet; the women taste of salt.

We go back to Florence on the 9th of this month, and leave for home on the 11th. I will wire you as soon as I know the time of our arrival in London. It will be very grand to stay with you, once more, for a couple of days.

We look forward to you both enormously.

Again, may the trouble not trouble you too long, or too deep. Tonight there is dancing in the streets.

And all our love.

Dylan

MS: Buffalo

MARGARET TAYLOR
August 3 1947   Albergo Elba   Rio Marina   Isola d'Elba

My dear Margaret:

The heat! Old Elbanites on their flayed and blistered backs whimper about the heat. Sunblack webfooted waterboys, diving from cranes, bleed from the heat. Old scorched mineral-miners, fifty years in the fire, snarl at the heat as they drag the rusty trolleys naked over the skeleton piers. And as for us! The children all sun-and-sea-rashed, Brigit peeling like the papered wall of a blitzed room in the rain. And I can hardly hold this pen for the blisters all over my hands, can hardly see for the waterfalls of sweat, and am peeling too like a drenched billboard. Oh, oh, oh, the heat! It comes round corners at you like an animal with windmill arms. As I enter my bedroom, it stuns, thuds, throttles, spins me round by my soaking hair, lays me flat as a mat and bat-blind on my boiled and steaming bed. We keep oozing from the ice-cream counters to the chemist's. Cold beer is bottled God. If ever, for a second, a wind, (but wind's no word for this snailslow sizzle-puff), protoplasmically crawls from the suffering still sea, it makes a noise like H.D.'s poems crackling in a furnace.[1] I must stop writing to souse my head in a bedroom basin full of curded lava, return fresh as Freddie Hurdis-Jones in Sodom, frizzle and mew as I sit again on this Sing-Sing-hot-seat. What was I saying? Nothing is clear. My brains are hanging out like the intestines of a rabbit, or hanging down my back like

1 Hilda Doolittle (1886–1961) wrote poetry under the initials 'HD'.

hair. My tongue, for all the ice-cold God I drink, is hot as a camel-saddle sandily mounted by baked Bedouins. My eyes like over-ripe tomatoes strain at the sweating glass of a Saharan hothouse. I am hot. I am too hot. I wear nothing, in this tiny hotel-room, but the limp two rivers of my Robins'-made pyjama trousers. Oh for the cyclonic Siberian frigidity of a Turkish bath! In the pulverescence of the year came Christ the Niger. Christ, I'm hot!

But the Island I love, and I wish I were not seeing it in one of the seasons of hell.

Today is Sunday. On Thursday we go back to Florence, which is said to be hotter. On Monday, we catch our incinerator home.

Thank you, so much, for the £5. I hope you got my euphemistic wire. It was so welcome. And more, perhaps in the post now, will be welcome, welcome again. You are good to, & for, me. And the house! You find it, furnish it, scythe the garden, soften the bureaucrats; we are known, before we go, to the coaled & carred publican. Salute Bob Russell!

I will ring you as soon as we get to London, on the evening of the 12th or the morning of the 13th, and we will meet.

My brains are hanging out like a dog's tongue. I must go, looking for God, ice, impossible air, blister-biting blimp-blue bakehouse sea.

Till the 13th, about, goodbye.

I have altered several words in my poem.

Dylan

MS: Texas

Texas also has a one-page draft of the foregoing letter, with small variants. The verso has Thomas's notes, evidently intended for letter-writing:

The drunk jumping fullyclothed in the fountain after clearing the bar, saying: 'I am alone, I live alone, I die alone, I drink alone'.

—

Rio occupied by Germans, Americans, English, Algerians, X kilometres from Corsica.

—

The one-eyed street-cleaner known as 'The Mister'

—

I read a poem to natives. They clap, say 'Molto Loud.'

—

Moscato. Cogna con uovo.

—

Via Claris-Appiani, where the fruit & fish market is. A parrot-house, from dawn till dusk.

—

The music. Nostalgic trumpet. The dancehall, suddenly like a Chelsea nightclub—Dutch dolls on the walls, coloured trumpeters, etc, painted by a 1st year art-student.

—

'erroino, the anarchist drunk for whom all cafés are closed.

—

Gigi, the translator. 'Plenty da fish-dog.' Translates V. Woolf & H. James.

—

Campi di Mirana, with the white, hot, long sand.

—

Fiesta at Cavallo (?)

—

The gabinetto under the pink church tower. The church itself destroyed by a landslide.

—

Rico in the Piembino boat, Rico, who said, after some said Elban wine would make him zigzag, 'Buono zig buono zag'.

—

Nanni, Elvio.

—

Street names.
Old men hawking chunks of — (?) minerals, no use except as paperweights.

—

The boiling nights. Drinking Late di Almondo (?) on the rocks round the little lighthouse. Eating winkles (get the name), the eggs of sea-urchins (get the name). The boys jumping from trolleybridges, tinroofs, cranes.

DAVID HIGHAM
August 6 1947   Elba

Dear David,
   I never received your note of 17th June with enclosed specimen page for *Doctor & The Devils*. But I like, certainly, the idea of printing the continuity matter in ordinary type, not in italics, so that it reads like a story.
   Has Donald Taylor sent you the other version of the script? It is *important* that Dent sees that before going on setting up.
   I'll be back in London, I hope, on the 13th of August, & will ring you. Perhaps we shd have a few minutes together.
                                        Yours,
                                        Dylan

MS: Texas

JEAN LEROY
19th September 1947   Manor House South Leigh Witney Oxon

Dear Miss LeRoy,
Your letter of yesterday. Please do accept on my behalf the fee of twelve guineas, plus one night expenses allowance of £1.7.6. for my part in the reading from Cervantes' THE DOG'S COLLOQUY on the 9th of October. But my return fare should now be from South Leigh, not from Oxford, as my permanent address is now the above. Will you see to that in future? Thanks very much.

Yours sincerely,
Dylan Thomas

MS: Texas

DAVID HIGHAM
19 September 1947   Manor House South Leigh Witney Oxon

Dear David,
Sorry, but I have only just returned from town to find your letter of the 10th trying to arrange a lunch between Bozman and myself for last Wednesday. I had a note from Bozman today, saying he would be in Oxford on Saturday the 27th, and I shall meet him then without fail.

Very glad that Roberts of N and Watson proved amenable, and that Dent are prepared to advance the necessary money to repay him. Never no more.[1]

I see from the last accounts-statement sent to me by you on September 17, that I have received, as my share re film rights 'The Doctor And The Devils', the sum of £91.5.0. And then occur the words: '3 instalments'. Does that mean that the £91 odd pounds constitute the *first* of *three* instalments? And that my whole share is eventually to be only £273.15.0? I thought Taylor promised something in the neighbourhood of £400. I shall see him about this anyway. But DON'T tell me that the £91 constitutes the whole of the *three* instalments. If—and there bloody well should be— there are another two instalments, each of £91 odd due to me, when will they be paid? At what intervals? Can you find out? I may not be able to see Taylor for a week.

The Atlantic Monthly, who are printing my new poem[2]—you sent on to me a request from the editor—have sent me the enclosed two Exemption Certificates, to be returned, signed, at once.[3] I enclose the

---

1 Nicolson and Watson had bought the rights of *Adventures in the Skin Trade* years earlier. Dent were now buying them back on Thomas's behalf.
2 'In Country Sleep', in the issue of December 1947.
3 The certificates were necessary to avoid tax being deducted, in the U.S., from Thomas's earnings on work sold for him by Williams.

covering letter also. I haven't completely filled the forms, as I did not know what to put for the address of 'trustee or agent'. Does that mean literary agent, too? And if so, would you fill it up? If I should put only my own personal address, would you mind filling that up and bunging the things off straightaway? Thanks.

I'll let you know what decisions, if any, Bozman and I come to when we meet.

Excuse the typing. I can use only one finger of my left hand.[1]

Yours,
Dylan

MS: Texas

GILBERT PHELPS[2]
September 24th 1947   Manor House   South Leigh   Witney   Oxon

Dear Gilbert,
Hundreds of apologies, all real, all late, for never having written from Italy about the Lawrence programme and about the poems and stories you were kind enough to let me read. I did enjoy them, a lot, and think it absurd they are not being published all over the place. There are so few magazines that pay anything and that get to enough people. Life & Letters, ed. Robert Herring, 430 Strand, W.C.2., is independent, I think, and imaginative. And what about a story to Argosy, which often prints intelligent ones and pays well too. I can let you have quite a long list of American little reviews, if you like, though probably the best are Partisan Review, Accent, Kenyon Review, and Sewanee Review. Give you the addresses when I can find them in the as yet unsorted muddle after moving into a new house: a fiveroomed cottage, lightless, waterless; the address is a credit-snarer.

I must apologise very much, too, for failing to return the mss. And I'm afraid I won't be able to for another week or so. They are with my own papers in a suitcase still in Italy, along with other vital luggage, which dirty Thomas Cook & Son Ltd. should have brought over for us but forgot, the international bleeder. As soon as the luggage comes, I'll send all your things off. Do try to forgive me.

About the Lawrence script. Yes, thank you very much, I should like to do it sometime very much. When will you be in London next? Will you drop me a line. I come up at least once a week. We could talk about all the things. Looking forward.

1 The McAlpines were not at home when the Thomases arrived from Italy to stay. Dylan tried to climb in through a window, slipped and broke his arm.
2 A BBC talks producer. He had sought Thomas's advice about some of his own writing.

Excuse this dreadful typing. I've broken my right arm, can't write, and have to type with one left finger.

Yours
Dylan

Regards to
your
wife

MS: Jim Martin

JOHN DAVENPORT
September 24th 1947   The Manor House   South Leigh   Witney   Oxon

My dear John,

The above my permanent address, until they find us out. Do please forgive my not writing. I can only tap with one finger of my left hand on this decrepit engine. And sorry about no copy of my poem—tossed off in Florence one evening between a Mass of Life and a little Crucifixion in oils—but found Roy Campbell had the last copy, which he was dragging around the thin puce belfries of the Third Programme.[1] Roy had been the only person I had told, after lunch that day, that you were going to ask Redgrave if he, Redgrave, might think, some time or another, of reading it if he liked it. Some of the words swirled into Roy's babble-box, a little of the highly hypothetical information strayed into that vague and thorny veldt, and the result must have been what Redgrave heard from the BBC: that he was quite definitely reading my poem. Do apologise to him for me, will you? I quite certainly had not misguided the BBC on purpose, nor mentioned R's name but in private maybe-ing conversation. I shall be in town next Wednesday lunch: a week today. Could we meet? twelve or twelve-thirty? pub, Lib or Authors? I'd love to. Last time there were so many people, and I myself was just about an inch and a half above the ground: I mean, in the air, not sticking out.

I'm so glad you thought of getting a copy of my little egg from Normal.

I have rather a good film idea, which also might interest Redgrave: a dark and fantastic romance of the German 1830's.[2] I'll try to type out a readable synopsis once I CAN USE TWO LEFT FINGERS AND HAVE A NEW RIBBON. Absolutely unexplained capitals!

Drop a line about Wednesday, can you?

Our Manor is a cottage, but only five minutes from Witney and exactly twenty five by train from Oxford. Do come down. Only one small single spare bed so far, but I think the new Davenport, that sveltie, could manage

1 Campbell was a BBC talks producer, 1946–49.
2 *The Shadowless Man*, a script based on a nineteenth-century German story about a man who sold his shadow. It was written in collaboration with Margaret Taylor, but never filmed.

quite comfortably. One weekend snag is that the pub isn't open on Sundays; but others are only two miles off.

DO forgive me for not having written long before.

Love,
Dylan

MS: Texas

R. N. CURREY[1]
25th September 1947   Manor House   South Leigh   Witney   Oxon

Dear Ralph,

Many thanks for Indian Landscape, and for your letter. I've had time only to read a few of the poems, and enjoyed them enormously, even more than I guessed I would—and that after reading, and liking so much, several scattered ones during and since the war. Those I have read seem to me right, true, just, exact, and exciting, and I'm looking forward, a lot, to reading them all.

About your Arlott Poetry Magazine: of course you may use my Fern Hill poem, and thank you for wanting to use it. I'd be glad to read it myself, but don't know how John Arlott will feel about this, as I have read the same poem in another of his programmes. However ... drop me a line if you both decide to want me to read it.

Hope to see you soon. At the Liberal, perhaps?

Yours
Dylan

and excuse long
delay.

MS: (the recipient)

DAVID HIGHAM
October 7th 1947   Manor House   South Leigh   Witney   Oxon

Dear David,

First of all, to tell you what Bozman and I talked about, unless he has already got in touch with you.

A book of poems, 1934–1947, and to include two new long poems hitherto unpublished in England, for next spring. This depends, of course, on whether the Fortune Press business can be settled satisfactorily before then.[2] I hope indeed that it can, and that you can soon start contract arrangements with Dent.

The Doctor And The Devils: Thank you for your note about this. I have

---

1 A schoolmaster and poet who also broadcast. His book *Indian Landscape* had just been published.

2 Fortune Press had bought the copyright of *18 Poems* in 1942. Thomas bought it back in 1949. But no book appeared until *Collected Poems* in 1952.

not yet got hold of Donald Taylor, but hope to see him in London this week. Dent want to make a big thing of this, with a lot of publicity. And to introduce it in a new way.[1]

My old, half-finished novel, *Adventures In The Skin Trade*, which Dent, with raised hands, refused to touch a few years ago, and which I then gave, under that ridiculous contract, to Nicolson and Watson, Bozman wants now to see again. He will give me, quickly, a final decision upon it; if Dent will do it, please go ahead, David; if not, then let us try to sell it, in its incomplete form, reputably, and not, as I did, by back doors and Tambis.[2] When Nicolson and Watson, on receipt of Dent's cheque, returned you the two contracts I had signed, did they also return the manuscript of the first half of *Adventures In The Skin Trade*, which I had given Tambi? If they did not return this, would you ask N. and W. straightaway for it, so that it can be shown very soon to Bozman? If Bozman doesn't want it, please bung it off somewhere, so that I can get some money and, thus encouraged, finish it. I think Graham Greene would be interested in it: more than anyone else, I should think. N. and W. have the only available copy at the moment.

Stories: Bozman favours the idea of putting the old fantastic stories, the new more-or-less naturalistic ones, *and* the Childhood Memories etc I did for the BBC, all into one book, and not to publish, even with good drawings, the Memories as a small single volume. I agreed. These stories to be collected together and arranged by me *as soon as possible*.[3]

It is, then: *Doctor and Devils*, if the Fortune Press business is cleared, and the *Poems 1934–1947* for next year, as early in the year as possible; and the *Stories* to follow. *Adventures*, when handed over to Bozman, to be given a quick decision upon—though, really, speaking for myself, I would rather Graham publish that particular one.

And now, lastly and quite as importantly, MONEY. I've done it again. With a little money behind me, I've settled in a nice new house, bought a few things for it, behaved a little extravagantly,—and now, yesterday morning, comes a letter from the bank saying that, not only am I not as well off as I imagined but that I am overdrawn and, unless something happens immediately, several cheques, made out to local tradesmen, will be returned. If they are returned, it will ruin us for ever in this village. Quite literally. It's enormously important, in a narrow tiny community like this, to keep frightfully well in with everyone, especially tradesmen, farmers, publicans etc. And unless you can pay in for me, at once, a cheque from Dent, we will forever be *out* with the tradesmen, farmers, publicans, etc. to all of whom I have given cheques.

So. You said, previously, that Dent will give me a hundred pounds advance on *Doctor and Devils*. I know there is, as you wrote me, some small stickiness about this from the film end, but Taylor assures that it will all come right. Can you get that hundred pounds *at once*, and send it to my bank. It really is a question of about two days. In about two days'

1 This was the film script in book form.
2 Tambimuttu had editorial connections with Nicolson and Watson.
3 For whatever reason, this failed to happen.

time, unless they get a cheque, they will return those damned cheques and bugger us up here for all time. I have wired to the bank saying money is on its way. Please help. If Dent can't give the hundred for D. and D., then perhaps for something else. QUICKLY PLEASE. I shall ring you on Thursday morning, from London.

Yours very urgently
Dylan

It's damnable, after, to us, a momentary affluence, to return to the old hand-to-mouth day-to-day living; but it would be worse if the hand refused to give the mouth anything at all. So do, please, get that hundred, David. Bozman seemed extremely friendly, & optimistic about the future.

MS: Texas

DAVID HIGHAM

7th October 1947   Manor House   South Leigh   Witney   Oxon

Dear David,

I've remembered one thing since writing you, so urgently, earlier this morning. About Donald Taylor and my share in the film rights of The Doctor And The Devils. Your secretary wrote to me, in your absence, on September 22 and told me that Taylor proposes to pay me my total amount of £365 in twelve monthly instalments. I have received, in one lump, the first three instalments. Could the next nine instalments be paid to me, as proposed, *strictly* once a month and not in irregular lumps. That is to say, can I be assured of a monthly cheque on a definite day of the month? This would ease matters for me considerably, and assure our rent etc. for the next nine months. I'd be very grateful if you would arrange this on a proper stated day of the month monthly basis.

Yours,
Dylan

But the really frightful *urgency* of my earlier letter this morning remains unabated.

MS: Texas

DAVID HIGHAM

12 Nov 1947   Manor House   South Leigh   Witney   Oxon

Dear David,

I've just got home to find Bozman's letter re *Adventures In The Skin Trade*, and also your note about it.

I shall write to Bozman, today, and tell him that I don't agree with his ideas about the book and intend to finish it, as I planned, symbolism and all, in the form of a short novel. So would you show what there is of it to Graham Greene—also telling Graham that there is a *strict* plot behind the book, that it is all planned out, and that, if he feels any interest in it, I should like very much to discuss the *rest* of the book with him. I don't want any one reading it to think of it as just a fragment of comic romantic taradiddle without a real structure & purpose.[1]

Perhaps if you'd let me know when Graham's had it, I could give him a ring about a lunch date? What d'you think?

Yours,
Dylan

MS: Texas

JEAN LEROY
12th November 1947   Manor House   South Leigh   Witney   Oxon

Dear Miss LeRoy,

Many apologies for not having answered several letters much sooner. I have been in London, and no letters were forwarded.

Perhaps I had, straightaway, [better] give you a London telephone number where I can always be reached before 10 a.m., and in the evenings, and where any messages can be left for me—in case anything urgent arises. It's a nuisance not being on the phone here. The number is RICHMOND 5582.

Going back to your first unanswered letter of 31st October. I am very glad indeed that you managed to get the BBC to pay twenty five guineas for my poem, *In Country Sleep*, broadcast in 'New Poems' on 28th October. And I presume that you have accepted. I note, too, that they won't be paying the same fee for repeat broadcasts.

About your letter of 5th November. I see that the BBC now agrees to pay my return fare of 19/11d, as well as 2.15.0 expenses, for each programme in the *'Paradise Lost'* series; and that they will be letting you have their cheque for £7.9.0 covering expenses due for *'P. Lost'* of October 19th and 26th. Good.[2]

About *Book 4* of *'P. Lost'*, mentioned also in your letter of the 5th. The rehearsals were on Friday (7th) Saturday (8th) & Sunday (9th); and this does definitely mean that I should receive *three* nights' expenses instead of two: our station here is on a very tiny, & inconvenient, branch-line.

1 Dent relinquished their interest in the book, and Graham Greene offered £200 for it on behalf of Eyre and Spottiswoode, who seem to have paid half. But the book remained unfinished, and the £100 was ultimately repaid and the rights reverted to Dent.
2 Douglas Cleverdon's serial production of Milton's *Paradise Lost* for the Third Programme was broadcast in the autumn, with Thomas reading the part of Satan, earning 120 guineas plus repeat fees. He replaced Paul Scofield, Cleverdon's first choice.

Your letter of November 11th: *'P. Lost' Book 5*, to be recorded on 15th November. Rehearsals for this, I see, are on Friday, Saturday, & Sunday. Therefore in this case also, I should receive *three* nights' expenses instead of two.

'P. Lost' Book 6 Rehearsals Friday (21st) & Sunday (23rd). I should come back to Witney after the Friday rehearsal, and return to London *Saturday* evening, as there is no train from Witney on Sunday morning that would get me to the studio by 10 a.m. Therefore, I should receive *two* nights' expenses, and *two* railway fares.

Hope I'm clear.

Yours sincerely,
Dylan Thomas

MS: Texas

MR TURNER
Dec 30th 1947   Manor House   South Leigh   Witney   Oxon

Dear Mr. Turner,
Please forgive me for not having answered your letter long before this. It got mislaid.

I'm afraid my broadcast 'Return Journey' hasn't yet been published, and unfortunately I have no copy myself to send you. I am very glad indeed that you liked it so much. It will be coming out in a book of my sketches & stories either this coming autumn or spring 1948.

You wanted to know about any other prose of mine. Apart from the stories which make up the second half of my book 'The Map of Love' (J. M. Dent), I have published only one book of stories, 'Portrait of the Artist As A Young Dog' (also J. M. Dent).

Thank you again for your letter. And, again, apologies for this long, rude delay.

Yours sincerely,
Dylan Thomas

MS: Texas

ROY CAMPBELL
30 Dec 1947   Manor House   South Leigh   Witney   Oxon

Dear Roy,
Thanks for the postcard. You said, 'what day suits you best to do 3 & 4 Instalments of the W. H. Davies *next* week?' You meant, didn't you, the week beginning Monday Jan. 5th? If so, *Monday 5th* itself would suit me fine. Any time you say. And what about *Tuesday 6th* or *Thursday 8th* for

Instalments 5 and 6?
    Please drop a line, or wire, me here if this suits.
    Had a good Christmas? My inside feels like a flooded tin-mine.
    Caitlin sends love to all. So do I.

                                                    Dylan
MS: BBC

JEAN LEROY
30 Dec 1947   Manor House   South Leigh   Witney   Oxon

Dear Miss LeRoy,
    The enclosed BBC cheque—for what I don't know, unless for the 2
instalments, already recorded, of the serial story, Autobiography of a Super-
Tramp; perhaps you could find out?—was, for some reason, sent to me.
Could you have it paid in, and a cheque sent to me as soon as possible,
please? I'm dead broke after an exhausting Christmas.
    Best wishes for New Year,

                                            Yours sincerely,
                                            Dylan Thomas
MS: Texas

JOHN ORMOND
Dec 30 1947   Manor House   South Leigh   Witney   Oxon

Dear John,
    What about my cheque? Can you hasten it up? I'm dead broke after a
loud, wet Christmas, and relying on P.P.[1] Do your best—*as soon as
possible. URGENT.*
    See you, I hope, in London sometime next week.

                                                    Yours,
                                                    Dylan
MS: Glenys Ormond

---

1 'Conversation about Christmas', in *Picture Post* dated 27 December. John Ormond had
  proposed he write it; the fee was £50.

DAVID TENNANT
Feb 7th 1948   Manor House   South Leigh   Witney   Oxon

My dear David,
    Alas! I lost my little notebook in which I had written down, at Virginia's invitation, the date of your party; and your letter, travelling via Roy Campbell, took days & days: the little romp in East Knoyle was over, when the letter came. We were both very very disappointed, but thank you both so much for asking us: we wanted, such a lot, to have a few little quiet innocuous drinks and demurely to throw an armchair or two. I do hope you'll give another party one day. And I do hope to see you soon. Have you regular London days? so that we could, maybe, meet on one of those mornings and begin our decline together—with or without Tommy Earp, as the case may be. Tommy's address is: 4 High St. Alton. Hants.
                                            Yours ever,
                                            Dylan

MS: Victoria

CAITLIN THOMAS
Sunday [?January or February 1948]   Blaen Cwm   Llangain

Caitlin, my own, my dear, my darling whom I love forever: Here it's snowbound, dead, dull, damned; there's hockey-voiced Nancy being jolly over pans and primuses in the kitchen, and my father trembling and moaning all over the place, crying out sharply when the dog barks— Nancy's dog—weeping, despairing. My mother, in the Infirmary, with her leg steel-splinted up towards the ceiling and a 300 lb weight hanging from it, is good and cheerful and talks without stop about the removed ovaries, dropped wombs, amputated breasts, tubercular spines, & puerperal fevers of her new friends in the women's surgical ward. She will have to lie, trussed, on her back with her leg weighted, for at least two months, and then will be a long time learning, like a child, to walk again. The doctors have stuck a great steel pin right through her knee, so that, by some method, the broken leg will grow to the same length as the other one. My father, more nervous & harrowed than I have ever seen him, cannot stay on here alone, & Nancy cannot stay with him,[1] so she [will] take him back with her to Brixham [to][2] stay, until my Mother can leave the Infirmary. My Mother will therefore be alone in the Infirmary for months.

1 Thomas's sister Nancy, now divorced from Haydn Taylor, was living in Brixham with her second husband, Lt-Col Gordon Summersby, who had bought a trawler and sold fish to local hotels. She had gone to Blaen Cwm to look after her father while her mother was in hospital in Carmarthen. Florence Thomas's injury, and her husband's increasing ill-health, made life difficult for Dylan and Caitlin through much of the year.
2 The paper is badly creased.

No-one here will look after the dog Mably, & Nancy cannot take him back to her tiny cottage as she has, already, a Labrador retriever: they didn't know what to do but to have Mabli destroyed, which is wrong, because he is young & well and very nice. So I have said that I will take him.

My darling, I love you. I love you, if that is possible, more than ever in my life, and I have always loved you. When you left, going upstairs in the restaurant with that old horror, I sat for a long time lost lost lost, oh Caitlin sweetheart I love you. I don't understand how I can behave to you senselessly, foully, brutally, as though you were not the most beautiful person on the earth and the one I love forever. The train hourly took me further & further away from you and from the only thing I want in the world. The train was icy, and hours late. I waited hours, in Carmarthen Station in the early snowing morning, for a car to take me to Misery Cottage. All the time, without stopping, I thought of you, and of my foulness to you, and of how I have lost you. Oh Cat Cat please, my dear, don't let me lose you. Let me come back to you. Come back to me. I can't live without you. There's nothing left then. I can't ask you to forgive me, but I can say that I will never again be a senseless, horrible, dulled beast like that.[1] I love you.

I am leaving here, snowbound or not, on Tuesday, & will reach London early Tuesday evening, with bag & Mably. I could come straightaway to you if—if you will have me. Christ, aren't we each other's? This time, this last time, darling, I promise you I shall not again be like that. You're beautiful. I love you. Oh, this Blaencwm room. Fire, pipe, whining, nerves, Sunday joint, wireless, no beer until one in the morning, death. And you aren't here. I think of you all the time, in snow, in bed.

Dylan

MS: (Maurice Neville)

JOHN ORMOND
6 March '48   Manor House   South Leigh   Witney   Oxon

Dear John,

A coincidence. I'm going down, with Caitlin, to spend a week in Laugharne—from March 29 (Easter Monday). Half for holiday (undeserved), half to see my mother in Carmarthen hospital—(she's broken her thigh).

Laugharne, as you know, I lived in for several years, sometimes with Richard Hughes. I know the little town intimately, and everyone in it, including the Portreeve (this time, a publican friend) and officers. (My photograph, even, looking repellent, is hung on the walls of Brown's Hotel.) It's an extraordinarily interesting place, and unique; the ceremony of Beating the Bounds is, so far as I know, practised nowhere else. The town

---

1 Violent quarrels became a feature of their lives. Rows and fist-fights were followed by moist reconciliations.

would make lovely pictures (especially from the tower of the Castle, and from St. John's Walk).

As I am going to Laugharne for a week on the 29th, *would* you ask Tom Hopkinson[1]—showing him this letter, if you like—if he would care for me to write an article: about the town itself, the Portreeveship (though that's not the word), the inhabitants, the customs including the Common Walk, etc. I really do know it intimately, love it beyond all places in Wales, and have longed for years to write something about it. (A radio play I am writing has Laugharne, though not by name, as its setting.)[2]

If Tom Hopkinson would care for me to do this, could I be paid my expenses? I'm terribly hard-up, and was going, with difficulty, to borrow enough money to take me down & keep me in the hotel for a week. I can promise no repetition of the disastrous PUCK FAIR VISIT! Indeed, I do so much want to 'pay a tribute' to Laugharne.

Let me know. If Tom H consents, the photographer need not, of course, be down there the same time as myself. (The Common Walk, as you say, doesn't take place till Whit Monday.)

Anyway, do ask about this, and let me know when you can.

See you soon?

Yours,
Dylan

MS: Texas

EDITH SITWELL
March 15 [1948][3]   Manor House   South Leigh   Witney   Oxon

My dear Edith,

I've been away, and have just seen your wire. So sorry.

No, of course I'll try to read the Smart, but I'm afraid I'll fail *miserably*. Thank you so much for suggesting an alternative. I shouldn't really, have bothered you with my fears about the Smart—(though they *do* exist. It's a wonderful poem).

Thank you *very* much for inviting Caitlin & me to lunch with you Wednesday 31st, too. It sounds so mysterious. We'd love to come, & look forward to seeing you a lot.

Only a very hurried note because I'm going to London almost at once to see about writing a film.

It will be lovely, for both of us, to see you so soon.

Did I thank you for my copy of 'Cain'?[4] I do now, anyway, most

1 The editor of *Picture Post*. No money was forthcoming in advance, and the article was not written.
2 The early stages of *Under Milk Wood*, though it had not yet acquired that title.
3 Thomas wrote '1947' by mistake.
4 Sitwell's *Shadow of Cain* ('Edith's vast bad poem' as he called it to Caitlin) had been published in book form.

gratefully. Will you write soon? perhaps?

Love,
Dylan

MS: Texas

VERNON WATKINS
April 17 48   Manor House   South Leigh   Witney   Oxon

Dear Vern,

I'm going to write an enormous letter, very soon, to make up for this long long but never unthinking silence. I haven't written a letter longer than a page for oh dear! years, I think. And I'll send my new poem too. The long one in Horizon had 16 misprints, including Jew for dew.[1] They are bringing out the poem as a broadsheet, to placate me, though I'm not cross.

This is only to say, *Of course*, please use my Man Aged A Hundred in your Old Age programme, and I'm glad and proud you want it, and that I shall definitely be one of the readers in the programme.[2] I'll love that.

Will you write & tell me when you will be in London, before or after Paris: preferably both. And I will come up, and we'll meet and talk and blare & whimper.

We're going to Paris at the end of May, for the British pretty Council. Wish it was when you were there.[3] We are staying, for no reason, at the Hungarian Embassy. Or perhaps I am someone else.

Llewelyn (to go, next term, to Magdalen School), Aeronwy, Caitlin, & me, who are all well, send our love to Gwen, Rhiannon, Gareth and you. There's names!

See you soon, and I'll write *enormously* soon, too.

Dylan

MS: British Library

AILEEN GOLDMAN
April 17th 1948   Manor House   South Leigh   Witney   Oxon

Dear Aileen Goldman,

Thank you, very much indeed, for your very very nice letter: I'm so pleased you liked the readings from 'Autobiography of a Super Tramp'. It's a lovely book, isn't it, and I'm glad I was allowed to make it known to such

1 'In Country Sleep', in the December 1947 issue.
2 Watkins was compiling a BBC programme of prose and verse. It was broadcast on 9 May, with Thomas as one of two readers.
3 Watkins was to read a paper on Yeats in Paris. Thomas was to read poetry there for the British Council, but the event was cancelled.

lots of people who had missed it before, and also to recall it, and try to bring it to life, to people who already knew & loved it. (On one of the readings, the 13th I think it was, I was suffering from gastric flu, and it sounded like it too, or even worse. I hope you missed that one, or blamed your set for bad reception.)

And thank you very much for saying you want to hear me broadcast again. I shan't be doing much for some time, as I am busy on film-scripts, having just finished a version of 'No Room at The Inn' and just started a filmstory about the South Sea Islands, called 'The Beach at Falesá', based on a short story by R. L. Stevenson.[1] But I shall do an occasional broadcast: my next is in one of the 'Time for Verse' programmes, on May 9th. I do hope you'll be able to hear it.

Thank you, again, so much, for writing. Delighted to get your letter.

Yours sincerely,
Dylan Thomas

MS: Texas

AUDREY WITHERS[2]
[April] 20 1948[3]   Manor House   South Leigh   Witney   Oxon

Dear Miss Withers,
Every apology under the sun, and I abase myself, I knock my head on the stones, I cut out my lying tongue. I can't do it. I just can't finish this damnable London article. I never knew it wd be *quite* so difficult, to try to rewrite something half from memory. Phrases I had used in the lost original kept floating up and then drifting away, tangled my brains, stopped me from scribbling anything new. I would have been better advised by myself had I begun afresh, taking no notice of old semi-remembered words and ideas; but now it is too late. Did my agents tell you? I gave, while hurrying to the train for Wales, my handwritten ms. to a most trustworthy friend to post, who has since told me that she, for the 1st time in years, got herself politely tipsy at a party of little, damp writers, went home, haphazard, in a taxi, and left my stuff on the seat or floor. I'm so dreadfully sorry for all the inconvenience my careless trust in a hitherto most trustworthy friend has caused you. I do not suppose you can ever let me write for you again; but do you mind if some time soon, I send you an

1 A new and lucrative career, writing feature films, had opened up briefly for Thomas. The domestic film industry enjoyed a few good years after the war. Thomas did some work for British National, rewriting dialogue; No Room at the Inn was one of the pictures. The Beach of Falesá was the first of three films he worked on for Gainsborough; the script was later published (New York, 1963; London, 1964). His remuneration for the Falesá script consisted of £250 at the outset, £20 a week for ten weeks' work, and £250 on completion. The other two scripts carried similar fees.
2 Audrey Withers was editor of British Vogue, 1940–61.
3 Thomas wrote 'May 20'. Someone, presumably the recipient, has altered this to 'April 20'.

illustratable article, all written, typed, completed? Try to forgive me. Honestly, I *have* been trying to finish this London piece, but the vanished original is far too distracting, and I would be days & days trying a new angle altogether and new words.

My most Spaniel-like apologies, & very sincerely.

Yours,
Dylan Thomas

MS: Fales Library, New York University

*T. C. H. PARRY[1]

April 20 1948   Manor House   South Leigh   Witney   Oxon

Dear Mr Parry,

I owe you a thousand apologies for what must appear my gross discourtesy in not writing to you, long before this, to explain my unavoidable absence on April the thirteenth. My mother, I learnt by wire, had been rushed into hospital, and I caught the next train for Wales, unfortunately leaving behind me my notebook and all the correspondence about my intended reading. I've got a shocking memory, and the actual date of the reading completely slipped my mind, and I had no means of checking up. I was shocked to see, on coming home here, that the date of my visit to you was well past, and that I could do nothing about it. I *do* hope that these seemingly thin and inadequate excuses will, at least, suffice to exonerate me from the severest charges: that I am careless and forgetful, although at a time of severe domestic strain, I cannot deny.

May I repeat my deep apologies for the inconvenience & annoyance I must have caused and is [it] too much to hope that, some time later, I could be invited again, this time to turn up punctually on pains of rack and excommunication?

Yours sincerely,
Dylan Thomas

MS: University of Wales, Bangor

CORDELIA SEWELL[2]

April 21st 1948 as from Manor House   South Leigh   Witney   Nr Oxon

My dear Cordelia,

Re. our conversation tonight on the telephone. You said that you agreed that my Mother and Father should, on Wednesday, the 28th April, come along to your cottage. My Mother will have to sleep, and stay, in the

1 Principal of Cartrefle Teachers' Training College, Wrexham.
2 Cordelia Sewell was a friend of the Thomases, and had a cottage in South Leigh.

downstairs bed. I am assuming that the rent of your cottage is three guineas per week, & am enclosing cheque for one month from Wednesday the 28th April. You will, by this time, have talked to Caitlin & worked out various things. The 'various things' include, naturally, your coming & going: Mary (ours, that is, Caitlin's, Mary) will look after my M & F & me, and Caitlin will be to and fro helping them (and you) as much as we can.

Yours ever,
Dylan

MS: National Library of Wales

CAITLIN THOMAS
Thursday [probably 22 April 1948]   In the Train to Brixham
[*written on reverse of letter from David Higham dated 19 April 1948*]

My own Cat my darling whom I love forever, my dear,

I'm writing this in the long train. Five hours of it. Steamed pig-fish and dripping cabbage and soapsud lager for mock-lunch. Three sleeping bores in the carriage, one with a bucket mouth. I tried to go yesterday, but was not called early enough, by Eileen, to catch the eleven morning train, which is the only good, or even reasonable, one. I phoned Nancy last night. My mother is coming out of hospital this coming Wednesday. No woman has been found. She & Dad, in an ambulance, will be coming to us on Wednesday. I also, as you probably know by this time, rang up Cordelia. Her cottage will be free—except for occasional visits by her & Black Beauty—on Wednesday, when Nicola & Vee return to school. So I am going to take the cottage temporarily for my people. Mary will have to look after them all. She can, aided by us. Please say you think this is a *brilliant* idea. I think it is. I will leave Brixham Saturday morning & be back in sweet Sow Lye Saturday night.[1] I love you more than ever. I think of you all the time. I love you, my dear dear. Here is an open cheque for Mags or [*illegible*—?Alice] Green to cash. I love you with my heart & my head & my body.

D.

If you want to ring me, the number is: BRIXHAM 3318. D.

MS: Andrew MacAdie

1 'Sow Lye', a surviving form of 'South Leigh'.

KATHLEEN GURNER
April 27 1948   Manor House   South Leigh   Witney   Oxon

Dear Miss Gurner,
   I'm so sorry there's been this bother about copyright permission for my
poem 'October' to be used in your Anthology for Schools. You certainly
have my own permission, & I suggest you write to my agent, David
Higham, Pearn, Pollinger, & Higham Ltd, 39–40 Bedford Street, London
W.C.2., saying that you have my permission & asking them to obtain
Dent's as quickly as possible. This they will do. What a nuisance it is!
                                             Yours sincerely,
                                             Dylan Thomas
MS: Texas

ROBERT POCOCK[1]
[?29th] April 48[2]   Manor House   South Leigh   Witney   Oxon

Dear Bob,
   11.30 George this Saturday. Nicholson's XXXXX or Younger's Scotch.
Lunch upstairs if greedy or faint.[3] Cricket, Oxford v. Gloucester. In the
evening, in Witney, Cordelia and two odd friends, the Colgroves, will
probably come with their van and take us to some country houses—public.
My father & mother arrive to stay with us on Friday, which will imprison
Caitlin, but she will be with us at least on Saturday morning. The landlord
of the Fleece has nearly lost his eye, our dog Mabli has eczema, our cat
Satan had mange and is now dead, Caitlin has gone to London with
Margaret Taylor & left me quite alone, the house beer has run out, I am 3
weeks behind with my filmscript, not having started it yet, my gas fire has
just exploded, I have flooded the kitchen with boiling soup, I am broke,
Caitlin has taken the cigarettes, I was suddenly sick in the middle of the
night, Phil has just sent me his 25 shilling book about Hampton Court,
rabbits have eaten the lettuce, and seven cows, who have opened the gate,
are trying to get into the lavatory. There is no news.
                                             Ever,
                                             Dylan
MS: Texas

1 A BBC producer and friend.
2 '29th' is crookedly written and could be some other date.
3 The George is in Oxford.

GEOFFREY GRIGSON
29 April 1948   Manor House   South Leigh   Witney   Oxfordshire

Dear Geoffrey,
   I didn't get your first letter, nor the one to Glyn Jones. Your letter, April 18, has just reached me. I've had lots of addresses lately. Yes, of course, do use the poem from my Eighteen Poems. What are you editing? Another Stuffed Owl?[1] I don't know Glyn Jones's address, but a letter sent c/o Gwyn Jones, Hillside, Bryn-y-Môr Road, Aberystwyth, would be sure to get him.
   Yes, I'm alive all right. And you?
                                                    Yours,
                                                    Dylan
MS: Texas

DAVID HIGHAM
May 3 '48   Manor House   South Leigh   Witney   Oxon

Dear David,
   No, Donald Taylor hasn't paid anything at all to me direct. I wondered what had happened. *Do* please go ahead with the *extraction*. I am, curiously enough, broke.
   About Denys Val Baker and his using my poem 'In Country Sleep' in his Little Reviews Anthology. Okay, of course, and thanks for getting a little more from him than he wanted to give, but, please, *insist* on my having a *proof* sent to me. The poem, as printed in Horizon, had something like *16* misprints, and that is the copy Val Baker will use.
                                                    Yours,
                                                    Dylan
MS: Texas

1 *The Stuffed Owl*, 'An Anthology of Bad Verse', edited by D. B. Wyndham Lewis and Charles Lee, was first published in 1930.

DAVID HIGHAM
14 May 1948   Manor House   South Leigh   Witney   Oxon

Dear David,
    Thanks for yours of 13th, and for straightening things out with Andrews
(who's a marvel, to get it down to £85).[1]
    I enclose, signed, the authorisation you wanted.
                                                        Yours,
                                                        Dylan

No word from Donald Taylor?

MS: Texas

C. GORDON GLOVER
May 25 1948   Manor House   South Leigh   Witney   Oxon

Dear Gordon,
    Thanks for 'A Poet In A Pub'. The titles you boys think up![2]
    Just a few points.
    I am 33, not 31.
    I don't think I used, of my father, the words 'the finest Shakespeare
reader of his day'. The phrasing seems foreign. If anything like it *is* needed,
couldn't it be: 'a great reader-aloud of Shakespeare'? or something like
that? As it stands, the phrase could mean that, of all people of this time
who read Shakespeare, he was the most indefatigable, omnivorous, etc. etc.
I meant only that his reading aloud of Shakespeare in class seemed to me,
and to nearly every other boy in the school, very grand indeed; all the boys
who were with me at school, & who have spoken to me since, agree that it
was his reading that made them, for the first time, see that there *was*, after
all, *something* in Shakespeare & all this poetry; and a great number of boys
have gone on reading poetry *after* school life, because of those readings. I
think that a phrase such as I suggested above would cover this point.
    I would not be surprised—you are quite right—if people said I was a sort
of modern Villon. But my lack of surprise would be caused *not* by the fact
that I think I resemble, in any way in the world, a sort of modern Villon,
but because I am used to listening to balls. I am about as much a modern

1 Leslie Andrews, an accountant, had given this estimate of Thomas's liability for arrears
  of income tax. He was brought in after Margaret Taylor visited David Higham the
  previous January, to discuss the growing muddle of Thomas's tax situation: for the first
  time in his life he was earning substantial fees as a freelance, and needed to provide
  against the Inland Revenue's day of reckoning.
2 Glover, journalist and broadcaster, had interviewed Thomas, and sent him the draft of
  an article for the magazine *Band Wagon*.

Villon—I cannot, incidentally, read French—as I am a modern Joanna Southcott, Raleigh, Artemus Ward, or Luther.[1]

I wasn't at Mrs Hole's kindergarten with either Dan Jones or Fred Janes (n, not m), whom I met later.

Do you think the extract, about 'Break break break', from my autobiographical sketches,[2] is confused by mixing it up with words not in the extract? Or not? I don't, myself, think that a reader would know that this extract came from my book; or, alternatively, I think that the reader would think the whole thing, including your interpolations, came from my book. It's very tiny, anyway, & doesn't really matter. Just a little point, sir.

It is true to say that I often cover perhaps a hundred sheets of paper in the construction of one poem. But what I said was, that I often covered more than a hundred sheets of paper with drafts, revisions, rewritings, ravings, doodlings, & intensely concentrated work to construct a single verse. Nor is this anything to be proud, or ashamed, of; I do not think any better of a verse because it takes weeks, and quires, to complete it. It is just that I work extremely slowly, painfully, in seclusion.

It was Aeronwy who was born in a blitz—as though it mattered!—not Llewelyn, who anticipated the war by more than 6 months.

Do, please, for old crimes' sake, cut out my spontaneous, and quite unbelieved-in, disparagement of village cricket. It was something I said for something to say. I'd be *awfully* pleased to see *all* references to cricket omitted. Let's leave cricket to Jack Squire; I have no ambition to join his jolly Georgian squirearchy.[3]

Finally, as a 'Profile', your admirable article should, I think, have taken, however parenthetically, other aspects of this impermanent, oscillating, rag-bag character into consideration: aspects, I admit, of which you, with great good luck, could have little first-hand knowledge: my basic melancholy; sullen glooms and black studies; atrocious temper; protracted vegetable comas; silences and disappearances; terror of death, heights, strokes, mice; shyness and gaucheness; pompous, platitudinary, repetitive periods of bottom-raking boredom and boorishness; soulburn, heartdoubt, headspin; my all-embracing ignorance; my still only half-squashed and forgotten bourgeois petty values; all my excruciating whimsicality; all my sloth; all my eye!

1 Joanna Southcott was a farmer's daughter (d. 1814) who claimed supernatural powers. She left a sealed box which was supposed to contain divine information if opened in the presence of twenty-four bishops. Opened in 1927, it contained a woman's nightcap and a pistol. Artemus Ward, pen-name of Charles Farrar Browne (1834–67), American humorous writer.

2 'The Fight', in *Portrait of the Artist as a Young Dog*:
'Dan kicked my shins in the silence before Mr Bevan said: 'The influence is obvious, of course. "Break, break, break, on thy cold, grey stones, O sea".'
'Hubert knows Tennyson backwards', said Mrs Bevan, 'backwards.'

3 Another disparaging reference to the poet John Squire, whose school of traditional writers was sometimes mocked as 'the Squirearchy'.

I enclose the article, with many thanks. What a fellow I sound! Thank God I don't have to meet myself socially, listen to myself, or except when reluctantly shaving, see that red, blubbery circle mounted on ballooning body, that down-at-soul hick, hack, hock-loving hake which now inscribes itself,

> Yours ever,
> Dylan

MS: Texas

HERMANN PESCHMANN

23 June 1948   Manor House   South Leigh   Witney   Oxon

Dear Mr. Peschmann,

Forgive my not answering your letter before this: I've been away on various jobs about the country, and on arriving home found my family all measled, and had to cook & char.

Thank you for inviting me to contribute a brief prefatory note to your anthology—which, by the way, I wish the best of luck.[1] But do you very much mind if, with reluctance, I say I'd rather not? I know your anthology's going to be very good; it isn't that; it's just that I'm laying off making any pronouncement about modern poetry, any comment, even, for the time being: for many reasons: I'm afraid this sounds more pompous than any pronouncement would, but I do hope you know what I mean. I'm not writing any poetry myself these days, & don't feel qualified to write about anyone else's.

I still feel very guilty, by the way, about that disastrous non-turning-up at your society. I hope to make up for that one day, if you still want me to.

> Yours sincerely,
> Dylan Thomas

MS: the recipient

MRS F. I. WEBLEY

June 25 1948   Manor House   South Leigh   Witney   Oxon

Dear Madam,

Please forgive me for not answering, before this, your letter of June 14.

I thank you very much indeed for your kind invitation to me to lecture to the Newport & Mon. Literary Club, but am afraid that, reluctantly, I must

1 *The Voice of Poetry*, 1930–50 (Evans, 1950).

decline. I am going abroad in the early spring of next year.

Thank you again for the invitation.

Yours faithfully,
Dylan Thomas

MS: Location unknown

DAVID HIGHAM

25 June 1948   Manor House   South Leigh   Witney   Oxon

Dear David,

As you see, from the enclosed, I want to open a quarterly credit account with Blackwell's.

Will you support me as a reference?

If so, will you either send enclosed back to me or bung it along to Blackwell's?

Hope you don't mind. If you do, doesn't matter. Let me know, though.

Yours,
Dylan

MS: Texas

HERMANN PESCHMANN

[?July 1948]   Manor House   South Leigh   Witney   Oxon

Dear Mr. Peschmann,

Sorry for the delay: I've been away.

Formal consent to print my four poems in your anthology, okay by me. But do you mind getting in touch with my agent, David Higham, of Pearn, Pollinger, & Higham Ltd., 39–40 Bedford St., Strand, London WC2, because I'm in a bit of a mess over copyright, especially that to do with the Fortune Press.

Thank you for your invitation to me to come along to the Reigate Poetry Club, in spite of my lapse last time. This time *definite*. Can you, sometime, fix an October date?

Yours,
Dylan Thomas

MS: Texas

HARALD SVERDRUP[1]
[?July 1948]   Manor House   South Leigh   Witney   Oxon

Dear Mr. Sverdrup,
    Sorry not to have answered before.
    My house here, though with such a dignified address, is a poky cottage
full of old people, animals, and children. And everyone I want to meet, I
have to meet outside somewhere: generally, and preferably, in a pub. So
can we meet one evening in Oxford in the bar of the George? It's large and
impersonal, nobody cares what you do or say, and the beer is better than
usual. Monday or Tuesday of next week would be fine for me. About 7
o'clock? Can you let me know? If neither evening suits you, let's fix one at
the end of next week. I look forward to hearing from you. I shan't by the
way be able to do anything about taking part in a BBC discussion as I am
nearly drowned under film work and daren't take a day off for some weeks.
                                        Yours sincerely,
                                        Dylan Thomas

MS: Location unknown

JAMES LANGHAM[2]
5 July 1948   Manor House   South Leign   Witney   Oxon

My dear James,
    Please forgive me. The most awful, but obvious, things happened, and I
couldn't get out of bed—no, not if *two* of you were waiting for me—till the
afternoon.
    I am coming up to London again early this week, & will ring you at once.
It won't be too late?
                                        Yours ever,
                                        Dylan

MS: BBC

CAITLIN THOMAS
Sunday [?July 1948]   [South Leigh]
Caitlin my darling, my own dear love, I love you forever & ever.
    How are you? I think about you *all* the time, every every hellish second
here.[3]

1 Harald Ulrik Sverdrup, Norwegian poet, translator of some of Thomas's work,
  then living in Oxford.
2 A BBC producer.
3 Caitlin and the children were with her mother, presumably in Hampshire.

And it *is* hell here, too. Margaret has driven my father nearly mad since we left, patronising, lecturing him on art & music, letting the house get filthy and children-scrabbled.

And since I came back on Friday night, she's been alternately duckeying and weeping.

Mary loathes her too, & is waiting for you—as I am doing, my dear, all night & day.

I am keeping away all I can, writing letters in the bedroom.

Yesterday, SHE asked me: Do you want me to go? and I couldn't say Yes, I was feeling too ill.

Were you ill too?

Oh, dear, my dear, come back on Monday. SHE will go then.

Alan came out yesterday on his bicycle. I didn't see him. He saw HER going on her way to Mrs. Green. There were SCENES on the road.[1]

And the bitch was red-eyed all evening, while my father talked about saucepans & operations and I trembled.

Come back, my love.

There are lots of huge lettuces, & I love you.

Love to Aeron, Llewelyn, & your mother etc.

Have you enough money?

I shall have to go town *twice* next week, over films, but will soon be settling down to writing them.

Oh Christ, it's awful here without you.

All the love
I have,
Dylan

MS: *(Maurice Neville)*

*MICHAEL SEWARD SNOW
July 15 1948   Manor House   South Leigh   Witney   Oxon

Dear Mr Seward Snow

Thank you very much for your letter. You must, please, forgive my not having written back at once: I've been away, hunting bread and butter.

And thank you, most sincerely, for asking me to be the President of the Ulysses Club.[2]

I am, of course, honoured & delighted to accept.

And may I wish the best of possible luck to the Club, and to all its members (and I hope there'll be lots of them).

---

1 Alan (A. J. P.) Taylor grew increasingly upset at the time and money that his wife lavished on the Thomases.
2 Seward Snow, later a painter, was a schoolboy when he planned the club in honour of James Joyce. Nothing came of it.

You will let me know, won't you, how the Club gets on?

And if there's anything I can do to help it, let me know and I'll do my best.

Thank you again.

And here is my stamp-sized book,[1] signed, Yours very sincerely,

Dylan Thomas

MS: the recipient

*CLIFFORD MUSGRAVE[2]

26 July 1948   Manor House South Leigh Witney Oxon

Dear Mr Musgrave,

Thank you for your letter of the 22nd July, which has just reached me. And, very much indeed, for your invitation to me to come & give a reading of my poems, under the auspices of the Brighton Public Libraries, at the Banqueting Room of the Royal Pavilion on October 7th or 28th.

I should like to come down exceedingly. May I choose the 28th?[3]

And how long do you want me to read for?

And must the reading be *all* of my own poems, or can I chuck a few of other people's in?

And what do I wear? dinner jacket? dark suit?

Thank you very much again: I'm delighted.

Yours sincerely,
Dylan Thomas

MS: Jim Martin

SYDNEY BOX[4]

26 July 1948   Manor House South Leigh Witney Oxon

Dear Sydney,

Perhaps you'll have heard, by this time, from agent Pollinger, that I shan't have to do that Welsh film I mentioned after all for Ealing: terms were no good, & time too short.[5] So if you'd care for me to start work

---

1 *Deaths and Entrances.*
2 Chief Librarian of Brighton.
3 Brighton Reference Library can find no evidence that the event took place. But Thomas's letter to Clifford Evans of 16 November (page 314) was written following a visit to Brighton, and implies they should have met on a Friday. 28 October was a Thursday.
4 Sydney Box (1907–83), film producer, then with Gainsborough.
5 See letter of 27 July to Clifford Evans.

for you as from *August 1*, rather than from *September 1*, as previously agreed, I'd love to.

Belatedly, I'm sending you, by separate post, 'Forgotten Story'. Done anything about it yet? I'd like to work on it, and, very much so, on that episodic idea, 'Me & My Bike'.[1]

And, last: though that hunk of work I did on 'Beach of Falesá' is not a shooting script, could I get the £250 that is still owing to me as the last instalment? I'm really broke: down to very small postdated cheque.

Hope to work with you soon.

Yours,
Dylan

MS: Texas

RALPH KEENE[2]
27th July 1948   Manor House   South Leigh   Witney   Oxon

Dear Bunny,

Thank you for letter and Revised Outline of *Me & My Bike*.

I don't know if *you* know, but it seems as though I shan't be doing this script for Ealing after all: disagreement on terms & on length of time (absurd) allowed for writing.

I have written to Sydney, telling him this, and saying also that I could start work for him, if he wanted it, as from August & not, as arranged, as from September. If he agrees, I could, perhaps, begin work on *M & MB* almost straightaway. There is, of course, *The Forgotten Story* as well, but he may have done something about that. I like that too.

But I'm *extremely* keen on the Bike. For me, as a supposedly imaginative writer, it's got wonderful possibilities, and I feel very enthusiastic about it. Sydney's carte blanche as to freedom of fancy, non-naturalistic dialogue, song, music, etc is enormously encouraging.

Yes, & whether I begin work for Gainsborough in August or September, I'll have a shot at one of the sequences almost straightaway: I've a lot to do, judging, my God, Poetry Festivals, & Third-Programming this week, & August Bank Holiday I devote to grossness. But after that, I'll get down to work at once: i.e. on Tuesday or Wednesday 2nd or 3rd of August. I've no preconceived ideas, but am so delighted with the *whole* idea that I hope to be able to produce something on the lines we all want.

I'll get in touch with you when anything has happened.

Yours ever,
Dylan

MS: Texas

1 *Me and My Bike*, which may have been Thomas's idea, was to be a 'film operetta'. The finale would be a cyclist pedalling into heaven to a chorus of bicycle bells. Only the opening sequence was written. This was published after Thomas's death, and formed the basis of a television film by Derek Trimby for BBC Wales.
2 'Bunny' Keene, a film director, then with Gainsborough.

CLIFFORD EVANS

Clifford Evans (1912–85), actor, had written a film story, and thought that Thomas might write the script. As a result Thomas attended conferences at the Ealing film studios. But the producer disagreed with him over ideas and finance. The film was later made as *A Run for Your Money*.

27 July 1948   Manor House South Leigh Witney Oxon

Dear Cliff,
    Disaster & apologies.
    First disaster: the Saturday evening appointment I failed to keep. I had to go, that day, to the hospital in Oxford to see about moving my mother, who's got a broken leg there. It was an awful rush, and I scribbled a wire to you and gave it to the station-porter here, a most reliable man except every now & then. That was one of the then's. Two days ago, he found the wire under a pile of Goods Vouchers on the station desk, apologised, and bought me a pint. I'm really deeply sorry, not being so irresponsible as all that, whatever They (whoever They are) might say.
    Second disaster. I heard, through agent, that Ealing was offering me £250 for a full treatment, this to be done under a month, the starting date to be that on which we met, with Frend, in Ealing (or perhaps a day after, I can't, for the moment, find the agent's letter).
    I wrote back to the agent, saying that he & I had agreed that I should work on this film for Ealing only if Ealing paid me what Sydney Box was prepared to pay me: i.e. £1000 for a shooting script. Also, I said that I *would* be agreeable to do a treatment only if I were given more time and, consequently, more money. To this, the agent replied that he had got in touch with Ealing who, on hearing that I had not accepted the £250 & the time-limit, considered the matter closed and would make other arrangements. That's the story from my side. And I was going to write to you in detail about it.
    In the meantime, I've heard that my agent, on receiving the definite CLOSURE from Ealing, had written to Box to say that I could begin work for him (Box) as soon as he (Box) wanted.
    So there it is, and I think that's where it will stand. I wanted, a lot, to work with you on *Nightingales*. But I told the agent, quite frankly what I thought: that the time allowed—it would have worked out at just over a fortnight, considering that we'd written nothing for nearly a couple of weeks after meeting, with Frend, in Ealing—wasn't enough to do justice to the story in. And I'm sure I was right.
    It's a stupid mess, isn't it?
    I'll ring you when I'm up next. Are you going down to Ealing August Bank Holiday week? Anyway, I'll know when I ring—which will be, I hope,

on Thursday or Friday of this week. I *was* looking forward, too, to our couple of Welsh days.

Yours ever,
Dylan

MS: National Library of Wales

SYDNEY BOX
August 5 1948   Manor House South Leigh Witney Oxon

Dear Sydney,
    Thank you a lot.
    I've heard from Jan Read[1] & from Bunny too, and I expect my agent will be hearing about contracts etc. soon.
    So glad to work for you from August 1.
    I'll have a shot, straightaway, now the holidays are over, at one of the sections of 'Me & My Bike', & will, anyway, be seeing Bunny about it early next week.
    Have good times away.

Yours
Dylan

MS: Texas

JEAN LEROY
6 Aug 48   Manor House South Leigh Witney Oxon

Dear Miss LeRoy,
    Re your letter Aug. 5.
    Yes, please do accept BBC fee of 6 guineas for my 'part' in programme 'Looking At Britain' recorded on July 30.[2] Best payment I've received: 2 short lines of verse spoken without rehearsal! More jobs like that.

Yours sincerely,
Dylan Thomas

MS: Texas

1 Jan Read was a script editor at Gainsborough.
2 The programme, about Radnorshire, was for the Overseas Service.

JOHN LEHMANN
7 Aug '48 [postcard]   Manor House   South Leigh   Witney   Oxon

Yes, please, of course use my poem 'Fern Hill' for the English number of 'Prisma'.[1] Shall one see a copy one day? Like to.

Yours,
Dylan

MS: Texas

DAVID HIGHAM
Tuesday [August] 10 '48   Manor House   South Leigh   Witney   Oxon

Dear David,
    Thanks for yesterday's letter. I enclose signed approved letter.
    I'm very glad Laughlin's bringing out a special limited selection. Sounds very fine.
    BUT   This is extremely important.
    I myself have no copy of my SELECTED VERSE which Laughlin brought out. I had my proper number of author's copies, but gave them away at once. Looking into a friend's copy the other day, I was horrified to see a number of glaring misprints: real stinkers: things like, in a love poem, 'coal' for 'cool'. And in another poem, one he will certainly reprint, one whole line left out, making havoc of rhythm & meaning. Mistakes all over the place.
    So, please God, before he, Laughlin, brings out this special edition, & before he reprints SELECTED VERSE, I *MUST* have *PROOFS.*
    Riddled with mistakes.
    Will you let Laughlin know *at once.*
    He mustn't print or reprint until these awful errors are rectified.
    It's a bit late in the day, isn't it? But it's got to be done now.

Yours,
Dylan

MS: Texas

JEAN LEROY
20 August 1948   Manor House   South Leigh   Witney   Oxon

Dear Miss LeRoy,
    Yes, please, do accept the BBC engagement for the reading of *Edith Sitwell's* poems on 28th September, in the 3rd Programme.

Yours sincerely,
Dylan Thomas

MS: Texas

1 *Prisma* was a book of contemporary verse that Lehmann was editing for the British Occupation authorities in Germany.

JOHN DAVENPORT
26 August '48   Manor House   South Leigh   Witney   Oxon

My dear John,
    I feel furtive & guilty about missing our last date at the Savage. As, perhaps, you noticed, I was not myself when we met in the Authors' and went out for wine; I wrote the Savage time down in my little book, and lost, later, my little book, my hat, my train, and had only a mist for memory. Then I should have written, but, at home, full of remorse, I could only potter gently in the garden, whimper, and hide, behind the runner beans, from tradesmen. Please forgive me.
    And thank you very much for putting me up, with Parry as seconder, for the Savage.[1] In a year, then, unless I am blackballed by Sir Jack or Kingsmill, I can give up the National Lavatory and be bad in worse company.
    The Stahls have gone to France, won't be back for three months. In case letters are forwarded to them, I will write their address at the end of this, when I get to a telephone book.
    I'm terribly sorry to hear about the money trouble. I cannot, at this moment, help in any way, and am, this morning, going to try a post-dated cheque at the village grocer's: well post-dated too. I haven't yet had my Gainsborough contract to sign, and have been living on little bits from the BBC. That's one reason I haven't been up to town. Also, an emissary of a man from whom I borrowed largely while in Italy has come to London—to the Italian Section, Bush House—and he wants, dear God, to meet me very soon. I am sunk. If the Box contract comes quickly through I shall save a little bit for you—very little it'll have to be, I'm afraid—before it all goes to Signor Furio Bianchini.[2] The box on which I write is vulgar with bills. Llewelyn must have a complete set of school-clothes for Magdalen C.S. next term. Caitlin wants a pressure-cooker & a nightgown. My mother & father will, I think, always be with us. I have given, months ago, a postdated cheque for £70 to Margaret Taylor, which is due September 1st. I am to go to read in the Edinburgh Festival on the 4th, & must hire a suit. Last week I fell down & broke my front tooth & have to have it taken out in Oxford by a German dentist called Mr. Pick. I wish you could come down for a few days: there's room, free, in the village. I do really wish so. I'll ring you at Bush House next Wednesday, and try to meet. Hope to God you can clear the bums. At the bottom of the garden, a man, at 3/- an hour, is digging a new shitpit & will dig on, he says, until he reaches water. By

1 Thomas was elected to the Savage Club (popular with writers and actors) in 1949. 'Parry': Parry Jones, principal tenor at Covent Garden.
2 Thomas borrowed £179 from a Mr Treves in Florence and Elba the previous year. The money was still unpaid in 1950.

that time I shall owe him this house, which is not mine. Love to all & to you. I do look forward to seeing you.

Ever,
Dylan

MS: Texas

CAITLIN THOMAS
[?2 September 1948]

My darling own dear dear Cat,
    I love you for ever & ever & think about you all the time always asleep & awake. I am sorry, my sweetheart, that these cheques are so late: I had no time, from the BBC, to get to Bank between 10 & 3. I go to Edinburgh Saturday morning. I love you.
    Be well, be good, be mine, dear

MS: (Maurice Neville)

JAN READ (Gainsborough Films)
September 9 1948 [telegram from Witney]

SORRY LATENESS REPLY BEEN EDINBURGH FESTIVALLING WHAT ABOUT CONFERENCE TUESDAY WEDNESDAY OR THURSDAY NEXT WEEK PLEASE WIRE MOST CONVENIENT. DYLAN THOMAS.

Oriignal: Texas

JOHN PURVES[1]
23rd Sept 1948   Manor House   South Leigh   Witney   Oxon

Dear Mr. Purves,
    Enclosed, at last, your book. You have every reason to cherish it; it's a most remarkable collection; and I can imagine how you must have felt when you thought that a nasty man, me, had lost it.
    I can't tell you how upset I was to realise how much I had upset you by my irresponsible carelessness; and I can only hope that the recovery of the

---

1 A university lecturer at Edinburgh who collected literary autographs.

book, all safe & sound, will perhaps help you, if only a little way, towards—one day—forgiving me.

The facts are simple. In a violent hurry to catch the London train, I gave both wire and parcel to the maid. She sent the wire, and brought the parcel back with her & put it on my desk. She is methodical in everything, even in her forgetfulness. I should never have entrusted her with so valuable a commission, but usually she is extremely able.

Since the sending of the wire, but not of the book, I have been partly in London and some of the time travelling about the country for the filmcompany who tolerate me; and no letters or wires were forwarded, as I had no fixed address.

Returning home yesterday, I found all your urgent letters and distressed, and distressing telegrams, and found the unfortunate truth out at once.

Nothing I can say can compensate for the anxiety I have caused you. But I would like you to believe that I am deeply sorry and regret, very bitterly, my unthinking carelessness.

I was very glad to be asked to write a poem in your book, among such distinguished company.

I offer every apology.

Yours sincerely,
Dylan Thomas

MS: National Library of Scotland

GRAHAM ACKROYD[1]

24 Sept 1948   Manor House   South Leigh   Witney   Oxon

Dear Graham Ackroyd,

Very sorry not to have answered your letter long before this. It was a long time being forwarded, I've been away, and I'm afraid I could read only about half of your handwriting. This is difficult to write mainly because I couldn't get, from what I could read, the general idea. It's going to be a comic novel? My Long-Legged Ballad, brash, barging, & violent as it may be, isn't a comic poem, though it *has* been laughed at; and I don't want bits of it to be used as chapter-headings for a book that's meant to make you laugh. This may sound priggish. The Ballad is a serious sexual adventure story; and I can't see how bits of it can add to a story about an eccentric puppet maker & his family buggering about and turning a bloody village upside down. Can you tell me more about the story, *your* story, please.

As for your p.p.s., which you've probably forgotten, I could read so little of this that all I gathered was: the puppet maker's youngest daughter, a fast

---

1 Graham Ackroyd, later a painter, was hoping in 1948 to be a writer. The novel, afterwards destroyed, was about a young poet's encounters with eccentrics.

from flaying the harp up school, wanted to read my old Ballad at the Oxford Festival, and that, for some reason, the great moment of her life was when I, God help me, visited her father for ship you are the custard only.

You will, I'm sure, understand that, although I am not one to stand on a non-existent dignity, I can't give permission for you to write into a novel such jabberwock sentences as I could translate.

Will you, in capitals, or on typewriter, tell me more about the novel, please? tell me what on earth, or sea, my Ballad, a serious, if chaotic, poem, has got to do with such antics as I can decipher? and finally tell me what queer ideas the youngest daughter might have about me, and in what character & in what capacity and to what length am I supposed to visit her no doubt delightful father?

Yours sincerely,
Dylan Thomas

MS: Texas

JAN READ
September 30 1948 [telegram from Chiswick]

STUFF ARRIVING MONDAY SORRY DELAY. DYLAN THOMAS.

Original: Texas

JAN READ
7 Oct 48   Manor House   South Leigh   Witney   Oxon

Dear Jan,
    Hope you've got revised script of *Falesá* by now.
    When you read it, you'll see, (I trust), that I've followed the main line of the suggestions on which the three of us agreed, and have tried to remember, & interpolate, all the chief points. One thing you'll notice is that I have cut out altogether the *two other traders* and stuck to one alone, calling him by the name of one of the other traders, Johnny Adams. This, I think, simplifies matters. We talk now about only *one* person whom we never see; our plot works back only to the *immediate* predecessor of Wiltshire. Perhaps you will think that the omitting of the French Priest's suggestion of 'poison', & the putting-in, instead, of 'driven mad with fear', lessens the tension: that Case *should* be rumoured as a murderer early on. But I can't agree with that; and think, anyway, that it's an improvement to cut out as many invisible characters as possible.
    As you'll see, I've cut all the introduction-by-the-waterfall cock about Uma. I've cut the Long Randall-&-burial-alive flash back. I've cut Namu, the renegade pastor.

I want to apologise for the dialogue I have given the French priest, & also for not attempting his real French. I am shockingly bad at French-English broken dialogue, & worse at the French original.

Apologies, also, for the long delay. I'm engulfed, as ever, in domestic mishaps & sicknesses.

I hope you & Ralph & I can meet soon: there'll be lots of things to disagree with in this version.

> Yours,
> Dylan T

MS: Texas

FRANCES HUGHES
October 10 1948 Manor House South Leigh Witney Oxfordshire

Dear Frances,

Thank you for your letter.

I'm giving this to Margaret Taylor to give to you in Laugharne. Unfortunately, I can't get away myself; I'm trying to write a musical comedy film, and am weeks behindhand. Margaret Taylor has come to Laugharne to see if she can find out, for me, exactly how the Starke-Hughes-Castle[1] case is going, and what chance there is of my getting the house for some years, and, if I did manage to, exactly what financial commitments I would be held to. Do, please, help her if you can. I can't explain my 'longing' to have the castle any more clearly than I did in my letter to Diccon.[2] I want very much to live in Laugharne because I know that there I can work well. Here, I am too near London; I undertake all sorts of little jobs, broadcasting etc., which hinder my own work. In Laugharne if I could live there, I would work half the year on my film-scripts, and half on my own poems and stories: cutting out all time-wasting broadcasts, articles, useless London visits.

I realise that there's a great difference between owning and renting a house, and that Mrs. Starke can be a querulous & annoying person to be tenant of. But, still, if anyone, *not* Mrs. Starke, is going to live in the castle, I'd like it to be Caitlin and me. So will you please, for both of us, let Margaret Taylor know how things stand? And if we *could* get the house, we'd like to buy, rent, or whatever, what furniture there still is in the Castle: that is, of course, if you are not going to take it away.

Anyway, we hope and we hope.

> Caitlin's love,
> Yours ever,
> Dylan

Only source: SL

1 Mrs Starke owned, or had owned, the house known as Laugharne Castle. There was a long-running row about alterations that Richard Hughes wanted to make.
2 'Diccon': Richard Hughes.

MARGARET TAYLOR
Thursday evening [?October 1948]   Manor

My dear Margaret,

Your letter, just arrived by winged messenger, has set us dreamily grinning, hopelessly shaking our heads, then beaming and gabbling together again as we think of the great house at the end of the cherrytreed best street in the world, bang next to the Utrillo tower, with its wild gardens and owly ruins, the grey estuary, forever linked to me with poems done and to be, flat and fishy below with Tom Nero Rowlands, the one last fisherman, who hates the water, trudging through it like a flatfooted cat; saying to ourselves, 'No no no, do not dream of it, never for us too ugly too old', and then once more saying, not too loudly, 'Perhaps and perhaps, if we try, pray, whisper, fear the God, abjure drink and fighting, be humble, write poems, do not bite our nails, answer letters, collect the fallen apples for economical pulping into glass jars, do not throw her crutches at my mother, be good, be patient, sing, love one another, ask God for peace, perhaps and perhaps one day one day the owly castle and the noble house will be ours for some of the seven most heavenly years since pride fell.'[1] Oh the kitchen for cooking & eating, for thinking Breughels! the room to the left as, praise be, you enter the house, that room for music and Caitlin dancing! the nursery for Aeronwy, that we must have more children to fill! the bedroom looking up at an unbalanced field, the field of infancy where even now we are all running so that, writing this in the rain, I can hear all our thin faraway children's voices glide over the plumtrees and through the ventilation skull-holes of this window! and the other bedroom looking out, happy as hell, at the clock of sweet Laugharne, the clock that tells the time backwards so that, soon, you walk about the town, from Browns to the gulls on the Strand, in the only Garden Age! the long cool once Dufy-hung living room: the only room in the world rightly described as one for living, and, at its end, the gravel path to the brass cannon pointing, as all cannons should point, uselessly out at the estuary air! the room, the velvet, padded room upstairs where poems are waiting like people one has always loved but never met, and O to sit there, lost, found, alone in the universe, at home, at last, the people all with their arms open! and then, but only through my tears, the hundreds of years of the colossal broken castle, owls asleep in the centuries, the same rooks talking as in Arthur's time which always goes on there as, unborn, you climb the stones to see river, sea, cormorants nesting like thin headstones, the cocklewomen webfoot, & the undead, round Pendine head, streaming like trippers up into seaside sky, making a noise like St Giles Fair, silent as all the electric chairs and bells of my nerves as I think, here, of the best town, the best house, the only castle, the mapped, measured, inhabited, drained,

---

1 Thomas's hopes of being able to live at Laugharne Castle were premature. That winter Margaret Taylor found them the Boat House instead.

garaged, townhalled, pubbed and churched, shopped, gulled, and estuaried one state of happiness!

Shall I tell you what I think when we meet? I have plans and stratagems, dreams & details, a head herring'd with ideas, I am weak and ruthless and exultant about this. I would do anything. I will. To Caitlin, it is as adorable and as impossible to conceive as it is to me!

Oh, *let's* do what we can, I had to write this to you.

And we'd like to come out on Saturday.

Dylan

MS: *Texas*

SYDNEY BOX
Nov 7 1948   Manor House   South Leigh   Witney   Oxon

Dear Sydney,

Sorry you were too busy for me to be able to see (and worry) you last Wednesday at the Studios. Perhaps, anyway, it would have been better for me to write.

The small (but not to me) point I wanted to see you about was, I'm afraid, a money one.

I'm in debt £150 to my bank. Until I pay them that sum, they will allow me to cash no more cheques. Until that sum is paid, I cannot carry on domestically day-to-day nor can I attempt to live normally on the weekly salary I get from Gainsborough.

So: My contract says I am to be paid £500 on the completion of each of this year's two scripts I do for you. Would it be possible for me to get £150 of this £500 on advance now? If it isn't possible, I'm sunk. Really sunk. One & all.

Please do what you can. And every apology for the embarrassing bother I'm making. But I can hold out against tradesmen etc (& the bank) only a few more days.

I do hope to see you for an unfinancial drink one day.

And, please, this nonsense is urgent.

Yours ever,
Dylan

MS: *Texas*

JEAN LEROY
Nov 16 1948   Manor House   South Leigh   Witney   Oxon

Dear Miss LeRoy,

I really don't feel that the fee and expenses offered by the BBC for my participation in the programme 'Trimalchio's Dinner', to be recorded on December 2, is at all adequate & I'm very glad you're questioning it.[1]

To begin with: £1.7.6. expenses for 2 days and *nights* seems to me absurd. I *do* have to pay for my bed on each of my London visits, & two hotel bills for bed alone come to more than £1.7.6.

Also I think the fee itself, fifteen guineas, to be extremely poor.

I hope you will go ahead fiercely & try to obtain a much better offer.

Sincerely,
Dylan Thomas

MS: Texas

JAN READ
Nov 16 48   Manor House   South Leigh   Witney   Oxon

Dear Jan,

Thank you for the copy of the 1st draft of 'Rebecca's Daughters'.[2]

I've now read all the stuff you gave me about the subject but haven't yet started getting down to the writing. I'll be doing this next week.

So glad Sydney was amused by the first chunk of *Me & My Bike*. I look forward to hearing more about it. Bunny wrote & said he was very Keene[3] on going on with it as it is.

See you soon.

Yours
Dylan

MS: Texas

---

1 The programme was *Trimalchio's Feast*, a play by Louis MacNeice. Thomas had the fee increased to 20 guineas.

2 *Rebecca's Daughters*, using material already owned by Gainsborough, was about the 'Rebecca Riots', widespread attacks on toll-gates in South Wales in the 1840s by farmers and other road users. Local ringleaders dressed as women and called themselves 'Rebecca', taking the name from Genesis 24:60, 'And they blessed Rebekah, and said unto her . . . let thy seed possess the gate of those which hate them.' It was the third and last of the Gainsborough scripts that Thomas worked on.

3 'Bunny' was Ralph Keene.

HERMANN PESCHMANN
Nov 16 48   Manor House   South Leigh   Witney   Oxon

Dear Hermann,
    So sorry not to have written before. And sorry we missed you on our way
back from Brighton: we had some friends with us, and were rather a large
party (though we could indeed have tried to bring you & your wife over for
a drink in Reigate or elsewhere). Brighton went very well, and noisily.
    About the Anna Wickham poem: I'm sorry, but I've scrapped all my
notes including, accidentally, most of the poems I'd so laboriously written
out. But you can find the poem in Richard Aldington's massive new
anthology.[1] I'm afraid I don't know if it was pre-1930—the poem, I
mean—but I rather think so.
    Thanks for the newspaper extract.
    Regards to you both.

                                            Yrs
                                            Dylan

MS: Texas

*CLIFFORD EVANS[2]
Nov 16 '48   Manor House   South Leigh   Witney   Oxon

Dear Clifford,
    So *really* very sorry not to have written as soon as we got home—home, I
hate the place. I wanted to write very much, to thank you and your wife for
being just as you were and for being friends at once and for not minding not
dining and for cashing my cheque and for liking the reading and the
afterwards.
    We missed you a lot at the Cricketers' that Friday, but hoped it *was*
because you were tied up with work or family and *not* because we were as
we were and are. (I knew you did not mind that, anyway, but it is polite to
say).
    I do hope we come to Brighton again soon, just to look at the sea and the
octopus-tank and be about, and then we'll ring you at once and let's meet if
we may, anywhere.
    Caitlin sends her wishes to both of you and to your son, and so do I.

                                            Yours,
                                            Dylan

MS: Robert Williams

1 *Poetry of the English-speaking World* (1947).
2 The ms has been crossed through with a diagonal line and may be a draft.

JOHN DAVENPORT
17 Nov 1948   Manor House   South Leigh   Witney   Oxon

My dear John!

O God, what a pickle, and I'm entirely useless. If only if only I could raise *ten* pounds, ten mean little pounds, to help you whom I owe so much from the past. If only, just for our sake, I could raise a guarantee from someone else. But my lady-patron no longer pays, at least not in money; a night at the opera, yes, ballets & cocktails whenever, but not one more crisp crunchy note can I drag from her unloved breast. My *own* foreign debt is pressing; the unanswered letters of the Italian lender grow briefer and less English. I have already borrowed in advance from my fee for my next unspecified filmscript in order to unfreeze *my* bank account so that I can write little overdraft cheques to tradesmen & the publican. And, crowning all this, Brigit's & Caitlin's mother & Brigit herself who is living with her have only this week written to say they are penniless and that they must appeal to rich, cigary filmtycoon *me*.

I am so sorry, John, that my letter to you is as full of woes as you to me. A wretched answer. I would to God I could send a better one. But I had to tell you how things are with me; if only they were one inch better, I could send some contribution. But all is stony here, & Christmas coming.

Can Helen & Bill McAlpine do nothing? They are the only people I know who might help. Augustus? Oh, but you must have gone through all the possible names in your great unhappy head, my beamishless boy. And flippancy doesn't help. Would you care for a drink on Friday lunchtime? I'm in town to wheedle. Henekey's downstairs 12.30 or 1? I'll ring & see anyway. I can at least buy some flat yellow pints, and we can whimper together. I'd love to see you. Why does your trouble coincide with mine? When I last saw you, at Brighton time, I was rolling in ready cash. Now I have to roll on credit. There's nothing here to sell. My soul's sold, my wits wander, my body wobbles, Aeronwy is too young, I won't let Caitlin, the only pictures on our walls are from Picture Post, our dog is a mongrel, our cat is half a mouse.

Small cheer for the needy in the old Manor House.

If you tackle McAlpines, do so quickly: they leave London next weekend to take a cottage in this cowpad village.

I have not yet managed to see Sidney B about our working together. He is always out, or out to me, or showing his great teeth to Rank. But I may see him Thursday evening.

I will ring on Friday morning. I do hope we can meet.

All my apologies for so abysmally failing you.

Love,
Dylan

MS: Texas

VERNON WATKINS
Nov 23 48   Manor House   South Leigh   Witney   Oxon

Dear Vern,
   Thank *you* for coming to the lunch. It was lovely to see *you*. Thank you
for writing and for remembering the book. Last week I bought it and left it,
at once, in a cab. Before I had opened it. I left also Robert Graves's
Collected Poems, Betjeman's Selected Poems, two library books about
sudden death, somebody else's scarf and my own *my own* hat. Now I must
wait till Christmas to read you. 'Cave Drawing', & 'Llewelyn's Chariot', I
have, and one of the Carmarthen poems in an anthology. But I want all. I'll
ask your godson about an annual when he comes back from school. It's
games morning. He hates it, can't kick or throw. All he can do is dribble.
Also he draws good engines, likes arithmetic, says Yah about poems, &
Wizard about aeroplanes, Dick Barton, Up the Pole,[1] tinned spaghetti,
walnuts, and the caravan where I now, dear help me, work.[2] Nothing
happens to me. I go to London and bluster, come back and sigh, do a little
scriptwriting, look at an unfinished poem, go out on my bicycle in the fog,
go to London & bluster. Mervyn Levy wrote to me yesterday. I wish Fred
would write. I would to him if I had his address. And to Dan. My mother's
no better, and will probably have to go to hospital again very soon. My
father's better & naggier. I wish you had heard my story about Rhossilli. I
wish I were in Rhossilli.[3] I wish we saw each other oftener. Next
Spring we will, in Laugharne and in Swansea. I'm so cold this morning I
could sing an opera, all the parts, and do the orchestra with my asthma.
   Write soon. Love to you all from us all.

                                                    Ever,
                                                    Dylan

MS: British Library

---

1 Popular radio programmes.
2 Margaret Taylor provided a caravan in the garden for Thomas to escape to.
3 Thomas read his story, 'Extraordinary Little Cough', about a childhood camping
   holiday in the Gower village of Rhossilli, on the radio on 27 October.

GRAHAM ACKROYD
November 24 1948   Manor House   South Leigh   Witney   Oxon

Dear Graham Ackroyd

I do apologise for not having answered your most understandable letter of nearly two months ago. I mislaid it, difficult though that was. Thank you very much for it.

Permission for poem etc. granted. I look forward to reading some Todd. (And I like the idea of the young man who is writing Todd's Life *and* Works. I wish someone would write *my* works. Then I could go out on my bicycle.)

I hope you write again, when you've got time and some railway posters.[1]

Yours sincerely
Dylan Thomas

MS: Texas

JEAN LEROY
25 Nov '48   Manor House   South Leigh   Witney   Oxon

Dear Miss LeRoy,

I've just today received, from your offices, the BBC cheque for my 'Extraordinary Little Cough'.

For One British Broadcast Use—   20.10.0.
   " One British Broadcast Performance—
   Reading   8. 8.0.
                                                                 ‾‾‾‾‾‾‾‾‾
                                                                 28.18.0.

I'm sorry, but I've mislaid your letter in which you detailed to me the fees of the contract for that story, but I *definitely* remember that the Performance, Reading fee was EIGHTEEN not EIGHT guineas. If it *had* been eight, I would have protested at once.

Do see, please, where the mistake has been made.

And thank you *very* much indeed for saying how much you liked the story.

Sincerely,
Dylan Thomas

MS: Texas

1 Stung by references to his handwriting, Ackroyd had replied on the back of a poster.

JEAN LEROY
Dec 6th 1948   Manor House   South Leigh   Witney   Oxon

Dear Miss LeRoy,
    Answering, late I'm afraid, your letter of Dec. 1st.
    Sorry about the typographical error. But thank you *very* much for getting the BBC to pay me 12 guineas for the reading. And *of course* it's acceptable.
                                        Sincerely,
                                        Dylan Thomas

MS: Texas

JOHN GAWSWORTH
7 Dec 48   Manor House   South Leigh   Witney   Oxon

Dear John,
    Awfully sorry, I've got nothing for your first number, really nothing, no poem nor prose. Soon, when I start writing again, I'd like very much to send whatever-it-is along. All the time now, I'm filming & radio-ing, reading, & worrying.
    I got the L.D.[1] (& cheque), thanks.
                                        Yours,
                                        Dylan

MS: Buffalo

JAN READ
13 Dec 48   Manor House   South Leigh   Witney   Oxon

Dear Jan,
    I hope that, by this time, you'll have heard from my agent Pollinger.
    This is only a personal note to thank you for the tone of your letter to Pollinger, and to assure you I am now working *hard* on Rebecca, having somehow managed to tidy over my domestic crisis, & will send it along as soon as possible.
    Apologies all round, to Sydney & Bunny.
                                        Yours,
                                        Dylan Thomas

MS: Texas

1 *Literary Digest.*

VERNON WATKINS
13 Dec 1948   Manor House   South Leigh   Witney   Oxon

Dear Vernon,
    Lovely book.[1] Thank you very very much. I am reading it from the
beginning, some every night, slow & light & lifted. I saw the review in the
Times Literary Supplement & liked its praise but not all its detail; & pre-
'Raphaelitism' is barmy. I'll write again when I've read all the (to me) new
beautiful poems. How good you really are!
    Llewelyn's Annual: he says there is something called 'Science &
Wonder' (Number 2. Very important, number 2.) Or anything, and he
thanks you from his rag-&-bone shop.[2]
    All well but poor and tired here. I am sorry, I do not mean my mother is
well, poor thing, she's as ill as a ward.

                              Love to all from us all,
                              Ever,
                                Dylan

MS: British Library

DAVID HIGHAM
Dec 21st 1948   Manor House   South Leigh   Witney   Oxon

Dear David,
    Please forgive delay. I have been in an accident, was knocked off my
bicycle by a lorry, and have badly broken arm & ribs. Also feeling shocked
& bruised all over & have a wonderful black eye.
    Thank you very much for at last successfully effecting an agreement
with the Fortune Press. I enclose Dent's agreement, signed.
    I can't, at the moment, find Laughlin's copy of my *Selected Writings* to
send on, proof-corrected, being too full of pain-killer to think or remember
clearly. But I hope to be better tomorrow and will find the book & send it
at once on.
    I wonder if you would do me a favour. I should write separately to
Pollinger but feel too battered to do so. Could you tell him of my accident
& ask him whether he thinks he should let Gainsborough know, as I'm
afraid my filmwork will be held up for—in the doctor's opinion—10 or
more days. Whimpering, I now lie down.

                              Yours,
                                Dylan

MS: Texas

1 Watkins's *The Lady with the Unicorn*.
2 W. B. Yeats, 'In the foul rag-and-bone shop of the heart' ('The Circus Animals'
  Desertion').

ROBERT MacDERMOT[1]
10 January 1949   Manor House   South Leigh   Witney   Oxon

Dear Robert,

Thousand apologies for not having answered at once your December letter about *Peer Gynt*. I've been laid up after an accident, with broken shoulder & ribs, too bloody and bowed to write a word or think of anything.

Thanks a lot for wanting me to do a new version of *Peer Gynt*. I really would *love* to, above anything, a great & favourite play, but I just daren't. I'm long behindhand with a filmscript for Gainsborough, and won't be able to finish it for the next three weeks or a month. Which makes it, to my grief, impossible to turn out a *P.G.* by the end of February.

I suppose you must now hand it to another chap—but if there ever was a chance of your postponing it, & of letting me have a shot in the Spring, I'd be more than delighted. Much more.

By the way, isn't 8 weeks a *madly* short time for anyone—I don't know a syllable of Norweigan[2]—to produce a really good version of a great play?

Do think of me in the future whenever anything as exciting as that turns up, will you, please? I *would* like to write for Television.

I've never seen a Television show. Could I come along as a silent, out-of-the-way looker-on one day?

Thanks again.

All the best wishes for New Year,

Yours,
Dylan

MS: BBC

---

1 MacDermot, the head of BBC television drama at a time when the service was more of a curiosity than anything else, had written to Thomas (20 December 1948), 'How allergic are you to *Peer Gynt*? I ask because we want to do a full-scale television version of it in late March or early April.' He wasn't happy with existing versions; nor was the producer, Royston Morley. This was the same Morley who commissioned programmes for Brazil early in the war. (In 1947 he had had plans for a TV adaptation of Euripides' *The Trojan Women*. Thomas was said to have been 'interested', though nothing happened.)
2 Thomas misspelt 'Norwegian' in all his letters about *Peer Gynt*.

DAVID HIGHAM
Jan 20 1949   Manor House   South Leigh   Witney   Oxon

Dear David,
  Since my enclosing note this morning, sent with the *Mardersteig Proofs*
& the corrected copy (to be returned to me) of the New Directions *Selected
Writings*, I have come across a copy of the poem, unpublished in book
form, which Laughlin wants to include in the Mardersteig edition.[1] So
he needn't bother about the Atlantic Monthly: here is the poem.
                                              Yours,
                                              Dylan

MS: Texas

ROBERT MacDERMOT
26 Jan 1949   Manor House   South Leigh   Witney   Oxon

Dear Robert,
  So glad you have been able to postpone the production of *Peer Gynt*
until, probably, the Autumn.
  And I should be delighted to have a shot at the adaptation & to try to
deliver it by the end of May. My cautious words 'have a shot' and 'try to
deliver' I use because I have never tried anything of this sort before, have a
great admiration for the play & no Norwegian, and am very awed by the
task ahead of me. But I'll do my very best.
  As a matter of fact, there is in Oxford now a young Norwegian poet,
Harald Sverdrup, whom I've met lately because he is preparing a talk on
my poems, and translations of them, for the Norwegian section of the
B.B.C. He seems a very nice chap & has marvellous English. Should I sound
him out next week—when I meet him—about the possibility of his helping
me—at any rate, in the first stages.
  You will, anyway, won't you, be able to give me a literal translation and
also let me have from the library all the available translations for
reference?
  I'm sorry this letter is, again, so late. I'm terribly busy on a script for
Gainsborough, and that reminds me: About my terms! My agents, Pearn,
Pollinger, & Higham, will be getting in touch with you and/or your
copyright people & I'm going to instruct them to ask for a *really* good fee.
It's a terrific amount of work, and extremely difficult too. Also, it will

---

1 A small issue of an *ad hoc* volume of Thomas's verse, *Twenty-six Poems*, printed by
  the Officina Bodoni, the hand press founded in Verona by Giovanni Mardersteig. James
  Laughlin and J. M. Dent were the publishers. The book is dated December 1949, issued
  the following year.

mean my setting aside work on another filmscript—and Gainsborough pays very well. So my agents will want all they can get, and more.

Do let me know what you think of the idea of attempting to co-opt the Norwegian poet, please.

And when shall I come up to see you or Royston?

Yours,
Dylan

MS: BBC

E. J. KING-BULL
26 Jan '49   Manor House   South Leigh   Witney   Oxon

Dear King-Bull,

Thanks for the letter. And for the commission. I understand now quite what is wanted: whether I can provide it is another matter. I'll try my best. And I'll get my agents to attack the copyright people straight away.

I shan't be able to get down to it for some time, though. I've got a filmscript in hand, and also am about to prepare to work on *Peer Gynt* for television. But I think I should be able to put something across the *Plain Dealer* by, as you suggest, mid-April.[1]

Perhaps we can have a word about it, over a drink in London, when I'm about to start on it & when I've got hold of a copy and read it several times—including backwards?

Yours,
Dylan

MS: BBC

JEAN LEROY
26 January 1949   Manor House   South Leigh   Witney   Oxon

Dear Miss LeRoy,

The BBC has approached me about two programmes.

First: Robert MacDermot, Head of Television Drama, has written asking me if I would do a new version of 'Peer Gynt', based on a literal translation from the Norwegian. This is for a full-scale television production in, probably, the autumn. And they would like, if possible, to have my version by the end of May.

I have written to Mr. MacDermot, telling him that I should like, very much, to do it, but that it entails a great deal of work of a high and concentrated order, as well as much & careful reading of all existent

1 See next letter.

versions in English and, probably, some initial work with a Norwegian translator. This being so, and also considering that I am under contract to Gainsborough Films and therefore will have to work *doubly* hard, I told MacDermot that I would need a good deal of money and that my agent would press like the devil, for the very maximum (and more) that Television can pay. So will you get in touch with them, please, and start this devilish pressing straightaway? I look forward, a lot, to having a bash at it, but obviously cannot do so, in light of my other work and of my film obligations, unless it is made *really* worth my while.

Second: E. J. King-Bull, of the Third Programme, has asked me to make a 'treatment', for the Third, of Wycherley's 'The Plain Dealer'.[1] What he requires is a 'personality treatment' of the play, including adaptation and cutting to a programme period as near to ninety minutes as possible. In King-Bull's words: 'Your interpolatory passages should either hasten or elucidate action which it would be tedious to broadcast, or point your general statement on whatever content of the play you choose to emphasise. Although there ought not to be more than a smallish proportion of exposition by you, it should maintain the personality stuffing and not often be mere "cut-to-narration"'.

Anyway, you'll be gather[ing] from King-Bull's rather curious phrasing, that it's quite a lively task. *And*, again, one that should be handsomely paid. Not only do I edit, adapt, & cut the play, but I introduce it, personally, on the microphone, and, throughout the play, interrupt, interpolate, & comment in my own sweet fashion. Thus the commission entails my working as editor, adapter, writer, and broadcaster. Will you see what money they offer—and then damn-near double it?

Hope to hear from you soon, & also that I've made things clear.

Yours,
Dylan Thomas

P.S. It is, of course, the Peer Gynt that is the *big* job.

MS: Texas

HECTOR MacIVER[2]
17 February 1949   Manor House   South Leigh   Witney   Oxon

Dear Hector,

I've often meant to write. But what's the good of meaning? (as your Dylanttantes might say).

I'll write at once to J. M. Dent, asking them to send to you, from me,

1 *The Plain-Dealer*, a romantic comedy by William Wycherley, was first performed in 1676.
2 Hector MacIver (1910–66), Scots teacher and writer. Probably Thomas met him during his visit to Edinburgh the previous year.

what in-print books of mine they possess. All, I think, are in print, except the first one and that soon should be: there's been some legal bother about it, something I don't understand about copyright. Anyway, some copies of the others will be reaching you. And I will not draw nasty pictures on the flyleaves.

Really I did mean to write, to thank you for whisky and ale, but work and sloth alternately kept me busy and then I lost your address. I wish I could speedily return to Scotland: here it is low and sodden, moley and owly, rheumatic, cloddish, gustless. In the Spring, we go to Wales to live, in a house on an estuary.[1] That will be nice, I do so hate it here in this toadish dungwilted valley among slow rabbits & sly cows. Oxford is near, but full of young men. Our pub is cold, and wild with dominoes.

I wish you would come South. If ever you do, do write or wire and I'll puff up to London full of the worst intentions. I appreciated a great deal your room, spirit, & company.

MacDiarmid is coming to lecture to the Oxford Poetry Society next month. Or is supposed to come. A party is being arranged.

I am working on a film which is trying to kill me.

Write when you have time & inclination. Anyway, to tell me if the books have arrived safely. And how they could arrive unsafely I don't know, unless a censor opens the parcel & Lallans them.[2]

It was good to hear from you.

Yours,
Dylan

MS: National Library of Scotland

[?February 1949]   Manor House   South Leigh   Witney   Oxon

Dear Idris Davies,

Glad to hear from you again, after so long. And glad, too, you used my name when you applied for a job with the BBC at Bangor—if it'll do any good at all. And if the BBC write to me, *of course* I'll speak up and bold and very sincerely too. I like your poems a lot—you know that.

I'm going to live in Wales in the Spring—in Laugharne, near Carmarthen. Perhaps we can meet in Wales then? Do hope so.

Yours ever
Dylan Thomas

MS: National Library of Wales

1 Mrs Taylor had bought the Boat House for £3,000.
2 Hugh MacDiarmid and others were trying to revive 'Lallans', or Scots dialect, as a literary language.
3 Idris Davies (1905–53), poet, began his working life as a miner and was later a schoolteacher.

JEAN LEROY
17 Feb 49   Manor House   South Leigh   Witney   Oxon

Dear Miss LeRoy,
    Thank you for your letter about the BBC's offer of £75 for my adaptation
of Wycherley's Plain Dealer. Perhaps we should close for that. And let's try
to get all of all we can for my actual speaking part in the broadcast, please.
                                                    Yours sincerely,
                                                    Dylan Thomas

MS: Texas

CAITLIN THOMAS
Saturday 6 o'clock [5 March 1949]   Hotel Flora   Praha[1]

Darling my dear Caitlin whom every moment—away from or with her—
I love more, my sweetheart Cat: I love you.
    I arrived in Prague about 24 hours ago, was met at the airport by an
elderly woman & a young man who took me at once to a reception in the
House of Parliament where hundreds of Czechs, Slovaks, Russians,
Rumanians, Bulgarians & Hungarians were drinking wine. After, dinner:
really incredibly bad food but nice people. After that a party to say goodbye
to two Greek film-men who were returning to the Greek War.[2] Today,
hours of Congress & translators. Lunch with an old Czech friend of
Norman Cameron's. After, more Congress & each guest made a speech.
Including me. Tonight, a Smetana opera. Tomorrow, more speeches, and a
broadcast. I love you. All this has nothing to do with writing—I mean, all
this multilingual congressing. But Prague is so beautiful. And bitingly
savagely cold; you, my love, would die of it. Tomorrow, I shall buy a small
fur hat here. All the insides of buildings are very very warm. I have, in spite
of all these appointments, a terrible loneliness. Even in 24 hours. And I
want to be with you. Do not be too sad; though it is stupid of me to say,
Don't. But please don't be, my own Caitlin. If I can get a seat in the plane, I
will fly back on Wednesday. If not, the next day. Nobody here so far allows
me to go into a café, pub, or dive. They prefer parties in the home. We don't
agree. But they are a wonderfully friendly people. I do do hope we can come
here together. Keep well. Give my love to A & L. And to you, my lonely
love, my true self, my undying faith, every dear wish. I think only, dream
only, *am* only you. Oh, Cat.
                                                    X   Dylan

MS: Tony Vilela

1 Writers from many countries had been invited by the Czechoslovak Government to see
  a writers' union inaugurated. The country had been under Communist control since a
  Russian-backed coup the previous year.
2 Greek Government forces were fighting Communist rebels.

MARGARET TAYLOR
[card, postmarked Prague, [?7] March 1949]

My hands are so dirty, excuse this scrubby note. I have just come, bludgeoned & flummoxed, from a Congress in 6 languages. [?Tonight] I go to the [?]. Cold & beautiful [?], but the lager thin.

Dylan

MS: Texas

ELWYN EVANS[1]
14 March 1949   Manor House   South Leigh   Witney   Oxon

Dear Mr Evans,
 Thank you very much for your letter, and please forgive me for not answering before: I've been abroad.
 And thank you for wanting me to give a talk on Hopkins in your new literary magazine; I only wish I could. But I've just got a new filmscript to write and a play-adaptation for the Third, and mustn't take on any other job, even a 15 minute one. But I would like, in the future, if I may, to talk in the magazine. And thank you very much for asking me.

Yours sincerely,
Dylan Thomas

MS: BBC

JEAN LEROY
March 14 49   Manor House   South Leigh   Witney   Oxon

Dear Miss Leroy,
 Thank you very much for your letter of the 11th. I think the new figure, £100, for my adaptation of the Plain Dealer & my performance in it is very good & please do accept it. I'll get in touch with the producer myself. Thanks.

Yours sincerely,
Dylan Thomas

MS: Texas

1 A producer with BBC Wales.

JEAN LEROY
March 18 1949 [telegram from Witney][1]

PLEASE ACCEPT PEER GYNT OFFER AND OBTAIN HALF IMMEDI-
ATELY THANK YOU VERY MUCH DYLAN THOMAS.[2]

Original: Location unknown

1 Copied in 1975 from the original at David Higham Associates.
2 The fee offered was 250 guineas (£262.10s).

Ways of Escape
1949–53

In the spring of 1949 the Thomases moved back to Wales, to the Boat House at Laugharne, bought and nominally rented to them by Margaret Taylor. Soon after, their third child, Colm, was born. The return to Wales, which Thomas seemed to anticipate as a solution, had little or no effect on the deepening chaos of his domestic life. He began to write poetry again, and worked, in the end successfully, on the 'play for voices' that became *Under Milk Wood*. But his life with Caitlin was stormy, and he was either unable or unwilling to make any serious attempt to live within his income. An invitation to read poetry in New York City led to a three-month tour of North America, when, for the first time, he had a taste of popular fame, and earned nearly £3000. The money went on expenses or otherwise ran through his fingers. The United States became, like the Boat House, a place of intended escape that led him back only to himself and a conviction that his powers were failing.

E. J. EVANS
8th May 1949   The Boat House   Laugharne   Carmarthenshire

Dear Sir,

Please forgive my not having answered your letter before this. I have just come back to Wales to live, and letters have been misforwarded.

I shall be most grateful if you will include my name in the list of those who are supporting the appeal to the Prime Minister for a Civil List Pension to be awarded to Huw Menai.[1] I have the greatest admiration for him—though I do not know him personally—for his work, and I think the Port Talbot Forum is to be congratulated on its sponsoring of the appeal—which I do most sincerely hope will succeed.

Yours faithfully,
Dylan Thomas

From a typescript. MS location unknown

DAVID HIGHAM
9 May 1949   The Boat House   Laugharne   Carmarthenshire

Dear David,

Very many apologies for not having sent back the Fortune Press agreement long ago. As you will see from the above address, I have moved back to Wales, & unfortunately forgot to leave a forwarding address in the South Leigh post-office so that nothing was sent to me here. I've arranged things with the P.O. now. But, for the future, my permanent (as possible) headquarters is as above. Enclosed, the Fortune agreement.

I also enclose letter & contracts from Columbia Records Inc., N.Y. These will explain themselves. If you think the contracts satisfactory, will you send them back to me to sign & I will send them to you, signed, by return.[2]

I hope to get a real *lot* of work done here, & have already started. I must get a book ready this year.

I will try to come up to London abt once a month, & will let you know

---

1 Huw Owen Williams (1888–1961), poet. E. J. Evans, of Port Talbot, had asked Thomas for his support.
2 Columbia were issuing an album of records, of poets reading their own work, under the title 'Pleasure Dome'. Thomas's contribution was to last five minutes.

beforehand so that, if possible, we can meet for a few minutes to discuss things.

Apologies again for great delay.

Yours,
Dylan

MS: Texas

DAVID HIGHAM
9 May 1949   The Boat House   Laugharne   Carmarthenshire

Dear David,

I want to buy some review-clippings from an American Literary Clipping Service. I enclose the forms as sent to me. The Service tells me they have, already, 70 American reviews awaiting me. I should like to buy what they call '250 Economy' clippings for 14 dollars, but do not know how to send the money to America. Can it be done by your office through Ann Watkins, & the price deducted from some future cheque of mine? I hope so. I shd very much like to see those 70 reviews.

Incidentally, I have been asked to America to lecture this coming autumn or next spring;[1] perhaps we can discuss this when we meet, as I hope, next month.

Yours,
Dylan

MS: Texas

MARGARET TAYLOR
Tuesday [postmarked 11 May] [1949]   Boat House

My dear Margaret,

I should have written. I have been meaning to write each day. I've been wanting to write, but have put it off and off. Oh, all those bells were cracked long ago! They ring like dustbins! But it's true that each day since coming to this place I love and where I want to live and where I can work and where I have started work (my own) already, I've been saying to my contemptible self, You must write to Margaret at once to say that this is *it*: the place, the house, the workroom,[2] the time. I can never thank you enough for making this fresh beginning possible by all the trust you have put in me, by all the gifts you have made me, by all your labour & anxiety in face of callous & ungrateful behaviour. I know that the only way to

---

1 See page 334.
2 The Boat House is below a cliff, almost at sea level. Thomas's workroom was a small hut, a former bicycle shed, adjoining the public path that ran along the top of the cliff.

express my deep deep gratitude is to be happy & to write. Here I am happy and writing. All I shall write in this water and tree room on the cliff, every word, will be my thanks to you. I hope to God it will be good enough. I'll send you all I write. And ordinary letters too, full of trees & water & gossip & no news. This isn't that kind of letter. This is only the expression of the greatest gratitude in the world: you have given me a life. And now I am going to live it.

Dylan

MS: Texas

DAVID HIGHAM

May 16 1949   The Boat House   Laugharne   Carmarthenshire

Dear David,
    I enclose the 3 Columbia contracts, signed by me, for you to send to Ann Watkins to see to &—eventually—to collect from. This shd go by air-mail, shouldn't it? It's been rather a long time (not all my fault).
    See you next month about things.

Yours,
Dylan

MS: Texas

ELWYN EVANS

May 21 1949   The Boat House   Laugharne   Carmarthenshire

Dear Mr. Evans,
    Thank you so much for your letter. I have, as you see, moved back to Wales to live, and I hope I'll be able, now, to broadcast occasionally in the Welsh Home Service.
    And I *would*, sometime, like to do that proposed talk on Manley Hopkins, but I daren't undertake any new work like that—for even a 15 minutes talk on a poet would take me a long time to write—for some time to come. I don't suppose you'd like me to give a reading from some poet connected with Wales—say Edward Thomas, or W. H. Davies? I'd love to do that—particularly Thomas—& could make a good selection with just a few notes or comments.
    Probably that isn't the sort of thing you want at all. In which case, I'm awfully sorry—& I do hope one day I can write a talk for you.

Yours sincerely,
Dylan Thomas

MS: BBC

WILFRED GRANTHAM[1]
28 May 1949   The Boat House   Laugharne   Carmarthenshire

Dear Mr. Grantham,

I owe you very many apologies for what must seem my appalling rudeness in never having acknowledged your letters about the previous scheduling of *The Plain Dealer*. I didn't receive your telegrams until well after the time you wanted the script, as I had been away from this address, moving all over Wales so that no letters or anything could be forwarded. And then I fell ill, & still am ill. But these miserable facts are, I know, no excuse for not having word sent to you. I can only say that I felt, & feel, so perfectly bloody that I just groaned at all my obligations & put my head under the blankets.

And now, the worst thing is that I really *dare* not promise my adaptation by June 9th. I can try, here in bed, to write but am so uncertain of my insides that I may fold up halfway through. Please do try to accept my apologies, difficult though that is in face of all the bother (& worse) that I have caused you. I *hope* to be fit again *very* soon, & to send you the script next month; but I daren't take the risk of promising it by this new date, & then, perhaps at the last moment, failing you. I hope this is clear, if regretful: I am full of doctor's dope.

And I do hope that the BBC will be lenient enough to give me a later date for this job—a job I very much want to do.

More apologies are useless, but, though unsaid, are nevertheless most genuine.

Yours sincerely,
Dylan Thomas

MS: BBC

JOHN MALCOLM BRINNIN
May 28 1949   The Boat House   Laugharne   Carmarthenshire   Wales

J. M. Brinnin (1916–98) was a poet and critic who in 1949 became director of the Poetry Center at the Young Men's and Young Women's Hebrew Association, New York City. Determined to make a name for himself as a cultural activist, he sent Thomas an invitation on 14 April, ten days after his appointment, to read at the Center for a fee of $500; he also helped arrange other readings. It was the invitation that Thomas had been hankering after since 1945.

Dear John Malcolm Brinnin,
Let me first of all apologise for not having answered your letter long before this.

1 Grantham was the BBC producer now in charge of the *Plain Dealer* project. Thomas had been paid part of the 100-guinea fee for adapting the play and acting in it. No script was written.

Secondly, thank you most sincerely for your letter.

And thirdly, [I] accept with great pleasure the invitation of the Poetry Center of your institution to come to the United States to give a reading of my poems.

About the first: I've been changing addresses, a lot, lately, and mail has been erratically forwarded. I had your letter only last week—but even then I should have answered it at once.

About the second: I feel extremely honoured to be the first poet to be invited from abroad, who was not already a visitor, and delighted too. I've wanted, for some time, to come to the States, and there couldn't be a pleasanter way of coming than this.

And about the third: I should like to come to New York to give my reading early in 1950, probably in January or February. I should be only too glad to accept your sponsorship and to read in other places, including California.

Now about the financial side of it: I quite understand that you, as a non-profit-making organisation, must work on a modest budget, and, apart from transatlantic expenses, I should be prepared to accept, for my reading at your headquarters in New York, any fee that you yourselves think adequate. I must, however, point out that I have no private money, that I will arrive in New York with almost none and therefore must, by other arrangements made by you, make money immediately. I myself am very inefficient at arranging any financial details, but I am seeing my London literary agent next month & will ask him to get in touch with Ann Watkins Ltd of New York, with whom he is associated: she will then get in touch with you.[1] I hope, also, that Ann Watkins will be able to fix up a few other jobs for me, outside of your sponsorship, so that I shall be able to bring back some money to England. I mention this—that I must bring back some money to England—because, in order to come to America, I shall, of course, have to refuse literary and broadcast commissions here for some months. And when I return to England, I shall be, more or less, starting off again, picking up scripts etc. here & there.

I hope I'm not writing confusedly: I've had influenza, and am full of injections.

I should like to stay in the States for about three months.

Does that cover most of the points? I hope so. And I hope I'll hear from you soon again.

And, again, apologies for this overdue reply; & many many thanks for the honour you have paid me.

Yours sincerely,
Dylan Thomas

MS: Delaware

---

1 Brinnin acted as agent and took a percentage of earnings from the first tour. In his *Dylan Thomas in America* he said that the costs he had to meet from his own pocket, such as phone calls and telegrams, meant he received only token payment.

DAVID TENNANT
July 3 1949   The Boat House   Laugharne   Carmarthenshire

Dear David,
   That was wonderfully good of you. It has made a chunk of peace. I can
now go out without my mask. Thank you sincerely, David. I'm sorry your
land's unsteady too, and doubly grateful that, at such a time, you could
throw me such a big bit of the landslide. It's sweet to be able to go out in
the daytime again. I have got terrible pains in my big toe, which I am too
poor to call gout but which feels very much like it. And it also hurts to pee,
about which I dare not think at all. I wish one day you could come down to
this part, a lovely part. There are three herons now in front of my window,
all looking like Edith Sitwell. I have to come to London next month, for a
broadcast, for only 2 days, & will look in, hoping very very much that you
will be there. Thanks again, and for always. It has made an *enormous*
difference.

Yours,
Dylan

MS: Victoria

ELWYN EVANS
July 3 1949   Boat House   Laugharne   Carmarthenshire

Dear Mr. Evans,
   Sorry not to have answered sooner. I've been away.
   I'll send along copyright details tomorrow.[1]

Yours sincerely,
Dylan Thomas

MS: BBC

DAVID HIGHAM
July 8 1949 [telegram from Laugharne][2]

LETTER IN POST EXPLAINING PEER GYNT ABSURD SITUATION
DYLAN

Original: Location unknown

1 Thomas had been asked to read and comment on poems by Edward Thomas in a BBC
  programme from Cardiff, 'Arts Magazine'.
2 Copied in 1975 from the original at David Higham Associates.

DAVID HIGHAM
July 9th 1949   The Boat House   Laugharne   Carmarthenshire

Dear David,
     Peer Gynt.
     I was told of no dead-line date.
     I have received, from Miss Ramsden, a literal translation of only *two* of *five* acts. Am I to learn Norwegian & translate the other three acts for myself?
     And, most important of all, I should like to bring this to the attention of the B.B.C.:
     Louis MacNeice is translating a work of similar stature to Peer Gynt: Goethe's Faust. For this, the B.B.C. has allowed him one whole year, during which time no other work is expected from him. On top of a special fee, he is, for that year, paid his usual B.B.C. salary, which means that he is not obliged, for that year, to do any other work.
     I, on the other hand, am expected to produce a five act play in a few months, for a fee not sufficiently large to allow me to devote *all* my time to this work. Far from it. And now the B.B.C. is cutting up rough at a time when not *half* of the literal translation has been given me.
     I bring in MacNeice's case only because I think that the BBC is treating him fairly and can expect a thorough & painstaking job. Peer Gynt is just as difficult to work upon as is Goethe's Faust. Both are enormous plays. Why should one have to be scamped through insufficient money & time?
     Perhaps I should have insisted, earlier, on a long & elastic period of time in which to do this work. But certainly I have to insist now. I cannot begin to work upon the play until the whole literal translation is in my hands. And then, by the very magnitude of the job, it is bound to take a long time.
     Also: MacNeice is translating Faust in the only way possible for a non-German scholar. He is going through the text, line by line, word by word, with the German expert who is supplying the literal translation. Only in this way can he appreciate the texture of the German; & do justice to its word-music.
     Maybe it is not in order for me to parallel MacNeice's case with mine. But I am certain that the way he is working upon Faust, & the time he is allowed for that work, & the money he is paid, should also be the way in which I shd work upon this important & complex play.
     If the BBC decide to cancel my contract, then they must. And somehow we must pay them back the £150 I have been advanced. But if they think that someone else can trot out a translation in the very short [?space] of time they have allowed me, then they must, of necessity, be content with an inferior job.
     Perhaps you can convey to them some of these—to me—most justifiable points?
     And forgive me if I am, for once, riding a high horse.
     I *want* to do Peer Gynt. But it *must* take a *long* time. It must because it is

a great play, and I am not prepared to hack it out to a ridiculous time limit.
Hoping to hear from you, & to see you later in the month.

Yours,
Dylan

MS: Texas

ELWYN EVANS

13 July 1949   The Boat House   Laugharne   Carms

Dear Elwyn Evans,
   Enclosed the brief E. Thomas script & also the Collected Poems. I've given page numbers in Script. Hope you will keep the book for me. What time do you need me on the night?

Yours sincerely,
Dylan Thomas

MS: BBC

JEAN LEROY

15 July 1949   The Boat House   Laugharne   Carmarthenshire

Dear Miss LeRoy,
   About the reading of Edward Thomas's poems for the BBC, from Cardiff on July 29th. Fee fine. The fare, return, from Laugharne to Cardiff will be £2.13.0. To get the most convenient train I have to go from Laugharne to St. Clears (the nearest station) by cab.

Yours sincerely,
Dylan Thomas

MS: Texas

HECTOR MacIVER

15 July 1949   The Boat House   Laugharne   Carmarthenshire

Dear Hector,
   Thank you for the school magazine. I was sorry to see no picture of you in charge of any athletic group, but enjoyed the 'Chant' and 'A Group of Trees'. K. M. certainly has something there; and the echoes, though I cannot place where they come from, seem to me not unpleasant. But, indeed, he might be very good. The Anonymous author of 'Chant' I would, myself, take to be a far older boy with a taste for Scotch, though I may be

entirely wrong. I read the Rector's letter, and am delighted not to be in his school.

Did the books from Dent reach you safely? Do let me know some time. If they didn't, I shall write Dent an indecent, but icy, card.

I don't know if I can be in London at the end of the month, but, if I can, very certainly will. *Would you send me a line to say when & where you'll be?* I'd like to know beforehand so that I could try to get a little job to do in London on or about that date to pay my fares & some, at least, of my expenses.

I am writing this with a vile Biro junior which cuts through paper & table-top, spits greased mock-ink at shirt, eye, and wall, and whose writing fades, sometimes conveniently, almost at once.[1]

My study, atelier, or bard's bothy, roasts on a cliff-edge.

My wife is just about to go to the infirmary to have a Thomas. There are not enough of them already.

And now I'm going to greet the unseen with some beer.

Don't forget the postcard.

Yours,
Dylan

I've just realised that I have a broadcast to do in Cardiff on July 29th, and could, if you were in England, join you in London on the 30th.

MS: National Library of Scotland

DAVID HIGHAM
15th July 1949   The Boat House   Laugharne   Carmarthenshire

Apologies for this dreadful Biro pen

Dear David,

Thank you for your long, & lucid, letter of the 13th.

I do agree that what we really want is a little more consultation, between you & me, before I commit myself to any major job with a time-limit on it. And in the future I'll see to it that we do have a chance to confer.

But now I'm afraid that, in spite of the BBC postponing their limit to Sept 30, I still have to say that I can't do it. The last 3 acts have just arrived from Miss Ramsden: I couldn't do the vast amount of work on them that is necessary in $2\frac{1}{2}$ months. I had begun to do preliminary work on Act One when your letter came. And I *had*, on the original receipt of the first 2 acts, written to Miss Ramsden about them.

Would the BBC allow me to keep Miss Ramsden's translation & work on it when I can throughout this year, setting no time-limit but allowing me

---

1 Ballpoint pens were coming into general use. Some of Thomas's letters, written with early models on cheap paper, are difficult to read.

to do the best job I *can* do on it *in my own time*? I should be most grateful if they could.

About the return of the money: I do not see how, at this moment, the matter can be arranged. Gainsborough Films still have £150 coming to me, but I would rather let them pay me this in due course rather than ask them, officially, now. I can, however, try unofficially, myself, through Ralph Keene.

I am just beginning the 1st treatment for Gainsborough of a technicolor film of 'Vanity Fair' (with, dear God, Maggie Lockwood) & there shd be lots in that eventually. But at the moment I don't see where the money to refund the BBC is to come from. My wife is just about to have another baby—it is a few days overdue[1]—and I'll need all I can get. What do you think?

I hope to be able to see you next week.

Yours,
Dylan

MS: Texas

WILFRED GRANTHAM
July 15 1949   The Boat House   Laugharne   Carmarthenshire

Dear Mr. Grantham,

I'm sorry as anything, but the reason you've had no word from me of the 'Plain Dealer'—&, what is worse, no script—is, still, this persistent gastritis of mine which I'm about to have X-rayed for many an ulcerous fear.[2] And I daren't promise it by August 15th in case I'm whizzed away to hospital. It's not such a long job, I know, but I do feel so bloody. I hope that, again, the BBC will be lenient with me & not, yet, demand back the half of my fee which I have already been paid. I may, indeed, be able to do the job by the required date, it may take a very short time to do, but what is that to the planners? I apologise for this useless letter, & plead for leniency.

Yours sincerely,
Dylan Thomas

MS: BBC

---

1 The child, a boy, was born at Carmarthen, 24 July 1949. He was named Colm Garan; the second name is Welsh for 'heron'.

2 It was becoming harder to distinguish Thomas's bouts of genuine ill-health from the excuses for editors that increasingly he had to make. By now the BBC was deeply suspicious.

JOHN DAVENPORT
30 July 1949   Boat House   Laugharne   Carmarthenshire

My dear John,

Arrived back, rather bruised, to find the financial situation here far worse than even I, in my tearful jags of the last week, cd have imagined. They've stopped sending coal, & will, any moment, stop sending milk: essential things in a baby-packed, freezing house. I'm summonsed for rates. No more meat. I cannot write a cheque, of course, so that we are—for the first time for years—literally without one shilling. Four cheques have been returned from the Savage, but without savage comment. And my father is dangerously ill with pneumonia; and I've had some sort of breakdown. Christ!

So if you do ever come across anyone—excluding Tony,[1] to whom I write separately, & about a different matter—with a single fiver to spare, it would make a difference. Or suggest anyone to whom I could write. The Tony-Liddel-Bank thing will work some time, for I shall be forced to go to America, God help me, my breakdown, & my guts, but it's *now*, at *once*, *temporarily*, the nine quid for milk, the ten for coal, six for builder, eight for summons, without mentioning cigarettes for Cat, sweets for Aeron etc. If you do see anyone interested, *please*, old boy. For any amount. To be paid after America. Can you also, please, send me Wyn Henderson's address?

How are you?

I'm on the *rim*.

Thanks to Marjorie[2] for her dinners & kindnesses.

Love,
Dylan

Am sending letter to Tony (which is only to corroborate the Liddel arrangement) care of you.

MS: Texas

MARGARET TAYLOR
Friday August 5 49   Boat House

My dear Margaret,

I haven't been up to the main street for over 2 days, ever since coming back, via Swansea & Vernon, from Cardiff. And your registered letter—though there *was* no letter, only those great green things I hadn't seen for so long—had arrived before I called at Brown's this morning. There I heard

---

1 'Tony' may have been an affluent acquaintance, introduced several years earlier by Mervyn Levy, with whom Levy served in the Army.

2 Davenport's second wife.

that you'd left me an urgent message to ring you: but this morning it was days too late, & so I must inadequately write. I hope the message wasn't terribly, [?stranglingly] important. And thank you ten times for this morning. I didn't know what to do, & one of the main reasons I didn't go out was fear of debts snapping at my heels. Thank you a great deal, & once I am again out of the money-wood, in the straight & pounded clear—though it will, as I said in nasty London, be ten weeks—may I be able to repay some of my now almost national debt to you.

Caitlin is awfully well. I do hope you got her letter. She gave me, just before leaving hospital, several letters—to mothers, sisters, & yourself—to post, but only yesterday I came across, in a pocket packed with fag-ends, a letter to Ringwood. I trust that was the only one that missed the letterbox.

Colum[1] Garan—Welsh for heron. Did Cat tell you?—looks just like any other baby I've seen, skinned and fragile, though Caitlin says he looks just like my father. Apart from the baldness, I see no resemblance.

Swansea was very noisy. Dan, Vernon, Fred, & I are to do a halfhour broadcast together from Wales some time next month.[2] I'll let you know when, in case you can pick up the station which is mostly preachers & choirs.

I'm writing this in the heaven of my hut. Wild day, big seas for Laugharne, & the boats of the Williamses lurching exactly like Williamses.

Write soon. I have no news. I am beginning to work hard again. Llewelyn goes to Lundy next week.[3]

And the thanks I can never express, again, for the help by which I can do the shopping, pay the girl, walk out at all into the best town.

Yours ever,
Dylan

MS: Texas

G. V. ROBERTS
5 August 1949   The Boat House   Laugharne   Carmarthenshire

Dear Sir,

Thank you for the invitation, from the Tenby & District Arts Club, to come along & read or talk sometime during your autum-winter session.

As you see, I live near to Tenby, and am very glad to accept your invitation.

If you could give me a choice of a few dates?

1 Thomas often gave the name, Colm, its phonetic spelling.
2 See page 803n. The broadcast wasn't until October.
3 Thomas's sister and her husband, Gordon Summersby, ran the ferry from the English mainland to Lundy Island. Dylan and Caitlin went there, too. Caitlin's friend Helen McAlpine was at the Boat House looking after the two younger children, Aeron (aged six) and Colm (aged four weeks).

Thank you very much for what you said about my reading from Edward Thomas last week.

Yours very truly,
Dylan Thomas

MS: National Library of Wales

PRINCESS CAETANI[1]
6 August 1949   The Boat House   Laugharne   Carmarthenshire

Dear Madame di Sermoneta,

I am very very sorry not to have answered, long before this, your letter of the end of June. I didn't want to say that I could send you a poem until I was quite sure I could; and I wasn't sure until I finished, only this week, the poem I enclose.[2]

The cheque you so very kindly sent on account of the poem—which I should, of course, have acknowledged—was more welcome than perhaps you could imagine. I had, myself, been ill and was, and am, in debt; and the cheque did really help. I would be most grateful if I could be sent any more small amount of money that is, maybe, due, on the poem, as soon as possible: I have a just-born new son, & there are so many things that are needed. I hope that this doesn't sound too grasping, especially after your first kindness and after my carelessly not replying to it.

Can I print this poem separately in an English magazine, or does your review also circulate in England?

Thank you very much for sending me a copy of the review, which had some magnificent poems.

Yours very sincerely,
Dylan Thomas

MS: Camillo Caetani Foundation

1 Marguerite Caetani (1880–1963), also known as the Duchess of Sermoneta. As Marguerite Chapin of Connecticut she married the Italian Roffredo Caetani, Prince of Bassiano, in 1911. A patron of the arts, she published important writers in two literary magazines that she financed and edited, *Commerce* (1924–32) and later *Botteghe Oscure*, which means 'dark shops' and was named after the district of Rome where she lived.

2 'Over Sir John's hill', published in *Botteghe Oscure IV* (December 1949). The Boat House faces the hill, half a mile away across the sands. Thomas wrote the poem, his first for two years, to celebrate his return to Laugharne.

DAVID HIGHAM
Monday [?August 1949]   The Boat House   Laugharne   Carmarthenshire

Dear David,
   Thank you very much indeed for the arrangement you have managed to make by which, for seven weeks, I can be paid £10 a week.[1] And for the first cheque. I haven't written before to acknowledge this, but did send a wire, fully approving the idea, last week—I do hope you got it, otherwise you must think me more careless than I really am.
   I hope, by the end of the 7th week—or is it eight weeks? I'm writing this on the sand in the sun, & your letter isn't to hand—that I shall [have] finished my final script for Gainsborough & that, if only temporarily, my financial position will be upright again.
   In the meantime, those cheques of £10 a week will save our lives. Thank you for making them possible.
   I hope to see you soon, in London, but not until the script is finished.
   Thank you for the Caton agreement,[2] which arrived separately.

Yours,
Dylan

P.S. I hope Mrs Taylor, for all her kindness, is not becoming a nuisance.

MS: Texas

*G. V. ROBERTS
18 August 1949   The Boat House   Laugharne   Carmarthenshire[3]

Dear Mr Roberts,
   Sorry not to have written before about the choice of dates you so kindly sent me.
   I think that October 28th would suit me best. And as for a title, I can think of nothing but 'Some Modern Poetry'. It will really be a reading with comments.
   And the fee of five guineas is very acceptable.
   October 28th, then, at 7.30.

With Best wishes,
Yours sincerely,
Dylan Thomas

MS: Victoria

1 Higham had withheld money in anticipation of tax demands, which may have proved less than expected.
2 The repurchase of rights in *18 Poems* for £150. N. Caton was a director of Fortune Press.
3 The letter was written from Lundy. So, probably, was the previous one.

PRINCESS CAETANI
11th October 1949   The Boat House   Laugharne   Carmarthenshire

Dear Madame di Sermoneta,

If I were to write down the number of apologies I owe to you, it would sound, I'm afraid, all too false and ridiculous:—nobody, one might think, *could* say that he was sincerely sorry so many times and still be sincere about it. So let me, for the moment, apologise only for not having answered your letter of September 23rd, nor acknowledged the very kind and very welcome cheque enclosed in it, nor even replied at once to your note of October 4th. There are lots and lots of reasons for all this appallingly rude delay of mine, but all so small, and contradictory, and confusing, I hardly dare name them. The letter to Witney, Oxfordshire, was long being forwarded to the above address in Wales, which is where I live; I have been away from home, unnecessarily broadcasting and lecturing; I have been ill, and depressed; I have missed the times of the post; I have carried letters around in my pockets for days; I have had so many really small, difficult, pokey, little jobs of work to do I have spent my time trotting and braying from one to the other and back again like a donkey stung by wasps. And there [are] many many more equally trivial, but momentarily insurmountable, obstacles to prevent my just being able to sit down calmly for a minute and write to you and thank you and to hope that we *will*, somehow, in spite of all the time that has frittered away, be able to meet in London before you leave.

You said, in your note of the 4th, that you wd be staying in London at least a fortnight. When—if you know it now—is the *really* last day on which we could meet? The 19th & the 20th are impossible to me: I talk to two Welsh societies on those dates—and about God knows what.

But I do so hope that somehow I may be able to come to London & meet you after that, or just before. Nothing is easy. This is eight hours from London. I am tangled in hack-work. Depression has me by the ears. And there are other reasons too, locusts of them. But, perhaps, it *may* still be managed.

I am very glad you liked the poem I sent you. Alas, I have not finished another: these damned little fly-paper jobs I have to do keep me stuck from my work. But when I manage to finish the poem now half completed,[1] it is yours to print. And thank you for what you said about the other poem.

Perhaps, if I'm ever forgiven, I shall hear from you soon about the possibility of our meeting?

And a sea of sorries again.

Sincerely Yours,
Dylan Thomas

MS: Camillo Caetani Foundation

1 'In the White Giant's Thigh'.

DAVID HIGHAM
11 Oct 1949　　　　　The Boat House　Laugharne　Carmarthenshire

Dear David,

Thank you for your summary of the points we discussed in your office.[1]

I enclose the first letter I had from John Malcolm Brinnin in America. The second I can find nowhere. All I remember of the second letter was that it said the fee for my recital at the headquarters of the Y.M.Y.W. Hebrew Association wd be 500 dollars: inclusive. This was written after I had said I would go to read there. I should very much like to know if the 500 dollars is supposed to include my fare out to the States. And also, of course, I must be absolutely sure of several other really worth-while engagements there before I *do* go. I want to come back to England with some dollars. Also, as I told you, I want to take my wife. I hope Ann Watkins is dealing with these points now.

Has that income-tax £10 a week I was receiving now come to an end? I didn't receive the usual letter & cheque today. I hope to God it hasn't: I can't continue without it: bills are *piling* up here: the worst bill is £50 for school-fees: and I'm afraid I was extremely optimistic when I said I would finish V.Fair ten days from our last meeting. It is going very stickily at the moment—though soon will, I hope, race ahead. *Do* please see what can be done: either a continuation, somehow, of that tenner a week or a possible advance on the Verona-printed poems (which I see advertised for February publication in Dent's catalogue. At the price of £5.0.0. Who'll buy?). Really, it's urgent.

No other point that I can think of.

　　　　　　　　　　　　　　　　　Yours,
　　　　　　　　　　　　　　　　　Dylan

MS: Texas

JOHN DAVENPORT
11 Oct 1949　　　　　Boat House　Laugharne　Carmarthenshire

My Dear John,

A scruffy note from a scruffy man. And, too, to tell you that I *haven't* finished that poem I promised for Arena: [*in margin*: Next number of Arena for certain][2] there's lots of work to do on it, and, instead of doing it, I've

1 Higham had tried to construct a plan of action for the conventionally successful freelance writer that he hoped Thomas had inside him, struggling to get out. It included *Vanity Fair* ('to be finished in about 10 days'), *The Plain Dealer* ('not to take more than a month'), *Peer Gynt* ('to be ready by the end of the year'), the U.S. visit (followed by 'a full year at your own work so far as possible, beginning with the completion of the *Skin Trade*'), 'the small effort required to collect material for the book for Dent', and Thomas's radio play.

2 *Arena* was a new 'literary magazine interested in values'. Davenport, Jack Lindsay and Randall Swingler were the editors.

been getting on with my awful script,[1] broadcasting from Swansea with Dan Jones & the boys[2]—Dan conducts the London Philharmonic in a performance of his 1st Symphony in the S'sea Festival of Music next week; this week, Wed or Thur, is conducting three tone-poems of his on the Welsh Regional (three!)—and being a pest up the wilds here, Mydrim, Brechfa, & Marble Town.[3] But, as soon as I finish it, I'll send it to you, Jack, & Randall whom I thank, v much, for their wire to which I should have replied had not etc.

I'm sorry I saw so little of you in London last, which sounds a compliment but is really a grief. I may be up in a fortnight & will write, ring, or just glaze in.

Ever,
Dylan

MS: Texas

JAMES LAUGHLIN
October 13th 1949 The Boat House Laugharne Carmarthenshire
Wales

(Thomas-hunting begins)

Dear Jay,
   Have you heard that I'm supposed to be coming to the States in February 1950? I've been asked, by John Malcolm Brinnin—what's he like?—to read, grandly and solemnly, like a man with the Elgin marbles in his mouth,[4] poems to the Y.M. & Y.W.H.A. at New York on, I think, February 23. Brinnin said that he could also fix up a few more readings in various parts, including California. Do you know of any people, places, institutions, etc. from whom or which, by reading aloud modern British poems and a few, as few as possible, of my own, I could get a handful of dollars? Ann Watkins is seeing to the Brinnin side: which, if his letters are any proof, is what he has. Perhaps, if anything occurred to you, you could have a word with, or drop a line to her? I'd be very, very grateful. I want to stay in the States for three months. And I want to be able to return to England with some money so that I won't, at once, have to chase again the hackjobs by which, dear

---

1 Probably *Vanity Fair*.
2 'Swansea and the Arts', a discussion—carefully scripted in advance—with Thomas as presenter. The others taking part were Vernon Watkins, John Prichard, Dan Jones and Fred Janes. Recorded in Swansea 6 October, broadcast (Welsh Home Service) 24 October.
3 Meidrim and Brechfa are villages in West Wales. 'Marble Town' is Swansea.
4 The Greek sculptures at the British Museum, and, in Thomas's joke, marbles as used in the game. The phrase became one of his standbys. 'Men from the BBC who speak as if they had the Elgin Marbles in their mouths', he said in his last radio broadcast, 'A visit to America'.

Christ, I live, have at once to set into motion again the insignificant, wheezy little machines that sausage out crumbs and coppers for me, scriptlings, radio whinnies. I don't want to find myself in New York with only two or three scantily paying engagements in front of me, and to return as broke as when I arrived. We have a new, three months' old son. I would, naturally, have to support him, my other two children at school, and my wife, for the three months of my absence. I should like to be able to bring my wife with me. Would that be possible, do you think? I don't want to load you with all my worries and apprehensions, but whom else do I load? The idea of the States puts the fear of Mammon in me, though I very much want to come. Briefly, can you help, in a practical way, to alleviate the worries of my visit? How, I don't know. But do write and tell me something soon, if you will. Maybe I should be writing like this to Brinnin, not to you. But you I know, all nine feet of you, as I remember, and me in my abbreviated coat, and Godfrey Winn popping out like a Jill in the Box.[1] If I cannot bring my wife, then I must leave with her money enough for three English (or Welsh) enormously costly months! And how the hell am I to do that?

Here, we can nearly carry on by my drivelling for films & radio. Without me, the Boat House sinks, the cormorants have it. Indeed, I can hardly, now, walk up the main street of this sad, lovely town without the bowler-hatted shags at my throat and ankles.

So please do write. Suggest what you can. Say what you like.

I have a couple of poems; and a few autobiographical sketches which, perhaps, you could try to place for me in the commercial magazines. I'll send them on when they are found, washed, and typed.

There are, I suppose, no chances of a reading on the radio? Why should there be?

I want to enjoy my visit, and come back rustling, if wobbly.

Yours,
Dylan

MS: Houghton

JOHN DAVENPORT

13 October 1949   The Boat House   Laugharne   Carmarthenshire

Dear John,

I've only now remembered that I addressed my yesterday's letter to you at Rossetti Mansions. It might not reach you. This, then, to make doubly sure, is to apologise for the fact that I haven't yet completed the promised poem for Arena, and to say that it will be ready for the next number and that the fee will be at least one crippling port, large, in the Savage or the

---

1 Godfrey Winn (1908–71), popular columnist, seen as effeminate.

Authors' now that Kingsmill is dead and being cut by Dickens. And please to thank Jack & Randall for the telegram, and yourself, of course. Things are appalling here, which can only mean one thing. Bills and demand notes, at me like badgers, whoosh! up the manholes, or gathered, grinning and panting round my bed, odiously familiar, like the little hyenas in Paphnutius's cell.[1] It is bad in a small community where everything is known: temporary insolvency goes the glad rounds as swift as a miscarriage. I owe a quarter's rent on my mother's house, Llewelyn's school fees (for last term), much to each tradesman. Yesterday I broke a tooth on a minto. There are rats in the lavatory, tittering while you shit, and the official rat-man comes every day to given them tidbits before the kill. Unfortunately for my peace of mind, the rat man has only one arm. Glyn Jones, the biggest prig in Wales, is coming to see me on Saturday about something priggish, with his wife like the backside of a chapel, and his little cool and collected moustache, and his thirstlessness, looking about him, prigbrows lifted, in my fuggy room like an unloved woman sniffing at the maid's linen on the maid's day out.[2] I am three months behind with my filmscript, a year behind with Peer Gynt. I have the hot & cold, rose-flush comings & goings after elderberry wine last night in a hamhooked kitchen with impossibly rich, and thunderingly mean, ferret-faced farmers who dislike me so much they treat me like a brother. At last the National Insurance has caught up with me who has never put a stamp on his card, having no card. If you see anyone likely, pinch his boots for me. I cannot come to London to hunt, for obvious reasons. Indeed, I dare not step out. This morning I had a toadstool for breakfast, and Caitlin called me a guttersnipe, though there seemed to be no connection. I'm sorry to write you such mournings. See you at the barracudas.

> Love,
> Dylan

MS: Texas

JEAN LEROY
16 October 1949   The Boat House   Laugharne   Carmarthenshire

Dear Miss LeRoy,
   Yours of the 14th. About the programme called 'Swansea & the Arts'. Twelve guineas seems alright, plus 2 return fares Laugharne–S'sea, & one night's allowance. The return fare Laugharne–S'sea is: 17/6. Two return fares make, according to me, £1.15.0.

> Yours sincerely,
> Dylan Thomas

MS: Texas

1 St Paphnutius, an Egyptian monk, much persecuted.
2 Glyn Jones wrote in his journal, 'My friendship with Dylan was bound to lapse because I represented all that he was trying to get away from.' He also remarked, 'I am not a prig, I am a puritan,' adding, 'So was Dylan, especially about homosexuals.'

PRINCESS CAETANI
2nd November 1949   The Boat House   Laugharne   Carmarthenshire

Dear Madame di Sermoneta,

I did enjoy, very much, meeting in London, though, to me, the meetings were all too brief and few. That, I feel, is entirely my fault. In London I am flustered, excited, unable to concentrate; I am so nervous, usually for no reason, that my nervousness too often turns to unintentional rudeness; I am stupid, shy, and garrulously arrogant in turn; all I seem to want to do is to get away from where I am and from what I am doing, however much I might like where I am and what I am doing; I can almost never say what I really mean to say; I am out of my world—though what that world may be, God knows—altogether. And it is for these reasons, and for many others, I am sure, which I am not, myself, perceptive enough to see, that our meetings *were* so brief, so very few.

So let me apologise, from this calm distance from London, for what must have appeared to be my vague and pointless behaviour and—what is worse—my ingratitude.

I wanted to talk to you about your magazine, and to hear you talk about it; I wanted to discuss with you several things in it that seemed to me to be of particular interest; I wanted to suggest to you the names of a few little-known English writers whose work I thought you might like to see.

And, instead of that, all I could do was to talk, disconnectedly, about myself, scatter you with ash, gollup your whisky-&-soda, make an inexact arrangement with you about a short story of my own, and then rush off into the London night I loathe.

But let me, anyway, and in writing, try to make exact the position of the story which I am to write for Botteghe. The next story I write is to be given to you immediately. In our conversation—if you can grace with that word a jumble of ineptitudes from myself and some kind words from you—you gave me no time-limit by which the story should reach you. If you care to give me a rough time-limit, I shall abide by that. The story I will try to make as good as I can.

And you, do you remember, agreed to pay me, in advance, for that story, the sum of £100. And there is, of course, no further money than that due to me from Botteghe for that story.

You gave me a cheque for £50, and said that you could send on the remaining £50 very soon.

I hope I am right in my interpretation of our agreement.

And now I come to the most shamefaced part of this shamefaced letter. I need that other £50 so very desperately, so very quickly.

When I came home, thank God, from London, I found my wife ill, really ill, with worry over the summonses for debt that had been pouring into the house during my absence. The amount needed to clear them is, to us, enormous, insurmountable. But if I *could* possibly have that £50 *straight*,

straight away, I could at least settle the most urgent and virulent debt of all.

I apologise for the horribly stilted manner in which I am writing to you. I, too, am too sick with money to feel, for a moment, free.

But all I mean is, I'm in a hell of a hole. I see no way of getting out of it. But that other money, if sent to me at once on the wings of the dove of the Air Mail from whatever country you are in, *would* help. (I was, of course, too careless, too conscienceless, to enquire from you where you were going when you left the Connaught Hotel. I can only hope this letter reaches you very soon.)

What self-pity I drench these pages in! How ghastly to read they must be! But all I can say, in any possible extenuation, is that, in all my moneyless days, I have never been more hopelessly engulfed in debt, that we can't sleep, and I can't work.

When I see you again, if ever, I can tell you, perhaps, what the hellish circumstances were. Now, however, there is no past tense: the hellish circumstances just *are*.

Thank you for your kindness in London.

> Yours sincerely,
> Dylan Thomas

MS: Camillo Caetani Foundation

*JOHN MALCOLM BRINNIN
[telegram, 7 November 1949, 2.36 pm, Laugharne]

PROPOSITION GRATEFULLY ACCEPTED PLEASE GO AHEAD LETTER IN MAIL DYLAN THOMAS[1]

Original: Delaware

BBC
November 7th 1949   The Boat House Laugharne Carmarthenshire

Dear Sir,

I'm afraid this is a very bothering request, but I do hope you can help me.

A few years ago—perhaps in 1944, or 1945—I broadcast a talk, for the Welsh Children's Hour, called '*Memories of Childhood*'. To the best of my

1 See page 355.

recollection, I broadcast it from Carmarthen, Mr Aneirin Talfan Davies producing.

Now I am making a collection, for publication in book form, of many of my old sketches and stories, and would like, very much, to include this particular one. Unfortunately, I have lost my only copy, and am wondering if you could dig out, from BBC files, the copy I used when broadcasting.

I'd be enormously obliged if you could help me. My publisher is waiting to get on with the book.

Yours faithfully,
Dylan Thomas

MS: BBC

HELEN AND BILL McALPINE

Saturday 12 Nov 49   Hut on Cliff

My dear two, Helen & Bill,

First, before apologies, messages of love, questions, and our tiny news, how more than pleased we are that the job's in the Billy-bag.[1] How sensible of them to recognise, when they saw him, the proper man. I'm always surprised when a bloody Body shows any sense at all. And how glad, too, will be your age-old friends in the township when, this Saturday night, I tell them in the great shining bars, the chromium Corporation, the Cross Club ('Dancing to Romaine & her Music'), the Back Room Hotel. But nobody could be as delighted as I am. Except Caitlin. Congratulations from my dirty eyrie, from the Columed house, from all the statues of the herons: relations on a monument.

How is the wrist? I can't say Helen's wrist, Bill's job, when I'm writing to both of you. I must suppose that you are one and the same person: you are a scientific officer, you fell arse over tip while skating, you have been writing stories, you are grieved because you cannot use your sewing machine, you old bisexual you. You are plastered, your wrist is plastered. How long will it be before you can type and stitch, button your flies and your brassiere? Does it INTERFERE? Send details at once, preferably illustrated, in plain envelope.

How are the stories? Is the book of them ready yet? And are there any new ones I could be sent?

And can you both manage to come down here for Christmas? We want you to, very much. And so does everyone else. Not a day potters by but I'm asked news of you, I'm commanded to send wishes, greetings, amiable insults, coarse remarks, love. Phil, Marie, Driver Raye, Frank who lays eggs with his mouth, Fleming, Tommy (Nero) Rowlands, Ivy of course, Texan Ebie, Dynamo Bill, Banjo Ned, the Irish teetotallers, fiend Aeron, Colum if

1 McAlpine was a scientific officer with the British Council.

he could, Llewelyn from his presumably masturbative dormitory, Jack Pierce, Billy Thomas, my father ('This is the end of civilisation!'), my mother ('Now don't think I'm interfering, dear, I just happened to be looking out of the window as you fell down Brown's steps'), people whose names I don't know, Tommy Gravel-Voice Williams, Up-it-Comes Gilbert, Ted and Norma (whose name should be spelt with a low whistle), Ivan, Shee, little battered men on Friday nights, the lecherous and patricidal ferrymen, dumb barber, all, all say, 'when are they coming down again?' and do not need to explain who they mean.[1] I forgot wren-legged Tudor; he too. So if you can come for Christmas, not only the Boat House but all the barmy town will cheer and drink your health, happiness, and unique contribution, if I may phrase it so, to the life of lazy Laugharne. Send answer by return, preferably on an incredibly obscene postcard, preferably of blonde Lesbians, preferably in sexicolor.

Early this week, Ebie, laying his pistol down,[2] and I went to Whitland Mart and bought three geese & a turkey. (Alas, only one goose is mine.) All alive. The buying took fifteen minutes, just after lunch, but, oddly, we didn't return till midnight, the birds in the boot savage and famished. Now they all live on the lawn back of Brown's, leering into the kitchen. We buy them Black Market grain at the Butcher's Arms, St. Clears: also, little wicked chops, but those for us. We had a very farmerish day, and came back covered in manure, slapping little sticks against our thighs, talking turkey and a lot of cock. Ebie didn't get up till teatime next day, and then rushed off to be given medicine by his fancy woman, the chemist. Next day he didn't get up at all.

My American plans are going ahead. I'm to read in the Museum of Modern Art, New York, & the Library of Congress, Washington, and several other places. I've been given a flat for my New York stay, in the centre of the city. The Gotham Book Mart is giving me a party on my arrival. I'm also to give a broadcast, & to spend a week at a Massachusetts Women's College oh my. I'm going to try to take Caitlin with me. Brigit has promised to have Colum for the 3 months, if necessary, and maybe Nancy & Gordon will take over the Boat House and look after Aeron, the innocents. So really all that stands in our way is money and red-tape permission. I hope Cat can come. She won't stay on in Laugharne if I do have to go alone, but can't think where to go. If I can't get permission to take her, perhaps she & Helen could fix up something together? Cat still isn't well, gets thinner and more nervous every day. I wish and I wish to

---

1 Among the well-wishers: Phil Williams was landlord of a pub, the Cross House; Frank was Frankie John, who had a superior accent; Fleming Williams was a former Portreeve of Laugharne and landlord of the Corporation Arms; Ebie (variously spelt) and Ivy Williams ran Brown's Hotel, and various other things; Gravel-Voice Williams was a fishmonger.

2 In 'Pistol Packin' Mama', a song of 1943 (by Al Dexter) that was still being played on radio, Mama was told to 'lay that pistol down'.

God she would be well again. America may help, though it's a queer place for a rest-cure.

I wish I had been to Burton, and to the Goose Fair. The ear-rings are *very* nice.

This morning, a photographer, John Deakin, came down from London to take pictures of me for the new American magazine, terribly tasty, terribly glossy, rich as rich, he says, called Flair. He told me he has seen a dummy of it. Its manifesto is written in white ink on silver paper. The captions to some of its photographs are invisible; heat has to be applied to the blanks before the words appear. The cover is by Cocteau. Deakin, a queer, took pictures of me in a high wind in the church cemetery, one of them inside the railings of a tomb,[1] my hair, uncut for months, either completely covering my face (I think he liked that) or blown up like a great, dancing, mousey busby. I look forward to seeing the pictures.

I have finished my poem, a hundred lines, but it may need a second part to it.[2]

Write soon & tell me everything. Our love to Fred. And very much to you both.

Dylan

MS: Buffalo

*PAUL REDGRAVE

Nov 14 1949   The Boat House   Laugharne   Carmarthenshire   Wales

Dear Paul,

Confusion upon confusion, as Frankie Howerd[3] says. I found, this morning, in a drawer, three unopened envelopes. Two contained bills, and I'm glad I never found them. The third had your letter, of the 24th of August. Last week I found a cheque, for one pound eleven & seven, in a slipper, dated July. A friend of mine once found a poached egg in his Blake. I'm *terribly* sorry to be so careless, you must think I'm a shit. And indeed I am, but not about things like that. It's miles too late now, I suppose, and your novel, I hope, has found a home. But, just in case, & to get in touch with when you have any new work, the agents are: Pearn, Pollinger, &

---

1 Thomas seems to be standing in the grave, with leaves to his waist; it is one of the best-known portraits. John Deakin, a Soho character, worked for *Vogue* and other magazines.
2 A 100-line poem suggests 'Poem on his Birthday', the only apparent candidate at that length. This may have been under way in 1949, but was not completed until 1951, when it was quickly sold and published. The reference here is probably to 'In the White Giant's Thigh', a poem that caused problems—Thomas told Vernon Watkins it took him three weeks to write the opening line—and got shorter as he reworked it.
3 British entertainer.

Higham, Ltd, 39–40 Bedford Street, Strand, London W.C.2. The man I know is David Higham.

How are you both? You'll be in St Catherine's now. Is Bill Morgan still there? If so, give him my love and say I lost his letter about a Welsh walking-holiday and hadn't got an address to write to. I am vile with everyone I know.

I was in Oxford a month ago, but only for one day & night. I Georged[1] it to great effect.

Our new child, Colum, a boy, is nearly 4 months old, very old and loud and lovable.

Best of luck with 'Murder is Honey',[2] & to you & Olwen.

I'll be seeing you in Oxford.

And I'll mention your name to Higham when I write to him this week.

Yours,
Dylan

MS: Location unknown

JOHN MALCOLM BRINNIN
November 23 1949   The Boat House   Laugharne   Carmarthenshire
Wales

Dear John Malcolm Brinnin,

First of all: Many apologies for this month-long delay in answering your extremely nice and helpful letter. My lying cable said, 'Letter in mail'. And I did intend to write at once, but had to go away, felt suddenly ill, clean forgot, put it off for a rainy day, was struck by lightning, any or all of these. And your cable about a second reading, my wife mislaid, found only this morning in a mousenest handbag.

Thank you profoundly for your letter. I can't tell you how pleased I am that you should have suggested you look after my American readings. I can think of nothing more sensibly pleasant. What an abominable phrase! Nothing I have ever enjoyed has been sensibly pleasant. I mean, I can think of nothing better. I was very nervous about my visit: that is, about the arranging of readings to make some money. I should have made a mess of things. My life here, in the deep country, is incredibly complicated; but, in a city, I spin like a top. And procrastination is an element in which I live. Thank you, very much indeed, for having, in the first place, made my visit possible, and for wishing to work with me. Naturally, I understand about the fee for expenses; I couldn't, anyway, allow you to work with me if you did not take a percentage. And the 15 per cent you mention is very, very moderate for all the troublesome work you'll have to do. I feel relieved

---

1 The George inn.
2 Later published as *Full Fathom Six*.

now; and can face the whole undertaking with only quite minor paralysis.

It's very very good of you to lend me your New York apartment for my stay there.[1] And the idea of a little rest cure in Saratoga Springs is also appealing: I think I shall need it.

As to the number of readings: you say that you will be able, you think, 'to arrange for, at least, fifteen engagements, and, very likely, considerably more'. How many jobs do *you* think I should do? I don't want to work my head off, but, on the other hand, I *do* want to return to England with some dollars in my pocket. And, of course, I want to get around the States a bit. I'll have to leave this to you. I have been asked to be one of the Kemball-lecturers-for-the-year at Mount Holyoke College, Massachusetts, at a fee of 150 dollars. I think I should accept this, don't you? And would it be possible to give a reading somewhere else near there—boring two birds with one stone? I should say, sometime in March for Holyoke. But you will know when to fit it in. I shall write today, to Holyoke, accepting, and saying that you will get in touch with them suggesting some dates, most possibly in March, which might be convenient for them. I enclose the Holyoke letter. Is that all right? Also: the Watkins agent has been writing to Robert Richman, of the Institute of Contemporary Art, about a reading & a lecture in Washington; together with a suggestion about a reading at the Library of Congress. I enclose Watkins' letter, to Richman. Would you care to write to Watkins about this? and arrange what you think best—if anything. I must say Richman wants a hell of a lot of the profits. I hand the baby over, with bewildered gratitude.

I should, incidentally, like *very* much to go to California.

I hope, I do hope, that in *most* of the cases you *will* be able to arrange that travelling expenses be paid in addition to the fee. It seems very important. And that leads me to the trickiest, to my mind, problem of all: Treasury permission from here to go over to the States. *And* the money with which to travel. I've no idea how to approach the Treasury about this, or what U.S. Departments I must approach. No idea in the world. Can you help in this? It's a kind of bureaucratic nightmare: *why* are you going? *who* wants you to go? *What* will you do when you get there? *Are* you a Communist? *Do* you have clean thoughts? And the question of travelling money: I want, if possible, to go by plane, not liking the big dull sea except to look at. This costs in English money about £80. How many dollars that is, since the devaluation of the pound, I have no idea.[2] I presume that the 500 dollars you offer me, through the Poetry Center, *includes* my travelling expenses to America. Is it possible for you to let me have an advance cheque to pay for the plane journey? And soon! I say 'soon', because I know I should book a plane trip well in advance. Whether you can or not, I've no way of telling—until you write. Do write quickly about this important point. And also about the Treasury etc. formalities, or what you know of them. I dare say my London literary agent can help a bit, but he's a stiff sod

1 Thomas stayed in hotels in New York City, and with Brinnin in Massachusetts.
2 The sterling exchange rate, fixed at £1/$4.03 since the early days of the war, was changed to £1/$2.80 on 18 September 1949.

and frightens the life out of me: I believe he is always waiting for an Enormous Novel, which he won't get.

I *do* wish we could talk these things over a drink.

Lloyd Frankenberg[1] has written to me, saying that he is to be in charge of a series of Poetry Readings at the Museum of Modern Art, & wanting me to give one. He said that, when he knew the dates & the fees, he would get in touch with the Watkins agents. I shall now write to him & tell him that, for my visit, you've very kindly undertaken to act as my agent etc. and will he arrange this through you.

About the readings themselves: Is there any strong reason why my readings should all be devoted to my own work? I most sincerely hope not. What I should like to do, more than anything else, is to read from a number of contemporary British poets, including myself. I far prefer reading other chaps' work to my own: I find it clearer. An hour of me aloud is hell, & produces large burning spots in front of the mind.

Will you be seeing Laughlin? He wrote to me about the same time you did, saying that 'to make any real money for you, things will have to be done hard and tough and business-like'. I hope you're an adamantine tartar. Laughlin also suggests that 'it might be well to get up a variant programme in which you would read the classic English poets'. What do you think? Personally, I shall be glad to read *anything*—& will certainly do my best to make it entertaining—except poems in dialect, hymns to Stalin, anything over 500 lines. Dare I, in my Welsh-English voice, read any American poets to American audiences? Over here, when I give broadcast readings, I quite often read some Ransom. But, whatever your opinion, I do very much want to read from *other* contemporary British poets. At the mere thought of reading only myself, I begin to feel hunted, invisible trolls shake hands with my Adam's apple.

There are so many urgent matters in this letter, I shan't now burden you with any more but will wait for your reply.

Very many thanks again, for what you have done and will do, for the apartment, for all the friendliness.

I hope to see you a few days before the 23rd of February, in N. York.

Laughlin says there will be a party for me at the Gotham Book Mart as soon as I get there: I shall polish up my glass belly.

With best wishes,
Yours sincerely,
Dylan Thomas

Will you, anyway, get in touch with Jay Laughlin who, I'm sure, will be very helpful about lots of things. He said, in his last letter, that he'd be going into details with Watkins & seeing what, between them, they could cook up. Perhaps he can cook up something with you now. About MONEY, pretty money.

MS: Delaware

1 Lloyd Frankenberg (1907–75), poet.

ANNA MILL[1]

Nov 23 1949   The Boat House   Laugharne   Carmarthenshire   Wales

Dear Professor Mill,

Please forgive me for not having answered, much sooner, your letter of October 22nd: it has—blame the Post Office—only now been forwarded from my old address.

Thank you very much indeed for the Department of English's invitation to me to be one of your Kimball lecturers for the year. I'm delighted to accept it.

I shan't be in the United States until the end of February: I give a reading in New York on the 23rd. So, would some date, most convenient to you, early in March be suitable? Mr. John Malcolm Brinnin has very kindly undertaken to act as my agent in the arrangement of American engagements, and I have today written to him to ask him to get in touch with you, as soon as he can, about the matter of the date.

I should certainly prefer to give a reading than to speak on English poetry. Could I be allowed to make my reading a small personal anthology of the work of contemporary British poets, including some of my own? I very much hope so.

Thank you, again, very much for your letter, and for the invitation. I look forward to my visit.

I hope you will be hearing from Mr. Brinnin very shortly.

Yours sincerely,
Dylan Thomas

MS: Mt Holyoke College

JAMES LAUGHLIN

Nov 23 1949   The Boat House   Laugharne   Carmarthenshire   Wales

Dear J,

Thank you, a lot, for your nice letter. It's good to think I have a friend your side, helping to Cook Things Up.

Perhaps Brinnin has already got in touch with you, and told you that he's undertaken to act as my agent, for readings etc., for my three months' visit? It seems quite a wise move; he says he's capable of looking after all details, of getting jobs and collecting the dibs, which I'm certainly not. I *do* want to dig up a few lucrative readings, as well as to get around and, in my mazy way, enjoy myself. I've asked Brinnin to see you, & be a co-Cook.

My wife, incidentally, won't be coming over, or trying to come over,

1 Professor in the English Department of Mount Holyoke College, Massachusetts.

after all. Since the birth of our last son—4 loud months now—she's been most unwell. All she wants is a long and sun-soaked rest cure, which is hardly what she would get in New York in February. If I can possibly manage it—it is only the tiny problem of Money—I'd like to send her, for 3 months, to Italy. She likes the little island of Elba, where she can live very well and cheaply. That would be nice. It is only money I have not got. (I have half a novel. Well, nearly half. The novel will not be more than 70–80,000 words. You wouldn't, I suppose, like to give me an advance on that? Well, I can but ask.)[1]

I hope you won't have gone on your European trip before I arrive. I'll try to get to New York about February 20. That is, if Brinnin, on behalf of the Y.M. & Y.W.H.A. Poetry Center, can advance me, from my 500 dollars for my first reading, enough for my plane fare. I don't want to, unless I have to, go by boat. I like it up in the air, having frequently lived there.

No, I haven't enough poems for a new book. Not for a year or more. I'll be publishing a collection of stories & sketches here in England, but several of the stories you've already printed, old ones, in The World I Breathe: J. M. Dent considered those particular ones to be, in parts, obscene. Now that I am better known here, they don't seem to mind so much. And the other stories & sketches that will make up the English book won't be enough to make a separate American one. I'll be sending some sketches to you for you to—as you very kindly suggested—bung across to Watkins to sell with aggression to the richer periodicals, I hope.

I'm having a tough time here at the moment. I want to write only poems, but that can't be. Never have I wanted to more. But debts are battering at me. I cannot sleep for them. Quite a moderate sum would clear them up & make the tradesmen twinkle. I wish I could sell my body to rich widows; but it is fat now and trembles a little. I'm sick of being so damned & utterly broke, it spoils things. I want to build poems big & solid enough for people to be able to walk & sit about and eat & drink and make love in them. Now I have only the scaffoldings of poems, never being unbadgered enough to put up roofs & walls. My table's heaped with odd lines, single words, nothing completed. (And this letter did not, oddly enough, begin as a whine of my woes.)

I hope Brinnin will keep you informed as to what arrangements he is making for me.

I look forward to my visit, to meeting you again. I like the idea of the Gotham Book party. I should like to go to New Orleans, but I suppose it is too far.

Is there anyone I should write to? Is there anything I should do? Oh, helpless baboon!

Thanks for Ruthven's address. Good old Ruthven, as you say. But I won't stay with him. Brinnin is lending me his apartment. Good old Brinnin, too.

What else? I can't think. I'm cold, it's raining on the sea, the herons are going home, the cormorants have packed up, I must go and play darts in

1 The ever-unfinished *Adventures in the Skin Trade*.

the cheerless bar, put my flat beer on the slate, listen to talk about swedes and bulldozers, Mrs. Griffiths's ulcer, what Mr. Jenkins said to Mrs. Prothero who is no better than she ought to be, the date of Princess Margaret's birthday, the price of geese, Christmas coming—oh, horrid thought! No presents for the unfortunate, importunate, devilish, trusting children! No Scotch or puddings or mincepies or holly! Just cold bills on toast, boiled writs, summonses on the spit!—the deaths of neighbours, the infamy of relations, the stature of Churchill, the invasion of water voles!

If you can help Brinnin in any way, I know you will.

Yours ever,
Dylan

I'll send odd sketches along when typed.

MS: Houghton

PRINCESS CAETANI
24th November 1949   The Boat House   Laugharne   Carmarthenshire
Wales

Dear Madame di Sermoneta, (is that what I *should* call you? You have so many names)

Please forgive me for this long delay in answering your very pleasant letter and acknowledging, with a thousand thanks, your generous and most welcome cheque: I have been away, giving readings of poems (not my own) to various societies in Wales and haven't had time to write a word. The cheque helped, greatly. I can see now over the boiling edge of my debts. Thank you, for replying so graciously, and so soon, though you were ill in bed. I do indeed hope you are well again, and back in Rome.

I see that you are wanting the story by March the first. And March the first it will certainly be, if I am not, before then, popped into the cooler, peeled, pipped, and sliced.[1] I have the skeleton of a story now, but so unpleasant that it should perhaps remain in its cupboard. I'll see. But a story, anyway, will come.[2] And, later, a poem. I am glad you like Fern Hill best of my poems to date. I also used to like it, & think it was among the, say, half dozen of mine which came nearest to what I had in heart and mind and muscle when first I wished to write them. I do not, now, read any of my poems with much pleasure, because they tell me I should be writing other poems *now*; because they say I should work on poems every day; because, when I see all their faults, I think that in the new poems I should be

1 The phrase was worked over, as in so many of Thomas's letters. A draft version at Indiana has, 'if I am not, before then, stoned to death by tradesmen', with 'tradesmen' crossed out and 'writs' substituted.
2 *Botteghe Oscure* published four poems by Thomas before his death, but only one prose work, part of the then unfinished *Under Milk Wood*: 'Llareggub, A Piece for Radio Perhaps', April 1952.

writing, *those* kind of faults, at least, would not occur again; because, falling so short of the heights I had wished them, they are cruel and not-to-be-gainsaid reminders of the fact that only through unceasingly devoted and patiently passionate work at the words of *always* new poems can I ever hope to gain even an inch or a hairslength. I do not like reading my old poems; because I *am* not working on new poems; because I must earn my living by bits and pieces of forced prose, by exhibitionist broadcasts, by journalistic snippets; because, nowadays, I can never spare the time to begin, work through, and complete a poem *regardless* of time; because my room is littered with beginnings, each staring me accusingly in the eyes.

Next year, in February, I go to the U.S.A. to give readings of poems and, I hope, to earn some dollars to bring, rustling, home. I shall spend 3 months there. Have you any friends there you would like me to see, or rather, whose addresses you would like to give me? I shall be going to, I believe, Washington, California, Massachusetts, as well as New York. But I know very few Americans.

And, when I return in the spring, I think I shall be offered quite a good job on the B.B.C., taking over Louis MacNeice's job when he goes, as British Council representative, to Athens.[1] This would entail only a few broadcast scripts for me to write, which I will enjoy, and those to be as imaginative & experimental as I like. So, perhaps, in the coming year my most horribly pressing problems will be solved. I now have only to live through the next few months, which include Christmas. And how I am to do that, I've no idea in the whole world.

I am glad you will be spending some of the summer in England, and that we can meet then somewhere in the country. I shall look forward to that, very much.

So thank you again.

It's a fine life, if you don't weaken.

Your letter helped me.

> In all friendship,
> Yours sincerely,
> Dylan Thomas

MS: Camillo Caetani Foundation

MARGARET TAYLOR
Nov 28 1949   City of Dreadful Night[2]

My dear Margaret,

Sorry not to have written over the weekend, as I said I would when we talked indistinctly on the telephone: on Saturday night I fell down again and cracked some ribs, how many and how badly I won't know till I'm

---

1 MacNeice went to Athens; Thomas didn't get his job.
2 'The City of Dreadful Night', by James Thomson, in which the poet seeks 'dead Faith, dead Love, dead Hope'.

Xrayed tomorrow. Don't tell Miss Isaacs, who thinks that I am rarely perpendicular. The pain is knifing, I cannot sit or lie, and I bellow. I wake the baby with my bullshouts. I cannot sleep. I can hardly write: this is written as I hang off a bed, yelling. Also I have gout in my toe, phlegm on my lungs, misery in my head, debts in the town, no money in my pocket, and a poem simmering on the hob. Caitlin is thin and pale, Aeron raucous, Colum okay.

Thank you for your letter. Perhaps something will come one day from the University of Wales, though I am not popular with the authorities, being non-Welsh speaking, non-rationalist, non-degreed, non-chapelgoing, & not to be trusted. It is very good of you to try.

I have the distinct possibility of being given a good job when I return from America—I can tell you about it later—and I am not over-worrying about next year. It is, as always, NOW that matters: NOW and approaching Christmas for which we are able to make no preparations & during which we will be penniless. I wish to the Lord I could finish this wretched script. I had decided, quite sternly, to finish it this week—I cd do it in ten days, anyway—but conveniently, and nastily, fell down. Week after week I have put it off, pulling out a poem instead once I got into the littered, great hut. Perhaps, when the hospital men have bound my diaphragm up tight, I can still get down in a fury & finish it. But, if not—& I may, after all, break my neck as a final procrastination—then these ravens are without Elijah.

I don't think Caitlin is coming to the States with me. It would be difficult, expensive, and, I think, bad for her. She wants a long & utter rest. New York, & huge journeys across the subcontinent, cold winter, parties, won't give her that. She would like to go to Elba, where it is cheap to live. But, now, the cheapest mouse-box is a Ritz to us.

Of course I should like to meet Glen George. When? Where? I'll be in London, ribs allowing, 12, 13, 14 December, to be a Raven in Louis's 'Dark Tower'.[1] A Raven: oh caw, what irony! Would you want me to meet him in London? or in Wales? I could go to Aberdare from here, if you thought it wise, if Glen George would like it, if I could afford it. I am still mobile—though down down in the sad world: and now I really do know that the earth is flat.

A dim bulbed letter. I hope you are well, & the little girls. We would have liked to come up for Christmas, but I couldn't stay in H. Ford. It is going to be chaotic, and worse, here.

Write about Aberdare.

My poem is now 80 lines long.[2]

Ever,
Dylan

MS: Texas

---

1 *The Dark Tower*, a Louis MacNeice play for radio.
2 'In the White Giant's Thigh' was getting shorter.

DAVID HIGHAM
December 1 1949   The Boat House   Laugharne   Carmarthenshire

Dear David,

America:—

I'm intent on going now, and had better straightaway acquaint you with what has been happening.

John Malcolm Brinnin has written to me at length, suggesting that he, as a wellknown lecturer, literary journalist, etc., in the States, and as Director of the Poetry Center of the Y.M. & Y.W.H.A. of New York, should become my secretary and agent for my stay there. He offered me, as well as his own peculiar knowledge of the American literary scene (if you'll excuse me), with particular reference to its poetry, a flat, or apartment, in the centre of N. York and a country cottage some little distance out in which to relax (or recuperate). He said that the Lecture Agencies, which prefer novelists anyway, have nowhere near his own acquaintanceship with the institutions etc. which like poets, and would take, for their services, anything up to 40%. He, although he would do it for friendship, as a fellow-poet (dear God!), cannot afford to do so, & would have to ask 15% of what I make on my appearances as a reader and lecturer. I cabled back & agreed, realising that Ann Watkins Inc are primarily literary agents, and believing that Brinnin will really do a good job for me. (I hear extremely well of him from Laughlin.) Brinnin wrote to me today, saying that he had already 'committed me to, or penultimately arranged, visits to (beyond the initial two Poetry Center readings) Harvard, Library of Congress, Bryn Mawr, Vassar, Amherst College, University of Chicago, Iowa State University, University of Michigan, Wayne University, Detroit, Smith College, Holyoke College, Massachusetts, etc.' And he says he can arrange as many readings elsewhere as I am prepared to give. These alone, on top of the reading (or readings) for the Museum of Modern Art, as mentioned in Lloyd Frankenberg's letter, make, for me, the prospect of my visit *extremely* worth while.

I wrote to Brinnin, before his letter arrived today, asking him to let me know, as soon as possible, what were the Treasury, Passport, etc. formalities through which I would have to go. And I expect to hear from him soon. But I should also like to have a clear word with you about all this. I understand *nothing* of it. Nothing at all. But surely a letter from Brinnin, acting as my secretary & Lecture-agent, and detailing all the arrangements he has made with such eminently respectable & excellent-sounding institutions such as Harvard, Vassar, Bryn Mawr, Museum of Art, Library of Congress, would mean something to the Treasury & to all the bureaucrats concerned? I shall be in London at 4.30 p.m. on the 11th of December, and will stay on the 12th, 13th, & 14th, rehearsing for a broadcast play of MacNeice's. So could I, either on the 11th, or at some lunchtime on any of those other days, meet you so that I can get some of my most pressing problems ('Where do I go to?' 'What do I have to say?' etc.) straight, or straighter? I must, I suppose, hurry everything up, as visas, travel-tickets, etc., cannot be too easy to procure.

Incidentally, MacNeice has written me a private, off-the-cuff letter, though on behalf of Laurence Gilliam, asking me whether I would like to take his (MacNeice's, of course) job over, on the BBC Staff, when he leaves to be British Council representative in Athens sometime in the New Year. I replied, enthusiastically, yes. MacNeice said I would get the same salary as himself, would not be expected to produce the scripts I write (so long as I *do* produce them), and could do most of my work in Wales. It sounds, doesn't it, ideal. It will be imaginative scripts, *of my own*, that will, on the whole, be required. I am only hoping that the job will be open for me until I return from the States at, probably, the end of May.

Let me know what you think of my *firm* decision to go to America. And when you can see me to advise me, if you will, about all the technicalities of Treasury & travel.

I enclose, signed, the 4 Exemption Certificates you sent.

Yours,
Dylan

MS: Texas

LORRAINE DAVIES[1]
1 Dec 1949   Boat House   Laugharne   Carms

Dear Mrs Davies,
Thank you very much for your letter. I do apologise for all the trouble my request is causing. I wouldn't have bothered you had there been any other copy in existence. It's a piece of luck [for] me that the discs weren't destroyed.

Thank you again, & I'll expect the teledephonication—what is the word?—in about a fortnight. It's extremely good of you.[2]

Yours sincerely,
Dylan Thomas

MS: BBC

---

1 Lorraine Jameson, who produced Thomas's 'Children's Hour' broadcasts, was now married.
2 The BBC had been unable to find a copy of the script Thomas wanted: his childhood reminiscences, presumably in Version II. But the recording had been kept, by mistake. A 'telediphone' was the BBC's word for a script transcribed from a recording.

SELDEN RODMAN
December 6 1949   The Boat House   Laugharne   Carmarthenshire
                                                                Wales

Dear Selden Rodman:

Many, many thanks for your letter, your wonderful invitation, and the
100 Modern Poems. I know your and Eberhart's *War and the Poet*, but
neither of your other anthologies.[1] I'll try to get hold of them when I reach
New York. I've had time to read, in a hurry, only a few beautiful strangers:
Ransom's Blackberry Winter, Lowell's 'Where the Rainbow Ends,' and 'The
Raid' by William Everson, whom I've never even heard of. So much of
Beyond Frontiers is new to me. This *is* a book.

Haiti . . . You could seduce me to visit Haiti easier than winking. I love
and long to go. But the dates are damnable. I'll be in New York at the end of
February. I'm booked up for readings right through March and early April—
J. M. Brinnin's fixing these up for me. So I've no chance of coming to Haiti
while you are there. When do you return? I don't think I'll leave the States
till the end of April. Will we be able to meet in N. York? I do hope so. And
does the Haitian invitation stand for another year? If my wife and I manage
to come to the States in 1951, can we—if we can raise the money—come
then to the island? Impossible to tell you how much I should like that.

How long does it take—N. York to Haiti? Even now, *perhaps, somehow*,
I can manage a little time.

Will you write? Anyway, with luck we'll meet some time in April.
Thank you again.

                                                    Sincerely
                                                    Dylan Thomas

From a typescript. MS location unknown

JOHN DAVENPORT
[?late December 1949]   Boat House   Laugharne

Dear Comrade,[2]

I was sorry to miss you when I was up in the smoke last week, I was
quite looking forward to a good chat about Arena in the 'local', but you
know how it is, I got caught up with rewording a petition against decadent
tendencies in the cultural field, I expect you'll be having a copy to sign any
day now, I hope you'll agree with subsection 4, it was my idea, I had the
hell of a job getting it past, I can tell you, they thought it was a bit

---

1 Rodman, a writer and critic, and the poet Richard Eberhart edited *War and the Poet*
  (New York, 1945). Rodman's *100 Modern Poems* (New York, 1949) included two poems
  by Thomas.
2 Some of Thomas's friends claimed him as a serious socialist. But after the 1930s he was
  happier parodying the Left than supporting it.

individualist, but that's them all over. Bert and I had a regular square-up, but he came over to my way of thinking once we got down the old Coal Hole, I had him almost laughing at the end. 'You poets'll be the death of me,' was all he could say. There's more to Bert than meets the eye, I happen to know as a matter of fact he often listens to the Third but for Christ's sake don't let on I told you, he's as sensitive as a kid about being tough and anti-pansy—remember when he threw his beer all over that chap with long hair in that boozer near Kew Gardens? Mind, I don't say he didn't deserve it, but it's his own hair, I said, remember, he can do what he likes with it so far as I'm concerned. But here I am rambling on, & there's work to be done. I've got a little meeting in the back room of Brown's tonight, Ivy Williams is going to be chairman, you wouldn't think she was with us, would you? She's hot, I can tell you. We're trying to organise a Left Library in the snooker room, I know it sounds small beer, but by God you don't know this burg or do you? It's true bloody blue to the core, even the workers vote Liberal and as for listening to a word against *dear* Winston[1]—a chap almost knocked me down last week for saying this was a slave state, and he was only a lorry driver, too, earning four quid odd, it's uphill work down here I can tell you, and there's hardly any time left to get on with the old poetry. But still I've got a new one ticking over, it's going to be something pretty big, I hope, a kind of colloquial Lycidas[2] set in the Rhondda valley.

I'll be painting London red again—& do I mean it—on Jan second. See you then.

Dyl

MS: Texas

CAITLIN THOMAS
[??1949] [on a fragment of paper; perhaps a postscript]

I love you
I'm hysterical & foulmouthed
All the baby's faults are mine not yours
I love you forever
You are all right

X
Dylan

MS: Maurice Neville

---

1 Winston Churchill.
2 'Lycidas' (1637), Milton's elegy on the death of a friend.

C. J. CELLAN-JONES[1]
10 January 1950   The Boat House   Laugharne   Carmarthenshire

Dear Mr. Cellan-Jones,

I owe you so many apologies I don't know where to begin, but as I must begin somewhere let me please say, shaggy forehead to ground and tail wagging in a desperate effort at propitiation, how very very sorry I was not to have been able to answer at once your kind and charming, censorious and forgiving, letter—which I did not deserve a bit but which I was deeply delighted to have. (Looking back, for a second, at what I've written, I see that an unfriendly eye—a Swansea doctor's eye, for instance—could interpret me as meaning that I think I did not deserve your censoriousness. That is far from the case. Indeed, I thought that your remark about having wished, on October 20th, to murder me in cold blood to be little short, or shorn, of lamb-like. I should have wished upon myself the Death of a Thousand Cuts; and especially if I were a surgeon.) But I'm apologising now, in the first place, for what must have seemed to you the final rudeness, the last straw, if you'll forgive me, that breaks the Cellan's back: I mean, the fact that I did not acknowledge straightaway your incredibly lenient letter of nearly a month ago. I plead that the collected will of the members of the Swansea Branch of the British Medical Association, working by a clinically white magic known only to their profession, drove me, soon after my inexcusable nonappearance at their Annual Dinner, into a bog of sickness and a cropper of accidents from which I have not yet fully recovered. The first effect of this malevolent mass medical bedevilment I experienced a week after the Dinner when stopping, heavily disguised, at Swansea in order to try to learn how really execrated I was in the surgeries and theatres, the bolus-rooms and Celtic lazarets, of a town I can approach now only in the deepest dark and where certain areas, particularly around the Hospital, are forever taboo to me. I felt sudden and excruciating pains, and when I whimpered about them to a friend he said: 'Whatever you do, don't you get ill in Swansea, it's more than your life is worth. Go in with a cough and they'll circumcise you'. So I knew what the position was, and I took my pains home. But even at home, word of my unworthiness had reached the doctors' ears, and I was treated like a leper (fortunately, a wrong diagnosis). Ever since then I have felt unwell. A little later I had an attack of gout—undoubtedly the result of some Swansea specialist sticking a pin into a wax toe—and a little later still was set upon by invisible opponents in the bogled Laugharne dark and fell down and cracked my ribs. So that when your very nice letter was forwarded to me—needing medical attention, naturally I could not spend Christmas in Wales whose every

---

1 A surgeon, secretary of the Swansea branch of the British Medical Association, at whose annual dinner, on 20 October 1949, Thomas was to have been guest of honour. His narrative of what kept him is a sanitised account of a drinking expedition with friends that ended, as he says, in Bristol.

doctor loathed my every rib—I was in bed, in London, feeling like hell, unable to write a word, unable even to answer you, to thank you for your forgiveness and for all you said about my part in 'Swansea and the Arts'. I want to thank you now, belatedly but most gratefully, for that letter. And I do hope you understand why I did not acknowledge it long, long before.

This leads me to try to make an apology for a far more serious breach of courtesy and good faith, and one of which I am profoundly ashamed. I felt, and knew, it to be a great honour when I was invited to be your chief guest and to propose the British Medical Association at your Annual Dinner. I looked forward a very great deal to that evening, though not without much knocking at the knees, and wrote a long, but not, I hope, too ponderous, address, and demothed my monkey-suit, and borrowed some proper shoes, which hurt, and went up to London a few days before, on a radio job, with all the good intentions in the world. The evening of the 19th, when about to set out for Paddington, an acquaintance of mine said: 'I have a new, a very fast, sportscar, a present from my mother'—who should know better—'and I will drive you down to Wales like winking. We will spend the night at Bristol'. The car *was* very fast, he *did* drive like winking, and we *did* spend the night at Bristol. Just outside Bristol, he drove his car into a telegraph post and buckled it, which I hope drove his Mother mad. And we spent the night, sick and shaken, in a hotel that frowned at our bruises and blood; and when I crawled out of bed, on the afternoon of the 20th, I could not find my acquaintance—the police, I was told, had called to see him—nor his buckled car in which I had left my bag in which I had left my strenuously worked-upon address, my suit, my borrowed hurting shoes. I looked round several garages: it wasn't there. And I was far too timid to dare to enquire at the police station the whereabouts of car, acquaintance, bag, suit, address, or shoes. And, anyway, by now, it was too late to catch a train which would get me to Swansea in time to deliver, in the suit I hadn't got, the address I couldn't find.

I should, I know, have informed you of this sad, sordid story the very next day. But I put such a confession off and off and off until it seemed too late to matter: by this time, I realised, I was among the doomed.

Written down cold, months after, it does, I agree, sound a thin tall story. The unfortunate fact is that I am one of those people to whom these stories really do happen.

I do hope you will be able, somehow, to accept this preposterous excuse, although it is so very lately given.

And I hope you will be able to convey my most heartfelt apologies to your colleagues for all the inconvenience, and worse, caused by my failure to attend their Dinner.

And I hope, last of all, that because one Welsh writer has proved himself unworthy of the honour they were so generous as to bestow upon him by their invitation, they will not, in future, think that no Welsh writer can be trusted. No Welsh writer can.

Thank you, again, for your letter and for the very kind things you said: I hope, one day, that I shall deserve them.

Yours very sincerely,
Dylan Thomas

MS: James Cellan-Jones

PRINCESS CAETANI
12 January 1950   The Boat House   Laugharne   Carmarthenshire

Dear Madame Caetani,

How extremely nice of you! Madame Subercaseaux sent us that lovely New Year's 'token'—and what an insufficient word that is—some time last week, and it arrived, not out of the blue, but of the pouring black. It arrived just at the very moment that the darling Bank wrote to me and said I must cash no more cheques, for however tiny amounts, until an overdraft (quite insurmountable) is paid. It arrived when I hadn't enough to buy cigarettes—what Lawrence called 'those tubular white ants'—and without these I feel naked and lost. It arrived when it was welcomer than the sun—and what a way to talk about money! Anyone would think that one couldn't get on without it! Thank you, most really, for your goodness. We are trying to live on that 'token' now—and that alone—until my raked and weather-sloshed, leaking, creaking, bit of a boat limps home. Thank you again, and for your sweet letter.

And thank you for promising me to send me letters to your sisters in New York & Washington. I shall be in New York on or about the 20th of February, and in Washington sometime in March, when I read poems at the Library of Congress. And I will certainly, with your letters and your permission, look them both up. And I will try not to be arrogant and awkward and unpleasant, as I was with you—but those apologies are over now, and next time we meet I shall, I hope, and since your recent letters, be at my ease with you, & therefore simple and natural. I shall like to meet your sisters. Are they like you? And, yes, I shall be going to Harvard; and so perhaps I can meet your friends there? I'm not sure if I go to Princeton, but I shall know when I reach New York and then, if I may, I shall write to you.

My story for you is only $\frac{1}{2}$ completed. I have been worrying so much lately, about all the usual things with one or two miserable additions, that I've found it hard to sit down every day in peace (as I must, if I'm to do my best) and write, without the little, prodding devils of responsibility at work behind my eyes. One of my newest worries is: how my wife is to live while I am away. This is a lonely place, & she has no-one to help with the children. I should like her to take a holiday somewhere, in the sun. She would like to go to Elba, which we love, but that is impossible. Somehow, I must claw up enough money just to keep her here—our house is warm & comfortable, and at the water's edge—until I return maybe with dollars enough so that, for some months, I need do nothing but write my own poems & stories.

It's a flat, dull day, with grey rain oozing like self-pity: in fact, a day like this letter. No more of it.

I will try, very hard, to finish the story before leaving—though, indeed, I cannot leave until my wife is provided for. But something will happen. It always does. And often it is nasty. (I said, 'No more of it'. And here the pity again is galloning down the drab sky.)

Please don't forget—I know you won't—your letters to your sisters.

I have about 40 readings to do in the States, which will keep me tearing busy.

Yes, I am frightened of drink, too. But it is not so bad as, perhaps, you think: the fear, I mean. It is only frightening when I am whirlingly perplexed, when my ordinary troubles are magnified into monsters and I fall weak down before them, when I do not know what to do or where to turn. When I am here, or anywhere I like, and am busy, then drink's no fear at all and I'm well, terribly well, and gay, and unafraid, and full of other, nicer nonsenses, and altogether a dull, happy fellow only wanting to put into words, never into useless, haphazard, ugly & unhappy action, the ordered turbulence, the ubiquitous and rinsing grief, the unreasonable glory, of the world I know and don't know.

Write soon, when you can; and forgive, if you can, the agitation of my letters, which is caused only by the superficial worries of mouth-to-mouth living & day after day; and thank you, with all my heart, for your New Year's gift and for the affection of your letter.

Yours sincerely,
Dylan Thomas

MS: Camillo Caetani Foundation

JOHN DAVENPORT
30 Jan [1950][1]   Boat House

Dear John,

Another point I forgot in my first letter:

You know when I was up last, at the end of my visit, I said 'To hell with America, to hell with my visa', and lurched home. Well, now it's quite obvious I have to go to America, so my visa's vital. The plane ticket, for Jan 20,[2] has just been sent to me. That doesn't give long for me to get a visa, especially as I can't come up to London at once because I have no money at all. Do you know of any high-up American who might help with getting a quick introduction to the American Consul or who might help speed

1 Thomas wrote '1949'.
2 Thomas meant 'Feb 20'.

things up? Sorry always to be wanting so much from you, & giving so little back. Just if you *do* happen to know how to quicken the visa-problem.

The problem of how I get to London to see the Consul remains.

Caitlin's just come in with the insuperable grocery bill for 2 months.

Love,
Dylan

MS: Texas

'CYRIL'[1]

January 31 1950   Boat House Laugharne Carmarthenshire

Dear Cyril,

Davenport told me, a few weeks ago, that the Hulton people would give me, in advance, £50 for an article which I'd write about the USA on my return. Is that true? And can you get it for me? And can you, please, get it at once? I'm desperate here, & for the first time for years have not got one single shilling. Coal & milk are both cut off, hell in this weather in this baby-packed house. I must get them put on again, & pay other terrible debts. Can you get the Hultons to send me £50 advance *at once*? I'll write them a lovely article. Can't tell you how wretched things are. It's all happened at once. There isn't even enough food in the house.

Yours ever,
Dylan

You *must* believe me.

MS: Carbondale

JEAN LEROY

31 January 1950   Boat House Laugharne Carmarthenshire

Dear Miss LeRoy,

Sorry not to have answered your letter of January 18th about my reading my poem Fern Hill, on February 16, in the Home Service Schools transmission. I think the terms are very generous, but I'm afraid I can't fulfil the engagement. As a matter of fact, I didn't know I'd been asked to do it: certainly I haven't by letter. I'd like to do it very much, but I'm leaving for America a couple of days after the 16th, & have a lot of things to settle down here, & a trip to London just at that moment would do me no good.

By the way: I see, from a letter of yours of January 27th, that the BBC will be rebroadcasting a selection, on the Third, of poems read by me, and you include a list of those poems & also the copyright charges the BBC will pay me. This rebroadcast is dated for February 7. Will you, please, see that the cheque for this is sent to me here, at the above address, & *not* to my

1 Unidentified recipient, presumably on the staff of a Hulton magazine.

Bank, with whom I am having a little overdraft trouble at the moment? Thank you so much: it's quite important to me.

Yours sincerely,
Dylan Thomas

MS: Texas

*CAITLIN THOMAS
[?February 1950]¹   Savage Club   1 Carlton House Terrace   London   SW1

Darling darling darling   Cat my own dear love I love you—
  I deserve to be hung up by my feet & flogged with bottles. I didn't remember till I was in the bloody train that I'd left both my chequebook (with only one cheque in it) in the desk, *and* my passport in the hut. Here is the hut key. The passport is, I believe on top of the bookshelves on the *right* of the hut as you enter. Please, darling, send it on at once: I can't go to the American Embassy without it, & I can't meet Tony²—even if he *is* in London—without the chequebook. London's awful. I've just arrived. I'm going to the cinema this evening, alone, to see Bicycle Thieves & then back, alone, to the Savage for supper, & then early to bed where I shall think of you, my own dear love, all night. I will try to come back Friday, but my forgetting chequebook & passport may hinder me & I may have to come back Saturday instead. But I'll try for Friday.
  I love you. Think of me as I think of you, with all my body & heart.

Your
Dylan
forever
X

MS: Berg

PRINCESS CAETANI
12 Feb 1950   The Boat House   Laugharne   Carmarthenshire

Dear Madame Caetani,
  This is only a very [?short] letter, to thank you, very much, for writing those notes to your sisters and to Archibald MacLeish. If things go well, I hope to be able to see them next month. It was awfully kind of you to write to them. And, too, to think of sending my wife a cheque on February 15: it will mean a very great deal to her, and she is as grateful to you as I am: if that is possible.

1 Evidently Thomas needed his passport to get a visa from the American Embassy. But his letters report anxieties about American visas in January 1952 and April 1953, as well as in 1950.
2 Perhaps Tony Hubbard. See page 409, to 'A Bank Manager'.

I am supposed to travel on the 20th. My visa is not yet through, though I have hopes of it tomorrow. All depends on that and on my ability to get enough money, before I go, to pay some outstanding, and howling, debts, and to leave, with my agent, a weekly sum for Caitlin & the children. That I have some chance of getting, from my publishers.

The only address I have, in the States, so far, is: c/o John Malcolm Brinnin, Valley Road, Westport, Conn. I shall be headquartered—and probably hanged and drawn as well—in New York, but that address will always find me.

I shall certainly try to see Samuel Barber, whose music I love—especially, perhaps, his setting of 'Dover Beach'—and Richard Wilbur.[1] Thank you, a lot, for their addresses.

I am, I think, supposed to be at Princeton on March the 6th, and I would indeed appreciate a word, to his friends, from your friend the attaché at the American Embassy in Rome. Though perhaps I have left things too late?

Perhaps I have left everything too late, & may never go at all. I have been too horribly worried to see, in the proper way, to all the necessary forms. And then my father has become dangerously ill, & there is only my mother, an invalid, to look after him. And now the damned roof is leaking all over this letter. I feel like an expurgated page of a Russian novel.

If I do get to the States, I will write you a long, long letter. And I hope to be able to correct my story for you there, & send it on. Forgive its lateness.

I wish you were to be in America.

Many thanks again for all, from us all. I shall, visa & money or not, write you very soon.

Yours,
Dylan

MS: Camillo Caetani Foundation

BILL McALPINE
Sunday 12 Feb 50   Boat House

My dear Bill,

I was right, I knew, to run to you weeping when things did, really, get too much. All the thanks there are, from Cat & me, for your kindness & quickness in helping us at one of the lowest—no, the very lowest, I think—downs of our seesaw life.

Now to say: Forgive me, Bill, for not writing immediately to thank you very very deeply. I've been in such a stygian depression, and so desperately flustered about visas, passports, inoculations, summonses, clanging overdraft, tradesmen, my father, Cat for the future, I couldn't do anything straight; I couldn't even write you back, as soon as your help came. Forgive me.

1 Richard Wilbur, poet.

Tomorrow I go to Cardiff to get, I hope, at last, my American visa. To get to Cardiff, I had to borrow from my mother: you'll realise from that that I'm still in an awful state of suffering brokeness. If the visa's okay—I expect nothing to turn out well—I will try to borrow money in Cardiff to go on to London to see a bankmanager to try to cash a postdated cheque. That sounds impossible, but I have got a plan afoot. I *can* do it, if the visa is okay. I think so, anyway. Then—after all these if's—I return to Laugharne to settle up vast bills & to try to provide for Cat when I am away. I have my plane ticket: for the 20th. If, if, if, if, visa & bank work out, then Cat & I will come to London to stay the weekend in Margaret's London house, where she wants to give a little Sunday party before I fly on Monday. If, if, if, if, visa & bank *do* not work, I shall have to fly anyway: but out of the window, into the sea.

Cat wrote a long letter to Helen today. Maybe it will arrive the same time as this. Presumably your old address forwards letters.

If I *am* in London this Tue or Wed, I'll ring the B.Council & try to find you.

My father is off the danger list. He had pneumonia as well, &, though the muck on the lung has not cleared up yet, the Doctors are optimistic. He is starting to grumble, though very weakly.

Thank you again, Bill, & I hope I see you very soon.

Keep your prayers crossed for us.

Ever, to you both,
Dylan

MS: Buffalo

CAITLIN THOMAS

[Letter card, postmarked 14 Feb 1950]　　　　　　　　　　　Savage Club
　　　　　　　　　　　　　　　　1 Carlton House Terrace　London　SW1

Darling I love you, darling.

Things have gone all right. Visa & bank okay. Am seeing posh dentist[1] tomorrow Wednesday so cannot come back at once. Will catch sleeper-train on Thursday night.

Here is 10 pounds. Will you please, my love, collect my suit from cleaners & send it *at once* to above address. Then I can be in Picasso play.[2]

I love you.
Thursday night.

X
Dylan

MS: Maurice Neville

1 Thomas had bad teeth. The American novelist Peter de Vries, who caricatured him as McGland in *Reuben Reuben*, made McGland commit suicide on hearing that he must have all his teeth out.

2 A reading of *Desire Caught by the Tail*, which Picasso wrote during the war, at the Institute of Contemporary Arts on Thursday 16 February.

*DAN JONES
[*Three undated items, placed together for convenience*]

Two telegrams from Laugharne to Jones at 22 Rosehill Terrace, Swansea

[1] CAN YOU MEET BUSH¹ 1.30 TODAY ON MY WAY TO AMERICA DYLAN

[2] CAN YOU MEET LUNCH THIS VERY SATURDAY 1.OCLOCK BUSH HOTEL DYLAN

On a small sheet of paper

A Bilingual Lyric for D J Jones

Aujourd'hui
I'll be
If je possibly can
Dans me Swansea
Avec me Dan

Location unknown

*JOHN MALCOLM BRINNIN
[22 February 1950]

Beekman Tower
On exclusive Beekman Hill
The only hotel overlooking
New Site of the United Nations
and the East River
3 Mitchell Place (at 49th
Street) New York 17 NY

Dear John,
    Gone to 3rd Avenue. See you at Costello's. Come at once. (I like this peremptory tone)

Ever,
Dylan²

MS: Delaware

---

1 A pub in the town centre.
2 Thomas had arrived at New York's Idlewild Airport on 21 February; it was his second day in America. A further note to Brinnin from the hotel says simply, 'Gone to Moiphys', ie Murphy's, another Third Avenue bar. Presently the Beekman Tower asked him to leave, for what Brinnin described as 'spectacular' behaviour.

CAITLIN THOMAS
Saturday Feb 25 '50   [headed paper: Midston House
                                    22 East 38th Street   New York 16]

My darling far-away love, my precious Caitlin, my wife dear, I love you as I
have never loved you, oh please remember me all day & every day as I
remember you here in this terrible, beautiful, dream and nightmare city
which would only be any good at all if we were together in it, if every night
we clung together in it. I love you, Cat, my Cat, your body, heart, soul,
everything, and I am always and entirely yours.

How are you, my dear? When did you go with Ivy back to Laugharne? I
hope you didn't racket about too much because that makes you as ill as
racketing makes me. And how is my beloved Colum and sweet fiend
Aeron? Give them my love, please. I will myself write to Llewelyn over
this weekend when I temporarily leave New York and go to stay with John
Brinnin—a terribly nice man—in his house in the country an hour or so
away. And how are the old ones? I'll write to them, too. I love you, I can see
you, now this minute, your face & body, your beautiful hair, I can hear
your lovely, un-understandable voice. I love you, & I love our children, & I
love our house. Here, each night I have to take things to sleep: I am staying
right in the middle of Manhattan, surrounded by skyscrapers infinitely
taller & stranger than one has ever known from the pictures: I am staying
in a room, an hotel room for the promised flat did not come off, on the 30th
floor: and the *noise* all day & night: without some drug, I couldn't sleep at
all. The hugest, heaviest lorries, police-cars, firebrigades, ambulances, all
with their banshee sirens wailing & screaming, seem never to stop;
Manhattan is built on rock, a lot of demolition work is going on to take up
yet another super Skyscraper, & so there is almost continuous dynamite
blasting. Aeroplanes just skim the tips of the great glimmering skyscrapers,
some beautiful, some hellish. And I have no idea what on earth I am doing
here in the very loud, mad middle of the last mad Empire on earth:—except
to think of you, & love you, & to work for us. I have done two readings this
week, to the Poetry Center of New York: each time there was an audience
of about a thousand. I felt a very lonely, foreign midget orating up there, in
a huge hall, before all those faces; but the readings went well. After this
country weekend, where I arrange with Brinnin some of the rest of my
appallingly extensive programme, I go to Harvard University, Cambridge,
Boston, for about 2 days, then to Washington, then back to New York,
then, God knows, I daren't think, but I know it includes Yale, Princeton,
Vassar—3 big universities, as you know, old know-all,—& Salt Lake City,
where the Mormons live, & Notre Dame, the Jesuit College, & the middle
West, Iowa, Ohio, Chicago—& Florida, the kind of exotic resort, & after
that the mere thought makes my head roar like New York. To the places
near to New York, Brinnin is driving me by car; to others I go by myself by

train; to the more distant places, I fly. But *whatever* happens, by God I don't fly back. Including landing at Dublin, Canada, & Boston, for very short times, I was in the air, cooped up in the stratosphere, for 17 hours with 20 of the nastiest people in the sky. I had an awful hangover from our London do as well; the terrible height makes one's ears hurt like hell, one's lips chap, one's belly turn; and it went on forever. I'm coming back by boat.

I've been to a few parties, met lots of American poets, writers, critics, hangers-on, some very pleasant, all furiously polite & hospitable. But, apart from on one occasion, I've stuck nearly all the time to American beer, which, though thin, I like a lot & is ice-cold. I arrived, by the way, on the coldest day New York had had for years & years: it was 4 above zero. You'd have loved it. I never thought anything could be so cold, my ears nearly fell off: the wind just whipped through that monstrous duffle. But, as soon as I got into a room, the steamed [?heat] was worse: I think I can stand zero better than that, &, to the astonishment of natives, I keep all windows open to the top. I've been, too, to lots of famous places: up the top of the Empire State Building, the tallest there is, which terrified me so much, I had to come down at once; to Greenwich Village a feebler Soho but with stronger drinks; & this morning John Brinnin is driving us to Harlem. I say 'us', you see: in the same hotel as me is staying our old New Zealander, Allen Curnow, & I see quite a bit of him.[1] I've met Auden, & Oscar Williams, a very odd, but kind, little man.

And now it must look to you, my Cat, as though I am enjoying myself here. I'm not. It's nightmare, night & day; there never was such a place; I would never get used to the speed, the noise, the utter indifference of the crowds, the frightening politeness of the intellectuals, and, most of all, these huge phallic towers, up & up & up, hundreds of floors, into the impossible sky. I feel so terrified of this place, I hardly dare to leave my hotelroom—luxurious—until Brinnin or someone calls for me. Everybody uses the telephone all the time: it is like breathing: it is now nine o'clock in the morning, & I've had six calls: all from people whose names I did not catch to invite me to a little poity at an address I had no idea of. And most of all most of all most of all, though, God, there's no need to say this to you who understand everything, I want to be with you. If we could be here together, everything would be allright. *Never* again would I come here, or to any far place, without you; but especially never to here. The rest of America may be all right, & perhaps I can understand it, but that is the last monument there is to the insane desire for power that shoots its buildings up to the stars & roars its engines louder & faster than they have ever been roared before and makes everything cost the earth & where the imminence of death is reflected in every last powerstroke and grab of the great money

---

[1] Allen Curnow, New Zealand poet.

bosses, the big shots, the multis, one never sees. This morning we go down to see the other side beyond the skyscrapers: black Harlem, starving Jewish East Side. A family of four in New York is very very poor on £14 a week. I'll buy some nylons all the same next week, & some tinned stuff. Anything else?

Last-minute practicalities: How does the money go? Have any new bills arrived. If so, send them, when you write (& write soon my dear love, my sweetheart, that is all I wait for except to come home to you) to the address on the kitchen wall. I enclose a cheque to Phil Raymond, & an open cheque to Gleed; pay that bill when you can.

Remember me. I love you. Write to me.

Your loving, loving Dylan

MS: Tony Vilela

D. J. AND FLORENCE THOMAS
Sunday 26th February 1950   [headed paper: Midston House etc]

My dear Mother & Dad,

How are you both? How are you keeping, Dad? Get stronger every day, please, so that when I come home to Laugharne, you'll be up and about and able to join me for one at Phil's. And Mother, too, by that time, must be spry enough to be able to run, like a goat, down the Boat House path. I was very sad to leave you at such a moment, with Dad so weak & with Mother not fit to do all the little things for him that must be done. I was very sad, driving away that morning, leaving you & Laugharne, but it had, God help me, to be done.

Caitlin's told you, I suppose, about our London visit and Margaret's house and party at which such a lot of old—& some new—friends turned up, so I won't add anything to that. Helen & Bill, by the way, send their fondest regards to you both.

The plane trip was ghastly. It seemed to go on for ever, and all my 30 fellow passengers seemed either actively unpleasant or moronic. The plane was stiflingly hot, & there wasn't any of the usual slight plane ventilation because of the height we travelled: in the stratosphere. We couldn't put down at the airport in Newfoundland because of icy weather conditions, so had to land somewhere in Canada. We got out for an hour: the cold was unbelievable, all the airport ground crew dressed up like Hudson Bay trappers and beating their great grizzly-bear-gloved hands together & stamping on the snow. And when we did, after several stifling eternities spent high as the moon, arrive in New York, it was to find it one of the coldest days there for years: when we got off the plane, it was four above zero.[1] Luckily I'd rather the cold than the heat, and my old duffle-coat was very helpful. John Brinnin, my agent, a terribly nice man, met me at the airport—about an hour from the centre of the city—& drove me to my hotel: right in Manhattan, among the unreal, shooting skyscrapers, and my room was on the thirtieth floor. Then we drove around the city, me gawping, like the country cousin I am, at this titanic dream world, soaring Babylon, everything monstrously rich and strange. That evening, I went to a party, given in my honour by the Professor of English at Columbia University: pack full of American dons, critics, writers, poets, all of the older & more respectable kind.[2] Then home to the 30th floor, to hear, all night, the roaring of heavy lorries, the hooting of ships from the East River—I could see the Queen Mary, or Elizabeth, from my window—& the banshee-screaming of police and ambulance sirens, just as on the films. There seems, at first sight, to be no reality at all in the life here: it is all an enormous façade of speed & efficiency & power behind which millions of little individuals are wrestling, in vain, with their own anxieties. The next day, Brinnin took me touring over half of this mad city: Broadway, Harlem, the Wall Street area, the East Side (where the Dead End Kids come from).[3] I drank huge icy milkshakes in the drugstores, and iced lager beer in the Third Avenue saloons almost every one of which is kept by an Irishman; I ate fried shrimps, fried chickens, a T-bone steak the size of a month's ration for an English family.[4] I went to the top of the Empire State Building, the tallest skyscraper in the world, had one look at the nightmare city, & came down quickly. That night I went to a party given to me by some of the younger writers. The next day Brinnin & I did little but prepare my itinerary, which seems to take me to every state in the U.S.A., & that evening I made my first public appearance before an audience of 800 people. The reading seemed to go very well. After that, a reception, so-called, in the flat of a young man whose name I didn't catch: flats are called apartments here, but this one had 20 rooms. The next day all over the city again, meeting many people, mostly, again, writers, painters, or actors. And yesterday, Saturday, my second appearance in the same hall as the first: 800 again, the full seating capacity. Today, Sunday, I go to the country, with Brinnin, until Tuesday when I make my way to Yale University & from there to Harvard, Boston. After that, I've got about 10 readings in 20 days. Don't you worry about me, now. I'm feeling tiptop. By the way, the first people to come along to the stage-door after my first reading were three people from Llanelly, utter strangers, now living in N.

1 4 degrees Fahrenheit, which is what Thomas meant, is minus 16 Celsius.
2 This sedate party is not mentioned in Brinnin's *Dylan Thomas in America*.
3 The Dead End Kids featured in the 1937 gangster movie about a New York slum, *Dead End*.
4 Meat remained rationed until 1954.

York. I'll write again next week. Tell me everything. *And Get Stronger.* My forwarding address is c/o John Brinnin, Valley Road, Westport, Connecticut. All my love to you both. I think of you. Give my regards to Billy & Mrs. Thomas.

D.

CAITLIN THOMAS
[about 11 March 1950][1]   [headed paper: 1669 THIRTY-FIRST STREET
                                                              WASHINGTON]

Kiss Colum again. Put   I shall write lots & lots
your hand on your heart   & lots to you from now, on
for me   the endless trains.

Caitlin my own own own dearest love whom God and *my* love and *your* love for me protect, my sweet wife, my dear one, my Irish heart, my wonderful wonderful girl who is with me invisibly every second of these dreadful days, awake or sleepless, who is forever and forever with me and is my own true beloved amen—I love you, I need you, I want, want you, we have never been apart as long as this, never, never, and we will never be again. I am writing to you now, lying in bed, in the Roman Princess's sister's[2] rich social house, in a posh room that is hell on earth. Oh why, why, *didn't* we arrange it *somehow* that we came out together to this devastating, insane, demoniacally loud, roaring continent. We *could* somehow have arranged it. Why oh why did I think I could live, I could bear to live, I could think of living, for all these torturing, unending, echoing months without you, Cat, my life, my wife, my wife on earth and in God's eyes, my reason for my blood, breath, and bone. Here, in this vast, mad horror, that doesn't know its size, or its strength, or its weakness, or its barbaric speed, stupidity, din, selfrighteousness, this cancerous Babylon, here we could cling together, sane, safe, & warm & face, together, everything. I LOVE YOU. I have been driven for what seem like, and probably are, thousands of miles, along neoned, jerrybuilt, motel-ed, turbined, ice-cream-salooned, gigantically hoared roads of the lower region of the damned, from town to town, college to college, university to

1 Thomas read in Washington DC on 9 March, then in New York on 13 March.
2 Katherine Biddle (1890–1977), one of Marguerite Caetani's two sisters (in fact, half-sisters), to whom Thomas carried letters of introduction. Her husband, Francis Biddle, belonged to a prominent Philadelphia family and was U.S. Attorney-General, 1941–5. Katherine Biddle gave money to cultural causes and herself wrote poetry. Thomas retaliated by stealing some of Biddle's shirts when his hosts had left for Bermuda.

university, hotel to hotel, & all I want, before Christ, before you, is to hold you in my arms in our house in Laugharne, Carmarthenshire. And the worst, by a thousand miles—no, thousands & thousands & thousands of miles—is to come. I have touched only the nearest-together of my eternally foreign dates. Tomorrow, I go back from Washington, hundreds of miles, to New York. There I talk to Columbia University. The very next day I start on my pilgrimage, my *real* pilgrimage, of the damned. I go to Iowa, Idaho, Indiana, Salt Lake City, & then a titanic distance to Chicago. All alone. Friend Brinnin leaves me at New York. And from Chicago I fly to San Francisco, & from there I lurch, blinded with smoke and noise, to Los Angeles. The distance from New York—where I shall be tomorrow—to Los Angeles is further than the distance from London to New York. Oh, Cat, my beautiful, my love, what am I doing here? I am no globe-trotter, no cosmopolitan, I have no desire to hurl across the American nightmare like one of their damned motorcars. I want to live quietly, with you & Colum, & noisily with Aeronwy, & I want to see Llewelyn, & I want to sit in my hut and write, & I want to eat your stews, and I want to touch your breasts and cunt, and I want every night to lie, in love & peace, close, close, close, close, close to you, closer than the marrow of your soul. I LOVE YOU.

Everything is not terrible here. I have met many kind, intelligent, humorous people, & a few, a very few, who hate the American scene, the driving lust for success, the adulation of power, as much as I do. There is more food than I dreamt of. And I want to tell you again, my Cat, that I still drink nothing but ice-cold beer. I don't touch spirits at all, though that is all that anyone else seems to drink—& in enormous quantity. But if I touched anything else but beer I just *couldn't* manage to get along. I couldn't face this world if I were ill. I have to remain, outwardly, as strong as possible. It is only in my heart and head that the woes and the terrors burn. I miss you a million million times more than if my arms, legs, head, & trunk were all cut off. You *are* my body, & I am yours. Holily & sacredly, & lovingly & lustfully, spiritually, & to the very deeps of the unconscious sea, I love you, Caitlin my wild wise wonderful woman, my girl, the mother of our Colum cauliflower. Your letter I read ten times a day, in cars, trains, pubs, in the street, in bed. I think I know it by heart. Of *course* I know it by heart. Your heart, alive, leaping, & loving, is in every word. Thank you, my dear, for your lovely letter. Please write as often as you can. And I will write too. I have not written since my first letter because never for a second, except for falling, trembling & exhausted thinking, thinking, thinking, of you, have I stopped travelling or reading aloud on stages and platforms. This is the first day on which I have had no work to do. I waited until I was in bed until I wrote to you. I can cry on the pillow then, and say your name across the miles that sever you from me. I LOVE YOU. Please, love & remember me & WAIT FOR ME. Keep the stew waiting on the fire for me. Kiss Calico Colum for me, & arrant Aeron.

I hope you got the stockings I sent you. I sent a pair to Ivy too. Today I

382 · THE COLLECTED LETTERS OF DYLAN THOMAS

had sent from a big shop in Washington lots of chocolates, sweets, &
candies, for you, for Aeron, for my mother. Darling darling, I am sorry I
could do nothing for dear Aeron's birthday. Dates & time were a maze of
speed & noise as I drove like a sweating, streamlined, fat, redfaced comet
along the *incredible* roads. But tell her many sweets & things shd reach her
in a few days. From N York tomorrow, I shall also send some foodstuffs.

About the Ungoed cheque: if my chequebook is in the bottom of my
suitcase, I shall write him a cheque & put it into this letter when I post it
tomorrow. If it is not in my suitcase, but in my other suitcase in Brinnin's
house, I shall send it separately tomorrow. I cannot look in the case now. It
is downstairs. The house is dark. I shall lie here & love you. I DO Love
You, Angel. Be good to me & ours.

What can I say to you that I have not said a thousand times before, dear
dear Cat? It is: I love you.

P.S. Always write me c/o Brinnin.

MS: (Thomas Trustees)

CAITLIN THOMAS
[15 March 1950]   c/o Brinnin   Valley Road   Westport   Conn

from your lost, loving Dylan.

Darling my dear my Cat,
    I love you.
    You're mine for always as for always I am yours. I love you. I have been
away for just over 3 weeks, & there's never been a longer & sadder time
since the Flood. Oh write soon, my love, my Irish, my Colum's mother, my
beautiful golden dear. There isn't a moment of any insane day when I do
not feel you loving and glowing, when I do not grieve for you, for me, for us
both, my sweetheart, when I do not long to be with you as deep as the sea.
Only three weeks! Oh God, oh God, how much longer. I wrote you last
from be-Bibbled[1] Washington. Then back I sweated to New York. Then I
read in Columbia University, New York. Then I flew to Cornell University, read, caught a night-sleeper-train to Ohio, arriving this morning. This
evening, in an hour's time, I do my little act at Kenyon University, then
another night-train, this time to Chicago. I never seem to sleep in a bed any
more, only on planes & trains. I'm hardly living; I'm just a voice on wheels.
And the damndest thing is that quite likely I may arrive home with hardly
any money at all, both the United States *and* Great Britain taxing my
earnings—my earnings for us, Colum, Aeron, Llewelyn, for our house that

1 Perhaps Thomas meant to write 'be-Biddled'.

makes me cry to think of, for the water, the heron, old sad empty Brown's. I am writing this in a room in Kenyon University, & can find no paper or sharp pencil & am too scared to go out and find somebody to ask. As soon as I raise the courage, I shall write Ungoed's cheque—it wasn't, of course, in my suitcase in Washington at all but in Brinnin's possession in N York—& address the envelope & have the letter air-mailed. I love you. Every *second* I think of and love you. Remember me. Write quickly. You are all I have on earth.

Did you get nylons & candy?

And please, when you write, tell me how the money's going at home, how you are making out.

Kiss Colum & Aeron for me.

Have you thought of having Mary Keene or Oxford Elizabeth down?

Tell me everything.

Love me, my dear love Cat.

Be good.

Write quickly. What can I send you?

I LOVE YOU XXX

Found a razorblade to sharpen my pencil, but no more paper. Out on the grounds—they call it the campus—of this College the undergraduates, looking more like bad actors out of an American co-ed film, are strolling, running, baseballing, in every variety of fancy-dress. Someone in the building is playing jazz on an out-of-date piano: the saddest sound. In a few minutes now I go out for cocktails with the President. I do not want to have cocktails with any President. I want to be home. I want you. I want you with my heart and my body because I love you. Perhaps, perhaps, perhaps, the door may suddenly open & in you will come: like the sun. But I do not think it likely. I love you, my pet

MS: Tony Vilela

CAITLIN THOMAS
[16 March 1950]   [headed paper: The Quadrangle Club   Chicago]

Cat: my cat: If only you would write to me: My love, oh Cat. This is not, as it seems from the address above, a dive, joint, saloon, etc, but the honourable & dignified headquarters of the dons of the University of Chicago. I love you. That is all I know. But all I know, too, is that I am writing into space: the kind of dreadful, unknown space I am just going to enter. I am going to Iowa, Illinois, Idaho, Indindiana, but these, though mis-spelt, *are* on the map. You are not. Have you forgotten me? I am the man you used to say you loved. I used to sleep in your arms—do you remember? But you never write. You are perhaps mindless of me. I am not of you. I love you. There isn't a moment of any hideous day when I do not say to myself, 'It will be alright. I shall go home. Caitlin loves me. I love Caitlin.' But perhaps you have forgotten. If you have forgotten, or lost your affection for me, please, my Cat, let me know. I Love You.

Dylan

The address is still Brinnin. He forwards all mail to my lost addresses. I love you.

MS: Maurice Neville

*JOHN MALCOLM BRINNIN
[telegram, 25 March 1950, 1.39 pm, Iowa City]

ARRIVING SAN FRANCISCO SUNDAY MARCH TWENTY SIXTH AND WILL STAY PALACE HOTEL WRITING FULLY. LOVE DYLAN

Original: Delaware

*JOHN MALCOLM BRINNIN
[telegram, 4 April 1950, 8.19 am, San Francisco]

ACCORDING TO LAST LETTER MY NEXT TWO DATES VANCOU-
VER APRIL 6TH SEATTLE 7TH INTEND ARRIVING VANCOUVER BY PLANE 850PM APRIL 5 PLEASE WIRE IMMEDIATELY CARE WITT DIMANT[1] 1520 WILLARD ST SAN FRANCISCO CONFIRMING ALSO HOW AND WHERE CONTACT HARRIS AND PRESS IGNORE NASTY CALDWELL WIRE[2] PROMISE WRITE TOMORROW LOVE DYLAN

Original: Delaware

*JOHN MALCOLM BRINNIN
[telegram, 5 April 1950, 3.16 pm, San Francisco]

JUST LEAVING FOR VANCOUVER HAVE ARRANGED FOR MILLS COLLEGE AND SAN FRANCISCO STATE FOR APRIL 17 AND 18 AND PROBABLY STANFORD SOME TIME THAT WEEK UTAH WANTS ME

---

1 Ruth Witt-Diamant (1895–1987) taught English at San Francisco State College. Thomas had a letter of introduction to her, which he showed to college students he met in a bar. When they telephoned her, she invited him to leave his hotel and stay at her house, and this became his refuge on the West Coast. In 1954 she founded the San Francisco Poetry Center.
2 Probably James R. Caldwell, Professor of English at the University of California at Berkeley, where Thomas spoke (to an audience of 1,000 in Wheeler Auditorium) on the evening of 4 April. Caldwell arranged the visit.

APRIL 25TH WILL YOU CORROBORATE AND IS IT POSSIBLE SEND
MY PROSE MANUSCRIPT TO VANCOUVER IN TIME FOR TOMOR-
ROW AFTERNOON IF NOT PLEASE SEND IT SEATTLE OR LOS
ANGELES LETTER IN POST LOVE DYLAN

Original: Delaware

CAITLIN THOMAS
[5 April 1950]   c/o Witt-Diamant   1520 Willard St San Francisco

My love my Caitlin my love my love
    thank you (I love you) for your beautiful beautiful beautiful letter and
(my love) for the love you sent. Please forgive, Cat dear, the nasty little
note I sent about your not-writing: it was only because I was so worried and
so deeply in love with you. This is going to be the shortest letter because I
am writing it on a rocking train that is taking me from San Francisco—the
best city on earth—to Vancouver in Canada. And with this tiny, but
profoundly loving, letter, I also send you a cheque to Magdalen College for
£50 & a cheque for £15 to you: that £15 seems an odd amount, but God
knows how much is in the Chelsea bank. I unfortunately can't find the
Dathan Davies bill you sent, so can you pay it out of this. Please, my own
sweetheart, send all the bills & troubles to me after this. And I hope the
cheques are met. The train is going so fast through wonderful country
along the Pacific coast that I can write no more. As soon as I get on
stationary land I will write longly. I said San Francisco was the best city on
earth. It is incredibly beautiful, all hills and bridges and blinding blue sky
and boats and the Pacific ocean. I am trying—& there's every reason to
believe it will succeed—to arrange that you & me & Colum (my Colum,
your Colum,) come to San Francisco next spring when I will become, for
six months, a professor in the English department of the University. You
will love it here. I am madly unhappy but I love it here. I am desperate for
you but I *know* that we can, together, come here. I love you. I love you. I
love you. I am glad you are stiff & staid. I am rather overwrought but am so
much in love with you that it does not matter. I spent last evening with
Varda, the Greek painter, who remembers you when you were fifteen. I
wish I did. A long letter tomorrow. O my heart, my golden heart, how I
miss you. There's an intolerable emptiness in me, that can be made whole
only by your soul & body. I will come back alive & as deep in love with you
as a cormorant dives, as an anemone grows, as Neptune breathes, as the sea
is deep. God bless & protect you & Llewelyn & Aeron & Colum, my, our,
Colum. I love you.

Dylan

P.S. Write, air mail, to the above address. I return to S. Francisco in a
week.
P.S.S. Darling, I realise fifteen pounds is inadequate, but let that big £50 get

thro' the bank alright & then I can send more. I can send you a cheque in dollars next week, which you can cash through the account of my poor old man or through Ivy.

I love you.

MS: Maurice Neville

CAITLIN THOMAS
7th April 1950

Caitlin. Just to write down your name like that. Caitlin. I don't have to say My dear, My darling, my sweetheart, though I do say those words, to you in myself, all day and night. Caitlin. And all the words are in that one word. Caitlin, Caitlin, and I can see your blue eyes and your golden hair and your slow smile and your faraway voice. Your faraway voice is saying, now, at my ear, the words you said in your last letter, and thank you, dear, for the love you said and sent. I love you. Never forget that, for one single moment of the long, slow, sad Laugharne day, never forget it in your mazed trances, in your womb & your bones, in our bed at night. I love you. Over this continent I take your love inside me, your love goes with me up in the aeroplaned air, into all the hotel bedrooms where momentarily I open my bag—half full, as ever, of dirty shirts—and lay down my head & do not sleep until dawn because I can hear your heart beat beside me, your voice saying my name and our love above the noise of the night-traffic, above the neon flashing, deep in my loneliness, my love.

Today is Good Friday. I am writing this in an hotel bedroom in Vancouver, British Columbia, Canada, where yesterday I gave two readings, one in the university, one in the ballroom of the Vancouver Hotel, and made one broadcast. Vancouver is on the sea, and gigantic mountains doom above it. Behind the mountains lie other mountains, lies an unknown place, 30,000 miles of mountainous wilderness, the lost land of Columbia where cougars live and black bears. But the city of Vancouver is a quite handsome hellhole. It is, of course, being Canadian, more British than Cheltenham. I spoke last night—or read, I never lecture, how could I?—in front of two huge union jacks. The pubs—they are called beer-parlours—serve only beer, are not allowed to have whiskey or wine or any spirits at all—and are open only for a few hours a day. There are, in this monstrous hotel, two bars, one for Men, one for Women. They do not mix. Today, Good Friday, nothing is open nor will be open all day long. Everybody is pious and patriotic, apart from a few people in the university & my old friend Malcolm Lowry—do you remember Under the Volcano— who lives in a hut in the mountains & who came down to see me last night.[1] Do you remember his wife Margery? We met her with Bill &

---

1 Malcolm Lowry (1909–57), British writer, had lived in British Columbia with his second wife, Margerie, since 1940.

Helen in Richmond, and, later, I think, in Oxford. She, anyway, remembers you well and sends you her love.

This afternoon I pick up my bag of soiled clothes and take a plane to Seattle. And thank God to be out of British Canada & back in the terrible United States of America. I read poems to the University there tonight. And then I have one day's rest in Seattle, & then on Sunday I fly to Montana, where the cowboys are, thousands of them, tell Ebie, and then on Monday I fly—it takes about 8 hours—to Los Angeles & Hollywood: the nightmare zenith of my mad, lonely tour.

But oh, San Francisco! It is and has everything. Here in Canada, five hours away by plane, you wouldn't think that such a place as San Francisco could exist. The wonderful sunlight there, the hills, the great bridges, the Pacific at your shoes. Beautiful Chinatown. Every race in the world. The sardine fleets sailing out. The little cable-cars whizzing down the city hills. The lobsters, clams, & crabs. Oh, Cat, what food for you. Every kind of seafood there is. And all the people are open and friendly. And next year we both come to live there, you & me & Colum & maybe Aeron. This is sure. I am offered a job in two universities. When I return to San Francisco next week, after Los Angeles, for another two readings, I shall know definitely which of the jobs to take.[1] The pay will be enough to keep us comfortably, though no more. Everyone connected with the Universities is hard-up. But that doesn't matter. Seafood is cheap. Chinese food is cheaper, & lovely. Californian wine is good. The iced bock beer is good. What more? And the city is built on hills; it dances in the sun for nine months of the year; & the Pacific Ocean never runs dry.

Last week I went to Big Sur, a mountainous region by the sea, and stayed the night with Henry Miller. Tell Ivy that; she who hid his books in the oven. He lives about 6,000 feet up in the hills, over the blinding blue Pacific, in a hut of his own making. He has married a pretty young Polish girl, & they have two small children. He is gentle and mellow and gay.

I love you, Caitlin.

You asked me about the shops. I only know that the shops in the big cities, in New York, Chicago, San Francisco, are full of everything you have ever heard of and also full of everything one has never heard of or seen. The foodshops knock you down. All the women are smart, as in magazines—I mean, the women in the main streets; behind, lie the eternal poor, beaten, robbed, humiliated, spat upon, done to death—and slick & groomed. But they are not as beautiful as you. And when you & me are in San Francisco, you will be smarter & slicker than them, and the sea & sun will make you jump over the roofs & the trees, & you will never be tired again. Oh, my lovely dear, how I love you. I love you for ever & ever. I see you every moment of the day & night. I see you in our little house, tending the pomegranate of your eye. I love you. Kiss Colum, kiss Aeron &

1 Thomas was in the running for an appointment at the University of California at Berkeley, where the Department of Speech wanted to offer him a post teaching the oral interpretation of literature. The university overruled the decision on the grounds that the poet was 'unstable'. See page 393.

Llewelyn. Is Elisabeth with you? Remember me to her. I love you. Write, write, write, write, my sweetheart Caitlin. Write to me still c/o Brinnin; though the letters come late that way, I am sure of them. Do not despair. Do not be too tired. Be always good to me. I shall one day be in your arms, my own, however shy we shall be. Be good to me, as I am always to you. I love you. Think of us together in the San Franciscan sun, which we shall be. I love you. I want you. Oh, darling, when I was with you all the time, how did I ever shout at you? I love you. Think of me.

Your
Dylan

I enclose a cheque for £15.
I will write from Hollywood in three days.
I will send some more money.
I love you.

MS: Maurice Neville

CAITLIN THOMAS
18 April [1950]   c/o Witt-Diamant   1520 Willard St   San Francisco

P.S. Sorry darling. Just been to bank &
50 dollars is only £17.15 shillings
(seventeen pounds fifteen shillings).
Will send another fifty dollars in
two or three days. *All* you have to do
with this cheque is to take it to
Barclay's Bank, Carmarthen. I love you.

Be good to me as I am good,
forever, to you, my love. I love you
every second of the day.

Darling my own, my Cat, my dear,
    Just returned from Los Angeles to S. Francisco to find your beautiful letter, my true love, & your very good, but heartbreaking, poem.[1] I know it must be a hell of a battle with the small amount of money I could leave; here is a cheque for 50 (fifty dollars) which you can take to any bank in Carmarthen & get cashed. It should be worth about £20 (twenty pounds) & will help a little. Perhaps it would be a good idea to see the man in the Laugharne little bank—he comes twice a week—& he may be able to cash this cheque himself. Anyway, he will tell you about it. I cannot send an English cheque as I have none left, so I have to give an American one & then have an American one written for me by my host or hostess. It's all

---

1 Caitlin Thomas, who would have liked a literary career of her own, wrote poems as a young woman and continued to write them throughout her life. Many are bitter or rebellious.

very complicated. This is a tiny letter which says nothing of my great love for you, & has no news. I just want you to have this small amount of money straightaway. I shall write tomorrow with all news—some of it good, none bad, except that I am without the one thing in life that matters to me, which happens to be a small unhappy blonde in Laugharne, Carmarthenshire. Went to Hollywood, dined with Charlie Chaplin, saw Ivan Moffat,[1] stayed with Christopher Isherwood, was ravingly miserable for you my true, my dear, my one, my precious love. I shall write to Llewelyn too tomorrow. Love to all our children. Regards to Elisabeth.[2] I'm glad she is with you.

I LOVE YOU   XXX   D.

MS: Tony Vilela

***JOHN MALCOLM BRINNIN**
[telegram, 18 April 1950, 4.58 pm, San Francisco]

TOO COLLAPSED TO GO TO FLORIDA CAN YOU WIRE BAROFF WILL EXPLAIN FULLY LATER REACH ME 1520 WILLARD STREET SAN FRANCISCO LOVE DYLAN

Original: Delaware

***JOHN MALCOLM BRINNIN**
[telegram, 20 April 1950, 8.19 am, Berkeley]

SORRY JOHN REALLY IMPOSSIBLE KEEP ENGAGEMENT 20TH FLORIDA HAVE WIRED BAROFF OFFERING ALTERNATIVE DATES 26TH OR 27TH LOVE DYLAN[3]

Original: Delaware

***JOHN MALCOLM BRINNIN**
[telegram, 21 April 1950, 8.24 am, San Francisco]

FLORIDA FIXED FOR 27TH ARRIVING 6AM MONDAY LAGUARDIA PLEASE RESERVE ROOM MIDSTON DYLAN

Original: Delaware

1 Ivan Moffat, an American scriptwriter, worked alongside Thomas at Strand Films in London during the war. It may have been Moffat who arranged the visit to Chaplin's (others have claimed the credit), when Thomas is said to have behaved badly. But no two versions agree.
2 Elisabeth Lutyens.
3 Brinnin had cabled Thomas, urging him to reconsider his decision.

CAITLIN THOMAS

May 7 1950   [headed paper: Hotel Earle   Washington Square NW
New York 11, NY]

My Darling

Darling darling dear my dear Caitlin, oh God how I love you, oh God how far away you are, I love you night, day, every second, every oceanic deep second of time, of life, of sense, of love, of any meaning at all, that is spent away from you and in which I only think of coming back, coming back, to you, my heart, my sacred sweetheart, Caitlin my dear one.

It will not be so long now, in terms of days & weeks, before I come back to the true world; but, in terms of lonely, sleepless nights, of heartbreak & horror, it is an eternity. I do not yet know when I can get a boat to sail back on; I know I cannot travel any more by plane. I have three more engagements, one in New York, the other two quite near, & then I am free. I am free from the 15th of May. But boats are hard to get, because of American tourists travelling to Europe, especially to Italy & Holy Year. I have good chances of getting a boat a few days after May 15, but dare not bank on it. So I have reserved a passage, anyway, for June 1st. But, by praying, perhaps I can leave a whole ten days or more before that. But I am coming to you. I love you. I knew, always, I loved you more than any man has ever loved a woman since the earth began; but now I love you more than that. I love you, my dear golden Caitlin, profoundly & truly & forever. Pray God you have not forgotten me. I love you. Pray God you are always good to me, as I to you. Pray God you love me still. I need you. I want you. Oh *dear dear* Cat! Oh my angel. Sometimes I think I shall go mad, & this time properly, thinking of you all day & night as I fly over the continent from university to university, hotel to hotel, stuffed-shirt to stuffed-shirt, heat to heat. It is getting abominably hot. Since I last wrote I have been in Florida, Wisconsin, Indiana, hell getting hotter all the time; I have been in Detroit, the worst city, the home of motorcars; & in and out of New York. I have been so exhausted I was quite incapable of writing a word. After readings, I fell into bed, into sweaty half-awoken nightmares. I couldn't write but I *do* hope you got the £17 cheque from San Francisco & the one last week from Boston. And I hope they helped a little. I think of you, my lovely dear, with all the children screaming in far Laugharne, with Oxford Elisabeth bitching on you, with Cordy[1] running away, with Mary & Alice arriving, with too little money, waking up alone in our beautiful bedroom—please Christ, my love, it *is* always alone[2]—waiting for me, for nothing, for something, listening to Ma Long,[3] hearing the curlews, seeing the herons, wailed at by old ill Thomases. Wait for me a little longer, my

1 Cordelia Sewell.
2 Dylan must have been aware by now of Caitlin's infidelities in Laugharne. According to her, in later life, he knew what was going on but chose to ignore it. Also he had infidelities of his own.
3 Dolly Long, general help and child-minder.

own true love. It was, you remember, the end of May on which I was supposed to return. How did I know 3 months could be like the distance from the sun to the earth, only infinitely lonelier. I love you.

I have heard nothing yet from San Francisco about our very possible year's visit there, but will hear before I leave for you. I have also been offered a lovely house in an orange ranch in Florida, but would be paid no money there. Whatever happens, we will return here for a year, you & I & Colm—kiss him for me—to California or the South. Kiss Aeron, too. And later on tonight—it is Sunday midnight in this little hotel in Greenwich Village—I will write to Llewelyn. I am lonely as the grave. This pen will not write. I want you. I love you.

I will write tomorrow to the parents. I have a whole day off before I commit my last few readings. If only *you* were here, we could be happy. I want you in my arms. I want to kiss your breasts! I want to make love to you, to sleep with you, to wake with you, us two in our house, warm, quiet, dear, & holy to one another. I love you.

I am glad Charlie Chaplin wired to you. He said he wanted to send his greetings. He's a very fine man. I was only 2 days in Hollywood, staying with Christopher Isherwood who took me along to Chaplin's to dinner. Chaplin danced & clowned all the time. I met also Ivan Moffat. Ivan says I could get a script to write almost any time. Once we are in San Francisco, we will see: it is not far away.

Next week I will send money again. Sorry it is always for such a curious amount: it is the English equivalent of 50 dollars.

Who is in our house now?

Think of me, my sweet wife, as I think of you.

I Love You. It Won't Be Long Before I am with you, God willing. I'll write very soon. Write to me dear, at this hotel.

I love you, dear dear *dear* darling Cat. I kiss your heart.

Dylan

MS: Maurice Neville

D. J. AND FLORENCE THOMAS
[unposted][1]
May 22 1950   [headed paper: Hotel Earle etc]

My Dear Mother & Dad,

How are you both? How, especially, is Dad? I think a great deal of you both, and very often, though I know you would hardly think so from my not-writing for so very long. But indeed, you are constantly in my mind; I worry very much about Dad's health, or lack of it; and, though I hear about you quite often from Caitlin, I still do not really get a clear picture of how

1 The letter was with Brinnin's papers. It has no alterations and doesn't appear to be a draft.

you are. Is Dad in bed all the time? Oh, I do hope not. And he doesn't still have to have injections, does he? And how is Mother walking now?

I am sailing for home on June the first, on the Queen Elizabeth. It will take four and half days. So, somewhere in the first week of June, I shall be seeing you. And I am looking forward to it terribly.

At last my tour is at an end. I have visited over forty universities, schools & colleges, from Vancouver, in British Columbia, to Southern Florida. I have travelled right through the Middle West, the North West, & on to the Western Coast of California. After a reading in Indianapolis, a man came up to me & said, in a strong Swansea accent, 'How's D. J. these days? He used to teach me English before the last war. I've been an American citizen now for 25 years.' And he sounded as if he'd just stepped out from Morriston. I didn't get his name, because just then I was captured by someone else. I've met Welsh people after every public reading I've given, several of them from Swansea, Carmarthen, & Pembrokeshire, and all of whom knew Laugharne—or, at least, Pendine. And was, in nearly every case, offered the hospitality of their homes: which I never had time to accept. It has been the time element in this tour that has been most tiring; and the reason, too, I have hardly written any letters at all. I have almost never had a moment to myself, except in bed and then I was too exhausted to do anything. And the varying kinds of climates and temperatures have lessened my energy, too. In Chicago, it was bitterly snowing; a few days later, in Florida, the temperature was ninety. And New York itself never has the same sort of weather 2 days running. So one of my greatest troubles has been to know what to wear; my second greatest trouble, as I flashed round the continent, was that of laundry & cleaners. Sometimes I have to buy a new shirt in each town.

I am writing this in bed, at about seven in the morning, in my hotel bedroom, which is right in Washington Square, a beautiful square, which is right in the middle of Greenwich Village, the artists' quarter of New York. Today I have lunch with my American literary agent, & supper with Anita Loos, who wrote a best-seller years ago called 'Gentlemen Prefer Blondes'. She is interested in a play in which I might appear, as an actor, sometime, though of course it is all very much up in the air.

> I am longing to come home.
> How is Caitlin *really*? And Aeron & Colm?
> Excuse this very bad pencil, & scrappy letter.
> > Love to you both,
> > Dylan

MS: Delaware

*TONY OSTROFF[1]
June 16 1950   The Boat House Laugharne Carmarthenshire Wales

Dear Tony Ostroff,
I never had a chance of seeing you again after our hurried few-minutes meeting just after my Berkeley reading. I very much wanted to, but was whisked away to rant in Los Angeles, Pomona, & Santa Barbara among other places and hardly had any time left, when I returned to San Francisco, before returning East.
I did manage to see Mr Marsh for lunch, and he seemed quite keen on the idea of getting me a temporary job—for 6 months or a year—in the Department of Speech, but didn't know, until he attended some official meeting, the attitude of those above: especially in regard to money. He did say he would get in touch with me before I left the States, but, unless the letter got lost or misdirected, never did. I don't know if I should write to him personally. Could you sound him out—and also Dick Hagopian,[2] to whom I send my greetings—about the possibility of my coming to Berkeley this autumn or sometime next year? I'd be very very grateful if you would.
I do really want to return to California, and think I could make a good job of whatever job I would be asked to do.
Do you mind trying to find out what the position is? And dropping me a line when you have time?
Perhaps I should write to Marsh? (What's his first name, by the way?) Or did I make an unfortunate impression upon him?

Yours,
Dylan Thomas

MS: Buffalo

MARGARET TAYLOR
Sunday June 18 1950   Boat House

My dear Margaret,
This is my first letter to you for a very long time. Too long. I should have written, for I wanted to, out of America, but was dizzily dippy most of my stay there that never stayed quiet. I was floored by my florid and stertorous spouting of verses to thousands of young pieces whose minds, at least, were virgin territory; I was giddy agog from the slurred bibble babble, over cocktails bold enough to snap one's braces, of academic alcoholics anything but anonymous; I was sick from the muted, boring thunder of planes in the stratosphere, an unlikely place of little interest; I was gassed and whimpering after the ministrations of all the sweet, kind hosts and hostesses who desired their guests to die, in delirium of only the very best

1 Anthony Ostroff taught in the Speech Department at Berkeley.
2 Gerald Marsh was chairman of the department; Richard Hagopian, another staff member.

Scotch. I managed to write a few times to Caitlin, mostly about domestic, that is, financial, matters, and once to the Pelican.[1] To Llewelyn I sent candy but, much to his disgust, no note. And nothing more. To you I wanted to send all the whirligig news of a three months'-and-longer hysterical, thumping chore-and-more, but couldn't get around to it for blather, haranguing, and rye, for the hospitable hawk-pounce, the gimlet questions, the dentist-drill telephone, the violent, tentacular intimacies of strangers who forget one's existence a moment later, and the jailing islands of hotel bedrooms from which one must escape at once even if it is into the hands and un-mercy of bewildered but energetic poets who sit, downstairs in the lobby, sweating into their lyrics and all nice as birds.

I met quiet people and had quiet times without Buchman, but with those and in those I wilted so gladly I hadn't the strength to lift a pen: all I could do was dawdle in powerful cars at seventy miles an hour tearing from Joe's Place to Mick's Steakery, from party to quiet party where almost nobody got hurt and the first guests to leave left, always, before dawn. I met contemplative people, brooding among the jukeboxes and hammering out their lonely poems, on typewriters big as tanks, to the accompaniment of television, traffic off its head, street fights & accidents, the deaths of dogs and babies, the iceman coming who cometh all the time, and the telephone insistent as a Jacques Tati hornet.[2] But, for the most part, things were loud; louder than people; and, Christ, the music that the police sirens sang!

So I couldn't write, not at all. And even now I can't write the kind of fruity farrago I would like (and you wouldn't) because I must try to answer the questions you put me, in your last letter, about the position of Poets in Universities.

The majority, the big majority, of poets in America *are* attached to universities. Quickly, I can, at the moment, think of only two well-known poets over there who are not: Wallace Stevens, Vice President of an Insurance company, and E. E. Cummings, President, Treasurer, Secretary, & all the shareholders of E. E. Cummings Ltd, a company that exports large chunks of E. E. Cummings to a reluctant public. If the name of a poet is mentioned in passing, someone is sure to say: 'Where does he teach?' But most of these poets are engaged as English lecturers & professors in the ordinary academic run of things. And it is, of course, with the others that you are concerned.

You mentioned Frost in your letter. Robert Frost, the G.O.M. of American poetry, is an exception to all rules, and isn't really to be considered. He is attached, in an honorary capacity, to several universities, but does little more there than give an occasional, perhaps, in some cases, yearly lecture. The universities just use his name, add lustre to their own reputations by *his* reputation, and also, of course, find it a way of paying him honour for his accomplishment and age.

The poets you are most interested in would be, I imagine, far younger

1 The house in Laugharne where his parents now lived, owned by Ebie Williams.
2 *The Iceman Cometh*, Eugene O'Neill's play, is set in a New York bar peopled with down-and-outs. Jacques Tati, French actor who made film comedies.

men. And a good example might be the young poet, Robert Lowell.

The Library of Congress, at Washington D.C., have, for some few years now, instituted a Chair of Poetry. This is held by a different poet each year, & those who have held it include Allen Tate, Louise Bogan, & Elizabeth Taylor. Lowell had this Chair last year. His job was to be a Poet in Residence, to be the temporary host of visiting writers to the capital, American & foreign, to introduce other writers to them, & to make recordings, many of them later to be issued in albums, commercially, of certain chosen poets.

This year, Lowell is running a Poetry Workshop in Iowa State University, there to 'discuss the demands of the craft, to criticise the individual works of student members of the workshop, and to foster enthusiasm for poetry & the sense of criticism among them.' He attends the workshop a few times a week. He is called a Poet in Residence. There is, in Iowa University, also a writer who runs a prose workshop—for fiction & imaginative writing only—along the same lines.

Lowell is paid the same salary as an Assistant Professor: in his case, between 5 & 6,000 a year. The disparity in incomes, & in spending power, between America & here is so great that this can, of course, give little or no indication of what money a similar post, if established here, would demand.

There are also, in many other universities, other Poetry Workshops. In some of these, the procedure is the same as in Iowa. In some of these, the Poet in Residence is engaged for one year only, to be followed by another poet. In other universities, the Poet is engaged for far longer periods, sometimes permanently. And in many cases, the Poet attends the university only for one, or for 2, terms a year. In other cases, he turns up only a few times a year, to give readings & lectures to all the students of English & to the English faculty.

I think that, for English universities, a plan might be arranged combining all of these different procedures. That is, perhaps the Poet would be in residence the whole of one term, on tap, as it were, to discuss the poetry of students & preside over the criticism of poetry by other students; & he would give occasional readings, lectures, etc, the other two terms. It should not be too difficult to arrange a scheme satisfactory to the poet & to the students alike.

Also, the Poet in Residence could arrange for other poets to come along occasionally as guests, & supervise the activities of the workshop (if it could be called that) for one session or more and/or to read or lecture.

And, also, students could be allowed, & invited, to send along their poems for criticism when the P. in R. is not present at the University.

The whole thing, I think, should be as informal & as give-and-take as possible.

There could, too—as there often is in the U.S.A.—[be] special provision for advanced students, certain periods being set aside when the P. in R. wd be available, for advice & discussion, either in the workshop or in his own rooms, to those who are most serious about being poets & who have produced some real stuff or, at least, the proper beginnings of it.

And I think the idea of a summer seminar for foreign, & U.S.A. students, should thoroughly be gone into.

Many universities, for example, run Writers' Conferences. I enclose the syllabus of one such Conference.

As you can see, I am vague, but extremely enthusiastic, about all this.

Yrs Ever, Dylan

For your benefit:

1) I visited about 40 universities, including Yale, Harvard, Princeton, Cornell, Columbia, Vassar, Brynmawr, Holyoke, Kenyon, Amherst, Illinois, Notre Dame, Iowa, Los Angeles, Pomona, Santa Barbara, San Francisco, Mills, Brandeis, Seattle, Chicago, Washington, Vancouver, Salt Lake City, Hobart, Florida, Detroit, Indiana, Philadelphia; and recorded poems, later to be made into an album and issued commercially, for the Library of Congress. Also, I recorded for the Library of Harvard, and read in the Museum of Modern Art, New York.

2) I read only modern British poems, from Thomas Hardy to today. I read Hardy, Binyon, Edward Thomas, W. H. Davies, Wilfred Owen, Edwin Muir, Robert Graves, Andrew Young, T. S. Eliot, W. H. Auden, David Gascoyne, George Barker, Alun Lewis, W. R. Rodgers, Vernon Watkins, W. B. Yeats, de la Mare, Louis MacNeice, Edith Sitwell, Alex Comfort, D. H. Lawrence, John Betjeman, James Stevens, all chosen carefully for what, I hoped, would be an immediate impact upon the audience. They were all, or should have been, clear at a first hearing: or, at least, *much* of their meaning would come immediately across. And it did. The audiences—in some cases, as many as a thousand—were all extraordinarily enthusiastic.

3) Before leaving for the States, I wrote out a large anthology in longhand. (This helped, of course, to get me thoroughly acquainted with all the poems.) And I never read the *same* selection at more than one place. Thus, I hoped to keep away from any staleness. I used to have all the poems on my lectern, & select from them, as I went on, according to the 'feel' of the audience.

4) Very often, at the end of a reading, I would meet a group, sometimes small, sometimes large, of interested students often in their common room, & talk, & answer questions informally. Sometimes I was invited to a students' party. Sometimes to a very small group in someone's house. I always tried to talk to the students,—never from the platform, this put too much of a formal distance between us—because the readings were for them. And from these meetings I got to learn what, of the poems I had read, they most appreciate, so that I often selected the poems for the next readings as a direct result of what I had learnt.

5) I always prefaced each poem with some prose comments. These, at the beginning of my tour, I wrote out in full; but as I grew more experienced

I dispensed with these notes & talked off the cuff, which was far more satisfactory all round.

6) I was invited by the University of California at Berkeley to join, for a year, their Department of Speech. I don't quite know what the function of this Department is, but my appointment wd be as Poet in Residence to discuss & criticise the poems of the students, to foster enthusiasm for poetry & for criticism. No date for my possible appointment was mentioned, but I gather that it is under discussion now.

7) And that's about all.

I hope this, & the preceding pages, will be of some little use.

I hope your & the Registrar's as-yet nebulous plans *will* come to something And, God, I need some stability.

Stability. You wanted to know some of the details of my—sweet words—financial embarrassments, so that your ravens may help.

Altho' I left Cat £10 a week—not in one sum, but to be delivered by the Bank—& also sent her several cheques from the States, the extravagant woman managed to chalk up, at the Chemist's, a bill for £150.[1] Also, I owe Llewelyn's school fees for this term, & Stanier *must* be paid the £50. And I owe Ebie for *many* taxis & for the Pelican. Say another £50. Altogether, £250. And I can raise, immediately, only £50 which I cannot send Stanier as we must manage to live here. I am starting to write some U.S.A. articles for Vogue, etc, but this will take a little time. Oh, ravens, come quick, come quick. Is there any hope? And desperately soon?

Write, please, M, anyway.

And I shall write again, & not all about Poets-in-Bloody-Residence and Work-Bloody-Shops.

Love,
D.

I had a very sweet letter from Dick. He, too, wants me to come to London & look about and try to cash in with newspapers & films. I'll go to London next week.

MS: Texas

JOHN F. NIMS AND MRS NIMS[2]
17th July 1950   The Boat House Laugharne Carmarthenshire

My dear Bonnie and John,

Remember me? Round, red, robustly raddled, a bulging Apple among poets, hard as nails made of cream cheese, gap-toothed, balding, noisome, a great collector of dust and a magnet for moths, mad for beer, frightened of

1 The Laugharne chemist's was more than a pharmacy, and sold groceries and liquor.
2 John Frederick Nims (1913–99), poet and teacher, had been Thomas's host at the University of Notre Dame, Indiana.

priests, women, Chicago, writers, distance, time, children, geese, death, in love, frightened of love, liable to drip.

I never managed to come back, although I so much wanted to. I never answered your nice letters, nor acknowledged the hollyhocks. My only damp excuse is that animal-trainer Brinnin ('Bring 'em back half alive') whipped me all over the wilds after I reluctantly left you, from British Columbia to Florida; I hardly ever knew where I was; I lost the ability to form words on paper; I ranted through my one-night stands like a ruined, sonorous mule; I spent one liquid, libidinous fortnight in New York and was wheelbarrowed on to the Queen Elizabeth by some resident firemen, a psychoanalyst's insane wife, Oscar Williams and *his* wife, whip-cracking Brinnin, a hosier from the Bronx, an eminent playwright (if anonymous), three unidentified men who came either from the Museum of Modern Art or from McSorley's Saloon, a lifelong friend of half an hour, a glossy woman who had made some mistake, and hairy people. Lots of hairy people, all sighing with relief. I shared a cabin with an inventor of a new kind of concrete, called, so far as I could gather, Urine—the inventor, not the concrete—and spent my days with salesmen at the bar. As a result, I have never felt physically better in my life, and go for long walks, healthy as a briar pipe, and sing in the bath (which does not exist), and have clear eyes and a new front tooth—which must have grown, for I have no memory of going to the dentist—and a spring in my step and a song in my gut and poems to write and no need to hurry to write them. I must ruin my health again: I feel so preposterously *well.*

But I do wish I had been able to return to Niles and Schmoo myself to sleep and meet your friends again. Not coming back was one of the things, in all my silly panting around, I most regret. But, if Caitlin and Colm and I come to the States next year—though how we shall achieve this, I don't know yet—may we stay for some days?

And if ever you manage to visit this country, beds, couches, cots, playpens, fish, cockles and mussels, flat warm Welsh bitter beer, affection, a dog as balanced and gifted as yours, sea and river, are all yours in this arsehole of the universe, this hymnal blob, this pretty, sick, fond, sad Wales.

Have you, John, a book of your poems to send me? I shall be giving some radio readings of American poetry, and want very much to read you and Lowell. In return I can send you an old bicycle or a new poem or a picture of Laugharne or any book you want.

Is there any news of the vague project you said you would work on for Caitlin and me and the hornless fiend who is playing at my feet with a scissors?

When you have time, will you write anyway & let me know how you are?

Love,
Dylan

Only source: SL

RUTH WITT-DIAMANT
[card, postmarked 27 July 1950, London NW8]
[Written jointly with Stephen and Natasha Spender. Only the sentence beginning 'And this' is in Thomas's hand.]

Dear Ruth, Dylan says he loves
you and is as grateful to you
as we are. We have been
meeting and singing your
praises. Stephen. And this is
to say how useless it is to say,
because you know it, that what
Stephen and Natasha say is true.
                Dylan

Elizabeth Matthew & I send lots
of love Natasha.

MS: Berg

JEAN LEROY
August Bank Holiday 1950   The Boat House   Laugharne
                                                          Carmarthenshire

Dear Miss LeRoy,
    In answer to your note of August 1st: The fee of ten guineas, plus
£2.15.0d expenses is okay for my part in the New Judgement on Edgar
Allan Poe programme broadcast on 23rd July, in the Home Service. My
fares in connection with this broadcast were: [*a blank space*]
    I'd be very much obliged if you would have the cheque sent to me at my
above home address, & *not* to my bank.
    In late reply to yours of 13th July, yes, please do let us close on the basis
that I am paid 50 guineas *on acceptance* of my script, *Letter to America*.[1]

                                            Yours sincerely,
                                            Dylan Thomas
MS: Texas

1 Thomas had proposed a 30-minute script about his U.S. trip for BBC radio's Home
Service. It was not written.

JEAN LEROY
21 Aug 1950   Boat House   Laugharne   Carmarthenshire

Sorry not to have included fare detail in my note about E. A. Poe programme. Return fare, Laugharne–Paddington, for this broadcast was £3.5.0.

I made a special journey to London for the John Donne broadcast of Aug. 14, & the fare was the same as above. Also there were the usual expenses for the day & accommodation overnight.

I hope you can get these cheques through quickly, & will you please send them to me at the above address & *not* to my bank.

Sincerely,
Dylan Thomas

MS: Texas

HELEN McALPINE
Thursday [postmarked 14 September 1950]   Boathouse

Helen,

A very special note, please, dear, to be destroyed straight after reading. I came back to find Caitlin terribly distressed, but managed to tell her that all that that grey fiend had pumped into her ear was lies and poison. And so it was. And Cat believed me. And now we are happy, as always, together again, and that other thing is over for ever.[1] So, please, Helen: remember for Cat's sake if not for mine: All, all, all that grey scum said was LIES. When Cat asks you, as she will, you must, please, say: 'It is all LIES. I met the girl with Dylan, & that is all there was to it.' You *must*, Helen, please. Don't answer this. I trust you with everything: which is Cat's happiness. And she is happy with me, though terribly miserable in Wales. We are coming, for a week or two, to London about the 24th of this month. Cat's mother is taking Colm & Aeron for that time, & Llewelyn returns to school. We'd love it if you'd put us up for that short time, but, if you can't, we'll see lots of you anyway. Will you write to Cat about this: I mean, *only* the putting-up part.

Do destroy this. I trust you & my dear Bill implicitly, as you know. All was

---

1 The Thomases were having a marital crisis. The 'grey fiend' was Margaret Taylor, who had hurried to Laugharne with the news that Dylan was involved with a New York magazine executive, Pearl Kazin. She and Thomas may have met for professional reasons. A memo from Ann Watkins, the New York literary agent, to David Higham (24 May 1950) said that '[Thomas] has personally sold a prose story to Pearl Kazin of *Harper's Bazaar* . . .' Kazin visited London in September 1950 and Thomas saw her again. Whether or not Caitlin was at first mollified, she later found letters from Kazin to her husband. Caitlin's extant letters to Helen McAlpine are anguished but say nothing about her own lapses.

JOHN DAVENPORT
[?autumn 1950]   *You know where*

John my dear,

How's everybody who's nobody in, dear, dead Chelsea these excruciating days? How's little Mary, the twenty-seventh Mews? and her oh so tantalising spraygun Michael? Still sculpting away? What a bore for the bronze! And, yes, do tell me, in words of one *shocking* syllable—how I *wish* I could speak in asterisks!—the faring of the Langhams, those conjugal double djinns. Has he found a complexion yet to match his shirt? And *credulous* my Mrs [?Smith]? we really *must* send her on a holiday to Prague: she'd love to see so many dishonoured Czechs all together! And Bunny too? that long, failed stoat? How *unfair* of him to have had piles! What will Persia give the dear fellow, I dare wonder? Maybe the mosques will get him yet! or am I confusing my religions?

Oh, how far, far away I feel, here in my *horribly* cosy little nest, surrounded by my detestable books, wearing my odious, warm slippers, observing the gay, reptilian play of my abominable brood, basking in the vituperation of my golden, loathing wife! How distant the trilling ripple of delighted laughter from the naughty Fulham inns as ebullient Beulah trapezes on a phrase! How *exquisitely* far off the rapier play of Ross, the Caspar sally, the limpid grace of that little silver lady who, even now, is delicately dropping down the mouth of a white telephone her perfect, pearl-like turds of ingenious insanity![1]

How adorably dim sound the great bar bells of London town!

How near is Brown's! How carcass dull! How slow! How higgledy! How me-embracing! And there I wend my day.

Ever yours,
You know who

MS: Texas

DOUGLAS CLEVERDON

Douglas Cleverdon (1903–87) was a bookseller and specialist publisher who joined the BBC in 1939 and after the war became the leading producer of literary features for the Third Programme. He made much use of Thomas as actor and reader, and hoped to produce his as yet unfinished radio play, whose title was not yet *Under Milk Wood*. On 20 October 1950 Cleverdon wrote to Thomas to say that the Third Programme 'have agreed to take The Town that Was Mad (or whatever title you prefer)'. On 3 November he was urging Thomas to press on with the script. Thomas's letter sending the 39 pages was no doubt near, or between, those dates.

1 A few of the references can be decoded. 'Bunny' was Ralph Keene, the film producer, with whom Thomas would soon be in Persia, making a film. Robert Beulah was a portrait painter. 'Caspar' is probably Rear Admiral Caspar John (whom the teenage Caitlin tried to seduce); he had a flat near the Davenports.

[late October 1950]   [headed paper: Savage Club]

> Many apologies for having forgotten
> the books. Tomorrow.

Dear Douglas,
    Here are the first 39 pages of the provisionally titled 'The Town That
Was Mad'. I hope it won't be too hard for whoever types it to follow. No
notice should be taken of the rings round several of the words.
    I've just read these pages over again & am very enthusiastic to finish the
thing. And quickly.
    The whole play will, I think, take more than an hour.
    See you Friday.

                                              Dylan

Quite a number of the short introductory bits will be extended.

MS: BBC

PRINCESS CAETANI
11 November 1950 27 Cranley Mews Cranley Gardens London SW7

My dear Madame Caetani,
First of all, and as too often in my miserably too few letters, apologies and
apologies to you for this long delay in writing. I had wanted to write at
once, to thank you forever, to say how deeply glad I was that you had liked
the poem. But I have been ill for several weeks, in and out of sick-beds in
several, and increasingly depressing, furnished London rooms and spiritual
orphanages. I caught lots of chills, and they jaundiced me, and I lay snarling
at the edge of pleurisy, and I couldn't write or read and I didn't want to
think. Caitlin went to an illicit hellhole to have her pregnancy killed
because she cannot and will not deal with another child in the topsy-turtle
life we reluctantly lead, and now is sad and weak. And I just couldn't thank
you for your great generosity, though it was upon that we built our breath
those days. Please, in your goodness, accept, once again, my saying: Forgive
me for the long, ill delay, and it was not caused by my lack of gratitude nor
by my not thinking of you with sincere affection. London I find bad, though
maybe only for me. So many of my friends here are friends only so long as I
am hopeless, lost, merry, and noisy. I want to be quiet and found, unhappy
at home or at anywhere but not here, not here—not in a borrowed room in
a crabbed and feckless house, all lumped together in a soya bean mock-
sausage, twanging on each other's nerves like Saint Vitus on a harp. It's
really the squalid devil, all in one London room with napkins and food and
spilt books and flung clothes and a baby rampant & all the radios of hell
turned on full moron-tilt. And there's that small house in Wales,

LIES. And, incidentally, it was. And incidentally, the girl has gone to France, not to return.

Ever,
Dylan

MS: Texas

RUBY GRAHAM[1]

15 September 1950   The Boat House   Laugharne   Carmarthenshire

My dear Ruby,

I should have written before—oh, how many letters start like that!—but I have been in London nearly all the time, trying to settle some of my grisly problems and sell myself to Metro-Korda-Odeon as a Celtic Noël Coward, a Welsh J B Priestley, a Swansea Rattigan, a Laugharne cockle. That is, I mean that my last filmscript contract has ended and I have been hunting another down the labyrinthine ways of the nasty studios. This takes a long time; each meeting leads to a conference, each conference to a dinner, each dinner to a hangover, and then in the morning nobody, including oneself, can remember anything and one has to start all over again. However, I have just landed a pretty good picture—good for me, though I never succeed beyond the B's—which begins quite soon.

And now the object of all this hoo-ha? It's to say: Please, Ruby, can I have a little time, quite a short time, before I pay you for all those marvellous fripperies and furbelows Caitlin bought in your shop?

Normally, I'm fixed well enough, in my sordid way, but now, on top of the death of my last contract, the Income Tax Dracula has now got me into such a corner that I've had to agree, through an accountant and agents, to hand him over every single penny I earn until what he wants is fully paid. So I live, temporarily, on nothing, while working hard for that fiend.

Can you wait a little? I'd be terribly grateful. We're all in such a money mess here, now, in our little howling home full of napkins and old poems.

I hope a lot to see you [. . .]—when I'm able once again to come to S'sea to show Caitlin the big world.

Sorry about all this, but I *do* hope you won't mind.

Love from both

Dylan

MS: (Clive Graham)

---

1 Mrs Graham was director of a dress shop. She and her husband Malcolm, who acted with Thomas in the Swansea Little Theatre in the 1930s, were old acquaintances.

PRINCESS CAETANI
[?mid September 1950]   9 Drayton Court   Drayton Gardens
                                                        London   SW10

My dear Madame Caetani,
   A very hurried, & late, note to apologise, profoundly, for all my past carelessness, & to thank you, from my heart, for the cheque you sent me. The cheque I have just received. We can pay some bills, and eat. Thank you, all my life.
   I hurriedly send you a poem, hoping you will like it. I have worked for a long time on it.
   Also I enclose a Note, for your possible interest, of where this poem will, one day, I hope, find its place.[1]
   All I want to do is to be able to write that long, intended poem.
   I will write, tomorrow, a letter of all my disastrous news. But not until tomorrow, though I could write, now, a little War & Peace—without much peace—about it. Not until tomorrow, because now I must go out, buy provisions, send off to a Welsh tradesman a months-old howled-for money-order. Because I must tell Caitlin.
   I will tell you, tomorrow, why the BBC job failed, why I came back from America without money but happy to have been.
   Our domestic life is a pit & trough. On top of it all, poor Caitlin is pregnant again & wants so much to stop it.
   When I write tomorrow, I will try to give you my news without too much grovel & self-pity.
   In the meantime, do read the poem.
   My *deepest* thanks, & apologies.

                                        Affectionately yours,
                                        Dylan

Do you think the poem could be typed before you read it properly? I think the difficulty of handwriting, and of my dreadful pen, hinder the reading a lot.

MS: Camillo Caetani Foundation

---

1 The poem was 'In the White Giant's Thigh', which Thomas had been writing for a year. The 'Note', published by *Botteghe Oscure* alongside the poem in November 1950, said that 'White Giant' would eventually form part of a longer poem, 'In Country Heaven'. Elsewhere Thomas implied that 'In Country Sleep' and 'Over Sir John's hill' would also be incorporated in this new work. The plan was never realised.

seemingly secure, snug, & all-to-be desired, from this distance, as a house in Trollope. But I can't return to it until I have finished some work here; then, with the money derived from the work, I'll be able to pay some, a few, of the bigger and fiercer Welsh debts; but here it's so hard to work. And Caitlin won't return alone, for the loneliness there is as dispiriting to her as the sardine-cluster here. My, my, what misery!

And all this is one of my old squeals. I shall fashion a morose bagpipe for it, and play all night in the rain.

I made money in America, but returned with very, very little. Firstly, the man who arranged my programme of lectures—I read & lectured only at Universities & Colleges, with three exceptions—arranged it, though kindlily, badly. I found I had enormous air-trips to make between engagements, and these, almost always, I had to pay myself. He'd omitted to make allowances for considerable travelling expenses. Secondly, I had, at the end of my engagements, over a month in New York. There I had to live, at my own expense, in an hotel. Thirdly, the American Income Tax took about 30 per cent of what remained. And, when I returned to England, I found that the broadcasting job I had been promised would not materialise after all.

Now, I am writing a long radio play, which will, I am sure, come to life on the printed page as well. I should like you to see this, when it is finished. With luck—I mean, if I can live till then—it will be finished early in the New Year. I am enjoying writing it enormously. It is not like anything else I have done, though much of it is poetry.

And I will have a new poem—part of the long poem—for you *by Christmas*.

Oh, & I forgot. Please do print the prose note about the long poem if you want to.

You'll try to forgive me, won't you, for not writing for so long & for not acknowledging the money which saved us from—I hear the squealing bagpipe of my woe again, so I'll say only that it saved us. Will you forgive me? I do feel still so beastly unwell.

Write when you can; and the Christmas poem is certain.

Thank you, very much.

Yours affectionately,
Dylan

MS: Camillo Caetani Foundation

BENJAMIN ARBEID[1]
December 7 1950 [draft]   The Boat House   Laugharne
                                                     Carmarthenshire   Wales

Dear Mr. Arbeid,

Will you forgive me, please, for not having answered your letter of months ago? It was extremely kind of you to write, and I must seem most ungrateful not to have answered at once. I've been away from this address for some time, and the local post office, while forwarding some letters, decided to slip others into the letter-box so that they might wait, unopened, on the mat for, so far as they cared, ever. I have just found your own letter today.

Thank you for reading my very briefly suggested treatment of 'The Shadowless Man'[2]—though it is so long ago now that very likely you may have forgotten it. And thank you for saying such very encouraging things about it. ~~I did, of course, realise at the time how impracticable a subject it was in the light of Wardour Street's reaction to it. But~~ Your suggestion that I should try it out on Cocteau, I shall certainly do something about.

~~You were~~ I also ~~kind enough to mention the~~ hope that the possibility of your possibility of you and your associates, sometime in the future, contacting me with regard to a possible film-writing consignment. I do hope this hasn't vanished into thin air. I'm about to go to Persia to write a filmscript for Anglo-Iranian Oil—some kind of technicolor documentary, though God knows what it will turn into—but I shall be returning to London in February.[3] Could we perhaps meet then? Or, anyway, I should be very glad if you could drop me a line.

                                                     Yours sincerely
                                                     Dylan Thomas

contacting me, in the near future, for some other filmwriting hasn't vanished into thin air.

MS: Texas

1 Ben Arbeid, later a film producer, was then a freelance production manager.
2 See n.2, page 279.
3 The film, directed by Ralph Keene, was part of the oil company's strategy to present itself as a friend of Iran, at a time when emerging nationalism was threatening company (and British) interests there.

HAROLD NICOLSON

Dec 7 1950   The Boat House   Laugharne   Carmarthenshire

Dear Mr. Harold Nicolson,

Will you please forgive me for not answering your letter at once? It was very very kind of you to write to the Secretary of the Royal Literary Fund about me, and I'm extremely glad you will put my name forward.[1] It must, I know, seem very rude indeed of me not to thank you a long time before this: I've been ill, too ill to do anything but moan about it and my difficulties, and there was a lot of trouble about changes of addresses and losing of letters, and then my wife brought me home to get well in the country, and then, at home, the difficulties came piling on me more heavily than ever, and I think I lost heart.

The Secretary of the Fund wrote to me, and sent me a form of application for a grant. This, too, I was unable to answer in time, and now I find that my application can't come up at the next meeting on December 13, as the Secretary has to have it, along with some letters supporting my case, at least seven days before the meeting. I've written him today, but my case must, I'm afraid, wait now until January 10. I do hope a grant will be made me. It's very urgent.

I hope you will forgive me for this long delay.

And thank you very much.
Yours sincerely,
Dylan Thomas

From a typescript. MS location unknown

*AUGUSTUS JOHN

8 December 1950   The Boat House   Laugharne   Carmarthenshire

Dear Augustus,

Will you do something for me, please? It only means writing a letter, but it means writing a letter to:

The Secretary, The Royal Literary Fund, Stationers' Hall, London, E.C.4.

Would you, in the briefest of letters, support my claim, which I have already made in an official application, that I am a person known to you to be in financial distress, and also that, in your opinion, I am a person whose

1 Once again Thomas turned to the Fund. The author Harold Nicolson (1886–1968) had written to the secretary, now J. G. Broadbent, in November to recommend him. On 8 December Nicolson wrote again: '. . . I should of course have to disclose to the Committee that he is a very heavy drinker . . . you may have encountered similar circumstances in which the money is paid in such a way as not to be spent entirely on drink . . . I gather that his wife is almost equally unreliable. On the other hand, he is one of our best poets, and if the Literary Fund exists for anything, it exists to enable such people to write a few more poems before they go completely to pieces.'

financial distress should rightly be alleviated by a grant from the Royal Literary Fund?

When I came back from London, I found that all my Laugharne cheques had bounced. You know what this means in a Welsh township not notoriously antipathetical to money. It is very painful here indeed.

Today I had a letter from the bank saying that all the London cheques had also been dishonoured. The English, too, are only nonchalant about money when you have it, and I expect London to be a painful place when I return.

I had thought there was money in the bank. There was; but none of mine.

This week, I have received a letter from Llewelyn's school at Oxford, saying that unless the last two terms' fees are paid he can no longer remain at that school.

And I owe, for the Pelican, Laugharne, which I rented for my father & mother, one year's rent. There is danger of their being evicted.

This little list of griefs does not include my long debts to every tradesman.

If I am not in 'financial distress', then I am dangerously near it.

I have lots of work to do next year, but can do nothing while these debts are dogging.

So *would* you write that letter, please? The Royal Literary Fund is a last hope.

See you on the Cross,[1]
Dylan

MS: National Library of Wales

UNKNOWN ADDRESSEE[2]
[?1950] [fragment; probably a draft]
The Boat House Laugharne
Carmarthenshire

Dear Sirs,

I am applying for a Grant because I most urgently need financial help so that I can go on working and be able to make enough money to keep myself and my family.

I am extremely badly in debt; these debts are pressing, and daily and horribly becoming more so; and it seems that I cannot think of anything else at all.

Surrounded by these debts, hurt and worried to despair in the very middle of them, and seeing and hearing my home crumble because of

1 As well as crucifixion, Thomas means the square at the foot of the town, with stone cross and Cross House pub.
2 The letter may have been connected with his Royal Literary Fund application.

them, I cannot write, they come between me and everything else I do. And, as I can't write, I can't make any money, and so new day-by-day debts arise; and I can't see any good end to this, and I would be insane if I could.

Less and less do I seem able to concentrate on anything except these worries and despairs—(the writing of this letter is a kind of torture, my mind keeps jerking painfully away to the thoughts of writs and tradesmen's bills)—and more and more important grow these beastly little griefs to me

MS: Texas

A BANK MANAGER
8 December 1950 [draft]   The Boat House   Laugharne
                                                         Carmarthenshire

Dear Sir,

Please forgive me for not being able, as I very much wanted, to come along & see you in London about my rather strained financial affairs. I was caught up with very frenzied preparations for my Persian visit, & also with domestic crises, including illness.

I am sorry that, through no fault of my own except carelessness— probably, to one's Bank Manager, one of the worst faults of all—I wrote, while in London, cheques for which there was [not] enough money in my account to provide for. I had been informed that a cheque for a £100 was on its way to your Bank, & accordingly, & foolishly, though not, I swear dishonestly, took premature advantage of it. I shall have, now, to come back to London early next week to see that that £100 is paid in at once.

Also, I should tell you now, as I shd have told you in our interview that, unfortunately, never took place, that I have seen Mr Anthony Hubbard about that cheque I made out to him, payable on June 1, & he has agreed that he & I shd deal with it privately.

And now, a most sincere plea: I have had to cash, locally, a cheque for £5, dated today, the 8th, & made payable to I. Williams. Will you *please* see that this is honoured. If it was dishonoured, I should be in a *very* painful situation here, & here is a very narrow & hidebound small Welsh town: my fellow countrymen are not, as you know, altogether antipathetical to money. Will you please do this for me? I *had* to cash the cheque. And I shall pay in a £100 this week.

MS: Texas

MARGARET TAYLOR
[?1950]   Laugharne

My dear Margaret,
I was so very sorry to have had to ask you, yet again, for money. I hate doing it; especially as I know how difficult it is now for you, with all your great kindness, to help me.
The coalmen would give us no more coal unless we paid their bill. This bill I had to pay by cheque. And there was, in my bank, no money to meet it. Therefore, the cheque would be returned. Therefore, the coalmen would be vile, & there would be no more coal. So, I had to have £20 to send in to the bank to say: 'Do what you must with other cheques, but *please* honour the cheque to Frank H. Brown'. If I get your cheque, by Saturday—I'll just save things. If I don't, we must, I suppose, leave Laugharne.
Thank you, *a great deal*, for trying to help; & I hope to God you can.
Sorry for my exhausted bloodiness the last day of my London visit.
I shall, I hope, if I can raise the fare, see you Monday.
                                                                           Yours,
                                                                           Dylan

MS: Texas

*DOUGLAS CLEVERDON
Dec. 8. 50   Laugharne

My dear Douglas
See you, then, in your office at 3.15 on Monday, the 11th. Have you a copy of 'Spoon River Anthology'[1] in case I have mislaid mine?
Mislaid is, I'm afraid, the word for the Faber Book of Comic Verse. I'm dreadfully sorry, and will attempt to right it.
I'll tell you about the Mad town when we meet.[2]
                                                                           Ever,
                                                                           Dylan

MS: Rosenbach Museum and Library, Philadelphia

CAITLIN THOMAS
5.30 Sunday [?10 December 1950][3]   On the Train

I'll wire you to tell you
what train I catch

1 See footnote, page 930.
2 Cleverdon had written on 5 December, 'Now that you are free from the distractions of this beastly cold metropolis, I hasten to urge you to complete "The Village that was Mad" ... Moreover, I can get the whole thing paid for immediately the script is approved.' It was three years before the play was finished.
3 Thomas was in London on Monday 11 December to record a BBC discussion with Roy Campbell, George Barker and W. R. Rodgers. This may have been the 'Celtic huddle of poets' referred to.

Leaving you, my love, without kissing you, or being kissed by you, hurt more than my legendary back, my ham of misery. And all the way, limping and squealing along the cliff, I hoped & hoped I was too late for the car. But go I would have to, whether then or Monday morning, so perhaps it wasn't too bad that I caught the train and now, in the buffet car, am writing to you to say: I love you for ever, day & night, all my life & death, I love you, Caitlin. Forgive my bellows when I'm hurt, my snarling recriminations which are really only against the weather, the world, God, bombs, penury, drink, myself, but *never* you. Never you, my dearest wife. The waiters in this buffet car are the same we met when you & Ivy and I went together to London on Sunday, nearly a year ago, and they all asked fondly after you. Everybody asks fondly about you, but I am the only one who loves you always; and you are mine.

The train is a horribly slow one, stops at every station. It won't be in Paddington until about 9.30, which will hardly give me time to have a drink with either John D. or Bob. I don't know yet whose house I grace: probably Bob, because he is nearer to the BBC & my Celtic huddle of poets. I'll tell Bob & Sheila[1] you are writing, and, myself, find out what they intend to do about Christmas. If they come, would they stay in the Pelican and eat with us? I love you. The waiters have just asked me to play cards, & so I will. One of them I told about my injured back, & he said, without interest, 'Too bad. Now *I've* got a little pimple just inside my nose—look here! you can hardly see it—and it makes me feel all nose. It's burning all the time.' I gave a cry as my back hurt me, & he said, 'That's what I feel like doing about my nose too.' People are very selfish. I love you for ever, my darling, my beautiful dear Cattle-Anchor, & I want you too.

Dylan

MS: Maurice Neville

CAITLIN THOMAS
[?1950] [on a torn scrap of paper]

Please my own Caitlin my dear darling I love you I love you my dear. And forgive my bad temper this morning: it was because I knew I had to leave you, in the vile cold. Caitlin my darling I love you forever.

Dylan

I might try to come back tonight. But certainly sometime tomorrow. I'll ring.

MS: (Thomas Trustees)

1 Bob Pocock and his wife.

CAITLIN THOMAS
[?1950] [on a piece of paper 23 x 17 cm]

I love you Caitlin, only you, now & forever, I love you with all my life. Oh, I love you so much, Cait.

Dylan

MS: Berg

JEAN LEROY
15 Dec 1950   The Boat House   Laugharne   Carmarthenshire

Dear Miss LeRoy,
    You asked me whether, in the programme 'Poetic Licence', recorded on the 11th December & broadcast on the 15th, I had any special expenses on top of my fee. Yes, I had returned to Wales a week before the recording, & had to travel to London for the recording. The fare is the usual return one, Laugharne to London.

Yours sincerely,
Dylan Thomas

P.S. Oh, & about that long-ago programme, 'Poems & A Commentary'. My expenses were: return fare Laugharne to London, plus one night's stay in London. Sorry not to have answered this before. Hope you can get the payments through before Christmas.

DT

MS: Texas

JOHN DAVENPORT
19 12 50   The Savage Club   1 Carlton House Tce   London   SW1

Dear Brother Savage John Davenport,
    It is a time-honoured custom of the Club to which we both have the honour to belong, to address one another fraternally thus. If this were not so, the appellation I should, in all honesty, be compelled to attach to your name would be one singularly lacking in camaraderie.
    Your cherished illusion is, I must suppose, that your fellow members remain in a state of ignorance as to the real purpose for which you joined the Club. May I point out to you that one member, at least, is under no illusion as to that purpose, which is to purloin from the Smoking Room the only copies of The Stage and The New Yorker?

If, as is obvious, you have no respect for other members who might wish to peruse those periodicals, have you none for Literature? This, as you well know, is a Club which regularly wines & dines such notable practitioners of that Art as Reginald Arkell, Alec Waugh, Tschiffeley, Louis Golding, Dale Collins, and L. I. F. Brimble.[1] Are you not letting down their good name, and the good name of all your fellow-scribblers—under which heading I humbly class myself—when you stoop so low as utterly and wantonly to disregard the injunction, Not To Be Taken Away, which is stamped upon every periodical in the Smoking Room?

Yours sincerely,
Dylan Thomas, F.R.S.L.

MS: Texas

JOHN DAVENPORT
19th Dec 1950   The Boat House   Laugharne   Carmarthenshire

Dear John,
   Many thanks for writing. The messages of good will were indeed welcome, and are reciprocated. I trust that the New Year will find us both in better financial fettle.

Yours,
Dylan

MS: Texas

*SHEILA AND BOB POCOCK
[December 1950]

Written on reverse of a photograph of the Boat House. An unsteady arrow points to the top left-hand window on the west side of the house. The writing is disordered.

to Sheila & Bob from Dylan
Sex marks the window where I sleep.
Follow the arrow thro' the wall & that's
where, I hope, you'll sleep together
one day soon.

MS: University of California, Los Angeles

---

1 Reginald Arkell wrote poems about gardening. L. I. F. Brimble wrote a book about trees. Alec Waugh and Louis Golding were popular novelists.

JOHN DAVENPORT
[?December 1950]   Boat House

My dear John,
   The Pococks are going back to London on the 27th. I am going to London
on the 2nd of January. Can you come down between those dates? We would
love to have you, & are looking forward immensely to it. *Do try.*
                                     Love to Margery & Hugo & Roger,
                                             Dylan

MS: Texas

J. G. BROADBENT (Royal Literary Fund)
January 1 1951   The Boat House   Laugharne   Carmarthenshire

Dear Mr Broadbent,
   Thank you very much for your letter, and please excuse my (once more)
very long delay in answering: I have been ill again, all over Christmas
unfortunately, & for some time before. I am afraid my recurrent illness has
set back a lot what hopes I had of being helped by the Royal Literary Fund,
but it was, quite obviously, unavoidable. I still do hope something may
come of my application when it is, as I so much trust it will be, brought to
the notice of the Committee on January 13.
   In your letter, you said you wanted to know the amounts of my various
debts. Well, here they are, & I am afraid they are enormous: written down,
they seem more frightening to me than ever.
   For my son's schooling, I am in debt £100. (He goes to Magdalen College
School.) For one year's rent of my own house—I mean, the house in which I
& my wife & children live—I owe another £100.
   And I owe yet another £100 for the rent of my parents' house.
   Tradesmen's bills in the town amount, approximately, to £60.
   And our clothing bills come to, approximately, £30.
   I know this amounts to quite a hideous sum, but there it is.[1]
   My present income is, as I think I tried to explain in my letter to the
Committee, frightfully erratic, coming only from my poems, occasional
stories, & some freelance work for the radio.
   My commitments for the near future—& I'm glad to be able to strike one
slightly happier note in all this woeful parade of debts—will be covered by
a film-writing job I am just about to do. But that job—very possibly the
only lucrative one I shall have this coming year—is meant to keep us while

---

1 Thomas was given a grant of £300, but it was instantly swallowed up by debts, which
   the Fund appears to have paid direct. Magdalen College School (where Llewelyn was a
   boarder) received £147; a girls' school (Aeronwy went to a day school in Carmarthen),
   £18; Savage Club, £15; Laugharne pharmacy and post office (with whisky and Guinness
   prominent on the bill), £50 on account of £117 owing.

I do more work at home to get money. What I just *cannot* do, by myself, is pay the past, & increasingly pressing, debts.

Sorry if this letter is vague: I still feel pretty groggy.

Thank you again for your letter. I hope that, by this time, you've received two letters to support my application: I wrote to Augustus John & Lord David Cecil, both of whom agreed to speak, or, rather, write for me.

Yours very sincerely,
Dylan Thomas

MS: *Royal Literary Fund*

CAITLIN THOMAS
[early Jan 1951]   c/o   Information Dept   Anglo-Iranian Oil Co
                                 Avenue Shah   (Naderi) Tehran   Persia

Caitlin my darling, dear, dear Caitlin, oh my love so far away I love you. All these strange, lost days I love you, and I am lost indeed without you my dear wife. This is so much further than America, and letters will take so much longer to travel to you and yours to me if you will ever write to me again oh *darling* Cat. And if you do not write to me, and if you do not love me any more, I cannot go on, I cannot go on sleeplessly thinking, 'Caitlin my Cattleanchor, my dear, does not love me, o God let me die.' I can't live without you; I can't go travelling with this long, wan Bunny[1] through this fearful, strange world unless I am sure that at the end we will be together as we are meant to be together, close & alone except for our cuckoo whom I miss very very very much, more than I could dream of. But you: I miss you more than I would miss my life although you *are* my life. I can see now, in this grand over-hot Oil-Company Guest House where we are staying, your smiling and your anger, your coldness with me, your once-love for me, your golden hair & blue eyes and our wedding ring from a cracker, I can see you coming to bed, I can feel your coldness turning, in my arms, to warmth and love, I can hear you so beautiful with Cuckoo Colm Colum Column, I can hear you saying, 'I love you', 'I hate you', 'Go away', 'Come close' to me all the blessed days of our life. Caitlin beloved, unless you write to say that we will be together again, I shall die. I love you I love you, day, night, waking, sinking into some kind of sleep. This letter may take a week to reach you, or it may take three days; however long or short a time, oh darling darling write to me. There will be nothing but pains & nightmares & howlings in my head and endless endless nights & forsaken days until you say, 'I am waiting. I love you.'

Forgive me, darling, for this business of money. I went with John D., as

---

1 Dylan had gone to Persia on the film-making trip, leaving Caitlin to brood on his infidelity. He left Laugharne on Tuesday 2 January, was the best part of a week in London, and flew to Persia on 8 January. With him was the director, 'Bunny' Keene.

you know, on Tuesday to London & left you ten pounds to last a week. Then, when I rang on Saturday, you said the money had gone & you must have more. I know, I know, it goes terribly quickly, but somehow ten pounds a week *must*, I'm sorry dear, see you through. You said, in your lovely letter that I picked up on Sunday from John, that the Princess had wired to say she was sending more money. But, until her cheque is in the Bank, I can't let you have a cheque for Dathan Davies. So: will you see which of the letters that has arrived for me bears Italian stamps, open it, and if it has the princess's cheque (probably for £50) in it, send it on to me at the c/o Information Dept address, and I will send a cheque for the whole amount to you *at once*. *Or*, you can sign the cheque on the back with *my name*, if you like, and put it through my father's account. *Or*, you can sign the cheque with my name, give it to Dathan Davies in payment of their account & then have the £10-odd change for yourself. Do one of these things *as quickly as possible*. And, please, forward my letters as quickly as possible too: there should be a cheque in one of them with which I can pay Llewelyn's school fees. Now, for the moment, all I can pathetically do is enclose a cheque to Eric Jones made out for £5. This sounds absurdly small an amount to send all the way from Persia, but it's all I dare do until I know there is some more money in the Bank: and the only way I can know that is to see the letters which have arrived since I left. You will be receiving, at the beginning of each week, ten pounds in notes from Bunny's firm, for five weeks—by which time I shall be back in England. By which time, if you will ever have me again, I shall be at home with you. I love you, darling darling, darling. I LOVE YOU. I know I should have written to you in the five days I was in London before I and that long drip flew away, but I knew I would phone at the end of the week. Oh, *please* forgive me. I love you so much, so very much I can think of nothing else. I love you. I love you Caitlin. Please write at once, please forward all letters. Please read carefully that bit about the Princess's cheque. The sun's shining, & I'm in darkness because I do not know if you will ever love me again. And I'll die if you do not. I mean that. I shall not kill myself: I shall die. Our life together is for ever & ever amen. I love you.

I have to go out to see the town of Tehran which, at a quick look, seems depressing and half-made. When I come back, I shall write you again today.

The plane trip took 24 hours &, on arriving, Bunny had a collapse.

I LOVE YOU, MY ONLY CAITLIN DARLING.

Love to our children.

Your husband in the darkness,
Dylan

MS: Tony Vilela

CAITLIN THOMAS
[January 1951] c/o Information Department   Anglo-Iranian Oil Company
Avenue Shah (Naderi)   Tehran Persia

I will write to
Llewelyn & Aeron, &
my mother & father
from Abadan. My love
Cat. Write to me quickly.
I love you.

Dear Cat Catlin darling, I love you. There's no meaning to anything without you. There's no meaning without us being together. I love you all the day and night, and I am five thousand miles away. Until I hear from you, Cat, every minute of the day and night's insane. I have to dope myself into nightmare sleep with tablets from Bunny's enormous medicine-chest. I wake up before it is dawn, in this great undersea bedroom under snow-mountains, and turn the echoes of your voice over and over in the dark, and look into your blue beautiful undersea eyes five thousand miles away: they're all that is real, the deepnesses of your eyes [. . .] the shadows of your voice, East, [. . .] or anywhere in the world.[1] Write [. . .] Cat dear. Say that you want me still, [. . .] you will wait for me. I love you. [. . .] of you all day and night: you in [. . .] saken seahouse in God knows what [. . .] misery and rain and hate of me: [. . .], in the snow & the sun, understanding nothing of the savage town around, wanting to know nothing of ugly, dirty, dinning Tehran with mosques and sores and disease and Cadillacs. I think of you always. I love you, Caitlin my wife for ever though you throw away my life. Write to me, Cat. My dear.

The long Bunny is still in bed, groaning: he has a 'little chill', he says, has a huge fire in his room, two hotwaterbottles, an array all over his bedside table of syrups, pills, syringes, laxatives, chlorodyne, liniments and compresses; he uses a thermometer every hour. And I? I go with horrible oil-men to interview horrible government-men; I sit in the lounge of this posh Guest-House for horrible oil-men and listen to Scotch engineers running down the Persian wops; I go, with a pleasant Persian guide, through endless museums, palaces, libraries, cou[. . .] law, houses of parliament, till my [. . .] and my boredom bleed. What for, what [. . .] for? Only the bazaar was wonderful [. . .] Tehran bazaar, the largest in Persia [. . .] all the things one's read about [. . .] bazaars, all the bits of films of [. . .] one's ever seen, haggling and cursing and grinning and smelling everywhere round one: miles of covered bazaar, smelling of incense and carpets and food and poverty. And women with only their eyes showing through tattered, dirty, cobble-trailing thin black sack-wraps; or lifting their wraps high to miss the mud and showing men's ragged trousers or baggy black bloomers; and lots of them with splayed and rotting high-heel shoes. Only

1 A corner is missing from one sheet.

the very poor—that is, the vast majority—of women wear these wrappings, not only of black but of grey, earth-brown, filthy white—and they wear them only to cover up their rags. They huddle their horrible poverty inside these chadurs as they slipslop through the foul main streets or the shouting, barging aisles of the bazaar. Often there are babies huddled in with the poverty. And beautiful dirty children in little chadurs slip-slop behind them. The poor in the streets & the bazaar wear every kind of clothing, so long as it's dirty and wretched. Men wear little green brimless bowlers, or caps like scavenging tram-conductors', and old army overcoats, British, German, American. Poor children all have cropped heads. Well-to-do children have their eyes darkened with kohl or mascara.

The only water for the poor in Tehran—the capital city of Persia—runs down the public gutters. I saw an old man pissing in the gutter, walking away a few yards, then cupping his hands & drinking from it. This running cesspool is the only drinking & washing water for the poor. I love you. I love you. I love you in this dirty city. I love you everywhere.

There is no nightlife at all in Tehran. Moslems are not supposed to drink, though some do. Only in one or two expensive hotels for Europeans can you buy a drink. There seems to be no fixed price for any drinks. I was charged six shillings for a bottle of beer, Bunny twelve shillings for a small whiskey. Only in welltodo houses—and in this Guest-house for oil-men—can one drink at all. In four days I have had eight pints of beer: all lager. I love you, I love you in this dry city. I love you everywhere.

Write to me quickly, darling. Tell me tell me. Shall I bring back Persian sweetmeats? (I cannot send them: they would evaporate or burst.) There are wonderful liqueur chocolates you would love. But not so much as I love you. I love you. I love you. I love you Cat.

D.

MS: Andrew MacAdie

CAITLIN THOMAS
16th January [1951]   [headed paper: Ahwaz   Persian Gulf]

Caitlin dear,

I do not know if this letter will reach you at all, or if my other two letters have reached you. I do not know if, whether any of these letters has reached you or will reach you, you will reply to them. I do not know anything, except that I love you. And I do not know if you love me. I love you enough for both of us, but I must know, still, if you are waiting for me, if you want me, if I may come home to you, if there is any cause for me to live. I love you, Caitlin darling dear. Perhaps my letters take very long to travel the miles between us, and so that is why I do not hear from you. Perhaps you have said: 'He is dead to me'. And, if you say that, indeed I will be dead. I love you, love you, love you, always, always, beautiful Cat my love. What I am doing here, without word of you, I just don't know.

Yesterday I left Tehran for Abadan, and am stopping here for the night, in an Arabian house, after a twenty-four [hour] train journey. By plane, the journey would have taken $2\frac{1}{2}$ hours. And so the powerful, tireless Bunny with his immense pharmacopeia, decided to go by train. It, of course, nearly killed him; and it has done me no good either. But, if I heard from you, if I knew, for one second, that you are mine, as I am yours, that you might again love me as I love you forever, I'd travel a thousand hours on the roof of the train. I grope through the nights and days like a blind man; even English around me is an unknown language; I am writing to you, my love, my wife, my darling dear Cat, the one soul and body in the world, as though I didn't know words: stiltedly, awkwardly. I love you. I can at least write that.

Yesterday morning, in Tehran, I went to a large hospital. In the children's wards, I saw rows and rows of tiny little Persian children suffering from starvation: their eyes were enormous, seeing everything & nothing, their bellies bloated, their matchstick arms hung round with blue, wrinkled flesh. One of them was crying: only one. I asked the English sister why. 'Poor little thing', she said. 'His mother went out every day begging in the streets, & he was too weak from hunger to go with her & she was too weak to carry him. So she left him alone in her hovel. The hovel had a hole dug in the earth floor where a fire always was; or at least hot cinders, ready for cooking. The child fell down into the fire & lay there *all day* burning till the mother came home at dusk. He is getting better, but he's lost one arm & all his toes.'

After that, I had lunch with a man worth 30,000,000 pounds, from the rents of peasants all over Iran, & from a thousand crooked deals. A charming, and cultivated, man.[1]

Now all the weather's changed. In Tehran, it was brisk, sunny spring. A wonderful climate. Here, 24 hours nearer the Gulf, I'm sitting dead still and panting & sweating. What it's like in the summer, Christ knows. In Tehran, they said: It will be cold down here. I brought a tweed suit & a duffle, & the temperature's nearly a 100. There are great palm trees in this garden, & buzzards overhead. At every station of this 24-hour journey—& the stations are very odd; they cater for no-one—children rushed up to the train from the mud-hut villages: three quarter naked, filthy, hungry, and, mostly, beautiful with smiles & great burning eyes & wild matted hair: begging for the smallest coins, pieces of bread, a sweet, anything. I gave the first lot my lunch, & woof! it went in a second. I love you. So write to me please, if you value me at all. Goodnight, my love.

Oh, it would be wonderful to be with you, to be in your lovely arms, my love. It's seven o'clock in the morning; I'm lying in bed; already it's awfully

1 If the tone of Thomas's letters is indicative, it is not surprising that no script by him was ever used by Anglo-Iranian, although he seems to have been paid £250. Iranian nationalists were already threatening the company, which was soon taken over. Fantasies later circulated that Thomas, far from sympathising with the poor, had been recruited by British Intelligence, which was anxious to see the status quo in Iran maintained.

hot; together we could be happy, we could go out into the garden in the sun, into the striped streets, on to the river banks. Yesterday evening, just before dusk, I saw four men, in long Arabian dress, squatting in a circle on a tiny mudbank in the middle of the river. The mudbank was just large enough to hold them. The sun was going down quickly, the river was rising. The four men were playing cards. Together here, or anywhere, in any dusty sunfried place, we could be happy, my dear love. I love you. I feel you & smell you, & hear you everywhere all around me. I see you in our pink house, so far away, I could yell till I die. Remember me, sweetheart. If I didn't think that, at the end of this wandering rubbish, I'd be with you again—and we could together prepare to be somewhere else; I wrote, last week, to San Francisco—I'd melt away, saying your name, into the hot sea. I love you love you love you love you, & I am yours & you are mine. Tell me, when, & if ever, you write, how you dealt with the Princess's cheque. If you forward letters, I will see if there is any money in the Bank & then I can send you some. BUT WRITE. I'm lost without you. Tell me about Colm, Aeron, & Llewelyn. I'll send Llewelyn stamps of Iran. My dear!

Dylan

MS: Tony Vilela

[PEARL KAZIN][1]
[about 17 January 1951] Abadan

[. . .]

I am writing this in a tasty, stifflipped, liverish, British Guest House in puking Abadan on, as you bloody well know, the foul blue boiling Persian buggering Gulf. And lost, God blast, I gasp between gassed vodkas, all crude and cruel fuel oil, all petroleum under frying heaven, benzola bitumen, bunkers and tankers, pipes and refineries, wells and derricks, gushers and super-fractionators and [?Shatt]-el-Arab and all. Today I was taken to see a great new black-towered hissing and coiling monster, just erected in the middle of the refinery. It cost eight million pounds. It is called a Cat-Cracker.

Abadan is inhibited almost entirely by British—or so it seems. There are thousands of young Britishers in the bachelor quarters, all quietly seething. Many snap in the heat of their ingrowing sex and the sun, and are sent back, baying, to Britain. Immediately, their places are taken by fresh recruits: young wellgroomed pups with fair moustaches and briar pipes, who, in the soaking summer, soon age, go bristled about, chainsmoke damp hanging fags, scream blue on arak, toss themselves tremblyall sleepless night in the toss-trembling bachelors' quarters, answer the three-knock knock at the midnight door, see before them in the hot moonlight

1 The only source of this incomplete item is a typescript used by FitzGibbon in *Selected Letters.*

wetmouthed Persian girls from the bazaar who ask, by custom, for a glass of water, invite the girls in, blush, stammer, grope, are lost. These old-young men are shipped back also, packed full with shame and penicillin. And the more cautious stay on, boozed, shrill, hunted, remembering gay wonderful London so white-skinned and willing.

I visited oil-fields in the mountains last week. By night, the noise of frustrated geologists howled louder than the jackals outside my tent. Utterly damned, the dishonourable, craven, knowledgeable, self-pitying jackals screamed and wailed in the abysses of their guilt and the stinking garbage pails. 'Rosemary', 'Jennifer', 'Margery', cried the nearmale unsleepers in their near-sleep. And the hyenas laughed like billyho deep down in their dark diseased throats. O evergreen, gardened, cypressed, cinema'd, oil-tanked, boulevarded, incense-and-armpit cradle of Persian culture, rock me soft before lorn hotel-bedtime. I have nostalgia and gout. [. . .] My toe pulses like a painful cucumber in the arraky bar. O city of Hafiz and Sad'i and Mrs. Wiltshire the Consul's wife, tickle me till my balloon toe dies [. . .] A lonely country. And so is stricken Persia, mosque and blindness, fountains and mudhuts, Cadillac and running sore, pomegranate and Cat-Cracker. Beer in an hotel bar costs ten shillings a bottle; whiskey, one pound a nip. There is no nightlife. Shiraz sleeps at nine. Then, through the dark, the low camel bells ring; jackals confess their unworthiness to live in an ignoble fury of siren howls and utter their base and gutter-breathed gratitude to the night that hides their abominable faces; insomniac dogs rumpus in the mountain villages; the Egyptian deputy-Minister of Education, who has the next hotel room, drunkenly gallumphs with a thin, hairy secretary; dervishes plead under my bed; there are wolves not far away. There is no night life here; the moon does what she does, vermin persist, camels sail, dogs defy, frogs gloat, snow-leopards drift, ibex do what they do, moufflon are peculiar, gazelles are lonely, donkeys are Christian, bears in the high hills hug [. . .]

Dylan

From a typescript. MS location unknown

CAITLIN THOMAS
[January or early February 1951]   Isfahan   Iran

Caitlin dear,

Your letter, as it was meant to, made me want to die.[1] I did not think that, after reading it so many times till I knew every pain by heart, I could go on with these days and nights, alone with my loneliness—now, as I know too well, for ever—and knowing that, a long way and a lifetime away, you no longer loved or wanted me. (After your cold, disliking letter,

1 Writing when drunk to Helen McAlpine on 20 January, Caitlin said she had cast Dylan out of her thoughts, was embittered and sexless, and felt trapped in Laugharne: whether he left her for good or came back to her from Persia, she would be the loser.

you wrote: 'All my love, Caitlin.' You could have spared that irony.] But the bloody animal always *does* go on. Now I move through these days in a kind of dumb, blind despair, and slowly every day ends. It's the nights I fear most, when the despair breaks down, is dumb and blind no longer, and I am only myself in the dark. I am only alone in an unknown room in a strange town in a benighted country, without any pretences and crying like a fool. Last night I saw you smiling, glad, at me, as you did a thousand years ago; and I howled like the jackals outside. Then, in the morning, it was the same again: walking, in despair, frozen, over a desert. It was even a real desert, the camels aloof, the hyenas laughing. I'm writing this, perhaps last, letter, just before I go to bed in an hotel full of brutes. If only I didn't have to go to bed. Nobody here, in this writing room, the wireless shouting Persian, can see anything wrong with me. I'm only a little fat foreigner writing a letter: a loving, happy letter to his wife 'waiting at home'. Christ, if they knew. If they knew that the woman I am writing to no longer needs me, has shut her heart & her body against me, although she is my life. I cannot live without you—you, always—and I have no intention of doing so. I fly back, from Tehran to London, on, I am almost certain, the 14th of February. I shall cable you from Tehran the time of my arrival. You said, before we parted, that you would come up to London to meet me on my return. You will not, I suppose, be doing that now? If you are not, will you please—it is not a great deal to ask—leave a message at the McAlpines. I will not come back to Laugharne until I know that I [?am] wanted: not as an inefficient mispayer of bills, but as myself and for you. If you do not meet me in London, I shall ring the McAlpines. If there is no message there from you, I shall know that everything is over. It is very terrible writing this such a great distance from you. In a few minutes I shall go to my bedroom, climb into bed in my shirt, and think of you. The bedroom knows your name well, as do many bedrooms in this country. 'Caitlin, Caitlin', I will say, and you will come drifting to me, clear & beautiful, until my eyes blur and you are gone. I love you. Oh, darling Cat, I love you.

Dylan

MS: Tony Vilela

CAITLIN THOMAS
Monday [?late February 1951]   4 St James Tce[1]

Cat darling dear, I miss you I miss you more, it seems, than ever before. Cat sweetheart my love, I love you. I love you for ever. You are everything that exists to me. You're my life and my love and I love you. London is

1 The McAlpines' current address. Dylan joined Caitlin there after the Persian trip, and they returned to Laugharne in disarray on Sunday 18 February. On 25 February Caitlin wrote to Helen McAlpine to say she had found more love-letters from Kazin in her husband's suitcase; adding that Dylan would be in London that week. This letter may have been written then.

terrible without you, and I know that Laugharne is terrible too. Since you left in the sun, leaving me broken and hollow and very near to crying, it has been dark yellow in the streets, with a fine thin dark yellow rain all the time as well. The days have been thousands of years long; the nights in our grandish but now almost pigsty McAlpine bedroom have been sleepless & feverish & sick and screaming with worry; I have had no money, and none—so far—of my appointments have led to any definite job. Tomorrow I meet Arbeid, who's been ill; he's going to Paris to see Dick & Hilda Sims;[1] he wants them in a film of his; and he wants me to write the film. But it isn't immediate. Whatever happens, I'll return on Wednesday even if it means coming back to London a week later to see Arbeid on his return from Paris. Also, I fell halfway downstairs here & cut my head and blacked my eye. I look repellent. Oh, Cat my Cat my true Cat my dear poor darling, I love you beyond any words, beyond the stars. I think of you all night & day. Everywhere you are with me, and not with me. I'm terribly sorry, darling, I can't send any money in this letter: I've only a few shillings. Somehow I'll get some to bring back on Wednesday. I want to be with you. I am lost without you. The already damned dark world darkens again. Every sun goes in. I love you & want to be with you always, until the end of time. You are my Caitlin, & I love you. Kiss the cuckoo for me. Love to Aeron. To you, all I have, which is bloody little. I love you love you love you. If you came into this posh musical room at this moment, I would cry & die I need you so. It is drizzling, afternoon. Helen is sewing downstairs. I am waiting till six o clock when I meet Ted Kavanagh again.[2] He's hopeful of us working together, but nothing is immediate. And it *has* to be. But please, my love, do know that I am trying everything I know. I am not drinking—I can't, anyway, but I don't want to. I am quiet, very sad, & wanting you all night and day. Please, dear dear Cat, try to endure the—I love you—long sad Laugharne end-of-the-world days for a little longer.

Dear Cattle anchor

Yours eternally affectionate,
black-eyed, profoundly
depressed

Dylan

MS: Tony Vilela

1 Hilda Simms, American actress.
2 Ted Kavanagh (1892–1958) was a radio scriptwriter whose wartime comedy show, the weekly *ITMA*, became a national event. He never repeated the success. In 1951 he hoped to collaborate with Thomas in a BBC comedy series, but it was not written.

TED KAVANAGH
[?February or March 1951]   The Boat House   Laugharne
                                    Carmarthenshire   Wales   Tel: *Laugharne 68*

Dear Ted,
Thank you for the Quid's Inn outline.[1] 'Rudest comments appreciated',
my black eye! I think it's a very very good idea indeed, lusty, twisty,
thirsty, and with enormous, almost frighteningly so, possibilities. It's a
whole new, old, rough and alive comic world you're thinking of conjuring
and gingering up: all the rich, rooted, fruity past of the rural gallimaufry
loud alongside with the world of to-now. (I'd like to see John Q. bring in the
stocks and the ducking stool again.) The whole thing is, to me, a wonderful
and exciting gamble—and, what's bettingly best about it, you can go wrong
from the very beginning. But I don't think you will. Everybody'll want to go
to Quid's Inn, in whatever village it is—Little Fiddle on the Grog or
anywhere, though not, by God, that—and I want to go myself. I want to
hear the village and the village singers—Al Rhubarb and his Glee, though
not, by God, that—noising in the upstairs Music and Recreation Room; and
the meetings of the local John O' London's, or Will O' Birmingham's,
Literary Society, or the P.E.N. or N.I.B. (National Institute of Bards?) Club,
and to hear, not sopping dance lyrics, but, affectionately guyed, such
ballad-concert favourites as 'Drake's Drum' and 'King Charles'. And, oh,
the societies of cranks!
I think, myself, by the way, that it would be wrong to use the Colonel
again.[2] A drunk, certainly, if you like, but a truly rural one: the last of the
red-faced squires, maybe, or the wicked, poaching Jack-of-all-trades, like
Bob Pretty in the W. W. Jacobs Cauliflower Inn stories. (And I want to hear,
very much, the medley of all English country accents, and the coming of
the Australian, and the frightful visitations of the enemies from over the
borders, the haggisy stone-snaffling Scotch[3] and the hymnal, leeky
Welsh.)
I want to go to Quid's Inn every week, and I'd like, if I could, to try to
help to make it the best, funniest, truest, and most exhilarating pub and
meeting place in the indestructible country. In fact, I really would like to
have a bang with you at all this, and do feel that I could add something. I
think it can be great stuff.
Will you drop me a line, or wire me, or phone me at Laugharne
(pronounced Larne) 68, whenever you feel like it? I'd be up the next
day, and perhaps we could have straightaway some drinks and/or
lunch.

1 'Quid's Inn' was the working title of the series.
2 'Colonel Chinstrap', an alcoholic character in *ITMA*.
3 On Christmas Eve 1950 a group of young Scots nationalists had broken into
  Westminster Abbey and stolen the Stone of Scone, the 'Stone of Destiny', on which
  sovereigns were crowned. They took it back to Scotland, where it came from in 1296.
  The stone was later recovered from outside Arbroath Abbey.

I've lots of ideas and suggestions and characters all floating about like kidneys.

> Yours,
> Dylan T

MS: *Texas*

PRINCESS CAETANI
March 20 1951   The Boat House   Laugharne   Carmarthenshire   Wales

Dear Marguerite Caetani,

I have been ill, with almost everything from gastric influenza to ingrowing misery. And only now my wife Caitlin has given me a letter that Davenport had forwarded from you nearly six weeks ago: She didn't know who the letter came from, and had half-mislaid and half-forgotten it in the general hell of sickness, children, excruciating worry, the eternal yellow-grey drizzle outside and her own slowly accumulated loathing for the place in which we live. I was distressed that the letter had remained unanswered for so long, and doubly distressed that you should have no letter from me after yours of December 14th. I wrote, at length and wildly, my thanks and affection and small mouse-on-a-treadmill news, at once to your Paris address. I suppose I put the wrong address. I am sorry that you should, through my apparent carelessness, have come to think of me as unmannerlessly grateful—as I am sure you must have come to think, for that long, hateful silence of mine, though unpremeditated, was the nastiest answer in the world to your great kindness to us and to the fond, nice way you are kind. I have a poem nearly finished, which will be about 50 or 60 lines long[1] and is coarse and violent: I will send it as *soon* as it is done—when I can, if I can, shake off this nervous hag that rides me, biting and scratching into insomnia, nightmare, and the long anxious daylight. But I won't mind a bit if you do not want to use it:—(of course, I shall mind a bit, but only in a hidden, unimportant way). I want to write poems so much—oh, the old pariah cry!—but I worry too much: I'm at my worries all day & night with a hundred crochet hooks. Will you forgive me for worrying you with my limp but edgy letters? And will you forgive me for the silence before this whimper? I did not mean it. Thank you again, and the poem will come: the crotchety poem not quite clean, but worked at, between the willies, very hard.

I wish I knew what to do. I wish I cd get a job. I wish I wish I wish. And I wish you a happy Easter, with all my heart. The sun came out this morning, took one look at wet Wales, and shot back.

> Yours affectionately,
> Dylan

MS: *Camillo Caetani Foundation*

1 'Lament'.

OSCAR WILLIAMS
25 March 1951   Boat House   Laugharne   Carmarthenshire   Wales

My dear Gene and Oscar,[1]

Ten months, nearly, since I saw you last, and longer, much, since I wrote. I meant and I meant and I meant, but somehow I never did write, although there was so very much to thank you for, fondness, beer, cheques, poems, paintings, a tooth. And books as well. I never thanked you for the new Modern Poetry which I recently took for a ride to Persia and read lots of in Isfahan and Shiraz and all the oily places. The Anglo-Iranian Oil Company sent me out to write a filmscript to show how beautiful Persia is and how little as a mouse and gentle is the influence there of that Company: my job was to help pour water on troubled oil. I got out just before martial law—a friend of marshall plan's[2]—and perhaps, disguised, will be sent back to write a script to show, now, suddenly, how beastly Persia is and how grandly irreplaceable is that thundering Company. Incidentally, the biggest thing in the Oil Refinery at Abadan is costing eight million pounds to put up, and is called a Cat-Cracker. I'd crack a lot of cats for that. Thank you a *great* deal, for selling that piece of cheese for such a splendid sum.[3] I'm enclosing the 2 Exemption Certificates, & hope I've filled them in correctly. I have a couple of poems, but can't find them; when I do, I'll send them on. I saw John Malcolm in London last summer, for a few revolving days. When I send the poems on, I'll write a longer letter with what grey and drizzly news I have. It has been raining in Wales since last June. I hope to come, with Caitlin, to the States next year: if there are any and if there is one. How are you both? Before a long letter, goodbye for a bit. And love, always, to you both.

                                                              Dylan

MS: *Houghton*

*MICHAEL FORTY[4]
7 April 1951   The Boat House   Laugharne   Carmarthenshire

Dear Michael Forty,

Thank you very much for your letter of December, 1950—which has just been given to me by Russell Williams.[5] He suggests a good date for me to come to Swansea to bellow would be Wednesday, April 25th. The time,

1 Oscar Williams was married to Gene Derwood, poet.
2 The 'Marshall Plan' (so-called, after G. C. Marshall, US Secretary of State) provided economic aid for postwar Europe.
3 The 'piece of cheese' was 'How to Be a Poet', a tongue-in-cheek article written for a British magazine, *Circus*, the previous year. Williams sold it to *Atlantic* for $250.
4 Chairman of the English Society at University College, Swansea, where he was a student.
5 A fellow student at the university college. He lived in the Laugharne area.

sometime in the afternoon. The 25th suits me, though I would really rather an evening date. Poems flag in the afternoon. But Russell says that it's difficult to get a crowd of people together in the evening, as they've gone, lots of them, or want to go, home to districts outside S'sea. If this is so, then let it be the afternoon.[1] R. also suggests I read to a lot of people, not to a small group. I don't mind either way. What I'd do would be to read modern poems, with a few silly comments. You could just call it 'Modern Poetry', which is vague enough. Anyway, will you let me know what you think? Fix anything, any time of day you like, for the 25th. By the way, I'll be in London & will have come down specially, so that my expenses will be return fare Paddington—S'sea. Is that all right?

Yours sincerely
Dylan Thomas

MS: West Glamorgan Archive Service

ALEC CRAIG
7th April 1951   The Boat House   Laugharne   Carmarthenshire   Wales

Dear Alec,
   Thanks for the letter. Yes, May 7th—7 o'clock programme—would suit me very well, and thank you for the invitation.
   I'd like to read other people's poems as well as my own, so perhaps it would be best to call my little do just 'A Reading of Poems,' which allows me to bring in what I like—especially poems by little-known modern British & American. Okay?
   It was nice to see you again.

Yrs,
Dylan

MS: (Thomas Trustees)

1 In the event, the meeting was held in the evening. Forty and another student met Thomas, who 'looked like a seedy commercial traveller in a shiny suit, carrying a little case,' at the station earlier in the day. Before and after the meeting, held in a basement room of the Students' Union building in Sketty Road, Thomas drank at the Uplands Hotel, once his neighbourhood pub, with students and staff from the university college. This was the evening sardonically described by Kingsley Amis, then a young English lecturer at Swansea, in the *Spectator*, 29 November 1957.

ANEIRIN TALFAN DAVIES
7th April 1951   The Boat House   Laugharne   Carmarthenshire

My dear Aneirin,
   Thank you for writing. I'd be delighted to do a Festival talk for the Welsh
Service; and I think the Festival Exhibition on the South Bank—or the
Festival Gardens & Funfair (what *is* the official title?) in Battersea—would
be grand. Which do you favour? And have you a rough date for the talk?[1]
                                                          Yours,
                                                          Dylan
MS: BBC

JOHN DAVENPORT
12 April 1951   Laugharne

Dear John,
   Sorry to have missed you my last London visit. What a word visit is for
my kind of occasional agitated bumbling in frowsy streets, unkind pubs,
deleterious afternoon boozers, snoring cinemas, wet beds! I stayed all the
time in the McAlpines', Bill frenziedly protecting his period furniture as
though I were going to lay an egg on it, Helen singing Irish ballads to West
Indians. And every day I was chasing money and jobs. I have found a job,[2]
and a very fishy one too I will tell you about when we meet over flat beer in
some chill emporium, but no money yet.
   And this job may make me stay in London for a long time, in which case
Caitlin will have to be with me too—and of course her cockalorum. That is
presumably what Mad Mags[3] meant when she told you about our giving
the Boat House up. She's wrong again, I've no intention of giving it up. But
we probably will want a flat or house in London, & M said she had found
half a house in Cheyne Walk by the chimneys which she was enquiring
about. Also, she *has* bought a cottage in Laugharne, in the downtown
square or Grist, for her & her horrors in the holidays. So has Mary Keene
bought a cottage there. We have reasons for leaving. It's like seeing a new
wing built, for obstreperous incurables, on to a quiet bin one has got used
to.
   I should be up next week, and will get in touch. And I'd love to meet
Canetti.[4] I'll look out for Richard Jones's letter.
   A pile of poems from Douglas Phillips, the butcher's son—remember?—

1 The Festival of Britain, centred on the South Bank of the Thames, was a national
   occasion, aimed at inspiring the nation as postwar 'austerity' faded. The talk was first
   broadcast on 5 June 1951.
2 Perhaps the script-writing with Kavanagh, of which Thomas had high hopes.
3 Margaret Taylor.
4 Elias Canetti, writer, Nobel laureate, 1905–94

arrived a few days ago. I haven't read them properly yet, but think they've got a lot. All about masturbation, sin, violent death, decay, wet dreams, impermanent love, hatred of Carmarthen, and—looking, at random, at the words of one poem—festering seashores, wet vulva lips, gaseous virgins, putrid flame, lewd men, raving swordfish, sensual whips, tortured women rending wedding-gowns, charred mates, smiling cream over lips' soft brim, lascivious farmers, shaven thighs, childhood captured in rubber sheaths, love's limpets sucking oval stones, rubber wives ripping blubbered membrane veils, plasmal fruit, burst plackets, fishes' bladders, bloated pelvis, vulpine fur, etcetera. I can't understand why he doesn't show them to his father. A few memorable lines:

1) '. . . the pus of sin
   That feeds each female with male cheer.'
2) 'The tiles are wreathed in smiles when chimneys copulate.'
3) 'O sexual scholar in masturbatory cell,
   Your writhing brain fictitious children sperms.'
4) 'What can I do when bugle-bellied wives
   Reveal the bedpan secrets of their lives?
   Can I bend down and crouch beneath their skirts
   To ease my bullying blow-boy where it hurts?'[1]

You never can tell now, can you?

But every now & then there are good bursting bits.

Stop press: M comes down on the midnight train tonight to discuss 'the Cheyne Walk Project'. If it comes off, I shall have a town house & a country house, and I have just borrowed 5/- from Ivy Williams to run them both.

Love,
Dylan

MS: Texas

JOHN MALCOLM BRINNIN
12 April 1951   Boat House   Laugharne   Carmarthenshire   Wales

Dear John,

How nice, nice, nice! Oh, my conscience, I had feared that you left London[2] breathing—no, I can't possibly mean that—had left London saying: 'No more of that coarsened looby and his backstairs drizzling town.

---

1 Douglas Phillips has pointed out that Thomas's summary of the poems, most of them part of a sonnet sequence, is not very accurate, although the quotations are. He also notes Thomas's generosity to a young writer—see Thomas's letters to him, pages 892 and 895. Two of the poems were later published, in *Dragons and Daffodils* (1960) and *Texas Quarterly* 1968.

2 Following Brinnin's visit the previous September.

Foul enough in my America, feebly lascivious in his pigsty in the Earle, puking in Philadelphia, burgling the Biddles, blackmailing psychiatrists' mistakes for radiosets and trousers, fanging through the lesbians, hounding poor Oscar, but there! there in that English sink, intolerable, dribbly, lost. And, oh, his so called friends! toadying slaves of the licensing laws, rats on a drinking ship'—or didn't we meet any friends? I can't remember. I remember I liked, very much, our being together, though you were in that Royal (was it?) jail and I in my false bonhomous Club. I remember meeting you at the station, and that was fine. And the London frowsty Casino, a memento of which I enclose: who are those perhaps-men, one bluebottle-bloated, one villainously simpering, with floral and yachting ties, so untrustworthily neat and prosperous with their flat champagne? I remember the Thames and old Pearl—whom I saw something of later but who, I imagine, left London, as I imagined you had done, rasping to herself: 'No more of that beer-cheapened hoddy-noddy snoring, paunched, his corn, his sick, his fibs, I'm off to Taormina where you know where you are: oh, his sodden bounce, his mistheatrical-demeanour, the boastful tuppence!' I haven't heard from her since she went away.

Now, for your letter. First: Next time I am in London I shall see what boys I know in the black rooms of the BBC and tell them that you are coming to London in July and that, if pressed in a vice, bribed heavily and dined, you might just possibly think of reading, on the Third Programme, your poems, the poems of America, or of assessing the contemporary literary situation in Massachusetts, Virginia, and the Whaler Bar. I'll do my very best. You couldn't, I suppose, persuade your publishers to send me the shiny anthology and the new book of poems? I'd like them, a lot, anyway. And I will talk to the Institute of Contemporary Arts. I am so glad, indeed, that you will be here in July; and I shall be less revolting than last time, whatever the sacrifice. And let us meet the tiny great for tea, and go to Oxford where I know a human being. Caitlin will be in London in July, which will not make things any quieter. We both will probably be living there for some time: I am about to take on a new job: co-writing, with the best gagman in England—he is an Irishman from New Zealand[1]—a new comic series for the radio. I have already thought of two jokes, both quite unusable. And may I come to Edith's party for you? Her parties are always brilliant opportunities for self-disgrace.

Give my love, if ever you see them or believe it, to Pearl, Lloyd & Loren, Marion & Cummings, Stanley Moss, Jean Garrigue, Gene Baroff, Jeanne Gordon, David Lougée, Howard, [a word is crossed out] the one I crossed out, Patrick Boland, and any ugly stranger in the street.[2] Have a thousand boilermakers for me, and send me your stomach: I'll put it under my pillow.

1 Ted Kavanagh.
2 The poet Lloyd Frankenberg and his wife, the painter Loren MacIver; the poet E. E. Cummings and his wife Marion Morehouse. Patrick Boland was Thomas's host in Detroit, and a poet, as were Jean Garrigue, Stanley Moss and Gene Baroff. David Lougée was an aspiring young writer.

I have written three new poems, one alright, which I will, if you like, send you when I can find them.

I have no news at all. I am broke and in debt. And that reminds me to thank you very much for sending to my, my, my! Chartered Accountants that quite legendary-looking account of my howl-for-my-supper earnings. The Accountants tell me I shall, probably, not have to pay any Income Tax on anything earned in the U.S.A. *except*:

(1) The amounts remitted by myself or by my Agent to this Country: i.e. remittances made to my wife, bank, or any other person.

(2) The amount brought in by me when I arrived back in this Country.

Can you help? I think, through you, I sent about three small sums to Caitlin. Can you remember? And I came home, I think, with about 200 dollars.

If you can remember what amounts of money I sent to Caitlin with your knowledge, would you be so kind as to write to Leslie Andrews & Co., 10 North Street, Horsham, Sussex, England, and let them know? And then that will really be the end of your agental duties *until next time*.

Now, next time: I would very much like (I'd adore it) to be imported to the States next year, 1952. The Poetry Center paying my passage and the first fee. I would bring Caitlin with me, if by that time I have made, as I intend to do, much money from my ha ha scripts. And would you, *could* you, act as Agent or Christ knows what for me again? I do not think I would wish to go through the Middle West, excepting Chicago, again, but anywhere, everywhere, else, unless I have quite ruined myself in all those places where you were not with me. Could you put out feelers, spin wheels, grow wings for me? I am so deadly sick of it here. I would bring great packages of new poems to read, and much more pre-written prose to pad them in. I would be much better than I was: I mean, sick less often. I mean, I would so much like to come. Could you write to any friends or acquaintances I might have made and see if they would help? Would you, now?

No, Persia wasn't all depressing. Beautiful Isfahan & Shiraz. Wicked, pompous, oily British. Nervous, cunning, corrupt and delightful Persian bloody bastards. Opium no good. Persian vodka, made of beetroot, like stimulating sockjuice, very enjoyable. Beer full of glycerine and pips. Women veiled, or unveiled ugly, or beautiful and entirely inaccessible, or hungry. The lovely camels who sit on their necks and smile. I shan't go there again.

No news. Still broke and in debt. I spent all the Persian money on beetroot vodka, glycerine beer, unveiled ugly women, and, as you conjectured, the camels, the camels, the camels are coming.

Yes, I *do* want to come to the States early next year. But I shall see you before then, & will do all I can do to make you a very little money on the BBC. But naturally don't count on that. You will be here during the Festival of Britain, though nobody here has any idea of what we have to be festive about. And mostly, I suppose, the BBC will be plugging homegrown poetry.

However, I know some unpatriotic people on the Third Programme, and they owe me something for the pleasure they've got in my not being on the Third Programme recently.

I'm sick of Laugharne. It has rained here since last June.

Write soon.

> Love to you,
> Dylan

MS: Delaware

ANEIRIN TALFAN DAVIES

1 May 1951   Boat House   Laugharne   Carmarthenshire

My dear Aneirin,

Sorry not to have answered long before.

Okay, make it a fixed date for June 5th. I am going to London next week & will see the Exhibition then, & will let you have the script as soon after as I can. 15 minutes?

> Yours,
> Dylan

MS: BBC

OSCAR WILLIAMS

[?May 1951] [postcard]

Can you see a X on postcard? That's us. Hope you'll see it closer, one day, soon.

> Dylan

MS: Houghton

PRINCESS CAETANI

17th May 1951   The Boat House   Laugharne   Carmarthenshire   Wales

My dear Madame Caetani,

First of all: all, all my thanks for your last letter and the cheque out of the great blue that made our life here temporarily bearable and made me, once more, so deeply grateful to you I should never, however long I lived, be able to say how much. It's fine to think that you think of me here, there in your Rome, & I love your letters. I wish I could write more often, with all my news, but all my news is bad & nervous and I'm sick of my always hurdygurdying these little griefs out and me like a monkey on the top of it all with my beggar's cap. But one day I shall write calm & at length, though, God, not now.

No, I'm sorry I never received the last number. It must have gone to a dead address. And I'm sorry I don't speak French.

Here is a poem you mightn't like at all, but do read it, please.[1] I hope you understand my painfully shaking writing. Though on the wagon now, I'm like a St. Vitus leaf. Tell me about the poem, anyway. It is, of course, yours if you want it. I have nearly finished two other poems, much slower & sadder than this, also yours, which I will send you as soon as I can.

I'm just beginning the beastly process of selling up my house here to pay debts etc, a very shaking thing to do because I am so fond of it. And we will have to try to get furnished rooms in London, if we can. But I'm going to keep my books anyway.

If you don't like *Lament*, please slam it back. And perhaps you'll like the ones-in-progress much better.

I'd like to have a copy, very much, one day, of the last Botteghe.

Now thank you, with all my heart, again.

Yours affectionately,
Dylan

MS: Camillo Caetani Foundation

EDITH CAPON[2]
27 May 1951 [draft]   Boat House   Laugharne   Carmarthenshire   Wales

Dear Sir,

I'm sorry I haven't been able to answer, before this, your letter wanting to know about the Writers Groups of the S.C.R. & my interest in it.

I, too, belong to no political party. I am a Socialist, and, so far as I know, there is no Socialist party.

MS: Indiana

OSCAR WILLIAMS
28 May 1951   Boat House   Laugharne   Carmarthenshire   Wales

Dear Oscar,

I'm afraid I'm sending you only one poem—and that only the first section of a poem, though nobody need know that. I mentioned the title and idea of this poem over a year ago, in pretty New York, but scrapped all

1 'Lament'.
2 The Capons, Edith and Eric, were acquaintances of Thomas with left-wing leanings and theatrical connections. Eric Capon produced the programme at the ICA on 16 February 1950 (see n.2, page 374). On the verso are draft lines, heavily corrected, from the fourth stanza of 'Poem on his Birthday'.

of it I had written on my return. I have only recently finished this version.[1] The other poems I found since last writing to you, I have sent to Botteghe Oscure. This means, I get paid by them *well*, first, & then can sell the poems (well again, I hope) in the States. If I publish the poems first in the States, Botteghe Oscure doesn't want them. So, when they're printed in Italy, I'll send them along. I've no spare copies now. And my newest poems aren't yet finished. Sorry I couldn't type this one out. A few words, on looking through it, seem hard to read. The first word on line 7 is PLEADING. The fourth word in the third line from the end of page one is LANES. On page 3, in the 3rd line, the word is ROISTER. In the 7th line of page 3, the word GAMBO means a farm-cart. In the last line but one from the end of page 3, it is THEY with the Simple Jacks. On page 4, line 7, RAIN and WRING are 2 separate words. I am sure this complicates matters. It's a conventionally romantic poem & perhaps you won't like it at all. But could you sell it for me for a LOT of money? I'm desperately in need of it. If you can get a cheque sent soon, will you see that it is made out on a *London* bank. Your last two lovely cheques took about 6 weeks to clear. I'm in such a state of debt & brokeness, I'm having to sell up my house as soon as I can & move to London which I hate.[2] The house—what I own of it—will all go towards debts—& then not all of them, by a hell of a long way. I hope to keep my books. Oh, oh, oh! Misery me. Do what you can about this lush poem. And please excuse rushed writing & no news.

Love,
Dylan

MS: Houghton

T. S. ELIOT
28 May 1951   The Boat House   Laugharne   Carmarthenshire

Dear T. S. Eliot,
   Very many thanks indeed for your letter & your cheque. It was extremely kind of you, and the cheque helped to ease my difficulties here. I was, as you know, very nervous in writing to you at all to ask your help; and especially since your recent reputation for wealth. It was in spite of this, that I managed to write my begging letter. I was, anyway, writing to the best poet I know, and not to a supposedly monied man.
   Thank you, again, most sincerely.

Yours,
Dylan Thomas

MS: Texas

1 'In the White Giant's Thigh'.
2 The house, which in any case belonged to Margaret Taylor, was not being sold. But she found the cost of upkeep a burden. The latest plan was to find the family another, temporary house in London, where Thomas would be nearer the sources of work and income, and so might not need to visit America again.

LAURENCE GILLIAM
28 May 51   The Boat House Laugharne Carmarthenshire

Dear Laurence,
About the possible Festival Fantasia. I couldn't get in touch with you—
my fault—on my last few London days.
Any suggestions about the F.F.? Treatment? Length?
And, *terribly* important to me, ADVANCE, IMMEDIATE?
I returned to find my local debts even more stridently urgent. I owe every
tradesman in town, and just can't think how I'm to pay them. I can't even
get down to work here unless I can pay them a little bit peace-offering.[1]
Can you do your best?
Or any other suggestions?

> Tremblingly, & very
> much in earnest,
> Dylan

MS: BBC

PRINCESS CAETANI
28 May 1951   The Boat House Laugharne Carmarthenshire Wales

My dear Madame Caetani,
I hope you've had, by this time, my brief, troubled letter and my rough,
untroubled poem.
I have just finished the short poem I enclose.[2] If you like the other one,
the 'Lament', well enough to print, I think this little one might very well
be printed with it as a contrast.
In spite of all the things that go with selling-up home, I am still trying to
work. (Indeed, I am still trying to sell up home, which has to be, and quick.)
And I hope to finish soon a longish play, as yet untitled, in verse and prose
which I have been thinking of for a long time. I will send it to you soon. I
do hope you will publish it—unless, of course, it is too long (or too bad)—as
I am, at the moment of working on it, pleased & excited with it. It is gay &
sad and sentimental and a bit barmy. So am I. I'm looking forward to
hearing from you.

> Affectionately,
> Dylan

---

1 Gilliam replied (30 May) to say that 'Third are very interested in the idea of a Festival
  Fantasia, but on checking with Copyright department I find that they have a working
  agreement with your agent that payment for commissioned work is only made on
  delivery of script. I am sorry, but I cannot get round this ruling . . .' Thomas's failure to
  deliver *The Plain Dealer* and *Peer Gynt* was to blame.
2 'Do not go gentle into that good night'. Published, with 'Lament', in *Botteghe Oscure*,
  November 1951.

The only person I can't show the little enclosed poem to is, of course, my father, who doesn't know he's dying.

MS: Camillo Caetani Foundation

ANEIRIN TALFAN DAVIES
[about 30 May 1951]   Boat House   Laugharne   Carmarthenshire

Dear Aneirin,
   Many apologies for this long delay in sending South Bank script. I've been ill.
   I'll ring you up Monday morning, to find out Tuesday rehearsal & recording times.
   Hope there's time to type the enclosed, & that you like it well enough.
                                                            Yrs,
                                                               Dylan

MS: BBC

DOUGLAS PHILLIPS[1]
June 24 1951   Boat House   Laugharne   Carmarthenshire

Dear Douglas Phillips,
   First of all, I want to say how very sorry I am not to have written to you a long time ago, when you sent me that packet of animal bombs by post: they burst all over the place, cocks and cunts and blood and stars and great green cabbages. I read the poems right through quickly, bits of them aloud and always with excitement, for it is exciting being in at the beginning of a new talent, however mixed-up it may be at the moment. Then I had to put the poems away and go to London. I should have written to you then, briefly, to say I'd had the poems and was enormously struck by them, and would write again about them. But I didn't, and I'm sorry.
   Now I've read the poems again, and will read them again. This is only to say what I should have said in March: I feel privileged to be allowed to read your poems in manuscript; you really have got a lot of something there, and a rage and a fire and (over-churning) movement of your own, and a weltering violence; and I'd like, if I may, to write about some of the poems in detail as soon as there's a proper lull between my bread-and-butter jobs.
   I hope you're writing now, and I'll be very glad to see anything new at any time.
   Soon I'll write a better letter.
   Congratulations!
   If any of this sounds like an elder poet writing, throw it in the fire.
                                                     Yours sincerely,
                                                        Dylan Thomas

MS: National Library of Wales

1 See letter to John Davenport, page 428.

OSCAR WILLIAMS
10th July 1951   Boat House   Laugharne   Carmarthenshire   Wales

Dear Oscar,

Many many thanks for selling my poem so quickly & for so much.[1]

I'm typing—or, rather, having typed—a few other ones which I'll airmail next week.

I enclose the Exemption Certificates, signed. I don't know what else to fill in.

Thank you for getting the cheque sent to a London Bank. I hope you can manage to send the $45 cheque to a London Bank too.

You are very good to me. (Even to the stamped envelope.)

I hope to come to the States early next year again, with Caitlin. Poetry Center & Museum of Modern Art (for whom I will read King Lear) will be helping.

I hope something will come of the possibility you mention: that of a group of midwestern colleges planning a good sum, or offer, for me.

I have to catch the post, but will write at length when I send on the new poems.

I read some of your poems aloud to a Welsh Society last week. Liked.
Love to you & Gene from C. & me.

Dylan

I think I'll be seeing J. M. Brinnin in London this month.
I'm going to live in London for the winter which I shall hate.

MS: Houghton

PRINCESS CAETANI
July 18 1951   The Boat House   Laugharne   Carmarthenshire   Wales

Dear Madame Caetani,

Many, many apologies. Of *course* I should have written at once to say: Thank you for your letter, for Botteghe Oscure, for the cheque which came zooming out of the Roman blue in time to pay a summons. But day after day I put off writing, because, each day, I hoped to finish the longish (about 100 lines) birthday poem I was—and still am—writing. I wanted to send it to you with my letter of gratitude: it is a much, much better poem than the 'Lament' & the villanelle to my father: I like it better than anything I have done for a very long time (which does not say a great deal: I do not like

---

1 'In the White Giant's Thigh'. *Atlantic* magazine paid $150 for first U.S. and Canadian rights. A steady stream of dollars was reaching Thomas via Williams, bypassing David Higham.

reading my poems at all; only writing them). But I couldn't finish the poem quickly enough, & now I *must* write to you without it. Today is Wednesday: I hope very much to finish it by this coming weekend, & will send it, arrogance, obscurity, & all, straightaway to Switzerland.

The play—did I say it was a radio comedy about Wales, & not a stage play?—I've temporarily shelved to write the poem which I have been wanting to write for a long time, ever, in fact, since my last year's birthday, which is what the poem is, in its way, all about. I'll send on the play, of course, as soon as it's finished. But the poem you shall have much first: in time, perhaps, (& if you like it) for the coming number (and perhaps if there is room). (and if there is time.) it was your fond mention of Cummings in your last letter that topples my punctuation about like this. And, yes, what a very fine man he is. I hope to see him again next year in New York, if ever I get there. The Museum of Modern Art has, for some erratic reason of their own, asked me to read King Lear; and Columbia & the Poetry Center have invited me over too. But I shan't go unless I can take Caitlin (who still, I believe, thinks that America is either all Hollywood or Senator McCarthy).[1] Did you, by the way, say that you would be in London this autumn for your daughter's wedding? (Will you give her my kindest regards?) If you do come, I very much hope we shall meet.

Thank you, deeply, again. And expect my new poem *very* soon. I trust, early next week.

Yours,
Dylan

PS I enclose the pale [?page] proofs, but there is nothing to correct. Only, please, make it a bigger dash than a hyphen after 'good bells jaw' at the end of the last-but-one line on the first proof page.[2]

MS: Camillo Caetani Foundation

GRAHAM ACKROYD
18 July 1951   Boat House   Laugharne   Carmarthenshire

Dear Graham Ackroyd,
Sorry not to have written much before this: I've been away, and didn't get any letters.

And I'm very sorry, too that my Miller letters are gone. Pinched. I'd kept them in a book of Miller's, and after a party I found that all the signed books were gone. And the letters.

About my visit to Miller at Big Sur: it was very short, nothing happened,

1 Joseph McCarthy (1909–57), whose political witch-hunts in search of crypto-Communists were in full swing.
2 'Lament': 'I lie down thin and hear the good bells jaw'.

and I remember v. little of what was said. But I could run out a very short, uneventful piece about it, if you *really* liked.[1]

Anyway, good luck with the book. And apologies again about this delay in writing. I can't apologise about the stolen letters: I can only think and curse.

Sincerely
Dylan Thomas

From a typescript. MS location unknown

JOHN MALCOLM BRINNIN
[telegram, 21 July 1951, 4.44 pm, Laugharne]

DELIGHTED YOU ARE IN LONDON RING LAUGHARNE 68 SUNDAY LUNCHTIME LOVE DYLAN

Original: Delaware

DOUGLAS PHILLIPS
Wednesday [July 1951][2]   Laugharne

Dear Douglas,

Thanks for the letter & the three poems. I like the first two poems very much, & think they contain some of the best lines, and brief passages, you have yet written. I am not sure, myself, of the third poem, but will read it very carefully again, as I also will the other two.

I'm writing to Botteghe Oscure this week, and will, with your permission, send the editor the first two of the new poems and tell her that I have many more to send her of yours if she likes these.

Don't worry about your behaviour here, it was alright. I'm a pretty silent person at home, too, & just go on dumbly & dully reading, but it doesn't mean anything. One should be able to be silent with one's friends, when one wants to.

Come down for a week-end when you can.

Yours,
Dylan

MS: National Library of Wales

1 Ackroyd commented: 'I must have had some daft idea about starting a literary magazine.'
2 Date supplied by recipient.

DONALD TAYLOR
31st August 1951   Boat House   Laugharne   Carmarthenshire   Wales

Dear Donald,

I had a foggy feeling, after our Lordly day[1] and the evening with the afflicted Americans, that you and I had fixed a date to meet, but, for the death of me, I couldn't remember if or no or, if, when and where. I hope I was mistaken, and that we hadn't arranged to meet, which sounds, maybe, discourteous, but you know what I mean. I tried to get in touch with Higham, but his nose was being scraped. If we did have a date, & I didn't (as was obvious) keep it, please forgive me. And, if we didn't, let's make another soon. I've such a lot to talk about, and that day (for me, at least) wasn't half long enough and was interrupted too much by bad cricket, indifferent drink, and mad women and fat men.

We come to London to live at the end of September, money willing and Caitlin's mumps gone—(she's moaning now, like a sad football). But, before I make that complicated move, I want to have, fixed as firmly as possible, if even only in the mind, a programme of work to keep me in creditless London. Have your plans moved any, and do they still, after a day in which I am sure I spoke very little sense, include me? (It was very good to see you, and I make no apologies for my senselessness: I was quite happy.) I must know as soon as possible—though I realise that nothing happens quickly, except disaster, in your and my world.

I told you about my American commitments. Today—one reason I am writing this—I heard from America the very final dates they have fixed for me. My first lecture is at Columbia on January 30th, & my last in the Museum of Modern Art in the last week of February. Therefore, my whole trip would take, at the maximum, six weeks. I *must* reply, in the next few days, to my American sponsors & say, quite definitely, Yes or No. Suppose—and, Lord, I hope so—you and I are working, soon, fully together: could I, then, take six weeks off from January, say, 20th on? Could you let me know how you feel about this? You know that, above everything, I want to work with you, again, on films, and exclusively, if possible, on feature films this time. And you know, as I told you at probably incoherent length in the Insipid Writers' Club, that I must have a regular job this winter. If six American weeks interfere with these two things—and I do so hope that both things are the same: i.e., that the regular job is to write scripts for and with you—then I'll cancel the lectures. But I must say Yes or No to Columbia University etc. straightabloodyway.

A pity we can't meet again very soon. I *could* come up to London; but I wish you could come to Wales: our house is almost childless now, and the weather, for the moment, windily good.

Have you any stories in mind which, perhaps, I could read or think about?

---

1 Watching cricket at Lord's.

Anyway, do please write quickly about these points.

I saw T.V. people a few days after seeing you. They're full of work to do, but offer lamentable pay. And, help us, we all do need so much these once-longed-for but execrable days.

I am writing a plotless radio play, first thought of as a film.

Two acquaintances of mine have committed suicide within the last fortnight; one of them was a painter, Ralph Banbury: do you remember him? A tall, languid man, friend & pupil of Cedric Morris, with a Chinese grandmother.

Love,
Dylan

MS: Buffalo

DAVID HIGHAM
August 31 1951   The Boat House   Laugharne   Carmarthenshire   Wales

Dear David,

Thank you very much for arranging, from your sinusoidal bed, for fifty quid to be advanced to me on future earnings. It was very kind of you, and I felt most callous to have had to ask you this when you were ill. I hope you're quite recovered now.

I hope, too, that the fifty quid can be paid back to you in a lump sum soon, and not taken, bit by bit, from small BBC cheques etcetera.

I wrote to Donald Taylor today, asking him if his film-plans were moving any, and telling him that I had just heard from America: the Poetry Center of New York *must* know, straightaway, if I can keep my dates there: the first is, Columbia University 30 January 1952, the last in the Museum of Modern Art the last week of February. Taylor will probably write to me directly about this; but, if you *do* happen to be getting in touch with him in the immediate future, perhaps you could stress the urgency of my knowing how soon to expect a regular contract job from him. As I told you when we briefly met, I'm coming to London to live at the end of this month, and really must have a regular job then to keep me there: or, at least, the tangible prospect of one very soon. There could, I suppose, be no question of Taylor giving me, from the end of September, a retaining fee until he starts his firm properly?[1] But perhaps I had better wait to hear from Taylor before you, possibly, put out any feelers in this direction.

Thanks again for the advance, which covered me over a particularly bad spot.

Yours
Dylan

MS: Texas

1 Taylor's plans came to nothing as far as Thomas was concerned.

JOHN MALCOLM BRINNIN
August 31 1951   Boat House Laugharne Carmarthenshire Wales

Dear John,
    A very brief note of apology and affection. Your letter, waiting for me in John Davenport's, I mislaid, and now don't know where you'll be or when, for a moment, you may come to London. (I've written to Reggie Smith, who's on holiday, but couldn't give him a date, except that I *thought* it to be early in September. I know he will fix a recording if he can: probably of verse.) But from your littler letter I see you will call at the American Express, Paris, around Sept 1–4. I *do* hope this will find you then. And I *am* so sorry I couldn't get up to London after you left Laugharne,[1] & that I lost your letter, & that I haven't written. I've been in a mess about money, and, in London, about trying to fix a film-job for the winter. Caitlin has mumps, badly, and oh! oh! oh! I'm vague & distressed about me and poems and Laugharne & London—and the States. But, of course, I'll be there for the Columbia date on January 30. I hope, very much, we can meet in London before you return: I want to ask you about these dates, about what sort of poetry you think I should read, what kind of prose I should write for the several occasions. Also, I should like very much to see you again, before next January.
    I hope you didn't have too muddled a time down here. Regards to Bill.[2]
    Please write soon, if ever you get this, and I'll write back fully.
    Try to make London.
    Caitlin sends you her love. And I send mine.
                                                    Dylan

MS: Delaware

PRINCESS CAETANI
31st August 1951   The Boat House Laugharne Carmarthenshire
                                                           Wales

My dear Madame Caetani,
    I owed you, before, a letter, a poem, and an apology. Now, Lord help us, I owe you a whole sackful of apologies; this letter must necessarily be sad and short; and there is no poem.
    I took the new poem—it is the first of three poems linked together by the occasion of a birthday—up to London with me on my last, just-over visit, meaning to typewrite it there and send it straight to you. Nothing, however, went right with my plans—it was my hope to arrange a job for myself for the winter, when we must move from here to London—and I decided to go, with no hopes, home. But I hadn't the money to go home,

1 When Brinnin was in Europe in July, he visited Laugharne for the first time.
2 Brinnin's partner Bill Read, later the author of *The Days of Dylan Thomas*, who came with him to Europe.

couldn't arrive home with no money, and was forced to sell my poem to a London magazine for ten pounds.[1] I don't think I need—I know you now, so well, from letters—tell you how ashamed I am. The poem, good or bad, was for you; I wanted, more than anything, for it [to] appear in Botteghe Oscure, the only periodical. But I had to have a little money at once; I knew no-one; and I had nothing to sell but this laborious lyric.

I will, of course, if you still want them, send to you the next two poems that will make the whole poem. But I would not be surprised if, after the breaking of my sincere promise, you found that you did not want them.

I do assure you that only the most drastic need would make me sell my work in this way.

You say that you will be in London for three weeks from the 15th of next month. I do hope we can meet during that time.

I am very sad about the poem; but I hope that, (somehow,) I shall be able to write the next two & make them better than the first.

Yours,
Dylan

MS: Camillo Caetani Foundation

DONALD TAYLOR
13 September 51   Boat House   Laugharne   Carmarthenshire

Dear Donald,
Thank you for the letter. I'm delighted you are making progress, and that we may be working together in a matter of a few weeks. I do hope so. This is only to tell you telephone number: Laugharne (pronounced Larne) 68, when you want to ring. I have severe gout, and am quite laughable, but not to me. Write or ring soon.

Love,
Dylan

MS: Buffalo

PRINCESS CAETANI
September 15 1951   The Boat House   Laugharne   Carmarthenshire
Telephone number: Laugharne 68

My dear Madame Caetani,
First of all: Thank you, very deeply, for your forgiving letter and for the money which you should not have sent me, because I had broken my word, but which I was so terribly glad you did, and surely that sentence is askew.

1 Presumably *World Review*, where 'Poem on his Birthday' appeared in October 1951. Thomas also sold the poem to the *Atlantic*. See letter to Oscar Williams, page 452.

The money saved my life again, or, rather, paid a horned and raging bill. Oh, how many times you've saved my lives now! I've as many, I suppose, as a Hallowe'en of cats. And the lovely letter of forgiveness was so good to have, though it made me feel only more ashamed that, in a moment of need, I had to sell my best poem for years to an aloof stranger.

Perhaps Davenport, who rang me this morning, will have told you how this came about. Day after day, in London, I tried to get settled some jobs which were (and still are, I hope) to support me this winter; and one of them, I was led to imagine, was to begin at once. So it didn't matter, then, in London, not having any money at all, nor not being able to send any home, because soon, very soon, I said to myself, tomorrow perhaps, or the rich day after, the job would just BE, like that, quick as a flick of the fingers, and then everything would be allright and the bills would be paid and the summonses silenced and we'd buy new clothes and the bells would ring fit to bleed; it was nice thinking this. But, of course, and a hundred of courses, the jobs, day after broke day, drifted further & further away. 'Oh, yes, they *would* materialise', the suave men said, 'Eventually. You must learn to take the long view. And, yes, yes, yes, we know you must come, at once, to London to live, because you can live no longer in your ivory Laugharne, but remember: home was not built in a day'. And the daft bellringing billpaying dreams, full of new suits and gold boots and flowers in the buttonholes and Something Coming In Every Week—(the wonderful wish words that sing like thrushes at night, out of the down-at-heel darkness, to the dispossessed in their little black beds)—they all faded. And there I was, not a potential man of affairs any more, solid shrewd and distinguished as a whiskey advertisement, with a smile that would float a merger, but a lost, plump bum with a bucket of words wailing 'Woe and woe' and nowhere to go. Or, at least, I felt as outcast as that. Or I romanticised myself into that shabby posture, and looked at the greasy, inviting Thames with wild (but, thank God, craven) eyes.

Caitlin was ill, at crumbling home, with, of all things, mumps. I almost wish it had been a more imaginative, and dolorous, illness. I had wired her to say, 'Okay, all in hand', meaning the work and the money was mine. And she had wired back to say how good that was and would I please come home that day and bring some money which was so much needed for the carping shops. But nothing was okay, and all was out of hand, and I couldn't even buy a ticket for the journey. I thought, then, of sending that beastly poem[1]—how over-important all this dreary business makes it! and it's no Paradise Lost!—straightaway to you and wiring you that it was on its way and could, would you, please, please wire me some money for it. But I couldn't. It was too damned abrupt. And it would take too long, however quick. I was quite sick with despair. So many days had come to this black blank. I had to get away. And so, having nothing else, I took the detested poem to a magazine and sold it there and then and bought a

---

1 'Poem on his Birthday'.

present, vainly to try to lessen the pennilessness of my arrival, and took the night-train back that said all the way: Welsh fool, Welsh fool.

I wrote to you a letter in a scrambling hurry. And then your letter came, and thank you again for it. I'm busy now piling up books and bits and pieces to take, when we can, to London, if there's anywhere there, and have lost your letter in this sad and grisly bustle, your letter that told me when, and for how long, you would be in England. Then, this morning, Davenport rang and said that you were leaving for France very early in the week of the 17th of September. I'd thought you were staying, oh, very much longer. And so now, I suppose I can't see you at all? There are several things I should like to talk to you about; and I do very much want to meet you. If there is any chance of your staying a day or so longer, could you wire me or ring me—my number is at the head of all this rigmarole—and then, perhaps, with luck and some scraping together I can come up to see you before you vanish again? I very much hope this can happen.

And thank you, once more. And I grieve that poem like hell.

Affect yours,
Dylan

MS: Camillo Caetani Foundation

FRANCIS BIDDLE[1]
15 September 1951   The Boat House   Laugharne   Carmarthenshire
Wales

Dear Mr. Biddle,

Only today I heard that you and Mrs. Biddle were in London, or, rather, that you had been in London, were on your way to Ireland, and would be returning to London in about a fortnight. I do hope this good news is true. I would so much like to meet you on your return. Would you, if we could meet, write to me and tell me when you'll be in London? I'm going up in about a week's time.

I'm awfully sorry I never wrote to you after Washington, and have no excuse, except that I had a very frantic & flying—oh how I loathe that endless air—two months after leaving you and ranted hoarsely all over the place, in California, Florida, and Canada, and never seemed to have any time to write & thank you for being so kind to me. I'm afraid I was very dim & shy.

My wife and I are going to the States in January, but I do hope I can meet you long before that, in London, and I'm looking forward a lot to seeing you both, if that is possible.

With all best wishes,
Dylan Thomas

From a typescript. MS location unknown

1 See n.2, page 380.

OSCAR WILLIAMS
31 Sep 51

Dear Oscar,
   In a frightful hurry for post.
   Permission slip signed & enclosed.
   'Immortal Poems'—my!
   Am sending you 3 new poems today.
   When do I get the 125 dollars? Am in trouble, serious.
   Will write with the poems.

                                        Love,
                                        Dylan

My 1st N. York date is January 30. I *shall* be free for a week in Feb.

MS: Houghton

ROBERT POCOCK
[postcard] 2 October 1951   Boat House   Laugharne   Carmarthenshire

Can you, will you, send me that ms of 'Adventures In The Skin Trade',
which I think you still have and which I want to work on and get money
from, at once. I'd be v. grateful; in fact, I shall die if you don't.
   We hope to be in our town residence in about a fortnight's time. There
will be a small, and disastrous, warming up.
   Love from us both to you both,

                                        Dylan

MS: Texas

RUTH WITT-DIAMANT
10 October 1951 The Boat House   Laugharne   Carmarthenshire   Wales

Darling Ruth,
   By this long time you will have, if not forgotten me—who *could* forget
that lordly, austere grace and grave demeanour, the soberly matured
wisdom, dedicate, reverend, chaste and aloof, that incorruptible ascetic,
that Santayana[1] of Wales?—at least have come most justly to loathe the
very hiccup of my name. (Of Tram's opinion of me, I daren't think. I found,
this week, a long, fond letter to him in a pile of socks and poems, unposted
since last Christmas. I am writing to him on bent knees, wagging my bum

---

1 George Santayana (1863–1952), philosopher and writer.

like a spaniel, but expect no answer. Give him my love. I very often think of him and Bill, of Gavin,[1] and, of course, of you who made my ranting holiday ridiculously happy, who showed me the exhibitionist floodlit seals and the pansied Pacific baths and the starry city and Miller's mountain, and gave me polar beer and artichokes, and laughed with me and at me till I felt more at home than at home where it's only at, and made me want more than anything to lurch back to the beautiful West where men are sometimes men and the bars are always exultantly open and the wind and sea and people are right and raffish and tins of fruit juice breed in the ice box.)

How could I not have written, when every week of the piggish year I mean to with all my heart, that poor bloody muscle? Oh, easy, easy. The son of a sloth and a turnip, either I hang by my whiskery toes, thinking of nothing and lust, or sit bigheaded in the wet earth, thinking of turnip poems; and time snails by; and San Francisco's six thousand lamenting miles away; and Wales is dead from the eisteddfodau up; and day after day I grow lazier and fatter and sadder and older and deafer and duller; grey grizzles in my dry hairmat; gout snarls in my big toe; my children grow large and rude; I renounce my Art to make money and then make no money; I fall in love with undesirable, unloving, squat, taloned, moist unlovely women and out again like a trout; I quarrel with Caitlin and make it up in floods of salt self pity; I fall downstairs; I frighten myself in the night, my own plump banshee; I celebrate other people's birthdays with falsely bonhomous abandon; I daydream of Chile, a place I never want to visit; I write poems and hide them before I can read them; and next week I shall be thirty-seven horrors old.[2] Does that, in any way, explain, dear Ruth, why I haven't written? Of course it doesn't. I've no excuse, but *please* try to forgive me. And are you well? and would you like to see me again? At the end of January, Caitlin and I are going to New York, financed by the Poetry Center, Columbia, and the Museum of Modern Art in collaboration, and I should hate it if I didn't, somehow, manage to get to California and (if you could bear it) stay with you for a week. Do you think some Universities would pay me enough, for readings, for us to be able to travel there from New York? And, if I am only but a little bit forgiven for my long and wicked silence, could you begin to try to find this out for me? My New York readings—at the Museum of Modern Art I read, Christ help me, scenes from King Lear, and a fine King Lear I'll look in my little shiny suit—will be over by the end of February, and I needn't return to England until the end of March. Will you see if anything can be done?

We're leaving Wales for London in a few weeks' time, to a house an insane woman has bought us. I'll hate to leave this sea but I must earn a living and will be writing filmscripts, class very B.

1 Tram Combs, a bookseller; Bill = William Swan; Gavin = Chester Alan Arthur III, grandson of a U.S. President. All were friends of Mrs Ruth Witt-Diamant. Information from notes by Tram Combs in the Berg Collection.
2 Thomas's birthday was not until 27 October.

How is your wonderful city? Is your son home? Will you write soon? And I'll write again, a letter full of woes and useless news and little dirty drawings in the margin.

I'll have a drink with you tonight in the forlorn pub where ragged, romantic, weatherbeaten fishermen talk about motorcars and the dollar crisis, and to your memory in, I'm afraid, tepid cat-sour beer. Have a drink with me, in your nice hill house, or in Gavin's tumbledown castle, or with Tram and his beard amen.

All my love to you,
Dylan

MS: Berg

PRINCESS CAETANI
October 1951   The Boat House   Laugharne   Carmarthenshire   Wales

My Dear Madame Caetani,
Thank you for your telegram from Paris. And I hope my letter, addressed to Brown's Hotel, was forwarded to you.

This is a difficult letter to write, because I am asking a great request of you.

But let me first explain. The enclosed manuscript is called, as you will see, 'Llareggub. A Piece for Radio Perhaps', though the title is most provisional.[1] And it is the first half of something I am delighting in doing and which I shall complete *very* shortly. Only very special circumstances—and I'll tell you of them in a moment, if I may—are preventing me from carrying on with it every minute of the working day.

I told you, as you may remember, that I was working on a play, mostly in verse.[2] This, I have reluctantly, and, I hope, only temporarily, abandoned: the language was altogether swamping the subject: the comedy, for that was what it was originally intended to be, was lost in the complicated violence of the words: I found I was labouring at each line as though I were making some savage, and devious, metaphysical lyric and not a play at all. So I set the hotchpotch aside, and am prepared to wait.

But out of my working, however vainly, on it, came the idea of 'Llareggub'. (Please ignore it as a final title.) Out of it came the idea that I write a piece, a play, an impression for voices, an entertainment out of the darkness, of the town I live in, and to write it simply and warmly & comically with lots of movement and varieties of moods, so that, at many levels, through sight and speech, description & dialogue, evocation and parody, you come to know the town as an inhabitant of it. That is an awkward & highfalutin way of speaking: I only wanted to make the town

1 Thomas had resurrected the joke-name that he first used in the 1930s.
2 If this is true, the work isn't known.

alive through a raw medium: and that, again, is wrong: I seem hardly able to write today, or, at least, to write *about* Llareggub: all I want to do is to write the damned thing itself.

Reading (as I hope you will) the first half of this piece as it stands, you'll see that I have established the town up to a certain moment of the morning. And the effect you will find, probably, rather jerky and confusing, with far too many characters and changes of pitch and temper. But the piece will develop from this, through all the activities of the morning town—seen from a number of eyes, heard from a number of voices— through the long lazy lyrical afternoon, through the multifariously busy little town evening of meals & drinks and loves & quarrels and dreams and wishes, into the night and the slowing-down lull again and the repetition of the first word: Silence. And by that time, I hope to make you utterly familiar with the places and the people; the pieces of the town will fit together; the reasons for all these behaviours (so far but hinted at) will be made apparent; & there the town will be laid alive before you. And only you will know it.

Let me particularise, & at random. As the piece goes on, two voices will be predominant: that of the preacher, who talks only in verse, and that of the anonymous exhibitor and chronicler called, simply, 1st Voice. And the 1st Voice is really a kind of conscience, a guardian angel. Through him you will learn about Mr. Edwards, the draper, and Miss Price, the sempstress, & their odd and, once it is made clear, most natural love. Every day of the week they write love letters to each other, he from the top, she from the bottom, of the town: all their lives they have known of each other's existence, and of their mutual love: they have seen each other a thousand times, & never spoken: easily they could have been together, married, had children: but that is not the life for them: their passionate love, at just this distance, is all they need. And Dai Bread the baker, who has two wives: one is loving & mothering, sacklike & jolly; the other is gypsy slatternly and, all in love, hating: all three enjoy it. And Mrs Ogmore-Pritchard who, although a boardinghouse keeper, will keep no boarders because they cannot live up to the scrupulous & godlike tidiness of her house and because death can be the only boarder good enough for her in the end. And Mr. Pugh, the schoolmaster, who is always nagged by his wife and who is always plotting her murder. This is wellknown to the town, & to Mrs. Pugh. She likes nagging; he likes plotting, in supposed secrecy, against her. He would always like plotting, whoever he lived with; she would always like nagging, whoever she lived with. How lucky they are to be married. And Polly Garter has many illegitimate babies because she loves babies but does not want only one man's. And Cherry Owen the soak, who likes getting drunk every night; & his wife who likes living with two men, one sober in the day, one drunk at night. And the cobbler who thinks the town is the wickedest place to live in in the world, but who can never leave it while there is a hope of reforming it; and, oh, the savour his cries of Gomorrah add to the pleasures of the little town wicked. And the old woman who every morning shouts her age to the heavens; she believes the town is the chosen land, & the little river Dewi the River of Jordan; she is not at all mad: she merely believes in heaven on earth. And so with all of them, all the eccentrics whose eccentricities, in these first pages, are but briefly & impressionistically noted: all, by their own rights, are ordinary & good; & the 1st Voice, & the poet preacher, never judge nor condemn but explain and make strangely simple & simply strange.

I daren't look back over what I have written: I wrote it v. quickly, & most probably it reads like nonsense. But I *terribly* want to finish the piece. And it *will* be good (of its own kind). And this is where my great request of you at last comes in.

Can you pay me—and, I am sorry, *at once*—for this half of 'Llareggub' just as though it were finished? For without being paid well and at once, I cannot finish it.

In the middle of next week, we finally leave Laugharne for London. I mean, we *have* to leave: the house is sold. But, still, I *cannot* leave without paying the whole of the debts I owe to this town. And they amount to about a £100. If I can pay this, we can leave for London, where I have borrowed a flat, and I can get on, at once, with the rest of 'Llareggub'. Oh, I want to so much. I can finish it in two weeks. But only if I can settle all up here.

I know the amount I am sending you of Llareggub (and, of course, quite possibly the quality: you may loathe the thing) is not worth a £100. But what I want is to be paid now for the *whole* piece in advance. Is that possible? I am pinning every bit of faith on to that.

Can you cable me your answer?

Wouldn't it be awful if you thought the whole thing bunk. My head is full of it, I *must* go on.

Please forgive this letter.

Ever,
Dylan

MS: Camillo Caetani Foundation

MARGARET TAYLOR
Wednesday [October 1951]   Laugharne

Yes, it *is* a long time since I wrote to you last. Before, perhaps, you housed us, so snug and beautiful, in Laugharne, in the imperishable Boat House down whose kitchen steps, some Saturday nights ago, I fell like a barrel?[1] I was in bed, then, for days, with a rumpled back, and gout came too, grinding gout, and went to bed in my toe, and a Summons arrived to

---

1 If this was the first letter Thomas had written Mrs Taylor since moving to Laugharne in 1949, it should come much earlier. But its references to the move to London and to other events date it to late 1951.

pay a firm of plumbers for the work they did, last December, in extricating, from the W.C. pipes of a London flat we were living in, a bottle of Hammerton's Stout thrown down by Colm. And, when I could walk again, I quarrelled and fought with Caitlin over something now forgotten but which I remember in every detail,[1] and huffed out of the house to Swansea where I stayed with a barrister who uses brandy like salt or sauce, pouring it over everything, meat, potatoes, porridge, and even boiled egg. And Caitlin & Lizzie Lutyens came & reclaimed me, and, though I am writing this in the upper room of the Pelican, (for my shed keys are lost once more, for I think the sixth time) I can hear Lizzie hissing and gushing and drooling & bubbling about Edward,[2] money, the BBC, twelve tones, Constant[3] & babies, men, men, men, all the way from her bed in the Boat House where she lies all day monologuing herself to death. Lizzie came into the Pelican yesterday afternoon, raving drunk, and gave my father a heart attack. Today, he is still shaking. Caitlin's black eye has just faded; a boy fell from a tree where he was picking conkers, quite near your Grist house, and his shoulderblade broke & pierced his lung, and at the postmortem in Carmarthen Infirmary they found he had been eating stamps; a white owl breathes on a branch right outside Phil the Cross's bedroom window, like a hundred people making love, and inflamed Phil so much he ran, for the first time in years, to his wife's bed and set about her so fiercely he nearly died of a fit of silicotic coughing and couldn't go to work next day; a printed form has just come that tells me I shall be prosecuted herewith unless I send in my National Insurance book fully stamped for 1950; Ivy's front teeth fell out one evening while she was playing skittles, and yesterday she told me she had been blind in one eye for twenty years; Colm's scalded chest is better, but he still has nightmares; there is little other news.

I do hope it will be possible for us to come up to London towards the end of next week. That is the date we had looked forward to, too. But, as you know, and as we said this morning on the telephone, It All Depends. I couldn't go into any details on the phone as weazel-eared Lizzie was lying in bed in the same room, reading a book on Erasmus Darwin upside down. After our conversation, I talked to Caitlin about the position, and she said—as, indeed, I do myself feel most sincerely—we shouldn't take any money from you who has already given us two houses and much, much more besides. I hope some other money will arrive before the end of next week, from America; some is due to come, but of course, it may take a month. Anyway, and in spite of my better feelings, and feeling every kind of calculating and ungrateful monster, I made out a careful and detailed list of my Laugharne & Carmarthen debts and found them far more dreadful than I had imagined. Ivy, I can stall, I think. I do not believe the Post Office will mind waiting. And my poor Mother, from whom I was obliged to

1 Their quarrels were getting worse. This one may have been about Caitlin's infidelity.
2 Edward Clark, Lutyens's husband.
3 Constant Lambert, composer and conductor.

borrow to avoid yet another prosecution, would wait until after the grave. But certain debts in the town are desperately urgent, and *must* be paid before I can leave; and I do not see how I am to pay them. *First*, there is that summons, Plumber v Colm, which I mentioned earlier: this amounts to £6.10.0. & must be paid in five days. *Second*, there is a bill of Sydney Heath, Carmarthen, for Llewelyn's new mackintosh & socks, & this must be paid at once as they do not know or trust us: £7. *Third*, there is a bill of Keene's, the Grocer, for £11. *Fourth*, there is a bill of Fred Phillips for £17, due since July. *Fifth*, there is a Turpin greengrocer bill of £10. *Sixth*, there is a personal debt to Phil of £4 which I am, in honour & friendship, bound to pay. These six items amount to £54.10.0., and, as I say, I cannot leave Laugharne for Delancey Street[1] without settling every single penny of it.

I shall be getting, for a poem, a small cheque, amount as yet unknown, which will take us up to London; and, after that, myself & London will see what we can do. That side of our gigantic move, I don't need help. This, the seaward, is the side that counts. We will both be terribly disappointed if we cannot come up next week to your/our new house.

Donald's film job is quite certain, as he wrote to me a few days ago, & will begin in 'some weeks'.

But, here in Laugharne & now, that doesn't mean anything, not to our summonses, grocers, greengrocers, clothiers, & candlestick makers.

Thank you for everything, for the beautiful Boat House, & for Delancey Street, for the caravan, for the Manor House, for the Little House, for a lot.

I shall show you my new poems in London—if ever, O God, we get there.

I am now going to borrow five shillings from someone for Woodbines & a Felinfoel.

Love,
Dylan

MS: Texas

OSCAR WILLIAMS
[October or November 1951] Boat House Laugharne Carmarthenshire
Wales

S. Howard Moss, of the New Yorker,[2] wrote to me asking for poems. This is no good for him, I suppose?

My dear Oscar,
Herewith a long new poem.[3] It's wonderfully good of you to take my bits and sell them so quick and so very well. I've spent months writing this

1 Where Mrs Taylor had bought a house, of which the Thomases were to occupy the basement flat; it was in Camden Town.
2 Howard Moss, poetry editor of the *New Yorker*.
3 'Poem on his Birthday'. The editor of *Atlantic*, Edward Weeks, was 'captivated' by it. He paid $200, grumbling slightly, and published it the following March.

poem, and hope you can squeeze out a real huge cheque from some moneyed illerate—it's me that's illerate, I meant illiterate—bastard for it. Months and months, and I think it's the best I've done. As always, I need money in a *terrible* hurry. Particularly urgently now, as next week we move to London, to stay in lodgings at the beginning & then to move into a house. I have gout, strained back, bronchitis, fits, and a sense of disaster, otherwise very ill. My love, and Caitlin's, to you & Gene whom we'll be seeing a lot (I hope) of in February. Please, old crazy friend, get me a lot of dough bloody bloody *quick*. And thank you a great lot for the 50 dollars.

Dylan

MS: Houghton

*LOREN MacIVER AND LLOYD FRANKENBERG
[1950–51] The Boat House Laugharne Carmarthenshire Wales

This quintessentially punning poem-as-letter was written for a married couple, a painter (MacIver) and a poet (Frankenberg), who were part of Thomas's small circle of New York friends as opposed to hangers-on. The manuscript is a fair copy without corrections except for the opening line, where Thomas began by saying that since he left America it was 'eleven weeks': then changed it to 'near seven months', 'near 14 odd months' and finally '15 odd months'. The letter was actually posted in November 1951, after 17 odd months. Assuming the chronology of composition is genuine, this doesn't explain why, in the version as sent, Thomas included the crossed-out dates when he made his fair copy from the earlier drafts that obviously existed: unless, as probably happened, he felt guilty about his long silence, and (in anticipation of his next visit to America, in a few months' time) wanted to show how hard he had been trying. Conceivably he faked the entire chronology: as Gwen Watkins believed he faked the appearance of a letter in 1944 (page 589).

Now 15 odd months have come to live in your dome
sweet dome[1] for the pleasure of dying with loren
    (hullo!) and long (thank you!) lloyd,
since in that titan's canoe I hiccupped for home
(I mean the queen e. where the limeys spoke foreign,
    to bowery me, as freud)
and shared my cabin with a minikin moron
who'd fifteen suits and was always milking his gnome
    with hairy cries in a com
    a, and a haggis embroid

---

1 'Pleasure Dome' (from Coleridge's poem, 'Kubla Khan', with its 'stately Pleasure-Dome') was the title of a book by Frankenberg; also of a collection of recordings that he edited, in which poets, among them Dylan Thomas, read their own works.

ering dominie who'd not behave as in rome
the romans behave but who thought me gomorrhan
    and (how the hell dare he!) hom
osexual too, an unsoberly fairy nom
an of probity'd deign to touch with his sporran.

And, cooped in that mastodon's sloop, I for the frank
enberg eyrie yearned for nearly a week and wept
    in deed for the scrapered shores;
and the pettylike pretties,[1] twotitted and swank
en, went esquired, and never their beds were slept
    in at all (at all!) by whores
truck me, though little I thought of but bribing cept
in god on the braided bridge for a chance to dank
    en their doors with the rank
    and file of their downers of drawers
and the borers off of their bras, or alone and drank
en or sober to enter and probe a much leapt
    in tallulah,[2] be she a lank
un or buttered with goosefat on breast, flank, bank
and brae. And never one word (the vicar's except

in) was asked but of gables, brown derbies, jane russell
's fables, minxes and sables, high balls (how heaver
    ly!), b. grables's pylons,
is m. west a lesbian, does bette d. hustle
in parties out there do the stars wear dishever
    ly? Did ever poor dȳlan's
onslaught on silence throughout his so clever
ly agented oddyssey raise any bustle
    in this cockles and mussel
    s town? No, not on your nylons![3]
'Tell us', they cried, 'of the boulevard tussle,
the bumdance of sunset, the strumpetting rever
    ly, hug, fug, and guzzle
in the chromium homes on the hills of bever
ly, hashish, hot splashes, nipple nibble and nuzzle.

Did you paint yale and harvard o'hara scarlet?
have a bash at the deans? did you maestro their broad
    s with a flash of cold mutton?
were holyoke girls all t. bara harlet

1 George Petty, American graphic artist, drew the stereotypical pin-up girls in the magazine *Esquire* from the mid-1930s.
2 Tallulah Bankhead (1902–68), flamboyant film actress.
3 In Thomas's caricature, Laugharne is interested only in what he has to tell them about American film stars: Jane Russell, Betty Grable, Mae West, Bette Davis.

s?[1] did you cry, "come into the garden, brynmawr maud
    s and act like betty manhutton"?
did you pluck the g strings (how your plectrum pawed!)
of vassar's[2] trig chippies and tiara'd starlet
    s and put in their belly button
        holes whole bowls and pink bord
ers of gypsy lee roses? did a harvard charlet
an, sweeny erect,[3] dance on those tse-tse-flied swards?
and did loopy chicago aquinasses rut on
poor sinused st thomas like capricorn hebawd

s?' Just as a blind man's nose gives a wriggle and twitch
as he passes a fish shop, he bowing and leery
    with, 'how d'you do, ladies?',
so some snobs' noses, that hang by their snot to the rich—
for the rich are of heaven, hail croesus and meary!—[4]
        writhe with a kind of sādis
tic joy at the name of some lionised, dreary
and serialised trilogist stuck in his saintly niche.
'Tell me, who did you meet?'—oh, the rabbity snitch
        es wiggle like nymphs with the itch—
        'not mere ritas and hedies'
(as though they wouldn't piss blood to meet either bitch)
'but somebody really, you know, I mean seri
        ous'. Prigs, fakes, and afraidies,
writers, backbiters, and, frothing, I ponder which,
till at last: 'well, I met Oscar Williams, deary.'

The inhaling bunion halfway between peepers
and chops does not wobble or whipcrack a bristle
        as this treasured name is struck—
(though down in derwood forest something stirs the creepers,
not robin hood, surely, and all his merry gristle,
        and it *cant* be friar tuck)—
no, from the cultural snozzle not one wet whistle!
I skim through a scum of vogues for a deep as
        charles morgan betrophied cuck
        old to buck these snout sleepers,
grope through the open fannies of flairs for a thistle
of fame but can find only vaselined weepers,

1 Some of Thomas's academic venues are listed: Yale, Harvard, Mount Holyoke. Scarlett
O'Hara is the heroine of *Gone with the Wind*. Theda Bara (1890–1955) was one of the
first silent-movie stars; her invented name is an anagram of 'Arab death'.
2 Bryn Mawr and Vassar: more venues.
3 The figure of 'Sweeney', a satiric analogue for modern man, occurs in several T. S. Eliot
poems, including one called 'Sweeney Erect'. John L. Sweeney of Harvard University
wrote the introduction to Thomas's *Selected Writings* (New York, 1946; see page 603).
4 'croesus and meary' = 'Jesus and Mary'. 'Meary' could be the literary entrepreneur
Meary James Tambimuttu.

then, ah! not oscar but tennessee williams, this'll
st vitus 'em! and indeed the pig vents sizzle!
'Didn't he write . . .?' He did, he did. A truck called fuck.[1]

In this pretty as a stricture town by the eel
y, oily, licking sea full of fish that taste like feet
        and feet that taste like fur,
under a bathwater sky where angels fly like teal
eaves, gritty I sit me down greeting on my fat seat,
        o faraway madam and sir,
and hear the goitred, scraggy swans deathsing like gigl
i, and the cow pouncing owls sneer in the groinpit heat.
        Here a whiskey whiskered seal
        wet barking virgin with spur
s on her teats gives birth to a mole in the main street.
Today we hunt babies (d'you ken your little john peel
        s right down to his marrow meat?)
Tomorrow's the day for the circumcision of bir
ds. And on cannibal sunday let's hope the vicar's sweet.

Nine hundred gabies; two chapels soprano with rat
s; five catafalque pubs licensed to sell enbalming gin
        and aconite tobacc
o: such is my home, and welcome is botched on the mat
of the excrementitious townhall with blood and spin
        ach, this rack a jack crack
a jill bug brained ball bearing year in the bloody vat.
And how long here shall my red market ration of skin
        and bone wait for the knack
        er yard?[2] shall I champ the slack
bit of these verses, this adjective gravied lack
a bone hunk of monkey beef skewered with winkle pin
        s and tureened with a comic hat,
until crabs strut straight and statesmen are sardined in
sacks, the moon beams black, and generals scream in the bin?

Must I stand in this public uranium ('please
adjust your bomb before leaving') until the back room
        boys find a ray to gamma
themselves alone? must I (to hell with my pis
an q's!) pound out these cuntos[3] on candystuck keys
        until orchidaceous, ama
rous oscar w. (a very watered street bloom)
discovers, at last, if women's elbows and knees—
        (to william blake I owe these

1 Tennessee Williams's play, *A Streetcar Named Desire*.
2 Meat was still rationed. 'Red market' is a play on 'black market'.
3 The pun is about 'minding one's Ps and Qs' and Ezra Pound's work, the *Pisan Cantos*,
here 'cuntos'.

            sacred bedpanorama
s}—are only glued together (as rare bits to cheese)?
must I strain out this mousecrap until damndom boom,
            until theodore reothke's seize
d with the king kong's evil and, searching his pomes for fleas,
snarls out, 'shit!' as he tarzans his way to the tomb?

Must I dree this wierd[1] that is drier than moth's wee
wee till miracles happen as often as rape?
            till stephen the seamen
's bender bullbellows and belches with me big chi
chi chief wigwam hamingway, stiff as a stewed ape?
            till sick of laying shemen
john lehmann the leman beds and bigbellies a fi
fi or mimi and grows a casanova shape?
            till peter lyrical tap
            ir tongued toryballed screamen
viereck turns russian red as a lobster? and e.
e. eimi gorblimey joyfarmer cummings goes pap
ist and shirty as trappissed merton[2] and t.
            t. too and writes in the then
dormouse room of respectable mountains?—(though gee
gee jesus defend us from canter! emen!)

But let rancour, like chancres, b off! penic
illin them both! rhymes of cantankerous malice
            and an epileptic beat,
no more, on my septic oath, shall spout their menace
into the idylls and oils of perry palace,[3]
            like a sewer on heat—
(O sixty one! o beer in a bishop's chalice!)
Please, nice penicillin, drip down! a nasty den is
            today my once tennys
            onian house, and excret
a whirls through the window, turdy as venice.
Blow away, naughty thoughts, like a mummy's phallus—
            (and isn't mummy complete!)
This mummery's over. The paunched, maudlin villain
in cloaca and dagger, bows. And says,
                              Love,
                              Dylan.

MS: Jeff Towns/Dylans Book Store

1 'Dreeing the weird' is a Scots dialect phrase for putting up with one's fate.
2 Various writers are brought into the verse: Stephen = Spender; Peter Viereck, who knew
   Thomas in America; Merton = Thomas Merton (1915–69), poet and Trappist monk.
3 The Frankenbergs lived at Perry Place in Greenwich Village, New York City.

DAVID HIGHAM

3 12 51   54 Delancey St   Camden Town   London NW1

Dear David,

Thank you for arranging that advance. And for writing to Leslie Andrews. If he still takes 75 per cent,[1] & you take your advance also, in bits, off the bits I earn, God alone knows how I'm going to live, and with bloody Christmas coming too.

Enclosed, is the Poem I imagined, incorrectly, was entitled 'Shabby & Shorten'.[2] Can you let Bozman have it? I saw him after leaving you & discussed the Collected Poems. He said also he would like to publish 'The Doctor & The Devils' at the end of next year. But—is there no chance of selling this *as a script* to a film company still?

Yours,
Dylan

MS: *Texas*

JOHN MALCOLM BRINNIN

3 12 51   54 Delancey Street   Camden Town   London   NW1

Dear John,

Your letter just forwarded from Laugharne to our new London house or horror on bus and nightlorry route and opposite railway bridge and shunting station. No herons here.[3]

Your letter, just read, has scared the lights out of me. First date in N.Y. January 23rd? I'll have to look lively. I'll also have to look like hell for money (£100) to keep girl & family here while Caitlin and I are junketing abroad.

Questions & answers:

(1) How long do we plan to stay? Between two & three months.

(2) Do we want to confine our movements to east & middle west or do we also want to go to the west coast?

We certainly want to go to California, after the other dates you have arranged. Ruth Witt-Diamant, of San Francisco, (address: 1520 Willard St, S.F.) has recently written asking us the same question, or roughly the same. She says she will, given due warning, be able to arrange some S. Francisco readings. I am sure that Hunter Lewis, of B.C. University, Vancouver, would also invite me again. He said so in a letter this year.

---

1 As provision against income tax.
2 'Once below a time'. ('The criers of Shabby and Shorten / The famous stitch droppers'.)
3 Caitlin, Dylan, Aeronwy, Colm and the family help, Dolly Long, had arrived in chaos on a winter's evening. Margaret Taylor, who had thought up the scheme, was in and out of the flat throughout their brief stay.

(3) I don't think Florida for a month. A Californian month (or less) for us after New York. And then New York at the end again. I would, incidentally, like to go to Washington. Would that club like me again? The shirtless Biddles[1] have invited Caitlin & me to stay with them there.

(4) Yes, yes, yes. I *do* want you please to be my little guide & agent.

On to other things. Oscar Williams, in his last letter to me, said that a group of mid-Western universities were getting together to invite me for a jolly week with them at a figure like one thousand dollars. He did mention mid-February, but I see that that now conflicts with my prearranged New York commitments. I shall write to him today; but do you think you could, as little agent, also get in touch with him and find out if the date—if it is a real date—can be moved to end of February or first of March. Then we could go on to S. Francisco in March sometime. I could leave Caitlin there while I went anywhere else on Pacific Coast where I was invited.

The Socialist Party in New York City—address 303 Fourth Avenue, N. York 10, tel. Gramercy 5-6621—have written to me to ask me for a poetry reading. They say they're a small body (like me) & can't pay much at all, but I would like to do it for them if you can arrange it. Oh, the chairman of the Finance Cte of the S. Party is, if you didn't know, a Jane Browne.

Next things you want to know: (1) Visa. I haven't got one yet. My passport is left in Laugharne, & I will try to go down & get it at the end of this week. Before I get the visa, I am almost certain to need—as before—papers from you, as my agent, explaining the purpose of my visit to the States and instancing some of my more worthy-looking engagements. Perhaps, if easily & quickly obtained by you, a letter from Columbia to you about me, from the Center, and from anywhere important else, would considerably help. Anyway, let me have some official papers of confirmation to show the scared baiters in power here.

(2) I have made no ship reservations for Cat and me, not knowing when I was due in N. York. I'll try to do this this week early, following your instructions about getting the steamship line to have their N. York office contact you at once at Poetry Center for payment.

(3) Caitlin will be coming with me, but *not* the baby.

(4) It's okay to say to the New School I'll do them a second programme of dramatic readings.

Now to *my* questions. What sort of poetry would, d'you think, most of my sponsors like me to read? Modern? including modern American, or is that presumptuous? Blake, Keats, Donne, Hopkins, Owen? And what about 'dramatic excerpts'? Marlowe, Shakespeare, Webster, Tourneur, Beddoes? Do tell me what, from your previous experience of 'my audiences', they

1 See n.2, page 380.

most would like from me. I don't want to read too much of my own, except for a few recent ones. Laughlin, by the way, is bringing out a pamphlet of new poems for my visit.[1]

What news of Pearl? I hope, God bless her, she's in Brazil. How are *you*? How goes Sidney G.? He was moaning for weeks about his companions, Raine & Gascoyne.[2] 'Och, there'll be wee orgies with those two sparocks.'

I'll get this off straightaway, without any news or affection; and will see about steamer bookings & visas *very quickly*.

Please you write quickly, too; & do let me know your suggestions as to the contents of my programmes. And do do something about West Coast. That's what Caitlin wants most.

Love,
Dylan

PS. Mebbe, after all, a bit of Florida would be good, if possible. Miami? Gainesville first, & then Miami?

PSS. A very important point I forgot. If we're to spend one whole month in N. York, *in an hotel*, we'll be desperately broke. Is there anyone who would put us up for, say, a week while we look around for someone else to put us up for the next week, and so on? It really's important. The money I earn we want for The Sights, not for board. Can you delicately hint around?

PSSS. I'm writing today to Ruth Witt-Diamant, but perhaps you could write as well—her address is on page one—to see what, if anything, she has done?

D.

MS: Delaware

ANEIRIN TALFAN DAVIES
3 December 1951 [postcard]   54 Delancey St London NW1

Yes, of course 'Dock Leaves'[3] can print my talk on the South Bank Exhibition. But please don't send them the typescript you have, as there [are] many misprints in it and I should also like to alter a few lines & words for publication.

I have a copy somewhere, which I will correct this week. Shall I send it on to you, or will you drop me a line to tell me Dock Leaves address?

Yours,
Dylan T

MS: Texas

1 *In Country Sleep and Other Poems* (a book, not a pamphlet), February 1952.
2 W. S. Graham, Kathleen Raine, David Gascoyne: all poets.
3 A shrewd literary magazine, founded in Pembroke Dock in 1949, later renamed *The Anglo-Welsh Review*. It persevered until 1988.

DAVID HIGHAM
Thursday [marked '14 Dec 1951 recd']   54 Delancey St   Camden Town
London NW1

Dear David,

When I was talking to Leslie Andrews' man the day before yesterday, I mentioned the fact that I was having an advance on a new book very shortly & that I very much hoped I could have this sum intact & that no tax deduction be made from it. He agreed to this, saying that the monies you had for him would keep the Income Tax wolf well at bay & that this advance need not be touched. So will you *please* let me have the American Diary £100[1] without any tax deduction &—*very* much please again— without deducting from it anything towards the money I owe your firm. This £100 will pay immediate debts & see my family over beastly, expensive Christmas. Can you see to it that I get this sum whole—(minus, of course, your usual agent's fee). I am doing two broadcast jobs just after Christmas, & the 50 tax per cent can be taken from those, which will, now, I think, nearly clear the Tax debt. Also from these can be taken the rest of what I owe you. But please (once more) let me have the *whole* of that £100. *It is urgent.*

I am posting Laughlin's proofs direct to him tonight.[2] Is that okay? I would have posted them sooner, but am going to read most of them tonight at the Institute of Contemporary Art & have no other copy.

Yours,
Dylan

I'll ring you about this, very briefly, tomorrow.

MS: Texas

JOHN MALCOLM BRINNIN
6 January 1952   54 Delancey Street   Camden Town   London NW1

Dear John,

Thank you for your two letters, official & not.

Thos. Cook have just written me to say you've paid for Caitlin's & my passage on the Queen Mary on January 15. Thank you. I only hope to the Lord I can make it. The difficulty is over my visa. The American Consulate would not revalidate it until they had 'investigated' me. They're presumably in the process of doing that now. The snag seemed to be a visit I paid to Prague in 1949—the year *before* I came to the States last. I'm *hoping* to

---

1 Higham had negotiated a £400 contract with the London firm of Allan Wingate for an 'American Journal' of 60,000 words, to be delivered on 30 June 1952. The first £100 was paid on signing. The book was not written.
2 Presumably *In Country Sleep and Other Poems*.

get the visa this week. Do you know anyone important your end who'd say a word to the Embassy, or Consulate, that I'm not a dangerous Red? I'll be seeing a British Foreign Office man myself tomorrow. But perhaps everything will work out okay. It's just that there's such very little time. If the worst comes to the worst, and my visa is withheld *after* the 15th, I'll cable. I'll cable you, anyway, if the Q. Mary sails with us. Will you meet us? Please?

Any hope of accommodation yet—or should we stay in a hotel for the first part of our visit?

Heard from Ruth Witt-Diamant about possible Californian readings?

I must read Lear again: haven't looked at it for years.

I enclose a letter from McGill University, Montreal. This letter seems, to me, to mean that McGill is prepared to transport me (I suppose at a good fee) all the way from Wales to Montreal. And (I suppose) back. They seem to know nothing about my coming to the States in January. *So*: as my transportation from N. York to Montreal will be so much less than from Wales to Montreal, the fee, surely, must be commensurately (or proportionately, I don't know the words) increased. I've written to Stors McCall, saying, 'Yes, delighted', & that I'd be in N.Y. the end of January. I told him that you, as my dear little agent, would be getting in touch with him as you, and you only, knew what my N. York commitments were, & when. Will you write to him, quickly? And as I don't particularly want to go to Montreal, soak McGill for twice (at least) as much as I get in the States— plus, of course, full expenses *by air*!

I'll be cabling you. Keep your fingers crossed for us.

I'm looking forward, a lot, to seeing you. And I hope I can.

Cat got her visa straightaway.

Love,
Dylan

MS: Delaware

JOHN MALCOLM BRINNIN
[telegram, 16 January 1952, SS Queen Mary]

SEE YOU PIER 90 SUNDAY BRING CARPET LOVE DYLAN CAITLIN.

Original: Delaware

MARGARET TAYLOR
10th February 1952

Hotel Chelsea 222 23rd St W
New York[1]

My Dear Margaret,
I've been meaning, & meaning, to write a letter, a proper letter, but this poor little scribble is so far the best I can do. (I've not even written to my parents, though Cat has.) It's the terrible speed & noise of this place, the parties piling, the faces blurring, the endless insistent killing kindness that's the reason I haven't, long before, said How are you? & how is dear Aeron? How is everything? I promise to write properly soon.

Dylan

MS: Texas

SOPHIE [?WILKINS]
Thursday [21 February 1952]

Dear Sophie,
I'm terribly, *terribly* sorry—and so is Caitlin, who sends her regards—that I can't come along tonight as I very much wanted to & looked forward to. I've been sick as hell all day, really physically sick in the most obvious & unpleasant way, & could only just get through a reading at the NYU.[2] Now the reading is over, & I'm going back to bed, hotwater bottle, & sleeping draught.
A great many apologies, & I hope, a lot, to see you soon. (We'll be in the White Horse,[3] at about [?4] o'clock on Sunday, on Hudson & 11th Street, & would like to see you & apologise in person—if you'll excuse the phrase.)

Fondly,
Dylan Thomas

MS: Location unknown

1 A large, economical hotel, beloved of writers, near the Greenwich Village district. Thomas and his wife arrived in New York on 20 January but he had no engagements for ten days.
2 Thomas read at New York University on Thursday 21 February.
3 A Greenwich Village tavern that Thomas made his drinking headquarters.

DAVID HIGHAM
26 Feb 1952   [headed paper: Hotel Chelsea, etc]

Dear David,

Caitlin & I are getting very anxious—to put it mildly. Today we heard from Dolly Long, 49 Orchard Park Estate, Laugharne, Carmarthenshire, the girl who is looking after our baby; she told us she had received no money from you in spite of my cable & Caitlin's letter. Do you remember, we arranged together that you would pay Dolly Long £3 a week for three months (or, if necessary, longer) out of the three monthly cheques for £50 each delivered you by Charles Fry?[1] I realised that I owed Pearn & Pollinger & Higham £50, so perhaps you have taken the February Fry £50 for that debt. If this is so, WILL YOU VERY MUCH PLEASE send to Dolly Long—I repeat the address, 49 Orchard Park Estate, Laugharne, Carmarthenshire—the WHOLE of the March Fry £50? And can you, please, *CABLE* me at the above address. If Dolly isn't paid—the main reason I arranged to write a book for Fry, a book which is shaping well, though roughly—then we shall have to return to England somehow rightaway, breaking all my university lectures etc., as Dolly Long is poor & cannot look after a child for nothing.

So, PLEASE: Send her the whole (minus, of course, ten per cent) of Fry's forthcoming *March* cheque. This is most urgent. Caitlin's breaking her heart about the baby. AND DO PLEASE CABLE TO RELIEVE OUR DEEP ANXIETY.

I've seen Helen Strauss, by the way, & Mike Watkins.[2] Mike wanted me to stay on with him, but, of course, I've followed your advice & instructions & told Helen Strauss that, along with your other writers, I have moved over to her. She is now in the process of settling some gramophone record contract for me.[3]

I'll write again when there is news. My lectures—readings, rather—are going extremely well. We start for the middle west in the middle of March.

But the main purpose of this very worried letter is:

Please Pay Dolly Long the whole March £50. AND *PLEASE* CABLE us you're doing so.

I'm sick with anxiety.

Yours,
Dylan

MS: Texas

---

1 Charles Fry, of Allan Wingate, had commissioned the 'American Journal'; further advances of £50 a month were due in January, February and March.
2 Strauss and Watkins were with the Ann Watkins literary agency.
3 Two young women, Barbara Holdridge and Marianne Mantell, had started the Caedmon record company. They recorded Thomas in New York, reading poetry and prose, in 1952 and 1953: a far-sighted investment.

RUTH WITT-DIAMANT

March 9th 52   c/o J. M. Brinnin   100 Memorial Drive   Cambridge
Mass

Darling Professor

Every day, since we arrived in the States, nearly three ulcering months ago, I've been meaning to write & say: 'Darling Professor, How are you? We will be in San Francisco towards the end of March. Can we stay with you for a week or two?' But I haven't been able to write a *single* letter. John Brinnin has again fixed me up with a breathless & bloody programme—though in S.F. there is little for me to do, thank the sunny Lord, but sit & like & be with you & see the seals & Big Sur & the Pacific baths. What a pity Tram & Bill are gone. And Elaine. I saw Donald Weeks in Washington a few days ago: he says she's getting married, lucky nasty man.

We are leaving New York on March 16, making our way to San Francisco & you via Chicago & Arizona, where for a few days we stay with Max Ernst. We will be in S.F. some time between the 22nd & the 24th of March. I'll wire you from the Ernsts[1] the *exact* date of our arrival. I'm longing to see you. And Caitlin sends her love.

John Brinnin, with whom we are staying for a few days while I rant at Harvard, says he will write to you tomorrow *in detail* about the Berkeley engagement etc. I think he needs a bit of assistance from you.

It's going to be grand.

Ever,
Dylan

MS: Berg

JOHN DAVENPORT

March 21 [1952] [postcard]

Am staying, very near here, for a few days with the Max Ernsts, though not in the villa in the foreground. A killer-diller of a journey so far. On our way, next week, to San Francisco. (By the way, Time Magazine will be approaching you in London about me. They're doing a piece, & wanted a London friend who Knew All.)

Love to you & Marjorie & the little others, from Caitlin & me.

Always
Dylan

MS: Texas

1 Max Ernst (1891–1976) and Dorothea Tanning, painters.

DANIEL JONES
March 21 [1952] [postcard]

Caitlin & I are buried in the Tuzigoot stone teepee
on the Other side of this card.
We were killed in action, Manhattan Island, Spring, 1952,
in a gallant battle against American generosity.
An American called Double Rye shot Caitlin to death.
I was scalped by a Bourbon.
Posthumous love to you & Irene & Dylan & Catherine[1] from
                                        Caitlin & Dylan

MS: Texas

*JOHN MALCOLM BRINNIN
[telegram, 21 March 1952, 3.47 pm, Flagstaff]

PLEASE URGENTLY WIRE ONE HUNDRED DOLLARS CARE OF
ERNST CAPRICORN HILL SEDONA D

Original: Delaware

OSCAR WILLIAMS
[postcard, with four signatures] [March 1952]

Wild & Western[2] Love to Gene and Oscar from—
            Max Ernst
            Dorothea
            Dylan
    and   Caitlin   X

MS: Houghton

---

1 Mrs Jones and their two children.
2 Sedona, where the Ernsts lived, is in a scenic valley of north Arizona, popular with
  film-makers because of its red-sandstone backgrounds.

BILL McALPINE
[card, postmarked 28 March, written earlier]

X marks where we are staying
I'm going to write you & Helen a long daft letter as soon as we arrive in San
Francisco after a (so far) tumultuously exhilarating & axe-splitting tour.
But for the moment, just this idea—though it's not, for a moment, as
sensational as the desert itself—of where we are on the 21st of March.
   Love to you both.

Always,
Dylan

MS: Buffalo

JOHN MALCOLM BRINNIN
4th April [1952]   c/o Witt-Diamant   1520 Willard Street   San Francisco
California

Dear John,
   Three letters lie—I don't, of course, mean that—before me: dated March
20, March 26, & April 1st. Here's a brief, but none the less stupid, reply to
them all.
   I'm awfully sorry, re March 20, that you've been sick. And not of us? A
mysterious illness; probably test-tubing out from M.I.T.—to whose English
students, & professor of English named maybe Fudge O'Dell, I owe a
forever unwritten apology for never turning up. But I'm very glad you're
better (April 1st) now, & on such a good day.
   Thank you for the damnably urgent & answerable letter from Higham.
I'm supposed, as perhaps you read, to write an introduction to the English
forthcoming edition of my Collected Poems, which, I suppose, entails my
reading them all. Daft I may be . . . .
   Now, re March 26th. Those 'ridiculous mishaps' that caused you to miss
my wire from Sedona proved agonising to us. Caitlin was frightfully ill all
the way from New York to Pennsylvania State College (where Phillip
Shelley was an old fool & more, but the audience gallant) and on the night-
train to Chicago. During the Chicago journey, my bottled up bottle illness
also grew severe; indeed, we were both so near to undignified death that,
on reaching Chicago, we just *could* not go straight across the city to catch
our next train to Arizona but *had* to lie down, dying, in an unrocking bed.
(Incidentally, a roomette is only for *one* traveller, & Christ help him. We
had to change to a bedroom. Dearer.) So we went to a cosy little hovel of an
hotel (the Sherman) & wept & sweated there until next day. The hotel was
fabulously expensive; the Pullman reservation for Tuesday, the 18th, fell
out of date; I had to buy a new one; & so we arrived at Flagstaff with less
than a dollar. The Ernsts were lovely, charming, & hospitable, but had no

ready money & none to lend. We stayed there, absolutely penniless, for 8 days, being unable to buy our own cigarettes, to post a letter, or stand with a beer at Sedona's cowboy bar, or even wire you again. We stayed there, saying 'Beastly John Brinnin', until help came from San Francisco. Arriving at San Francisco, we found your 2 letters, & 2 cheques, & also a letter from the headmaster of Llewelyn's school saying he would be thrown out unless a £100 were paid by April 5. I then wired you again. You sent a cheque for 200 dollars. And so I had 400 dollars altogether. 300 dollars I wired to Llewelyn's school. The other 100 I spent on a Vancouver ticket. So (again) *HELP*.

(On top of this, Caitlin had carefully arranged for some laundry to be sent on from New York to San Francisco. This cost 40 dollars.)

I can just manage to get to Vancouver, & I'll leave Caitlin the fee for my S.F. State College reading which is tonight & which will be only 50 dollars.

About other engagements: Is the date, on April 26, at the University of Chicago the *same* as that, on April 24, at the Northwestern University, Chicago? Or can't I read?

It's summer here, not spring. Over 80. At Easter we go to Carmel & on to see Miller at Big Sur. We are both well.

Please write very soon, [*the remaining words form a large circle*] with any news, some love & a *Bit of Money*. Caitlin sends her love. And, as always, so do I.

Yours, Dylan

MS: Delaware

HENRY MILLER

[early April 1952]   1520 Willard [St]   San Francisco

Dear Henry,

I'm back here once more, staying with Ruth Witt-D for a week or so. This time my wife Caitlin is with me.

We're driving out your way next—Easter—weekend. Shall we call & see you? I'd love to. It would be on Easter Saturday or Sunday.

If it's no good to you, perhaps you wouldn't mind dropping a card to me? But I hope it is all right.

Yours,
Dylan Thomas

From a typescript. MS location unknown

JEAN GARRIGUE[1]
April 5 1952   c/o 1520 Willard St   San Francisco   California

Dear Jean,

Your letter's just come from the Chelsea. I *did* miss seeing you in New York; though I knew, from Stanley Moss, that you were teaching at Bard:— I hoped you might visit the city some weekend, & that we could meet. But even hearing from you I like very much.

Look: To whom do I say what I'd like to say about your poems for the Guggenheim you *must* get? To you? or to the, to me, nameless & addressless Guggenheim people themselves? I can do either, or both.

As perhaps you know, should know, or don't know, I think your poems are beautiful; they are subtle & exciting; they're the work of a deeply serious poet with a fine ear and a lovely, dangerous, voice of her own.

Isn't that awful, when all I mean is that I like them a *lot*, that I re-read them, remember them, & was moved, & made full of wonder, by the new poems in Botteghe Oscure.

To whom shall I say something like that? or something, I hope, much better said?

Write, if you will, to the address above, which I leave on April 17. After that, my best address, as I'm moving quickly all over the place, is c/o John Brinnin, 100 Memorial Drive, Cambridge, Mass.

Caitlin & I get to New York on April 30, & leave for England on May 16. Any chance of meeting between those dates?

Always,
Dylan

MS: Berg

KARL SHAPIRO[2]
[early May 1952]   [headed paper: Hotel Chelsea, etc]

Dear Karl,

Thank you for the Rhyming Dictionary. I'll write something so soon as I get back to England, doom, & duty.

Had the bad news, on arriving here, that my son had been thrown out of his school because past fees had not been paid. Also, that the rent on my parents' house was so overdue that they, too, (crippled, blind, etc) may be thrown out.

Will this melt a rich bitch heart? Can you try?

Caitlin (who sends her love to you both) seems to imagine that Mrs (Meat) Prince[3] would be sympathetic. Do you?

1 Poet. She taught at Bard College, 1951–2.
2 Poet. He edited *Poetry* (Chicago).
3 Perhaps Ellen Borden Stevenson (former wife of the politician Adlai Stevenson), patron of the arts.

Anyway, can you try to do something for us? Otherwise, we'll arrive back with nothing but debts & gloom & nowhere to go & no time to write. We leave on May 16th. You were both fine to us in Chicago.

Ever,
Dylan

[*printed at foot of page:* LARGE and SOUND-PROOF ROOMS]
[*written beside it:* Don't you believe it]

MS: Carbondale

*JOHN MALCOLM BRINNIN
[about 16 May 1952]   Holland-America Line

My dear John,
I'll be writing very soon, from the Boat House, Laugharne, where we hope to be by the end of the week. This is just to thank you for everything: I wish we cd have been more together. Will you send what money there is on to Laugharne? And thank you for cabling to me.

Ever,
Dylan

[*A postscript in Caitlin Thomas's hand says that Brinnin can keep America and adds that she will never again be called a 'sweet wife'. Caitlin was rowdy and aggrieved for much of the time in America.*]

MS: Delaware

GENE DERWOOD
[card, written at sea, postmarked 23 May 1952]

So sorry we didn't manage to say Goodbye to you—Terrible [*illegible*] and muddly as usual. Tell Oscar will send manuscript to him when I can get him something decent together.
Very rough & rocky in mid ocean.

XXX   Love Caitlin & Dylan

MS: Indiana

P. H. NEWBY[1]
4 June 1952   The Boat House   Laugharne   Carmarthenshire   Wales

Dear Mr. Newby,
Thank you very much for your letter about 'Personal Anthology'. It was waiting for me when I returned from the States to London last week, but, in travelling home to Wales, I'm afraid I somehow mislaid it. Would it be an awful nuisance for you to tell me once more the details of time, length, date etc? I'd like, a lot, to do a 'Personal Anthology', & can put it together very quickly. What about an Anthology of modern American verse?
Sorry about the delay, & my carelessness in losing your letter.
Hoping to hear from you soon,

Yours sincerely,
Dylan Thomas

MS: BBC

DAVID HIGHAM
28 June 1952   The Boat House Laugharne Carmarthenshire

Dear David,
Thousands of apologies. That's so easy to write, but I mean every one. Though small, I must be one of your most infuriating thorns.
When in London, I spent a lot of time in Lord's—(where lazy thorns go, when they're not pricking their agents)—bareheaded and balding in the sun. I developed what I thought to be sunstroke, and, by kind daft friends, was put, moaning, into a sleeper and trained home. But it wasn't sunstroke: I had pleurisy, and I'm only just recovered. Not *serious* pleurisy, except to me whom the States have taught an obsessive, and intriguing, hypochondria. But serious or not, I couldn't write. Now I'm resuming what I imagine to be work.
1) I saw Bozman, and got fresh proofs from him.[2] I promised him the preface in a week, but illness supervened. And now I have to confess that I can't write an ordinary prose-preface at all, having no interest whatsoever in it. What I *am* doing, and doing quickly, is writing a Prologue in verse: not dense, elliptical verse, but (fairly) straightforward and colloquial, addressed to the (maybe) readers of the Collected Poems, & full (I hope) of references to my methods of work, my aims, & the kind of poetry I want to write. I hope it will be interesting; I know I'm interested in writing it. It will be about 160 to 200 short lines of verse, of which I have written about 80 so far.
2) I saw Donald Taylor. But far from *my* charming him out of his attitude, he, with his airy-fairy lackadaisical blarney charmed *me* into a

1 Percy Howard Newby, novelist, who joined the BBC as a talks producer in 1949.
2 Of *Collected Poems*.

kind of acquiescent and doped silence. 'Just leave everything to me. Everything will be all right. I'll see (or write to) Higham & Bozman. Just don't you worry. I'll do what's best for us both', is, I dreamily believe, what he told me.[1] Have you heard? Should I drop him a line? I can be much more definite with written words than I can in pleasant, lulling, and responsibility-procrastinating company.

The script work he has for me is still vague, though he is, of course, most optimistic.

3) I didn't see Fry. I rang him up to put off our lunch-date till the evening; &, by the evening, was, as I thought then, struck dumb & giddy by the sun. I'm writing to him this week-end, however, with explanation, and to give him an idea of how I intend to do the book.

4) A letter came to me from Kilmartin, so I didn't need to see him. He was keen on having articles on America for the Observer.[2] These articles, however, cannot now be chunks of the Wingate book, as that will be mostly of a fantastic nature & quite unsuitable for a newspaper. But I hope to be able to write, for Kilmartin, separate, straight pieces.

5) I've written to P. H. Newby about 'Personal Anthology', & will finish the anthology (of American modern poetry) as soon as a couple of books I am waiting for arrive from London. This is a quick job.

6) I couldn't of course take part in the MacNeice programme, which took place when I was ill.

I shall be in London for the Newby recording in the middle of July, & will ring you then. I have bought a panama hat for Lord's, to keep off the pleurisy.

Hope to hear soon about Laughlin.

And all my sincere apologies again. Don't despair of me.

Yours, Dylan

PS. By the way I forgot to give you my home phone number. It is: LAUGHARNE (pronounced Larne) 68.

MS: Texas

DAVID HIGHAM
21 July 1952   The Boat House   Laugharne   Carmarthenshire

Dear David,

I had a nice letter from Fry, and an enthusiastic one from Bozman about the verse prologue to the Collected Poems. I posted, today, a short note to Donald Taylor, telling him I'd be in London this week—for a recording of

1 *The Doctor and the Devils* was still unpublished. Dent wanted Dylan Thomas to be shown as the sole author; Donald Taylor complained that it was he who 'initiated, constructed and partly wrote' the script. As published (1953), it is 'by' Thomas, 'from the story by' Taylor.

2 Terry Kilmartin, literary editor of the *Observer*.

American poems—and want, very much, to see him about Hedgerley Films (whatever they might be) and, in view of Bozman's final refusal to print it unless it bears my name alone, about the ill-fated Doctor & the Devils.

Now the verse prologue should have been finished by this time, and *would* have been hadn't a London visit and two Welsh university lectures cropped up. The London visit was for various recordings for the 3rd Programme, and was interrupted by an urgent call to return to Carmarthen to meet the Income Tax Commissioners along with Leslie Andrews who was contesting their right to tax me, for my 1950 visit to the States, on £1,907.[1] Andrews was defeated, & now it's up to me & him to plug in lots more expenses. Whatever happens, there's going to be a lot deducted from this coming winter's earnings. And the university lectures, in North Wales, an area harder to get to from S. Wales than Ireland would be, took up a lot of time; I had to do them, though, as they made a few necessary pounds. I have to come to London again this week, to continue the recordings that were interrupted by the Income Tax trolls; but, immediately on my return at the end of the week, will hurry up & finish the prologue for Dent.

Which leads me to a very urgent matter: Last week, right after the horror of the Tax tribunal, an inspector called here from the Ministry of National Insurance. I'd filled up only one of my insurance cards since the scheme began, and had put off and forgotten, in about equal parts, the whole thing until this Inspector came. And now I have to pay £50. 12. 6d at once—last day tomorrow, Tuesday, 22nd July,—or they will prosecute me & Make A Warning of me. So can you *please, please,* pay £50 into my bank—Lloyd's Bank Ltd., 164 Kings Road, Chelsea, S.W.3.—tomorrow, the 22nd? That is, can you, please, advance me £50 on the strength of the Dent Collected Poems & on the various BBC jobs I'm now doing? There is nowhere else to approach in such a terrible hurry as this, & you've always been wonderfully good to me (better than I deserve) in the past.

If you could ring me up here, at Laugharne 68, when you have received this letter, and say that you can do this for me & that the £50 is on its way to my Chelsea bank, then I can write a cheque for that amount and take it in to the National Insurance office that day. That very Tuesday, the 22— or I am *done for.* The Inspector, otherwise, will prosecute *from that moment.* Please, David.

And once the verse prologue is finished, I can get down, fast & properly, to the American fantasia.

Yours,
Dylan

I'll wait in all morning for your *prayed-for* call.

MS: Texas

1 Thomas's earnings on the 1950 tour were £2800 (worth £53,000 half a century later), but his accountant had claimed successfully that £900 of this was spent on travel, hotels and other business.

R. D. SMITH[1]
22 July 1952   Boat House   Laugharne   Carmarthenshire
                                                         Laugharne 68

Dear Reggie,
   Did you get that sketch of mine typed? If you did, thanks very much my
boy & will you send it to me so that I can make it better? And if it isn't
typed, don't bother a bit but do please [send] the ms on just as it is: it's not
too good as it stands, but I *can* make something of it if I work more
carefully at the end. It's hot & lovely here, and I'm sitting in my pink skin
in a garage, writing this, and looking hellish.
                                                     Love
                                                     Dylan

MS: (Dr Cyril James)

DOUGLAS CLEVERDON
19 August 1952   Boat House   Laugharne   Carmarthenshire

Dear Douglas,
   At long last—and with many apologies—'Spoon River Anthology'.[2]
   You will see that I have chosen too many poems, probably, but I think it
worth duplicating too many in the script for you to work on with the
readers. The order need not be kept in the way I have indicated, but can—
and should—be changed about, according to voice, mood etc. I'm sorry I
couldn't arrange the poems better—that is, make a real programme of
them, alternating grim & (fairly) gay, etc—but I had only that one
afternoon in the library with the book. I didn't write much then, only got
engrossed in the poems until 6 o'clock.
   I hope the introduction isn't too long and/or tendentious.
   Will you drop me a line about this?
   And, if it *is* possible to get a little money soon, could it be got, somehow,
straight to me, & not through my agents, d'you think? I'm in a hell of a
money mess, sued on all sides; trying to finish several things, including
'Llarreggub' & a long poem, but worried to death; ill with it.
                                                     Ever,
                                                     Dylan

I remember, when we last talked of this programme, your suggestion that
there shd be a few words by me between each poem. This, really, isn't any
good. After the introduction, the poems, I think, *must* come one after the
other, with only the pause when the Narrator says 'Joe Smith'.

MS: BBC

1 Reggie Smith, BBC producer.
2 Thomas was compiling a radio programme from the book, *Spoon River Anthology*, a
  collection of short poems by the American writer Edgar Lee Masters, first published
  1915.

DOUGLAS CLEVERDON
23 Aug '52   The Boat House   Laugharne   Carmarthenshire

My dear Douglas,

Thank you very much for your letter. I enclose a formal note about (I hope) BBC payment for 'Spoon River'. And, *please*, make it come, if at all, terribly quickly.

Delighted to think you might be coming here about the middle of September. There is, of course, a bed for you here.

I'm glad you and Laurence[1] & all want to get 'Llareggub' on the air. I want, myself, to finish it more than anything else. I'm longing to get to work on it again. I have only to finish one job, which I should do by the end of the week of the 25th, and then I can—BUT: I can't without money.

This is the position. I'll want a month or 6 weeks to complete it, working on it every day: I write very slowly when I'm very much enjoying it. And I can't work on anything for a month, without the money to keep us going during that time. I have to write little things & pack them off straight away for money by return; and this is obviously death to any project that needs a month or six weeks' full concentration. If the BBC could pay me a weekly sum, (not less than £10 a week, for the period of 6 weeks) I could shove all other small jobs aside & work on 'Llareggub' only; and guarantee the script complete at the end of that time. That's really the only way it can be worked.[2]

Could you talk to Laurence about this?

I could devote my time, with the greatest enjoyment, to writing imaginative full-length things for the radio if I could be paid a weekly wage. Otherwise, it's bits & pieces for me all the time; this does not get me enough to live on; & is in every way unsatisfying.

Will you do what you can?

And, in the meantime, *please* do try to get me some 'Spoon River' money. I'm being sued by the National Insurance people, among other people.

                                 Yours ever,
                                   Dylan

MS: BBC

---

1 Laurence Gilliam.

2 Cleverdon, knowing that advance payment was impossible, proposed to his superiors that the BBC give Thomas five guineas (£5.25) for every thousand words of the script he delivered. Cleverdon even offered to have the money deducted from his own salary, should the BBC suffer any loss. 'It will be a tragedy for the Corporation, no less than for himself,' he wrote, 'if he cannot bring to fruition the works of creative imagination of which he is capable.' The plan was agreed, but had little effect. *Under Milk Wood* was completed hurriedly in 1953 for stage readings in the United States. It was not broadcast until after Thomas's death.

DOUGLAS CLEVERDON
[enclosed with previous letter]
23 August 1952   The Boat House   Laugharne   Carmarthenshire

Dear Mr. Cleverdon,
   This is to authorise the B.B.C. to make their payment for 'Spoon River Anthology' direct to me at the above address.

                                        Yours truly,
                                        Dylan Thomas

MS: Texas

MARGED HOWARD-STEPNEY

Another Thomas benefactor, Marged Howard-Stepney (1913–53) came from a wealthy Anglo-Welsh family. She was an eccentric who dismayed her advisers by handing out presents to the needy, and spent much time drinking with Thomas. This letter-as-poem is taken from a heavily-altered worksheet, and probably was never sent.

[?1952] [draft]

My dear Marged, You told me, once, upon a time, to call on you when I was beaten down, and you would try to pick me up. Maybe I should not have remembered

> You told me, once, to call on you
> When I was beaten down . . .

                    Dear Marged,

> Once upon a time you told me,
> I remember in my bones,
> That when the bad world had rolled me
> Over on the scolding stones,
> Shameless, lost, as the day I came
> I should with my beggar's cup
> Howl down the wind and call your name
> And you, you would raise me up.

> The same very same time I told you,
> And swore by my heart & head,
> That I would forever hold you
> To the lovely words you said;
> I never thought so soon I'd lie
> Lonely in the whining dust;
> My one wish is to love and die,
> But life is all mustn't & must.

> I mustn't love, & I must die
> But only when I am told,
> And Fear sits in the mansioned sky
> And the winged Conventions scold,
> And Money is the dunghill King
> And his royal nark is the dun;
> And dunned to death I write this jingling thing
> Dunned to death in the dear sun.
> This jingling thing

MS: *Texas*

CAITLIN THOMAS
[?1952]

Two conjectures are involved in trying to place this despairing letter. 'That Marged gin woman' suggests it was written after Caitlin had found and read the previous piece of doggerel. And 'the Insurance thing summons' places it near similar references in letters to David Higham of 21 July and Douglas Cleverdon of 23 August.

Caitlin,
   Please read this.
   That letter you saw was horrible, it was dirty and cadging and lying. You know it was horrible, dirty, and cadging and lying. There was no truth in it. There was no truth meant to be in it. It was vile, a conscientious piece of contrived bamboozling dirt, which *nobody* was supposed to see—not you, or that Marged gin woman. I wrote it as I will tell you. The fact that you read it has made me so full of loathing & hatred for myself, and despair, that I haven't been able to speak to you. I haven't been able to speak to you about it. There was nothing I could say except, It isn't true, it's foul, sponging lies. And how could I say that when you'd *seen* it? How could I tell you it was all lies, that it was all made up for nothing, when you'd seen the dirty words? You'd say, If you didn't mean the dirty words, why did you write them? And all I could answer would be, Because I wanted to see what foul dripping stuff I could hurt myself to write in order to fawn for money. I'd as soon post that muck as I'd swim, I was going to tear it up in a million bloody bits. Marged told me, when she was drunk with that Pritchard,[1] to write to her about what I owed the Insurance things & others, or that's what I gathered—as much as anyone could gather. Or perhaps that's what I wanted to gather. Anyway, I put the Insurance thing summons in an envelope & explained, in a note, that I'd spent the other half of the money she'd given us for that, & that there were other real debts too. Then I went on writing something else—those endless rotten verses of mine, which I

1 Cyril Pritchard was solicitor to the Howard–Stepney estate.

almost agree with you about—and then, when I came to a dead bit, to a real awful jam in the words, I saw—on the other broken table—when I'd written to Marged & started writing a proper sycophantic arselicking hell letter, putting in pretentious bits, introducing heart-throb lies, making, or trying to make, a foul beggar's lie-book of it. I only just avoided tuberculosis & orphans. There's no excuse for my writing this. I'd no idea it would go further than the floor of this shed. I was all wrong to drivel out this laboured chicanery. So wrong, & ashamed, I haven't been able to say a word to you about it. The misery I'm in can't make up for, or explain the misery I've made for you by my callous attempt at a mock-literature of the slimiest kind.

I love you.
Dylan

MS: *(Thomas Trustees)*

BBC
5th Sept 1952   The Boat House   Laugharne   Carmarthenshire   Wales

Dear Mr Layton,[1]
    Thank you for yesterday's letter. I enclose the Talks Contract, signed.
    I do hope you can let me have your cheque for 20 guineas as soon as possible.[2] That, indeed, is the reason I asked, in this particular case, for you to negotiate directly with me instead of with Pearn, Pollinger, & Higham, in the usual way: I thought it would be a bit quicker, as I'm going through one of those times when all the bills are coming in together and I want whatever money's due to me with all the speed possible.
    When, however, it comes to negotiations about the feature programme 'The Town That Was Mad', that I have been asked to write, I should like you, please, to deal with P.P. & H., my agents.
    Thanks very much.

Yours sincerely,
Dylan Thomas

MS: BBC

1 The addressee was Miss E. M. Layton, Copyright Department.
2 For *Spoon River Anthology*.

*HUMPHREY SEARLE[1]

6 Sept 52   Boat House Laugharne Carmarthenshire

Dear Humphrey

Thanks for the note. Yes, Nov 16 for 'Shadow of Cain' is fine. And the rehearsal the previous Friday. I'll probably be living again in Camden Town[2] by that time.

Sorry I shan't be in London before September 15th, unless called up by some urgent job—in which case I'll let you know. But it's unlikely, I'm afraid.

I mean to write to Edith every week, and next week *will*.

Yours
Dylan

MS: British Library (Searle papers)

E. F. BOZMAN

10 September 1952   Boat House   Laugharne   Carmarthenshire

Dear Bozman,

More apologies than there's paper, for this crippling delay.

I intended, as you know, to write a more-or-less straightforward & intimate prose preface, and then funked it. And then I began to write a prologue in verse, which has taken the *devil* of a time to finish. Here it is, only a hundred & two lines, and pathetically little, in size & quality, to warrant the two months, & more, I've taken over it. To begin with, I set myself, foolishly perhaps, a most difficult technical task: The Prologue is in two verses—in my manuscript, a verse to a page—of 51 lines each. And the second verse rhymes *backward* with the first. The first & last lines of the poem rhyme; the second and the last but one; & so on & so on. Why I acrosticked myself like this, don't ask me.

I hope the Prologue *does* read as a prologue, & not as just another poem. I think—though I am too near to it now to be any judge—that it *does* do what it sets out to do: addresses the readers, the 'strangers', with a flourish, and fanfare, and makes clear, or tries to make clear, the position of one writer in a world 'at poor peace'.

---

1 The composer Humphrey Searle (1915–82) had written a setting for a long poem by Edith Sitwell that was inspired by the bombing of Hiroshima, 'The Shadow of Cain'. The work had a public performance at the Palace Theatre, London, on 16 November 1952, with the verse read by Thomas (who didn't like the poem; see page 678) and Sitwell.

2 Where Margaret Taylor had the house with the basement flat. There is no evidence that Thomas went back there.

I will have a proof of this, won't I?

I'm writing to Higham, to say that the Prologue and the proofs are at last in your hands. And I'm begging him to have my contract with you settled *as quickly as possible*. Though the result does little to show it, I've spent 2 months at this poem, working hard at it every day and doing no other work-for-money at all. And consequently I've got very badly into debt, am faced with summonses, and cannot even now buy myself a beer and cigarettes. And daily it gets worse. So, please, do do all you can to let me have my advance royalties on the Collected Poems really quickly. It's very urgent. I'm in quite a desperate position, even to a few pounds, and day-to-day wants & needs.

You asked me, in a previous letter, about possible interviews with the press when the book comes out. Of course, I'd be pleased & will do whatever you can arrange.

All my apologies again.

Yours,

Dylan Thomas

PS. I shd, if possible, like a dedication: just

To Caitlin.

Proofreading the Collected Poems, I have the horrors of 'Paper & Sticks' on page 116. It's *awful*. I suppose it's *quite* impossible to cut it out? I shd so like it, somehow, to be omitted.[1]

D. T.

MS: (J. M. Dent)

GILBERT PHELPS

3 October 1952   Boat House Laugharne Carmarthenshire

Dear Gilbert,

First I heard that I was taking part in 'New Soundings'[2] was in your letter yesterday. But I do remember that my agent was sending my new poem, Prologue, to Lehmann, so I suppose that's it. I've just come back from London, & can't come up again until October 16. I'll be travelling

---

1 'Paper and Sticks' was first published in the magazine *Seven*, Autumn 1939. It was reprinted in *Deaths and Entrances*. The poem was deleted from the 1952 collection, and replaced by 'Do not go gentle into that good night', at proof-stage the last-but-two poem in the book, but as published, nearer the middle of the volume. It contained a misprint, 'has' for 'had' in line 5.

2 'New Soundings' was a Third Programme literary magazine, broadcast monthly. Gilbert Phelps was the producer. Thomas recorded 'Prologue' for it on 24 October and the broadcast was two days later.

down to London from Oxford the morning of the 16th. Is that day possible? I don't quite know how long the poem takes—ten minutes or more. Do let me know. I want, if possible, to catch the night train back to Wales on the 16th.

Want to see you about Personal Anthology too.

Yours,
Dylan

MS: BBC

E. F. BOZMAN
6 Oct 1952   Boat House   Laugharne   Carmarthenshire

Dear Bozman,

Hope this is satisfactory, & that you can get it in in time. *Do* try, please. And apologies again for my terribleness.[1]

Sincerely,
Dylan Thomas

MS: (J. M. Dent)

---

*E. F. BOZMAN
[telegram, 7 October 1952]

DO REALLY THINK MOST VITAL USE NEW NOTE WHATEVER DELAY.

Only source: Davies and Maud edition of Collected Letters, *in 'Textual Preface', page 173.*

GILBERT PHELPS
8 October 1952 [postcard]   Boat House   Laugharne   Carmarthenshire

Good. October 16th then. And yes let's have lunch. I'll meet you in the Cock, Great Portland Street, at one? Okay? The Cock's to avoid wicked friends in other pubs. Unless I hear from you, then.

Dylan

MS: BBC

---

1 The publishers had prepared a brief 'Note' to the 'Author's Prologue', as the introductory poem was then titled. It explained that the Prologue was 'in two verses of fifty-one lines each, and the second verse rhymes *backwards* with the first'. The information had come from Thomas himself, in his letter to Bozman of 10 September, but evidently he was not keen to have it emphasised. He deleted it from the rewritten Note he returned to Bozman on 6 October and added new material, including the much-quoted remark that 'These poems ... are written for the love of Man and in praise of God, and I'd be a damn' fool if they weren't.'

OSCAR WILLIAMS
October 8 1952   Boat House   Laugharne   Carmarthenshire   Wales

Dear Oscar,

How are you and bless you you Little Treasure.[1] Our love from us, looking over wet sand at nothing with some birds on it, to you eagled there looking out at the Statue of—what's its name? I think it has something to do with what Our Side gives to people after it has napalmed them. If anyone in any uniform said to me, 'Now we're going to make you free', I'd cut my throat with a blunt cunt. How are you, you label-less red hot red potato you, I salute you from this bronchial heronry.

Thank you, very, very very much, for the two letters and the two cheques, they arrived in the old nick of time when every lane was mantrapped for me and grocers were armed to their sandy fangs and I couldn't even afford to go to the brewers' annual picnic which, everyone assured me afterwards, was the best for years, chaos, blood, disaster, singing, from beginning to end.

Thank you, *very* much, for working so hard to get me some of that money, damn and blast it with a great big kiss. And I'm terribly glad you think you might be able to send along, from Miss Gardner[2] (whom God wing!) the balance in full of a hundred and fifty dollars this month. I'm very poor now. I've been working on a poem, and it takes so long, and I've no time, then, to do any other jobs for our bread, marge, and gristle, so the money'll be wonderfully welcome. I'm sorry not to have written long before: I've had pneumonia etcetera and the etcetera was worse. But it's not through not thinking of you, cock, and that's a cockney expression and doesn't mean balls.

I saw John Brinnin and Howard Moss off on their backbound train, Howard being kissed goodbye by an adolescent boil with simper and spindles attached. I see Gene Baroff in London, who is so Anglicized, who corsets and straitjackets his vowels so cruelly, he faints. I'm giving a reading on the BBC 3rd Programme of Roethke this week, and of Robert Lowell next week. Half an hour each. I'm trying to arrange a Williams (not WC).[3] Good news about Poetry. (I mean, of course, Poetry Chicago. What *could* good news about poetry be? Bishop Eliot defrocked?) Oh, yes, and I'm introducing & arranging a half hour of Spoon River, and also a Personal Anthology—the B.B.C. has been running a feature called this for about six months now—devoted to Masters, Lindsay, Robinson & Sandburg,[4] a fine

1 Among the anthologies Williams edited was *A Little Treasury of Modern Poetry*.
2 Isabella Gardner, patron and poet, purchased many Thomas manuscripts. A receipt (at Indiana) dated 15 October shows her paying Williams $250 for 143 worksheets of 'Poem on his Birthday', a holograph ms of the poem, and a letter.
3 WC = the American poet William Carlos Williams.
4 Edgar Lee Masters and (probably) Vachel Lindsay, the 'jazz' poet; E. A. Robinson; Carl Sandburg.

old four for a programme and a boozeup. But going back to Karl[1] and Poetry Chicago: Thank you—this is thankyous today, and about bloody time—for suggesting and making possible that number you talked about. I'm sorry I can't send on my new poem, myself, for that number, but my agent here, David Higham, will be doing so, direct to Karl. You see, the poem is a 'Prologue' to my Collected Poems, due to be published any moment now, and, had, therefore, to go through Higham's hands. I told him that Poetry, Chicago, wanted a poem, so perhaps Higham has already sent it along.[2] (The Prologue, by the way, is a complete poem by itself, not just something written especially for a collected volume.) Any money coming from that Prologue will have to go through Higham, of course; but any other money from Karl—for the printing of the manuscript pages, for the possible prize you hinted at—can come, thank God, direct to me. And do I need it! And do I need it now! We are entirely without money, & want some more urgently, if that is possible, than ever before. Here, as you know, we are not as we are in the States, where we don't think or care about what we spend. Here, we have nothing to spend, and think and care about it all the time. So please, cock. (I've asked for a copy of Collected Poems to be sent to you.) I've another vast wodge of working-sheets for the Prologue Poem: want them, for sale? I'm enclosing a copy of that poem, too, for you yourself: on fine, thick paper it can take the place of a window pane, can be a very small tablecloth, or you can race cockroaches on it. How is Gene? Caitlin's & my love to her and to you, always.

Dylan

The copied-out poem is really in 2 verses. I forgot, & have drawn in a line. Unnecessarily, & with great trouble, I have, as you might notice, rhymed all the way back from line 51 to line 1.

MS: Indiana

DOUGLAS CLEVERDON
9 October 1952   Boat House   Laugharne   Carmarthenshire
Laugharne 68

My dear Douglas
   Oh, dear dear! I've been so looking forward to your coming down here, and the very date you manage to get away I'll be in London. I'm going to lecture in Oxford on Wednesday the 15th, & on Thursday the 16th I'm recording a new poem of mine for John Lehmann's programme in London with Gilbert Phelps. I want to return to Laugharne on the Thursday night

1 Karl Shapiro.
2 'Prologue' appeared in the *Atlantic*, January 1953. Nothing appeared in *Poetry* (Chicago).

train, arriving there Friday (17th). Is it possible for us to do something about this? (You must, of course, stay with us.) Could you ring me at number above, or drop a card? Surely, we can fix something somehow. I do hope so. (Going to start work on Llarregub today.)[1]

Ever,
Dylan

MS: the recipient

JOHN ALEXANDER ROLPH[2]
October 9th 1952   Boat House   Laugharne   Carmarthenshire

Dear Mr. Rolph,
Thank you very much for your letter. Indeed, I remember your talking to me about a bibliography of my writings—how could I forget? It seems such a fantastic project—and I'm glad, & amazed, it's actually made progress. Yes, of course, I'll help you all I can about dates & placings of early poems etc, but I must warn you I won't remember much. I know I did quite a lot for the New English Weekly—poems & stories—which I've never gathered together or reprinted. But, anyway, I'll do all I can, & I'm sure it can be done by correspondence.

I'm very grateful to you for the trouble you are taking in such a peculiar cause, & for your very nice letter.

Very sincerely,
Dylan Thomas

MS: Texas

GUGGENHEIM FOUNDATION
October 17 1952   Boat House   Laugharne   Carmarthenshire   Wales

Gentlemen:
I write in behalf of Mr. Oscar Williams who has applied for a Guggenheim this year. He is without doubt a very real and important American poet and the help and encouragement a foundation like yours can give should do a great deal to keep his creative powers alive. His

---

1 An engagements book that Thomas used in 1952 is at Texas. Cleverdon is shown as visiting Laugharne on 17 and 18 October. On 19 October Thomas wrote 'SOLID WEEK ON LLAREGGUB TO FINISH IT'. Then he altered 'WEEK' to '16 DAYS'.
2 J. A. Rolph, bookseller; author of *Dylan Thomas: A Bibliography*.

powerful imagery and unique personal idiom will add a permanent page to American poetry, I feel sure. I don't know of any poet in America, who has not yet received a Guggenheim, who deserves it more than Mr. Williams. I fervently pray that you will see your way clear to awarding him a fellowship so that he can write his new book of poems.

Sincerely yours,
Dylan Thomas

MS: *Indiana (typescript, signed by Thomas)*

GWYN JONES
October 28 1952   Boat House Laugharne Carmarthenshire

Dear Gwyn Jones,
Thank you & your wife very much indeed for asking me to stay with you when I come up to read poems to the Arts Society on November 12th.[1] I'd love to. Looking forward to seeing you again after so many cruel, fattening, short, delicious, or abysmal, years.

Sincerely,
Dylan Thomas

MS: *National Library of Wales*

E. F. BOZMAN
28 Oct 1952   Boat House Laugharne Carmarthenshire

Dear Bozman,
You wanted me to send back this written copy of the Prologue: for an Exhibition of Books. Sorry I haven't anything else but stacks of worksheets.

Sincerely,
Dylan Thomas

MS: *(J. M. Dent)*

PRINCESS CAETANI
6 November 1952   The Boat House Laugharne Carmarthenshire
Wales

My dear Marguerite Caetani,
It was beautiful to have your letter, and it made me a hundred times more ashamed, if that were possible, of my wretched, long, dark silence. Your letter was so warm, and good, as though I had never been barbarously

1 Gwyn Jones was then Professor of English at University College, Aberystwyth.

bad to you at all, and as though, almost, I was forgiven for the breaking of promises, the filthy discourtesy incomprehensible to me also, even the whole dead year's dumb insult itself. It was beautiful to hear from you. I don't deserve one warm word but only bashing on the head and then forgetting cold as ice. I don't understand why I never wrote, why I never wrote if only to *explain*, to explain why I could not, at that time, in spite of my promises, finish the second half of my piece for you. Many times I began a letter, and then put it aside because the piece was not finished. And the drafts of letters piled up, and time lapped on and thickened, putting on skins of distance, and daily, and even more so nightly, I grew more ashamed of my silence and more angry with my procrastination until, at last, I couldn't write at all. I buried my head in the sands of America: flew over America like a damp, ranting bird; boomed and fiddled while home was burning; carried with me, all the time, my unfinished letters, my dying explanations and self-accusations, my lonely half of a loony maybe-play, in a heavy, hurtful bunch. These ostrich griefs were always with me, and whispered loudest in the late night when, indeed, I was all sand. 'Put it off, put it off', 'It's too late now', 'You can never be forgiven', 'The past is as dead as you'll be', 'Burn the daft drafts, unwind the half-play in your head so that nothing's left', 'Forget, you damned Welshcake, for doom'll nibble you down to the last loud crumb', 'Strangle your litter of wits in a sack, and splash!'—these agenbite-deadeners[1] did their long-night worst, but the little voice in the dark, oh, throb, throb, throb it went across Kansas and in all the ovens of the hotel bedrooms. (These pages, I think, are wilting in the grey nearly permanent drizzle that sighs down on to this town and through the birdscratched matchboard roof into my wordsplashed hut. It isn't rain, it must be remorse. The whole fishy bay is soaked in guilt like the bad bits of poems-not-to-be oozing to the marrow on the matchsticked floor, and the half-letters curling and whining in the warped drawers. I'm writing this guilty noise in a cold pool, on a November afternoon, in mists of depression. Forgive me even for this, if you can. I find my pitiful wallow in the drizzle of regret an indulgence I can't pity. This weather gets me like poverty: it blurs and then blinds, creeps chalky and crippling into the bones, shrouds me in wet self, rains away the world.)

I can't explain why I didn't write to explain why I couldn't finish the piece. (No, I can't explain. When I try to explain my fear, the confused symbols grow leaden and a woolly rust creeps over the words. How can I say it? I can't. I can say: One instinct of fear is to try to make oneself as little, as unnoticeable, as possible, to cower, as one thinks, unseen and anonymous until the hunt is past. My fearful instinct is to bloat myself like a frog, to magnify my unimportance, to ring a bell for a name, so that, as I bluster and loom twice my size, the hunt, seeing me monstrous, bays by after different & humbler prey. But that is not what I mean: the symbols have wet-brain, the words have swallowed their tongues.)

1 'Remorse-deadeners'. See page 449, Vol I.

All that I can't explain. But why I didn't finish the piece there and then, as I said I would, is another matter. I was, as you know, leaving home—though, am, miraculously, home again now in this tumbling house whose every broken pane and wind-whipped-off slate, childscrawled wall, rainstain, mousehole, knobble and ricket, man-booby-and-rat-trap, I know in my sleep. I was leaving for ever, it seemed, had nowhere to go, nothing to go with, and, after you had wonderfully helped me to pay off some of my many debts here, I went to London, which, to me, is nowhere, and lived by odd reviews—and they were odd, too—odder broadcasts, pretending to women's clubs, putting off, putting off, all the nasty time, the one thing I wanted to do: finish my piece for you, and make my peace. But nothing could happen. Then I went to the States with my luggage of dismays and was loudly lost for months, peddling and bawling to adolescents the romantic agonies of the dead. I made money, and it went, and I returned with none; and once more, with the unfinished letters, poems, and play weighing much more heavily now on a mind nearly out of its mind with its little, mountainous anxieties and aches, reviewed, begged, lectured, broadcast, waited, with no hope, for the time when I could come back here and write truly again. I waited, and I put off, full of fear and wishes.

It is all a very inadequate explanation, and it cannot call itself an excuse, and indeed my fears are inexcusable though very real to me in their mean, mad way. And my talk, though terribly but weakly true, of 'putting off' all the time, is terribly putting off, I know.

These are the reasons, however—and expressed in depression and with little hope of them being believed or thought worthy—for my silence and my broken promises. About John Davenport and René Char I had heard nothing until your letter; and, even if I had heard, how could that, in any way in the world, affect you and me: your goodness to me, your faith in me, and my affection and gratitude kept, so it would appear, so obstinately secret?

I'm trying to work again now, and faithfully promise you the rest of the thing, and whatever other work I have, by, at the latest, the first of February. I won't fail you. Or have I joined forever the folds of the snarling and letting-down black once-friendly sheep? Oh, I do hope not.

It is so difficult for me to live and keep my family alive. There are many petty jobs which would make me just not enough money for tradesmen and rent, for clothes and school, for parents, shoes, and cigarettes, but these petty jobs, by their nature and by the time they claim, stop me writing as I would wish to write. But how, without these jobs, am I to live, to write, at all? These problems keep me treadmilling small nightmares all the waking nights.

About another visit to the States, I don't know. Though I can only play a poet there, and not make poetry, yet there I can, if only for a few months, live and send money home. I may have to go again. I cannot go on thinking all the time of butchers and bakers and grocers and cobblers and rates and rents until I bleed. After I have finished what I am now working on, I may have to give up writing altogether. (My need—as I imagine it—to write, may be all conceit. The bellows that fan the little flicker is nothing but wind, after all. And writing is certainly not one of the ancient secrets of the head-shrinking tribes. Ach, my endless bleating of private woes because I am not 'allowed' to write, as though the trees would grow inward, like toenails, if I renounced this passion for self-glorification. 'Peace, let me write. Gag the tradesmen, I must write. Alms, for the love of writing.' Perhaps I should be better off pulling teeth. But even this momentary disgust I blame upon the weather. And even this disgust is 'material for writing' just as trees, and toenails, and glorification, and teeth.) I think it's time to stop this. I wanted, at first, only to say that I am profoundly ashamed of my silence and of my broken promises, and that I will not fail you again, and that I do, with all the bloody muscle of my heart, ask for your forgiveness. But the letter got caught up with my despairs, though, always, I want, one day, to write you a happy letter. Because I am very often happy, and not always, here by the sea, without cause.

Please forgive me, and try to trust me again.

The old, cold pool of the day is a little warmer now.

Yours ever,
Dylan

MS: Camillo Caetani Foundation

MIMI JOSEPHSON[1]

7 Nov 1952.   Boat House   Laugharne   Carmarthenshire
                                              Laugharne 68

Dear Mimi Josephson,

I was, honest to God, and in spite of my 'idiosyncracy' that I do not answer letters, about to write to you. You'll see, from the word in quotes, that Dent's have passed on your letter to me.

And isn't it awful, but I'm afraid I *won't* be staying in London after Monday the 17th. I'm going up to London on the 14th, and will be about that night and on the night of the 15th. If you could be in town then, let's have a drink. Otherwise, what about coming down here—not really to be recommended—or to Swansea some time soon. Yes, Swansea best, as I love any excuse for going there. That sounds ungallant, but I don't mean it. The thing, anyway, would be to have a drink together, in Swansea or in London 14th or 15th (evenings). Do let me know which is best for you, and I'm sorry I didn't write before.

Sincerely,
Dylan Thomas

MS: Location unknown

1 Mimi Josephson was a freelance journalist in Cardiff, interested in poetry and poets.

MIMI JOSEPHSON
[telegram, 15 November 1952, Laugharne]

FRIGHTFULLY SORRY IMPOSSIBLE LAST MOMENT MEET SWANSEA
TOMORROW WRITING. DYLAN THOMAS

Original: Location unknown

MIMI JOSEPHSON
Fri 21 [November] 52   Boat House   Laugharne

Quickly, and with much disappointment: I can't turn up this Saturday in
S'sea as I'm in bed with bronchitis I caught—if it is a thing you catch—in
London from which I've only just returned. Many apologies & regrets.
Thank you, a lot, for the poem and the terrifying things it says. As soon as
I'm audible again—I can't speak at all now, only croak,—& out & about, I'll
get in touch with you. And this will be quite soon, I hope. Awfully sorry
again.

Dylan Thomas

MS: Location unknown

GWYN JONES
21 Nov 1952 [postcard]   Laugharne

Thank you both, a lot, I loved being there, you were awfully kind, I had a
fine audience at the reading, and the memories of Icelandic firewater[1]
lasted well until Shrewsbury. I've just come back from a loud week in
London, with bronchitis and an overpowering sense of fear. I hope never to
move again from this wet lost spot—except, of course, to Aberystwyth and
Iceland. Hope to see you again soon,

Dylan

MS: National Library of Wales

1 Gwyn Jones was an authority on Icelandic literature.

A. G. PRYS-JONES[1]

21 November 1952   Boat House   Laugharne   Carmarthenshire

Dear A. G. Prys-Jones,

First of all, do please forgive me for not answering your dizzyingly kind letter long before this, and for not acknowledging the typescript of the review—a review I am quite dumb before. I've been away in London, no letters were forwarded from Laugharne, and in that ghastly city I caught so much cold I'm still croaking and snuffling about the house like an old, slippered crow.

It was extremely good of you to send on the full copy of the review,—but in face of its staggering praise of my poems, what can I say? Cold 'thank you', even, could sound damnably immodest, as though perhaps I were thanking you for something which I expected, something I thought my due. Which is light years from the case. I was amazed at the praise; honoured by the constructive work and care which had gone into the appreciation of these often absurdly difficult poems; and, of course, delighted by the fact that you understood, so deeply, the underlying purpose and direction of the stuff itself—even though some of the poems, and many of the passages and lines, I had, I know, made impenetrable to others by my own tortuous ignorance of the particular dark in which I was trying to move.

Yes, amazed, honoured, & delighted, that's all I can say. And thank you, too. (But I could have written so much more freely if you had damned the book to little wild bits.)

I'm hoping to have a Collected Stories, including some new ones and many that have appeared only in small, forgotten magazines, at the end of next year. My next book will be pretty awful: a film-scenario I wrote some years ago, which no-one would film, and which Dents seem to think is worth printing, as a story in itself. I just don't know: it's a long time ago & all over to me. It will be called 'The Doctor & The Devils'. And I'm also hoping to bring out an extravagant play, as yet unfinished & maybe the radio will do it first, about a day's life in a small town in a never-never Wales. It sounds very ordinary, but it isn't that anyway, it's odd as anything, & I'm enjoying writing it. No title yet, only an unprintable one.

Once again, but never finally, all my thanks and regards.

Very sincerely yours,
Dylan Thomas

MS: Texas

1 Arthur Glyn Prys-Jones (1888–1987), educationist and writer, reviewed Thomas's *Collected Poems*, published 10 November, in the Cardiff *Western Mail*.

STEPHEN SPENDER
22 November 1952   Boat House   Laugharne   Carmarthenshire

Dear Stephen,

Were you at Edith's on Monday? I couldn't turn up, I was sick and wretched though I wanted very much to see you and Natasha again and to say goodbye to Edith, and now that I'm more or less home again I'm wretcheder than ever. I seem to be finally caught and tangled. I knew, when I was in London helping to raise Cain,[1] that I had left scores of unsettled debts behind me and that there were several summonses on the way. Then, on Monday morning, more dreadful letters were forwarded. I got back here to more bills, and to hear that the bailiffs will be moving in unless I pay what I can never pay because I have no money at all, even for bread or cigarettes but have to borrow the shillings for these. The bailiffs will be moving in because I can't pay enough, on account, of the income-tax I owe on money I earned, and spent, in America in 1950. And I have nothing to go on with day to day.

There's no need to write out a hideously long list of all I owe and all I must pay at once at once because I'm not asking you for anything but—*Do* you know anyone who could help me *now*? I don't know anybody. I can't write properly. I can't write anything anyway, I can't work or sleep because of this. From all I earn, anyway, the Income Tax, for that damned American trip, take 75 per cent & will now take everything. Of course I've no savings, and this house isn't mine to sell. Only immediate help can save me from I don't know and I can't say because I have never been so full of despair nor Caitlin neither. Do you know anyone you can ask? I can provide that anyone with a real long row of my debts so that he can see that it isn't for me to spend. I can't go on like this. I'm used to living up and down and mostly down, but this is over the edge and the end. I've been helped before, in the past, & that was wonderful. But I've never needed it as I need it now. I'm sorry that my first letter for so long to you should be like this, but I don't know who to turn to and perhaps you do know someone. *Surely* there is someone—though I'm sure I don't know why. It's nice, I suppose, to be overpraised, as I've been recently, but it makes this despair much worse, if that were possible and I suppose it always is, to know that those over-words were about somebody quite else, somebody I don't know at all, and not about who I am and what I am and the hating, unwanting where-I-am, and all the misery because I haven't a couple of hundred pounds or so and never bloody will. (Here they are, and I did want to keep them out, near-hysteria and rage and selfpity.) Please help if you can. And *surely, surely* there's someone somewhere, I'll keep on saying to myself till I hear from you.

Love to you and Natasha,
Dylan

I'm sending this to John Raymond at the New Statesman to send on to you.

MS: Houghton

1 Sitwell's 'Shadow of Cain'.

A. J. HOPPÉ
22 Nov 1952   Boat House   Laugharne   Carmarthenshire

Dear Mr. Hoppé,

Many apologies for not returning, & commenting on, the rough design & blurb for 'The Doctor & The Devils' long before this. I've been away in London, unfortunately no letters were forwarded to me there, & since my return I've been in bed with bronchitis.

I think the rough design is adequate, if not exciting. But the sub-title doesn't seem [what] we want at all. I've been trying to think of others— such as, A Film Without Pictures—but none was successful. But I don't think, anyway, the suggested subtitle should stand. What is a film scenario anyway but a story written for films, as the script of a play is a story for the stage. One might as well say, 'A Story In A Stage Play'. I may be wrong indeed, & scenario may mean something else. But the subtitle on this jacket does seem to me, at least, awkward & repetitive.

Wouldn't it be possible to have the jacket without any subtitle *at all*? and let the blurb say in what form 'The Doctor & The Devils' is written?

I know you want to sell this to general readers of fiction, & perhaps readers of thrillers, & that some suggestion, on the jacket, that [it] *is* fiction would be a help. But I think myself that if you're going to try to combine 'story' & 'scenario' on the jacket you're going to find it very difficult; & reviewers will have a fairly easy time picking whatever subtitle you choose to bits.

Yes, really, for me, no subtitle on the jacket. The blurb straightaway *does* say, 'D & D' is written in such & such a form, & is 'a gripping' story about murder. So much for readers of general fiction & thrillers.

I notice that in neither the blurb nor the brief note for the half-title is there any mention of Donald Taylor. I know that he & Dents have come to some arrangement as to the use of his name, but shouldn't it be referred to, even in passing, in the blurb? In the 3rd paragraph of the blurb, for instance, if you put after 'two things stand out . . . in this scenario', just the words, 'which is based on a story-line of Donald Taylor'—wouldn't that meet the case? I don't, of course, know what sentence Dent's & Taylor had arranged to cover his share in the thing: mine was merely a suggestion.

What a pity, by the way, the *second* name for Robert Knox, the name thought of after the ms was in Dents hands, hadn't been used throughout. Thomas Rock is so much rockier, & nearer the original, than the wet, lame William Salter. It *would* make an awful difference, I think, to the whole story if its principal figure had a dynamic kind of name you could believe in & credit him with.[1]

But this letter's already too long.

Sorry again for the long delay.

                                        Yours sincerely,
                                        Dylan Thomas

MS: (J.M. Dent)

1 Dent deferred to Thomas's suggestions.

ELLEN KAY[1]
[late November 1952]

Dear Ellen,

Will this ever reach you? There's one of your names missing, too, and the typed poems I have of yours, with all your names, are somewhere else.

It was lovely to see you, if only for a moment, after I'd helped to raise Cain that Sunday. I had to go off with a lot of awful people because I'd promised.

I shall be in London, on this Friday evening, the 28th. Would you like to meet me? I wish you would. I shall be in a pub. Now which pub? Do you know the Salisbury, next door to the New Theatre in St. Martin's Lane? I'll wait there from six till seven.

Or, if you get this and can't come, will you ring Primrose 0529 some time on Friday. I won't be there but you can leave a message. And I'll ring up there as soon as I arrive in London from Cambridge, where I'm just going.

This sounds so complicated; and it would be so simple if you *could* come to the Salisbury, this Friday evening, between six and seven.

Yours,
Dylan

MS: Pierpont Morgan Library

JOHN BELL[2]
2nd December 1952   Boat House   Laugharne   Carmarthenshire

Dear Mr. Bell,

Thank you very much for your letter. I'm very interested indeed in your suggestion that I should write for children, a book of the old stories of Wales; and though I've never written for children, or thought about it, I really would like to try: especially on such themes.

My trouble is one of time. I've a prose-book to finish for a publisher—I've only very recently begun it—before I can touch anything else. The book's overdue, badly, already, and I must get down to that and nothing else. This will take me some months; I'm afraid I can't say exactly how many. After that, I'd be delighted to start on the Welsh legends: to start, anyway,

---

1 Ellen de Young Kay (b. 1930) was an aspiring poet, who met Thomas when he read at Mills College in Oakland, California, April 1950. She saw him a number of times over the next year or two, in America and London, and said that perhaps she was 'the only woman who went out with him in two continents but never went to bed with him'. She was later an Episcopalian nun of the Order of St Helena.
2 Of Oxford University Press. The proposal was for a book of 'Welsh Fairy Tales', but it was never begun.

reading the old collections of them, gathering & selecting. But all this may be far too vague for you.

My agent, by the way, is David Higham, of Pearn, Pollinger, & Higham, 39–40 Bedford Street, Strand, W.C.2. And details—if you felt, after this unsatisfactory letter, that you could wait until I'd finished this commissioned book I'm working on now—would have to be gone into with him. But I *would* appreciate it if you would let me know, too, what you think. Could you? Thanks again.

Yours sincerely,
Dylan Thomas

MS: Oxford University Press

JAMES JONES[1]
2 December 1952   Boathouse Laugharne Carmarthenshire

My dear Jim,
    It was fine to hear from you after the centuries that have passed since Warmley, the impromptu chambermusic, complete with Woolworth whistles & saucepan lids, the great unknown composer Dr. Percy, your wonderful hot jazz, and the banging on the wall of the Careys (wasn't it?) next door. I don't often see Dan, though we're less than fifty miles apart: when I do get to Swansea, we drink champagne, go to horror films, and (sometimes) have a little nap on Constitution Hill on the way back to Rosehill Terrace. I wish we all could have met when you were down in Swansea last summer. Fred Janes I see even less often than Dan; and Tom Warner has disappeared, to me, altogether. I often see, in the Evening Post, pictures of the Rev. Leslie Norman,[2] Vicar of St. Somewhere, who—remember?—had a cleft palate and was an authority on tramcars.
    I'll be listening to Dan's Symphony on the 17th.
    Thanks a lot for writing. Your telephone exchange is, I notice, rather reminiscent of Warmley.
    Hope to be seeing you,

Ever,
Dylan

MS: Texas

1 Dan Jones's brother, a journalist.
2 Vicar of Christchurch and the chaplain at Swansea Prison. The cleft palate seems to be an invention.

MR EVANS[1]
3 December 1952   Boat House   Laugharne   Carmarthenshire

Dear Mr. Evans,

I can't tell you how very deeply disappointed I am not to be able to make my visit, as President, on Friday; and I do wish it had been possible for me to let you know this miserable news far sooner, so that any preparations could have been postponed. As it is, I'm afraid I've left it to the last moment. I could not be more sorry. My father, who lives in the same village, has been blind and very ill for a long time; but, in the last few days, his condition has grown desperate, and I cannot possibly leave him, as my mother is a permanent invalid and cannot take care of him at all.[2] I *had* hoped that perhaps a slight improvement in his extremely serious illness would allow me to make my visit to Bangor, and, with that in mind, put off writing to you until this last moment. But he is weaker than ever today, and delirious, and his doctor has just told me that I should be on hand day & night. I know you will understand; and I do hope you know, too, how much I was looking forward to the whole evening.

Is it possible for the Dinner & Address to be postponed, and not cancelled? I could come up any time you suggest in the New Year.

My deep apologies again,

Yours sincerely,
Dylan Thomas

MS: National Library of Wales

CAITLIN THOMAS

For Caitlin Thomas on Her Birthday[3]
8th December 1952, from her Husband.

Caitlin I love you
And I always will.
I love you in Brown's Hotel,
The Cross House, Sir John's Hill,
London, New York, bed.
In any place, at any time,
Now, then, live, dead—

1 Thomas's host-to-be at an unidentified function in North Wales.
2 Jack Thomas's eyesight began to fail at the end of his life, although his son had been describing him as blind for months. As with the 'blind eyes' and 'dying of the light' in 'Do not go gentle', the poem written to his sick father almost two years earlier, Dylan was rearranging events to suit his purpose.
3 Caitlin Thomas was thirty-nine.

> This is all that I
> Have to say
> On your birthday,
> My Caitlin:
> As sure as death is sure,
> So is my love for you everlasting[1]

MS: *Maurice Neville*

ELLEN KAY
9 December 1952   Boat House   Laugharne   Carmarthenshire

My dear Ellen,
   I hoped that that was what had happened. I don't mean I hoped my letter would be too late for you to come to meet me, but I mean that I hoped it was the lateness of the letter and not anything else, such as your just not wanting to come and meet me. I mean—but you know what I mean. I was very sorry to miss you, and moped, and snarled at every one I saw, and cursed America—and especially San Francisco—and drank limitless pints of liverish liquorice unlibidinous Guinness, and was melancholy, tragic, and a bit sick—like an old, round adolescent. But, even if my note had reached you, it would have given you very little time. As soon as I know I'm going to London next, I'll give you plenty of warning, and if you don't come I'll cut my throat on a rusty poem. I don't know if I can get to London before Christmas. I want to, very much, but am too poor now. By poor, I mean, simply, I have no money at all. If I had, I would come to London. What is maddening is, that usually I am in London, where I do not want to be, every couple of weeks; and now that I want to be there, I can't. (It makes me cross, too, to think that you have been in England so long, and that I never knew it. You said you wrote. Did you write to the Savage Club? I haven't been there this year. I am a fool. I should die.) Thank you for your sonnet. I really did like it a lot, and it was lovely to have it, and to know that it is mine. 'Esq.' looks wonderful, like a little silk hat. I liked the way the poem moves; and most of all, perhaps, the movement of the first six lines. I hope I can somehow see you very soon. If not, then in January.
                                         Yours
                                         Dylan

MS: *Pierpont Morgan Library*

1 Caitlin kept a draft version of this poem in her handbag (the Berg Collection acquired it after her death). It has no dedication. In the draft line 4 of the second verse has 'My darling Caitlin'. The last two lines appear as four draft lines:
> As ~~cert~~ sure as death,
> So is my undying love for you.
> As ~~man's~~ sure as death is sure,
> So is my love for you everlasting.

STEPHEN SPENDER
9 December 1952   Boat House   Laugharne   Carmarthenshire

My dear Stephen,

This isn't about the same miserable subject as my earlier letter—though the situation is, if that were possible, worse than it was then, and it certainly looks as though it's going to be worms and water for Christmas— but only to thank you, very much indeed, for your notice, of my Collected Poems, in the Spectator.[1] You were, as you know, the very first person ever to write to me about a poem of mine; and this is now the clearest, most considered and sympathetic, and, in my opinion, truest, review that I have ever seen of my writing. I mean, that your statement of understanding of my aim and method seems to me to be altogether true; and no critic has attempted, in writing about my most uneven and unsatisfactory work, to set out, plainly, the difference between the writing of poetry towards words and the writing of poetry from words—though that's, of course, oversimpli- fication. No writer before you; and I do want, please, to thank you again very much.

I do hope, by the way, that my first, almost despairing letter, wasn't a dreadful nuisance to you, and didn't seem an impertinence. I had, & have, no-one to turn to, and felt sure you would understand my present, beastly difficulties.

Please thank Natasha for her telegram. I will write her separately, if or if not this wretchedness is somehow lifted or even eased.

Oh, & I forgot. I'm not influenced by Welsh bardic poetry. I can't read Welsh.[2]

Yours,
Dylan

MS: Houghton

JOHN ALEXANDER ROLPH
11 December 1952   Boat House   Laugharne   Carmarthenshire

Dear Alexander Rolph,

So very sorry not to have written long before. Thank you, a lot, for your letters, and your awfully kind offer to try to get hold of any difficult-to-get items for me should I need them: I won't forget that. You said you were

---

1 Spender called him 'a romantic revolting against a thin contemporary classical tendency ... In [his] poetry the reader feels very close to what Keats yearned for—a "life of sensations" without opinions and thoughts'.
2 Spender: 'His poetry is not so much influenced by, as soaked in, childhood experiences of the Bible, and doubtless, also, Welsh bardic poetry.'

moving to Weybridge in the new year. When? I don't think I'll be in London until about the 12th or 13th of January: about that date I'm helping to raise Cain again, or his Shadow rather, this time without Edith S. and at the Albert Hall. If you haven't moved by that time, do let's fix up to meet for some drinks one evening round then.

I'm afraid I'm going to be nearly no good at all to you in answer to these questions about when & where etc. My memory's bad, I keep no files or old numbers of periodicals.[1]

New English Weekly. Yes, perhaps I did contribute to it *after* 1935, though I'm not sure. I seem to remember 2 poems and another prose piece than 'After the Fair'. And a regular novel review in, about, 36, 37, or 38.

Of the periodicals you mention, all, I think, are finished. And 'Caravel' was the only one I believe to be not British. If you like, I could put you in touch with Ruthven Todd, in New York, whose knowledge of these fly-by-night magazines *used* to be enormous.

Do you know my American selection of poems & stories called 'The World I Breathe', brought out by New Directions in 1939. There are 4 stories in that that don't appear in 'Map of Love'. Of these, one, 'A Prospect of The Sea', was, I think, printed in a Penguin of Modern Welsh Stories. Again, I don't know if it was reprinted from a periodical: I rather think I sent, on request, the manuscript to the editor. 'The Burning Baby', also in 'The World I Breathe', was published in Roger Roughton's 'Contemporary Prose & Verse', just before the war.

A London magazine called 'Janus' published a story of mine called 'The Horse's Ha', which hasn't been in book form yet. And another little magazine, called 'Yellow Jacket', edited by Constantine FitzGibbon (who's brought out a couple of novels fairly recently) printed 2 stories, called, as far as I remember, 'The Vest' and 'The True Story'.

Robert Herring's 'Life & Letters ToDay' printed, I think, 2 or 3 stories, including one called 'The Lemon', which also has not yet been in a book.

The Booster was edited by Henry Miller in Paris before the war: I'm afraid I don't know when. (Miller's address is, I think, quite simply Big Sur, California.) There were certainly very few numbers of it brought out under Miller. It was, I think, originally a little 'organ' run by, or for, American business-men visiting Paris, full of rotarian-like gossip. Miller, as an American exile living in Paris, somehow got temporary hold of this bit of hail-fellowry, & immediately printed Alfred Perlès, Lawrence Durrell, very odd drawings, himself, & one contribution by me—all to the surprise of the subscribers.

The Map of Love. My memory's almost gone here. *Some* of the stories, I believe, *were* printed in periodicals. One of them, at least, I am sure appeared in 'New Stories', a brown magazine, & was later reprinted in one of E. J. O'Brien's Best Stories of The Year, or whatever he called it. 'The Orchards' was, I think, published in Elizabeth Bowen's 'Modern Short Stories', which was an early Penguin, though whether she reprinted it from

1 There are some errors in Thomas's account.

the 'Map of Love' or from a magazine I can't remember.

And I feel pretty certain 'The Tree' was published somewhere. Maybe in the N.E. Weekly.

Any other things I can remember about poems & stories—especially about stories in The Map of Love—I'll send you.

Oh, I do remember. 'The Mouse & The Woman', in 'The Map of Love', was, I'm fairly sure, published in 'transition' just before the war.

Enough to go on with?

Let me know about the date of your going to Weybridge, & whether we can meet in London round about Jan. 13.

> Yours,
> Dylan Thomas

PS. Some prose was printed by Keidrych Rhys in his 'Wales', now also defunct. 'Prologue To An Adventure', printed in 'The World I Breathe' appeared in one of the New Directions yearly anthologies—& also somewhere, forgotten, else. 'The Holy Six' & 'The School For Witches', in the same 'W. I Breathe', haven't been published in periodicals.

MS: Texas

MARY DAVIES[1]
16 December 1952

Dear Miss Davies,

You will, I know, be very sorry to hear that my father died today. It was a very peaceful death.[2]

You will excuse my mother not writing personally to you, at this moment. She is bearing up, however, wonderfully well, and sends her fondest love to you.

> Yours
> Dylan

MS: Location unknown

*HETTY AND KEN OWEN[3]
16 December 1952   The Pelican   Laugharne   Carmarthenshire

Dear Hetty & Ken,

You will, I know, be very sorry to hear that Dad died today. It was, thank God, a very peaceful death.

Dad will be cremated at Pontypridd. I'm afraid I don't yet know exactly

1 A family friend in Carmarthen.
2 D. J. Thomas was seventy-six.
3 Friends of Florence and Jack Thomas.

when, but will put a notice [in] the Western Mail. Mother, who is bearing up wonderfully well and bravely, says that she doesn't want any flowers. But she would, I know, *very* much love to see you.

> Affectionately,
> Dylan

MS: Reginald Evans

*HUMPHREY SEARLE
[postcard] 29 December 52   Boat House   Laugharne   Carmarthenshire

Fine for the 13th[1] I'll come up to London on the 11th or 12th and will ring you then. Do you really think it best for me to be on the stage this time? One of the many advantages of being off-stage with a mike last time was that the separate conductor of ours had time to slow & speed us up when necessary. But of course I don't mind, & will willingly speak on the stage if thought best. I hardly think I can do without the loudspeaker system in the Albert Hall, as quite a lot of the words have got to come through terrifically loud noise. But of course we'll try, see, & hear. Incidentally, I haven't heard yet from the orchestra's secretary about my fee, although in reply to him, I wrote quite a long & reasoned demand (though not for a specific sum). Thanks a lot for writing to me about my father.

> Yours,
> Dylan

MS: British Library (Searle papers)

VERNON WATKINS
29 December 1952   Boat House   Laugharne   Carmarthenshire

Dear Vernon,
    Thank you so much. I miss him a great deal.
    This is only a little—after, years?—to say Happy New Year to you & Gwen & the children.
    I hope I'll see you soon. I am going to read 3 ballads of yours from Swansea on the 14th of January. Can we meet for lunch that day?
    It will be wonderful to see you again.

> Ever,
> Dylan

MS: British Library

1 Another performance of 'The Shadow of Cain', this time at the Royal Albert Hall.

E. F. BOZMAN
29 December 1952   Boat House   Laugharne   Carmarthenshire

Dear E. F. Bozman,

You wrote me, on the 11th, about John Alexander Rolph, modern rare bookseller, who's planning a bibliography of my writings and wants to know if you would publish it. And you wrote back to him, you said, & told him you'd prefer to wait a few years. I shd think so, too. Let's have something to bibliographize first. But as to his wanting to 'establish a priority on his own behalf' to be my bibliographer, I shd certainly say, Yes. I've been in correspondence with him for quite a time, have met him once or twice, and he seems excellent, to me, & very keen. He knows more than almost anyone wd want to know about the scores of fly-by-night little reviews of the thirties, in which such a lot of my stories etc. appeared; & I think that when and if ever the time comes when a bibliography of my at-present all too meagre writings could be considered saleable, then Rolph is the very man.

Thank you again for your Christmas greetings, for the Fables, and for your kindness in allowing me to anticipate such a *very* welcome chunk of my next spring's royalties.

By the way: Have you thought again of having that insipid 'William Salter' changed to rugged 'Thomas Rock' in the 'Doctor & The Devils'? I know the expense wd be considerable; but the script wd, in my opinion, gain *enormously* in strength & distinction just from that alteration. I do think it important.

Yours sincerely,
Dylan Thomas

PS. Donald Taylor sent a copy of 'Doctor & Devils' to James Bridie once, for his opinion, & because Bridie had dealt with *exactly* the same theme in that wellknown play of his whose name I've now forgotten. Bridie liked it, but the first thing he said, as far as I remember, was: *Do* change Knox's name to something good & strong. I shd, of course, have done it before the manuscript was submitted to you. But I'm mentioning this now only because of my great respect for Bridie's opinion on anything, big or small, of dramatic value.

D. T.

PSS The name of Bridie's play was, of course, 'The Anatomist'. I had not read it when I helped to write Doctor & Devils, but, reading it later, I found a *great* deal of resemblance in the treatment.

D. T.

MS: (J. M. Dent)

W. MORGAN JAMES[1]
30 December 1952   The Boat House   Laugharne   Carmarthenshire

Dear Mr. Morgan,

   My mother has asked me to write to you, to thank you, very deeply, for your kind and consoling letter on my dear father's death. I and my family wish to join her in thanking you. Your tribute to my father's teaching I very much appreciate and shall always remember. I was taught Shakespeare and Milton by him in the old Grammar School, and owe my first love of poetry to him. He had been suffering for a long time, and towards the end of his life was nearly blind.

   Uncle Arthur died in 1947, and my father's ashes were buried with his.

   It was good to hear from one who had known not only my father but my grandfather as well, whom I never knew.

   Thank you again for your letter, and your prayer that we may be blessed & sustained in our sorrow.

Yours very sincerely,
Dylan Thomas

MS: National Library of Wales

OSCAR WILLIAMS
Jan 5 1953   Boat House   Laugharne   Carmarthenshire

Dear Oscar,

   Love to you & Gene from Cat & me, always.

   This is only a little note, because Christmas here has been so confused that I'm still $\frac{1}{2}$ daft with it. My father, in great pain, & blind, died a few days before Christmas, & I had a lot of sad business to attend to: I'm the only one left, if you exclude, as well you may, a sister in Bombay.[2] The children have been ill. Caitlin's pregnant again. The water pipes have burst & the house is flooded, etc. etc. And the etceteras are almost worse than the rest. So this, before a real letter, is only to say: Thank you, thank you, for the cheque for 150 dollars, previously unacknowledged, and for the last, December 8, cheque for 100 dollars. Oh, Mrs. Stephenson, would you were the first lady of the land, you old bag![3] *And, please,* I *would* like, *straightaway,* the balance due to me, on that piece of Chicagoanery, of 200 dollars. Without those cheques you've been whistling across the water, we couldn't have lived through these foul months.

   New York I am supposed to come to end of April; alone, maybe, at first, to be joined by Cat in the early summer.

1 An acquaintance of Jack Thomas, evidently not known to Dylan.
2 Nancy, aged forty-six, was seriously ill.
3 Ellen Borden Stevenson, misspelt by Thomas.

I return, signed, the Golden Treasury slip. You do me over-proud.
The 'Prologue' sheets I shall send this week, along with a short story.
Also, I received the Skin-Trade 198 dollars, praise be.[1]
(And am *longing* for the last Stephenson 200 dollars.)
No news now; just thank yous, please send, & all love.
Doctor & Devil is a bad book: an old commissioned filmscript. Let's all forget it.
What Guggenheim news?

> Again,
> Yours,
> Dylan

MS: Houghton

ALFRED JANES

5 Jan [1953]   Boat House   Laugharne   Carmarthenshire

Dear Fred,
Thank you, very very much indeed, for writing on my father's death. Poor old boy, he was in awful pain at the end and nearly blind. The day before he died, he wanted to get out of bed & go into the kitchen where his mother was making onion soup for him. Then, a few hours afterwards, he suddenly remembered everything, & where he was, & he said, 'It's full circle now'.
My mother is very good & brave about it; and she wants to thank you very much, as well, & to wish you a good New Year.
I do hope to see you soon.

> Ever,
> Dylan

MS: Location unknown

REV J. OLIVER STEPHENS

5th January 1953   Boat House   Laugharne   Carmarthenshire

Dear Professor Stephens,
My mother wants to thank you and your sister very very much indeed for your sympathy on my father's death and for your warm, consoling letter; and may I and my family join her too in thanking you with all our hearts. My father was in great pain and distress at the end, and nearly

---

1 The previous year, New American Library had bought rights in *Adventures in the Skin Trade* for $397.50. This was precisely calculated, 15,900 words at 2½ cents a word. The $198 was a 50 per cent payment.

blind; but though we wished him peace and rest, his death was a terrible loss to us all.

My mother knows you will forgive her for not, at this time, writing to you herself.

I do hope we shall meet again one day. I remember, with very much pleasure, our last all-too-brief meeting.

Thank you again, both of you, from all of us.

Yours sincerely,
Dylan

From a typescript. MS location unknown

E. F. BOZMAN
6 January 1953   Boat House   Laugharne   Carmarthenshire

Dear E. F. Bozman,

Thank you for your last letter of the 2nd of January, in which you mentioned the possibility of an autobiography, especially in relation to my early years. Well, of course, I have produced a more-or-less autobiography in my 'Portrait of The Artist As A Young Dog'. And I really haven't enough desire, or material, to try to write another. And the childhood broadcast you mentioned—I'm afraid I don't know which one it was—is one of only six similar broadcasts: not nearly enough for even the smallest book. These six were, incidentally: Two on *Memories of Christmas*,[1] one on *Memories of August Bank Holiday*, one called just *Memories of Childhood* & the other *Early One Morning*, and the other, in dramatic radio form, called *Return to Swansea*.

I have also a recent short story, about the adolescent period, called *The Followers*.[2]

In an American book of mine, published by New Directions, called 'The World I Breathe'—a book of verse and prose—there are five stories which haven't appeared in an English book: 2 of them haven't appeared in any periodical. These five are:

The Holy Six,
A Prospect Of The Sea,
The Burning Baby,
Prologue To An Adventure
The School for Witches

and are all very young & violent and romantic.

---

1 Only one radio essay was about Christmas; the companion piece, 'Conversation about Christmas', was written for *Picture Post*.
2 Published in *World Review* October 1952. It is a not very successful attempt to repeat the *Portrait* formula.

There are also, in periodicals, 4 stories of a similar kind:

> The Lemon,
> The Horse's Ha,
> The Vest,
> The True Story.

I think that the broadcast reminiscences, all fairly riotously innocent, *together* with the death-&-blood other group typified by the Burning Baby, would make an interesting volume: especially if somehow, through a longish introduction, through an introductory story, or through some as-yet-unthought-of prose-links, I could explain their origins & bring them closer together.[1]

If you would be interested in this, I could have the five stories from 'The World I Breathe' typed out, write to a friend on the B.B.C. to gather together the reminiscent broadcasts, of which, unfortunately, I have no copy, and ask John Alexander Rolph, my bibliographist-to-be, to find the four stories in the old, fled periodicals. Perhaps we could discuss this on the 20th or 21st.

> Yours sincerely,
> Dylan Thomas

This wd, I realize, be a hotchpotch of a book, but the separate items cd be introduced, in some way, so as to make them cohere into a kind of oblique autobiography: *a growing-up told (a) in stories written while growing up, and (b) in memories of childhood written when grown up.*

MS: (J. M. Dent)

*HUMPHREY SEARLE

[postcard] 6 Jan 1953   Boat House   Laugharne   Carmarthenshire

Thanks for the letter. John Croft wrote a couple of days ago, offering 25 guineas (plus $12\frac{1}{2}$ guineas for the broadcast) and, of course, I've written off accepting this. There has been no question of expenses from Wales–London & back mentioned as yet. The main reason I thought my presence on the stage unnecessary was the reaction of the audience, & the press, last time. No-one, for a moment, suggested that not seeing Edith & me was any loss. The whole piece is so hideously dramatic that the sight of a little fat speaker on the stage would, I think, detract from the dramatic value— (though it may, of course, add to the horror).[2] Anyway, I'll see you on the

---

1 Bozman, like Church before him, still found some of the early stories unpalatable. See note, page 586.

2 According to Searle in his memoirs, 'Quadrille with a Raven' (published on the internet), Thomas did appear on the stage. At a party afterwards he 'danced wildly . . . and stuffed sausage rolls down the ladies' cleavages'.

11th or 12th; will be staying with Bill,[1] I hope.

> Yours,
> Dylan

MS: British Library (Searle papers)

GWYN JONES
6 January 1953   Boat House   Laugharne   Carmarthenshire

My dear Gwyn,

Thank you for the letter and Adelphis,[2] and I'm very sorry not to have written much sooner. My father died last month, and the children were whining sick, and there was black wet Christmas, and I've been terribly busy failing to write one word of a more or less play set in a Wales that I'm sad to say never was, and as for money I've been up and down up and down for weeks like a prick in a box.

I liked the three stories very much indeed: real stories in wonderful words. And I hope to be able to say so, in a review, when Shepherd's Hey[3] comes out—along with a few carps about characterisation. Thank you a lot for sending them. Caitlin loved them too.

I haven't anything yet to send Ifor Evans, but will *as soon* as I have. It's good of you of both of you to want me to (as Fowler puts it).

I'm reading some poems of Vernon Watkins from S'sea on the 14th, if you ever listen in. And of course if you don't, I'll still be reading them. What do you think of his poetry? I forgot, sipping that Faxafloi water,[4] to ask you.

> All good wishes to both,
> Yours,
> Dylan

MS: National Library of Wales

A. G. PRYS-JONES
6 February 1953   Boat House   Laugharne   Carmarthenshire

Dear Prys,

Of course you can persuade me to come to the Cardiff Literary Society— but, oh, what a long time away! If living, then I'll boom, with pleasure, on December 10th, and thank you for asking me. Fee fine.

1 Bill McAlpine.
2 The magazine *Adelphi* was edited by a Welshman, Sir Ifor Evans (referred to later in the letter), who was seeking contributions.
3 A collection of stories by Gwyn Jones.
4 Faxafloi, Faxi's inlet, in Iceland. Gwyn Jones was serving schnapps.

Yes, the Foyle prize was certainly better than a slap in the belly with a wet poet.[1]

Looking forward to meeting you again; though before the end of the year, I hope. If in Cardiff at any time, may I give you a ring?

And thank you a lot, for sending me the two books. I like your own verse, and the Bible isn't bad either.

Very sorry I couldn't write to you much sooner than this: I've been in London, and letters weren't forwarded. Perhaps you have left Porthcawl by this time, but I'll take a chance.

Yours,
Dylan

MS: Texas

JOHN ARLOTT
6 Feb 1953   Boat House   Laugharne   Carmarthenshire

John,

Very many apologies. I've been away, missed your letter until today, and now am ill with flu, bronchitis, etc. croaking and snuffling. Thank you very much for the letter, for thinking about me, for suggesting that piece, & for pushing up the price. I'm awfully sorry I can't do it: not because I don't want to, but because I *daren't* promise that I could turn it out by mid-February: I'm in a tangle of doubts & debts, as well as shoved to the eyebrows with frogs' catarrh, and am disastrously behind in two commissioned jobs. But thanks a *great* deal for the offer of the job, which I'd like to do, & the money, which, dear, I'd simply adore.

Did I ever thank you for that bit of practical help you sent along so kind & so quick? If not, I should have very much indeed; and if so, I do it again.

Dylan

From a typescript. MS location unknown

DAVID HIGHAM
6 February 1953   Boat House   Laugharne   Carmarthenshire

Dear David,

From a sickbed of bronchitis and doubts, I croak my sincere apologies for not having answered letters. I feel awful. I've been away for some little time, trying to think straight, returned feeling more crooked than ever, tried to do 4 recordings from the S'sea BBC, failed entirely because of lack

---

1 The Foyle's Poetry Prize, worth £250, was awarded to Thomas for *Collected Poems*.

of voice, & coughed back to bed where I now am. I'll try to do the recordings (I suppose Jean Le Roy knows about them) again on Monday.

a) I'm writing, *really*, a *really* explanatory letter—& one which I hope will allow me grace—to Charles Fry this weekend; as soon as I get up.
b) Yes, please do go ahead with the O.U.P. agreement.[1] I want very much to do it.
c) My 'affairs in general' are in a hell of a mess, and thank you, very very very much, for being so willing to try to help me with them.[2] As soon as I possibly can—very soon; next week, I hope—I'll come up to London to see you. Could we meet outside the office, d'you think? For lunch somewhere? or a drink at the Savage?

Oh, splutter & bark, I'm full of toads & Friar's Balsam.

Apologies once more.
Dylan

MS: Texas

GLYN JONES
15 February 1953   Boat House   Laugharne   Carmarthenshire

My dear Glyn,
    Thanks very much for writing. So sorry not to have been able to answer at once: I've been away, in Swansea & in London. But I'm writing to Idris today. I've known him, off & on, and always, unfortunately, in little bits, for years & years; and I was terribly sorry to hear from Vernon, & from you, about his illness. I think he's a fine chap and a real poet, God bless him.[3]
    I'm so glad you liked being in Vernon's company. So do I. I saw him in Swansea only a few days ago & he talked about you then: a real sign of affection: as you know, he usually talks about nothing but poetry and its synonym, Yeats. Keidrych is, I see from the correspondence column in the Western Mail, ranting in Llandilo now. I don't know what happened to him & our Dumb Friends. Do you think something similar happened to his little charges as did to Carlyle's dog? Carlyle used to talk to it for hours, week after week, year after year, and at last it could bear it no longer &

---

1 The 'Welsh Fairy Tales'.
2 Higham had written on 8 January: 'If there is a crisis in your affairs that you would like to talk over with me, I'd be more than ready to do so.' Burdened by debts and broken promises to publishers, desolated by what he feared was a decline of his creative powers, Thomas had entered the last and bleakest period of his life. A letter that Caitlin Thomas wrote to their American friends, Oscar Williams and his wife Gene Derwood, on 9 February, gave a gloomy report. Dylan, she said, now preferred performing to writing. All he had to sell was either his rehashed adolescence, or promises for the future.
3 Idris Davis was dying of cancer.

threw itself out of the window. Have you read anywhere recently of a mass animal suicide?

By the way, is the poetry society you mentioned in your letter anything to do with Prys-Jones? Because if it is, I've agreed to go & read poems in Cardiff—invitation from Prys—some time in October. So perhaps we *will* get our annual hour. But I hope it's sooner.

> Ever
> Dylan

MS: Carbondale

JOAN BOWLES
15 Feb 1953   The Boat House   Laugharne   Carmarthenshire

Dear Miss Bowles,

Will you forgive me, please for not having answered your extremely kind and very welcome letter long before this? It's nearly a month since you sent it; but since then there have been all kinds of illnesses and little disasters happening here, and I really haven't been able to do anything much but grieve and sneeze. It was very good of you to write to me after I helped to raise Cain in the Albert Hall before such a tiring audience. And thank your friend for me, too, for encouraging you to write to me. I felt encouraged as well to think that you were so moved by the whole performance. Yes, the Radio Critics (whom I didn't hear, except at second hand, when they dug their little claws in me) are a mealy, genteel drawl and giggle of parasites. Glad you dislike them too.

Thanks again for all the nice things you said.

> Yours sincerely,
> Dylan Thomas

From a typescript. MS location unknown

CHARLES ELLIOTT[1]
15 February 1953   The Boat House   Laugharne   Carmarthenshire

Dear Mr Elliott,

Thank you very much for your letters. And will you thank the committee of the College English Society for their kindness? It was good of them to forgive me for mislaying, somehow, the original letter, & very nice of them to say that an early meeting cd be arranged—even one in the afternoon. I think poetry aloud sounds better (& often louder, too) in the

---

1 Secretary of the English Society at University College, Cardiff, where he was on the staff of the English department.

evenings; and so could you tell the committee I'd be glad if they could arrange a meeting, at the *usual* time for meetings, in the evening, about the middle of March some time? About money: it's not that my time's precious, but that money is to me. Can you pay ten guineas, plus Laugharne return-fare? Thanks again for writing. Will just a return of poems do, by the way, with a few comments?

Sincerely,
Dylan Thomas

MS: Columbia University

*IDRIS DAVIES
16th February 1953   The Boat House   Laugharne   Carmarthenshire

My dear Idris,

First Vernon Watkins in Swansea, only a few days ago, told me you'd been ill for a long time; and then, when I got home, there was a letter waiting me from Glyn with your address in it—an address which Vernon, of course, had lost in a bus or a teashop or a dream. (How has old Vernon managed to stay as a cashier in a Bank for twenty years? He told me he was often making little mistakes of a £1000 or so. 'They get frightfully annoyed', he said, 'but I can still add up three columns of figures at once, and I still play hockey for Mumbles, *and* I met Yeats.') I was terribly sorry to hear about your long illness. And God knows why I hadn't been told, by someone, about it before. If I was ill myself, and old friends and fellow-countrymen and poets like yourself didn't write me a line, I'd be furious. Please be furious with me for not writing before to say Hullo after such a very long time—railway station, 1946—and to send my greetings and to ask you if there is anything I can do at this beastly time. Books, bottles, old poems, bad advice? No, no, can I help in any way, especially about books? If there are any books you want and can't get hold, tell me, please: if I can't find them myself, I know a horrible man in London, whom people call, for obvious, and obscure, reasons, Auntie Jack, who can get one anything from Watson's unwritten poems to an indecently signed photograph of Matthew Arnold dead-drunk and naked. Don't forget, Idris: if there's anything, let me know, by letter or card or Rhymney pigeon or Glyn.

I said, a moment ago, that I just met Vernon in Swansea. I was there to record a series of four small selections of modern poetry for Aneirin Talfan, to be broadcast once a week from St. David's Day on. The first selection is, naturally, from Welsh poets—to hell with the Anglo-Welsh; I mean, in this case, Welshmen who write their poems in English—and I do hope you'll hear it. It's made up of: Vernon's 'The Collier'; your Bell-Poem from 'Gwalia Deserta'; Edward Thomas's 'Child On The Cliffs'; Alun Lewis's 'Letter from Sacco to his Son'; my own 'Ceremony After A Fire-Raid'; W. H. Davies's 'Child Lovers'; and Owen's 'Strange Meeting'. (Not in that order, though the programme does begin with Vernon and you). There are lots of objections to be made against this choice of poems, I know. 'The Collier' is not V's best poem by any means, and I myself prefer those of much thicker texture. I would rather read, of yours, a longer and—though these are almost certainly the wrong words—a more polemical and rhetorical piece, most likely from Angry Summer,[1] (though indeed the Bell Poem, for want of a proper title, is angry enough indeed). Edward Thomas is only somewhat of a Welshman, even though 'Child On The Cliffs' is experienced in Wales; Alun Lewis's Sacco poem is unlike anything else he wrote, and probably I should have read, instead, one of the Indian poems. I shouldn't include one of my own, specially a long & loud one; I know what people are apt to think & feel when an anthologist includes himself at grandiose length; and I remember only too well Oscar Williams's American anthology, 'Immortal Poems of the English Language', in which he put three big poems of his own, three of his wife's (Gene Derwood), and his own photograph on the back, facing Tennyson, Burns, Keats, Wordsworth, & Donne. And any claim we may make to Wilfred Owen as a Welshman has been repudiated, Anglo-Saxonly and indignantly, by his brother and, I think, his mother. I can defend this choice of poems only by saying that I think they all *sound* well, and that very much of them can be appreciated by a large public at a first hearing. I can't defend my patriotic annexing of Thomas & Owen; I like them very very much indeed, & that's all. I'm afraid you'll find the reading aloud of the poems inadequate—and I don't blame you if you use a much biting-er word than that: I was nervous, I had laryngitis, there was too little time, the studio was hot as a Turkish broth, this was the first of the series, I plead in semi-honest excuse. Perhaps the other three readings, mostly Yeats, Hardy, Lawrence, Auden, will sound less bumbling and breathless. Another perfectly good criticism of the choice of poems by Welshmen is: why didn't I put in more stuff by younger poets, such as Glyn Jones, John Ormond Thomas, R. S. Thomas. And to this I whimper, 'There wasn't room'. And, again, Irish or no, Graves should have appeared, or sounded, as well. And, for St. David's Day, why 'modern' at all? What about Vaughan, Traherne, Herbert, pretty 'Grongar Hill',[2] and the Welsh-influenced poems of Hopkins? And why not Keidrych & Lynette?[3] One answer, of course, to that last is, Why?

I hear your new book is coming out with Faber's this year; which is splendid. I'm going to order a copy straightaway; or even write for one free, if I can beg any periodical to let me review it—: (my review would be, there it is, read it; a chunk of genuine praise; and then a *lot* of quotations).

1 *The Angry Summer* (1943), a long poem about the General Strike of 1926, seen through the eyes of 'the workers'.
2 A topographical poem by John Dyer (1699–1757), of Llangathen, Carmarthenshire, about a nearby hill.
3 Lynette Roberts, Keidrych Rhys's ex-wife.

I have a not-very-good melodrama coming out in the spring, called 'The Doctor & The Devils'. And, in the autumn probably, a new, as-yet-title-less collection of stories & sketches.[1] And next year a sort of play with a title to be read backwards, called 'Llareggub'.

We—that is, Caitlin, Llewelyn, Aeron, Colm, & me—will be moving from Laugharne fairly soon. We're losing our love for the place, which is just as well for we're losing the house we live in too. I don't know where we're going—to people with no money in a split, warring, witch-hunting passported world the possibilities are small—but, with any luck, it may be Rhossili, where an old & ratty rectory owned by a batty farmer is empty at the moment.[2] But the Laugharne address will always find me, if, as I hope, you some time decide to get in touch. Wish I could call on you. And perhaps I can soon.

All my very best wishes for everything, Idris. And I'm looking forward to the book & any word from or of you.

Ever,
Dylan

MS: National Library of Wales

CHARLES FRY[3]
16th February 1953   The Boat House   Laugharne   Carmarthenshire

Dear Charles,
First of all, a *tremendous* number of apologies, profound, very very nervous, terribly late, too late perhaps. These apologies, we both know, are childsplay to make and we're not children (though I feel, sometimes, even now, as useless as a fat child in a flood) and contracts and the writing of books aren't playing. And what perhaps kills trust between persons most, is silence: that dead, muffling, insistent, insolent silence of which I've been guilty for so very long. All I can say at the beginning of this inadequate, breathless, and honest-as-I-can-be letter is: my apologies come from my head and my heart. And the silence, which I hate, came from no intended insolent carelessness or any desire to dishonour a promise I was longing to keep, but from one tortuous cause alone, which I will try to explain: a cause that, aggravated by guilt and grief and illness, became daily more intolerable to me until now, at this most urgent moment, I can still hardly write at all.

---

1 See the letter to E. F. Bozman, 31 March 1953.
2 The Old Rectory at Rhossili, in the Gower peninsula, is three-quarters of a mile from the village (which had no licensed premises in 1953), down a steep path to the sea. The Thomases stayed where they were.
3 Of the publishers Allan Wingate.

Let me straightaway apologise, please, for never having had the courtesy to answer a letter, or the courage to write directly to you and to try to explain my one real problem which has, for a year now, nagged and savaged me and made me lose nearly every shivering ounce of faith in myself. The reasons I didn't answer, I couldn't answer, your kind and justifiably firm letter of December were, mostly, all circumstantial ones, though magnified and distorted, no doubt, by my small, deep hell of the last year. These 'circumstantial' reasons were: my father died that month, blind, of cancer, and everything that had to be done was done by me: this included the care of my mother, who is a permanent invalid, and her maintenance, for the pension she and my father existed on died with him. The children got sick, and I had no money. Early this year, my best friend in the world, a woman of my own age, died of drink and drugs.[1] And I've been ill too. So far, so very obviously bad, a mockRussian whine or drab borrowed slice of Gissing.[2] Perhaps these recent happenings *could* just about pardon my not writing letters. But they have, of course, nothing to do with your chief worry and mine: why the book I promised, and so very much want to write, is not yet written. These happenings can't pardon that, and my detailing of them is not intended to. The 'nagging, savaging, destroying' problem, the real reason why the book is as yet unwritten, *that* is what you want explained. And how can I write that reason down? *That* is the thing itself: for a whole year I have been able to write nothing, nothing, nothing at all but one tangled, sentimental poem as preface to a collection of poems written years ago.

Perhaps it doesn't seem and sound—that phrase, 'I have been able to write nothing'—the throttling bloody hell it's been to me for this whole waste of a twisted year. And this letter is sure to be silly and pretentious enough without my griping on about words being the light and reason of my life etcetera. I went to America, as you know, about this time last year, and kept a jungle of a diary[3] which I felt quite certain that I could, on my return to this wet idyllic tomb on the coast, shape and order into a book neither you nor I would be ashamed of; and I was excited, as I still am, at the thought of wheedling and hacking a proper work out of the chaos of places and people I'd scrawled in planes and trains and bedrooms-like-boilers. I went on all over the States, ranting poems to enthusiastic audiences that, the week before, had been equally enthusiastic about lectures on Railway Development or the Modern Turkish Essay; and gradually I began to feel nervous about the job in front of me, the job of writing, making things in words, by myself, again. The more I used words, the more frightened I became of using them in my own work once more.

---

1 Marged Howard-Stepney, 'that Marged gin woman', died in London on 22 January. The inquest was told that she suffocated after a dose of sleeping pills; the verdict was misadventure. She meant to take over the Boat House from Margaret Taylor and pay its expenses for the Thomas family, but her financial advisers were making difficulties.
2 George Gissing (1857–1903), writer and pessimist.
3 If Thomas kept an American diary, it has never been seen.

Endless booming of poems didn't sour or stale words for me, but made me more conscious of my obsessive interest in them and my horror that I would never again be innocent enough to touch and use them. I came home fearful and jangled. There was my hut on a cliff, full of pencil and paper, things to stare at, room to breathe and feel and think. But I couldn't write a word. I tried then to write a poem, dreading it beforehand, a few obscure lines every dumb day, and the printed result shook and battered me in any faith in myself and workman's pride left to me. I couldn't write a word after that. These are the most words I have written for a year.

And then, because I wouldn't write at all, I got broke—I'd brought little or no money back from the States—and kept the wolf just a hairy inch from my door and my sleep by croaking poems, and such, on the air: an appalling retrogression to an American habit that had gone bad on me. I didn't croak enough to keep me going, and lectured, then, to English women: less intimidating, maybe, but less profitable, too, than American. And all the time I couldn't, I really couldn't, do the one thing I had to do: write words, my own words, down on paper.

Now I can understand what one ordinary, I suppose, reaction would be to this endless jumbled dull confession: Here's somebody who read aloud and lectured too much too often and too long in a too-hospitable place and who became sated with public words and with his own exhibitionism.[1] On his return, he couldn't get down to work; he missed the willing audience, the easy, but killing, money; as time went on, he became frightened of his failure to meet his literary commitments and now, groaning as though all disinterested heaven were lurching on to his head, conjures up, to a squeal of Welsh bagpipes, some vague psychological hoo ha to account for his timidity and sloth.

I know it goes deeper than that, I've lived with it a long time, or so it seems, and know it horridly well, and can't explain it. I haven't been able to write a word, of anything. Behind me, all the time, I heard, And you'll never be able to write a word again. I thought it would break me up into little self-pitying bits.

But an odd thing's happened, and only now. Or perhaps it isn't odd, and time alone has done it. Whatever the reason, since the disasters, big and midget, I mentioned some time ago, on page 93 of this letter, I've got unknotted. Now for God's sake I can't explain that; but there it is. And Higham is going to get lots of other difficulties straightened out, so that I can get down to those ogre words again without nightmares of doubt and debt, and my dear diabolic family shall be protected for a time. And I'll write that American book, or die.

I'm coming to London Monday next. Higham, I hope, has fixed up a time to meet you. (For me to meet you, I mean.)

I daren't read back over these pages, in case I scream with denial & embarrassment.

It *must* be time alone that's done its work.

1 This was the charge that Caitlin made, to his face and to others.

Please try to forgive me for my mean, tortured silence; and for this letter.

Yours ever,

Dylan

MS: Texas

E. F. BOZMAN

18 February 1953   Boat House   Laugharne   Carmarthenshire

Laugharne 68

Dear Bozman,

So very sorry to be so late with these proofs. I've been ill, & unable to do much; & when I got better I lightheartedly—or lightheadedly, rather—thought I could get through the Doctor & the Devils in half a day. It's proved gruelling, & I've just finished. It looks an awful mess, I'm afraid; & do you think I shd have a quick look at a second proof? If you do, I guarantee to let you have it back the next day. Of course, changing Salter to Rock throughout has helped to botch the pages; & then the whole typographical form is difficult too.

I shd have most of the material for the next book in hand this month. I'm coming up to London on Monday, & will give you a ring.

Yours,

Dylan Thomas

Yes, I *do* think I should have a look at a second proof, don't you? I certainly might have missed a few things in all that mess.

MS: Andrew MacAdie

GRAHAM ACKROYD

20 February 1953   Boat House   Laugharne   Carmarthenshire

Dear Graham Ackroyd,

Thank you very much for sending Philip Callow's 'In the Wonder', along to me: I was interested to read it, but don't by any means agree with what you say about it.[1] He's obviously a man of some deep feeling; but there is, to me, no sign, in these pieces, that he is a poet at all. He appears to believe that all he has to do is to scribble down, on separate lines, a few soulful sentimental stale-phrases in the lack-of-rhythm of weak back-broken prose, utter a few passionate bleats, throw in an ill-assorted handful of abstractions, sew on, most untidily, a few threadbare coloured ribbons from old bad half-remembered twilight verses, and wind up cosy and mysterious with God—and there, by God, is a poem. This is probably

1 Philip Callow, better known as a novelist and biographer, also wrote poetry.

horribly, and cheaply, unfair to someone of sincerity and conviction; but he must know, sooner or later, that poems are made out of living words; and that his words are all dead. 'In The Wonder' is, in my nasty opinion, tepid and spineless gush. Don't, please, show this to your friend, who may be all you say: perhaps this is a blind day to me.

How are you these days? And when are we going to have a drink in London together? Sorry I've still lost the Miller letters. How is he? and how's the picaresque novel—I'd like to see it a lot.

Sorry I can't help with Philip Callow's stuff.

Yours,
Dylan Thomas

MS: Texas

JEAN LEROY
20 Feb 1953   The Boat House   Laugharne   Carmarthenshire

Thanks for letter about BBC Welsh Home Service contract for my four Anthology programmes. You wanted to know the cost of two railway journeys Laugharne–Swansea. It is £1.6.6.

Sincerely,
Dylan Thomas

MS: Texas

OSCAR WILLIAMS
27 February 1953   Boat House   Laugharne   Carmarthenshire   Wales

Sending work-sheets
separately
D.

Dear Oscar,

The New American Library cheque has just arrived.[1] I cannot take my sticky eyes from it, and I remember that great line: 'the heel's wide spendthrift gaze towards paradise'. Thank you, so very much, for the bother and speed & business of it. And forgive me, please, for the asthmatic brevity of this. I'm about to catch a bus to catch a train to catch a film-man and, almost certainly, to miss the bus. I'm so fat now I can't hurry; I have elephantiasis: a huge trunk and a teeny mind. It's full-moon time, & the town is baying. And I'm awfully worried about my scheduled visit to the States. I have to write a book by June, & haven't begun it. We're being thrown out of this house—though only we would live in it, over-run by rats: us *and* the house.[2] I hardly dare write to Brinnin to say it is all too

1 See page 503.
2 Margaret Taylor found it increasingly difficult to finance the Boat House. But the Thomases continued to live there.

difficult, but must do so quickly or he will need a hundred new kinds of pills all big as roc eggs. Perhaps if Caitlin were settled in some new warren, I could fly over for a few dates: but we're moving to Christ knows where by the sea. I want very much to meet the mogul you mentioned & to find out about that 4000 a year each etc: it sounds wonderful: we could go anywhere on that, except Laughlin's heart and ski-run. But I don't know how I'm going to see you at all this year, with the commissioned book yapping at me, the house being pinched, and all my depression at the thought of ever moving again except into my long and dirty home. I'll write you again when I hear from John Malcolm once he has heard from me in a re-balding letter.

I enclose the signed note for the Prologue poem; also the work-sheets. I do hope you can sell them for an impossible sum. My agent here has said he will help me with my debts but allow me no money: so I must have some of the stuff on the side. You must take some money yourself from whatever you can get for these messy sheets—poems won't change the sheets for their guests—so that we can both celebrate. Please.

The trivial short story I can't find but will. It was published in World Review.[1]

Caitlin's no longer pregnant: it cost five broadcasts and a loan, and I wish I could have announced, on the air, the reason for these broadcasts.

The bus is getting up steam.

Love to you & Gene from us all, and thank you deeply.

I look forward to a letter.

> Yours Ever,
> Dylan

I'll be doing a broadcast of your poems some time this spring. Will let you know when. The BBC doesn't much like doing American copyright poems: they hate spending dollars. I *may* have to put some English poems in the same programme: if I have to, I'll choose very good ones.

MS: Indiana

KEITH KYLE[2]

27 February 1953   The Boat House   Laugharne   Carmarthenshire

Dear Mr. Kyle,

Thank you for your letter of February 19th, and I'm sorry not to have answered straightaway.

I read, with great interest, the four scripts, in the 'This I Believe' series,

---

1 'The Followers'. Oscar Williams sold it to the New American Library, to use in an anthology, *New World Writing*, for $150.
2 A producer in the BBC's North American Service. He sent scripts by Viscount Kemsley, John Lehmann, Peter Ustinov and Aneurin Bevan. Thomas didn't contribute to the series.

you enclosed. Thank you for asking me to contribute to the series: I'd very much like to, and will send you the 3½ minute script as soon as possible. Perhaps you could let me have a recording date—or even one or two to choose from?—when you have the script? Is it, by the way, possible to record from the Swansea studios?—only an hour or so away from me. Anyway, I'm in London often.

Yours sincerely,
Dylan Thomas

MS: BBC

CHARLES ELLIOTT

27th Feb 53   Boat House   Laugharne   Carmarthenshire

Dear Mr Elliott,

So sorry not to have answered your letter: I've just come back from London. Yes, March 10, Tuesday, 6.30's fine. I can't think of a title, as I'll probably be reading some modern poets & also a chunk of a kind-of-play of mine. 'Some Recent Writing' might do.

I'd like to spend the night in Cardiff. Anywhere. And I'll send you a wire to say time of my arrival.

Very many thanks for all the *great* amount of trouble you're taking; & your kindness in arranging things.

Sincerely,
Dylan Thomas

MS: Columbia University

DAVID HIGHAM

March 2 1953   Boat House   Laugharne   Carmarthenshire

Dear David,

Thank you very much for lunch & for the consoling talk about my wretched affairs. Sorry I was so out-of-sorts that day: I don't know: I'd only just arrived in London, the place that usually out-of-sorts me but takes some days to do so. I hope you'll have lunch with me soon, and that I'll be brighter. But, in spite of my dimness then, I do hope I managed to make you understand how grateful I am to you for the bother you're taking to more or less take care of me—so far as debts go &, of course, so long as I work like a beaver. You asked me to send you a list of my local debts: I enclose the largest: far larger, by the way, than I had, even at my gloomiest, expected. If more details of the bill are wanted, they can be provided: I think the house rent[1] comes to about 165 & the hiring of taxis, over a long period, makes up the rest. Ebie Williams is a friend of mine & will be

1 Of The Pelican, where his mother lived.

satisfied, to begin with, with whatever you can send him from the kitty. I have two other bills here, for about £20 each. What shall I do with them? The rest are small bills I'd like to pay myself *if I had the money*. Could you put something in the bank for me straightaway, so that I can pay these. 25? I've a weekly girl to pay, as well, apart from my own day-to-day expenses. (Ebie Williams, of our local Brown's Hotel, is very pleased, by the way, that his bill is being sent to you, however slow the payment of it might be. He's my friend, as I said, & therefore he knows me.)

I went to see Charles Fry, & arranged to deliver manuscript by end of June.

Thank you for sending the old magazine material. I'm dealing with it. Bozman wants to bring the book out in October. No title yet.

I wrote to Michael Powell.[1]

Thank you again, sorry for my dyspeptic vagueness at our lunch, & I hope you can put a sum in the bank right away & also let the owner of the Pelican House (where my mother lives) have something. Also, shall I send the two other £20 bills?

Yours,
Dylan

MS: Texas

OSCAR WILLIAMS
March 3 1953   Boat House   Laugharne   Carmarthenshire

Dear Oscar,

Work sheets of 'Prologue'. Perhaps a typed copy of the final poem, on top of the sheets, wd look well to a maybe buyer, I don't know. I've tried to keep the sheets in some sort of order, from the very first germ of the poem—it was going to be a piece of doggerel written to someone in the States on my return from there to Wales, but soon grew involved & eventually serious.

Hope you can sell this.

Hope you've had my letter.

I've got gout today. God, that reads like GOAT. I mean, the one in the toe.

Every time a bird flies by, I yell, thinking it might land on my toe. All I can think about is TOE.

Hope you're having a good toe.

Toe to you both.

I'll write soon properly long.

Ever,
D.

MS: Indiana

1 A short film on a classical theme, to be written for the director Michael Powell, seems to have been mooted.

E. F. BOZMAN
16 March 1953   Boat House   Laugharne   Carmarthenshire

Dear E. F. Bozman,

Sorry to be late with the enclosed proofs: I've been away, broadcasting.

I'm afraid I don't know how to answer the proofreader's queries about Donald Taylor's account (page 135).[1] But I do suggest that the penultimate paragraph be deleted: it seems a little smug & apt to forget that this film is only a melodrama & much of it probably wildly inaccurate. I have also ventured to correct Taylor's grammar on page 136 & insert one or two commas. I was very sorry not to have been able to see you during my last London visit. I had to hurry home after only a day & a half. The gathering of material for the new book of stories is going on well: I am waiting, however, for some more stuff from Rolph the bookseller. And, as you suggested very kindly, it would be a great help if the material could be typed for me when it is ready so that I could go through it carefully in typescript rather than in proof.

I hope to see you when I am next in town.

Yours,
Dylan Thomas

MS: (J. M. Dent)

DAVID HIGHAM
17 March 1953   Boat House   Laugharne   Carmarthenshire

Dear David,

I do hope you got my last letter, written just after we met in London. I've been expecting an answer, and am worried about it. I hope you aren't ill; or that anything, in my letter or at our lunch, offended you: I'm awfully sorry if it did.

If you got that letter you'll remember I enclosed with it a bill from our local Brown's Hotel, mostly for the letting of a house, for £190. Now that—though it must, of course, be paid, eventually, however slowly—is not, at this moment, nearly so urgent as other quite small ones which have cropped up in the town and which I really *must* pay at once. (Friendly Brown's can wait. These tradesmen and rates-men can't.) And the most urgently pressing bill is one for £35 to Magdalen College School, Oxford. As soon as I won that Foyle's award, the very first cheque I wrote was to the School, for that amount; but they kept the cheque, without presenting it, for so long that when they *did* present it it was returned by the Bank, the

---

1 *The Doctor and the Devils* included a brief essay by Taylor, 'The Story of the Film'.

Foyle's money being by that time finished. This is really distressingly important for me to pay *now*.

I don't know how my account stands with you, but you should have received, from the BBC over £100 for four Personal Anthologies I recorded in the Swansea studios several weeks ago and which have been broadcast, on the Welsh Region, week by week. Also, I recorded a Childhood Reminiscences sketch for the Welsh Region, from Swansea, last week, for £20 (twenty pounds) and this coming Friday am to record two more, at, I believe, the same fee.[1] So that there should be a £100 in the kitty, and £60 coming. The £100 should *certainly* be there by now. Can you, therefore, let me have the money for Magdalen College School, or arrange to pay it, at once? And can you, *please*, pay into my Bank all you possibly can, *at once* as well. I need £50 for various small bills here which simply *must* be paid this week. I have no money at all.

I'll ring you, at your office, in the morning, hoping that you will have read this by that time and that you will be able to let me have £50 directly in the Bank & enough to pay the School. The Income Tax *must*, this time, wait for its share.

And, also, when I ring I do hope I'll find that you aren't ill or offended.

Yours ever,
Dylan

MS: Texas

JOHN ALEXANDER ROLPH
17 March 1953   Boat House   Laugharne   Carmarthenshire

Dear John,

Very many apologies for this delay. I shd have written weeks ago, to thank you for the letter & for all you're doing to try to get these scraps & stories of mine together. And to say, Sorry, too, that our evening in town—or our hour, rather—was such a mess. I do hope we'll have another evening soon without so many people & so much confusion. The thin, pale woman with us—Marged Howard-Stepney—who drank sherry very quickly, died the next evening of an overdose of sleeping drug.

Since seeing you, I've managed, myself, to get hold of *Janus* (May 1936) and *Yellowjacket* (May 1939), with my stories, 'The Horse's Ha', 'The True Story', & 'The Vest', in them. Also I've found two forgotten ones: 'Prologue To An Adventure' in *Wales*, Summer 1937; and 'Adventure From A Work in Progress' in *Seven*, Spring 1939.

What I wd, & urgently, like from you is: 'After the Fair', N.E.W. March

---

1 These talks were some of the old reminiscences, being rebroadcast.

1934; & any other N.E.W. story. And 'Quite Early One Morning', the only copy of which I've lost. Is it possible for me to have them soon? Then I can let Bozman have at least 17 items towards that book, which he wants to bring out as soon as possible. Do let me know.

Yours,
Dylan

MS: Texas

CHARLES ELLIOTT
17 March 1953   The Boat House   Laugharne   Carmarthenshire
Laugharne 68

Dear Charles Elliott,
Thank you for my evening at Cardiff, all the kindness & hospitality. It was a wonderful audience.
I wonder if I can ask one more favour of you. Do you remember that I had with me a suitcase & a briefcase, & that I transferred, some time in the evening, some of the contents of the briefcase into the suitcase? Well, anyway, I left the briefcase somewhere. I *think* it must be in the Park Hotel. I've written to the manager; but could you possibly, when & if passing by, drop in & see if it is there? It's very urgent to me: the only copy in the world of that kind-of-a-play of mine, from which I read bits, is in that battered, strapless briefcase whose handle is tied together with string.[1]
If the thing isn't there, do you think you *could* find out where the hell I left it? I didn't leave with it on Wednesday morning when I caught the train.

Thank you again, & sorry for all this.
Dylan Thomas

MS: Columbia University

JOHN MALCOLM BRINNIN
18 March 1953   Boat House   Laugharne   Carmarthenshire   Wales

I shall be applying for a visa next
week: in Cardiff, this time. I do not
think they are quite so screening-
strict there as in London. URGENT,
& just remembered: Let me have, at
once, a formal and official Poetry

1 This may have been the first time an audience heard parts of *Under Milk Wood*. In the spring Thomas lost the manuscript again, in America, and a third time in October, in London, when Douglas Cleverdon found it in a pub.

Center letter Dear Mr. Thomas-ing
me and saying what cultural &
important engagements you have
fixed up for me.

Dear John,
    After all sorts of upheavals, evasions, promises, procrastinations, I write,
very fondly, and fawning slightly, a short inaccurate summary of those
events which caused my never writing a word before this. In the beginning,
as Treece said in one of his apocalypses, was the bird; and this came from
Caitlin, who said, and repeated it only last night after our Boston-
Laugharne babble, 'You want to go to the States again only for flattery,
idleness, and infidelity'. This hurt me terribly. The right words were:
appreciation, dramatic work, and friends. Therefore I didn't write until I
knew for certain that I could come to the States for a visit and then return
to a body and hearth not irremediably split from navel to firedog. Of course
I'm far from certain now, but I'm coming. This unfair charge—flattery,
idleness, etcetera—kept me seething quiet for quite a bit. Then my father
died, and my mother relied on me to look after her and to stay, writing like
fury, pen in paw, a literary mole, at home. Then a woman—you never met
her—who promised me a real lot of money for oh so little in return died of
an overdose of sleeping drug and left no will,[1] and her son, the heir, could
hardly be expected to fulfil *that* kind of unwritten agreement. Then a
publisher's firm, which had advanced me money for an American-Impres-
sions book of which I never wrote a word, turned, justly, nasty, and said I
had to do the book by June 1953 or they would set the law on me. Then
Caitlin was going to have another baby and didn't want it. Then Margaret
bloody Taylor said that she was going to sell the rickety house we wrestled
in, over our heads and live bodies. So this was the position I was in, so far
as my American visit was concerned:—Caitlin was completely against it,
and was going to have a baby; my mother was against it, because I should
be near her and working hard to keep the lot of us; and I was reluctantly
against it, because I was without money, owing to an unexpected suicide,
and I could not, naturally, leave a mother and pregnant wife and three
children penniless at home while I leered and tubthumped in Liberty Land;
and the publishers were legally against it, because I had to write a book for
them quickly; and on top of all that, the final reason for my knowing I
could not come out this spring was the prospect of the rapid unhousing of
dame, dam, chick-to-be, and the well-loved rest. (I write like a cad. I should
whip myself to death on the steps of my Club for all this.) Well anyway: I
won a prize, for the book of the year, of £250 (pounds), which put paid to
baby through the wicked good will and skill of a Pole like Conrad Veidt.[2]

1 Marged Howard-Stepney.
2 Conrad Veidt, German actor, first seen in the early horror film, *The Cabinet of Dr
  Caligari.*

And a brother-in-law in Bombay said he would look, from a distance, after my mother's welfare. And Margaret bloodiest Taylor has, temporarily, relented.[1] And I think I can give the demanding publishers the script of 'Under Milk Wood' (when finished) instead of, for instance, 'A Bard's-Eye View of the U.S.A.' And Caitlin's hatred of my projected visit can be calmed only by this: that after no more than 6 weeks' larricking around I return from New York with enough money to take Colm, her and me for three winter months to Portugal where all, I hear, is cheap and sunny. Or, alternatively, that I find, in a month, a house for us, in your country, and can send for Caitlin to join me in the early summer and keep us going, through summer and autumn, by work which is not cross-continental reading and raving. Of the alternatives, she would far prefer the first. So do you think it possible? Do you think I can earn a lot in six weeks: enough, that is, for a Portuguese winter? I do not care, in those six weeks, how much I read, or how many times, or where. I think, for economy, it would be best for me to stay in a New York hotel—the Chelsea, I trust—for only a little time and then to move in, manias and all, on to friends. I am hoping that perhaps my old friend Len Lye,[2] who lives in Greenwich Village, near Ruthven Todd, will put me up: I am only small, after all, and alone, though loud. I haven't his address, but will get in touch with him once in Chelsea'd New York. So, friend and agent, as much as I can do in six weeks please is perhaps best for us all.

I have put down, in more or less true detail, all the above little hells to show why I have been unable, till now, to write and say: 'It is fine. Go ahead.'

About 'Under Milk Wood'. I shall not have the complete manuscript ready until the week of my sailing. I have, anyway, some doubts as to the performance of it by by myself and a professional cast. Some kind of an approximation to a Welsh accent is required throughout, and I think I could make an hour's entertainment out of this myself. Shall we discuss it later? I shall have the m.s. with me, embarking from the liner, and if you still think, after reading it, it needs other and professional voices, then I don't believe it would need all that 'careful preparation' you mention. I should be *very* glad, by the way, to hear from you, as soon as possible, about any ideas you might have as to what I shd read aloud in my general verse-reading programmes. What poets, and of what centuries? I'd like a wide repertoire. Caitlin sends her love to your mother.

Yours always, dear John
Dylan

MS: Delaware

---

1 Margaret Taylor, whose own marriage was threatened by her mission to save Dylan, had been insisting that the Thomases pay two pounds a week rent.
2 The New Zealander Len Lye (1901–80) was a sculptor, painter and film-maker, who lived in London before settling in New York.

JEAN LEROY
30 March 1953   The Boat House   Laugharne   Carmarthenshire

Dear Jean LeRoy,
   You asked about a piece which has just appeared, in Paris, in the new literary magazine, Les Lettres Nouvelles: a piece called Le Bébé Ardent. This, I suppose, is a translation of a story of mine called 'The Burning Baby'. I've got an awful memory, but I *do* just seem to remember hearing from a new French magazine about this story; but I very much doubt if I answered it; if it *did* ever come, I lost it immediately. Anyway, I've had no copy of the magazine. Sorry to be so useless.

Yours,
Dylan Thomas

MS: Texas

E. F. BOZMAN
30 March 1953   The Boat House   Laugharne   Carmarthenshire

Dear E. F. Bozman,
   Enclosed are some of the books & magazines in which appear 12 of the stories & sketches for the new book. I do hope it won't be too much of a nuisance to have these typed. And could I have the typescript as soon as possible? Also the books & magazines. I'm leaving for New York, for a month's lecturing, on April 16th, and would like to read through the typed 12 stories before then. Also before then I hope to get together the other 9 or so items to make the book complete. What of a title? As it is a book about, & mostly by, adolescence, perhaps the title of one of the sketches would do: 'Quite Early One Morning'. Otherwise, I suggest 'The Burning Baby'. What d'you think?
   I will be seeing you before I leave for N. York.

Yours,
Dylan Thomas

MS: (J. M. Dent)

E. F. BOZMAN
31 March 1953   Boat House   Laugharne   Carmarthenshire

Dear E. F. Bozman,
   I hope that by this time the first quite big chunk of material for the new book has reached you, & also the accompanying letter. I don't remember, however, if I indicated, in my letter, what material exactly was to be typed

(& it was extremely kind of you to suggest that you might get it typed for me). In case I didn't, the list is:

The Followers (World Review)
Holiday Memories
Quite Early One Morning } (typescript)
Adventure (Seven)
The Vest
The True Story } (Yellowjacket)
The Horse's Ha (Janus)
The School For Witches
The Holy Six
The Burning Baby } (This World I Breathe)
Prologue To An Adventure
A Prospect of The Sea

I've heard today from friends of mine who've helped me collect the above that I can expect to have nearly all the rest next week. This will include 'Return Journey', a long piece, 'Memories of Childhood', and 'Memories of Christmas', all originally broadcast: that is, written to be *spoken* aloud but also, very much, to be read. 'The Crumbs of One Man's Year', that was broadcast one New Year's Day & is, I hope, quite a good piece. A short story of the fantastic kind, called 'The Lemon'. Another Christmas piece. And a little very early story called 'After The Fair', which appeared in the New English Weekly many years ago. My bibliographer-to-be, John Rolph, has tracked this last down to the files of a public library but is not allowed to take the copy out and, having no shorthand, cannot easily copy it. I shall have to think how to get hold of this as—whatever its literary merits; I can't remember a thing about it now—I *should* like to include it: it's the earliest story of mine & will take its place next to some little piece describing the author just about that time of his life.[1]

I'll write again; & I do hope we can hurry a contract up. I'm going to the States, for 6 weeks lecturing, on April 16th, and *must* have some money to keep my family going while I am away and to settle some outstanding debts before I leave. I'm desperately broke.

Yours,
Dylan Thomas

MS: Andrew MacAdie

1 Many of the stories and radio talks listed by Thomas were collected in book form, in the UK, soon after his death: in *Quite Early One Morning* (1954) and *A Prospect of the Sea* (1955). But the more violent and sexual stories remained under a cloud as far as his British publishers were concerned: a reader's report dated January 1954 said 'The Burning Baby' was 'a horrible fantasy', 'Prologue to an Adventure' a 'welter of pornographic filth' and 'The Horse's Ha' 'disgustingly obscene'. It was 1971 before these and similar stories from Thomas's list appeared in a British book, in *Dylan Thomas: Early Prose Writings*: more than thirty years after they were written.

KEITH KYLE
31 March 1953   Boat House   Laugharne   Carmarthenshire

Dear Mr. Kyle,
Thank you for your letter, & the enclosure from Cecil Day Lewis. Yes, certainly I'll write to David Higham, my agent, asking him to waive that ban in this particular case and to get in touch with you immediately. I didn't know the ban existed, myself.[1]
I've written Day Lewis to the same effect.
Sorry not to have sent my script 'This I Believe' much sooner. I've had bronchitis. I'll send it on in the next few days.

Sincerely,
Dylan Thomas

MS: BBC

DAVID HIGHAM
31 March 1953   Boat House   Laugharne   Carmarthenshire

Dear David,
I enclose a letter from Keith Kyle of the BBC, and a note from Cecil Day Lewis. I think we should, if possible, waive that ban they refer to, in this particular case. (I didn't know the ban existed.) As Day Lewis says, if he can't get my permission he'll go no further with the project. And I think those talks *shd* be heard in the U.S.A. If you agree, could you let Kyle know?
Writing soon at more length about other things.

Yours,
Dylan

P.S. Both letters in sad disrepair, I'm afraid.

MS: Texas

---

1 C. Day-Lewis had included Thomas's poem 'A Refusal to Mourn' in a radio programme that was to be distributed in the U.S. by the BBC's Transcription Service. Thomas's agents didn't allow this use of his material.

THEODORE ROETHKE[1]
31 March 1953   Boat House Laugharne Carmarthenshire Wales

Dear Ted,

Sorry not to have written before to thank you for sending the Dancing Poems. I think they're wonderfully good. I kept putting off writing until I knew when I'd be in the States, so that I could say, See you, I hope, in the so-and-so. Now so-and-so is April 21st, and I'll be in and around New York until June 5. Any chance of seeing you for a few hours, evenings, days? A line to me c/o Brinnin, saying, Yes, or even, Yes, perhaps, would be fine to look forward to.

I asked the BBC, officially, about getting hold of a copy, for you, of the recording I made of the three poems of yours, but the BBC said, We never, we never, we never. Which is not true. Now I'm climbing into the BBC by the back door, and falling over the slimy accents, and hope to get a copy soon. I'm glad and proud you want one: I hope I haven't boomily buggered the poems up. The recording got several letters: 'terrific poems', 'gibberish', etc, and one or two simple serious & passionate ones from people I didn't know of that did show how disturbed they were by the strange things that had happened to them across the air. You still have a grotesquely small audience here, but very fierce.

Had your wedding card. Congratulations. Best wishes, & sympathy, to your wife. Hope you had a nice, loud, elbowy, dancing time and fell on some guests.

I haven't seen a copy of Poetry Chicago yet with your piece about my book.[2]

Are you writing poems? I want very very much to see them. And do try to meet; New York or Chicago. Or anywhere.

Yours,
Dylan

MS: Washington

---

1 Thomas and the American poet Roethke (1908–63) became friends during the American visits.
2 A review, in the December 1952 issue of *In Country Sleep and Other Poems* (New Directions, 1952), under the pseudonym 'Winterset Rothberg'.

*CHRISTOPHER HASSALL[1]

3 April 1953   Boat House   Laugharne   Carmarthenshire

Dear Christopher,

I've asked Denis Mathews to hand this to you.

Thank you very much indeed for your postscript to his letter, and for wanting me to write something about E.M.[2] for the book: I'm very proud of being asked. But I really don't see how anything I could write would be of any use at all; or, indeed, how I *could* write anything. The length of my personal acquaintance with him could not be more than one minute; I met him twice, after Apollo readings, in a crowd of people & only to say, Good evening. I've always, naturally, had a great respect for him, and should like to have met him properly; but that's all I could write down. I'm awfully sorry to be so useless about this—but I know you couldn't bear a tribute that would be, of necessity, pious & impersonal.

Thank you again for writing. And I *do* wish I had known him.

Yours,
Dylan

MS: Cambridge University Library

E. F. BOZMAN

April 6 1953   Boat House   Laugharne   Carmarthenshire

Dear E. F. Bozman,

I'm sorry our telephone conversation was obscured by the failure of my telephone apparatus to make my really great gratitude heard. Thank you very very much for saying that you would arrange for £250 to be paid to me, this Tuesday, tomorrow, on advance of our contract: things have been difficult for me lately, indeed stopping me writing at all because of nagging and bewildering financial worry; and this considerable kindness on your part will ease them all. I could not have left for the States without paying some of my outstanding debts in this tolerant village, nor without leaving my family enough money to live on in my absence. Thank you again. I am writing, after writing this, to David Higham, to ask him to send on immediately as much of that generous advance as he, and the Income Tax, allow.

Your letter, about the stories & sketches which I sent you, did not really surprise me; I realised, I think beforehand, that the early violent stories *were* very raw. I myself thought that their rawness would, in contrast to the maturer, remembering, sketches, be acceptable; but I do appreciate all

1 Author and librettist, 1912–63.
2 Probably Edward Marsh, who died in 1953; Hassall was to be his biographer. There are letters from Thomas to Marsh, as a 'patron of letters', in 1939 and 1940.

you say. I *would* like, one day, to have those other stories printed in book form, but I shall leave them now, and I look forward to talking with you about them before, visa willing, I set out on my short, and maybe vain, in both senses, American tour.

I shall send along the rest of the acceptable material as quickly as possible.

Yours very sincerely,
Dylan Thomas

MS: (J. M. Dent)

DAVID HIGHAM
April 6 1953   Boat House   Laugharne   Carmarthenshire

Dear David,

I sent the first big chunk of the material towards the new proposed book of short stories for Dent's, to Bozman a few days ago. The later ones he liked, but the early ones he considered 'too raw for publication under the Dent imprint'. This was a disappointment to me, as I had considered that the juxtaposition of the early violent stories and the calmer prose-memories would make an interesting book. However. Bozman wants now to make a volume of the later sketches & stories, although these do not, as yet, number more than 8 altogether, including the 3 which Bozman is now having typed. And I am persuaded, by him, to leave those early stories alone at the present moment.

Two days ago, Bozman phoned me to say that—perhaps in view of the fact that he had to turn these raw stories down—he was prepared to advance me, on my contract, the sum of £250 immediately. This seems extremely generous, and I have written very thankfully to him. He will be in touch with you tomorrow (Tuesday), and promises to let you have a cheque, at once, for this amount. I do hope you will be able to let me have, for myself, the most substantial part of this cheque: indeed, all that is possible out of it. I am due to sail, visa willing, for New York on Thursday the 16th of this month, for a reading-tour, in the Eastern States, of about 5 or 6 weeks, probably six. And I can't leave without settling outstanding debts & arranging for my family to live in my absence. So that: please do let me have nearly all of that advance—sent to my bank. I'm in an awful mess, as usual, and in a frightful flap about leaving: visas, ticket, etc. I have a television show, from Cardiff,[1] & two recordings—one from London, for

---

1 'Home Town—Swansea. A programme in which viewers meet some of the interesting people who live in this old Welsh town.' 9 April 1953. Alfred Janes, Dan Jones and Vernon Watkins took part with Thomas. Wynford Vaughan-Thomas introduced it.

Cleverdon, & one from Swansea—before leaving; and a packet of small debts, etc., to see to; and a quick script to write.

I'll ring you in the morning. I have written to my bank telling them to expect a good deal of money by Wednesday, and am already drawing on this.

Yours,
Dylan

MS: Texas

DAVID HIGHAM
16 April 1953[1] as from   The Boat House   Laugharne   Carmarthenshire

Dear David,

Thanks for everything you're doing. This is just to give you my American address: c/o J. M. Brinnin, 100 Memorial Drive, Cambridge, Mass. And to say: will you, for the next 5 weeks—i.e. until I come back from the States—send whatever monies come in to me (I mean, the 50% of them) direct to Caitlin, at Laugharne, and *not* to my bank? Please.

Yours ever,
Dylan

MS: Texas

CAITLIN THOMAS
Monday 20 April 53   [headed paper: United States Lines]

Oh Caitlin Cat my love my love, I love you for ever & ever, I LOVE YOU CAT, if only I could jump over this rocking ship-side into the awful sea and swim to you now, I want to be with you all the time, there isn't one moment of the endless day or night on this hell-ship when I'm not thinking about you, feeling through the dark and the rolling and the wind for you and talking to you. Don't be lost to me, darling; forgive me for all my nastiness, mad-dog tempers, of the last days & weeks: they were because I didn't want to go, I didn't want to leave you in old dull Laugharne with children and loneliness, I didn't want, I promise you before God, to move at all, except with you. I longed to be with you, terribly close as we very often are, as we nearly always are, sitting in the shed and writing, being with you, & in your arms at night. And here I am, on this huge hot gadget-mad hotel, being tossed and battered; the sea's been brutal all the time; I can hardly write this at all, in the tasteful, oven-ish, no-smoking library-room, for the rattle & lurch; everybody's been sick every day; for one whole day,

1 The letter was written just before Thomas left on his third trip to the U.S.

full of dramamine, I groaned in a fever in the cabin which I do not share, alone in my horrible rocking hothouse where there's no time, no night or day; occasionally now I manage to rock, like a drunk, to the bar where a few pale racked men are trying the same experiment as me, and then, after an ice-cold couple, stagger back to my room, to pray that I was with you, as I always wish to be, and not on this eternal cocktail-shaker of a ship—or if I *have* to be on it, which God knows I don't have to be, then oh Cat oh my sweetheart, then why why aren't you with me too. I've spoken hardly a word to anyone but one stout barman; the people who share my table— when any of us is well enough to appear—are a thousand times worse than those dumpling (Dolly's kind of dumpling) Dutchmen: there's a middle-aged brother & sister, and a little sophisticated German woman; the little German woman's beastly, and told me, when the brother & sister weren't there, that she'd thought of asking the purser to move her to another table: 'I don't like', she said, 'having my meals in the company of a woman who reminds me of my cook'—which seems one of the oddest things I ever heard said. There is also a German count, or mock-count, with whom I have exchanged half a dozen words: he looks, speaks, & acts like Charles Fisher. Otherwise, not a word to anyone. Every one is very clean & well-dressed and moneyed; the only one possible thing I have in common with them is that we all feel ill. It is nine o'clock in the morning; tomorrow we dock at New York; breakfast has been & gone. I love you, Caitlin, oh my darling I love you. To think that *I* was angry because *you* did not want me to go away. I was angry, really, only with myself, because I did not want to go away and yet was going. But I shall bring money back & we will go [to] the sun very soon: that is sure. I'll write properly when I'm on land: this rocking is getting unsteadily worse. And I'll send some money in the letter, just as soon as I get any. Higham's number is TEMPLE BAR 8631 in case you feel like ringing him about the letter I wrote to him on the morning of my going away: I told him then to send any money coming to me *direct* to you. I love you. Please, my darling, try to love me, and wait for me. Wait for me, dear, I'll hurry like hell through this sad month-and-a-bit. I can see you now. You're more beautiful than ever, my own true love. Kiss the children and beat them to death. I hope the sun is out, and that you can buy the canoe. Be good to me: you are everything. Why did I snarl when you only wanted me to stay? I love you.

Now I am going to the bar for a cold beer, then back to the bloody cabin to lie on the unmade bed & to fall into a timeless dream of you and of all I love— which is only you—and of the sea rocking & the engines screaming and the wind howling and the despair that is in everything except in our love.[1]

Oh, Cat,
I love you
Dylan

MS: Maurice Neville

1 When she received this letter, Caitlin wrote to Helen McAlpine to say that he sounded like a lost soul; adding that now he was in America, she was leaving him to the wolves.

CAITLIN THOMAS
April 22 [1953]   as from 100 Memorial Drive   Cambridge
                                                                Massachusetts

Darling,
   Arrived in Newfilthy York two days ago. Staying in Chelsea for 3 days, in
small room exactly under our old one. Chelsea staff very disappointed you
didn't come. If *they* are, what do you think I am? I love you my love for
ever & for ever and wish to be with you always on earth & in heaven.
   Oscar & I are together at this moment in a post-office, so this is very
short. Here's a cheque for 100 dollars—about 37 pounds. I'll write a letter
from John B's at Memorial Drive, where I go tomorrow.

                                                 I love you,
                                                 Dylan

MS: (Thomas Trustees)

*CAITLIN THOMAS
May 7th 1953   [headed paper: Hotel Chelsea   New York West
                                   Twenty third Street at Seventh Avenue
                                                   New York 11 NY]

Darling Caitlin Caitlin my love my love, where are you & where am I and
why haven't you written and I love you every second of every hour of every
day & night. I love you, Caitlin. In all the hotelbedrooms I've been in in
this two weeks, I've waited for you all the time. She *can't* be long now, I
say to my damp miserable self, any minute now she'll be coming into the
room: the most beautiful woman on the earth, and she is mine, & I am
hers, until the end of the earth and long long after. Caitlin, I love you. Have
you forgotten me? Do you hate me? Why don't you write? Two weeks may
seem a small time but to me it's old as the hills & deep as my worship of
you. Two weeks here, in this hot hell and I know nothing except that I'm
waiting for you & that you never come. *Darling* Cat, my wife, my beautiful
Cat. And in two weeks I've travelled all over the stinking place, even into
the deep South: in 14 days I've given 14 readings, & am spending as little as
possible so that I can bring some money home and so that we can go into
the sun. John Brinnin has a book all about good sunny places, & exactly
how to get there, & exactly how much money is needed to live there; & the
best & cheapest seems to be Majorca, where we can, I hope, rent a house &
have servants for very very little. I'm going to find out more about it before
I leave. I'm coming back, by plane, on the 26th of May, & will tell you later
just when the plane arrives. Will you meet me in London? I'm enclosing a
cheque for 250 dollars (which is well over 80 pounds) for bills and things.
David Higham wrote & said he was sending you some money. Has any

come? Did you get my letter from the horrible ship? And the little letter with the 100 dollar Oscar cheque? I don't know what's happening, because you don't write. I love you, I want you, it's burning hell without you, I don't want to see anybody or to talk to anybody, I'm lost without you. I've been staying with John & his mother in Cambridge; they were very nice, & she sends you her love. But that's a different kind of love. I love your body & your soul & your eyes & your hair & your voice & the way you walk & talk. And that's all I can see now: you moving, in a light. I love you, Caitlin. I've been to foul Washington, stayed with Beatrice Rudes; I've been to Virginia & North Carolina and Pennsylvania & Syracuse & Bennington & Williamstown & Charlotteville; and now I'm back in New York, for two days, in the same room we had. That was the last love & terror, because I *know* you are coming into this room, & I hide my heaps of candies, & I wait for you—like waiting for the light. Then I suddenly know you are *not* here; you are in Laugharne, with lovely Colm; & then the light goes out & I have to see you in the dark. I love you. *Please*, if you love me, write to me c/o John at 100 Memorial Drive, Cambridge, Massachusetts. Tell me, dear dear Cat. There is nothing to tell you other than that you know: I am profoundly in love with you, the only profundity I know. Every day's dull torture, & every night burning for you. Please please write. And try to be in London on the 27th when I come back. I'm enduring this awfulness with you behind my eyes. You tell me how awful it is, & I can see. But I *will* have Majorca money. Look Majorca up in the Encyclopedia in the Pelican. (I shall write to my mother). You think I don't understand grief & loneliness; I *do*; I understand yours & mine when we are not together. We shall be together. And, if you want it, we shall never be not together again. I said I worshipped you. I do; but I want you too. God, the nights are long & lonely.[1]

I LOVE you. Oh, sweet Cat.

Dylan

MS: Berg

---

1 Caitlin was now writing to Helen McAlpine to report tormenting visions of Dylan lying in scented bowers, surrounded by concubines. Meanwhile Thomas had just begun, or shortly would begin, an affair with Elizabeth Reitell, Brinnin's assistant at the Poetry Center. He also had a last encounter with Pearl Kazin.

*JOHN MALCOLM BRINNIN

[20 May 1953]   [headed paper: The Lord Jeffery [Inn] Amherst
Massachusetts]

11.30.

John,
   Have gone to have a drink with Joe Barber at 692-W (tel).[1]

                        Dylan

MS: Delaware

CAITLIN THOMAS

[about May 23 1953]   [headed paper: The Poetry Center]
          as from 100 Memorial Drive Cambridge Mass

        P.S. If you write again to [*an arrow points to Brin-
        nin's address*], darling please put c/o J. M. Brinnin.
        Letters to me just at 100 Memorial Drive don't get
        delivered, it's such a huge building, and one letter
        from you, love, to me, has been sent back to England.
        XX I kiss you.

Cat sweetheart,
   Caitlin my love three thousand miles away darling Cat you are so near.
And your beautiful letter tore all the time and distance away and I was
with you again, again in our bed with the beating seaweather, as I read the
words of the letter over & over and as I saw your hand writing it and as I
could see your face & hair and eyes my darling darling. You are with me
always, Cat, as God is with the devout; other people around me are lousy
with their personal interests, are unhappy & lost, but I am certain in my
body & my heart & that makes all the miraculous difference. I'm certain
that we are together; I am sure that I love you; I know that you are Caitlin;
and I am smug about it. But always through the smugness comes the
terrible fear: Caitlin may always be distant, perhaps she or I will die, my
true incredibly-lovely Cat doesn't, can't, love me any more. I love you,
Caitlin Macnamara, I love & love you. People here know that, although I
would never say it. They can see the love for you around me; they can
know I'm blessed. I'm damned if I'm blessed, but all the eyes of the
strangers can see that I am in love with you. I love you. I'm writing this
again in Brinnin's Memorial Drive; Brinnin is away; his mother is
shopping, I suppose. And I love you.
   This trip is nearly over. There is one foul thing, though. The aeroplane I

1 Mentioned in Brinnin's *Dylan Thomas in America*. Barber was in the English
department of Amherst College, where Thomas gave a reading.

was to have caught on May 26th has been removed from the passengers' list because of the Coronation: that is, so I understand, rich bitches have bought it out so that they can get to London to look at the Queen. And so I have to get the next poor-available plane, which is on June the first, arriving on June the second, the day of the Coronation.[1] I'm sorry, my love, my own, Caitlin my Cat, but there is no other way. I shall telegram the exact hour of my arrival in London on June 2nd to Laugharne & to Helen's address in case you are there. Meet me, Cat: oh, what [am I] without you? I love you. It is only 4 days later.

June the 2nd, then in London. And may Laugharne stop raining. And then: can you—this is important—make plans well-beforehand to be away with me the whole of July. Alone, without Colm or Aeron. You & me. I know that at the end of July, Llewelyn comes out of school, but somehow it must be arranged. You and me must, at the beginning of July, go together to Hollywood. We can get a boat from London, direct but slow, to San Francisco, & then fly to Los Angeles in an hour or so. Outside Hollywood, in a huge easy house in the hills, we're to stay for the month with Stravinsky. I've seen him, just now, in Boston, and we've thought of an opera and it is—for me—so simple that the libretto can be written in the time we're there.[2] That's not just optimistic: it *can*, & will be. In advance, I'll be given 500 pounds & our passage, firstclass, & then another £500—& then royalties until we die. We'll go back from Hollywood to Laugharne, &, in the winter, we'll go to Majorca. There'll be plenty of money. This time it's working. Majorca seems to be the cheapest place in the sun there is: I've got lots of information about it. We can stay at a pension, & then get a house & two servants. It sounds mad but I think it's true & can be done. I love you.[3]

Biddy rang me up & came along & gave me a rather moth-eaten camelhair coat for you. I'm going to send Ivy a lot of rich sweets; buy a shirt for Phil; something cowboy for Ebi; bring along a piece of finery for my mother. For you, Caitlin, only my eternal untouched love, my wonder at *your* love, my heart & my gout. I'm going to buy Welly a leather travelling-bag to go with his travelling rug. And whatever I can think of for darling Colm & dear Aeron. I am sick damp drivelling *and* strong with my love for you. Oh, Cat, this letter sounds so cheery & so silly. I'm desperate really to be with you. The pictures of you & me on John's walls here make me shout & cry and weep.

1 Of Elizabeth II.
2 Boston University's Opera Workshop cabled Thomas on 21 May, to ask if he would consider writing a libretto for Stravinsky. He met the composer briefly at an hotel in Boston. They discussed a story about a world reborn, perhaps colonised from outer space after a holocaust: a new Eden. But it was a tentative plan, not a commission. Boston still had to raise the money.
3 Plans and dreams hovered at the Boat House that summer. At one point Caitlin even wrote to her friend Giovanni Chiesa, the hotel proprietor on Elba, to suggest they visit the island in September. Chiesa replied to say that if her husband went to America, perhaps she would come alone, and 'Dilan' could join her later.

Is my sister dead?[1]

I'll try to write to my mother.

I've finished that infernally eternally unfinished 'Play' & have done it in New York with actors.[2]

I've seen Dave & Rose.[3]

But it's *I* who love you, even though Rose says she does.

I love you.

I love your oh I don't know just everything of you.

I'm going back to New York tomorrow to do the 'PLAY' again. Tomorrow I'll send some money. It will come in 4 or 5 days. About sixty pounds, for bills.

Why am I here? I want to be with you. We will never again be not together.

> I love you I love you I love you I love you
> I love you
> Oh Cat.

And please do, carefully, the preparations for Hollywood July.

> I love you my Cattleanchor my dear
> dear dear

MS: (Maurice Neville)

IRENE JONES

[postmarked 14 June 1953]   Boat House   Laugharne
                                                      Laugharne 68

Dear Irene,

Here are the addresses & names of 3 of the best bone-boys in the country.

Sir H. A. Thomas Fairbank
6M Hyde Park Mansions
Marylebone Rd.
H. Osmond-Clarke
80 Harley St.
Sir Reginald Watson-Jones
82 Portland Place.

The last is the best but all are top.

> Yours, with love,
> bottom.

MS: Texas

1 Nancy had died 16 April.
2 *Under Milk Wood* had its first performance at the Poetry Center on 14 May.
3 Rose Slivka, then married to the sculptor Dave Slivka, was Caitlin Thomas's closest friend in America.

ELIZABETH REITELL
June 16 1953   Boat House   Laugharne   Carmarthenshire   Wales,
                                        but as from, privately, The Savage Club
                                        One Carlton Terrace   London SW3

Elizabeth Reitell (b. 1920), was a wartime lieutenant in the U.S. Women's Army Corps, then
an artist, and from 1951 to 1953 worked with J. M. Brinnin as assistant director of the Poetry
Center. There she met Thomas in the spring of 1953, helped him prepare *Under Milk Wood*
for production, and fell in love with him. She had been married twice.

Liz love,
    I miss you terribly much.
    The plane rode high and rocky, and over Newfoundland it swung into
lightning and billiard-ball hail, and the old deaf woman next to me, on her
way to Algiers via Manchester, got sick in a bag of biscuits, and the bar—a
real, tiny bar—stayed open all the bourbon way. London was still glassy
from Coronation Day, and for all the customs-men cared I could have
packed my bags with cocaine and bits of chopped women. All my friends,
including the Irish ones I stay with, were, early that morning, in the middle
of Coronation parties that had already lasted a week, and did not seem to
think that I had been away: my broken bone, of course they took for
granted, and they showed me an assortment of cuts, black eyes, & little
fractures to prove that they too had suffered for Royalty. I came back here,
to the always sad West drizzle, the following week, the candies running in
my bag, and have just been sitting around, getting accustomed. These are
the first words I've written, and all they mean to say is: I miss you a great,
great deal. We were together so much, sick, well, silly, happy, plagued, but
with you I was happy all the time.
    No, don't send that stupid Prologue to Richman, but please to me. And
also, if you can, any other reviews and also some of the poems among the
papers.
    I saw my Welsh solicitor, and he did not appear to know why I had gone
to see stuffy Maclean O.B.E. I told him he had written to me to ask me to
go, but he said no. Who is right, if anybody, can you remember? Now he
says that he intends to go on with the anti-Time case only in Europe whose
libel-laws he understands, and to leave the American side altogether.[1] I
told him about that New Directions digest of reviews, on yellow paper,
that you were going to send Maclean. If you haven't already sent it to
Maclean, would you send it to me to give to the Welsh solicitor. If Maclean

---

1 *Time* magazine published an article about Thomas on 6 April 1953. Thomas objected
to a passage that said he guzzled beer and smothered truth and fact in 'boozy
invention'. The article continued: 'He borrows with no thought of returning what is
lent, seldom shows up on time, is a trial to his friends, and a worry to his family.' His
solicitor (and friend) in Swansea, Stuart Thomas, issued a writ on 30 April. *Time*
responded by putting a private detective on Dylan Thomas's tail when he made his
next and final visit to the U.S.

has it, he, Welsh solicitor, will write Maclean for it. All this is disjointed & probably confusing. Hope you can disentangle it. And I'm sorry, Liz dear, that, all these miles away, I am still worrying you over such small things. I wish I was worrying you, very near.

Later today—this is the wet, gray morning, all seabirds & mist and children's far-off voices and regret everywhere in the wind & rain,—I'll write to Stravinsky, and then soon may know a bit more of where I shall be & what I shall do this fall. I've been asked to go to an International Literary Conference—oh God, oh Pittsburgh—in October, with Eliot, Thomas Mann, Forster, Elizabeth Bowen, Camus, Hemingway, Wilder, Faulkner, and my agent in London says I certainly should and I probably shall. With those boys' names, there *must* be money. Oh, and Arthur Miller will be there too, so he and I can be avant-garde together and write a play in which *everybody* takes his clothes off in a sewer. It's a shame our sweet little David couldn't have had that bunch all together in his party. Remember me to little sticky-fingers if ever you see him. And to Ruthven, please? With thanks for housing my cases of rubbish. And to Mr. Campbell in the bucketing rain in F. Street, and to the so liberal party, and to Herb at the Crucible, and to Charlie Read chasing you—which is more than Herbert will do this year at Harvard.[1] And always to John, to whom I shall write this long, trembling week.

My arm is still in plaster: new Welsh plaster. I haven't yet found a Doctor like Milton, nor will I ever. All my best wishes to him: he picked me out of the sick pit with his winking needle and his witty wild way.[2]

Oh, I miss you, Liz.

I've put 2 addresses at the top of this letter. The first is for Poetry Center. The second—deep as a grave full of comedians—for you and me should you write, one day, from you to me.

I'm sending this to Charles Street. Next month I'll write to you at Dundee.[3]

What are you doing?

> Love, love, to you,
> Dylan

MS: Jeff Towns/Dylans Book Store

---

1 Herbert Hannum, an architect, was later Elizabeth Reitell's third husband.
2 Milton Feltenstein, a fashionable New York doctor, had treated Thomas for a broken arm, caused by a fall down stairs when drunk. Feltenstein also gave him injections of cortisone, then a new 'wonder drug', to ease the discomfort caused by gout and gastritis. It was Feltenstein's 'winking needle' that injected Thomas with half a grain of morphine on 4 November 1953, and led directly to his death.
3 Reitell claimed to have other letters from Thomas, but said they couldn't be published without 'terrible harm to feelings of living people'.

JOHN MALCOLM BRINNIN
16 June 1953   Laugharne

My dear John,

Just arrived back here, fractured and barmy, to torpor and rain and Ivy's dungeon, and I've nothing to tell you except a thousand thankyous and how much I miss you. In spite of Milk fever, bonebreak, some nausea, Carolina and Richman, old Captain Oscar Cohen,[1] I enjoyed myself an awful lot, especially in Cambridge & Boston. And thank your mother too for every kindness.

I haven't heard yet from Sarah Caldwell[2] about the opera, and wrote to Stravinsky only today, so I don't know yet any autumn plans. But there's an International Literary Spender-less Conference at Pittsburgh in October, to which I've been invited, and, though to hell with Conferences, I shall quite likely go there on the way (I hope) to California via (somehow) Memorial Drive; and with Caitlin, too.

I'm going to start work tomorrow and shall revise Milk Wood for publication and broadcasting here. I'll also be seeing David Higham soon, and will get Milk Wood copyrighted as a play for public performance. Could you, then, d'you think, do something, with Tom Brockway and with the woman of Wolfe & influence, whose name I've forgotten, about getting it done across the States? And then, after finishing 'In The Skin Trade', I want to begin on a new, and, in one sense, proper-er, play. About this I'll tell [you] in—is it?—August. Do write to me, however briefly, though please not shortly; and could you let me know Sarah Caldwell's address at Boston University?

The very best to Joe.

> Ever,
> Dylan

MS: Delaware

IGOR STRAVINSKY
16th June 1953   The Boat House   Laugharne   Carmarthenshire   Wales

Dear Mr. Stravinsky,

I was so very very glad to meet you even for a little time, in Boston; and you and Mrs. Stravinsky couldn't have been kinder to me. I hope you got well very soon.

I haven't heard anything yet from Sarah Caldwell, but I've been thinking a lot about the opera and have a number of ideas—good, bad, and chaotic.

---

1 'Captain Cohen' is Oscar Williams. Richman is probably Robert Richman, who founded the Institute for Contemporary Arts in Washington DC.
2 Of the Opera Workshop.

As soon as I can get something down on paper, I should, if I may, love to send it to you. I broke my arm just before leaving New York the week before last, and can't write properly yet. It was only a little break, they tell me, but it cracked like a gun.

I should like very much—if you think you would still like me to work with you; and I'd be enormously honoured and excited to do that—to come to California in late September or early October. Would that be convenient? I do hope so. And by that time, I hope, too, to have some clearer ideas about a libretto.

Thank you again. And please give my regards to your wife and to Mr. Craft.

Yours sincerely,
Dylan Thomas

MS: Paul Sacher Foundation, Basle

THEODORE ROETHKE
19th June 1953   Boat House   Laugharne   Carmarthenshire   Wales
Telephone: Laugharne (pronounced Larn) 68

Dear Ted,

I missed, very much, seeing you in America, heard you were with your wife, you normal old thing, in Wystan's in Ischia,[1] and hoped, a lot, I'd be back in time to see you hereabouts. I returned, on June the third, just missing the crowning horror, with a broken arm and rhubarb eyes and feeling like the Island of Bourbon—which, according to the Encyclopaedia Britannica of 1810, the only work of reference in Laugharne, has fpiders of the fize of a pigeon's egg, moft enormous bats, and a burning mountain which throws out vaft quantities of bitumen, fulphur, and other combuftible materials and makes all about ufelefs. And I got somehow back to our very small house in the grey perpetual rain with a party of Liverpool-Irishmen who insisted on carrying my crippled and fear-dumb mother (who lives nearby), down the dangerous cliff-path, dropping her every now and then with cries of 'Watch out, Ma', and who all fell asleep on the floor and then, fully clothed, went riding the children's rubber animals and birds on the rough sea: none was drowned, but one very nearly, and the village's opinion of him was, 'He wasn't fit to be on a swan'.

I had a good bad enough time in Mew York [*sic*] and in Cambridge too where I met some old and fond friends of yours whose names I never caught, suffered in Syracuse and Carolina, made them suffer in Amherst, was called a Red in Washington but so was Mr. Taft, felt curiously thwarted in Bennington which talks of you with a reverent terror, Winterset, and signed an excellent paper-back book contract—copies in

1 W. H. (Wystan) Auden had a villa at Ischia.

every drugstore, with a suggestive cover—for the story you read a bit of in New World Writing.[1] That story is what I'm about to work on now. I haven't tried to write poetry since last October. *Your* new poems—written in Europe? not, I suppose, that it matters where—I think are beautiful. I'd like to hear you read them, and to go through them very carefully with you. Perhaps we can learn a little from each other, and anyway it will be very enjoyable if we learn and know nothing and only blunder loud about. I'll find out what I can about publishers in England for the Waking Poems, and we'll see Louis MacNeice together, a very good chap, about a rant at the BBC. And so: when *can* we meet? I shall be in London, taking up the revised version of the kind-of-play to the publishers, at the very beginning of July, and then have to come back, on July 6, to Llangollen in North Wales to report, for the Welsh BBC, on an International Eisteddfod there, which lasts until the 11th. I have a suggestion for after that. You said you were going on to Ireland after London. Caitlin, who comes from County Clare, and I want to go to Ireland, too. So, if I can raise enough money, shall we all go together? Laugharne is only about 30 miles from Fishguard from where the boats cross to Rosslare. And from Rosslare we could go into County Cork by train, eat and drink a bit in the West, and wind up in Dublin. Perhaps you and your nameless wife—my very best to her—would spend a day or two here on the way from London to Fishguard, before all setting off. Can we talk about this in London—if you can be in London anytime from July 1 to 5 or 6? If you can't, do write please. Ireland together would be wonderful, I hope.

Here—for any news & nonsense I have can keep until London, Laugharne, or/and Ireland—are two songs, from the play, to fill up the page.

1st Song

Johnnie Crack and Flossie Snail
Kept their baby in a milking pail
Flossie Snail and Johnnie Crack
One would pull it out and one would put it back
O it's my turn now said Flossie Snail
To take the baby from the milking pail
And it's my turn now said Johnnie Crack
To smack it on the head and put it back

Johnnie Crack and Flossie Snail
Kept their baby in a milking pail
One would put it back and one would pull it out
And all it had to drink was ale and stout
For Johnnie Crack and Flossie Snail
Always used to say that stout and ale
Was *good* for a baby in a milking pail.

---

1 *Adventures in the Skin Trade.*

2nd Song

I loved a man whose name was Tom
He was strong as a bear and two yards long
I loved a man whose name was Dick
He was big as a barrel and three feet thick

And I loved a man whose name was Harry
Six feet tall and sweet as a cherry
But the one I loved most awake or asleep
Was little Willie Wee and he's six feet deep

Oh Tom Dick & Harry were three fine men
And I'll never have such loving again
But little Willy Wee who took me on his knee
Little Willy Weazel was the man for me.

Now men from every parish round
Run after me and roll me on the ground
But whenever I love another man back
Johnnie from the hill or Sailing Jack
I always think as they do what they please
Of Tom Dick & Harry who were tall as trees
And most I think when I'm by their side
Of little Willy Wee who downed and died.

Oh, Tom Dick & Harry were three fine men
And I'll never have such loving again
But little Willy Wee who took me on his knee
Little Willy Weazel was the man for me.

Now when farmers' boys on the first fair day
Come down from the hills to drink and be gay
Before the sun sinks I'll lie there in their arms
But I always think as we tumble into bed
Of little Willy Wee who is dead dead dead.

Oh, Tom Dick & Harry were three fine men
And I'll never have such loving again
But little Willy Wee who took me on his knee
Little Willy Weazel was the man for me.

From us both to you both,
Dylan

MS: Washington

JOHN ALEXANDER ROLPH
20 June 1953   Boat House   Laugharne   Carmarthenshire

Dear John,

Thank you for your last letter. Sorry I haven't written before: I've been back from America only a very short time, with a cracked arm and the quivers, and have only just come to. Come to what, I don't know yet. And thanks for trying to dig out more stories from old magazines: an awful job, I know, & I don't wonder it's failed. The copy of 'Wales', by the way, was very useful.

The paragraph John Davenport referred to in his Observer review of my bad 'Doctor & Devils'[1] came, as you guessed, from an 'Horizon' questionnaire. The questionnaire is, I believe, quoted in full in Connolly's new 'Ideas & Places'.[2] I can't remember a word of my own contribution to it.

How is the new business coming on? Hope to see you in London one day.

Yours,
Dylan

MS: Texas

DAVID HIGHAM
June 20 1953   Boat House   Laugharne   Carmarthenshire

Dear David,

Sorry not to have got in touch with you as soon as I came back. I broke my arm just before catching a New York plane for London, and it's rather hindered me. 'Under Milk Wood' is finished; it was performed, twice, in the Poetry Center, New York, with a cast of six, as a 'play for voices', to two audiences of a thousand each—mostly theatrical audiences, including lots of producers & playwrights—& went down extremely well. And I also gave a shortened reading of it, by myself, at Harvard. I've got three good notices of it, from the New York Times, the Saturday Review, & the leading Boston daily, which I lent to some woman who's doing an article on me for John O'London's weekly. I've written to her, today, to send the notices directly on to you so that you, if you will, may send them along to Charles Fry. He might like to see that, anyway, it *has* been well thought of. I'm busy now revising the play, but will have it ready by the end of this month. It definitely does need revising for publication; many phrases & whole passages I had to alter for dramatic performance, & will now have to change them back. Also, the two performances have shown me several

---

1 *The Doctor and the Devils* had been published, at last, on 14 May.
2 *Ideas and Places* (1953) reprinted Connolly's essays from *Horizon*.

weaknesses in the writing which I am now going (I hope) to better. I'll be up on the 30th of June myself, and will ring you at once. Either then, or on the 1st of July. And either I shall bring the ms. with me or send it on to you beforehand. I'm afraid there will only be one copy, & that not perfectly typed by any means: it will be the copy I used on the stage, with alterations & many new passages in writing (but clear writing).

Thank you very much indeed for looking after Caitlin, & all the other things, so wonderfully well when I was away.

Looking forward to seeing you.
Dylan

I saw the S'sea solicitor.

MS: Texas

CYRILLY ABELS[1]

June 20 1953 [draft][2] Boat House Laugharne Carmarthenshire Wales

Dear Miss Abels,

Thank you very much for writing to me. I did enjoy meeting you, and Miss Bolster, and the very pleasant cameraman, for that very short time in the hotel; and I only wish I cd have been more helpful to your guest-editor. I felt like an old pudding with feet. Perhaps I shall be able to meet you again in New York. We might be doing 'Under Milk Wood' once more at the P.C. in October of this year: a revised and, I hope, a much better script. I'm working on it now.

And thank you for photographs; it was nice of you to let me have a set for myself. My wife said one of the pictures looked a bit blurred, but I said it was me; and indeed it was. The pictures were awfully good.

I got the little interview, and there was of course nothing wrong. I'll look forward to seeing the feature.

Thank you again.
Yours

[*on reverse, draft lines from* Under Milk Wood: Captain Cat, at his window thrown wide to the sun and the clippered seas he sailed long ago when his long-ago eyes were blue & bright, slumbers & voyages;]

MS: Texas

---

1 Cyrilly Abels was managing editor of *Mademoiselle*. She had sent Thomas text and photographs of an article in their August feature 'We Hitch Our Wagons'.
2 When *SL* was in preparation Abels supplied a photocopy of the letter as received by her. This is lost, Abels is dead, and all that remains is Thomas's draft.

JOHN DAVENPORT
20 June 1953   Boat House   Laugharne   Carmarthenshire

Dear Brother Sly Boots,

I shall listen in, twice, tomorrow, Sunday, to hear the midday rats at my cheese, and, later, Miss Powell. Thank you. I saw a review by Bonhomie Dobbin in the Spectator.[1] I wish I'd seen yours in the Observer.

It was lovely to see so many of you in London and in Bach's-a-poor-man's guineapig-catty flat. I'll be up again on July 1st about, to deliver a ms, and will ring the BBC for you.

Ted Roethke will probably be in London at the same time. He's been staying in Wystan's nest in Ischia. He wants to know if he can have a pitch on the BBC all for himself to read some of his own poems. He reads awfully well. Can you do anything?[2]

So Bill & Helen are going to Tokyo in October. Helen comes back with an Irish accent after a week in Kerry. I can't phrase or illustrate the gesture needed to describe the effect upon her of four Japanese years.

Love
Dylan

MS: Texas

MIMI JOSEPHSON
June 20 53   Boat House   Laugharne   Carmarthenshire

Dear Mimi Josephson,

It was very pleasant to see you in Laugharne, even for such a short time, and I do hope we'll meet again when I'm in Cardiff: I'll be there sometime in August to do a television story, and, if you'll give me your number, I'll ring you up, if I may.

I realise that you felt you couldn't, with Fitzgerald & the cameraman there, ask me as many, or the sort of, questions you wanted to; and I find I'm no good talking to on the telephone: I know I give the impression of being terse and in a hurry, when indeed I'm anything but. So, if there's anything you want me to say, do write me a line and I'll answer by return.

Two things: one, will you let me see the article?[3] and, two: will you, *please*, send on the 3 cuttings about 'Milk Wood', from the American papers, which I lent you, to my agent, David Higham, of Pearn, Pollinger, & Higham, Ltd., 39–40 Bedford St., Strand, W.C.2. Can you do that *straightaway*? Sorry to be a nuisance, but he wants them at once to show

---

1 Dilys Powell was reviewing *The Doctor and the Devils* for the BBC. Bonamy Dobrée had reviewed it in the *Spectator*.
2 Davenport was working for the BBC.
3 Mimi Josephson was preparing an article about Thomas for *John O'London's Weekly*. It appeared on 7 August, 'Poet in the Boat House'.

to the publisher (Allan Wingate) who'll be printing the play this year. You've probably picked out what lines, if any, you want to use from those notices by this time. Can you let Higham have them as soon as you receive this? Thanks a lot.

And don't forget to write if there's anything I can do. I look forward to seeing you again.

Yours,
Dylan Thomas

P.S. Caitlin told me you just rang up. The photograph of the man with the striped tie, on the fire-escape of his New York apartment: W. H. Auden. Other photographs in my hut are of D. H. Lawrence & Thomas Hardy, there's a big photograph of Walt Whitman over my table, just under the roof, and a portrait of Blake. There are also, pinned about, pictures of monkeys & naked women.

MS: Location unknown

OSCAR WILLIAMS
June 22 1953   Boat House   Laugharne   Carmarthenshire   Wales

Dear Oscar, Little dear Honourable Treasurer of mine, how are you? Did you discover Columbus well? and give my best to Long Don Drummond the Potent Man? I missed you a lot my last days, and was Lizzed away to the plane alone. I almost liked the plane-ride, though; it was stormy and dangerous, and only my iron will kept the big bird up; lightning looked wonderful through the little eyeholes in its underbelly; the bar was open all the way from Newfoundland; and the woman next to me was stone-deaf so I spoke to her all the way, more wildly and more wildly as the plane lurched on through dark and lion-thunder and the fire-water yelled through my blood like Sioux, and she unheard all my delirium with a smile; and then the Red Indians scalped me; and then it was London, and my iron will brought the bird down safely, with only one spine-cracking jar. And, queasy, purple, maggoty, scalped, I weak-wormed through festoons, bunting, flags, great roses, sad spangles, paste and tinsel, the million cardboard simpers and ogrish plaster statuettes of the nincompoop queen, I crawled as early as sin in the chilly weeping morning through the city's hushed hangover and all those miles of cock-deep orange-peel, nibbled sandwiches, broken bottles, discarded vests, vomit and condoms, lollipops, senile fish, blood, lips, old towels, teeth, turds, soiled blowing newspapers by the unread mountain, all the spatter and bloody gravy and giant mousemess that go to show how a loyal and phlegmatic people—'London can break it!'—enjoyed themselves like hell the day before. And, my God, wouldn't I have enjoyed it too! In the house where I stay in London, a party was still going on, at half-past seven in the wet, beige morning, that had started two nights before. Full of my news, of the latest American gossip from the intellectual underworld, of tall goings-on, of tiny victories and disasters, aching to gabble I found myself in a company of amiable, wrestling, maudlin, beetleskulled men, semi-men, and many kinds of women, who did not know or care I had been so far and wildly away but seemed to think I had been in the party all the whooping time. Sober, airsick, pancaked flat, I saw these intelligent old friends as a warrenfull of blockish stinkers, and sulked all morning over my warm beer as they clamoured and hiccupped, rolled rodgering down, fell gaily through windows, sang and splintered. And in the afternoon, I stood—I was the only one who could—alone and disillusioned among the snorers and the dead. They grunted all around me, or went soughing and green to their Maker. As the little murdered moles in the Scotch poem, like sma' Assyrians they lay. I was close to crying there, in the chaotic middle of anticlimax. It was all too sordid. Oh how I hated these recumbent Bohemians! Slowly, I went upstairs to bath. There was a man asleep in the bath. And tears ran down my cheeks. Two creatures stretched dead in my bed. And, now, rain was boo-hooing too all over London.

P.S. I am sorry to add to this that by the end of the day I was happy as a pig in shit myself, and conducted the singing of hymns with my broken arm, and chased people and was caught, and wound up snug as a bugger in Rugby. Oh, my immortal soul, and oh, my tissues!

I returned to Laugharne ten days later; and now, in my left mind again, I shall begin to go on with the Adventures In The Skin-Trade. It is still raining here, just as when I left, but the sun hops in and out between the drizzles and fish skip in the sea and the old people are dying off like moths and our murderer goes around with an axe hanging by a string from his belt and white owls wheeze in the castle and there was a fight in the churchyard last night and I can hear now the cries of the village idiot being tortured by children in the Square and Aeron my daughter rides the waves proud on a rubber swan and Colm on a red duck and Ted Roethke is coming down in three weeks and we're going to Ireland together and Caitlin's brown as a berry from the bits of the sun through the West rain and I've revised 'Under Milk Wood' for an English publisher, adding many pages, and here comes the sun again and things, all said and done, all dead and gone, are just about liveable, praise bloody be!

I could find no silver belt, but, before leaving, commissioned someone to search for and buy one and I know she will; so any day now, Gene will have it, with my love. I hope she is well again.

Thank you very much for the photographs of you, Cecil Scott, and me: we all look like vampires full of breakfast.

Did I see you before I recorded for the Hairies?[1] I took your advice, and read only my poems on both sides of the disc. The Yeats I had no time to do—my own recording lasted all night long—but I will record when I

1 Thomas's nickname for the founders of Caedmon, Barbara Holdridge and Marianne Mantell.

return. I may be returning—though my Californian plans are still cloudy—in October. Another performance of Milk Wood has tentatively been dated for October 6 or 7, and I've been invited to an International Literary Conference at Pittsburgh a few days later. So I may see you quite soon, with Caitlin too, and see more of you, and clearer, than this last muddled time.

I am giving some radio readings of American poets in August, but cannot find the copy you gave me of your book of American Poetry. Could the publishers send me one, do you think? I do hope so: it is a fine book, and I should like it very much, and it will be useful.

And I would, a lot, appreciate Mrs. beautiful Adlai's[1] last hundred dollars (minus expenses) as there are hundreds of debts to settle here. Could you, *quickly*?

The murder of the Rosenbergs should make all men sick and mad.[2]

Yours always,
Dylan

Thank you for everything you did for me, Oscar, during my stay, before & after, for the Mentor contract[3] & countless kindnesses, and for being in New York and for being at all. Caitlin sends her love.

MS: Houghton

MEREDITH JONES
22 June 1953 [draft]   Boat House   Laugharne   Carmarthenshire

Dear Meredith Jones,
    Thank you very much for your letter. I'm so glad I'm not too late to come & talk at the Summer School, & I'll look forward to Porthcawl on the 5th of August. And many thanks for your kind invitation to stay with you that night: I'd be very glad to.

As to a fee: I suggest 15 guineas, plus return railway fare from Laugharne. If this is considered *too* handsome, I'll not bite the hand that gives me ten. But naturally I prefer 15, & do consider it appropriate for an hour's fairly strenuous reading of poems with comments. If you want a title, would just that do: 'A Reading of Poems, With Comments'? I think of reading a collection of modern British & American poems, with passages of introduction, explanation, & criticism, etc. Wd that do?

I hope to hear from you again about further details.

And once more, I'm very pleased I'll be able to come along.

Yours

MS: Texas

1 Ellen Stevenson.
2 Julius and Ethel Rosenberg, convicted of spying against the United States for the Soviet Union, were executed on 19 June 1953, despite international appeals for clemency.
3 The *Skin Trade* paperback contract.

LLEWELYN THOMAS
23 June 1953 [draft, incomplete]   Boat House   Laugharne

Dear Llewelyn,

I've been back here now about three weeks, as Mummy probably told you, with a broken arm. I managed this just before catching the homeward plane in New York. When we all came back from Italy, I did at least wait till we had got to London before tripping over a wire. This time, it was in an hotel bedroom in the dark: I woke up & couldn't find the light and got out of bed & tripped over my suitcase—crack! I screamed and screamed, but nobody came so I had to go back to bed.

I may be returning to America this autumn for another month or two, to write the libretto of an opera. But what I really want to do is to go with you & Mummy to Majorca for a holiday. I don't know about the others. Try to find out what

MS: Texas

LLEWELYN THOMAS
[?] [draft]

My dear Llewelyn,

What are you doing, always catching colds? You are the coldest boy in England! You should be an Eskimo

living in a

and fishing in a

MS: Texas

*DAVID HIGHAM
July 6 1953   Boat House   Laugharne   Carmarthenshire

Dear David

Sorry: I couldn't come up, as promised: I was—and still am—revising 'Under Milk Wood'. It'll take about another week. It would take less, but I am going to North Wales, to Llangollen for the International Music Festival, for the Welsh B.B.C. for 3 days this week, starting tomorrow.

In the meantime, I enclose a copy of the thing *unrevised*.[1] This is the version which was performed—or, rather, spoken in performance—in New York. I am now *adding* quite a lot to this, and changing quite a bit which is more effective on the stage, I think, than it would be on the printed page. The greatest amount of *addition* will take place late in the script, after page 47. The play (for voices), as you know is an evocative description of a Welsh town-that-never-was from, roughly, midnight to midnight. And, in *this* version, it will be seen that *dusk* arrives too sharply & suddenly and that the whole of the day *up to* the dusk much overbalances, in emphasis & bulk, the day *after* dusk. This was all right on the stage: the thing ran an hour & twenty minutes, straight dramatic reading with no intervals, & it was about as much as, in my opinion, an audience could be expected to take. Now, however, I am paying as much attention to the evening as, say, to the morning; & I hope to improve 'Milk Wood' very much structurally by this.[2]

I hope Charles doesn't despair over this, dislike it too much, or consider it preposterously short. It's extremely concentrated—in parts, anyway—and *has* to be short anyway. It can be made to *look* quite a nice book, I think. And I've got a lot of faith in it myself—perhaps because I enjoyed it so much, & am still enjoying the additions & alterations.

I shall come to London the week of the 13th, I hope, & will ring you at once.

Yours,
Dylan

P.S. Cyrilly Abels, editor of 'Mademoiselle', saw 'Milk Wood' performed in New York & was much taken by it. I let her have a rough copy—that is,

---

1 Higham sent the script on to E. F. Bozman at J. M. Dent. Bozman, who was evidently worried that the play was improper, passed it to the proprietor, Martin Dent, who replied to his editor-in-chief on 10 July, 'As you say it's a bit broad in places but I'm sure it's too good, too authentic Dylan Thomas to let it go . . . It's not at all like a pornographic novel.' Mr Dent added that 'to turn it down might be to lose the author'. When the play came to be published, posthumously, in 1954, the joke-name 'Llareggub' proved too much for Bozman. He managed to convince Dan Jones, the literary trustee, that Thomas himself had intended to change the word—an unlikely story—and Jones proposed 'Llaregyb', a bowdlerism that survived for years.

2 Thomas's plan to extend the 'evening' section was not much developed, or perhaps had been abandoned, when he died.

one similar to the enclosed—& she's just written to say she would like to print a much-shortened version, or digest, of it in 'Mademoiselle', taking just a few of the front pages & not—as most of her fiction does—continuing on at the back. For this very shortened version she will pay 750 dollars. Shall we talk about this when I see you? What do you think about it? It's good money, isn't it.

Dylan

PSS Please take no notice of the dim red lines on the enclosed script. They are just suggestions made by Cyrilly Abells.
PSSS This, looking at it again, will be quite a *lot* altered in small detail.

MS: Texas

P. H. NEWBY
15 July 1953   Boat House   Laugharne   Carmarthenshire

Dear Mr. Newby,
    I'd be delighted to read Sir Gawain and the Green Knight—(did J. R. R. Tolkien write a very good children's book, The Hobbit?)—and thank you very much for asking me.[1]
    Yes, I *was* going to America this month, but have put it off now until October. More than likely I'll be back before Christmas—but, anyway, would it be possible to do the recordings any time before October?
    I'm coming to London next week. Shall I give you a ring? Perhaps we could have a drink together. And could I get, then, a copy of the translation?
    I must apologise to you—& to my friend, Gilbert Phelps—for never having done anything about that Personal Anthology. I'd still like to do a reading of modern American poets. Perhaps we can talk about that when—as I hope—we meet? Anyway, I'll ring you early next week. And thank you again.

Sincerely,
Dylan Thomas

MS: BBC

1 Tolkien had made a new translation of the medieval poem. Newby wanted six 30-minute readings.

EDWARD RIORDAN[1]
15 July '53   Boat House Laugharne Carmarthenshire

Dear Mr. Riordan,

Please forgive me for not having answered your letter much sooner: I've been away and no letters were forwarded.

Yes, most certainly you have my permission to use those extracts from poems of mine as chapter-headings for your novel: I'm glad they come in useful.

Yours sincerely,
Dylan Thomas

MS: Texas

J. G. DAVIES[2]
July 16 1953 [draft]   Boat House Laugharne Carmarthenshire

Dear Mr Davies

I'm so sorry not to have answered your letter long before this: I've been away, and unfortunately no letters were sent on. And I'm sorry, too, I'm not the chap you thought I was. After such a charming letter, I feel I really should be, but I just *can't* change Swansea Grammar to Pencader Grammar School however hard I try. The time is right, about 25 years ago; it's the place that's the trouble. But it's strange that photograph that rang a bell in your belfry. My parents never told me of a twin brother banished to Pencader—I apologise for the word 'banished': that other boy's parents wd have considered Swansea the place of banishment—and I have, I'm *very* glad to say, never as yet seen any human being look quite like me. (Even *I* don't look like me half the time, which is some consolation.) So I'm afraid it's a mistake. But thank you indeed for being so very pleasant to me, & I'm delighted that you like my writing. I do hope you've thoroughly recovered from your operation now.

With all best wishes,

Yours sincerely,
Dylan Thomas

(of S'sea, I'm almost sure, not Pencader. You see that grain of doubt you've planted in my mind?)

MS: Texas

1 Riordan, of Harrogate, Yorks, asked to use lines from 'I have longed to move away' and 'The hand that signed the paper'.
2 J. G. Davies of Coventry, who was brought up on a farm at Pencader, in west Wales, had seen a photograph of Thomas in a newspaper, and written to ask if he had been at the local grammar school.

THEODORE ROETHKE
17 July 1953   Boat House Laugharne Carmarthenshire
                    Telephone Laugharne (pronounced Larn) 68

Dear Ted,

Thank you for your letter & enclosures. I liked the revision of the fine poem, and the other two poems, Squeeze & Dinky, are better, or nicer anyway, than Goethe.

I don't think damn it I'll be able to raise enough lovely to get to Ireland in the *very* near future—bills suddenly stormed in, and the Eisteddfod cost a tiny fortune and my health—but I'll try. I'll try all right.

I'm coming to London on Monday the 20th. I don't know where I'm staying yet, as where I stay isn't any more, but will you *please* leave a message at the Savage Club, 1, Carlton House Terrace, London, S.W.3.— the number's in the telephone book.

If you haven't found one yet, a pretty good hotel is the Royal Court, Sloane Square, Chelsea—but just a little stuffy.

The BBC Third Programme is *longing* for you—the word is the word of the old fat friend, John Davenport, I got hold of on the BBC—& we'll see him when we meet & fix up a torrential recording.

Hope this reaches you at the American Express.

I'm glad your wife was Beatrice O'Connell & is now Roethke. My wife was Caitlin Macnamara and is now unfortunate.

All the best to you both from both of us.

                                        Dylan

MS: Washington

THEODORE ROETHKE
[July 1953]   Laugharne 68

                    Dylan,
                    Boathouse,
                    Laugharne,
                    Carmarthenshire,

                    Book
                    From Paddington
                    Station
                    To
                    Fishguard
                    ———
                    (I think
                    you get
                    tickets all the

way through to
Dublin at
Paddington)

———

Stop at St. Clears
Station in Wales, where
[*illegible*] will meet you for Laugharne.

MS: Washington

ELI MORTLAKE[1]
18 July 1953 [?draft][2]   Boat House   Laugharne   Carmarthenshire

Dear Eli Mortlake,
   Yes, I had heard about Helen's death, and was very sad. I would have
written you, but had no address.
   Certainly I would like to write something—'anything', as you say—
about Helen, but it is extremely difficult: I knew Helen very little indeed,
though the little I knew made me most fond of her; and I hadn't seen her
for years. Also, I'm awfully bad at remembering times and places. I know
the first time I met her was in Glasgow, and the other times must have
been in London—usually, I imagine, with Sydney Graham and Colquhoun
& MacBryde.[3] But the details are irredeemably blurred, and all I
remember really, from these occasions, was Helen's sweetness, strength,
and humour. I wish there [was] something of use that I *could* write.
   I shall be in London very soon. Would you care to meet and have a drink?
If you'll let me know, I could drop you a line to say just when I'd be there.
   Thank you very much for the letter.

Yours,
Dylan Thomas

MS: Texas

1 Unidentified correspondent.
2 The writing is unclear. Another draft at Texas is dated '18th July'.
3 The painters Robert Colquhoun and Robert MacBryde.

JEAN LEROY
28 July 1953   Boat House Laugharne Carmarthenshire

Dear Daphne Richards,
I mean, Dear Jean LeRoy,
   Sorry not to have written before: I've just got back here. And back to find
I haven't a spare copy of 'Under Milk Wood' to do the Mademoiselle cuts
on.[1] The copy I have I'm working on, slowly, in a quite different way: I'm
adding to it. The only other copy, Bozman of Dent's has. I think he'd part
with it. If you let me have it then at once, I could send it back by return or,
if you wished, airmail it direct to Cyrilly Abels. It's all a nuisance, I know,
but it's not all my doing: the number of typescripts was, in the first case,
very limited, most of these going to the cast that read it in New York;
Cyrilly Abels returned her copy to Poetry Center, New York, where the
thing was performed, asking them to let me have it to cut. This copy was
sent to me, & I sent it to Higham who gave it to Bozman. I cut the end of
the page as I'd added yet another complication which is best, at the
moment, forgotten.
   Can you do anything?
   About Muggeridge & Punch.[2] I *haven't* written any satirical verses
about America, but only a piece of satirical prose, which I used as an
introduction to some poetry readings there and is (a) unsuitable, (b)
incomplete as a piece. By 'unsuitable', I mean I don't think it's good
enough for Punch. But I would very much like to write a piece, or pieces,
for Punch as soon as I can.
   And please thank Mr MM for asking me.

                                        Yours,
                                        Dylan Thomas

MS: Texas

OSCAR WILLIAMS
[28 July 1953]   Boat House Laugharne Carmarthenshire

Our Dear Oscar,
   Very many thanks; which always begins every letter to you. For your
own letter; for the Selected Williams—thank you for sending the *right*
Williams; and for the American Anthology. This is very brief because I
have just come back from London, rain, despair, Roethke, publishers,
agents, wee brawls, schoolboards, snubs, snobs, ulcerous luncheons, and
am depressed here & insolvent in Wales and rain. I'm enclosing, signed, the
note of permission. 14 poems! Dear God, we'd better not become any

1 Extracts from the play appeared in *Mademoiselle* in February 1954.
2 The writer Malcolm Muggeridge was editor of *Punch*, 1953–7.

better friends, even if we could. And it's wonderful of you to say you think you can manage to get the * 'round fee' for me straightaway. Oh, I *do* hope so. I'm down the drain again, and have arranged to send Aeron to a boardingschool next term, which is hideously expensive, and what with taxes and the immortal soul it's hardly worth keeping your head above the shit. (Surely, by the way, I did, didn't I, damn me, acknowledge the last lovely manuscript hundred you sent? If I didn't, I do now most gratefully. If I did, I do again.) And another by-the-way, though a furious one this time: the Caedmon Hairies, Marianne & Barbara, paid me only 200 dollars of the 500 dollars they were supposed to pay me—on signing of contract—for that last recording of my own poems. They promised to send me—personally, not to my agent—the other 300 by July 1st. I'm writing this, rot them, on July 28. I want their hairy money.

I read American poems, including, of course, yours, to the University of Wales a week or so ago. And will be broadcasting some soon again. I'll let you know details.

Caitlin sends her love to you & Gene and so do I.

I do hope (again) you can airmail that cabbage back (see asterisk on first page).

Ever,
Dylan

Just finishing final revision of 'Under Milk Wood'. It's quite a bit better. Would you like the ms? or, rather, bunches of the working sheets?

D.

Do you know—I mean, can you get for me—the Hairies' address? I'll send them the crabs of a letter.   D.
I'll write *fully* next time, v soon.

MS: Houghton

RALPH WISHART[1]
July 28 1953   Boat House   Laugharne   Carmarthenshire

Dear Ralph,

I'm really terribly sorry about the misunderstanding and you've every right to think I'm a dirty dog. Well, I am, if you like, a middle-aged dog with a dirty mind, but of course I was coming to see you, and still am, and always will, and the reason for my not coming in on Monday or afterwards is very simple. I was driven up from Laugharne on the day of that broadcast, arriving in good time—good time, that is, for a quick one in the King's Head—about seven o'clock in the evening. You were, of course,

---

1 Ralph Wishart (1911–75), 'Ralph the Books', a Swansea character, had been a second-hand bookseller in the town since the 1930s.

shut. After the broadcast was, to the relief of thousands, over, I was driven straight back to Laugharne—if you can call it straight, stopping about thirty times—and I haven't been to Swansea since.

I didn't write to explain, as perhaps I should, because I knew I was coming up to Swansea any time to call on the B.B.C. and I would be meeting you then. Now I'm coming up, for the first time since I saw you after my Llangollen visit, tomorrow, Thursday, to see D.J.T.V. Thomas.[1] I'll drop in after lunch—with, I hope to God, a cheque.

How's Dan? I'll be seeing him too, I hope. Thanks for everything, & sorry again.

All the best,
Dylan

Only source: SL

FELIX GERSTMAN[2]
28 July 1953 [draft]   Boat House   Laugharne   Carmarthenshire   Wales

Dear Mr Gerstman,
Very many thanks for your letter, which interested me considerably. I'm grateful to Mr Watson Pierce for introducing us.

I hope to be in New York for a short visit in October, and would very much like to get in touch with you then. There are a number of things I would like to discuss. I'll let you know well beforehand my New York dates so that—as I hope—we can arrange to meet. Thank you again.

Sincerely yours
Dylan Thomas

MS: Texas

DANIEL JONES
Monday August 24 1953   Laugharne

Dear Dan,
Will you be in Swansea this week? John Ormond came down here, warbling and nut-fed, a few days ago, and said you were in Cardiff. If you aren't, and are home again, will you let me know quickly? I don't want to come to adanabandoned Swansea.

I owe you some money, and hope to give it to you when I see you. Did you see Stewart[3] after his intentional and contemptuous failure to turn

1 David J. Thomas was the BBC producer in charge of 'A Story'. Thomas performed it on 10 August in a makeshift studio, set up in the Dean's Library at St Asaph Cathedral, North Wales; it was his only solo appearance on television.
2 An agent with whom Thomas hoped to arrange a more lucrative U.S. lecture tour.
3 The Swansea solicitor Stuart Thomas.

up? or had he forgotten? I can only suppose he never meant a word of it, and thought it fun. I still need fifty pounds *terribly*, which should make him laugh his head off.

I have to see T.V.D.J. Thomas in Swansea, *and* Aneirin, but will get that over quickly and then—oh, to bask unasked in a Bass cask, etc!

Isn't life awful? Last week I hit Caitlin with a plate of beetroot, and I'm still bleeding. I can't finish a poem, or begin a story, I chew my nails down to my shoulders, pick three-legged horses with beautiful names, take my feet for grey walks, moulder in Brown's, go to bed as though to an office, read with envy of old lonely women who swig disinfectant by the pint, think about money, dismiss it as dirt, think about dirt.

Do write a postcard, if you're at home, or telephone Laugharne 68.

Ever,
Dylan

MS: Texas

MIMI JOSEPHSON
25th August 1953   Laugharne

Dear Mimi Josephson,

Thank you so much for sending me John O'London. Naturally, I liked your article a lot, and thought it awfully well done and full of fun and sense. 'Naturally', because it made such a splendid rumbustious figure of this melancholy bad-natured slob mouldering away in his mud-hole by the wish washy water. But I think you did a really warm, and lively, and imaginative job. The portrait was excellent, and depressing. Caitlin says, by the way: we have *six* rooms and a kitchen; but that is another storey. Many thanks again.

Yours,
Dylan Thomas

From a typescript. MS location unknown

PETER DAVIES
25th August 1953   Boat House   Laugharne   Carmarthenshire

Dear Peter Davies,

Thank you for your letter. I'm sorry I couldn't answer it before this: I've been away from Laugharne. Of course I'll be very pleased to sign any books, and to meet you if you come down here. I'll be away all the week of the 31st of August, but before then and after will be at home nearly all the time.

Yours sincerely,
Dylan Thomas

From a typescript. MS location unknown

ALAN HODGE[1]
August 25 1953   Boat House   Laugharne   Carmarthenshire

Dear Alan,

So sorry not to have written long before this. I lost your letter almost as soon as I got it, and didn't know where to write you. I found the letter this morning.

I'm very glad you and Robert Graves are hoping to get a publisher to bring out a collected Norman. And of course I'd like to write down some of my memories of him. I was awfully young when I first knew Norman in the early 30's, and so bloody full of myself, or full of my bloody self, that that wonderful time is mostly vague and muddled now; I remember all the feel of it, but not many happenings or details. But I'll try, I'll try all right.

I'm coming to London next week. Would you meet and have a drink? Perhaps you'll make me remember some more. I'm even dim about Night Custard, though I was there at its first stirring. I remember better the Unpopular Man, that Old Normal and I made together.

Shall I give you a ring at History Today?

Yours ever,
Dylan

MS: Buffalo

*G. V. ROBERTS
25 August 1953   Boat House   Laugharne   Carmarthenshire

Dear Mr Roberts,

So sorry not to have answered your letter well before this: I've been away and unfortunately no letters were forwarded.

Thank you very much for the invitation to come along to the Tenby & District Arts Club on October 2nd. I'd like very much to come, but the trouble is: I shan't know until about September 6 or 7 whether I shall be in this country or not in October. Can I let you know definitely, on the 6th or 7th, or would that be too late? Perhaps you could drop me a line to tell me, or 'phone me at Laugharne 68.

Thank you again, & I do hope I'll be able to manage it.

Yours sincerely,
Dylan Thomas

MS: Victoria

1 Alan Hodge (1915–79), writer and historian. He had written to ask Thomas for his recollections of Norman Cameron, who died earlier in 1953.

STEPHEN SPENDER
August 25th 1953   Boat House   Laugharne   Carmarthenshire

Dear Stephen,

Sorry not to have written much sooner about *Encounter*:[1] I mislaid your letter.

I'm glad you want something of mine, and wish I had something to send straightaway. I'm working on a small poem now, and will let you have it when ready.[2] As for that extract of a novel you saw in New World Writing: do you remember which extract it was? Two have been printed in New World Writing so far. The first extract, 'A Fine Beginning', has been printed in England. But the second—which appeared in the last number of N.W.W.—called 'Four Lost Souls' hasn't been printed anywhere except there & I'm sure you could get permission to use it. I hope you do.[3]

Yours,
Dylan

MS: Houghton

CYRIL CONNOLLY
5 9 '53   Boat House   Laugharne   Carmarthenshire

Dear Cyril,

Here's *my* permission to include the three poems you wanted in The Golden Horizon.[4] The book-publishers of the three poems were, in England, J. M. Dent, &, in America, New Directions.

Yours ever,
Dylan

MS: Texas

*CLIFFORD DYMENT[5]
7 Sept 1953   Boat House   Laugharne   Carmarthenshire

Dear Clifford,

I've put off writing to you in the hope that, when I did write, I would have a little good news. Now, I'm afraid, the news, if it can be called that, is vague and unsatisfactory. I put off writing because John Malcolm

1 Spender was a founding editor (with Irving Kristol) of *Encounter*, first published October 1953.
2 Perhaps the unfinished 'Elegy'.
3 'Four Lost Souls' didn't appear in *Encounter*.
4 *The Golden Horizon* (1953), an anthology of extracts from the magazine.
5 English poet, Welsh by adoption, 1914–70. He met Thomas during the war when both were working on propaganda films.

Brinnin, who is the Director of the Poetry Centre of the Y.M.H.A. in New York—the organization you spoke of in your letter—was coming to spend a few days with me down here. Now he's told me that the Poetry Centre doesn't any more bring poets over from abroad. The last they did finance to go to New York were a weird trio, Gascoyne, Sydney [W. S.] Graham, & Katheleen Raine, & then the Centre promised them only one public reading: the rest they had to get themselves. Apparently, the thing was a flop, & the Governors of the Association wouldn't hand out any more money like that again. But Brinnin knows and admires your work, & says that *if only* you can get to New York he will give you a reading at the Poetry Centre—they pay extremely well—and do all he can to get you other engagements: and I know, from experience, that he's very good at that. Also, he says that in America there should be many more chances of your making some money than in England, & in this he would help. And *also*: he assures me that you could go, any time of the year, to a place called Yaddow, of which you probably know, and live there free for some months. Yaddow is a large country house outside Saratoga Springs. Many, many writers go there to work: they have comfort, peace, etc, a place of their own to live & write in, & nothing to pay but their laundry bills. Brinnin & some of his friends would see to it that you got there, *once you were in America*. And, of course, the other awful snag, you wd have to be alone: Yaddow doesn't take married couples: it's supposed to be just a place for a writer to rest or/and write.

Summing up: Get to the States, & you can get some profitable readings, maybe other jobs & engagements, & a celibate free spell in the country. That is, of course, according to Brinnin. I'm afraid he has no ideas as to *how* you get out there. Isn't there some sort of fellowship that gets writers out there & gives them small living expenses per-day for some limited period? If anybody knows about this, it is John Davenport, who's now on the BBC 3rd Programme. I think it wd be worth ringing him & finding out. And also seeing him. I wish to hell I myself could help, but I'm in an awful state of debt & near-despair. I daren't answer the phone or the door, & am drowned in undone work & writs.

I hope to the Lord something useful happens to you soon.

Yrs ever,
Dylan

I think Yaddow's spelt Yaddoe now I come to think of it.

MS: Victoria

E. F. BOZMAN
11th September 1953   Boat House   Laugharne   Carmarthenshire
                                                              Laugharne 68

Dear E. F. Bozman,

I was sorry I wasn't able to see you when I came to London last: I'd a very short time there—just for a little broadcast, and to see about my daughter's new school—and David Higham told me that, so far as he knew, there was nothing very urgent to discuss. I wanted to meet you anyway; and I do hope now we'll be able to lunch together before I go to the States early in October.

Well before I leave, I'll have finished the final corrections and amplifications of 'Under Milk Wood'. I think it's much better now—(it sounds as though it had been ill). One of the reasons I'm going to America is to take part in three public readings of it, with a professional cast, at the Poetry Center, New York. (The other, and main, reason is to go to California to begin work with Stravinsky on a new opera.) And, when I return some time in December, I hope that it can be given one or more reading-performances, most likely on a Sunday night, in London; with any luck, I'll be able to get firstrate Welsh actors to read it. Higham, in the meantime, and as soon as he has my complete version, will see to it that someone like Sherek[1] has a chance of reading it with this in mind. 'Under Milk Wood' will also be broadcast next year, in full, and it should be possible to arrange this broadcast to happen about the same time as publication. I myself have good hopes altogether of the success of Milk Wood; and I'm *very very* grateful to you for taking it over.

About the *Book of Stories*—I suggest, tentatively, the title of 'Early One Morning', the title of one of the stories:—I have reckoned out that there are now eleven of these, including a very recent one that will, I think, be appearing in next week's 'Listener'.[2] And I want to write two or three more, still on a childhood theme, to complete the book. In spite of what you very rightly say about the 'rawness' of the other, and earlier, stories I sent you some time ago, I still think that one, and one alone, of these 'A Prospect of The Sea' could well take its place in the volume. Perhaps, when you have the rest of the stories together, you would consider this again? (Though I may very well be completely wrong about it.) And, thinking back, yes, 'Early One Morning' does seem to me a good title.

Higham told me that you were prepared to consider again the short novel, 'Adventures In the Skin Trade'. I'm so glad. When I come back from America, I intend to settle down & finish it. And, after that, another 'Play for Voices', using the same form as in Milk Wood.

Now to a much more difficult part of this letter. Straightaway, I just *must* say that I'm in money trouble again, and this time quite seriously

---

1 Henry Sherek (d. 1967), theatre producer.
2 'A Story', the television broadcast.

again. And I'm wondering, and hoping terribly much, that somehow you can help me. I really do need help at this very moment. As perhaps you know, David Higham has taken over what I suppose I must call my 'financial affairs' in .a very expert way. As well as seeing to my eldest children's school-fees—my daughter will be beginning boarding-school next week—he also keeps money aside for income-tax and allows me a sum per month for personal expenses. But I'm afraid that that sum isn't enough to pay tradesmen's accounts etc. and now I'm being pressed to pay at once some most urgent debts I have simply had to incur over recent months. I cannot ask Higham to help me with these: he is doing all he possibly can with the money at his disposal. And I do not know what on earth to do. I'm trying to put this down as simply and flatly as I can; but, really, I'm *sick* with anxiety, and find it terribly hard to work. What's particularly infuriating is, that I'm about to make quite a lot of money in the States. The Stravinsky libretto is, in itself, an assurance of that. (I hope one day you'll publish the libretto.) And I'm going to give a short series of very well paid commercial lectures—(I mean by that, not to universities, as on my previous visits, but in town halls & to large unacademic paying audiences. The lectures, incidentally, won't be lectures, but readings of poetry). There money is, a lot of it, so near; and here I am in the most awful position, owing money to everywhere here and the debts mounting every day nightmarishly. I can't say 'Stravinsky' to tradesmen, insurance, etc. etc. Oh Lord, I am in a mess.

Can you help? I don't know how. And really, I need help without Higham's—no, I can't say 'knowledge', that sounds like working behind his back; perhaps I mean his friendly superintendence. He thinks me extravagant, as perhaps I am. But my debts are all for unextravagant country living, & they've mounted up horribly. Have you any suggestions? Could Dent advance me any good sum on 'Milk Wood',[1] or on 'Early One Morning'. Or could I somehow borrow money & pay it back from my American earnings in October & November? It's so hard for me to think. We haven't, now, even enough to take Aeronwy & Llewelyn to their schools next week; & it seems so silly; but the silliness is frightening in this remote place. Or in any place, I suppose, except that here nearly everyone is very poor: certainly, all my friends. Now I am beginning to gabble.

Can you write me, or ring me?[2]

When I rang this afternoon, I felt too awkward to say anything. I couldn't even *ask* for your private address, which is what I had rung for. Forgive me. And for this letter.

I just realised: in one breath I talk of going to the States in a very few

---

1 Some time previously, Dent had paid an advance of £250.
2 Bozman sent a stern but kindly reply, refusing to cheat Higham. 'You have every reason, Thomas,' he wrote, 'to look forward to a brilliant and successful future, not only in fame *but FINANCIALLY*!' On Bozman's letter Thomas drew a gargoyle with a squint, and wrote the name of a horse for the 4.30.

weeks, probably three weeks or less, & in the next breath say we cannot afford the trains to London. This sounds absurd. My American ticket is, of course, paid for by the Poetry Center New York. But before I go, I *have* to clear up everything here & leave it (almost) sweet & smiling.

Yours,
Dylan Thomas

And I daren't look back over the last part of this letter in case I cross it all out in horrified embarrassment.

MS: (J. M. Dent)

PRINCESS CAETANI
[?1953] [incomplete draft][1]

Dear Marguerite Caetani,
    What can I say?
    Why do I bind myself always into these imbecile grief-knots, blindfold my eyes with lies, wind my brass music around me, sew myself in a sack, weight it with guilt and pig-iron, then pitch me squealing to sea, so that time and time again I must wrestle out and unravel in a panic, like a seaslugged windy Houdini, and ooze and eel up wheezily, babbling and blowing black bubbles, from all the claws and bars and breasts of the mantrapping seabed?
    Deep dark down there, where I chuck the sad sack of myself, in the slimy squid-rows of the sea there's such a weed-drift and clamour of old plankton drinkers, such a mockturtle gabble of wrecked convivial hydrographers tangled with polyps and blind prawns, such a riffraff of seabums in the spongy dives, so many jellyfish soakers jolly & joking in the smoke-blue basements, so many salty sea-damaged daughters stuffing their wounds with fishes, so many lightning midnight makers in the luminous noon of the abysmal sea, and such fond despair there, always there, that time and time again I cry to myself as I kick clear of the cling of my stuntman's sacking, 'Oh, one time the last time will come and I'll never struggle, I'll sway down here forever handcuffed and blindfold, sliding my woundaround music, my sack trailed in the slime, with all the rest of the self-destroyed escapologists in their cages, drowned in the sorrows they drown and in my piercing own, alone and one with the coarse and cosy damned seahorsey dead, weeping my tons.'

1 There is no version of this letter in the Caetani archive. It was probably drafted at Laugharne during Thomas's last summer there, and left unfinished to be found by one of the collectors who descended on the Boat House after his death. Texas has several sheets, covered with trial phrases: 'babbling and blowing bubbles, like a wheezy Houdini', 'don't I smell fishy as I ooze webfooted', 'arse over head', 'dandruff over corns', 'up to their sockets in snails', 'up to their skulls in crabs', 'spare me a copper for a cuppa for my supper'. And 'down at eel'.

What can I tell you? Why did I bray my brassy nought to you from this boygreen briny dark? I see myself down and out on the sea's ape-blue bottom: a manacled rhetorician with a wet trombone, up to his blower in crabs.

Why must I parable my senseless silence? my one long trick? my last dumb flourish? It is [not] enough that, by the wish I abominate, I savagely contrive to sink lashed and bandaged in a blind bag to those lewd affectionate raucous stinking cellars: no, I must blare my engulfment in pomp and fog, spout a nuisance of fountains like a bedwetting [?whale] in a blanket, and harangue all land-walkers as though it were their shame that I sought the sucking sea and cast myself out of their sight to blast down to the dark. It is not enough to presume that once again I shall weave up pardoned, my wound din around me rusty, and waddle and gush along the land on my webbed sealegs as musical and wan and smug as an orpheus of the storm: no, I must first defeat any hope I might have of forgiveness by resubmerging the little arisen original monster in a porridge boiling of wrong words and make a song and dance and a mock-poem of all his fishy excuses.

The hell with him.

MS: Texas

PETER DAVIES
15 Sept 1953   Boat House   Laugharne

Dear Mr. Davies,
Sorry not to have answered straightaway. Yes, do come down if you want to this week: any day except Thursday. I won't be at my house, as all the family's gone to London: but you can leave a message for me at Laugharne 13: the pub.

Sincerely,
Dylan Thomas

From a typescript. MS location unknown

*G. V. ROBERTS
September 15 1953   Boat House   Laugharne   Carmarthenshire

Dear Mr Roberts,
Sorry not to have answered by return. I spoke, however, to the owner of the Salad Bowl on the telephone & we arranged a time for me to be picked up here: it's very kind of everyone. No objection, of course, to Mr Houling's

playing the piano; I hope he doesn't mind me, either. I look forward to coming to Tenby on Friday October 2nd.[1]

Sincerely,
Dylan Thomas

MS: *Victoria*

IGOR STRAVINSKY
September 22 1953   The Boat House   Laugharne   Carmarthenshire
Wales

Dear Igor Stravinsky,
   Thank you very very much for your two extremely nice letters, and for showing me the letter you had written to Mr Choate of Boston University. I would have written again long before this, but I kept on waiting until I knew for certain when I would be able to come to the States; and the lecture-agent there in New York, who makes my coming across possible, has been terribly slow in arranging things. I heard from him only this week. Now it is certain that I shall be in New York on the 16th of October; and I'll have to stay there, giving some poetry-readings and taking part in a couple of performances of a small play of mine, until the end of October. I should like then, if I may, to come straight to California to be with you and to get down together to the first stage of our work. (I'm sure I needn't tell you how excited I am to be able to write down that word 'our'. It's wonderful to think of.)
   One of my chief troubles is, of course, money. I haven't any of my own, and most of the little I make seems to go to schools for my children, who will persist in getting older all the time. The man who's arranged my readings in October, at a few Eastern universities and at the Poetry Center, New York, is paying my expenses to and from New York. But from there to California I will have to pay my own way on what I can make out of those readings. I do hope it will work out all right. Maybe I'll be able to give a few other readings, or rantings, in California to help pay expenses. (I'd relied on drawing my travelling expenses etc from the original Boston University commission.) I want to bring my wife Caitlin with me, and she thinks she can stay with a friend in San Francisco while I'm working with you in Hollywood. Anyway, I'll have to work these things out the best I can, and I mustn't bother you with them now. Money for California will come

---

1 Thomas fulfilled the engagement, probably his last in Britain before his death. Ken Hewlings gave a piano recital at the meeting, which was held at a local café, the Salad Bowl. The fee was handed over in an envelope on which a shaky hand has written 'With the compliments & thanks of Tenby Arts Club'. Three names of horses have been added in Thomas's hand, 'Cardinal Star', 'Siren Light' and 'Starry View'. (*Envelope: Thomas Trustees*)

somehow. I'll pray for ravens to drop some in the desert. The *main* thing, I know, is for me to get to you as soon as possible, so that we can begin— well, so that we can *begin*, whatever it will turn out to be. I've been thinking an awful lot about it.

I was so sorry to hear you had been laid up for so long: I hope you're really well again by this time. My arm's fine now, and quite as weak as the other one.

If you don't write to me at Wales before I leave, about October 7th, then my American address will be: c/o J. M. BRINNIN, POETRY CENTER, YM-YWHA, 1395 Lexington Avenue, New York 28. But anyway I'll write again as soon as I reach there.

I'm looking forward enormously to meeting you again, and to working with you. And I *promise* not to tell anyone about it—(though it's very hard not to).

Most sincerely,
Dylan Thomas

MS: Paul Sacher Foundation, Basle

*AERON THOMAS
September 22 1953   Laugharne

Darling Aeron,

We all miss you here very very very much: Mummie, Grannie, Colm, Dolly, Sheila, Desmond, Ma-ma, Tibby. Oh yes, and me too of course. The Boat House is very empty and *very quiet* since you and Welly[1] went away, and there doesn't seem to be anybody for me to shout at any more. I'll just have to shout at myself.

Mummie and Grannie showed me the letters you wrote to them, and I liked them very much. I didn't know you wrote so well. Will you write me a letter one day? *and* Dolly? *and* Colm? *and* your Grannie at Blashford? Well, some time in the term anyway, or you won't have any time to do anything else but write letters. I'm glad it's nice at school and that you've got friends and that you do a lot of dancing.[2] You must teach me to dance ballet when you come home—or will I go through the floor?

Mummie's going to Carmarthen tomorrow, which is Wednesday, to buy some things for you, and I'm going to the dentist to scream the house down.

When you write to me, tell me what you would like me to bring you from America. (Colm, of course, wants an aeroplane: a real full-size one).

---

1 Aeron's brother, Llewelyn. Other names: Dolly was Dolly Long, the family help; Desmond, her son, Sheila, her niece.
2 Aeron, now aged ten, had recently gone to the Arts Educational School in Hertford-shire. Llewelyn, fourteen, was still at Magdalen College School.

What time do you get up in the morning? and what time do you go to bed? I'd like to know *everything* and all the news.

Mummie will write tomorrow.

> All my love to you,
> Daddy

And we think about you
all the time, you old silly.

MS: Aeron Thomas

*JOHN MALCOLM BRINNIN
[telegram from Laugharne, 6 October 1953, 9.40 am]

VISA AWAITING APPROVED PETITION PLEASE HAVE AUTHORITIES CABLE AMERICAN CONSULATE CARDIFF DYLAN

Original: Delaware

CLIFFORD ROBERTS
9th October 1953 [?draft] The Boat House   Laugharne   Carmarthenshire

Dear Mr. Roberts,
    Thank you very much indeed for your kind invitation to me to attend the Port-Reeve's Annual Breakfast this coming Sunday. Unfortunately, I am going to London today, & from there to America, and will have to miss the pleasure of the Breakfast. I am indeed sorry, but wish you a very successful Sunday morning & the best of wishes over the coming year.

> Yours sincerely,
> Dylan Thomas

MS: Thomas Trustees

JOHN MALCOLM BRINNIN
[telegram, 17 October 1953, from London]

TICKET ARRIVED COUPLE DAYS TOO LATE NOW CATCHING PLANE 7.30 PM MONDAY 19TH DESPERATELY SORRY. DYLAN.[1]

Original: Delaware

---

1 The original flight was booked for Tuesday 13 October.

ELLEN STEVENSON
[telegram, 25 October 1953, 9.51 pm, New York]

DEAR ELLEN OSCAR WILLIAMS HAS TOLD ME THAT YOU WOULD
LIKE ME TO PRESENT MY PLAY ENTITLED 'UNDER MILKWOOD' IN
CHICAGO I SHALL BE DELIGHTED TO DO SO WITH OR WITHOUT
CAST BUT NOT WITHOUT CASH SOME TIME BETWEEN NOVEMBER
12TH AND NOVEMBER 15TH ON MY WAY TO HOLLYWOOD
WOULD YOU KINDLY GET IN TOUCH WITH MY MANAGER JOHN
BRINNIN 100 MEMORIAL DRIVE FOR FULL DETAILS THANK YOU
VERY MUCH LOOK FORWARD TO SEEING YOU WITH WARM
REGARDS DYLAN THOMAS

Original: Texas

Dylan Thomas's last public engagement was a lunchtime reading at the
City College of New York on Thursday 29 October 1953. He spent much of
the next few days with Elizabeth Reitell. He seemed exhausted and unwell,
and drank heavily. The detective hired by *Time* magazine padded along
behind him and his friends. On the night of Saturday 31 October, Thomas,
in a bar on 7th Avenue, was heard to say that all women were only
substitutes for Caitlin. He was also seen to be taking benzedrine. On the
night of Wednesday 4 November the assiduous detective noted a 'get-
together' at the Chelsea. The friends left; Elizabeth Reitell remained. Dr
Milton Feltenstein, summoned to the hotel late that night, injected
Thomas with half a grain of morphine, apparently to relieve the symptoms
caused by alcohol, gout and gastritis. Between midnight and 1 am on 5
November, Thomas collapsed and went into a coma: breathing difficulties
caused or exacerbated by the morphine had led to brain damage, which in
turn was the probable cause of the raised sugar levels that were found,
although some have interpreted these as evidence of diabetes. He died in
hospital four days later without recovering consciousness, at midday on
Monday 9 November 1953.

Index of Recipients

Index